PROGRAMMING FOR PEACE

Advances in Group Decision and Negotiation

Volume 2

The book series, Advances in Group Decision and Negotiation — as an extension of the journal, *Group Decision and Negotiation* — is motivated by unifying approaches to group decision and negotiation processes. These processes are purposeful, adaptive and complex – cybernetic and self-organizing – and involve relation and coordination in multiplayer, multicriteria, ill-structured, evolving dynamic problems in which players (agents) both cooperate and conflict. These processes are purposeful complex adaptive systems.

Group decision and negotiation involves the whole process or flow of activities relevant to group decision and negotiation – such as, communication and information sharing, problem definition (representation) and evolution, alternative generation, social-emotional interaction, coordination, leadership, and the resulting action choice.

Areas of application include intraorganizational coordination (as in local/global strategy, operations management and integrated design, production, finance, marketing and distribution – e.g., as for new products), computer supported collaborative work, labor-management negotiation, interorganizational negotiation (business, government and nonprofits), electronic negotiation and commerce, mobile technology, culture and negotiation, intercultural and international relations and negotiation, globalization, terrorism, environmental negotiation, etc.

Programming for Peace

Computer-Aided Methods for International Conflict Resolution and Prevention

Edited by

ROBERT TRAPPL

Vienna Medical University and Austrian Research Institute for Artificial Intelligence, Vienna, Austria

Springer

A C.I.P. Catalogue record for this book is available from the Library of Congress.

ISBN-10 1-4020-4377-5 (HB)
ISBN-13 978-1-4020-4377-2 (HB)
ISBN-10 1-4020-4390-2 (e-book)
ISBN-13 978-1-4020-4390-1 (e-book)

Published by Springer,
P.O. Box 17, 3300 AA Dordrecht, The Netherlands.

www.springer.com

Printed on acid-free paper

Printed in the Netherlands.

Contents

Preface

From its beginning in the fifties of the last century, Artificial Intelligence was heavily supported by "defence agencies" in order to make "better warfare".

But, if an AI researchers assumes that her/his discipline really can deliver results—otherwise s/he would be a dishonest researcher—then why not try to use it to help decision-makers in government or concerned groups outside goverment who want to prevent the outbreak of war or want to end it?

Therefore, already in the eighties, the Austrian Research Institute for Artificial Intelligence (OFAI), often in cooperation with the then Department of Medical Cybernetics and Artificial Intelligence of the University of Vienna, tried to use AI methods first on a more conceptual base but then increasingly by using conflict-, crisis- and conflict management-databases to either find, by case-based reasoning methods, similar cases in order to see which conflict management methods were successful or by computing decision trees with machine learning methods to find the conflict management strategy with the greatest chance of success in a new crisis situation (for more information, please see Chapter 11 and its references).

Our research efforts were supported both by the Jubilee Fund of the Austrian National Bank and by the Austrian Federal Ministry of Science and Research / Science, Research and Culture / Science and Transport / Education, Science, and Culture (the same Ministry but with, successively, four different names). The Ministry opened, in 2000, a tender for research projects for "Promoting Peace and Preventing Violence". 22 project proposals were submitted, an international jury selected 3, and we were happy to be among those chosen.

This project enabled us to organize a two-day workshop to which we could invite leading scientists from countries all over the world, to present and discuss their recent results. The participants of the workshop concluded that the interesting discussion papers, elaborated by the authors and enriched by contributions of scientists who were not able to particpate, would be of interest and of use to a larger audience. This volume is the result of this endeavour. I therefore want first to thank the authors who took great pains to enhance their original position papers to book chapters by including new material and by considering the comments in and outside the discussions.

Second, I want to thank the successive Federal Ministers in charge, namely Heinz Fischer, Erhard Busek, Caspar Einem and Elisabeth Gehrer, and the very helpful state officers in their Ministry, especially Sigurd Höllinger, Ilse König and Christine Lutter.

Third, I want to thank Dan Druckman who established the contact to Mel Shakun, the editor of the series "Advances in Group Decision and Negotiation" at Kluwer Academic Publishers, now Springer, and Mel Shakun himself for accepting this book in his series.

Welmoed Spahr and Marianna Pascale of Springer were always very cooperative partners.

Fourth, my thanks go to Isabella Ghobrial-Willmann and Ulrike Schulz for their help in the organization of the Workshop and their very useful secretarial help.

I am especially indebted to Sabine Payr: she not only laboriously converted all submitted chapter manuscripts to the formatted camera-ready book manuscript and prepared the two indices, she also diligently improved the English of the contributions wherever necessary. And the title of this book is also her creation. I look forward with pleasure to future joint endeavours.

Finally, I want to thank the Austrian taxpayers whose money enabled us to work as a group for two years, to enlarge the Confman database with conflict management attempts in the years 1995 to 2000, to pay for the travel and hotel expenses of the particpants of the Workshop, and finally to prepare this volume.

It is my sincere hope that this volume can contribute, at least a little bit, to reduce the suffering of humans.

ROBERT TRAPPL

Chapter 1

Introduction

Robert Trappl
Medical University of Vienna and Austrian Research Institute for Artificial Intelligence, Vienna, Austria

> *"Even by the standards of war, some of the atrocities in eastern Congo are shocking. Zainabo Alfani, for example, was stopped by men in uniform on a road in Ituri last year. She and 13 other women were ordered to strip, to see if they had long vaginal lips, which the gunmen believed would have magical properties. The 13 others did not, and were killed on the spot. Zainabo did. The gunmen cut them off and then gang-raped her. Then they cooked and ate her two daughters in front of her. They also ate chunks of Zainabo's flesh. She escaped, but had contracted HIV. She told her story to the UN in February, and died in March."*
>
> —© The Economist Newspaper Limited, London (June 11th, 2005).

After reading this passage from a recent issue of The Economist, can one go back to "normal"? Not easily. And even if one thinks that the research on computer-aided methods for conflict resolution and prevention can only contribute a tiny bit to help preventing such horrible events, one has to work on that. The more so as there are already programs available which calculate the risk of losses for a potential aggressor, e.g. the Tactical, Numerical, Deterministic Model (TNDM), developed by the Dupuy Institute (http://www.dupuyinstitute.org/tndm.htm, last checked 23 Sept 2005); even though programs of this kind sometimes may encourage an intervention in an unjust war.

But "Programming for Peace" should not mean "peace at any price". It even could mean "war" in order to establish "long-term peace". The title invites misinterpretation. But, to take a historic example, (nearly) all Europeans wholeheartedly welcomed the decision of the USA to enter the war against Hitler's Germany and its allies.

Researchers of international relations soon became aware of the potential of computers for their work. Already in the Eighties of the last century data sets were compiled, such as the Correlates of War (COW) by David Singer (e.g. Leng, 1987), focusing on 30 crises selected from the 1915-1975 period, or the World Events Interaction Survey (WEIS, Schrodt, 1991). But also in Europe, in Germany, to be precise, the *Arbeitsgemeinschaft für Kriegsursa-*

R. Trappl (ed.), Programming for Peace, 1–8.

chenforschung (AKUF) compiled a database covering "all martial conflicts" between 1944 and 1984 (AKUF, 1987).

For the analysis, Mallery (1988) and Alker et al. (1991) attempted to use natural language processing methods to create semantic networks ("text models") from texts related to political problem solving (the RELATUS project). Thorson and Sylvan (1982) and Anderson and Thorson (1982) described an interactive cognitive model that supported counterfactual simulation of President Kennedy's decision process during the Cuban Missile Crisis.

UNCLESAM (Job and Johnson, 1991) was a rule-based simulation of the US decsion-making regarding the Dominican Republic between 1961 and 1965. Another study focused on the analysis of responses of the Soviet Union to crises in Eastern Europe, specifically the "Czechoslovakian Crisis" of 1968 (Mefford, 1986). His program matched histories against cases to assemble composite precedents representing courses of action leading from the present into the future. In this area of the Cold War also specific Artificial Intelligence projects were proposed, in order to reduce the likelihood of having a "hot" war: the joint development, i.e. by scientists both of the USA and the USSR of an intercultural knowledge base, an English-Russian/Russian-English translation program, and a crisis handling expert system (Trappl, 1986).

A more detailed overview of the research in this time period can be found in Trappl and Miksch (1991), an edited volume of contributions from leading researchers in Hudson (1991).

Present-day computers allow for the development of larger databases with much more variables, sometimes with automated updates, statistical analyses of far higher complexity, elaborate simulation models, and even interactive uses of these databases. It may, sometimes, be of interest to investigate why some complex methods, developed and/or applied in the Eighties, were phased out and others entered the scientific arena. An overview of current research can often be found in the special issues of the *Journal of Conflict Resolution*, and a comparison of different research methodologies for studying conflict in international relations is given in the book by Maoz et al. (2004).

This volume, however, is focused on one specific task: the study and application of computer-aided methods for international conflict resolution and prevention. Since conflicts are a world-wide phenomenon, the majority of the contributors to this volume still come from the USA—no wonder!—but also scientists from Austria, Canada, Germany, New Zealand and Switzerland have contributed.

This volume is structured into three parts according to only slightly overlaping categories:

- Part I: the collection of information or the development of databases and their analyses by statistical means,
- Part II: the application of complex analytical methods like wavelet analysis, hidden Markov models, multi-layer perceptrons, self-organizing maps, decision trees, case-based reasoning, and rule learning,
- Part III: complex theoretical studies but with a strong application component.

All of the contributions are aiming at preventing or ending conflicts.

Part I

In chapter 2, “Conflict Resolution by Democracies and Dictatorships: Are Democracies Better in Resolving Conflicts?”, Frank R. Pfetsch computes, among others, using the KOSIMO database developed under his guidance, a ranking of 162 individual countries with regard to their endangerment, security, and potential to resolve conflicts, with the result that democracies rank distinctly higher in the resolution index than dictatorships. The much smaller number of violent conflicts of democracies compared to autocracies and compared to the total sum of conflicts indicates that democracies can resolve conflicts better. This is also valid for belligerent encounters. The calculations also show which states are especially endangered and which are specially secure.

In chapter 3, “Trade Liberalization and Political Instability in Developing Countries”, Margit Bussmann and colleagues study, in a dataset of 90 developing countries for the time period 1978-1997, whether free trade reduces the risk of political instability and whether the process of liberalization increases this risk. With regard to political violence, free trade has a conflict reducing effect in the long term—but no effect in the short term. Furthermore, the suspicion that countries on their way to a more open economy are more susceptible to instability cannot be supported. Their results suggest, among others, that free trade has a conflict-reducing effect especially for political violence. The results are supplementary to the findings of the liberal peace on the interstate level.

In chapter 4, “Computer Assisted Early Warning—the FAST Example”, Heinz Krummenacher introduces the political early warning system FAST. FAST is a German acronym which stands for early analysis of tensions and fact-finding. This system aims at enhancing political decision makers’ ability to identify critical developments in a timely manner so that political strategies can be formulated to either prevent or limit destructive effects of violent conflicts or identify windows of opportunity for peace building. FAST combines field investigation by annual fact finding missions, a weekly event data analysis and a daily qualitative analysis, i.e. constant monitoring, with permanent external expertise by an expert network.

In chapter 5, "Country Indicators for Foreign Policy: Developing an Indicators-Based User Friendly Risk Assessment and Early Warning Capability", David Carment and colleagues present this project, acronym "CIFP" as an ongoing effort to identify and assemble statistical information conveying the key-features of the political, economic, social and cultural environment of countries around the world. The data provides at-a-glance global overviews, issue-based perspectives and country performance measures. The foundation of CIFP methodology is the use of structural indicator analysis of latent conflict potential.

In chapter 6, "The Confman.2002 Data Set: Developing Cases and Indices of Conflict Management to Predict Conflict Resolution", Jacob Bercovitch and Robert Trappl present this dataset which was initiated at the University of Canterbury under the direction of the first author in the mid-1980ies. The main concern has been to provide a comprehensive, chronological account of international conflict between 1945 and 2000 and to shed some light on its occurrence and management. The international conflict management dataset is an extension of this work and focuses on the conditions that make international mediation and negotiation successful and on the application of sophisticated data-analysis methods to identify and predict conditions of conflict management. In this chapter an operational definition of conflict and different variables, especially those related to the parties and to conflict management as such, are introduced. Furthermore, the many results of statistical analysis are presented.

Part II

In chapter 7, "Events, Patterns, and Analysis: Forecasting International Conflict in the Twenty-First Century", Devika Subramanian and Richard J. Stoll stress at first the importance of anticipating conflict: if conflicts cannot be anticipated, what chance do we have to prevent or stop them? They propose a research project to improve the ability to anticipate serious international conflict by using a combination of online media sources, analytic techniques and knowledge derived from research in international conflict. After a thorough theoretical analysis of the topic the authors focus on the primary building block of their research, the event, and they propose to automate the extraction process from media sources. In their research they will pursue two paths of analysis: the first will involve attempting to predict the onset of serious international conflict strictly from patterns in previous events. The second path will involve building models that will increase the understanding of the process by which conflicts escalate. As an exploratory task, they chose the ebb and flow of the Cold War, in the period 1966-1978, and analyze human-coded data with a wavelet, the result being a high correspondence to historic key events in this period.

In chapter 8, "Forecasting Conflict in the Balkans Using Hidden Markov Models", Philip A. Schrodt attempts to forecast conflicts in former Yugoslavia for the period January 1991 to January 1999 by using political and military events reported in the lead sentences of Reuters news service stories. These sentences were coded into the World Events Interaction Survey (WEIS) event data scheme. The forecasting scheme involves randomly selecting eight 100-event "templates" taken at 1-, 3-, or 6-month forecasting lags for high-conflict and low-conflict weeks. A seperate HMM is developed for the high-conflict-week sequences and the low-conflict-week sequences. Forecasting is done by determining whether a sequence of observed events fits the high-conflict or low-conflict model with higher probability. The author describes the outcome of his experiments, summarizing that, among others, it is possible to use models with substantially fewer parameters without markedly decreasing the accuracy of the predictions; in fact, predictions of the high-conflict periods actually increase in accuracy quite substantially.

In chapter 9, "Analyzing International Conflict Management by Neural Computation", Georg Dorffner and colleagues report about the application of pattern recognition methods from the area of neural computation exploring their capabilities for finding structure in the CONFMAN database. Two methods were tested, namely, so-called Multi-layer Perceptrons (MLPs), nonlinear classifiers, and so-called Self-organizing Maps (SOMs), a clustering and visualization method. A thorough analysis of this non-linear classification revealed only minor differences as compared to linear classifiers, yet classification performance significantly above chance could be reached. Self-organizing Maps revealed clusters and substructure in the data. In a third exploration it could be shown with these methods that there are significant differences in the two subsets 1945-1989 and 1990-2000; conflict management outcome is also more predictable after 1989 using an MLP.

In chapter 10, "Modeling International Negotiation: Statistical and Machine Learning Approaches", Daniel Druckman and colleagues study the question of which factor(s) is(are) the best predictor(s) or discriminator(s) of the outcome in an international negotiation. In this chapter statistical findings, primarily correlation analyses, were compared with two types of machine learning approaches, decision trees and rule learning. The analyses were conducted on a dataset of 42 cases where each case was coded in terms of 16 features and in the 5 categories of international negotiation objectives. Comparing the results, the authors conclude that the combined approaches of statistical and machine learning analyses yield a larger picture of what is happening in negotiations.

In chapter 11, "Machine Learning Methods for Better Understanding, Resolving, and Preventing International Conflicts", Robert Trappl and colleagues want to answer the question if it is possible to aid decision makers or their advisers who want to prevent the outbreak of hostilities/wars or to end them through negotiations or mediation, by giving them recommendations as the result of applying artificial intelligence, especially machine learning methods, to existing war/crisis/mediation databases. Using the CONFMAN database, they start with showing a decision tree, presenting the most important factors for successful outcome of a conflict management attempt. By differentiating between the cases before and in 1989 and the ones in 1990 and after—in 1989 the fall of the Berlin Wall marking the transition from two superpowers to one—they obtain a decision tree with better prediction accuracy than the overall one. Computing decision trees for different world regions shows that some of these trees have an even higher predictive value. Furthermore, two interfaces are presented which were developed by the authors in order to enable decision makers to find out cases similar to a given crisis situation, for the purpose of either investigating which conflict management methods are most likely to be successful, or helping to assess the risk of its escalation in order to more efficiently prepare humanitarian aid.

Part III

In chapter 12, "New Methods for Conflict Data", Will Lowe explores some of the methods international relations researchers apply to event data and to conflict databases. Probabilistic reformulations and developments are proposed for their improvement. State space models should allow more realistic models to be fitted to event data and probabilistic expert systems should extend the range of theories testable with conflict databases.

In chapter 13, "Information, Power, and War", William Reed employs a simple ultimatum game of bargaining to evaluate two traditional power-centric theories of world politics, balance of power and power transition theory. The formal and empirical analyses demonstrate that as states approach power parity, information asymmetries are greatest, thus enhancing the probability of militarized conflict. Uncertainty is a central cause of conflict emergence and is correlated with the distribution of observable capabilities. Recognizing the relationship between the distribution of power and uncertainty offers a more sophisticated interpretation of power-centric explanation of world politics.

In chapter 14, "Modeling Effects of Emotion and Personality on Political Decision-Making. Application to International Conflict Prevention and Resolution", Eva Hudlicka describes a generic methodology for representing the effects of multiple interacting emotional states and personality traits on decision making and an associated computational cognitive architecture which implements this methodology. She presents results of an evaluation experiment that demonstrates the architecture's ability to model individual tactical decision-making and to produce observable differences resulting from distinct individual profiles. She then discusses how the methodology and architecture could be extended to model strategic, political decision making, and how it could support a variety of activities geared towards international conflict prevention and resolution. She concludes with specific theoretical and pragmatic challenges associated with this approach to computer-aided conflict prevention and resolution.

In chapter 15, "Peacemaker 2020: A System for Global Conflict Analysis and Resolution; A Work of Fiction and A Research Challenge" Kirstie Bellman uses the approach of designing a complex system by starting with a solution and working backwards. Her story takes place in the year 2050, when a lecture is given about the analyses of 30 years of performance of the Peacemaker System 2020. She continues with the discussion of the technology and the issues underlying the system, especially pervasive computing, sophisticated "de-Babeling", new database construction and analytic techniques. Role-playing simulation, social worlds and story logics as a fundamental key to analyses could be three new issues for peacefare.

This chapter of Kirstie Bellmann would be a perfect conclusion of this volume if it were not that the important current threat, terrorism, was not treated in any of the chapters. Therefore one more, short chapter was added.

In chapter 16, "Concluding Remarks: And Terrorism?", Robert Trappl shows first why the standard databases in international relations are of hardly any use with respect to terrorism and briefly gives three examples of databases developed for terroristic events. He furthermore presents examples of computer-aided methods applied to those databases, namely the analysis by time-series and modeling networks of terroristic groups in order to find better means for their destabilization.

The final remark in Kirstie Bellmann's chapter is the best conclusion for this introduction:

"Hopefully, this paper and its companion papers in this volume will start the discussion towards both experimentation and experience in Peacefare."

References

Anderson, P. A., and Thorson, S. J., 1982, Artifcial Intelligence based simulations of foreign policy decsion making, *Behavioral Science* **27**:176-193.

AKUF, 1987, Verzeichnis der Kriege nach dem Zweiten Weltkrieg, in Steinweg, R. , ed., *Kriegsursachen*, Suhrkamp, Frankfurt/Main.

Alker, H. R. Jr., Duffy, G., Hurwitz, R., and Mallery, J. C., 1991, Text modeling for international politics: a tourist guide to RELATUS, in Hudson, V. M., ed., *Artificial Intelligence and International Politics*, Westview Press, Boulder, CO.

Hudson V. M., ed., 1991, *Artifical Intelligence and International Politics*, Westview Press, Boulder, CO.

Job, B. L., and Johnson, D., 1991, The Application of a Rule-Based Model of U.S. Foreign Policy Making, in Hudson, V. M., ed., *Artificial Intelligence and International Politics*, Westview Press, Boulder, CO.

Leng, R. J., 1987, *Behavioral Correlates of War, 1816-1975*, ICPSR.

Mallery, J. C., 1988, *Thinking about Foreign Policy: Finding an Appropriate Role for Artificial Intelligence Computers*, Annual Meeting of the International Studies Association, St. Louis, MI.

Maoz, Z., Mintz, A., Morgan, T. C., Palmer G., and Stoll, R. J., eds., 2004, *Multiple Paths to Knowledge in International Relations. Methodology in the Study of Conflict Management and Conflict Resolution,* Lexington Books, Lanham, MD.

Mefford, D., 1986, Analogical reasoning and the definition of the situation: back to Snyder for concepts and forward to Artificial Intelligence for method, in Hermann, C. F. et al., eds., *New Directions in the Comparative Study of Foreign Policy*, Allen and Unwin, New York.

Thorson, S. T., and Sylvan, D. A., 1982, Counterfactuals and the Cuban missile crisis, *International Studies Quarterly* **26**:539-571.

Schrodt P. A., 1991, Artificial Intelligence and international relations: an overview, in Hudson, V. M., ed., *Artificial Intelligence and International Politics*, Westview Press, Boulder, CO.

Trappl, R., 1986, Reducing international tension through Artificial Intelligence: a proposal for 3 projects, in Trappl, R., ed., *Power, Autonomy, Utopia: New Approaches Toward Complex Systems*, Plenum, New York.

Trappl, R., and Miksch, S., 1991, Can Artificial Intelligence contribute to Peacefare?, in *Proceedings Artifcial Intelligence AI'91*, Technical University, Prague, 21-30.

PART I

Chapter 2

Conflict Resolution by Democracies and Dictatorships: Are Democracies Better in Resolving Conflicts?

Frank R. Pfetsch
University of Heidelberg, Germany

The chapter deals with the capacities of various regimes to master conflicts. Does the regime character make a difference? Are democratic regimes better in resolving conflicts than autocratic or transitory regimes? The study draws from a wide range of indicators for the independent variables 'challenges' and 'support' (both are put together in order of ranking with indices as to their management capacities) for each existing state. Besides these explanatory factors, regime factors are calculated independently. The dependent variable 'conflict' draws on the data set Kosimo in two ways: first, with the number of conflicts occurring between 1945 and 2000; and second, with the weighted number of internal and neighboring conflicts only. These conflicts are then confronted with the management capacities of each state. Cross-calculations show that, not surprisingly, on the whole democracies have had a better record in the management of conflicts than other regimes.

1 INTRODUCTION: FORMULATION OF THE PROBLEM

The discussion about the so-called 'democratic peace' has been going on for some decades.[1] What is at stake is not the observation that democracies are not going to war against democracies. The 'democratic peace' comes "as close as anything we have to an empirical law in international relations" (among many others Levy, 1988: 662; Bremer, 1992; Maoz and Russett, 1993; Gleditsch and Hegre, 1997; Raknerud and Hegre, 1997). The discussion concentrates rather on the theoretical foundation of that "law".[2]

1. Foremost in the journals *Journal of Peace Research*, *International Security*, *Zeitschrift für Internationale Beziehungen*, and *Journal of Conflict Resolution*.

R. Trappl (ed.), Programming for Peace, 11–47.

Three approaches can be distinguished in this debate: one position holds that internal factors cause democratic behavior (Mousseau and Shi, 1999). Realists (among others Layne, 1994; Russett et al., 1995) put forward external factors that cause such behavior. A third position states that both internal and external factors equally cause peace between democracies (Czempiel, 1996). According to a variant of this position the international environment is responsible not per se but through democratic institutions (Moravcsik, 1998; Randall and Peceny, 2002).

In these camps differentiations are being proposed: on the domestic side, structural factors such as parliaments, checks and balances, public opinions, elites (Owen, 1994; Russett et al.,1995) or the media (van Belle, 1997) are responsible for the peaceful behavior, and on the normative side factors such as culture, democratic values or the media (Layne, 1994; van Belle 1997) are mentioned.

As to the external factors, studies related to the following themes have been made: the perception of states of each other (Owen, 1994), the disposition towards military interventions (Kegley and Hermann, 1996; Tures, 2001), the diffusion of democracy through democracies (Randall and Peceny, 2002). Does the intensity of trade relations between states guarantee peace? (Gowa, 1994; Mansfield, 1994; Hegre, 2000). What is the role of the power status, of alliances and international regimes or of the existence of a hegemon (Weede, 1983; Bremer, 1993; Maoz and Russett, 1993; Henderson, 2002)? Are existing power constellations and their perception of any importance (Owen, 1994)? In these debates, realists and liberalists confront each other. The realists question the 'democratic peace' approach by stressing anarchy, competition and self-help instead.

Some authors look at the relationships between internal and external factors: external threats tend to lead to authoritarian structures (Hintze, 1975; Baade, 1962); some argue that external crises do not change democratic structures (Mousseau and Shi, 1999). Another area of concern is the adequacy of Kant's propositions in his philosophical sketch "Zum ewigen Frieden" (Layne, 1994; Robinson, 2001; Randall and Peceny, 2002).

As against these studies, my investigation proposes the following steps of inquiry:

First, we deal with the *explanandum*, i.e. the conflicts that have occurred during the fifty years of the second half of the 20th century; this investigation

[2]. Some other formulations read as follows: Democracies do not start wars against each other; democratic nations are rarely, if ever, on opposite sides in wars, democracies join other democracies in case they are at war (Hegre, 1997). "Democratic dyads are far more peaceful than non-democratic and mixed dyads" (van Belle, 1997: 405). However, democracies are on the whole not more peaceful than other regimes; most of the wars after World War II have been fought by democracies but not against one another.

is based on a very broad information base on conflicts including violent as well as non-violent, internal as well as external behavior.

Secondly, this article suggests that the *explanans* for observable conflict behavior is the result of the difference between potential threat and potential support of states: a country's insecurity/endangerment and security/support as well as—deduced from this—its ability to resolve conflicts (empowerment) are operationalized and transformed into measurable quantities. It is the empowerment and governance capability that explains success in conflict management. As a result, countries are ranked according to their specific threat and security index.

Thirdly, the data base on regimes is rather comprehensive and is calculated independently of the measures mentioned before; it allows the identification of countries according to their regimes. As a final result, I present a list which ranks most of the countries of the world according to their specific capabilities to deal with conflicts in order to identify the regimes that are better equipped to settle conflicts. At the same time, the index serves to identify specifically endangered states and, through pointing out the supporting factors, to discuss the possibilities of non-violent ways to resolve conflicts.

This chapter takes into account the above mentioned studies about internal and external determinants and tries to combine these approaches and to test them against a broad range of conflicts that have occurred during the fifty years since 1950. Which states can best handle conflicts and which have a greater capacity to resolve them? Does the character of the regime (democratic, transitory, or autocratic) and the quality of governance make a difference in resolving conflicts?

2 THE MODEL

The *explanandum*, resolving conflicts, is the result of institutional realities (structural level) and political capabilities (operational level) of states and constellations of states (*explanans*). The action of a government is seen as dependent on three determining factors: the conflict-generating factors, the oppositely working conflict-mitigating factors and, additionally, the regime factors.

The basic model assumes that actions of governments depend on three groups of factors: firstly, governments have to master demands, challenges/endangerments or risks[3]. These factors indicate the insecurity of a country. Secondly, governments, as a response, receive support, legitimation and

3. I use these terms as interchangeable.

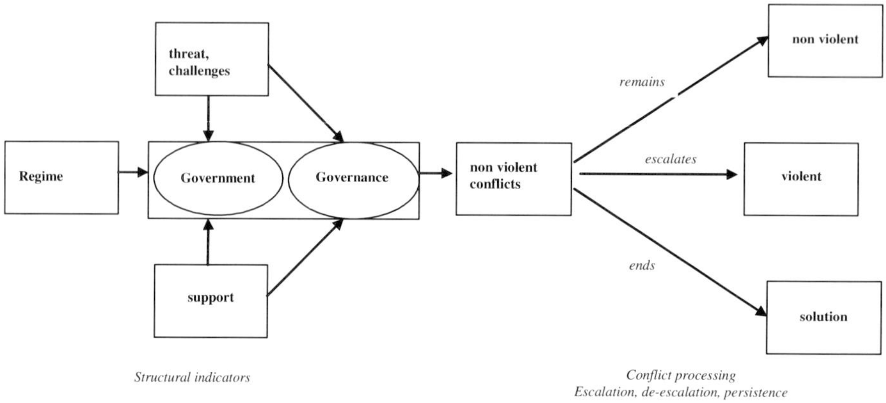

Figure 2.1. Dynamic phase model

capacities to act. These factors indicate the security. Thirdly, and in addition, the character of the regime also determines its ability to manage conflicts. The discrepancy between endangerment/challenge-indicating factors and support-indicating factors reflects the freedom of action of a given government. If a regime is confronted with a challenge leading to a conflict, then the conflict develops violently or non-violently according to the regime's action and/or reaction. The way a regime handles a conflict depends on its capacity to dynamically process the conflict, on the management (governance) of it, on the issue involved and on the actions of the opposing side, etc.

3 CONFLICT-PROMOTING AND CONFLICT-MITIGATING FACTORS

The theoretical literature mentions numerous factors of individual actors, society, state and behavior between states that could lead to peace-endangering situations. I will list here some important theoretical approaches that can be found in the literature on the history of ideas:

As factors that *endanger peace* the following can be found in the literature: fear, threat, ambition of rulers and non-ruling elites, power politics, the calculus of power, power rivalry, misperceptions, aggression, fanaticism, ideology, belief of a conspiracy, autistic behavior, military ambition (militarism), proliferation of (nuclear) weapons, escalation of conflicts through rivalry (security dilemma), interests of a power cartel, so-called 'rogue states' (weak states, absence of centrally effective and responsive institutions), increase of the number of states on a global scale, collapse of systems and regimes, imbalanced development of states, economic interests (access to raw materials and sales markets), expansive ideologies (fascism, communism), proximity of countries to one another (contiguous countries), fragmentation, segmentation, discrimination (nationalities, minorities, and ethnic and religious groups), economic inequality, exhaustion of resources, and finally the character of a regime (dictatorship).

As *peacekeeping factors*, the literature mentions the perception of security (no threat), cooperative strategies in negotiating conflicts, open foreign politics without aggressive intentions, calculated restraint in the use of weapons (politics of deterrence), disarmament, end of territorial expansion, social justice, free commerce, geographic distance, international organizations, alliances, integrated regimes, actions of non-governmental organizations, good conflict management, balance of powers, the existence of a hegemonic power, good governance, codification and suability of human and civil rights, world opinion (international forums, media, so-called ‘CNN factor’), and finally the character of the regime ('democratic peace'). (Pfetsch, 1994: 255f.)

From this unqualified list of factors, I have chosen those which allow for operationalization and transformation into measurable quantities. I assume that, by this, I capture the most relevant factors. The dynamic model can serve as orientation for the interdependence of actions and effects, and for logical argumentations respectively.

4 STATES

The goal of my study is to present data on every state (non-state actors are not considered in this analysis) in the form of an index which makes possible the creation of a ranking of states according to the degree of endangerment, security and susceptibility to conflicts, as well as their ability to resolve conflicts. Which states are the most endangered and which states enjoy security?

All states with available data[4] and of a certain size (having a population of at least 500,000) were included. According to these criteria, there are at least

4. When establishing the list of states and their regime type the following has to be taken into consideration: The number of states has not remained stable in the course of fifty years. There are many states that were added after their independence. There are states that have changed their economic potential and political regime. Some states have been newly created after larger units have dissolved (Yugoslavia, USSR, Pakistan, Ethiopia, Czechoslovakia; UAR, etc.) or through unification (Germany, Yemen, Vietnam, Tanzania), and some have remained divided (North and South Korea). Some states have changed their names (Rhodesia now Zimbabwe, Burma now Myanmar, Zaire now Congo, Dahomey now Benin, Upper Volta now Burkina-Faso) or carry different names in different languages (White Russia or Belarus). Finally, there are areas that are not at all or only partly recognized by the world community (West Sahara, Northern Cyprus).

30 states that did not enter the calculations, leaving 162 states. The states were divided into three regime categories: democratic, transitory and autocratic regimes. Transitory ones can, in some cases, be understood as a residual factor.

I have tried to accommodate changes by forming a time series of decades for the most important indicators. In this way, one can see how many types of regimes predominantly existed within the different decades, and how many conflicts appeared and with what intensity.

Independently from the previously considered index calculation, the states are now defined according to their regime character. Therefore, an array of quantitative and qualitative studies is taken into account each of which emphasizes various criteria for political regimes. The criteria mentioned most often for democratic regimes are the following:

- All political power emanates from the people and remains in its control (participation).
- Those who exercise power are duty-bound to present to the voters their programs and leadership (openness of the selection process).
- Elections are to be held under competitive conditions between at least two parties (competition in elections).
- Political parties must be democratic in their structure and must be led as voluntary organizations and not as instruments of the government.
- Individual rights and fundamental freedoms must be guaranteed (political and civil liberties).
- Public opinion is not allowed to be unilaterally determined through the manipulation by the government (civilian division of powers).
- Rule of law must be recognized.
- The power of the political center must be constitutionally limited and controlled (limitation of power, division of powers) (Pfetsch, 1985: 176; Beetham, 1995; Dahl, 1999; Schmidt, 2000).

Three quantitative studies on democracy (Vanhanen, 1984, 1990, 1997; Freedom House, 2001; Polity IV: Marshall and Jaggers, 2000) take into account the most important characteristics of such an understanding of democracy, e.g. competition, participation, the guarantee of civil and political individual rights and fundamental freedoms as well as the limitation of power.

The Finnish researcher on democracy Tatu Vanhanen (Vanhanen, 1984, 1997) chose two variables for his index of democracy (D-Index), namely competition and participation.[5] In addition and as a correction to this simple democracy index the more normative approach by Freedom House on political rights (PR) and civil liberties (CL) should be included.[6] As a third and more reliable study, I draw on the Polity IV Project by Monty G. Marshall and Keith Jaggers (2000) which consists of three indicators for democracy and autocracy: the degree of competition and political participation; openness of the selection process for political personnel; and the limitation of executive power. The decade value for the regime character was calculated with these data (see Table 2.1.) because the data collection was done according to a unified, all-embracing criterion of three regime types and is available for the complete time period of five decades. In contrast, the other two sets of data are formed either according to a dichotomized criterion (Vanhanen) or the data are not available for all five decades (Freedom House).

All three sets of data on regime types indicate the general trend of an increasing number of states and of an increasing number of democratic states. Until the eighties, the number of autocratic states increases, too. It is only in the nineties that there are more democracies than autocracies. All sets of data show this important finding: that the number of democratic states has a tendency to increase, with the exception of the seventies bringing an end to decolonization.

Table 2.1. Political regimes according to different sets of data (Marshall and Jaggers, Vanhanen, Freedom House), decades 50s to the 90s

Regimes of countries	50s			60s			70s			80s			90s			End of 90s
	Marshall&Jaggers	Freedomhouse	Vanhanen	Marshall&Jaggers	Freedomhouse	Vanhanen	Marshall&Jaggers	Freedomhouse	Vanhanen	Marshall&Jaggers	Freedomhouse	Vanhanen	Marshall&Jaggers	Freedomhouse	Vanhanen	Combined regime-index
Democracies	37	-	32	41	-	37	37	34	33	47	41	56	78	52	98	75
Transitory regimes	14	-	-	24	-	-	18	44	-	17	49	-	34	61	-	29
Autocracies	38	-	45	59	-	73	80	59	78	71	49	81	44	45	62	58
Total of countries	89	-	77	124	-	110	135	137	111	135	139	137	156	158	160	162

For the nineties the three sets of data (Marshall and Jaggers, Vanhanen, Freedom House) were calculated into a combined index according to the most possible concordance (see Table 2.1.). This combined index is included in the calculation of conflict susceptibility and is contained in the list in Appendix 2.

5. See Survey of indicators in Appendix 1.

6. See Survey of indicators in Appendix 1.

5 FIFTY YEARS OF CONFLICT BEHAVIOR (1950-2000)

I present the panorama of conflicts by using the database Kosimo[7]. Each state is presented in its empirically observed conflict behavior, whereby two different sets of data are required: first, the absolute number of observable conflicts over five decades, independent of their internal composition and their external environment, of their intensity and their geographic location so that their overall involvement can be determined; and second, a qualified number of incidences of internal and neighboring conflicts so that relationships to the potential measurements could be established. This measurement includes the intensity, i.e. the weights given to the conflicts with the factors 1 for latent conflicts, 2 for crises concerning conflicts that show no or little violence, 3 for serious crises and 4 for wars concerning violent conflicts. The first set thus contains the absolute number of all conflicts, non-weighted, national, neighboring and international, the second set the weighted number of internal conflicts plus conflicts with neighboring states, weighted according to intensity.

5.1 Absolute Numbers

Chart 2.1 shows the increase in the absolute number of conflicts that are recorded over five decades from 1950 to 2000. The differentiation between violent and non-violent conflicts shows that until and into the seventies violent conflicts increased dramatically. Afterwards, the number of non-violent conflicts is prevalent. With autocratic regimes, the dominance of non-violent and violent conflicts changes as an average over decades. After the eighties, non-violent conflicts are prevalent also in these regimes.

5.2 Weighted Numbers

The picture changes when we consider the conflict intensities: In course of five decades, democracies and dictatorships both have waged more violent than non-violent conflicts. In contrast to democracies more violent conflicts are attributed to dictatorships. This finding not only holds for absolute figures but also in relation to the existing number of regimes. The intensity of vio-

7. Kosimo is a conflict data bank developed by the Institute of Political Science of the University of Heidelberg and contains, in its first version, 661 conflicts that can be reduced to 287 basic conflicts occurring between 1945 and 1995, with 28 descriptive variables. Further information in: F.R. Pfetsch and Ch. Rohloff, 2000. The extended relational data bank Kosimo 2.0 contains 630 conflicts with five categories of intensity and 3300 intensity codings altogether; thus each conflict changed, on the average, five times in intensity. See: www.kosimo.de.

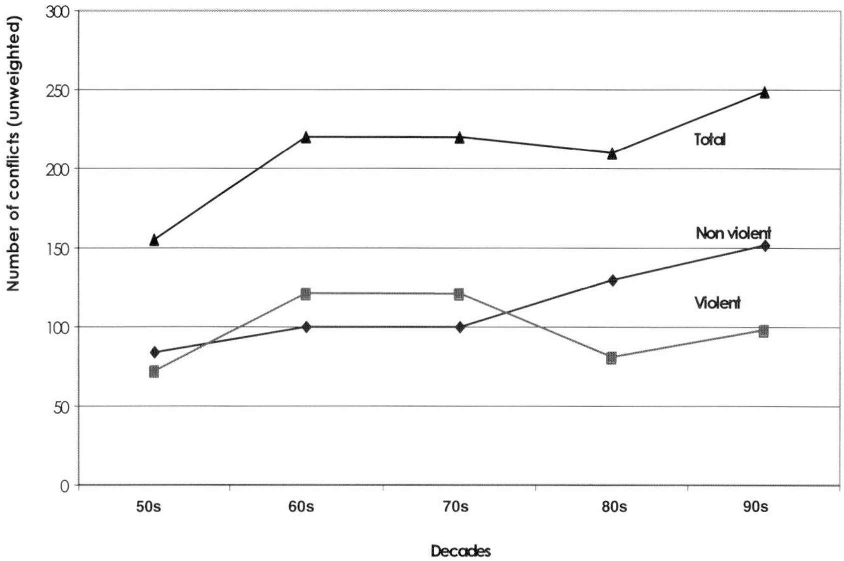

Chart 2.1. Conflicts (non-weighted) violent and non-violent, by decades

lence (number of violent conflicts in relation to existing regimes) is twice or three times higher in dictatorships than in democratic regimes (see Table 2.2., next page, and Chart 2.2., page 31).

Table 2.2. Intensity of violence according to decades and regimes

Decades	50	60	70	80	90
Dictatorships	0,97	1,37	1,01	0,62	1,00
Democracies	0,47	0,29	0,32	0,32	0,36

Sources: Kosimo for conflicts and Polity IV for regimes
Number of violent conflicts in relation to existing regimes

6 THE POTENTIAL DANGER FOR STATES

In the beginning, I ask the question whether the internal composition and the external environment of a state indicate the danger of violent conflict behavior. From the many factors that trigger or promote conflicts, five indicators have been selected.

First of all, there is the internal composition of a state. The pressure by minorities, various groups and communities put on the central government as well as rivalries among various sub-nationalities have led to most of today's conflicts (Pfetsch and Rohloff, 2000: 101). Ethnic conflicts for independence, autonomy, self-determination or secession of minority groups and power rivalries for governmental positions have been most frequent since the seventies. “Ethnic conflicts have become especially widespread” (Donal Horowitz, 1985: xi) and “ethnic groups fight all the time” (Daniel P. Moynihan, 1993: 5). James D. Fearon and David D. Laitin (1996; 2003) however remind us that, among ethnic groups, cooperative relationships can be found more often than violent encounters. This observation has to be taken with reservations since the empirical basis is very small and selective. In the future, the ethnic-religious conflicts will dominate since there will hardly be any more violent conflicts between states. Western states (Spain, Great Britain, etc.) will be affected as well as autocratic (Iran, Iraq, etc.) and transitory regimes (Bosnia, Turkey, Russia etc.).

The collection of data on minority groups in a country is highly problematic. There is no universally accepted definition of a minority. Nevertheless, the U.N. have given a definition of the term mentioning three criteria. It states that a minority has to be a) of a non-ruling group of the population that possess stable ethnic, religious or linguistic traditions; b) it has to be large enough in order to develop such characteristics; and c) it has to be loyal towards the respective state. However, this definition does not capture the fact that, first, there are minority groups that are not necessarily and/or only partially loyal to the state; and second, that with regard to the question of their potential endangerment, nothing is said about their behavior. There exist a large number of minority groups, whether defined ethnically, religiously, culturally, linguistically, etc., which despite all their heterogeneity do not raise claims to change their situation. As to the drawback which exists in the difficulty to distinguish between rebelling from non-rebelling groups, Ted Gurr, with his *Risk of Minority Index,* considers the behavior of such groups shown in the past (Gurr, 2000). Still there is the shortcoming that population groups are included in the risk index which are without a territorial basis and are to be grouped under Kymlicka’s term of multiculturalism (Kymlicka, 1997). One should therefore compare Gurr’s data with the data on groups which are living in communities that have a coherent territory within a given country. Only these minorities should be counted, because only such groups can develop a potential of action.

As another approach to measure the heterogeneity of a country indicator, Tatu Vanhanen’s ethnic homogeneity indicator was tested. It lists the proportion of the largest groups in a country. I transformed this indicator into a heterogeneity index by calculating the difference to one hundred. The greater the difference, the more groups exist in a country and the more heterogeneous it is.

Second, when citizens flee a country for a neighboring one or one that is considered to be secure for refuge, this expresses the political and economical instability of that country and its government. The number of refugees who flee their country of origin for a destination country offers such evidence. In both countries the political stability is affected by refugees: those fleeing from their country because its insecurity has become so crucial, and those fleeing to the destination country because the native population feels or could feel threatened and this could lead to xenophobic riots. The flight of the Hutus from Rwanda to Zaire, Tanzania and Burundi, caused by civil war, destabilized also the destination countries. This also happened with the Palestinians seeking refuge in Lebanon and Jordan, and the Salvadorian civil war refugees in Honduras as well as the Nicaraguan Indios in Honduras and the Tamils in Sri Lanka. As a measurement for the proportion of political refugees to the entire population, we have chosen to count only political and not economic refugees. The refugees in destination countries are weighted by a factor of 0.33 because it can be assumed that refugees indicate more the instability of the country from which the refugees come than to which they go.

Third, the real or alleged threat with which a government is confronted can indicate a perceived danger. Christopher Layne (1994) found that the perception of threat determines the actions of governments in situations of crises. The threat that a government perceives can be measured by the relative amount of military expenditure, because the countries that arm themselves are mostly those that feel threatened and are in regions of tension, such as Greece and Turkey, Pakistan and India, Israel and neighboring Arab states, etc. Thus, I take the consequences of a threat as an indicator of threat itself. Operationally, this potential of endangerment is represented by the percentage of military expenditure in GDP; for it is empirically proven that governments that feel threatened try to compensate this by the increase of their armaments. By this they trigger the so called security dilemma: neighbouring countries feel threatened as well and increase their armaments, thus escalating the arms race.

Fourth, another indicator for instability is the irregular changes of government which show, on the one hand, that there are no constitutional provisions for a peaceful change from one government to another; and, on the other hand, that there are parties, groups or individual politicians who are willing to use forceful means to conquer power positions. A study by the World Bank (2002) has, therefore, taken into account such irregular governmental changes. I have chosen the number of putsches and attempted putsches in a country as an indicator. Many countries in Africa, South America and the Middle East experience or have experienced such violent changes of power. After 1950 the list of the coups d'états or attempts is headed by Bolivia with 18, followed by Syria with 17, Iraq with 14, Sudan with 12 and Nigeria with 11. In Europe, Greece with six putsches or attempted putsches has had the most (Pfetsch and Rohloff 2000: 140-147).

Fifth, endangerment can result from the external and inter-state environment. The geo-political situation of a country and the bordering countries can determine the potential for conflict. Our empirical research shows that external threats to security mostly stem from neighbouring countries (Pfetsch and Billing 1994: 110). Also regional or universal powers can be threatening but only in times of imperialistic politics. Thus, as indicator for external threat I choose the number of neighbouring countries. The more a country has borders the higher can be the potential threat to its security.

These five variables, indicating the endangerment a country is exposed to, are normalized to a scale with hundred points. The index value (shown in Appendix 2) is calculated as a tenth of this average value. It shows the degree of endangerment of a country. In other words, the more discriminated a group/minority in a country is or perceives itself to be, the more a government perceives threat, fear to be replaced by irregular means, the more people are forced to flee, and the more neighbouring countries a country has, the greater is its potential degree of endangerment. Thus the equation reads as follows:

> Potential endangerment = F (minorities + instability/crisis + threat + non-constitutional change of government + neighbouring countries).

Hypothesis 1: It is expected that endangerment is independent from the regime type and is distributed somewhat equally among countries regardless of the type of political regime. Each regime type could be equally endangered.

Empirical test: The list of the most highly endangered states is led by Afghanistan, Angola and Bolivia followed by Uganda, Nigeria, Eritrea, Iraq, Congo (Democratic Republic of the Congo), etc., i.e. states that are not democratic. The countries with the lowest endangerment index are found among democracies (except North Korea and Moldova), e.g. Iceland, Japan, Malta, Taiwan, Ireland, Moldova, North Korea, Norway, Denmark, etc. (see lists in the appendix). The endangerment index shows on both extremes of the scale democratic and autocratic regimes, even so when the list of endangered states is led by non-democratic states and democratic regimes are found among those least endangered.

The list of countries that are ordered according to their endangerment index shows a relatively wide range of endangerment of various regimes across the three groups of countries that can be found in the first, the second and the third part of the list with 54 states in each. The Chi Square test for the entire distribution results in χ^2 (4, N = 162) = 11.857, $p < 0.05$. This means that the distribution of the regime types in all three groups with respective endangerment indices differs significantly from an accidental distribution. In other words, in terms of endangerment democracies and autocracies differ significantly from one another. The statistical test does not support hypothesis 1. However, the individual comparisons of pairs show a more differentiated picture: between the dyads democratic and transitory regimes and between autocratic and transitory states there is no statistically significant difference with regard to the index of endangerment.[8] This statistical test delivers, therefore, only limited confirmation of hypothesis 1. Diagram 2.1 shows the high average endangerment of autocratic regimes compared to transitory and democratic ones.[9]

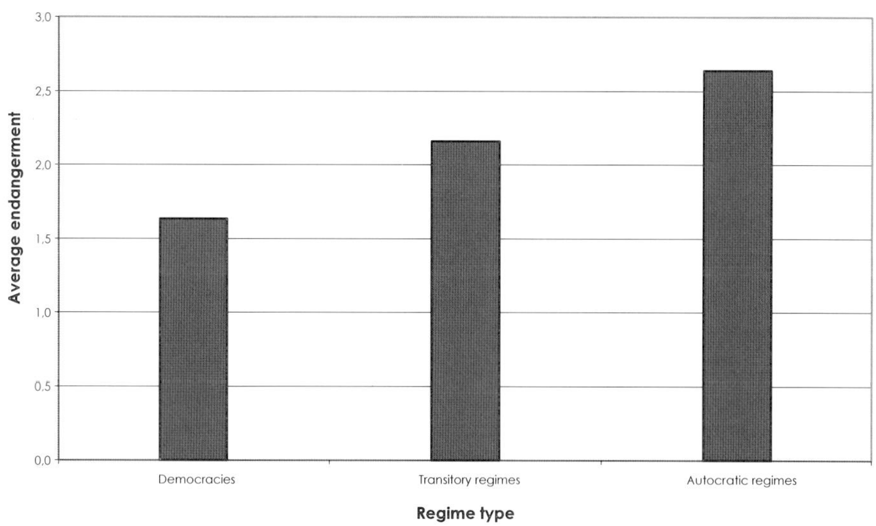

Diagram 2.1. Insecurity by regime types

The countries that show the greatest potential insecurity among the OECD states are Greece, Mexico, Switzerland, Germany, Spain, The Netherlands, as well as Turkey. The countries with the least endangerment are Japan, Ireland,

8. The Kolmogorov-Smirnov tests are calculated as individual pair comparisons that correspond to the classic Mann-Whitney U-test (See Basic Statistics Tutorial, www.conceptstew.co.uk), but are also fitting for the bound ranges as they are given.

9. Average means the sum of the endangerment values of each regime type divided by the number of states of each regime type.

Norway, Slovakia and Italy. According to the resolution index, however, Luxembourg, Ireland, Denmark, Finland, Portugal, Belgium and Norway are on top of the list. The countries with high endangerment no longer appear at the top of the list of resolution indices. They can presumably better compensate for their endangerment through better security and support, and higher legitimacy and performance. Germany for example is ranked position 22 (of 162 states) on the resolution scale, possesses relatively good resources and is ranked at position 8 on the support scale with high legitimacy and support and at rank 23 on the endangerment scale, the country has only a medium-sized danger to master.

7 SECURITY-PROMOTING FACTORS—SUPPORT

Next I attempt to measure the security potential of individual states. To what degree do states and their governments possess the capacity (resources) to resolve conflicts? The resource potential can be operationalized with indicators of the internal and external characteristics of a given regime. Four indicators have been selected as security promoting factors.

Firstly, as an indicator for the internal stability of a political regime, the degree of acceptance of a particular regime by its citizens can be mentioned. This input legitimacy can be operationalized by surveys. Also election turnouts can be taken as an indicator for acceptance. Since survey data are not available for a sufficient amount of time for all states, I have decided to use Vanhanen's (1997) collected data on voter turnout (participation) that he measured as the proportion of active voters of the entire population (not just for eligible voters). In addition, I have taken the internet data from "Election World" as an alternative indicator for legitimacy.

Secondly, as a measure for the security of a state, I take the support of states being members of an alliance or a regional union. According to the neo-idealist school, international regimes reduce the probability of wars. Interstate conflicts correlate negatively with alliances (Ostrom and Hoole, 1978; Wayman, 1990). States that are members of several organizations have better safeguards than other states. The membership in international organizations and integrated systems can thus serve as an indicator of support. Some authors therefore suggest the forming of international organizations or integrated systems as a political strategy (Hasenclever, 2002: 336). The integration in a system of leagues, alliances or systems of integration has led to the reduction of violent encounters between the members of such organizations. The empirical fact that there are hardly any more wars between countries (see Pfetsch and Rohloff, 2000) can be attributed to the existence of regional and/or universal organizations. This integration factor can be operationalized with the number of memberships a country has in international and regional organizations. It makes sense to weight the membership according to the degree of integration. Universal political (such as the U.N.) or economic organizations (such as the OECD) are weighted with factor 1, while regional organizations (such as the OAS or the OAU) are weighted with factor 2 and memberships in integrated regional organizations such as the EU with factor 5.

Thirdly, for the avoidance or mitigation of outbreaks of violence economic interrelationships can be taken as an indicator. The higher the economic interdependence between states, the less likely they go to war against each other (Henderson, 2002: 43-45; Hegre, 2000: 17). Classic economic liberalism has pointed out and numerous theoreticians have emphasized (Kant, Mill, Schumpeter, even Kautzky) that intense trade relationships are a prerequisite for and make possible peaceful coexistence (Rosecrance, 1986). The intensification of trade relations correlates negatively with the occurrence of interstate wars (Polacheck, 1980; Gowa, 1994; Mansfield, 1994; Hegre, 2000). Dyads of industrialized states with intense trade relations show much less war potentialities than dyads with less intense trade relations. Despite some reservations (exceptions included, Barbieri and Levy, 2003) this relationship can be considered robust. As a measure for the degree of economic integration I take trade relations expressed by export quotas (export as a part of GDP).

Finally, data on governance can serve as an indicator for output legitimacy. As a source of information I use the study commissioned by the World Bank. Kaufmann, Kraay and Zoido-Lobatón (2001) define governance as "the traditions and institutions by which authority in a country is exercised. This includes (1) the process by which governments are selected, monitored and replaced, (2) the capacity of the government to effectively formulate and implement sound policies, and (3) the respect of citizens and the state for the institutions that govern economic and social interactions among them" (Kaufmann, Kraay and Zoido-Lobatón, 2002: 4 5). To these groups of indicators for governance the following are added: 1. the process of electing, controlling and change of a government (voice and accountability); 2. the ability of a government to make decisions and to carry them out (political stability[10] and government effectiveness); 3. the acceptance of institutions that regulate the economic and social relationships (rule of law and corruption). I chose those indicators for political stability and for government effectiveness because data on legitimacy and acceptance have already been taken into account in the par-

10. The indicator "political stability" of the World Bank's data comprises, among others, non-constitutional changes of government.

ticipation index. Political stability refers to the perception of non-constitutional changes of government, whereas the group of indicators for effectiveness refers to the perception of the quality of the government's action and its apparatus (bureaucracy). In other words, the governance indices express how stable a government is and how well it is in a position to implement its program. One can argue that one of the characteristics of governance, the interrelationships between state and private actors, is not sufficiently taken into consideration. The concept encompasses more than merely the effectiveness of lobbies, and also does not show the close relationship of a corporate system.[11] This aspect, however, is included in the indicators for acceptance, legitimacy and effectiveness. The equation expressing the security potential reads as follows:

> Security potential (support) = F (legitimacy/regime acceptance, membership in international regimes and/or organizations, economic integration in the world economy, „good governance")

Hypothesis 2: It is expected that states differ from each other as to their security potential depending on their internal (regime type) and external capacities.

Empirical test: The list of countries (Appendix 2) with a great deal of support is headed by Luxembourg and Singapore, followed by Belgium, The Netherlands, Ireland, Denmark, Malta, Germany and Finland as well as Sweden (see appendix). These countries are democratic. The countries that experience the least amount of support are the non-democratic states of Afghanistan, Rwanda, Myanmar, Bhutan, Eritrea, Somalia, Burundi, etc. The security index clearly discriminates between democratic and non-democratic regimes. The group of democratic states shows a much higher value according to the non-parametric analysis of the variance of ranking than the non-democratic states (Kolmogorov-Smirnov test: $z = 1.835$, $p < 0.005$). Thus, the democratic states in their support potential are significantly different from the non-democratic states. The list of the security index shows a clear concentration of democratic states in the first third and of autocratic states in the last third of the list. The Chi Square value amounts to χ^2 (4, N = 162) = 24.138). This value is highly significant ($p < 0.01$). Hypothesis 2 can, therefore, be considered as confirmed.

The comparison of different regimes as to their endangerment and security leads to relationships that run in the opposite directions: from "democratic" to "dictatorial" regimes the amount of support decreases, but the degree of

11. Another definition states: Governance is „the manner in which power is exercised in the management of a country's economic and social resources of development" (Webster's dictionary).

endangerment (see Diagram 2.1, page 23) increases. Autocratic regimes tend to not only be more endangered than democracies, but possess, above all, a smaller support potential (see Diagram 2.2).

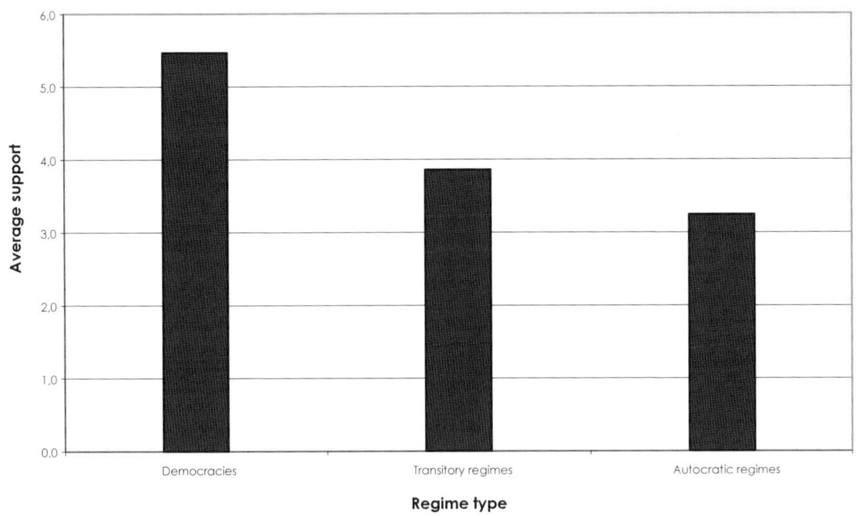

Diagram 2.2. Support by regime types

8 THE POTENTIAL FOR CONFLICT RESOLUTION

The political potential for conflict resolution can on the one hand be linked to indicators of support (input indicators), and on the other hand to the achievements a political system is able to produce (output indicators). The equation reads:

> Potential for conflict resolution = F (security/support potential – insecurity/endanger potential)

A political system has more to manage when it is confronted with a high degree of endangerment that can be compensated by support. Resolution, then, results from the difference between the security-promoting and security-endangering factors. The polynomial trend curve for all 162 states shows an increase in endangerment and a decrease in support.[12]

12. The trend assumes the following values: $y = 0{,}0596x^2 - 1{,}0449x + 6{,}2291$ with a value of $R^2 = 0{,}2578$

As to the output approach, three factors of conflict management can serve as measuring units: decrease in violence, durable treaties and the ending of war.

> Actual resolution of Conflict = F (de-escalation of conflicts; a lasting, contractually fixed agreement or treaty and the victorious conclusion of a war.

The list of countries (see Appendix 2) that show higher indices of support than indices of endangerment is led by the democratic states of Luxembourg and Ireland, followed by Denmark, Singapore, Malta, Iceland, Finland, Portugal and Belgium, then follow Norway, Sweden and Italy. These countries, with the exception of Singapore, are classified as democratic.

Countries with higher degrees of endangerment than support are Afghanistan, Eritrea, the Democratic Republic of Congo, Bhutan, Bolivia, Nigeria, Uganda, etc. These countries are autocratic with the exception of Bolivia.

From the list of countries ranked according to their management capability one can form two groups, a group of highly endangered states whose resolution indicator lies in the negative area, and a group of states that are less endangered and have positive resolution indices. The group of states that are highly endangered is smaller and shows above all more dictatorial regimes than the states that are less endangered. The statistical backing of this over-representation of autocracies is highly significant (χ^2 [2, N = 178] = 14.172, $p < 0.01$).

Using another method, the distribution of countries can be divided into two halves of equal size. The value dividing the "endangered" and the "secure" halves is 2.0. States with a resolution index smaller than this value are considered to be endangered; states with a value of 2 or higher are considered to be secure. Democratic states are found more frequently on the "secure" side. Dictatorial states, on the other hand, are on the non-secure side. The Chi Square test yields a highly significant difference ($p < 0.01$) with χ^2 (2, N = 178) = 22.288. Democracies are clearly rated higher in their resolution index than dictatorships.

While the endangerment index scale shows a larger representation of non-democratic regimes in the upper portion, the democratic states are clearly located in the portion of the security index scale that shows better support (see Diagram 2.1. and Diagram 2.2.). According to this difference we see a higher potential for resolution in democracies than in dictatorial or transitory regimes. The hypothesis that democracies have a higher potential for resolution than dictatorships can, therefore, be supported by the statistical test.

9 CONFLICT MANAGEMENT

Once conflicts have occurred, there are three different ways they could continue or end. First, they can last at low intensity; second, they could escalate to violent conflicts; and third, they could end temporarily or for a long time (see Figure 2.1. on page 14).

As mentioned, conflict resolution is on the one hand a result of the relationship between the potentials for endangerment and security. On the other hand successful conflict management can also be the result of three processes: first of de-escalation of a conflict to a lower level of intensity, second, of the conclusion of an agreement between the disputing parties and third of a victorious end of a war. Victory in a war that beats back the aggressor can signify the accepted end of the conflict. However, in such cases only a political, not military solution remains the ultimate ratio. Armistices or dictated peace agreements ("Diktatfriede") cannot be subsumed here. In a strict sense, a conflict is resolved when it leads to a "lasting agreement" of at least five to ten years. However, the conclusion of an agreement or peace treaty is not necessarily a guarantee of a solution. On the contrary, numerous agreements are either not implemented or are not worth the paper on which they are written. A legal document signed by the parties only indicates an intention to change and to achieve an arrangement. Such rather formal documents must be supplemented with more detailed analyses in order to estimate their value. Under what circumstances and under what conditions were the agreements concluded? We refer to the considerations that are published elsewhere and that formulate the conditions under which a lasting solution can be reached (Pfetsch, 2000: 127-155). Thus, the far-reaching definition of a solution to a conflict refers to a document that is signed voluntarily and without reservation by all participating and/or effected states, including all relevant issues and whose declarations of intent are fulfilled and endured.

10 EMPIRICAL TEST OF HYPOTHESES OF THE BEHAVIOR OF RESOLUTION POTENTIAL AND CONFLICT FREQUENCY

In the beginning, we asked the question whether the different ways a state behaves in a conflict could be observed according to its regime; and if yes, if it was possible to find an explanation for this by way of measuring indicators. Do democracies have a higher potential for the resolution of conflicts than dictatorships and can this be shown by their conflict behavior? To answer this question we started with the description of conflicts as they occurred over the last fifty years in absolute and weighted numbers. Then, the frequency of internal and interstate conflicts was confronted with the respective potential of endangerment, support and resolution capacities of the countries involved together with their regime characteristics. As to the calculation of external conflicts only neighbouring countries have been taken into account, not geographically distant countries in order to make them compatible with the indicators for security and insecurity.

Hypothesis 3: Democracies have shown to be more peaceable than autocratic regimes. With the increase in the number of democratic states, it can be assumed under *ceteris paribus* conditions that the world can become more peaceful.

Empirical test: The hypothesis cannot be confirmed in the present form because of discrepancies that occur in the account of the conflicts in terms of absolute and weighted figures. In absolute numbers, democratic states are at the top of participants in conflicts. Between 1945 and 1995, Great Britain participated most frequently not only in violent and non-violent conflicts but also in international conflicts (Pfetsch and Rohloff, 2000: 76). The USA lead the list of external participation in conflicts. The permanent members of the U.N. Security Council (in the rank order besides Great Britain the USSR, the USA, France and China) were the states most frequently involved in conflicts during this time. Only with regard to internal conflicts Indonesia, Ethiopia and Iraq rank next to the USSR. Consequently, democracies in general were not more peaceful by virtue of their international status than other regimes. They waged, however, more non-violent than violent conflicts over the five decades after World War II.

As to endangerment/insecurity, support/security and the capacity to master conflicts (resolution), the following hypotheses can be formulated:

10.1 Insecurity

Hypothesis 4: The higher the susceptibility to endangerment, the more likely conflicts will arise, especially violent conflicts.

It can be expected that countries exposed to high threat would also show a high rate of conflicts. As shown, the number of conflicts increases with the degree of endangerment. As a tendency, hypothesis 4 can be considered as confirmed, even if the correlation coefficient is of medium value. Violent conflicts increase at a higher rate than those that are less violent (see Chart 2.1 on page 19). The correlation coefficient is 0.474; this means that, statistically, 47 percent of conflicts are explained by the endangerment index. This corresponds to a medium statistical correlation. The endangerment index contributes, therefore, to the explanations of up to almost half of the conflict behavior. Some of the democratic "breakaway" states such as Georgia, Israel,

India or Turkey (by itself not the best democratic candidates) are ranked higher than the average with regard to the frequency of conflicts in comparison to their endangerment. These states are either young democracies or democracies that are exposed to higher threats. In the group of transitory regimes, the deviating cases are Russia, Yemen and Bosnia and Herzegovina; within the category of dictatorial regimes, we find Iraq, Sudan and Yugoslavia.

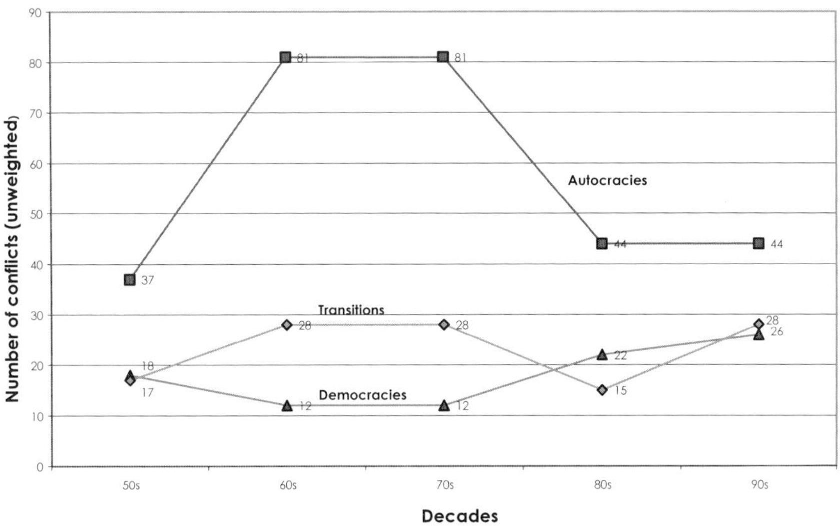

Chart 2.2. Violent conflicts according to regimes

10.2 Support

Hypothesis 5: The higher the potential security (support) of a country, the less likely it is that conflicts will arise.

Chart 2.3 clearly shows this relationship. The number of conflicts increases with the degree of endangerment and decreases with support. The polynomial trend curves show developments that run in opposite directions. The negative relationship between the indices of support and the number of weighted conflicts show a medium correlation coefficient of -0.369. Also in this case there are deviant cases. In relation to their security the frequency of conflicts in democratic or quasi democratic countries such as Georgia, India, Israel, Turkey, Columbia, Sri Lanka and South Africa is higher than the average. The same holds for the transitory states like Russia, Yemen, Bosnia and

Herzegovina, as well as for the autocratic states of Iraq, Sudan, Afghanistan or Yugoslavia.

10.3 Resolution

Hypothesis 6: Democracies' greater potential for conflict management explains their less violent conflict behavior and their higher efficiency in carrying out conflicts.

As mentioned before the greater ability to resolve conflicts can be measured with three indicators: fewer acts of violence, negotiated treaties and victories in wars.

Empirical evidence of fewer acts of violence by democracies is given in Table 2.2. and shown in Chart 2.2. Autocracies show a higher frequency of violent conflicts with lesser support (security potential).

As a tendency, all regimes show a decrease in frequency of conflicts with an increasing capacity for resolution. The correlation coefficient between the resolution index and the frequency of conflicts is -0.471. This expresses a decreasing frequency of conflicts with increasing potentials for resolution with a medium statistical explanatory power. As regards autocracies, the values of the resolution index lie more frequently in the negative area and the number of conflicts is remarkably higher (see Charts 2.3 and 2.4).

The indicator "negotiated treaties" does not lead to a discriminating result between democracies and autocracies in our count of agreements. What has been said about formal documents may explain this finding. In the fifty years between 1950 and 1999, autocracies—as the majority of the then existing states have—with the exception of the fifties and the eighties, concluded more agreements than democracies (see Table 2.3.). The interpretation, however, is possible only when we know more about the conditions under which they have been reached. At present no studies are available.

Table 2.3. Treaties according to regimes

	50ies	**60ies**	**70ies**	**80ies**	**90ies**	**Total**
All States	89	122	135	68	162	576
Democracies (A)	40	39	31	33	68	211
Transitional Regimes (B)	12	21	20	10	43	106
Autocracies (C)	37	62	84	24	51	258

Reiter and Stam (2002) have shown in their empirical study that on the basis of interstate wars occurring between 1816 and 1992 democracies were more successful in carrying out wars. These countries pursued wars of shorter duration, with fewer losses, and they showed better military leadership. Above all, they are more dependent on public opinion than dictatorships and make decisions with greater circumspection (Reiter and Stam, 2002: 198-199). As belligerent and defender, democracies reach better results than dictatorships or oligarchies (Table 2.4.). Of the wars that democracies initiated, they won 93 % (compared to 60 % by dictatorships) and as the defending state, they have won 63 % (compared to 34 % by dictatorships). The ending of the two world wars may serve as examples for the plausibility of these statements.

Table 2.4. Victory and defeat in wars according to regimes (according to Reiter/Stam, p. 29)

	Dictatorships	*Oligarchies*	*Democracies*	*Total*
War initiating country				
Wins	21	21	14	56
Losses	14	15	1	30
Winning percentage	60%	58%	93%	65%
Targeted country				
Wins	16	18	12	46
Losses	31	27	7	65
Winning percentage	34%	40%	63%	41%

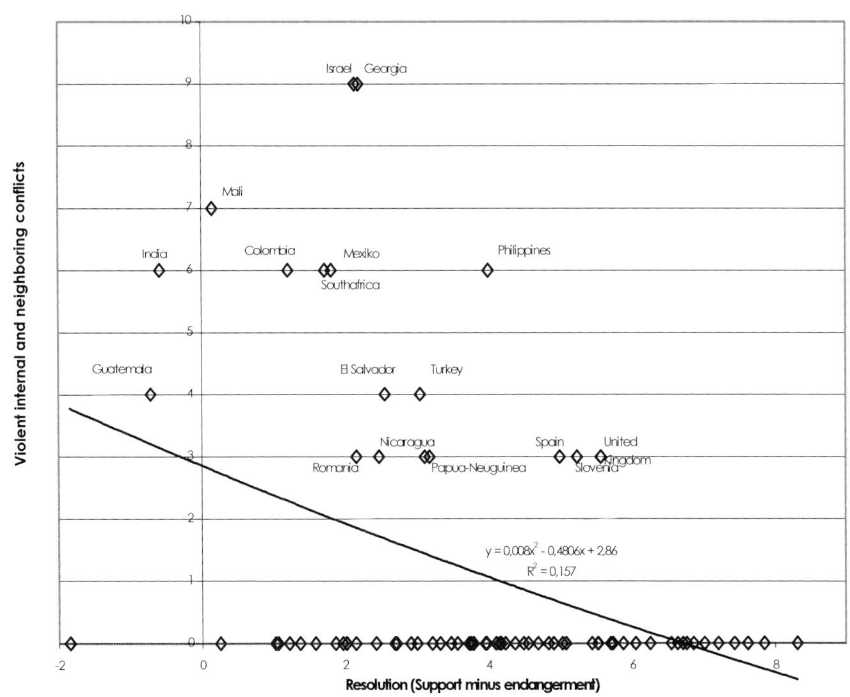

Chart 2.3. Resolution, by violent conflicts (democracies)

If one compares the structural conditions of each country (endangerment, support) with the conflicts that occur within, one would expect that the countries with a high support potential would have a better performance, above all, if they are democratic regimes. The curve that describes the security component of conflict development is convex with regard to democracies and transitory regimes. That means: the higher the security index, the smaller the

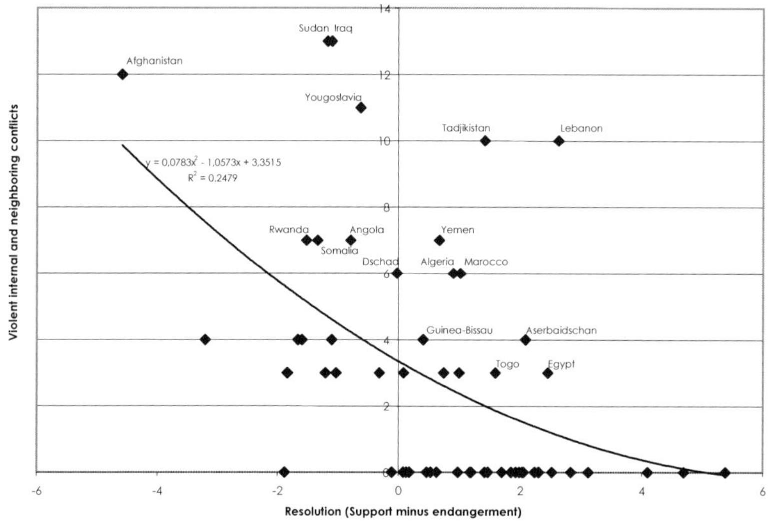

Chart 2.4. Resolution, by violent conflicts (autocracies)

number of conflicts. With regard to autocratic regimes, the trend is concave. The thesis that conflicts are less likely to arise in states that have higher resource capacities can, therefore, be considered to be confirmed in its tendency. If one applies the character of the regime to the ability to resolve conflicts, then all regimes show, at first, fewer conflicts with an increase in the ability to resolve them, with the difference, however, that autocratic regimes are found to be more numerous in the negative area of conflict resolution. As calculated for all the states the trend curve of conflicts with resolutions on the x-axis and conflicts on the y-axis increases slightly. That means that conflicts are more frequent where there is a higher degree of endangerment and less support. When comparing regime types, this trend is more obvious with democracies than with transitory and autocratic regimes. The frequency of conflicts cumulates less with democracies in the area of endangerment than in security, while with regard to autocratic and transitory states, conflicts are spread over a greater area of endangerment. There are also deviations from the average values that lie in the trend (see Charts 2.3 and

2.4). The ability to resolve conflicts is less developed in democratic states such as Georgia, Israel, Mali, India, Columbia, Mexico, the Philippines, South Africa, or Turkey (some of which are young democracies), and in non-democratic states like Russia, or Bosnia and Herzegovina (transitory) as well as Iraq, Sudan, Afghanistan, Yugoslavia, Lebanon, or Tajikistan (autocratic).

11 CONCLUSIONS

The important finding of this exercise consists in the calculation of the rank position of each of the 162 individual countries with regard to its endangerment, security and potential to resolve conflicts (see Appendix 2). The central question which states or regimes resolve conflicts better, and which explanation can be given for this, can be answered through the empirical findings: democracies rank distinctly higher in the resolution index than dictatorships. The much smaller number of violent conflicts of democracies compared to autocracies and compared to the sum total of conflicts indicates that democracies can resolve conflicts better. This is also valid for belligerent encounters. The higher values for their security and potential for resolving conflicts can help explain this differing conflict behavior. The calculations also show which states are especially endangered and which are especially secure.

The following results can be mentioned as a summary of tested hypotheses:

- The hypothesis that the endangerment of states is independent of the type of political regime is not confirmed for the dyad democracy-autocracy but only for the dyads democracies-transitional regimes, and dictatorships-transitional regimes.
- The hypothesis that states differ according to their security potential according to their capacities and their type of regime can be considered confirmed. Democracies and autocracies differ significantly with regard to their security potential.
- The hypothesis that considers democracies to be more peaceful than autocratic regimes is confirmed with modifications. What confirms the hypothesis is the fact that autocracies have used more violence. In all five decades, the proportion of violent conflicts is higher with regard to autocracies than to democracies. What disproves the hypothesis is the fact that the participation of democracies in violent conflicts was not less than that of autocracies. On the contrary, the three democracies among the permanent members of the Security

Council show the highest participation in conflicts all together. Democracies, however, have not fought wars against each other.

- The hypothesis according to which conflicts, and especially violent ones, are more likely to occur in states that are highly susceptible to endangerment is, to say it cautiously, not refuted by the correlation analysis.
- The hypothesis according to which conflicts are less likely to arise in countries with a large potential of security (support) can be considered confirmed. The correlation analysis confirms the negative relationship.
- The hypothesis that democracies' greater potential for resolution explains their reduced use of violence in carrying out conflicts can, under given premises, be considered confirmed by the correlation analysis. The correlation analysis confirms the negative relationship whereby autocracies lie more frequently and with higher values in the negative area (higher endangerment than support) than democracies.

Within an extended research design, these results could be tested with inference statistical methods. The rich material of the Kosimo databank invites such an endeavour.

References

Baade, H. W., 1962, *Das Verhältnis von Parlament und Regierung im Bereich der auswärtigen Gewalt der Bundesrepublik Deutschland*, Hansischer Gildenverlag, Hamburg.

Barbieri, K. and Levi, J., 2003, The trade disruption hypothesis and the liberal economic theory of peace, in *Globalization and Armed Conflict*, Schneider, G., et al., eds., Rowman and Littlefield, Lanham, MD, pp. 277-298.

Beetham, D., 1995, *Defining and Measuring Democracy*, Sage, London.

Belle, D. A. van, 1997, Press freedom and democratic peace, *Journal of Peace Research*, **34**:405-414.

Bremer, S., 1992, Dangerous dyads: conditions affecting the likelihood of interstate war, 1816-1965, *Journal of Conflict Resolution* **36**:309-341.

Bremer, S., 1993, Democracy and militarised interstate conflict, 1816-1965, *International Interactions* **18**:231-250.

Czempiel, E.-O., 1996, Kants Theorem. Oder: Warum sind die Demokratien (noch immer) nicht friedlich?, *Zeitschrift für Internationale Beziehungen* **3**:79-101.

Dahl, R. A., 1999, *On Democracy*, Yale University Press, New Haven.

Fearon, J.D. and Laitin, D. D., 1996, Explaining interethnic cooperation, *APSR* **90**:715-735

Fearon, J.D. and Laitin, D. D., 2003, Ethnicity, insurgency, and civil war, *APSR* **97**:75-90

Fischer Welt Almanach, 2002, Fischer, Frankfurt/Main.

Freedom House, 2001, *Comparative Survey of Freedom. Freedom in the World Country Ratings. 1972-73 to 2000-01*, http://www.freedomhouse.org/research/freeworld/2001/index.htm

Gleditsch, N. P. and Hegre, H., 1997, Peace and democracy: three levels of analysis, *Journal of Conflict Resolution* **41**:283-310.

Gowa, J., 1994, *Allies, Adversaries, and International Trade*, Princeton University Press, Princeton, NJ.

Gurr, T. R., 2000, *Peoples Versus States. Minorities at Risk in the New Century*, United States Institute of Peace Press, Washington.

Hasenclever, A., Sie bewegt sich doch, *ZIB* 2/2002:331-364

Hegre, H., 2000, Development and the liberal peace: what does it take to be a trading state?, *Journal of Peace Research* **37**:5-30.

Henderson, E. A., 2002, Neoidealism and the democratic peace, *Journal of Peace Research* **36**:203-231

Hintze, O., 1975, The formation of states and constitutional development, in F.Gilbert, ed., *The Historical Essays of the Otto Hintze*, Oxford University Press, New York.

Horowitz, D., 1985, *Ethnic Groups in Conflict*, University of California Press, Berkeley, CA.

Kaufmann, D., Kraay, A., and Zoido-Lobatón, 2002, *Governance Matters II: Updated Indicators for 2000/01*, World Bank Policy Research Paper no. 2772.

Kegley, C. W. Jr., and Hermann, M. G., 1996, How democracies use intervention: a neglected dimension in studies of the democratic peace, *Journal of Peace Research* **33**:309-322.

KOSIMO, http://www.kosimo.de.

Kymlicka, W., 1996, *Multicultural Citizenship. A Liberal Theory of Minority Rights*, Clarendon Press, Oxford.

Layne, C., 1994, Kant or Cant: the myth of democratic peace, *International Security* **19**:5-49

Levy, J., 1988, Domestic politics and war, *Journal of Interdisciplinary History* **18**:653-673

Mansfield, E., 1994, *Power, Trade, and War*, Princeton University Press, Princeton, NJ.

Maoz, Z., and Russett, B., 1993, Normative and structural causes of democratic peace, 1946-1986, *American Political Science Review* **87**:624-638.

Marshall, M. G., and Jaggers, K., 2000, *Polity IV Project*, http//www.bsos.umd.edu/cidcm/inscr/polity.

Moravcsik, A., 1998: *The Choice for Europe: Preferences and Power in European Integration*, 1955-1991, Cornell University Press, Ithaca, N.Y.

Mousseau, M., and Shi, Y., 1999, A test for reverse causality in the democratic peace relationship, *Journal of Peace Research* **36**:639-663.

Moynihan, D. P., *Pandaemonium: Ethnicity in International Politics*, Oxford University Press, New York.

Ostrom, C., and Hoole, F., 1978, Alliances and war revisited: a research note, *International Studies Quarterly* **22**:215-236

Owen, J. M., 1994, How liberalism produces democratic peace, *International Security* **19**:87-125.

Parish, R., and Peceny, M., 2002, Kantian liberalism and the collective defense of democracy in Latin America, *Journal of Peace Research* **39**:229-250.

Polacheck, S. W. 1980, Conflict and trade, *Journal of Conflict Resolution* **24**:55-78.

Pfetsch, F. R., 2000, Kreatives Verhandeln in Politik und Wirtschaft, in R. M. Holm-Hadulla, ed., *Kreativität*, Heidelberger Jahrbücher 2000 XLIV, Heidelberg, pp. 127-155.

Pfetsch, F. R., 1994, *Internationale Politik*, Kohlhammer, Stuttgart.

Pfetsch, F. R., 1985, *Verfassungspolitik der Nachkriegszeit*, Wiss. Buchgesellschaft, Darmstadt.

Pfetsch, F. R., and Billing, P., 1994, *Datenhandbuch nationaler und internationaler Konflikte*, Nomos, Baden-Baden.

Pfetsch, F. R., and Rohloff, C., 2000, *National and International Conflicts, 1945-1995*, Routledge, London/N.Y.

Raknerud, A., and Hegre, H., 1997, The hazard of war: reassessing the evidence for the democratic peace, *Journal of Peace Research* **34**:385-414.

Randall, P., and Peceny, M., 2002, Kantian Liberalism and the Collective Defense of Democracy in Latin America. In: *Journal of Peace Research* 39, March

Reiter, D. und Stam, A., 2002, *Democracies at War*, Princeton University Press, Princeton.

Robinson, E., 2001, Reading and misreading the ancient evidence for democratic peace, *Journal of Peace Research* **38**:593-608.

Rosecrance, R., 1986, *The Rise of the Trading State*, Basic Books, New York.

Russett, B., Layne, C., Spiro, D. E., and Doyle, M. W., 1995, Correspondence. The democratic peace, *International Security* **19**:164-184.

Schmidt, M. G., 2000, *Demokratietheorien*, Leske&Budrich, Opladen.

SIPRI, 2001, *Yearbook 2001. World Armaments and Disarmament*, Oxford University Press, Oxford.

Tures, J. A., 2001, Addressing concerns about applying the democratic peace arguments to interventions, *Journal of Peace Research* **38**:247-249.

Tures, J. A., 2001, Democracies as intervening states: a critique of Kegley & Hermann, *Journal of Peace Research* **38**:227-235.

UNHCR, 1998, 1999, 2000, *Refugees and Others of Concern to UNHCR. Statistical Overview 1998, 1999, 2000*, Geneva, http://www.unhcr.ch.

UNHCR, 2001, *2000 Global Refugee Trends*, Geneva, http://www.unhcr.ch.

UNHCR, *Statistical Overviews*, Geneva, http://www.unhcr.ch.

Vanhanen, T., 1984, *The Emergence of Democracy. A Comparative Study of 119 States, 1850-1979*, Helsinki.

Vanhanen, T., 1990, *The Process of Democratization. A Comparative Study of 147 States, 1980-88*, Crane Russak, New York.

Vanhanen, T., 1997, *Prospects of Democracy. A study of 172 countries*, Routledge, London/N.Y.

Wayman, F., 1990, Alliances and time-series analysis, in C. Gochman and A. Sabrosky, eds., *Prisoners of War?* Lexington, Lexington, MA., pp. 93-113

Weede, E., 1983, Extended deterrence by superpower alliance, *Journal of Conflict Resolution* **27**:231-254.

Weltbank, 2000/01, *Weltenwicklungsbericht 2000/01*, January 2002 htto://www.worldbank.org/wbi/governance/govdata2001.htm.

APPENDIX 1

Survey of Indicators and their Operationalization

Indicator	*Operationalization*	*Source*
Regimes 1.Democracies, subset OECD-States 2.Transitory regimes 3.Autocratic regimes	For the typology at the end of the nineties: Index of democracy by Vanhanen, Freedom House, and by Marshall & Jaggers. For the typology covering decades 40 to 2002 there are polity-values by Gurr and the index of democracy by Vanhanen. **Marshall & Jaggers** (Polity IV Project): For democracy: Competition about political participation; openness and competition about the recruitment of political staff; limitation of the executive. For autocracies: Competition about political participation; rule of participation; openness and competition about the recruitment of political staff; limitation of the executive. Values between +10 (highly democratic) to –10 (highly autocratic) **Vanhanen**: The D-Index is calculated by multiplying competition and participation divided by 100. Competition: 100 minus of the percentage of votes of the strongest party. Participation: Part of active electors of total population. Index of democracy (ID) **Freedomhouse** uses a scale from 1 to 7 for Political Rights (PR) and Civil Liberties (SL), whereby 1 is the highest degree of freedom and 7 the lowest. The resulting status of freedom is divided into three categories: in F=free (with scale values between 1.0 and 2.5) in PF = partially free (with scale values between 3.0 and 5.5) and NF = not free (with scale values between 5.5 and 7.0). This 7-degree scale for PR and CL is ordinal scaled, whereby, indeed, the characteristic specification creates a natural ranking order, but no qualification between the distances is possible. Since the D-value deals with an ordinal-scaled measurement, the ordinal scale had to be transformed into an interval scale to make an aggregation possible.	Vanhanen 1997/ Marshall & Jaggers 2000/ Freedomhouse 2001

Potential danger	• Minorities according to *Vanhanen*: Heterogeneity = 100 minus the part of the largest group in a state; *Marshall & Jaggers*: The index of Gurr covers values between –7,03 to 2,10. –7,03 stands for the lowest, 2,10 for the highest probability concerning further rebellions of minorities or the escalation of existing rebellions of minorities (degree of protest/ rebellion). For the index of endangerment the figures have been transformed in a proportional scale where –7,03 means an endangerment of 0% and 2,1 one of 100%. • Political instability / crisis: number of refugees related to total population; refugees of country of origin are weighted with factor 1, those of country of destination with factor 0,33 • Endangerment: Military spending related to GNP • Neighbouring countries: Number of neighbouring states • Non-constitutional change of government; number of coups/ attempted coups	Vanhanen 1990 UNHCR: Statistical Overviews, different volumes SIPRI 2001 Fischer Weltalmanach 2002 KOSIMO
Security-causing factors	• Acceptance of regime: voter turnout in % of total population • Political integration: Number of memberships in alliances and systems of integration (weighted) • Economic integration: export share • Governance, conflict management: political stability of regimes and effectivity of governments (work)	Vanhanen 1997 Fischer Weltalmanach 2002 Worldbank: World development report 2000/01 D.Kaufmann/ A.Kraay, P.Zoido-Lobatón 2002

Potential for resolution	Security potential minus endangerment potential, reduction from one level of escalation to another; win in a defensive war	KOSIMO
First set: All Conflicts: Absolute number of conflicts, without weighting, violent and non-violent conflicts		
Second set: Conflicts: internal + neighbouring conflicts, weighted by intensity	Number of internal and neighbouring conflicts. Weighting with factor 4 for wars, factor 3 for serious conflicts, factor 2 for conflicts and factor 1 for latent conflicts according to KOSIMO. Data are related to indices	
Treaties	International political (not economic) treaties concerning peace, armistice, independence, international arbitration, court decisions, constitutional amendment/new constitution, internal armistice, peace treaties	
Date	All data for conflict resolution apply to the nineties. Conflict data and regime data are there for the five decades 1950 to 2000.	

APPENDIX 2

162 States with Indices of Endangerment, Support and Resolution, Conflicts (end of the 90s)

Rank	States	Comb. Regime-Index	Endangerment
1	Afghanistan	C	5,5
2	Angola	C	5,1
3	Bolivia	A	5,0
4	Uganda	C	4,8
5	Niger	C	4,6
5	Eritrea	C	4,6
6	Iraq	C	4,5
8	Congo, DR	C	4,4
9	Russ. Fed. (USR)	B	4,2
10	Liberia	B	3,9
11	Kenya	C	3,8
11	Ethiopia	B	3,8
11	India	A	3,8
12	Sudan	C	3,7
12	Djibouti	C	3,7
13	Syria	C	3,6
13	Peru	B	3,6
14	Chad	C	3,5
14	Senegal	C	3,5
14	Indonesia	B	3,5
15	Central Africa Rep.	B	3,4
15	Sierra Leone	C	3,4
16	Nigeria	C	3,3
17	Tanzania	C	3,2

Rank	States	Comb. Regime-Index	Support
1	Luxemburg	A	9,5
2	Singapore	B	8,8
3	Belgium	A	8,5
4	Netherlands	A	8,3
5	Ireland	A	8,2
6	Denmark	A	8,0
7	Malta	A	7,7
8	Germany	A	7,6
8	Finland	A	7,6
9	Sweden	A	7,5
10	Portugal	A	7,4
10	Austria	A	7,4
10	United Kingdom	A	7,4
10	Spain	A	7,4
11	Italy	A	7,3
11	Island	A	7,3
12	Czech. Republic	A	7,1
12	Norway	A	7,1
13	Greece	A	7,0
13	France	A	7,0
14	Slovakia	A	6,7
15	Canada	A	6,6
15	Malaysia	A	6,6
16	Hungary	A	6,5

Rank	States	Comb. Regime-Index	Resolution	Non-Violent Conflicts	Violent Conflicts	Total Conflicts
1	Luxemburg	A	8,3	0	0	0
2	Ireland	A	7,8	0	0	0
3	Denmark	A	7,6	0	0	0
4	Singapore	B	7,5	0	0	0
5	Malta	A	7,4	0	0	0
6	Iceland	A	7,2	2	0	2
7	Finland	A	7,0	0	0	0
8	Portugal	A	6,9	0	0	0
9	Belgium	A	6,8	0	0	0
10	Norway	A	6,7	2	0	2
11	Sweden	A	6,6	0	0	0
12	Italy	A	6,5	1	0	1
13	Netherlands	A	6,2	0	0	0
14	Austria	A	6,0	0	0	0
15	Slovakia	A	5,9	2	0	2
16	Czech. Republic	A	5,7	2	0	2
16	France	A	5,7	1	0	1
17	Great Britain	A	5,6	1	3	4
18	Mauritius	A	5,5	1	0	1
18	Hungary	A	5,5	2	0	2
19	Canada	A	5,4	2	0	2
19	Cuba	C	5,4	1	0	1
20	Slovenia	A	5,2	0	3	3
21	Costa Rica	A	5,1	0	0	0

17	Botswana	A	3,2
17	Thailand	A	3,2
17	Yugoslavia	C	3,2
17	Cameron	C	3,2
17	Bhutan	C	3,2
17	Guatemala	A	3,2
18	South Africa	A	3,1
18	Jordan	C	3,1
19	Ghana	B	3,0
19	Burkina Faso	C	3,0
20	Algeria	C	2,9
21	Myanmar	C	2,8
21	Guinea	C	2,8
21	Greece	A	2,8
21	Honduras	A	2,8
21	Kuwait	B	2,8
22	Ecuador	A	2,7
22	Mexico	A	2,7
22	Switzerland	A	2,7
22	Iran	C	2,7
22	Somalia	C	2,7
22	Rwanda	C	2,7
23	Latvia	A	2,6
23	Mali	A	2,6
23	Germany	A	2,6
24	Macedonia	B	2,5
24	Bangladesh	A	2,5
24	Chile	A	2,5
24	Guinea-Bissau	C	2,5
24	Burundi	C	2,5
24	Malaysia	A	2,5
25	Pakistan	B	2,4
25	Mozambique	B	2,4

16	Cuba	C	6,5
17	Mauritius	A	6,3
17	Equatorial Guinea	C	6,3
18	Estonia	A	6,2
18	Slovenia	A	6,2
18	Guyana	A	6,2
19	Costa Rica	A	5,9
20	Uruguay	A	5,8
21	Switzerland	A	5,6
21	Cyprus	A	5,6
22	USA	A	5,5
22	New Zeeland	A	5,5
22	Australia	A	5,5
23	Tunisia	B	5,4
23	Poland	A	5,4
24	Croatia	B	5,3
25	Chile	A	5,2
26	Bulgaria	A	5,1
26	Latvia	A	5,1
26	Vietnam, N.+S.	C	5,1
27	Korea, S. (Rep.)	A	5,0
27	Turkey	A	5,0
27	Trinidad u. Tobago	A	5,0
27	Gambia	C	5,0
28	Swaziland	C	4,9
29	Namibia	A	4,8
29	Rumania	A	4,8
29	Lithuania	A	4,8
29	Belize	A	4,8
29	South Africa	A	4,8
29	Argentine	A	4,8
29	Russ. Fed. USR)	B	4,8
29	Mongolia	A	4,8

22	Germany	A	5,0	0	0	0
22	Spain	A	5,0	2	3	5
23	Uruguay	A	4,9	0	0	0
24	Estonia	A	4,8	2	0	2
24	Tunisia	B	4,8	0	0	0
25	Australia	A	4,7	0	0	0
25	Equatorial Guinea	C	4,7	1	0	1
26	Korea, S. (Rep.)	A	4,6	1	0	1
27	Taiwan	A	4,5	2	0	2
28	Japan	A	4,4	1	0	1
29	Greece	A	4,2	3	0	3
29	Mongolia	A	4,2	0	0	0
29	Poland	A	4,2	0	0	0
29	Lithuania	A	4,2	0	0	0
30	Malaysia	A	4,1	1	0	1
30	Swaziland	C	4,1	0	0	0
31	Philippines	A	4,0	0	6	6
31	Bulgaria	A	4,0	0	0	0
31	Moldova	B	4,0	2	0	2
31	Namibia	A	4,0	0	0	0
32	Croatia	B	3,9	0	4	4
33	Guyana	A	3,8	3	0	3
33	Belize	A	3,8	1	0	1
34	Cyprus	A	3,7	1	0	1
35	New Zeeland	A	3,6	0	0	0
36	Jamaica	A	3,5	0	0	0
37	USA	A	3,3	2	0	2
37	Fiji	B	3,3	0	0	0
38	Trinidad u. Tobago	A	3,2	0	0	0
38	Papua-New Guinea	A	3,2	0	3	3
39	Nicaragua	A	3,1	1	3	4
39	Gambia	C	3,1	0	0	0
39	Turkey	A	3,1	5	4	9

25	Brasilia	A	2,4
25	Congo, Rep.	C	2,4
25	Tajikistan	C	2,4
25	Panama	A	2,4
25	Saudi Arabia	C	2,4
25	Paraguay	A	2,4
25	Guyana	A	2,4
25	Spain	A	2,4
25	Rumania	A	2,4
26	Cambodia	B	2,3
26	Kyrgyz Rep.	B	2,3
26	China, VR	C	2,3
26	Israel	A	2,3
26	Uzbekistan	C	2,3
27	Morocco	C	2,2
27	Vietnam, N.+S.	C	2,2
27	USA	A	2,2
27	Gabon	C	2,2
27	Libya	C	2,2
27	Turkmenistan	C	2,2
27	Kazakhstan	C	2,2
28	Zambia	B	2,1
28	Togo	C	2,1
28	Dominican. Republic	A	2,1
28	Bahrain	C	2,1
29	Argentine	A	2,0
29	Netherlands	A	2,0
29	Turkey	A	2,0
29	VAE	C	2,0
29	Bosnia Herzegovina	B	2,0
30	New Zealand	A	1,9
30	Cyprus	A	1,9
30	Columbia	A	1,9

30	Taiwan	A	4,7
30	Philippines	A	4,7
31	Fiji	B	4,6
31	Panama	A	4,6
31	Mexico	A	4,6
32	Israel	A	4,5
32	Ukraine	B	4,5
32	Kazakhstan	C	4,5
32	Japan	A	4,5
33	Ghana	B	4,4
33	Papua-New Guinea	A	4,4
33	Jamaica	A	4,4
34	Angola	C	4,3
34	Moldova	B	4,3
34	Brasilia	A	4,3
34	Thailand	A	4,3
34	VAE	C	4,3
34	Botswana	A	4,3
35	Nicaragua	A	4,2
35	Syria	C	4,2
36	Dominican. Republic	A	4,1
36	Honduras	A	4,1
36	Gabon	C	4,1
37	Turkmenistan	C	4,0
37	Kyrgyz Rep.	B	4,0
37	Paraguay	A	4,0
37	Oman	C	4,0
38	Ecuador	A	3,9
38	Malawi	A	3,9
38	Macedonia	B	3,9
38	Indonesia	B	3,9
39	Tajikistan	C	3,8
39	Cap Verde	A	3,8

40	Cap Verde	A	3,0	0	0	0
41	Switzerland	A	2,9	0	0	0
42	Ukraine	B	2,8	2	0	2
42	Vietnam, N.+S	C	2,8	4	0	4
43	Argentine	A	2,7	1	0	1
43	Chile	A	2,7	2	0	2
44	Lesotho	B	2,6	1	0	1
44	Lebanon	C	2,6	0	10	10
44	Comoro	B	2,6	2	0	2
44	El Salvador	A	2,6	1	4	5
45	Brunei	C	2,5	0	0	0
45	Rumania	A	2,5	2	3	5
45	Egypt	C	2,5	0	3	3
46	Latvia	A	2,4	1	0	1
47	Kazakhstan	C	2,3	1	0	1
47	VAE	C	2,3	1	0	1
48	Oman	C	2,2	2	0	2
48	Israel	A	2,2	1	9	10
48	Panama	A	2,2	0	3	3
48	Malawi	A	2,2	0	0	0
48	Georgia	A	2,2	2	9	11
49	Azerbaijan	C	2,1	2	4	6
49	Mauritania	C	2,1	0	0	0
50	Belarus	C	2,0	0	0	0
50	Dominican. Republic	A	2,0	0	0	0
50	Ivory Coast	C	2,0	0	0	0
50	Venezuela	A	2,0	2	0	2
51	Gabon	C	1,9	0	0	0
51	Sri Lanka	B	1,9	0	8	8
51	Brasilia	A	1,9	0	0	0
51	Turkmeni-stan	C	1,9	0	0	0
52	Mexico	A	1,8	0	6	6
52	Bosnia Herzegov-ina	B	1,8	0	15	15

30	Madagascar	B	1,9
30	Gambia	C	1,9
31	Yemen	C	1,8
31	Great Britain	A	1,8
31	Armenia	B	1,8
31	Trinidad u. Tobago	A	1,8
31	Malawi	A	1,8
32	Belgium	A	1,7
32	Laos	C	1,7
32	Mauritania	C	1,7
32	Oman	C	1,7
33	Ukraine	B	1,6
33	Nepal	B	1,6
33	Equatorial Guinea	C	1,6
34	Albania	B	1,5
34	Zimbabwe	B	1,5
34	Sri Lanka	B	1,5
35	Azerbaijan	C	1,4
35	Georgia	A	1,4
35	Estonia	A	1,4
35	Egypt	C	1,4
35	Venezuela	A	1,4
35	Austria	A	1,4
35	Czech. Republic	A	1,4
36	Fiji	B	1,3
36	Croatia	B	1,3
36	Ivory Coast	C	1,3
36	Singapore	B	1,3
36	France	A	1,3
37	Poland	A	1,2
37	Canada	A	1,2
37	Papua-New Guinea	A	1,2
37	Bulgaria	A	1,2

39	Egypt	C	3,8
39	Algeria	C	3,8
39	Mauritania	C	3,8
40	Guinea	C	3,7
40	Bosnia Herzegovina	B	3,7
40	Kuwait	B	3,7
40	Togo	C	3,7
40	Jordan	C	3,7
41	Mozambique	B	3,6
41	Lesotho	B	3,6
41	Cambodia	B	3,6
41	Congo, Rep.	C	3,6
41	Senegal	C	3,6
41	Comoro	B	3,6
41	Bahrain	C	3,6
41	Georgia	A	3,6
41	Saudi Arabia	C	3,6
41	El Salvador	A	3,6
42	Azerbaijan	C	3,5
42	Brunei	C	3,5
42	Chad	C	3,5
42	Iran	C	3,5
43	Laos	C	3,4
43	Djibouti	C	3,4
43	Iraq	C	3,4
43	Sri Lanka	B	3,4
44	Venezuela	A	3,3
44	Cameroon	C	3,3
44	Armenia	B	3,3
44	Tanzania	C	3,3
44	Peru	B	3,3
44	Albania	B	3,3
44	Uzbekistan	C	3,3

53	Albania	B	1,7	2	0	2
53	South Africa	A	1,7	2	6	8
53	Kyrgyz Rep	B	1,7	0	3	3
53	Zimbabwe	B	1,7	0	0	0
53	Laos	C	1,7	0	0	0
54	Togo	C	1,6	2	3	5
54	Paraguay	A	1,6	0	0	0
55	Armenia	B	1,5	2	4	6
55	Bahrain	C	1,5	5	0	5
56	Tajikistan	C	1,4	0	10	10
56	Korea, N.DVR)	C	1,4	1	0	1
56	Ghana	B	1,4	2	3	5
56	Honduras	A	1,4	1	0	1
57	Macedonia	B	1,3	1	0	1
57	Cambodia	B	1,3	0	0	0
57	Madagascar	B	1,3	1	0	1
58	Ecuador	A	1,2	1	0	1
58	Columbia	A	1,2	2	6	8
58	Nepal	B	1,2	2	0	2
58	Congo, Rep.	C	1,2	2	0	2
58	Mozambique	B	1,2	0	0	0
58	Saudi Arabia	C	1,2	9	0	9
59	Thailand	A	1,1	2	0	2
60	Botswana	A	1,0	0	0	0
60	Morocco	C	1,0	2	6	8
60	Uzbekistan	C	1,0	0	3	3
60	Guinea	C	1,0	2	0	2
60	Kuwait	B	1,0	3	7	10
61	Algeria	C	0,9	0	6	6
62	Zambia	B	0,8	2	0	2
63	Iran	C	0,7	6	3	9
63	Yemen	C	0,7	9	7	16
64	Jordan	C	0,6	1	0	1

38	Luxemburg	A	1,1
38	Cuba	C	1,1
38	Nicaragua	A	1,1
39	Belize	A	1,0
39	Comoro	B	1,0
39	Lesotho	B	1,0
39	Brunei	C	1,0
39	El Salvador	A	1,0
39	Slovenia	A	1,0
39	Hungary	A	1,0
40	Sweden	A	0,9
40	Namibia	A	0,9
40	Jamaica	A	0,9
40	Slovakia	A	0,9
40	Uruguay	A	0,9
41	Swaziland	C	0,8
41	Belarus	C	0,8
41	Cap Verde	A	0,8
41	Costa Rica	A	0,8
41	Mauritius	A	0,8
41	Australia	A	0,8
41	Italy	A	0,8
42	Philippines	A	0,7
42	Lithuania	A	0,7
43	Lebanon	C	0,6
43	Tunisia	B	0,6
43	Mongolia	A	0,6
43	Portugal	A	0,6
43	Finland	A	0,6
44	Korea, S.(Rep.)	A	0,5
45	Denmark	A	0,4
45	Norway	A	0,4
45	Korea, N.(DVR)	C	0,4
46	Moldova	B	0,3
46	Ireland	A	0,3

44	Ivory Coast	C	3,3
44	Morocco	C	3,3
45	Liberia	B	3,2
45	Lebanon	C	3,2
45	Zimbabwe	B	3,2
45	India	A	3,2
45	Burkina Faso	C	3,2
45	Madagascar	B	3,2
46	Bolivia	A	3,1
46	Columbia	A	3,1
47	Zambia	B	3,0
48	Uganda	C	2,9
48	Guinea-Bissau	C	2,9
48	Belarus	C	2,9
49	Nepal	B	2,8
49	Ethiopia	B	2,8
49	Niger	C	2,8
49	Bangladesh	A	2,8
49	Kenya	C	2,8
50	Mali	A	2,7
51	Libya	C	2,6
51	Central Africa Rep.	B	2,6
51	Yugoslavia, BR	C	2,6
51	Sudan	C	2,6
52	Yemen	C	2,5
52	Guatemala	A	2,5
53	China, VR	C	2,2
53	Pakistan	B	2,2
54	Nigeria	C	2,1
55	Congo, DR	C	2,0
56	Korea, N.(DVR)	C	1,8
57	Sierra Leone	C	1,7
58	Somalia	C	1,4
58	Burundi	C	1,4
58	Eritrea	C	1,4

64	Russ. Fed.(USR)	B	0,6	14	16	30
65	Syria	C	0,5	2	0	2
65	Libya	C	0,5	1	0	1
66	Guinea-Bis-sau	C	0,4	0	4	4
66	Indonesia	B	0,4	2	5	9
67	Bangladesh	A	0,3	3	0	3
68	Burkina Faso	C	0,2	0	0	0
68	Mali	A	0,2	0	7	7
69	Cameron	C	0,1	2	0	2
69	Senegal	C	0,1	0	3	3
69	Tanzania	C	0,1	0	0	0
70	Chad	C	0,0	0	6	6
71	China, VR	C	-0,1	10	0	10
72	Pakistan	B	-0,3	0	3	3
72	Peru	B	-0,3	2	4	6
72	Djibouti	C	-0,3	2	3	5
73	India	A	-0,6	5	6	10
73	Yugoslavia, BR	C	-0,6	2	11	13
74	Liberia	B	-0,7	2	0	2
74	Guatemala	A	-0,7	1	4	5
75	Angola	C	-0,8	5	7	12
75	Central Africa Rep.	B	-0,8	0	3	3
76	Ethiopia	B	-1,0	4	4	10
76	Kenya	C	-1,0	0	3	3
77	Iraq	C	-1,1	8	13	21
77	Burundi	C	-1,1	1	4	5
78	Sudan	C	-1,2	2	13	15
78	Nigeria	C	-1,2	3	3	6
79	Somalia	C	-1,3	0	7	7
80	Rwanda	C	-1,5	0	7	7
81	Myanmar	C	-1,6	2	4	6
82	Sierra Leone	C	-1,7	0	4	4
83	Uganda	C	-1,8	0	3	3
83	Niger	C	-1,8	1	3	4
83	Bolivia	A	-1,8	1	0	1

47	Taiwan	A	0,2
47	Malta	A	0,2
48	Japan	A	0,1
48	Island	A	0,1

59	Bhutan	C	1,3
60	Myanmar	C	1,2
60	Rwanda	C	1,2
61	Afghanistan	C	0,9

84	Bhutan	C	-1,9	0	0	0
85	Congo, DR	C	-2,4			10
86	Eritrea	C	-3,2	8	4	12
87	Afghanistan	C	-4,6	2	12	14

Legend:

A Democracy

B Transitory Regime

C Dictatorial Regime

Indices range from 0 to 10, with 10 being the highest and 0 the lowest value

Chapter 3

Trade Liberalization and Political Instability in Developing Countries[1]

Margit Bussmann, Harald Scheuthle, Gerald Schneider
University of Konstanz, Germany

1 INTRODUCTION

When in spring 2002 thousands of Argentineans protested against their government's economic policy, their anger was directed against, amongst other issues, the economic liberalization of the 1990s. After decades of protectionism, the Latin-American state followed the recommendation of the IMF, as did its neighbors, and systematically opened its markets of goods and capital. Critics of globalization considered the Argentinean crisis as an affirmation of their skepticism towards the "Washington consensus", namely the recipes of liberalization and deregulation. According to their interpretation, economic integration instigates socio-political conflicts because of the redistributive effects of liberalization. While capital owners and multinational firms profit from the renunciation of import substitution and other protectionist measures, the working population and the local industry are, in this perspective, the losers of the new policy.

This view suggests that increasing social and political instability will accompany the "Rush to Free Trade" (Rodrik, 1994) onto which many developing countries have embarked within the past two decades. Although this thesis plays a central role in the debate on globalization, it was not systematically tested until now. The majority of the economic literature deals with the *causes* but not with the *consequences* of economic interdependence. The increasingly professional research on the causes of civil war refers only partially to economic conditions as potential explanations of intrastate conflicts.

1. We would like to thank the participants of the workshop on "Computer-Aided Methods for International Conflict Resolution and Prevention" at the Austrian Research Institute for Artificial Intelligence, Vienna 25-26 October 2002, for comments. Margit Bussmann and Gerald Schneider gratefully acknowledge the German Foundation for Peace Research for financial support of this project. In this chapter, we present a translated and slightly revised version with complementary analyses of Bussmann, Scheuthle, and Schneider (2003).

R. Trappl (ed.), Programming for Peace, 49–70.

The availability of natural resources deserves special mention (Collier, 2001; de Soysa, 2002). However, a state's interlacing with the world economy is attributed at the most the role of a control variable. This is in sharp contrast to the dependency school, which was prominent in the 1970s and 1980s. Their representatives repeatedly pointed at the destabilizing effect that foreign direct investment allegedly has.

Academic research has dealt with the economic causes of protests since a long time already (e.g., Jagodzinski, 1983). However, the relationship between economic openness and political instability was ignored, although Ronald Rogowski (1989) raised the issue already some fifteen years ago. He showed with a standard trade model how free trade may affect class differences and conflict. Other researchers also find a connection between trade liberalization and regime change or economic crises (Fernandez and Rodrik, 1991: 1147), whereas Alesina and Drazen (1991) point out how the "war of attrition" in which contending social groups engage because of their unwillingness to pay the adjustment costs delays necessary reforms.

Although they are hardly inspired by these findings, opponents of globalization have repeatedly emphasized the destabilizing effects of economic integration. According to their point of view, a state that undergoes socially painful reforms such as trade liberalization significantly runs the risk of increased political instability. In principle, economic openness can influence the unity of a society in the long and in the short run. In this study, we distinguish between the two effects and examine them separately. A society possibly experiences social and political unrest shortly before and after measures of economic liberalization are implemented. In the long run, conversely, the economic growth resulting from economic openness might render exactly these conflicts harmless. For a better understanding of how measures of openness work, we will differentiate between various forms of instability, namely non-violent mass protests, political violence, and state failure.

Our chapter will be organized as follows. Based on foreign economic policy, we will first portray under which conditions and in which time frame measures of economic liberalization could meet domestic resistance. For this purpose, we will derive hypotheses on the long-term and short-term effects of openness from recent research in the field of political economy. The hypotheses will be compared to alternative explanations from the literature on the causes of civil war. In the description of our research design, we will lay out the operationalizion of the variables and introduce our method of estimation. We present our bivariate and multivariate results in section 4. The article concludes with a summary and suggestions for further research steps.

2 FOREIGN ECONOMIC OPENNESS AND DOMESTIC POLITICAL INSTABILITY: THEORY AND HYPOTHESES

2.1 The long-term effects

No economist is in doubt about the positive effects of trade for the national economy welfare (for example Krugman and Obstfeld, 2000). According to the neoclassical perspective, trade renders the division of labor between states more efficient. States that have opened up to international competition use their comparative advantage, and thus can produce and consume more goods than autarkies. In free trading states, prices approach world market prices. Protectionist measures, by contrast, increase the wedge between the national and the international price of a good. Sachs and Warner (1995) show that economically open developing countries grow faster and can better prevent balance of payments crises than comparable closed economies. Plümper (2001) qualifies this argument but does not deny that reducing trade barriers has a positive effect. In order to benefit from the welfare gains, regulative conditions have to be present for flourishing free trade. The degree to which a state shields its economy against foreign competition largely determines to what extent it can realize welfare gains from free trade.

Free trade can minimize the risk of domestic conflict in two ways. First of all, trade increases the welfare for the general population, and thus reduces factors that can lead to instability, as stated by the theory of deprivation (Gurr, 1971). According to the Stolper-Samuelson theorem of international trade, the abundant factors in a country profit from free trade. In developing countries this is, depending on how factors are divided, either labor or unskilled labor (Wood, 1994). In any case, it is the masses of the population that benefit from trade liberalization. However, the question arises whether economic openness increases income inequality. Here the empirical evidence is split. According to Fischer (2001), income inequality declined after economic liberalization in South East Asia, while at the same time it increased in Latin America. Other studies found either no relationship between the two variables or they arrived at the conclusion that countries experienced a fairer distribution of income through openness (Bourguignon and Morrisson, 1990; Bussmann et al., 2002; Edwards, 1997). If free trade really leads to more income equality, we can expect an additional reduction in the risk of political conflict. Rich and satisfied citizens are, according to the theory of deprivation, less involved in protests than poor and disadvantaged people.

Furthermore, gains from trade increase the interest in maintaining a free trade regime. Violent conflicts would be a hindrance to this commercial spirit.

Thus, it is in a country's interests, as well as in that of its citizens, to guarantee domestic peace and stability. This second line of reasoning is an extension of the liberal and democratic peace literature. In accordance with Immanuel Kant, several researchers argue that democratic states and states that are integrated into the world economy have a lower risk of fighting each other. War disrupts trade flows between countries, and therefore is too costly for a state and its citizens (Russett and Oneal, 2001). In addition, trade enforces liberal norms that are opposite to war and violent conflicts (Kant, 1795 [1987]). This argumentation, as applied to interstate wars, is widely discussed and finds considerable empirical support (Barbieri and Schneider, 1999; Russett and Oneal, 2001; Schneider et al., 2003). The same logic could be transferred to intrastate conflicts. Extreme forms of domestic instability are an obstacle to free trade and reduce potential gains that could be achieved through foreign economic liberalization in the long run. The relevant actors will include free trade in their cost-benefit calculations when they consider domestic strategies. An escalation of quarrels about the foreign economic orientation of a country is thus counterproductive for all participants because it deters foreign investors and trading partners. In case of an escalating domestic conflict, the parties —unions and employers, export-oriented and import-substituting industries— are all in the same boat.

Concerning the long-term effects of economic liberalization, we assume that economic openness helps to enhance economic development. The incentives for political opponents to find a peaceful solution for the conflict will be higher. Besides, liberal norms of conflict resolution are widespread, as postulated by transactionalism for half a century already (Deutsch et al., 1957). Based on the above arguments, we hypothesize that more open states are less susceptible to political instability.

2.2 The short-term effects

Whereas in the long-term the welfare increasing effect of economic openness is important, the distributive effect of the process of liberalization is decisive in the short run. A closed economy's opening up to free trade is a serious interference in existing economic and social relations. This is especially true for developing countries that largely rely on the development strategy of import-substitution. Liberalization might be accompanied by important economic changes that could affect large parts of the population.

The assertion that the process of opening an economy to international trade increases the risk of instability can be related to two classical models of international trade theory, the Ricardo-Viner model and the Stolper-Samuelson model. An example of conceptualizing the conflict centering on the free trade orientation is provided by the widely acknowledged work of Rogowski

(1989). In his model, the coalition patterns activate a change of the trading regime in such a way that the society becomes less stable. He distinguishes, based on the Stolper-Samuelson model, the factors *capital*, *labor*, and *land*. In case of a turn to free trade, the holder of abundant factors will benefit, whereas the owners of scarce factors will lose. The losers want to stop this change and the winners are interested in accelerating the reforms in order to enlarge their power. Rogowski derives the lines of conflict for countries that are in transition from protectionism to free trade. The cleavage runs between urban and rural areas in countries where land is the abundant factor, and between labor and capital in countries that have abundant labor.

Frieden (1991) presents a similar model. He argues, based on the Ricardo-Viner model, that sector-specific factors are not completely mobile between the sectors. In this model, the lines of conflict do not run between the different classes but, in case of trade liberalization, between the export-promoting and the import-substituting sectors. The more specific a factor and the more cohesive a sector, the higher is the pressure on politics and thus the larger its political clout.

The political economy of developing countries is determined by state regulation and rent-seeking, both aiming at the enrichment of the elites and the stability of the ruling regime, instead of at the welfare of the population (Tullock, 1980; Weede, 1990). An economy regulated by the government has the goal of earning foreign exchange through the export of resources and agricultural products to raise money in support of the import-substituting industries. Followers of the government manage these industries often inefficiently, rendering them internationally uncompetitive. To save these firms the markets are closed. This way the ruling elites can earn rents and in return they promise loyalty and support to the government. In the medium-term this system is stable because neither the government nor the elites have an incentive to change the existing order. In the long run, however, the national economy suffers, and reforms become eventually inevitable.

Foreign economic liberalization destabilizes the existing social system because the profiteer of a closed economy loses a large share of income. Economic liberalization enhances national welfare, but the distributive effect is immense. Rodrik (1994) estimates that the cost-benefit ratio is larger than five; this means for each currency unit of additional income from liberalization five currency units will be redistributed. A change in trade policy presumably has a direct impact on the income of the import-competing sector which has to bear the total costs while the general population (through low prices) and the export sector are the winners. Until the 1980s the industries in most developing countries were protected from competition; they could produce inefficiently and sell their products more expensively than the world market price, i.e. with a higher margin of profit. With open markets this is no longer possible. Consequently, the import-competing sector is always opposed to foreign trade liberalization.

The state has to expect losses from liberalization as well. Due to an inefficient tax system, many developing states relied on the income from tariffs and the sale of licenses in order to finance their budget (Rodrik, 1994). Liberalization reduces this source of income. Because taxpayers might fear that the government seeks compensation, they have some reason to oppose the reforms.

Another problem of trade reforms results from the fact that differently structured groups are affected by the gains and losses of the reform. As the general public is the winner, individual gains are small. Because the losers are a small group, which often coincides with the political and economic elite, the individual disutility is large. This divergence creates an important asymmetry. According to Olson (1965), it is much easier for a small homogeneous group to organize itself, whereas a large heterogeneous group suffers from the problem of collective action. Every individual wants to use a public good but has no incentive to contribute to its provision. As a result the public good is not or only insufficiently provided. In the case of trade liberalization, this means that, unlike the small group, the large group is badly organized, and thus not efficient in its fight for the public good "liberalization". The beneficiaries of the previous system, however, could show their resistance to liberalization in order to maintain their privileges. If the government decides to open the country to free trade, it has to expect massive opposition from the import-competing sector but can count on only limited support.

Foreign liberalization is a difficult undertaking, especially because the supporters of the government are potential losers. An additional problem results from the long-term character of the costs of liberalization, as it is not possible for protectionists to seek the rents after the reform. This source of income dries up completely through liberalization. Especially neo-patrimonial governments have increasing difficulties to compensate its followers because they lose a source of income as well.

In this situation the state is susceptible to political instability. On the one hand, the government has to improve the economic situation in order to avoid turmoil in the population and to weaken the opposition. On the other hand, the government is afraid that the elite will organize a coup in order to prevent or reverse reforms. These contradictory goals put pressure on the government, what Plümper and Schneider (2000) call the trilemma of the protectionist autocrat. The autocrat has to maximize his own income and that of his followers and simultaneously, in times of crises, he has to make concessions to the liberal opposition or to the population in order to maintain regime stability.

This situation is problematic for the autocrat as he can only achieve two of the three goals at the same time. Thus, it is obvious why a long lasting socio-political conflict often prevents the timely implementation of reforms (Alesina and Drazen, 1991).

In addition to the hypothesis on the long-term effects of economic openness on political stability, we will examine short-term effects. We assume that the liberalization of the economy directly increases the risk of domestic conflict because this process is accompanied by a far reaching redistribution, which polarizes between the economic and political winners and losers. This is especially true in times of reforms, as the welfare gains that the government promises remain uncertain. We expect, in sum, that in the short term the process of foreign economic liberalization increases the risk of instability.

2.3 Control factors

Whereas our focus is on the relationship between economic liberalization or openness and political violence, we will also control for other factors that are spelled out as potential causes of instability. There are essentially two strands of literature that deal with the causes of political violence. One theory emphasizes economic dissatisfaction and the other considers political incentives as root causes of rebellion (Schock, 1996). Representatives of the theory of economic dissatisfaction, also called relative deprivation, start with the assumption that the population's perception of the difference between expectations and actual economic conditions leads to violence (Gurr, 1971). The distinction between absolute and relative deprivation is common. In case of absolute deprivation, a group becomes rebellious if it possesses very little of a certain good (Lipset, 1959), whereas in case of relative deprivation, a group compares itself with another group. Frustration emerges because the group has less of a good than the group with which it compares itself (Gurr, 1970, 1994). A high degree of economic and political inequality within the population leads to these processes. In addition, factors of identification, such as ethnicity or religion, can justify violence against other groups (Ellingsen, 2000).

Identity and frustration are not sufficient factors to start a rebellion; the group needs in addition a good opportunity. The group is accordingly supposed to calculate if the rebellion is likely to be successful (Tilly, 1978). For the representatives of the theory of political opportunity, it is less the economic conditions that are important. The political context and the opportunity to overcome collective action problems are more salient. Factors that contain a potential for violence are present in every society, but only in certain situations will potential violence turn into actual violence (Tilly, 1978; Tarrow,

1989, 1998). Here, especially the characteristics of the political system play a role.

A high level of development is expected to reduce the risk of instability because the population attributes its economic well-being at least partly to the government (Henderson and Singer, 2000). Lipset (1959) showed that economic welfare leads to achievements like education or better access to information which in turn reduces instability. Furthermore, Gurr (1979) considers economic development as a means to reduce political violence without reducing protests because rich countries are predominantly democracies and democracies tolerate non-violent protests. A micro-level version of this explanation is offered by Collier and Hoeffler (1998). According to their study, the costs for a rebellion go up with a higher level of development because a rich individual has more to lose from a rebellion than a poor citizen. We assume that economic welfare renders the conditions that might lead the population to become involved in a rebellion less attractive. Economic welfare is thus expected to reduce the risk of political instability.

Liberalism as a theory within the field of international relations postulates that democracies are especially resistant against violent political conflicts. The two underlying causal mechanisms that this approach puts forward relate to the competitive elections on the one hand and the non-violent norms of conflict resolution on the other hand that shape democratic systems. If the majority of the population is dissatisfied with the government, it can vote for another party in the next election. The threat to be moved out of office functions, in the liberal view, as a deterrent against the use of force. The democratic norms allow for a generally peaceful conflict resolution and a non-violent way of dealing with political questions (Russett, 1993; Gleditsch, 1995; Rummel, 1997). The thesis that democracies are more peaceful political systems is, for the most part, empirically supported. However, we cannot assume a linear relationship between the two variables but rather an inverse U-curved relationship between democracy and political violence (Muller and Weede, 1990; Boswell and Dixon, 1993; Schock, 1996; Auvinen, 1997; Benson and Kugler, 1998; Ellingsen, 2000; Henderson and Singer, 2000; Hegre et al., 2001). This means that the risk of political instability is rather low in democracies as well as in autocracies, whereas it is high in semi-democracies. In contrast to democratic politicians, autocrats are not dependent on the support of the population but are generally backed up by a very small winning coalition. In exchange for their support the group expects to receive rents from the government (Frey and Eichenberger, 1994; Pritzl and Schneider, 1997). The small size of a winning coalition makes the survival of the autocratic ruler relatively independent from the performance of the economy (Bueno de Mesquita et al., 2000). In addition, autocrats have the possibility to suppress resistance by force. The risk of instability is assumed to be higher in semi-autocratic regimes than in democracies or autocracies. An economic crisis weakens the government in many ways making a country more susceptible to rebellions. Reduced income from taxes limits the abilities to silence a potential opposition (Plümper and Schneider, 2000). Second, an economic crisis increases dissatisfaction among the population who has to bear the main burden and holds the government responsible. In a democracy the government counts on losing the next elections; in a dictatorship political violence might erupt if the government can no longer distribute rents to its supporters who might consider overthrowing the government by force. As Collier and Hoeffler (2000) point out, an economic crisis increases the risk of a domestic conflict but not because certain groups in the population feel deprived of their rents. Instead, a bad economic situation reduces the costs of recruitment for the rebels because they can offer higher incomes to potential members than the wages to be earned on the regular labor markets. Economic growth should reduce the risk of political instability.

The size of the population needs to be taken into account, especially in connection with foreign economic liberalization. The assumption is that large states are more susceptible to conflict. Populous states are more heterogeneous which increases the probability that individual groups expect an advantage from successions (Collier and Hoeffler, 1998: 564), a relationship that a broad literature supports (i.e. Rothgeb, 1990; Collier and Hoeffler, 1998, 2000; Zanger, 2000). In addition to a direct effect of a country's size, there is an indirect effect. Large countries are less strongly integrated into the world economy because they can satisfy the need of the population within the domestic market, whereas for small states integration in the world economy gives access to a larger market (Alesina et al., 1997; Alesina and Wacziarg, 1998). This advantage comes at the price of higher cultural heterogeneity which minimizes the efficiency of political institutions. We can easily deduce from this argument that in small countries economic liberalization will be more welcomed in the population because it brings more direct benefits to the citizens. In large countries the advantages of liberalization are less pronounced. In these countries economic liberalization might provoke a strong reaction and thus increases the risk of instability.

3 RESEARCH DESIGN

We examine the hypotheses of a relationship between political instability and foreign economic openness and liberalization with data for 90 developing countries for the time period from 1978 to 1997. As *protest, political violence,* and *state failure* are dichotomous dependent variables, we choose logistic regression as method of estimation. This statistical approach estimates the probability that an event occurs, i.e., the probability that the dependent variable takes the value 1. We conduct all tests with White-corrected standard errors in order to deal with the problem of heteroscedasticity; this releases the condition that the single observations, at least within a state, have to be independent. The panel structure of the data set bears another problem, the problem of temporal dependence, and thus an additional violation of the assumption of independence of observations. We controlled for temporal dependence with the approach taken by Beck et al. (1998) of adding a variable that measures the stability in the past. Stability in the past is calculated as the number of years since the last outbreak of instability with the program Binary Time-Series-Cross-Section Data Analysis Utility Version 4.0.4. (Tucker, 1999). What follows is the description of how we operationalized the individual variables and of the corresponding sources of data.

3.1 Dependent variable: Political instability

Our dependent variable is political instability which we operationalize in three different ways: as *mass protests*, *political violence*, and *state failure*. By using different indicators of instability we want to ensure that our results are robust to the operationalization of the dependent variable, especially in light of the lacking consensus in the research community on how to measure political instability (Auvinen, 1997; Kimenyi and Mbaku, 1993; Boswell and Dixon, 1993; Sidell, 1988).

For the first two indicators we use information on various forms of political instability from the Cross-National Time-Series Database (CNTS Archive 2001). All variables in the CNTS database count the events per year. The combination of different events into an additive index is problematic because the ordinal character of these variables is questionable. Instead we use indicators that take the value 1 if one or more of the described events happened and 0 otherwise. This means the indicator variable *mass protest* takes the value 1 if a country experienced one or more demonstrations, general strikes and/or revolts within a given year. Revolts are violent demonstrations. General strikes and anti-government demonstrations are peaceful and are aimed against government policies. The variables are 0 if none of these events happened. We calculate *political violence* similarly, using the CNTS-data about revolutionary wars, guerilla wars, and political assassinations. Revolutions are instirred with the goal of overthrowing the government. Guerilla wars account for activities of illegal rebel groups. Political assassinations are killings or attempted killings of high ranking civil servants or politicians.

In addition to *mass protests* and *political violence*, we examine *state failure* with data from the State Failure Task Force (Esty et al., 1998; King and Zeng, 2001). The State Failure Project divides the variable *state failure* into revolutionary wars, ethnic wars, and genocides. In order to be classified as a civil war, a conflict has to break out between the state and a rebel group of at least 1000 members and the conflict has to have a threshold of at least 100 victims per year. Revolutionary wars aim at overthrowing the government, whereas in ethnic wars the dispute occurs between the government and an ethnic group that wants to change its status, for example seceding from the state. Genocides are mass killings organized by the state and that last at least six months. State failures are abrupt and violent changes in the state's structure or a change to an autocratic regime. They are defined by a change of at last three points on the Polity-scale or through a long period of missing state institutions. As before, we use state failure as a 0-1 indicator.

3.2 Independent variables

3.2.1 *Foreign economic openness and liberalization*

We distinguish between economic openness and economic liberalization. The former variable stands for the extent to which the state is actually integrated into the world economy; the latter concept is the process with which the government creates the regulative conditions for free trade. In order to estimate the long-term effects of economic openness we rely on a measure that calculates the sum of exports and imports divided by GDP with data from the Penn World Tables version 6.0. A problem with this measurement is that trade flows do not necessarily provide information about trade policy (Martin et al., 2001: 3).

Foreign economic liberalization denotes the regulations that are necessary for free trade, i.e., the absence of tariffs, quotas, import and export limitations, and a freely convertible currency. Liberalization signifies the withdrawal from regulative obstacles for free trade. For a country to benefit from the advantages of trade, the political conditions favorable for free trade have to be present. In order to investigate the short-term effects of the process of economic liberalization, we will use the CACAO-indicator of Martin, Plümper and Schneider (Martin et al., 2001). This indicator of openness measures trade institutions and barriers on an ordinal scale from 0 for open to 7 for closed. This index is based on a combination of trade policies and institutional arrangements taken from the IMF's *Report on Exchange Arrangement and Exchange Restrictions*. The process of liberalization will be measured as the CACAO's difference to the previous year.

3.2.2 Level of development

The negative relationship between the level of development and political instability or civil war was empirically supported in several studies. The GDP per capita is a standard variable in every regression on this topic (Auvinen, 1997; Collier and Hoeffler, 1998, 2000; Elbadavi and Sambanis, 2000; Fearon and Laitin, 2003; Henderson and Singer, 2000; Zanger, 2000). Others arrived at the same result by using the energy consumption per capita (Jagodzinski, 1983; Ellingsen, 2000). We add the GDP per capita in logarithmic form to our regressions to account for the skewed distribution of this variable.

3.2.3 Economic growth

Few studies have tested the influence of economic crises on instability. Jagodzinski's (1983) study revealed a negative or no effect of economic growth. Auvinen (1997) found a positive relationship between inflation and political conflict and a negative effect of economic growth per capita. Based on GDP per capita, economic growth will be measured as $(GDP_t - GDP_{t-1})/GDP_{t-1}$.

3.2.4 Level of democracy

We operationalize, as indicated, the type of regime with the widely used Polity IV-index (Marshall and Jaggers, 2000). Polity combines various institutional characteristics of a political system—openness and competitiveness of executive recruitment, constraints on the chief executive, regulation and competitiveness of political participation—to an index ranging from -10 for autocracies to +10 for democracies. We add the index of regime type to our model of instability in its linear form as well as its squared term to examine whether the relationship has the form of an inverted U-curve.

3.2.5 Population

To account for the size of the population we use data from the World Bank (1999). The variable will be used in its logarithmic form.

For the variables *economic development*, *economic growth*, *democracy*, *openness*, and *liberalization* we take the values from the previous year in order to avoid that the variables are influenced by instability. For *population* this is not necessary because this concept does not vary greatly over time. Table 3.1. summarizes our basic models and indicates the signs that we expect for the independent variables.

Table 3.1. Expected influence of different variables on political instability

Independent variable	*Expected influence on political instability*
Openness	-
Liberalization	+
Economic growth	-
Level of development	-
Democracy	+
Democracy squared	-
Population	+

4 RESULTS

As a first approach to the research questions we will examine whether economically open countries are more stable than closed states by looking at a simple cross tabulation of *openness* and *instability* (see Table 3.2.). For this purpose *openness* is divided into three categories: from closed (0 to 2 on the CACAO-openness scale) over an intermediate category (3 to 4) to open (5 to 7). As *instability* we use collective protests and political violence.

Table 3.2. Cross-tabulations of trade openness and instability

Protest	*Trade openness*			
	1 - closed	*2*	*3 - open*	*total*
0 – no protest	831 67,18%	97 62,58%	49 70,00%	977 66,83%
1 – protest	406 32,82%	58 37,42%	21 30,00%	485 33,17%
Total	1237	155	70	1462

Pearsons Chi-Quadrat (χ^2)=1,65 df(2)

Political Violence	*Trade openness*			
	1 - closed	*2*	*3 - open*	*total*
0 – no violence	749 63,69%	101 69,66%	52 88,14%	902 65,36%
1 – violence	427 36,31%	44 30,34%	7 11,86%	478 34,64%
Total	1176	145	59	1380

Pearsons Chi-Quadrat (χ^2)=16,15** df(2)

We can detect a significant χ^2 difference between the categories only in the case of political violence. This means open countries experience less instability. For the closed and intermediate categories the proportion of non-violence and violence is about 2:1, whereas for the open states this proportion is 9:1. In the case of protests the differences could happen by chance. Here we can see that the distribution for all categories of openness is throughout about 2:1. A simple bivariate examination leads us thus to conclude that *openness* is not related to *protests* but does vary systematically with *political violence*.

In our multivariate regression analyses we examine the relationship between *openness* and *instability* while holding other influences constant. For the tests we use different indicators of instability.

The first column in Table 3.3. shows the long-term effects of *openness* on *mass protests*, i.e., the incidence of demonstrations, strikes, and/or unrests. *Openness* is negatively related to *mass protests* at a level of statistical significance of .06. The null hypothesis of no relationship between the two variables cannot be rejected. In the second column, we substitute the long-term variable of *openness* with *liberalization*, the variable measuring the short-term effects of the process of opening an economy. We can observe a negative relationship but it is clearly not significant. In our tests, we could not confirm short-term effects of foreign economic liberalization on the protest behavior in developing countries.

In both models the control variables have the expected direction. The results of *economic development* indicate that the hypothesis of rich countries having fewer conflicts than poor countries is not warranted, at least not concerning protests. Instead, we can observe that protests are more likely in rich countries, a result that is statistically significant. The variable *economic growth* as indicator for economic crises points, as predicted, to a conflict reducing effect. It seems that economic crises can significantly destabilize a country. The lacking significance of the squared term of *democracy* suggests a linear relationship between *protests* and *democracy*. In democracies we can observe more protest behavior, which has to do with lower levels of repression and more freedom of expression in democracies. This is consistent with Prezeworski et al.'s (2000) findings. *Population* shows a highly significant and positive relationship with *instability*; this means that large countries are less stable than small countries. This finding is in agreement with the hypothesis that large countries are more heterogeneous and thus have a higher potential for conflict. The variable accounting for the history of protests is, as expected, highly significant. The more years without protests a country experienced, the less likely it will undergo a protest now.

Table 3.3. Foreign economic openness and liberalization and various indicators of political domestic instability, 1978-97.

	Protest		*Political violence*		*State failure*	
	Model 1	*Model 2*	*Model 3*	*Model 4*	*Model 5*	*Model 6*
Openness $_{t-1}$	-0.0072* (0.0038)	-	-0.0062* (0.0037)	-	-0.0073 (0.0058)	-
Liberalization $_{t-1}$	-	-0.071 (0.122)	-	-0.0031 (0.164)	-	-0.065 (0.389)
Economic development $_{t-1}$	0.405*** (0.127)	0.308* (0.119)	-0.046 (0.116)	-0.044 (0.123)	-0.223 (0.206)	-0.151 (0.212)
Economic growth$_{t-1}$	-2.17* (1.06)	-3.77* (1.23)	-0.946 (1.01)	-1.13 (1.36)	-1.84 (1.22)	1.56 (1.72)
Democracy $_{t-1}$	0.042*** (0.011)	0.030* (0.012)	0.045*** (0.013)	0.048*** (0.014)	0.067*** (0.021)	0.076* (0.056)
Squared Democracy $_{t-1}$	-0.0019 (0.0024)	-0.001 (0.0029)	-0.0084* (0.0034)	-0.0061* (0.0037)	-0.012* (0.0053)	-0.0075 0.0057
Population	0.32*** (0.08)	0.38*** (0.07)	0.093 (0.08)	0.13* (0.06)	0.39*** (0.10)	0.211* (0.12)
Years since last Instability	-0.818*** (0.141)	-0.801*** (0.155)	-1.25*** (0.156)	-1.207*** (0.181)	-1.89*** (0.21)	-2.00*** (0.22)
Constant	-7.69*** (1.61)	-8.33*** (1.29)	-0.011 (1.65)	-1.06 (1.51)	-2.44 (2.26)	-0.026 (2.42)
N	1442	1052	1345	988	1445	1052
Wald Chi^2	208.34	166.69	176.97	138.13	347.31	276.55
Prob. > Chi^2	0.0001	0.0001	0.0001	0.0001	0.0001	0.0001
Pseudo R^2	.20	.21	.20	.20	.56	.66

Note. The first numbers in each cell are the coefficients, the number in parentheses are the semi-robust standard errors. The asterixes are the level of significance (* P < .05; ** P < .01; *** P < .001).

In models 3 and 4 we substitute *protests* with *political violence* as indicator for instability. As expected, in autocracies and democracies the risk of instability is smaller, whereas in semi-autocratic regimes the risk is higher. The *democracy* variable in its simple form has a positive sign and the squared democracy term has a negative coefficient, thus referring to the relationship of an inverted U-curve. Both variables are jointly significant at the .001 level. In model 4, we can detect a positive relationship between *population* and *political violence* as well. The variable for the violence history is again significant. Between *openness* and *political violence* we have a negative relationship with a probability of less than 10 % that this relationship occurred by chance. On the other hand, foreign economic liberalization has no effect on political violence in model 4.

Finally, we consider instability operationalized as *state failure*, a dependent variable that is based on data from the State Failure Project. The inverted U-curve between level of *democracy* and *state failure* can be confirmed; both variables are jointly highly significant. We find, with a high level of significance, that large countries are more susceptible to instability. The level of development has the expected negative sign but is not statistically significant. Economic growth also turns out to be insignificant. The variables *openness* and *liberalization* have both a negative coefficient without statistical significance.

To sum up, we can conclude from the tests so far that in the long term an open economy is related with political stability, a finding for which we detect some support. In the short term, the process of liberalization does not appear to affect instability.

4.1 Tests of robustness

In the next series of tests, we examine additional control variables that were emphasized in the literature. We want to reduce the omitted variable bias and to ensure that our results are robust to the model specification. The following analyses are based on the model of political violence, the variable we are primarily interested in. The literature frequently mentions income inequality as a possible cause of political violence. The predominant and widely spread opinion is that an unequal distribution of income increases the risk of political instability (Muller and Seligson, 1987; Boswell and Dixon, 1993; Alesina and Perotti, 1996). Poor people perceive inequality as unfair and demand a more just distribution of resources. Therefore, we examine the additional hypothesis that an unequal distribution of income increases the risk of political conflict by using the Gini coefficient to measure the income distribution. Data are available from Deininger and Squire (1998). Theoretically, this control variable is very important; however, our results show that it is statistically not significant. With the inclusion of the Gini index the number of observations drops to 589 in our model. Its addition has no impact on the trade variables.

Besides income inequality, ethnic fractionalization is frequently pointed out as a reason for political instability. The research community does not yet agree which form this relationship has. On the one hand, there is the assumption that the danger of conflict is highest when there are two equally strong groups because each one of them believes that it will be the winner in a conflict but also because the costs of coordinating and founding a rebel group are smallest. (Henderson and Singer, 2000; Collier and Hoeffler, 1998). The other side argues that a group's ethnic dominance is most dangerous because the group has an incentive to take advantage of its strength and to exploit other groups (Auvinen, 1997; Collier, 2001). We examine the hypothesis that ethnic fractionalization increases the risk of political conflicts.

Ethnic fractionalization is constructed as the Herfindahl-index by summing up the squared proportions in the population and subtracting it from 1. Small values stand for homogenous and large values for heterogeneous societies. We use data from Collier and Hoeffler (2000). Changes in the ethnic composition of a population are very small and therefore, we took the last values for all the years until 1997 to avoid missing values. The variable has in both models a negative sign but is not significant and does not influence the results of the other variables. *Openness* remains marginally significant and *liberalization* insignificant.[2]

We examined our basic model of political violence for collinearity of *openness* or *liberalization* with any of the control variables to see if this influences our results. For example, one could expect that the variable *democracy* influences the effect of *openness*, because democratic states presumably have a higher involvement in free trade (Bliss and Russett, 1998). Excluding the level of development and economic growth does not affect the results of *openness* or *liberalization*. However, when suppressing the *democracy* variables from the equation, *openness* loses its significance. The violence reducing effect is thus not completely independent from the regime type.[3] If *population* is excluded, the level of significance rises dramatically ($p < .001$). In this case however, *openness* accounts for the fact that small countries are more open.

5 SUMMARY

In this study we examined, with a dataset of 90 developing countries for the time period 1978-97, the two questions of whether free trade reduces the risk of political instability and whether the process of liberalization increases this risk. We wanted to shed light on the long-term and short-term effects of free trade with regard to instability in form of mass protests and political violence. Neither long-term openness nor short-term measures of liberalization

2. We also added the squared term of ethnic fractionalization in order to account for Ellingsen's (2000) argument. Both variables had the expected signs but were insignificant.

3. The inclusion of an interactive term between openness and democracy does not provide further insight as it is insignificant.

seem to have an impact on the protest behavior in a population. With regard to political violence, free trade has a conflict reducing effect in the long term but no effect in the short term. The suspicion that countries on their way to a more open economy are more susceptible to instability cannot be supported. The results of our regression analyses rather lead to the conclusion that countries that are more open economically seem to be more stable. This supports the basic idea that integration into the world economy reduces the risk of domestic conflicts. In this regard our results are supplementary to the findings of the liberal peace on the interstate level. The results suggest that free trade has a conflict reducing effect especially for political violence and that it can affect the preferences and norms of conflict regulation. The second important result of our study is that the process of foreign economic liberalization does not increase the risk of instability.

High economic growth, interpreted here as an absence of an economic crises, reduces the risk of mass protests. In democracies and large countries we can observe a higher probability that protest will happen. The inverted U-curve effect of democracy, which postulates that democracies as well as autocracies are less susceptible to political violence, can be confirmed.

This work was a first attempt to make the debate on the effects of globalization more objective. We laid a bridge between the literature on economic openness and reforms and the research on conflict and civil war. The influence of foreign economic liberalization on instability was not systematically examined yet in the empirical social sciences. In this regard our work is a contribution to this shortcoming. It introduces a new potential cause of conflict into the theoretical debate and, at least partly, confirms this effect empirically.

A major problem with our empirical tests was the quality and incompleteness of the data. Missing values result in the complete exclusion of some countries and years. This impairs our results and does not allow us to draw generalizations as the missing values are not random. New and more complete data have to be collected. In particular an extension of the data set on income inequality would be very valuable with regard to the causes of political instability. Case studies can help to clarify the causal relations in a next step. In addition, international factors, such as interstate conflicts, have to be included in an analysis. We are confident that by extending our research, the central finding will be maintained: Foreign economic liberalization has triggered in many countries what could be called the "peace dividend" of globalization.

References

Alesina, A.and Drazen, A., 1991, Why are stabilizations delayed?, *American Economic Review* **81**: 1170-88.

Alesina, A. and Perotti, R., 1996, Income distribution, political instability, and investment, *European Economic Review* **40**: 1203-28.

Alesina, A., Spolare, E., and Wacziarg, R., 1997, Economic integration and political disintegration, NBER Working Paper Nr. 6163.

Alesina, A., and Wacziarg, R., 1998, Openness, country size and government, *Journal of Public Economics* **69**: 305-321.

Auvinen, J., 1997, Political conflict in less developed countries 1981-89, *Journal of Peace Research* **34**(2): 177-195.

Barbieri, K., and Schneider, G., 1999, Globalization and peace: Assessing new directions in the study of trade and conflict, *Journal of Peace Research* **3**(4): 387-404.

Beck, N., Katz, J. N., and Tucker R., 1998, Taking time seriously in binary time-series--cross-section analysis, *American Journal of Political Science* **42**(4): 1260-1288.

Benson, M., and Kugler, J., 1998, Power parity, democracy, and the severity of internal violence, *Journal of Conflict Resolution* **42**(2): 196-209.

Bliss, H., and Russett, B., 1998, Democratic trading partners: The liberal connection, 1962-1989, *The Journal of Politics* **60**: 1126-47.

Boswell, T., and Dixon, W. J., 1993, Marx's theory of rebellion: A cross-national analysis of class exploitation, economic development, and violent revolt, *American Sociological Review* **58**(5): 681-702.

Bourguignon, F., and Morrisson, C., 1990, Income distribution, development and foreign trade: A cross sectional analysis, *European Economic Review* **34**: 1113-1132.

Bueno de Mesquita, B., Morrow, J. D., Siverson, R. M., and Smith, A., 2000, Political institutions, political survival, and policy success, in: *Governing for Prosperity*, B. Bueno de Mesquita and H. L. Root, eds., Yale University Press, New Haven and London, pp. 59-84.

Bussmann, M., de Soysa, I., and Oneal, J. R., 2002, The effect of foreign investment on economic development and income inequality. ZEF-Discussion Paper on Development Policy no. 53, Bonn.

Bussmann, M., Scheuthle, H., and Schneider, G., 2003, Die 'Friedensdividende' der Globalisierung: Außenwirtschaftliche Öffnung und innenpolitische Stabilität in den Entwicklungsländern, *Politische Vierteljahresschrift* **44** (2003), 302-324.

CNTS Archive, 2001, Cross-National Time-Series Archive; http://www.databanks.sitehosting.net/www/main.htm.

Collier, P., 2001, Implications of ethnic diversity, *Economic Policy* **16**(32): 127-166.

Collier, P., and Hoeffler, A., 1998, On economic causes of civil war, *Oxford Economic Papers* **50**: 563-573.

Collier, P., and Hoeffler, A., 2000, *Greed and grievance in civil war*, unpublished manuscript, World Bank.

Deininger, K., and Squire, L., 1996, A new data set measuring income inequality. *World Bank Economic Review* **10**: 565-91.

de Soysa, I., 2002, Paradise is a bazaar? Greed, creed, and governance in civil war, 1989-99, *Journal of Peace Research* **39**(4): 395-416.

Deutsch, K. W., et al, 1957, *Political Community and the North Atlantic Area: International Organization in the Light of Historical Experience*, Princeton, N.J.

Edwards, S., 1997, Trade policy, growth, and income distribution, *American Economic Review* **87**(2): 205-210.

Elbadawi, I., and Sambanis, N., 2000, How much war will we see? Estimating the incidence of civil war in 161 countries, unpublished manuscript, World Bank.

Ellingsen, T., 2000, Colorful community or ethnic witches' brew? Multiethnicity and domestic conflict during and after the cold war, *Journal of Conflict Resolution* **44**(2): 228-249.

Esty, D. C., Goldstone, J., Gurr, T. R., Harff, B., Surko, B. T., Unger, A. N., and Chen, R. S., 1998, The state failure project: Early warning research for U.S. foreign policy planning, in: *Preventive Measures. Building Risk Assessment and Crisis Early Warning Systems*, J. L. Davies and T. R. Gurr, eds., Rowman and Littlefield Publishers, Inc., Lanham, MD, pp. 27-38.

Fearon, J. D., and Laitin, D. D., 2003, Ethnicity, insurgency, and civil war, *American Political Science Review* **97**(1): 75-90.

Fernandez, R., and Rodrik, D., 1991, Resistance to reform: Status quo bias in the presence of individual-specific uncertainty, *American Economic Review* **81**(5): 1146-1155.

Fischer, R. D., 2001, The evolution of inequality after trade liberalization, *Journal of Development Economics* **66**: 555-579.

Frey, B. S., and Eichenberger, R., 1994, The political economy of stabilization programmes in developing countries, *European Journal of Political Economy* **10**: 169-190.

Frieden, J. A., 1991, *Debt, Development, and Democracy. Modern Political Economy and Latin America, 1965-1985*, Princeton, NJ.

Gleditsch, N. P., 1995, Democracy and the future of European peace, *European Journal of International Relations* **1**(4): 539-571.

Gurr, T. R., 1971, *Why Men Rebel*, Princeton University Press, Princeton, NJ.

Gurr, T. R., 1979, Political protest and rebellion in the 1960s: The United States in world perspective, in: *Violence in America: Historical and Comparative Perspectives*, H. D. Graham and T. R. Gurr, eds., Sage, Beverly Hills, CA.

Gurr, T. R., 1994, *Minorities at Risk. A Global View of Ethnopolitical Conflicts*, United States Institute of Peace Press, Washington, DC.

Hegre, H., Ellingsen, T., Gates, S., and Gleditsch, N. P., 2001, Toward a democratic civil peace? Democracy, political change, and civil war, 1816-1992, *American Political Science Review* **95**: 33-48.

Henderson, E. A., and Singer, D. J., 2000, Civil war in the post-colonial world, 1946-1992, *Journal of Peace Research* **37**(3): 275-299.

International Monetary Fund, Various Years, *Report on Exchange Arrangements and Exchange Restrictions*, IMF, Washington D.C.

Jagodzinski, W., 1983, Ökonomische Entwicklung und politisches Protestverhalten 1920-1973. Eine kombinierte Quer- und Längsschnittanalyse. *Politische Vierteljahresschrift Sonderheft* **14**: 18-43.

Kant, I., 1795, 1986, *Zum ewigen Frieden: ein philosophischer Entwurf*, Engelholm Verlag, Stuttgart.

Kimenyi, M. S., and Mbaku, J. M., 1993, Rent-seeking and institutional stability in developing countries, *Public Choice* **77**: 385-405.

King, G., and Zeng, L., 2001, Improving forecasts of state failure, *World Politics* **53**: 623-58.

Krugman, P. R., and Obstfeld, M., 2000, *International Economics: Theory and Policy*, 5th ed., Addison-Wesley, Reading.

Lipset, S. M., 1959, Some social requisites of democracy: Economic development and political legitimacy, *American Political Science Review* **53**: 69-106.

Marshall, M. G., and Jaggers, K., 2000, *Polity IV project: Dataset users manual*, http://www.bsos.umd.edu/cidcm/inscr/polity/index.htm.

Martin, C. W., Plümper, T., and Schneider, G., 2001, *Economic openness in developing countries: An empirical investigation using CACAO*, unpublished manuscript, Universität Konstanz.

Muller, E. N., and Seligson, M. A., 1987, Inequality and insurgency, *American Political Science Review* **81**(2): 425-452.

Muller, E. N., and Weede, E., 1990, Cross-national variation in political violence. A rational action approach, *Journal of Conflict Resolution* **34**(4): 624-651.

Olson, M. Jr., 1965, *The Logic of Collective Action*, Harvard University Press, Cambridge, MA.

Plümper, T., 2001, *Weltwirtschaft und Wohlfahrt. Die politischen Determinanten des Wachstumsbeitrages der außenwirtschaftlichen Offenheit*, Unpublished habilitation thesis, University of Konstanz.

Plümper, T., and Schneider, G., 2000, The trilemma of the protectionist autocrat: Assessing the link between democratization, governmental divisions and foreign economic liberalization, paper presented at the *APSA Conference*, October 1-5, 2000.

Przeworski, A., Alvarez, M. E., Cheibub, J. A., and Limongi, F., 2002, *Democracy and Development. Political Institutions and Well-Being in the World, 1950-1990*, Cambridge University Press, Cambridge.

Pritzl, R., and Schneider, F., 1997, *Zur Politischen Ökonomie autokratischer politischer Systeme. Ein theoretischer und empirischer Ansatz*, Arbeitspapier Nr. 9713, Institut für Volkswirtschaftslehre, Johannes Kepler Universität Linz.

Rodrik, D., 1994, The rush to free trade in the developing world: Why so late? Why now? Will it last?, in: *Voting for Reform: Democracy, Political Liberalization, and Economic Adjustment*, S. Haggard and S. B. Webb, eds., Oxford University Press, New York, pp. 61-88.

Rogowski, R., 1989, *Commerce and Coalitions. How Trade Affects Domestic Political Alignments*, Princeton University Press, Princeton, NJ.

Rothgeb, J. M. Jr., 1990, Investment dependence and political conflict in third world countries, *Journal of Peace Research* **27**(3): 255-272.

Rummel, R. J., 1997, *Power Kills. Democracy as a Method of Nonviolence*, Transaction Publishers, New Brunswick, NJ.

Russett, B., 1993, *Grasping the Democratic Peace*, Princeton University Press, Princeton.

Russett, B., and Oneal, J. R., 2001, *Triangulating Peace: Democracy, Interdependence, and International Organizations*, Princeton University Press, Princeton, NJ.

Sachs, J. D., and Warner, A., 1995, Economic reform and the process of global integration, *Brookings Papers on Economic Activity* **1**: 1-118.

Schneider, G., Barbieri, K., and Gleditsch, N. P., 2003, *Globalization and Armed Conflict*, Lanham, MD.

Schock, K., 1996, A conjunctural model of political conflict. The impact of political opportunities on the relationship between economic inequality and violent political conflict, *Journal of Conflict Resolution* **40**(1): 98-134.

Sidell, S. R., 1988, *The IMF and Third-World Political Instability. Is There a Connection?*, Macmillan Press, Houndmills.

Tarrow, S., 1989, *Struggle, Politics, and Reform: Collective Action, Social Movements, and Cycles of Protest*, Ithaca, NY.

Tarrow, S., 1998, *Power in Movement: Social Movements and Contentious Politics,* New York.

Tilly, C., 1978, *From Mobilization To Revolution*, Random House, New York.

Tucker, R., 1999, BTSCS: *A Binary Time-Series--Cross-Section Data Analysis Utility*. Version 4.0.4. Harvard University, Cambridge, MA. http://www.fas.harvard.edu/~rtucker/programs/btscs/btscs.html.

Tullock, G., 1980, Rent seeking as a negative-sum game, in: *Toward a Theory of the Rent Seeking Society*, J. M. Buchanan, R. D. Tollison, G. Tullock, eds., Texas A+M University, College Station, pp. 16-36.

Weede, E., 1990, *Wirtschaft, Staat und Gesellschaft*, Mohr, Tübingen.

Wood, A., 1994, *North-South Trade, Employment and Inequality: Changing Fortunes in a Skill-Driven World*, Clarendon Press, Oxford.

World Bank, 1999, *World Development Indicators 1999 CD-ROM*, World Bank, Washington, DC.

Zanger, S., 2000, A global analysis of the effect of political regime changes on life integrity violations, 1977-93, *Journal of Peace Research* **37**(2): 213-233.

Chapter 4

Computer Assisted Early Warning – the FAST Example

Heinz Krummenacher
swisspeace—Swiss Peace Foundation, Berne, Switzerland

1 INTRODUCTION

FAST is a German acronym which stands for early analysis of tensions and fact-finding. It is a political early warning system that aims at enhancing political decision makers' ability to identify critical developments in a timely manner so that political strategies can be formulated to either prevent or limit destructive effects of violent conflicts or identify windows of opportunity for peacebuilding. Thus, FAST is not merely an academic exercise but tries to impact decision making processes. FAST products are tailored to the needs of practitioners and while we strive for sound intellectual analysis, academic rigor is not an end in itself. We also refrain from using one single methodology but strongly believe in a comprehensive approach using multiple methods. While qualitative analysis is considered to be essential for maintaining a context-specific understanding of the target countries, FAST uses quantitative techniques to manage the huge flow of information and thus to reduce complexity. Figure 4.1. shows how different qualitative and quantitative methodological parts feed into FAST's core products

2 DEFINITION OF EARLY WARNING

According to a generally accepted definition "early warning consists of [...] the collection and analysis of information about potential and actual conflict situations, and the provision of policy options to influential actors at the national, regional and international levels that may promote sustainable peace (FEWER, 1999)".[1] According to this definition, in the FAST scheme com-

1. For an in-depth discussion of the early warning concept see Krummenacher et al. (1999) and Krummenacher and Schmeidl (1999).

R. Trappl (ed.), Programming for Peace, 71–80.

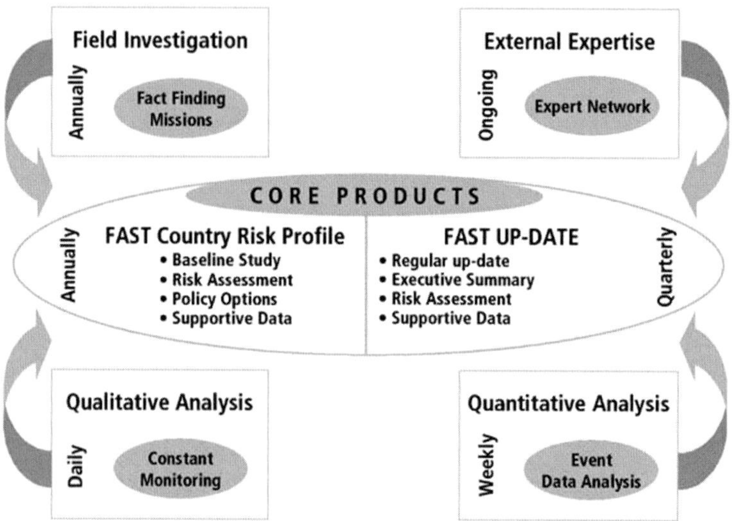

Figure 4.1. FAST - Methodological Overview

puter assisted research techniques play a role during the initial first two steps: the systematic collection of data and the interpretation of the data. While electronic data processing could in many ways be helpful in the decision making process as well and thus encompass all three steps or dimensions of early warning, we have so far restricted our ambitions to data collection and analysis.

3 EVENT DATA ANALYSIS

Methodologically, we rely on event data analysis, one of the most common types of methods used in quantitative international relations research.[1] Event data analysis is basically a three step process content analysis: First we determine a source or sources of news about salient political interactions in the countries under study. This could be an internationally-oriented newspa-

[1] see http://www.ukans.edu/~keds/intro.html and Krummenacher and Schmeidl (2001) and Schmeidl and Bond (2000).

per such as the "Financial Times" or the "New York Times", regional newspapers and newsmagazines, a news summary such as the "International Security Network's" Weekly Wrap (ISN) or "Jamestown's Chechnya Weekly", or a newswire service such as "Reuters" or the "Associated Press". Second according to a specific coding framework, we code the relevant events, note the initiator and the recipient of an action, the action itself, the time and scope of action and other parameters. Eventually, each action corresponds to a specific event-type (indicator) and, depending on whether it is cooperative or conflictive in nature, is assigned a certain numeric value. Third, by aggregating all relevant events on a weekly or monthly basis, an accurate picture can be drawn of the overall conflict potential or stability in a given country as well as the patterns of conflict and cooperation between selected actors over time.

4 DATA COLLECTION

In research based on event data it has become popular to use news wires (either "Reuters" or "Associated Press") as the source of information, mainly because machine coding seems to make this a prerequisite.[1] FAST, however, after using "Reuters" for quite an extended period of time (1998—2000), has chosen a different approach because Reuters news service has important draw-backs, the major one being lack of satisfactory coverage in many parts of the world due to the following reasons (for more detail, see Schmeidl and Bond, 2000):

- At present parsers can only read English-language news wires.
- Event-data analysis is based on the principle of daily logging, while news dispatches often tend to be based on the principle of interval reporting. The intensity of coverage may increase as a crisis occurs ("blood sells") but is weak or non-existent during more peaceful times, thus not all important events leading up to conflict escalation may be reported (see also Siegfried, 2001).

1. While in the early days of event data analysis, existing soft- and hardware did not allow any other method than time intensive and expensive human coding, in recent years both the Program on Nonviolent Sanctions and Cultural Survival (PONSACS) in Harvard and the Kansas Event Data System (KEDS) have made substantial progress towards machine coding. Using pattern recognition and grammatical parsing they have developed highly sophisticated tools which greatly enhance the possibilities of this method. Recent studies show that automatic coding is not only faster and less expensive but also at least as reliable as human coding. The problem, however, is not that automatic coding does not perform well, the problem is the inadequacy of the input in those systems (i.e. international news wires).

- International journalism is based on the principles of covering events believed to be of general interest to the rest of the world (not all countries and regions are).
- As a guiding principle, Reuters only needs to report those events with a greater connotation at the national level. Yet this eliminates possible important events at a district or provincial level that often precede a crisis on national level.

The border-conflict and later war between Ethiopia and Eritrea was the turning point when we realized that FAST could not longer rely on newswires if it ever wanted to go beyond descriptive analysis and actually forecast conflict escalation or de-escalation processes. The war in the Horn of Africa literally came out of nowhere—at least for event-data analysis based on "Reuters". The number of coded events jumped from zero in April 1998 to 31 in May of 1998 when the border dispute began and from six in January 1999 to 53 in February 1999 when the border war broke out. This illustrates that the event-data principle of no report meaning no event does not hold true in countries or regions of lesser interest to (English-speaking) news-services. It may simply mean that no English-speaking journalist was present or that on-going events were deemed to be of no particular international interest or importance.

FAST had to tackle precisely these problems, as many countries it monitors find themselves not—or only temporarily—in the limelight of world politics and media attention. Central Asia, for example, is covered well by media in the Russian language, but this would require analysts (or machines) to read Russian. Similarly other language news-wires (French, Portuguese) may be more relevant for certain parts of Africa than English ones are. Thus the English-language requirement for current parsing is clearly something event-data analysis can improve upon. However, other language news sources may nevertheless adhere to the same principle of English-language news – "blood sells"—so it might be difficult to overcome this particular problem of sensational information production in general; unless one uses other input than news services. Hence FAST chose a second option to improve upon "Reuters" data feed. In collaboration with Virtual Research Associates (VRA) it created an alternative news-feed in the form of local information networks (LINs) of field-monitors that log relevant information according to the same coding rules as the VRA parser (to allow for compatibility of data).[1] All Central Asian and selected Southern African countries which are monitored by

1. Virtual Research Associates (VRA) is a Harvard-based group of academic analysts who at the same time are also involved with PONSACS (see http://vranet.com).

FAST have such a network, and additional LINs are being currently set up in the Balkans, in the North Caucasus, in Central Africa, and in Nepal.[1]

Experience gained so far gives ample evidence that FAST-LINs perform much better than Reuters. Not only is the overall event coverage higher in numerical terms, as the following graphs show, FAST LINs also report a wider variety of event types.

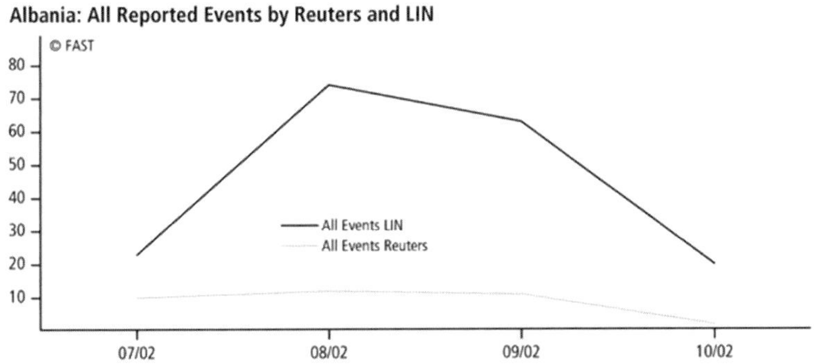

Figure 4.2. Reuters versus FAST-LIN (number of coded events in Albania)

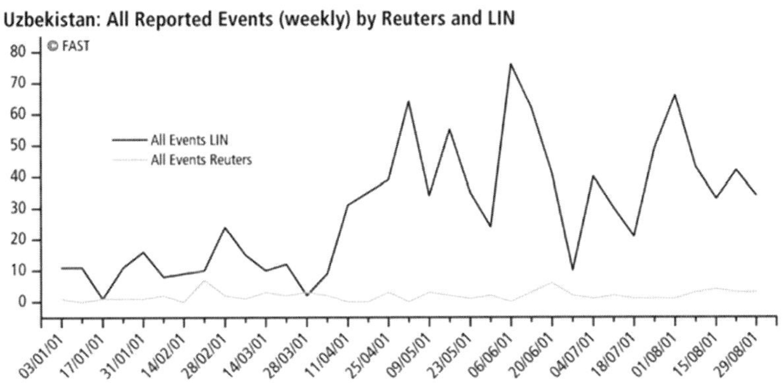

Figure 4.3. Reuters versus FAST-LIN (number of coded events in Usbekistan)

1. For additional information regarding the individual countries that are to be covered and the timetable see www.swisspeace.org.

5 DATA ANALYSIS

Instead of developing a coding system of its own, FAST uses the "Integrated Data for Event Analysis" (IDEA) approach for coding and analyzing the data. IDEA has been co-developed by VRA[1] and specifies

a. what types of political interactions constitute an "event,"

b. the categories of events and their codes, and

c. any other information to be coded in addition to the basic event.

There is a set of 186 individual events depicting conflict and cooperative behavior within and between state and non-state actors. These events feed into tension barometers as raw data but also as composite measures (some merely a compilation of indicators while others are based on more complicated analyses). Non-standardized graphs show fluctuations depending on the current numerical value of events coded as well as the number of events within a given time-period. In order to allow for cross-country comparison, standardized graphs rely on the current numerical value of a given set of events in proportion to the total number of events. As the number of graphs based on single indicators is rather large (based on WEIS [World Event Interaction Survey] and now extended into IDEA [Integrated Data for Event Analysis] categories (for more detail, see Bond *et al.*, 1999), only the summary graphs currently used by FAST are listed here:

- *Goldstein Cooperation*: captures various forms of accommodative or cooperative behavior between diverse domestic or international actors. Such behavior can vary from verbal agreements, meetings to specify joint efforts, or operations to promote mutual benefits between domestic actors (based on Goldstein, 1992).
- *Goldstein Conflict*: captures contentious or conflictive interactions (e.g., antagonism, contradictory action, or disagreement) between diverse domestic or international actors. The type of conflict can vary from verbal antagonism, disagreements, or contradictory action to outright physical force with various levels of intensity (based on Goldstein, 1992).
- *Conflict Carrying Capacity (CCC)*: reflects the stability of the system or polity rather than a particular regime or administration; a CCC

1. Other scholars involved are Joshua Goldstein, Craig Jenkins, and Charles Lewis Taylor (see http://vranet.com).

trend line approaching 1.0 suggests 100% stability (based on Jenkins and Bond, 2001).

- *Forceful Action (FA)*: refers to the proportion of any and all uses of physical force and any associated manifest violence by any actor (based on Jenkins and Bond, 2001).

The graphs on the following page are examples of tension barometers generated for FAST early warning reports. Event data for selected countries is aggregated weekly or monthly for some of the most frequently used indicators. For the sake of being able to make comparisons between graphs based on FAST-LINs and those depicted from "Reuters" news wires, both sources are included. The result is remarkable as LIN-based graphs reveal much greater variance in the data and thus provide more insight in the development of conflict and cooperation than "Reuters" curves do.

6 CONCLUSION

In light of the above, we conclude that event data analysis is a viable tool for early warning purposes. The advantages are:

- Event data - especially if coupled with automated or semi-automated coding - allows speedy tracking of specific violent or cooperative incidences over time.
- A multitude of information is broken down in its component parts and depicted in easy-to-read graphs, demonstrating aspects of conflict and cooperation within and between countries.
- Event data counts and respective graphs provide checks – and balances against a desensitization toward violence and/or media hypes.
- Event-data analysis challenges the analyst's perception so that he or she might become aware of his or her own "blind spots", biases, and preconceived notions.
- Event data analysis, if further developed, eventually will enable us to forecast trends in conflict and cooperation.

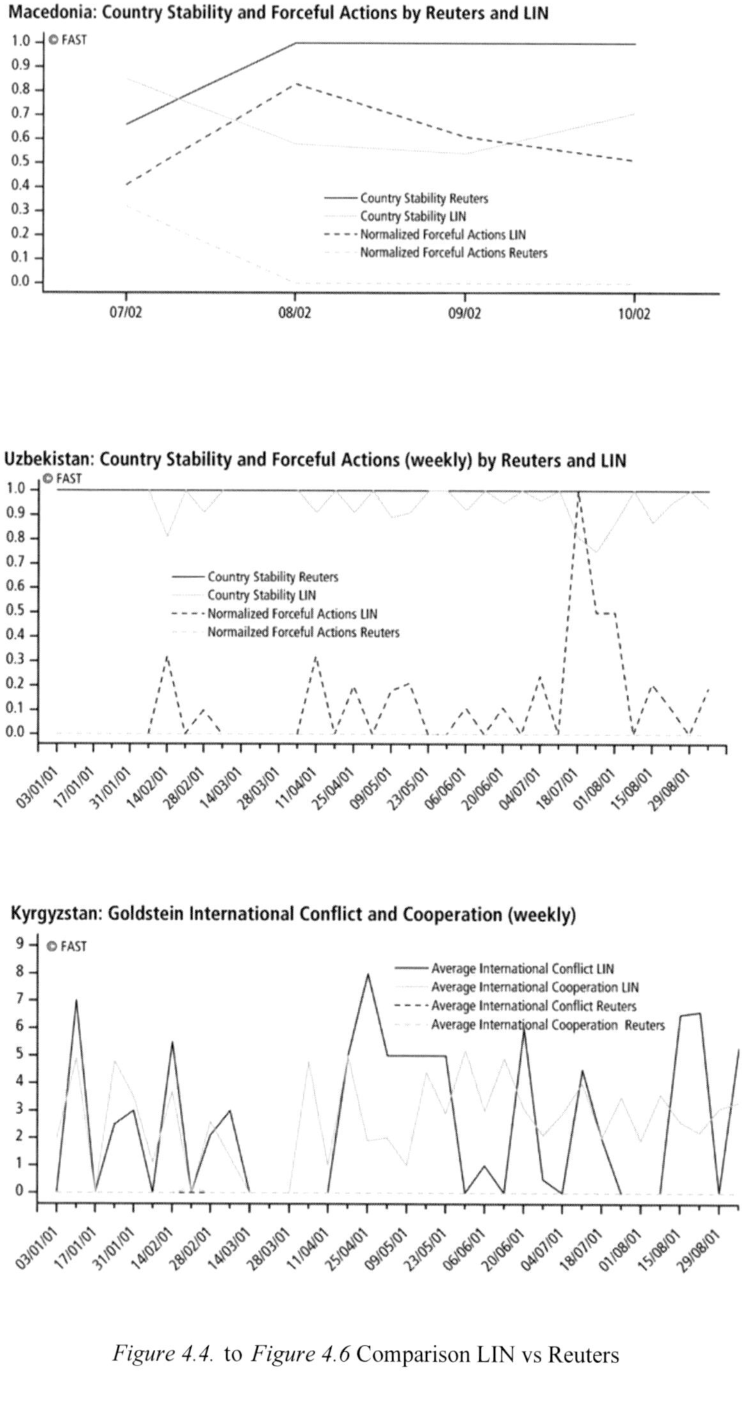

Figure 4.4. to *Figure 4.6* Comparison LIN vs Reuters

However, two major reservations need to be stressed. First, in areas with low media coverage event data based early warning efforts are to no avail without the existence of Local Information Networks that provide reliable information and maintain a certain flow of information at all times. While we clearly see the benefits of automatic coding of news wires (high-speed information digestion and impartiality), we strongly urge researchers to make only prudent use of this tool. In the Middle East, where media coverage remains constantly high, it makes perfectly sense to rely on the system, but in most parts of the world, a semi-automated approach based on locally gathered information as applied in FAST promises better results. Event-data generation based on LINs actually seem to be an excellent solution to the early-warning information problem and we should not abandon the idea simply because it is far more expensive than using news wires.

Second, in the past event data based early warning was basically confined to descriptive analyses of conflictive trends and analysts still have to rely on their qualitative judgement to make conflict assessments. There is little evidence that automated event data efforts have had any significant benefit for forecasting crisis escalation or de-escalation. Thus FAST's future goal is to improve its forecasting ability by developing quantitative methods that help (a) to verify if developments are significantly different from those in the past and (b) to propose trends for the future. While VRA has begun to work with FAST on an interim solution that involves tracking the mean of event-data inputs over time (mainly through use of Z-scores to establish threshold values), a more sophisticated approach needs to be developed yet.

References

Bond, J., Bond, D., Silva, J., Oh, C., 1999, *The VRA Reader*, VRA Press, Weston, MA.

FEWER, 1999, *Conflict and Peace Analysis and Response Manual*, FEWER, London.

Goldstein, J. S., 1992, A conflict-cooperation scale for international events data, *Journal of Conflict Resolution*, **36**:369-385.

Jenkins, J. C., Bond, D., 2001, Conflict carrying capacity, political crisis, and reconstruction: A framework for the early warning of political system vulnerability, *Journal of Conflict Resolution* **45**:3-31.

Krummenacher, H., Schmeidl, S., 1999, FAST: An integrated and interactive early warning system: The example of Central Asia, *The Soviet and Post-Soviet Review* **24**:147-161.

Krummenacher, H., Baechler, G., Schmeidl, S., 1999, Beitrag der Frühwarnung zur Krisenprävention: Möglichkeiten und Grenzen in Theorie und Praxis, in *Krisenprävention: Theorie und Praxis ziviler Konfliktbearbeitung*, Österreichisches Studienzentrum für Frieden und Konfliktlösung, ed., Rüegger, Chur, Zürich.

Schmeidl, S., Bond, D., 2000, Assessing the implications of automation in event data analysis: An examination of the conceptual and empirical differences between human-assisted and fully-automated coding, paper presented at the *Annual Convention of the International Studies Association*, Los Angeles, USA.

Siegfried, M., 2001, *Patterns in the Escalation Process of Armed Conflicts*, unpublished MA Thesis (available at swisspeace).

Chapter 5

Country Indicators for Foreign Policy

Developing an Indicators-Based User Friendly Risk Assessment and Early Warning Capability

David Carment and Caroline Delany, with Susan Ampleford, George Conway, and Angelica Ospina[1]

Norman Paterson School of International Affairs, Carleton University, Ottawa, Canada

1 INTRODUCTION

The CIFP project was initiated by the Department of Foreign Affairs and International Trade (DFAIT) in partnership the Norman Paterson School of International Affairs at Carleton University, in Ottawa Canada. The project represents an on-going effort to identify and assemble statistical information conveying the key features of the political, economic, social and cultural environments of countries around the world.

The cross-national data generated through CIFP was intended to have a variety of applications in government departments, NGOs, and by users in the private sector. The data set provides at-a-glance global overviews, issue-based perspectives and country performance measures. Currently, the data set includes measures of domestic armed conflict, governance and political instability, militarization, religious and ethnic diversity, demographic stress, economic performance, human development, environmental stress, and international linkages. In an effort to address the need for a dynamic and comprehensive capability CIFP developed an innovative approach that emphasizes the need for transparent, easy to interpret, open source early warning information. The foundation upon which CIFP's methodology is based is the use of structural indicators of latent conflict potential. CIFP analysts complement structural indicator analysis with global overviews, country performance measures, and issue-based perspectives on political, military,

1. The authors would like to thank Robert Trappl and Daniel Druckman for helpful comments on draft versions of this chapter and the anonymous reviewers of this volume. They are also indebted to the Canadian International Development Agency, The Security and Defence Forum of the Department of National Defence and The Social Sciences and Humanities Research Council of Canada for their support in this research

R. Trappl (ed.), Programming for Peace, 81–113.

demographic, social, economic and environmental factors. In doing so, CIFP's methodology offers an accessible quantitative and qualitative approach to conducting early warning reporting and analysis. This type of information can be included in best practice early warning analysis together with events data and local field analysis, making it a very effective, and methodologically sound approach to early warning and conflict risk analysis.

The CIFP database currently includes statistical data in the above issue areas, in the form of over one hundred performance indicators for 196 countries, spanning fifteen years (1985 to 2003) for most indicators. These indicators are drawn from a variety of open sources, including the World Bank, the United Nations Development Programme, the United Nations High Commissioner for Refugees, the Stockholm International Peace Research Institute, and the Minorities at Risk and Polity IV data sets from the University of Maryland.

2 EARLY WARNING SYSTEMS: A GOOD PRACTICE

The Forum on Early Warning and Early Response (FEWER) was initiated in 1997 in response to the genocide in Rwanda and ceased to exist in 2004. During its brief lifetime a number of pilot early warning activities were undertaken around the globe. In addition, research was carried out to survey and define "good" practice in the conflict early warning field. From its applied experience and research, FEWER arrived at the assessment that effective early warning requires the use of a range of data sources and analytical methods, including (i) local analysis (i.e. analysis of events and perceptions not covered by the media), (ii) monitoring of newswire reports (or "events data") and (iii) structural data (such as economic and developmental indicators of country performance).

The "good practice" early warning system underscores the role played and value added by different organizations participating in the FEWER network. CIFP was identified as playing an important role in providing structural data and analysis on both conflict and peace generating factors. Events data monitoring systems, such as those provided by FAST at the Swiss Peace Foundation (see Chapter 4 in this volume), can provide real-time perspectives on the flow of events. Local member organizations in regions of concern are in a position to assess the importance of different indicators and understand the agendas and grievances of key stakeholders. Such a "good practice" early warning system is illustrated in Figure 5.1.

Figure 5.1. Early Warning Systems: Emerging Good Practice

3 RISK ASSESSMENT AND EARLY WARNING:

As part of its contribution to these new networks, CIFP produced structural risk assessment reports for the two target regions. These reports are intended to precede and serve as a ground for subsequent country-specific early-warning reports that will integrate the various data sources and analytical methods (local analysis, events data, structural data). In this respect, "risk assessment" and "early warning" are viewed as complementary but distinct modes of analysis that can be distinguished in several important respects. For example, Gurr and Marshall (2000) make the distinction between early warning and risk assessment as follows:

> Risk assessments… identify situations in which the conditions for a particular kind of conflict… are present. They are not predictions in the sense that is usually meant by the terms "forecast" or "early warning" because risks are assessed on the basis of background and intervening conditions— the conditions that establish the potential for conflict. Whether or not risks are realized depends on whether the preconditions remain unchanged and on the occurrence of accelerating or triggering events. Early warnings by contrast are derived from monitoring the flow of political events, with special attention to actions that are likely to precipitate the onset of conflict in high-risk situations. Risk assessments provide the context. Early warnings are interpretations that the outbreak of conflict in a high-risk situation is likely and imminent.

Risk assessments precede and complement early warning, through identifying background and intervening conditions that establish the risk for potential crisis and conflict. They focus monitoring and analytical attention on high risk situations before they are fully developed and they provide a framework for interpreting the results of real-time monitoring of events.

While the primary goal of risk assessment is to diagnose a situation rather than devise solutions, early warning is a process designed to pinpoint appropriate, forward looking, preventive strategies. Accordingly, FEWER defines early warning as the systematic collection and analysis of information for the purposes of anticipating the escalation of violent conflict, developing strategic responses to these crises, and presenting options to critical actors for the purposes of decision making and response.

The policy relevance of early warning stems directly from the fact early warning systems are not restricted to analysing a crisis, but also assess the capacities, needs, and responses for dealing with a crisis. The central purpose of early warning is thus not only to identify potential problems but also to create the necessary political will for preventive action to be taken. Accordingly, early warning represents a proactive political process whereby networks of organizations conduct analysis together in a collective effort to prevent likely events from occurring.

4 STRUCTURAL INDICATORS OF CONFLICT POTENTIAL

In order to establish a framework for analyzing the emergence of violent conflict, it is necessary to understand how crises typically develop and which possible avoidance efforts can be effective. In general terms, the factors that contribute to conflict escalation are categorized as "structural factors," "accelerators," and "triggers."

1. "Structural factors" or "root causes" are those factors that form the pre-conditions of crisis situations, such as systematic political exclusion, shifts in demographic balance, entrenched economic inequities, economic decline and ecological deterioration;
2. "Accelerators" or "precipitators" are factors that work upon root causes in order to increase their level of significance; and,
3. "Triggers" are sudden events that act as catalysts igniting a crisis or conflict, such as the assassination of a leader, election fraud, or a political scandal.

As FEWER's "good practice" schema above indicates, local analysts and events-monitoring systems are best positioned to monitor and provide analysis on "triggers" or "catalysing events" that are likely to precipitate the onset of conflict in high-risk situations. CIFP is positioned to provide data and analysis focusing on the "structural" level, in order to assess the degree of risk in given country-contexts, and to assess whether shifts in country performance indicators (such as ameliorating or worsening economic performance) are increasing or mitigating the severity of this risk.

In this framework, "risk" refers to presence of conditions that inform the likelihood that some outcome will occur. Risk assessments therefore have the objective of developing knowledge of the causes that produce specific effects. Given that the primary dependent variable of CIFP risk assessments is "conflict potential," these causes, for example, can either be conflict-engendering or peace-engendering, with their effects being either negative (such as an outbreak or intensification of violent conflict) or positive (such as the cessation or abatement of violent conflict).

In order to assess the conditions underlying conflict potential, it is necessary to identify a set of associated indicators. Often a crisis has no single cause and furthermore the different contributing causes vary in importance—variables may at times reinforce each other, while at other times they may neutralize one another. Thus, analysis of conflict potential requires an assessment of the relative importance of different indicators and their interrelationships.

The selection of structural indicators for the CIFP risk assessment reports was informed by a number of factors. It is based largely on the results of FEWER's collaborative work with local early warning analysts and their understanding of the type of information needed to effectively assess conflict potential. In addition, indicators have been included on the basis of evidence in the conflict analysis literature of their being strong crisis predictors.[2]

The structural indicators included in the CIFP risk assessment reports cross nine interrelated issue areas identified as potential "problem areas:" History of Armed Conflict; Governance and Political Instability; Militarization; Population Heterogeneity; Demographic Stress; Economic Performance; Human Development; Environmental Stress; and International Linkages. Table 5.1. cites a number of indicative concerns within each "issue area," and includes specific indicators that can be used to assess the relative severity of these issues. Accordingly, CIFP rates a country's degree of "risk" in terms of "structural instability." "Structural instability" is considered high in cases where a country has an enduring history of armed conflict, is politically unsta-

2. See in particular: Esty, D. C., Goldstone, J. A., Gurr, T. R., Harff, B., Levy, M., Dabelko, G. D., Surko, P. T., and Unger, A. N., 1998, "State Failure Task Force Report: Phase II Findings," *Science Applications International Corporation*, McLean, VA; van de Goor, L. and Verstegen, S., 2000, "Conflict Prognosis: A Conflict and Policy Assessment Framework, Part Two," Discussion Paper, Clingendael Institute, The Hague.

ble or has unrepresentative or repressive political institutions, is heavily militarized, has a heterogeneous and divided population, suffers from significant demographic and environmental stresses, has had poor economic performance and low levels of human development, and is engaged with the international community in ways that detract from, rather than contribute to, peaceful conflict management.

On the other hand, "structural stability" is considered high in countries that have developed stable democratic political institutions, that respect fundamental human rights, that have successfully managed conflict without resorting to violence, that invest less in the military, that lack profound ethnic or religious cleavages or demographic stresses, that have achieved sustainable levels of economic development as well as healthy social and environment conditions, and that are free from serious external conflicts and threats.

5 OPERATIONALIZATION OF INDICATORS: CIFP "RISK INDEX"

CIFP assesses country risk by means of an overall country risk index. The higher the risk index, the greater the assessed risk of conflict that country faces. The risk index consists of the weighted average of nine composite indicators, corresponding to the nine issue areas outlined above: armed conflict, governance and political instability, militarization, population heterogeneity, demographic stress, economic performance, human development, environmental stress, and international linkages. Each of the nine composite indicators is derived through averaging the individual risk scores for a number of leading indicators within each issue area (included in the third column of Table 5.1.). The weighting of each of the nine composite indicators is discussed below.

Leading indicators within each issue area are themselves assessed in terms of three separate scores: the country's performance for a given indicator relative to other countries (global rank score); the direction of change for a given indicator, be it improving, worsening, or remaining level (trend score); and the degree of fluctuation in a country's performance for a given indicator (volatility score).

Table 5.1. Issue Areas

Issue Areas	*Indicative Issues of Concern*	*Leading Indicators*
History of Armed Conflict	• Indicates conflictual political culture, with higher risk of parties continuing to resort to violence as a means of airing grievances • Indicates inability of the state to resolve conflicts through institutional channels, and a greater inclination for armed forces to engage in political disputes • Indicates low state capacity to provide basic security, potentially resulting in the loss of popular confidence in state institutions and state legitimacy • Refugees or Internally Displaced Persons produced by past or ongoing violent conflict can have destabilizing effects within affected regions and countries, potentially spiralling into larger problems	• History of Armed Conflict, including Annual Conflict-Related Deaths • Number of Refugees Produced • Number of Refugees Hosted, Internally Displaced Persons (IDPs) or other Populations of Concern
Governance and Political Instability	• The lack of representative and accountable political institutions through which to channel grievances can aggravate the risk of outbursts of violent conflict • Transitional states are at higher risk of experiencing abrupt or violent change, as are new or unconsolidated democracies • The denial of civil and political liberties, such as the rights of expression, assembly and association, or the censorship of media, increases the likelihood dissenting views will be expressed through violence • Endemic corruption of political elites can result in the loss of popular confidence in state institutions	• Level of Democracy • Regime Durability (years since regime change) • Restrictions on Civil and Political Rights • Restrictions on Press Freedom • Level of Corruption
Militarization	• Excessive military expenditures can indicate general militarization of the state apparatus and potential for increased military involvement in political affairs • Excessive military expenditures reduce investment in the social sectors, indicating state priorities focused upon military rather than developmental solutions to potential crises, which can in turn influence state legitimacy • Fluctuations in military spending can create tensions or resentment within the armed forces • Shifting military expenditures and arms imports/exports can destabilize regional balance of power	• Military Expenditure • Military Expenditure (% of GDP) • Fraction of Regional Military Expenditure • Total Armed Forces • Armed Forces per 10,000 persons

Population Heterogeneity	• Potential for tensions and cleavages is greater in ethnically or religiously heterogeneous populations • Issues of governance are further complicated by diverse and often competing group expectations and demands • The historical loss of group autonomy can serve as a motivation for ethno-political protest and secessionist movements • Political or economic inequalities along group lines can give rise to communal or separatist mobilization and aggravate the potential for conflict • Restrictions on specific groups' cultural practices limit opportunities for expression of grievances through non-violent means • The greater the strength of a group's identity, the greater its potential for mobilization • External support for communal groups can be a major determinant of the magnitude of ethno-political rebellion	• Ethnic Diversity • Religious Diversity • Risk of Ethnic Rebellion • Lost Autonomy • Economic Discrimination • Political Discrimination • Cultural Discrimination • Strength of Ethnic Identity • Mobilization of Militant Orgs. • Support from Kindred Groups
Demographic Stress	• High population density and growth rates can accentuate the risk of conflict by heightening competition for physical and social resources • Economic conditions can result in migration to urban centres, increasing the burden on municipal services and resulting in worsening scarcity and urban living conditions • Young, unemployed populations can be political volatile and prone to violence, and may place far less trust in political institutions and patterns of authority	• Total Population • Population Growth Rate • Population Density • Urban Population (% of Total) • Urban Population Growth Rate • Youth Bulge

Economic Performance	• Economic decline (including declining incomes, inflation, exchange rate collapse, and declining levels of foreign investment) affects material living standards, and can aggravate dissatisfaction with government performance, or cause scapegoating of economically privileged minorities • High debt burdens negatively affect social investments, fuelling popular unrest and other preconditions of conflict • Low involvement in international trade is associated with higher risk of state failure, given that the conditions that inhibit high levels of international trade and foreign investment (such as rampant corruption and poor infrastructure) also contribute to the risk of political crises • High levels of economic inequality can contribute to social fragmentation and declining state legitimacy	• GDP • GDP Growth Rate (Annual %) • GDP Per Capita • Inflation rates • Exchange rates • Foreign Investment • Debt Service • Trade Openness (Trade as a % of GDP) • Inequality Score (GINI Coefficient)
Human Development	• Poor material living standards correlate strongly with higher risk of violent conflict and state failure; poverty is a fundamental cause of civil strife • Lack or decline in public services such as health services, education, safe water and sanitation indicate weak state capacity to distribute and allocate vital services that can decrease popular confidence in the state leading to political instability and social unrest • Unmet expectations regarding educational opportunities or other opportunities for social advancement increase discontent and the likelihood and severity of civil strife	• Access to Improved Water Source • Access to Sanitation • Life Expectancy • Infant Mortality Rate • Maternal Mortality Rate • HIV/AIDS • Primary School Enrolment • Secondary School Enrolment • Children in Labour Force
Environmental Stress	• The degradation and depletion of renewable resources can generate effects such as constrained economic productivity and growth, poverty and migration, which underlie social or political instability • Scarcities in natural resources can result in increased demand and/or unequal distribution, raising the potential for conflict • Environmental factors interact powerfully with demographic shifts such as population growth and density, and scarcity risks sharpening existing disparities between groups or regions	• Rate of Deforestation • People per Sq. km of Arable Land • Access to Fresh Water

Interna-tional Link-ages	• Countries with fewer diplomatic, political, commercial, trade or cultural linkages with regional organizations and neighbouring states are less likely to profit from constructive engagement with outside actors, in areas such as developmental assistance, mediation, or support in peace processes • Participation in international regimes and organizations can help decrease security risks by codifying broad rules and processes by which to resolve disputes peacefully • Frequent or intense inter-state political or territorial disputes can undermine regional security • Prevalence of armed conflict in neighbouring states can have a destabilizing effect on national stability, through cross-border refugee flows or movement of rebel forces, or through their contribution to regional war economies • Prevalence of non-democratic or transitional regimes across the region can impact national security through heightened risk of regional instability	• Participation in Regional and International Organizations, including: **1** Economic Organizations **2** Military/Security Alliances **3** UN Organizations **4** Multipurpose Organizations **5** Miscellaneous Organizations • Interstate Disputes, including: • Resource and Territorial Disputes • Political and Cultural Disputes • Prevalence of Armed Conflicts across Region • Prevailing Regime Types Across Region

5.1 Global Rank Score

"Risk potential" is a relative term that has meaning only with respect to a country's performance and risk *vis à vis* other countries in the international system. Accordingly, each lead indicator is converted to a 9-point score on the basis of its performance relative to a global sample of countries. This global sample of countries is ranked from highest to lowest level of performance, divided into nine equal categories, then assigned score numbers ranging from 1 to 9 based on their rank position within the sample. This scoring procedure is intended to facilitate the identification of key areas of concern, and as a way of directing attention to potential problem areas.

In general, a higher score (in the 7 to 9 range) indicates that the country is performing poorly relative to other countries (i.e. high levels of armed conflict, autocratic governments, poor economic performance, low levels of human development) or that a country's standing is a cause for concern (i.e. significant youth bulge, high levels of ethnic diversity). A lower score (in the 1 to 3 range) indicates the country is performing well relative to other countries (i.e. no or little armed conflict, democratic governments, strong economic performance, high levels of human development) or that a country's standing is less of a cause for concern (i.e. no youth bulge, low levels of ethnic diversity). Values in the middle 4 to 6 range indicate moderate levels of performance approaching the global mean.

Since relative country performance can vary significantly from year to year (as in the case of economic shocks), averages are taken for global rank scores over a five-year time frame. The most recent five years contained in the CIFP data set are used for this index (generally 1996 to 2000). The 1 to 9 Global Rank score forms the "base scale" upon which individual indicator risk scores are calculated. (See Table 5.2., Column 1)

Table 5.2. Calculation of Risk Scores for Leading Indicators

Global Rank Score[a] *(Base Scale)*		*Trend Score (Modifier)*		*Volatility Score (Modifier)*		*Indicator Risk Score (Sum)*	
High Concern	9	Worsening	+1	High	+2	Very High Risk	12
	8	No Change	0	Moderate	+1		11
	7	Improving	-1	Stable	0		10
Moderate Concern	6					High Risk	9
	5						8
	4						7
Low Concern	3					Medium Risk	6
	2						5
	1						4
						Low Risk	3
							2
							1
							0

a. Global rank scores and resulting Indicator Risk Scores are on a grey-scale according to severity of risk, where 1-3 = low concern / risk (light grey), 4-6 = medium concern / risk (grey), 7-9 = high concern / risk (dark grey).

5.2 Trend Score

In addition to a relative measure of a country's performance within the international system, an assessment of risk also requires consideration of the absolute development of a state's performance demonstrated by changes over time. The direction of change, whether worsening or improving, indicates whether a country's performance for a given indicator is even more likely to contribute to conflict potential (i.e. increasing restrictions on civil and political rights, worsening economic conditions, increasing demographic or environmental stresses) or detract from it (i.e. greater respect for civil and political rights, improving economic conditions, decreasing demographic or environmental stresses).

While both long term trends and shorter term trends are relevant to assessing shifts in a country's performance, the CIFP risk calculation places emphasis upon short term (five year) trends, given that these are assumed to have a more immediate and determining impact upon the processes of conflict development. CIFP calculates a trend score based on an ideal linear "least-squares" regression line, where the slope of the trend line (whether positive, negative, or zero) is used as a measure of the direction of change. The trend score modifies the base scale by adding a value of 1 to the base scale if the direction of change is worsening, and by subtracting a value of 1 from the base scale if the direction of change is improving. In cases where the trend line has a slope of 0, the base scale is not modified. (See Table 5.2., Column 2.)

5.3 Volatility Score

While the trend score assesses whether the short-term trend of a given indicator is improving, worsening, or remaining level, a single linear trend score can in some cases mask high levels of variation in country performance. For this reason, the CIFP risk calculation includes a third measure of "volatility," which measures the degree of variation from the ideal linear trend line. The degree of volatility is a critical component of the risk assessment calculation, considering that instability across a given indicator (i.e. regime transitions, a massive influx of refugees, fluctuations in military expenditure or foreign direct investment) can have a profoundly destabilizing effect and sharply increase the potential for conflict.

While different statistical measures of variance could be employed for this purpose, CIFP has opted to use a qualitative assessment of the degree of volatility, based on the observed deviation of the actual year-by-year trend over a five year time series from the ideal linear trend line derived for the trend score. As in the case of the trend score, the volatility score modifies the base scale by adding a value of 2 to the base scale if the degree of volatility is assessed as being "high" and adding a value of 1 to the base scale if the degree of volatility is assessed as being "moderate." (See Table 5.2., Column 3.) If there has been little or no volatility, the base scale is not modified.

5.4 Weighting of the Nine Composite Indicators

As Table 5.2. illustrates, indicator risk scores on a 13-point scale (0 to 12) are derived for each leading indicator within each of the nine issue areas. In order to arrive at composite indicators for each of the nine issue areas, leading indicator risk scores within each area are averaged. These nine composite issue area scores are themselves averaged to determine a country's overall risk index. However, in order to further elaborate the relative impact of each of these issue areas upon the conflict development process within a country, composite indicators are assigned weights. CIFP derives these weights deductively, based on inferences about the causal relationships between issue areas (James and Brecher, 1986).

Given there are nine issue areas that could conceivably be related in a causal manner to any or all of the others, there exists a maximum of 72 potential linkages. Accordingly, the weight assigned to each composite indicator is based on the number of direct causal linkages it is postulated to have with the others, thereby reflecting the magnitude of each issue area's impact upon overall risk. Areas to which no direct causal linkages are postulated are considered independent of its effects. Note that, in order to preserve the clarity of the CIFP risk index, only direct causal relationships figure into the operationalization of the composite scores, and that no effort is made to incorporate indirect linkages in this risk calculation (which could multiply the number of causal linkages exponentially). Table 5.3. describes these postulated linkages, and lists the resulting weightings. Figure 5.2. illustrates these linkages and weightings graphically.

Table 5.3. Weighting of Composite Indicators Based on Linkages

Issue Areas	*Linkages*
History of Armed Conflict (Weighting = 8)	Armed conflict can directly increase a state's level of (1) *Political Instability* and create or aggravate problems of governance. To the extent that armed conflict can result in excessive military expenditures and a disproportionate allocation of a country's budget to the military, it has an impact on (2) *Militarization.* (3) *Population Heterogeneity* is affected by armed conflict to the extent that ethnic and other divisions within a society become rigid and deeply cleaved through warfare. (4) *Economic Performance* and (5) *Human Development* are affected by armed conflict since the allocation of funds to fuel conflict can result in the growth of a black market, corruption and skewed or declining incomes. Armed conflict can also cause economic instability, increased inflation, and declining levels of foreign investment, having an impact on material living standards. Prolonged warfare can cause (6) *Demographic Stresses* and imbalances though its impact on gender ratios or age distributions. It can also compound (7) *Environmental Stresses* through direct damage to natural resource stocks, and through over-exploitation of resources to fuel the conflict. (8) *International Linkages* are directly affected by armed conflict, to the degree that spillage can affect neighbouring states, undermine regional security, and compel or invite external intervention.

Gover-nance and Political Instability **(Weighting = 5)**	Regime structures can directly contribute to the potential for (1) *Armed Conflict* if regimes are perceived as providing differential advantages to regions and ethnic groups rather than pursuing policies that are broadly distributive; political instability can also provide openings for revolutionary or secessionist groups to try to effect change. Highly authoritarian regimes often achieve high levels of (2) *Militarization* as a means of consolidating political control. Ineffective, kleptocratic or collapsed governments are unlikely to provide the macroeconomic and fiscal environment required for sound (3) *Economic Performance*, or to provide for the well-being of their population through provision of public services such as education and health care, having a severe impact on (4) *Human Development*. (5) *International Linkages* are directly affected by governance and political stability since democratic and stable governments are more likely to adhere to prevailing international norms of reciprocity and peaceful negotiation.
Militariza-tion **(Weighting = 5)**	High levels of militarization and the prevalence of arms (particularly small arms and light weapons) are likely to increase the inclination of parties including the armed forces to engage in (1) *Armed Conflict*. Excessive military expenditures can also indicate a militarization of the state apparatus and the potential for increased military involvement in political affairs, leading to (2) *Political Instability and Governance* problems. High levels of military expenditure can reduce investment in social capital and productive sectors, affecting both (3) *Economic Performance* and (4) *Human Development*. Shifting military expenditures can destabilize the regional balance of power, affecting (5) *International Linkages*.
Population Heterogene-ity **(Weighting = 4)**	Population Heterogeneity can have affect (1) *Governance and Political Stability* by introducing or aggravating competing group expectations and demands, and motivating the emergence of secessionist groups challenging the territorial integrity of the state. Population heterogeneity affects (2) *Armed Conflict* and (3) *Militarization* by increasing the potential for tensions and cleavages that can break into violent conflict and incite military responses. (4) *International Linkages* are directly affected by population heterogeneity, as ethnic cleavages and conflicts can have a demonstration effect on, or spill over into, neighbouring states, causing regional instability.
Demo-graphic Stress **(Weighting = 5)**	High population densities and growth rates can accentuate (1) *Environmental Stress* by heightening competition for natural resources. (2) *Economic Performance* and (3) *Human Development* are also affected by heavy populations placing burdens on local services, resulting in increasing scarcity and worsening living conditions. Young unemployed populations can be politically volatile and prone to violence, thereby having an impact on (4) *Political Stability* and increasing the likelihood of (5) *Armed Conflict*.

Economic Perfor-mance **(Weighting = 8)**	Poor economic conditions can cause dissatisfaction with government performance and contribute to the potential for (1) *Violent Conflict* and (2) *Political Instability and Governance* problems. Economic differentials can also accrue along group lines in countries with high (3) *Population Heterogeneity*, increasing ethnic cleavages. Declining incomes, inflation, exchange rate collapse, declining levels of foreign investment and high external debt affect material living standards and levels of (4) *Human Development*. Poor economic conditions can result in inter-regional or rural-urban migration, creating additional (5) *Demographic Stresses*, as well as compelling the movement of peoples into ecologically sensitive areas, thus having an impact on (6) *Environmental Stress*. A state's ability to finance its military is also directly contingent upon economic performance, and fluctuations in state revenues can result in uneven support for armed forces, thereby affecting (7) *Militarization*. Economic performance affects (8) *International Linkages* to the degree that a state's ability to participate in international fora or to benefit from international support often depends upon its ability and willingness to pursue macroeconomic or fiscal reforms.
Human Develop-ment **(Weighting = 3)**	Poor material living standards and unmet expectations regarding opportunities for social advancement can cause civil strife and higher risks of (1) *Armed Conflict*. The lack of, or decline in, public services such as health, safe water and sanitation can decrease popular confidence in the state leading to (2) *Political Instability and Governance* problems. (3) *Economic Performance* is restricted by low levels of Human Development; low levels of investment in human capital hinder the development of a skilled labour force, necessary for increasing productivity and incomes.
Environ-mental Stress **(Weighting = 5)**	The degradation and depletion of renewable resources can generate effects such as constrained economic productivity and growth, poverty and migration, thereby affecting (1) *Economic Performance* and (2) *Human Development*. Scarcities in natural resources can have an impact on (3) *Demographic Stress* by causing migration, increasing demand and unequal distribution, and also raises the potential for (4) *Armed Conflict* by heightening competition over increasingly scarce resources. Resource scarcities can alter and affect relations between states, thus directly influencing (5) *International Linkages*.
Interna-tional Link-ages **(Weighting = 5)**	International linkages influence (1) *Militarization*, (2) *Economic Performance* and (3) *Human Development*, as countries with fewer diplomatic, political, economic or cultural linkages with regional organizations and neighbouring states are less likely to profit from constructive engagement with outsides actors in the areas of economic co-operation, development assistance, military aid, mediation and support in peace processes. The prevalence of armed conflict in neighbouring states can have a destabilizing effect on (4) *Governance and Political Stability* and spill over into local (5) *Armed Conflict*, through cross-border refugee flows and the movement of rebel forces.

Figure 5.2. Linkages Between Issue Areas and Resulting Weights

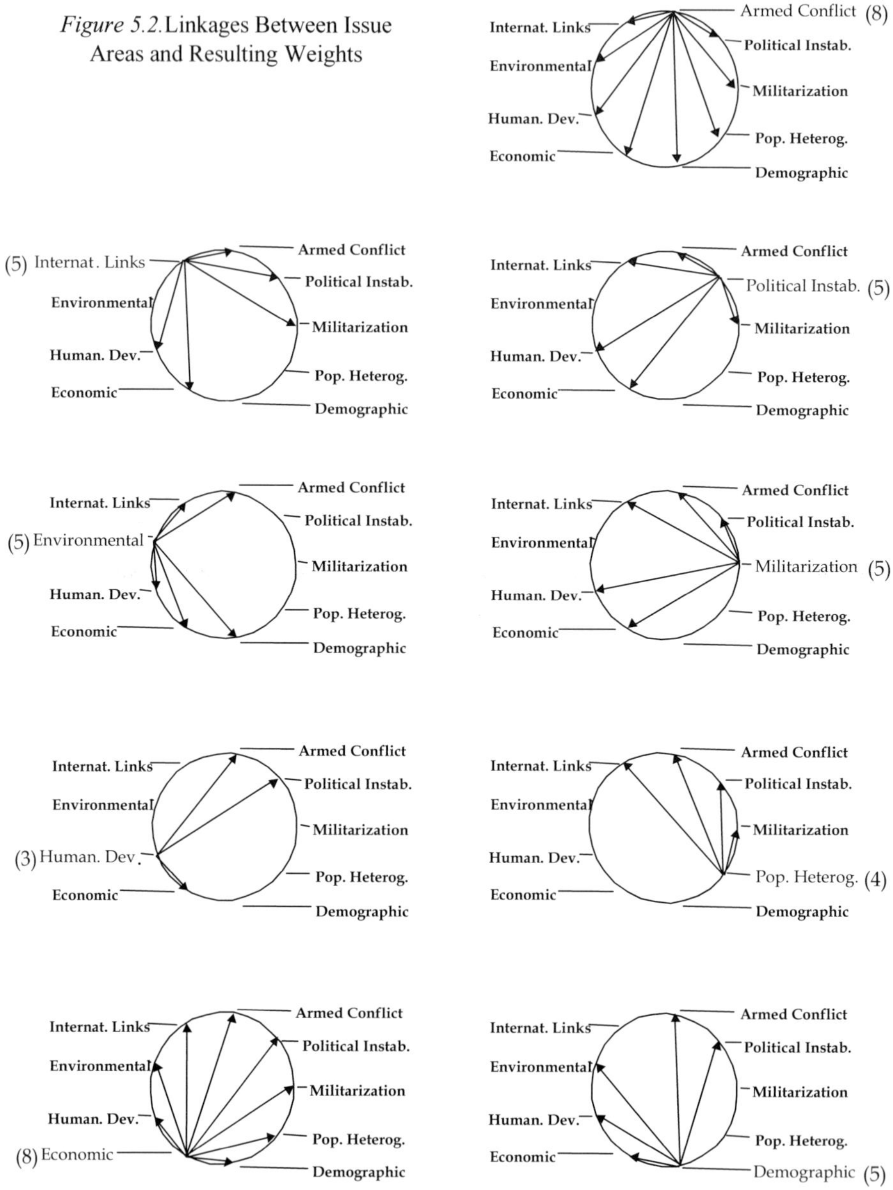

5.5 *Calculating the Index*

As indicated above, a country's overall risk index is calculated on the basis of the weighted mean of the nine composite issue area scores, employing the weighting scheme elaborated in Table 5.3. and Figure 5.2.. The formula for calculating this weighted mean is as follows, where xn are the values of the nine composite issue area scores, and wn are their corresponding weights:

$$\text{Overall Risk Index} = (w_1x_1 + w_2x_2 + ... + w_9x_9) / (w_1 + w_2 + ... + w_9)$$

Table 5.4. presents the composite issue area ratings and scores, as well as the overall risk index scores for the West African countries of the Mano River Basin and Senegambia (Guinea, Liberia, Sierra Leone, Gambia and Senegal). The values for each of the individual indicators that compose the nine issue area scores (including their global rank scores, trend scores and volatility scores), can be found in the "Conflict Assessment Report: West Africa: Mano River Union and Senegambia", which can be found at http://www.carleton.ca/cifp[3].

Table 5.4. Risk Assessment Calculation for Mano River Basin and Senegambia

GAMBIA	*Composite Issue Area Risk Rating*	*Composite Issue Area Score*	*Weight*	*Weighted Average*
History of Armed Conflict	Low	3.2	8	25.6
Governance and Political Instability	High	6.9	5	34.4
Militarization	Low	2.3	5	11.3
Population Heterogeneity	Medium	4.0	4	16.0
Demographic Stress	Medium	6.4	5	31.8
Economic Performance	Medium	5.2	8	41.4
Human Development	High	7.4	3	22.2
Environmental Stress	High	6.5	5	32.5
International Linkages	High	6.6	5	33.0
Unweighted Sum		48.6		
Unweighted Average		5.4		
Sum of the Weights			48	
Weighted Sum				248.9
Risk Index (Weighted Average)		**Medium Risk**		**5.0**

3. Indicators for which only a single year is available are measured only in terms of global rank, without trend and volatility modifiers. Indicators for which this is the case are marked as "single measure". Also note that in cases where absolute and relative measures are both provided in the CIFP data set (i.e. GDP and GDP per capita), only relative measures are used for this calculation.

GUINEA	*Composite Issue Area Risk Rating*	*Composite Issue Area Score*	*Weight*	*Weighted Average*
History of Armed Conflict	Medium	3.7	8	29.3
Governance and Political Instability	High	7.7	5	38.4
Militarization	Low	2.6	5	12.8
Population Heterogeneity	Medium	5.3	4	21.3
Demographic Stress	Medium	5.6	5	28.0
Economic Performance	High	6.8	8	54.6
Human Development	High	7.7	3	23.0
Environmental Stress	High	7.0	5	35.0
International Linkages	Medium	5.6	5	28.0
Unweighted Sum		51.8		
Unweighted Average		5.8		
Sum of the Weights			48	
Weighted Sum				269.0
Risk Index (Weighted Average)		**Medium Risk**		**5.6**

LIBERIA	*Composite Issue Area Risk Rating*	*Composite Issue Area Score*	*Weight*	*Weighted Average*
History of Armed Conflict	High	7.1	8	57.1
Governance and Political Instability	High	7.5	5	37.6
Militarization	Medium	4.5	5	22.5
Population Heterogeneity	Medium	6.0	4	24.0
Demographic Stress	Medium	6.3	5	31.3
Economic Performance				0.0
Human Development	High	7.0	3	21.0
Environmental Stress				0.0
International Linkages	Medium	6.2	5	31.0
Unweighted Sum		45.6		
Unweighted Average		5.1		
Sum of the Weights			35	
Weighted Sum				227.5
Risk Index (Weighted Average)		**Medium Risk**		**6.3**

SENEGAL	*Composite Issue Area Risk Rating*	*Composite Issue Area Score*	*Weight*	*Weighted Average*
History of Armed Conflict	Medium	5.4	8	43.2
Governance and Political Instability	Medium	5.0	5	24.8
Militarization	Medium	4.3	5	21.7
Population Heterogeneity	Medium	4.3	4	17.3
Demographic Stress	High	6.1	5	30.7
Economic Performance	Medium	5.8	8	46.4
Human Development	High	6.0	3	18.0
Environmental Stress	Medium	5.0	5	25.0
International Linkages	Medium	5.0	5	25.0
Unweighted Sum		49.3		
Unweighted Average		5.5		
Sum of the Weights			48	
Weighted Sum				261.3
Risk Index (Weighted Average)		**Medium Risk**		**5.2**

SIERRA LEONE	*Composite Issue Area Risk Rating*	*Composite Issue Area Score*	*Weight*	*Weighted Average*
History of Armed Conflict	High	9.3	8	74.1
Governance and Political Instability	High	8.3	5	41.3
Militarization	Medium	3.8	5	18.8
Population Heterogeneity	High	6.7	4	26.7
Demographic Stress	Medium	6.1	5	30.3
Economic Performance	High	9.6	8	76.4
Human Development	High	7.9	3	23.6
Environmental Stress	High	8.5	5	42.5
International Linkages	Medium	5.4	5	27.0
Unweighted Sum		65.4		
Unweighted Average		7.3		
Sum of the Weights			48	
Weighted Sum				360.7
Risk Index (Weighted Average)		**High Risk**		**7.5**

6 CIFP RISK ASSESSMENT REPORTS

The intent of CIFP risk assessment reports is to provide in-depth analysis, based on the component indicators of the risk index as well as relevant supplementary data, of the structural conditions within a country that underlie that country's potential for conflict. The reports are structured in a similar fashion to that employed in the risk index calculation, addressing the nine issue areas and their component leading indicators. At this stage, CIFP risk assessment reports are regional in focus, under the premise that "risk potential" is a relative term, and that a regional comparative focus allows not only the identification of areas of concern within target countries, but provides a means of assigning relative priority to different areas of concern on a regional basis. CIFP is currently producing risk assessment reports for West Africa and Southeast Asia, with a particular focus upon the countries of the Mano River Basin (Guinea, Liberia, Sierra Leone) and Senegambia (Gambia, Senegal) in the former region, and the countries of Cambodia, Indonesia, and the Philippines in the latter.

6.1 Identification and Interpretation of Areas of Primary Concern

The risk assessment calculation allows an identification of areas of primary concern within each country, as well as the comparison of areas of relative priority across the region. A useful guideline for the identification of areas of primary concern is to highlight those areas that score high on the three component risk scores—i.e. indicators for which a country is performing poorly relative to other countries (high global rank score), indicators for which a country's absolute performance trend has been worsening (trend score), and/or those indicators that have demonstrated a high degree of irregularity (volatility score). Individual indicators that have scored highly in any of these scores—and particularly indicators in which two or more risk scores are high—are likely candidates for further and more detailed attention.

While the CIFP risk index calculation provides a heuristic measure allowing for the identification of areas of primary concern, the task of CIFP risk assessment reports is to provide analysis and interpretation of high risk indicators, prominent trends, and area linkages. Since the goal of CIFP risk assessment reports is to provide a basis upon which response-oriented early warning reports can be built, the identification and interpretation of areas of primary concern, trends and linkages can serve to focus analytical attention, and to provide a framework for interpreting the results of real-time monitoring of events. In addition, these can serve as a ground for linkages with particular policy fields and instruments, in order to develop logical policy options in subsequent early warning reports.

The analytical component of CIFP risk assessment reports is critical. While many indicators may "speak for themselves" to a certain degree, this is not always the case, nor is the manner in which data points or trends can be explained always self-evident. CIFP risk assessments are intended to provide key contextual information, for example, describing the circumstances of regime transitions underlying trends in Governance and Political Instability indicators, or of economic shocks impacting economic performance indicators, and so on. The provision of contextual information is especially important for indicators that rely on previously coded assessments of country performance, such as the indicators of democracy and regime durability derived from the Polity IV data set, the "risk of ethnic rebellion" measure built upon the Minorities at Risk data set, and the indicators of conflict intensity, derived from data from the Conflict Data Project/SIPRI.

In addition, it is important to bear in mind that similar trends or patterns in indicator data may signify different things in different countries, especially with regards to their potential impact on the processes of conflict development. In different contexts, for example, both increasing and decreasing levels of military expenditure may aggravate the potential for conflict: on the one hand, increasing levels of military expenditure in certain cases may indicate increasing militarization of the state apparatus as a regime strives to consolidate political control, thereby aggravating the potential for militant oppositional activity; on the other hand, abrupt reductions in military expenditure can create tensions or resentment within the armed forces, potentially inciting the armed forces to withdraw support from prevailing regimes. What is most important is that interpretations of indicator trends must bear in mind contextual and country-specific information when making assessments. So too for the identification and interpretation of linkages between different indicators and issue areas.

While the CIFP risk assessment calculation incorporates a weighting scheme that is based on pre-coded assessments of the prevailing forms of linkage between different issue areas, it is the task of the risk assessment reports to draw out and elaborate upon linkages as they arise in particular country and regional contexts. Thus, while the risk assessment calculation posits recursive causal linkages between environmental stress, demographic stress and economic performance, the precise nature of these linkages—and the direction of causality—are likely to manifest differently in different countries.

As an example, Table 5.5. identifies indicators that should be highlighted for additional attention and analysis in the Mano River Basin and Senegambia regional risk assessment report. The selection is based on the risk index scoring tabulation outlined above, and on the notion that where trends are worsening and or there is a high degree of volatility within the recent five year time period, particular attention must be paid to analyse the dynamics of this structural evidence.

Table 5.5. Comparison of High Risk Indicators (for Mano River Basin and Senegambia)

Country	*High Risk Issue Areas*	*Individual Indicators Of Special Concern (Scoring High in Two or More Categories of Risk: Global Rank of 7-9, Trend of +1, and/or Volatility of +2)*
Guinea	Gov. and Political Stability Human Development	Restrictions on Press Freedoms (High Concern and Worsening Trend)
Sierra Leone	History of Armed Conflict Gov. and Political Stability Population Heterogeneity Economic Performance Human Development Environmental Stress	Armed Conflict (High Concern and Worsening Trend) Refugees Produced (High Concern and Worsening Trend) Level of Democracy (High Concern, Worsening Trend, High Volatility) Regime Durability (High Concern, Worsening Trend, High Volatility) Civil / Political Rights (High Concern, High Volatility) Press Freedoms (High Concern and Worsening Trend) GDP Growth Rate (High Concern, Worsening Trend, High Volatility) GDP Per Capita (High Concern, Worsening Trend) Inflation (High Concern, Worsening Trend, High Volatility) Exchange Rate (High Concern, High Volatility) Foreign Direct Investment (High Concern, High Volatility) Trade Openness (High Concern, Worsening Trend)
Liberia	History of Armed Conflict Gov. and Political Stability Human Development	Refugees Produced (High Concern, High Volatility) Refugees Hosted (High Concern, High Volatility) Population Growth Rate (High Concern, Worsening Trend) Urban Population Growth Rate (High Concern, Worsening Trend)
Gambia	Gov. and Political Stability Human Development International Linkages	Refugees Hosted (Worsening Trend and High Volatility) Restrictions on Press Freedoms (High Concern and Worsening Trend) Youth Bulge (High Concern and Worsening Trend)
Senegal	Demographic Stress Human Development	Population Growth Rate (High Concern and Worsening Trend) Secondary School Enrolment (High Concern and Worsening Trend)

Noteworthy in the above tabulation in Table 5.5. are the regionally endemic low levels of Human Development, as well as the prevalence of high levels of concern in the areas of Governance and Political Stability. The region is also plagued with high levels of refugees, returning refugees, and internally displaced persons. These countries also face specific challenges, such as the histories of violent conflict in Liberia and Sierra Leone, the worsening record of civil and political liberties in Guinea and Gambia, and the relatively higher levels of demographic stress in Senegal.

The identification and interpretation of the primary areas of concern is the first stage in the preparation of the regional risk assessment reports. Subsequently, the analyst must evaluate whether the data available from the global sample is sufficient in order to provide an accurate assessment, and in which areas complementary data must be obtained for the purposes of evaluating the underlying conditions. In certain cases it may also be useful to examine other specific issues areas not represented within the global data sample—for example, specific issue areas such as diamonds and small arms in the case of West Africa.

6.2 Assessment of Complementary Data

While the intent of CIFP risk assessment reports is to provide in-depth analysis and assessments based on the risk index calculation and its component data, the reports also provide an opportunity to incorporate and assess relevant supplementary data. A key aspect of the current CIFP data set is that it only incorporates data from reliable sources that are global in scope, and that have methodological consistency both across time and across countries in order to ensure that data it is truly comparable. This means, however, that data for some countries is absent if it does not meet the condition of global comparability, or if it does not have a high enough level of reliability.

The case of Liberia is indicative here. The CIFP draws a majority of its economic data from the World Bank, which bases its data on national accounts statistics collected from national statistical offices. Given the lack of reporting capacity in Liberia during the country's civil war and since its end, the World Bank provides very little by way of current economic data for the country. While data does exist – currently in the form of estimates, such as those assembled by the IMF in coordination with Liberian authorities in an effort to begin the reconstruction of national income accounts data[4] -- this data is not built into the CIFP data set or risk calculation because the data is not necessarily comparable with that used for the global sample in the CIFP data set. Accordingly, analysts are encouraged to seek out regional or coun-

4. See for example IMF Staff Country Report No. 00/50 "Liberia: Selected Issues and Statistical Appendix" (2000).

try-specific data sources that can complement the data provided by the CIFP data set, in order to fill in data gaps in cases where they do occur.

6.3 Preparation of Regional Risk Assessment Reports (3 Elements)

1. Country overview including a map of the region	2. Analysis of 9 issue areas including charts and graphs representing the data in comparative formats (approximately three pages per issue area). Assessment of complementary data where appropriate.	3. Summary of conclusions and overall risk ratings

7 REGRESSION ANALYSIS OF CIFP

As has already been discussed CIFP risk assessment reports examine nine issue areas (History of Armed Conflict, Governance and Political Instability, Militarization, Population Heterogeneity, Demographic Stress, Economic Performance, Human Development, Environmental Stress and International Linkages). Each of these nine issue areas include a variety of variables which are used to determine the nine composite indicators. These nine composite indicators are then weighted and averaged to determine a state's risk index. This section will examine the relative importance of each variable in determining the composite indicators, and the relative importance of the composite indicators in determining the Risk Index. In order to do this, data from a CIFP risk assessment report on Sub-Saharan Africa, was put through regression analysis.[5]

7.1 *Risk Index*

The CIFP methodology gives each of the nine issue areas a weight, which is then used to calculate the Risk Index (see sectiion 5). This weighting scheme generally corresponds to the correlations between Risk Index and each issue area composite score, for the Sub-Saharan Africa data, although there were some surprises. Table 5.6. compares the variance explained (the

5. See "Conflict Risk Assessment Sub-Saharan Africa – Appendix A" (2002). A sample country table from the Sub-Saharan Africa report can be found in Appendix A. The full report can be found on the CIFP website: http://www.carleton.ca/cifp/risk.htm

correlation of each issue area to the Risk Index score) to the weight assigned by the CIFP methodology.

Table 5.6. Issue Area Correlation to Risk Index (Sub-Saharan Africa)

Issue Area	*Variance Explained (Correlation to Risk Index)*	*Weight*
History of Conflict	61 %	8
Militarization	43 %	5
Governance and Political Instability	33 %	5
Environmental Stress	23 %	5
Economic Performance	17 %	8
Human Development	15 %	3
Demographic Stress	11 %	5
Population Heterogeneity	1 %	4
International Linkages	0 %	5

By far the issue area that was had the strongest correlation to the risk index is History of Armed Conflict. This is consistent with Fig. 2, which shows that this issue area has linkages to all other issue areas. In addition, it is common sense that a history of armed conflict will be strongly associated with a risk for further conflict. The issue area Militarization has the second strongest correlation to the Risk Index, however Militarization and History of Armed Conflict are not only strongly correlated to the Risk Index, but also to each other. The explanatory power for all the composite scores, without that of History of Conflict is 89 % and the explanatory power for all the composite scores, without Militarization is 98 %. The correlation between these two issue areas could be explained by the fact that a state with a history of conflict will likely be highly militarized.

In fact, there are a number of strong correlations between the composite scores for each issue area. Figure 5.3. is a sample of some output from the statistics software SPSS. The figure shows all the correlation numbers for the weighted composite scores for each issue area. By eliminating composite scores that have a correlation greater than .300 it was possible to find a small subset of issue areas which have a strong correlation to the Risk Index. Together, the explanatory power of History of Armed Conflict, Economic Development and Demographic stress is 87 % percent.

The following sections will look at the explanatory power of the variables that determine the composite score for each issue area.

		Weighted Demographic	Weighted Economic	Weighted Environment	Weighed Governance	Weighted History Comp	Weighted Human Development	Weighted International	Weighted Militarization	Weighted Population
Pearson Correlation	Weighted Demographic	1.000	.120	.510**	.296	.159	.127	-.118	.121	.117
	Weighted Economic	.120	1.000	.261	.267	.126	.235	-.175	-.052	.286
	Weighted Environment	.510**	.261	1.000	.170	.235	.265	.000	.400**	-.035
	Weighed Governance	.296	.267	.170	1.000	.544**	.170	.228	.162	.000
	Weighted History Comp	.159	.126	.235	.544**	1.000	.091	.194	.638**	.066
	Weighted Human Development	.127	.235	.265	.170	.091	1.000	.309*	.269	.120
	Weighted International	-.118	-.175	.000	.228	.194	.309*	1.000	.239	-.364*
	Weighted Militarization	.121	-.052	.400**	.162	.638**	.269	.239	1.000	.040
	Weighted Population	.117	.286	-.035	.000	.066	.120	-.364*	.040	1.000

*Figure 5.3.*Correlations between Composite Scores

7.2 History of Armed Conflict

There is a strong correlation between all three independent variables in the issue area History of Armed Conflict, and each of them has strong explanatory power for the composite score. The variable History of Armed Conflict has the strongest correlation to the composite score, with 68 % explanatory power. Together with the variable Refugees Produced, History of Armed Conflict has a 90 % correlation to the composite score.

7.3 Governance and Political Instability

The variables with the most explanatory power in this issue area are Level of Democracy and Level of Corruption, which have a 72 % and 71 % correlation to the composite score, respectively. However, all the independent variables in this issue area are strongly correlated to the composite score (the lowest correlation is Regime Durability at 42 %). This can be explained by the fact that many of these variables are strongly correlated to each other. The only pairs of variables which are not, are Level of Democracy and Regime Durability, Regime Durability and Restrictions on Civil and Political Rights, and Regime Durability and Restrictions on Press Freedom. These pairs also each have the most explanatory power in regards to the composite score, with a correlation of 89 %, 92 % and 90 %, respectively.

7.4 Militarization

Military Expenditure (% of GDP) is the independent variable with the most explanatory power in this issue area (69 %). The other variables also have high correlations to the composite score with the lowest being Military Expenditure (43 %). As with the previous issue area, the independent variables in Militarization are closely correlated, so it is possible to narrow down the variables to find just a couple which are strongly correlated to the Risk Index. Military Expenditure (% of GDP) and the variable Total Forces have an explanatory power of 94 %, while the variables Military Expenditure and Armed Forces (per 1000 persons)[6] have an explanatory power of 91 %.

7.5 Population Heterogeneity

Unlike the previous issue areas, the independent variables in Population Heterogeneity are not closely correlated (except perhaps for Ethnic Diversity and Religious Diversity, which have a correlation of .336). The variable most closely correlated to the composite score is Religious Diversity, with an explanatory power of 60 %. Ethnic Diversity and Religious Diversity has a combined explanatory power of 84 %.

6. For the Sub-Saharan Africa report this variable is per 1000 persons, rather than 10000 persons as in the CIFP template.

7.6 Demographic Stress

Alone, the independent variables in the issue area Demographic Stress, each have only a modest correlation to the composite score. Population Growth Rate and Urban Population Growth Rate have the strongest correlation to the composite scores at 37 %. The variable with the least correlation to the composite score is Urban Population (% of Total) at 7 %. There are also some correlations between the variables in this issue area. When closely correlated variables are separated it is possible to find a smaller subset of variables which have a strong correlation to the composite score. The three independent variables Total Population, Population Growth Rate and Population Density have a combined explanatory power of 87 %.

7.7 *Economic Performance*[7]

Independently, the independent variables in this issue area have only moderate correlations to the composite score. The variable with the strongest correlation is GDP Per Capita (56 %). Second is Trade Openness (35 %). The variables Inflation, Debt Service and Inequality Score have very little correlation to the composite score, with explanatory power 8 %, 4 % and 0 % respectively. Inflation and Inequality Score, on further regression analysis, were also shown to add little explanatory power even when grouped with other variables. This was not the case with Debt Service, which, when grouped with other variables, added to the explanatory power of the variables.

In this issue area there are several correlations between the independent variables (see Figure 5.4.). For example, GDP per capita was closely correlated to GDP Growth Rate, Exchange Rates, Trade Openness and AID (% of GNI). When the variable set is GDP Per Capita, Trade Openness and Debt the explanatory power is 75 %, while the variable set GDP per Capita, FDI and Debt Service had an explanatory power of 80 %. These are substantial numbers considering that this issue area has nine independent variables.

7.8 Human Development[8]

The variables in this issue area each have fairly low independent correlations to the composite score. The variables with the highest explanatory power are Access to Improved Water Source, Infant Mortality Rate and Chil-

7. Please note that the variable GDP was not included in the Sub-Saharan Africa Data, and an additional variable (AID - % of GNI) was included.

8. Please note that the variable Secondary School Enrollment was not included in the Sub-Saharan Africa Data.

Correlations

		gdp_growth	GDP_CAP	Inflation	exch_rate	FDI	DEBT	TRADE_OP	AID	INEQUALI
Pearson Correlation	gdp_growth	1.000	.394*	.133	-.190	.231	.013	.094	-.092	.479*
	GDP_CAP	.394*	1.000	.196	.348*	.261	-.097	.480**	.609**	.042
	Inflation	.133	.196	1.000	.195	-.239	.204	-.129	-.112	.145
	exch_rate	-.190	.348*	.195	1.000	.264	.057	.358*	.370*	-.261
	FDI	.231	.261	-.239	.264	1.000	-.230	.464**	.281	-.187
	DEBT	.013	-.097	.204	.057	-.230	1.000	-.195	-.193	.116
	TRADE_OP	.094	.480**	-.129	.358*	.464**	-.195	1.000	.401*	-.397*
	AID	-.092	.609**	-.112	.370*	.281	-.193	.401*	1.000	-.224
	INEQUALI	.479*	.042	.145	-.261	-.187	.116	-.397*	-.224	1.000
Sig. (2-tailed)	gdp_growth	.	.012	.434	.239	.146	.939	.563	.577	.013
	GDP_CAP	.012	.	.245	.030	.104	.556	.002	.000	.840
	Inflation	.434	.245	.	.247	.154	.232	.452	.523	.488
	exch_rate	.239	.030	.247	.	.096	.732	.025	.022	.199
	FDI	.146	.104	.154	.096	.	.153	.003	.083	.359
	DEBT	.939	.556	.232	.732	.153	.	.233	.244	.572
	TRADE_OP	.563	.002	.452	.025	.003	.233	.	.013	.045
	AID	.577	.000	.523	.022	.083	.244	.013	.	.272
	INEQUALI	.013	.840	.488	.199	.359	.572	.045	.272	.
N	gdp_growth	41	40	37	40	41	40	40	39	26
	GDP_CAP	40	40	37	39	40	39	39	38	26
	Inflation	37	37	37	37	37	36	36	35	25
	exch_rate	40	39	37	41	41	39	39	38	26
	FDI	41	40	37	41	42	40	40	39	26
	DEBT	40	39	36	39	40	40	39	38	26
	TRADE_OP	40	39	36	39	40	39	40	38	26
	AID	39	38	35	38	39	38	38	39	26
	INEQUALI	26	26	25	26	26	26	26	26	26

*. Correlation is significant at the 0.05 level (2-tailed).

**. Correlation is significant at the 0.01 level (2-tailed).

*Figure 5.4.*Correlations between Independent Variables in Economic Performance

dren in the Labour Force (28 %). The variables with the least explanatory power are Access to Sanitation (6 %) and Life Expectancy (8 %).

This issue area also has numerous correlations between the independent variables (see Figure 5.5.). For example, Access to Improved Water Source had correlations to Access to Sanitation, Maternal Mortality Rate, HIV/AIDS and Children in Labour Force. Other interesting correlations were those between Maternal Mortality Rate and Access to Improved Water Source, Primary School Enrollment and Life Expectancy. The two variables Access to Improved Water Source and Children in Labour Force have an explanatory power of 64 %. This is quite high considering that they are only two of nine independent variables in this issue area.

7.9 Environmental Stress

For this issue area there are only three independent variables (Rate of Deforestation, People per Sq. km. of Arable Land and Access to Fresh Water). These variables do not have a strong correlation between each other, except for People per Sq. km. of Arable Land and Access to Fresh Water (.314). The variable with the most explanatory power on its own is Access to Fresh Water (68 %), and paired with People per Sq. km. of Arable Land these two variables have an explanatory power of 85 %, however the other two combinations of two variables are not much lower (at 74 % and 78 %).

Correlations

		WATER	sanitation	LIFE_EXP	INF_MORT	MAT_MORT	HIV/AIDS	prim_enrol	child_labour
Pearson Correlation	WATER	1.000	.516**	-.216	.043	.542**	-.335*	.105	.393*
	sanitation	.516**	1.000	-.448**	-.199	.217	-.488**	.109	.139
	LIFE_EXP	-.216	-.448**	1.000	.295	-.281	.539**	-.154	-.015
	INF_MORT	.043	-.199	.295	1.000	.254	.196	.281	.136
	MAT_MORT	.542**	.217	-.281	.254	1.000	-.215	.564**	.395*
	HIV/AIDS	-.335*	-.488**	.539**	.196	-.215	1.000	-.142	-.075
	prim_enrol	.105	.109	-.154	.281	.564**	-.142	1.000	.392*
	child_labour	.393*	.139	-.015	.136	.395*	-.075	.392*	1.000
Sig. (2-tailed)	WATER	.	.001	.200	.801	.001	.043	.582	.019
	sanitation	.001	.	.006	.245	.218	.003	.572	.434
	LIFE_EXP	.200	.006	.	.054	.088	.000	.386	.925
	INF_MORT	.801	.245	.054	.	.123	.208	.107	.396
	MAT_MORT	.001	.218	.088	.123	.	.196	.001	.016
	HIV/AIDS	.043	.003	.000	.208	.196	.	.422	.639
	prim_enrol	.582	.572	.386	.107	.001	.422	.	.027
	child_labour	.019	.434	.925	.396	.016	.639	.027	.
N	WATER	37	35	37	37	35	37	30	35
	sanitation	35	36	36	36	34	36	29	34
	LIFE_EXP	37	36	43	43	38	43	34	41
	INF_MORT	37	36	43	43	38	43	34	41
	MAT_MORT	35	34	38	38	38	38	31	37
	HIV/AIDS	37	36	43	43	38	43	34	41
	prim_enrol	30	29	34	34	31	34	34	32
	child_labour	35	34	41	41	37	41	32	41

**. Correlation is significant at the 0.01 level (2-tailed).

*. Correlation is significant at the 0.05 level (2-tailed).

*Figure 5.5.*Correlations between Independent Variables in Economic Performance

7.10 International Linkages

In this issue area the independent variable Military and Security Alliances is a constant for the Sub-Saharan Africa data, so it was not included in the regression analysis. For the other independent variable, there is a strong correlation between all of them, except for Interstate Disputes. Alone, this variable has little explanatory power (5 %), but when included with other independent variables it adds substantial explanatory power. The pair of independent variables with the most explanatory power are Multipurpose Organizations and Interstate Disputes (74 %), which increases to 90 % when the variable Economic Organizations is included.

8 CONCLUSIONS

Due to its open source nature, the methodology outlined could contribute to a more effective open source early warning system. Several challenges lay ahead. First, the conflict prevention field is young and there is an inadequate "know-how" of how to do good early warning and early response, and limited understanding of how to tackle complex conflict factors (e.g. dismantle the political economy of war). While there are "pockets" of know-how and expertise, there is limited synergy and sharing in the field. This hampers the ability of conflict prevention practitioners to draw on research for improved field operations.

Second, early warning and response are still characterised by "extractive" practices through an interventionist paradigm. Northern institutions analyse conflicts in the South and define and implement responses. There is still limited support to Southern early warning and response initiatives, or to the inclusion of Southern perspectives into Northern decision-making processes.

Third, conflict prevention activities are often not informed by regular and locally prepared situation analyses. Where such analyses are factored into programming, it is often a "one-off" exercise or an external analysis that does not reflect local perspectives. Given the dynamic and complex nature of conflict, systematic monitoring and analysis, as well as local input into that analysis, are prerequisites for appropriate and sustainable action.

Fourth, the impact of conflict prevention activities is reduced because of a lack of co-ordination and strategy. Frequently, key conflict prevention actors (NGOs, governments, multilateral organisations, civil society groups, etc.) operate in isolation or do not co-ordinate activities across sectors. This often results from a lack of common analysis and the lack of multi-agency planning forums for the development of joint conflict prevention strategies.

References

Gurr, T. R., and Marshall, M., 2000, Assessing the risks of future ethnic wars, in *Peoples Versus States: Minorities at Risk in the New Century*, Gurr, T. R., ed., US Institute of Peace Press, Washington, DC, Chapter 7.

James, P., and Brecher, M., 1986, *Crisis and Change in World Politics*, Westview Press, Boulder.

APPENDIX

Sample Country Table from CIFP Conflict Risk Assessment Sub-Saharan Africa

Angola	*Global Rank Score*	*Trend Score*	*Volatility Score*	*Sum*	*Avg.*	*Weighted Avg.*
History of Armed Conflict					**9.03**	**72.27**
Armed Conflicts	5.7	1.0	1.0	**7.7**		
# of Refugees Produced	8.2	1.0	0.0	**9.2**		
# of Refugees Hosted, IDPs, Others of Concern	7.2	1.0	2.0	**10.2**		
Governance and Political Instability					**8.80**	**44.00**
Level of Democracy	7.4	0.0	1.0	**8.4**		
Regime Durability	8.6	0.0	1.0	**9.6**		
Restrictions on Civil and Political Rights	8.0	0.0	0.0	**8.0**		
Restrictions on Press Freedom	8.0	1.0	0.0	**9.0**		
Level of Corruption	9.0	single measure	single measure	**9.0**		
Militarization					**7.48**	**37.40**
Military Expenditure (Constant 1998 US$ millions)	6.5	-1.0	2.0	**7.5**		
Total Military Expenditure (% of GDP, Constant 1998 US$)	9.0	0.0	2.0	**11.0**		
Imports of Maj. Conv. Weapons	6.2	1.0	2.0	**9.2**		
Total Armed Forces	5.7	-1.0	0.0	**4.7**		
Total Armed Forces (per 1,000)	6.0	-1.0	0.0	**5.0**		
Population Heterogeneity					**7.67**	**30.67**
Ethnic Diversity	9.0	single measure	single measure	**9.0**		
Religious Diversity	8.0	single measure	single measure	**8.0**		
Risk of Ethnic Rebellion (Single Measure)	6.0	single measure	single measure	**6.0**		
Demographic Stress					**5.93**	**29.67**
Total Population	7.0	exception	exception	**7.0**		
Population Growth Rate (Annual %)	8.6	-1.0	0.0	**7.6**		
Population Density (people per sq km)	2.0	exception	exception	**2.0**		
Urban Population (% of Total)	3.0	exception	exception	**3.0**		
Urban Population Growth Rate (Annual %)	8.2	-1.0	0.0	**7.2**		
Youth Bulge (Pop. Aged 0-14 as a % of Total)	8.8	-1.0	1.0	**8.8**		
Economic Performance					**7.10**	**56.80**
GDP Growth Rate (Annual %)	2.4	1.0	0.0	**3.4**		
GDP Per Capita (PPP, Current International $)	6.6	-1.0	2.0	**7.6**		

Inflation [Consumer prices (annual %)]	9.0	-1.0	2.0	**10.0**		
Official exchange rate (LCU/US$, period avg.)	7.6	-1.0	2.0	**8.6**		
FDI [Net inflows (% of GDP)]	1	1.0	1.0	**3.0**		
Total Debt Service (% of GNP)	9.0	1.0	0.0	**10.0**		
Trade Openness (Trade as a % of GDP)	2.0	1.0	2.0	**5.0**		
Dependence on Foreign Aid (Aid as % of GNI)	7.2	0.0	2.0	**9.2**		
Inequality Score (GINI Coefficient)	..	single measure	single measure	..		
Human Development					**9.04**	**27.11**
Access to Improved Water Source (% Tot. Pop.)	9.0	single measure	single measure	**9.0**		
Access to Sanitation (% Tot. Pop.)	7.0	single measure	single measure	**7.0**		
Life Expectancy (Years)	9.0	1.0	0.0	**10.0**		
Infant Mortality Rate (per 1000 live births)	9.0	1.0	1.0	**11.0**		
Maternal Mortality Rate (per 100,000 live births)	9.0	single measure	single measure	**9.0**		
HIV/AIDS (% of Adult Population)	7.5	1.0	0.0	**8.5**		
Primary School Enroll (% Relevant Age Group)	8.8	-1.0	2.0	**9.8**		
Illiteracy rate, adult total (% of people ages 15 and above)	..	..	..	..		
Health expenditure per capita, PPP (current international $)	..	..	..	..		
Child Labour (% Children aged 10-14)	7.0	1.0	0.0	**8.0**		
Environmental Stress					**5.00**	**25.00**
Rate of Deforestation (Percent)	6.0	single measure	single measure	**6.0**		
People per Sq. Km. of Arable Land	5.0	1.0	0.0	**6.0**		
Freshwater Resources (cubic meters per capita)	3.0	single measure	single measure	**3.0**		
International Linkages					**6.30**	**31.50**
Economic Organizations Index	8.0	single measure	single measure	**8.0**		
Military/Security Alliances Index	9.0	single measure	single measure	**9.0**		
UN Organizations Index	5.5	single measure	single measure	**5.5**		
Multipurpose and Miscellaneous Orgs. Index	7.0	single measure	single measure	**7.0**		
International Disputes (# of)	2.0	0.0	0.0	**2.0**		
Unweighted Sum					**66.35**	
Unweighted Average					**7.37**	
Total Weighted Sum						**354.41**
Risk Index (Weighted Average)						**7.38**

Chapter 6

The Confman.2002 Data Set

Developing Cases and Indices of Conflict Management to Predict Conflict Resolution

Jacob Bercovitch
University of Canterbury, Christchurch, New Zealand

Robert Trappl
Medical University of Vienna and Austrian Research Institute for Artificial Intelligence, Vienna, Austria

1 INTRODUCTION

There can be no doubt that conflict in general and international conflicts in particular are amongst the most important phenomena that we should study. Tens of millions of people have died as a result of conflict in the last century, untold destruction was wreaked on many societies, and millions of people lost all and became refugees as a result of some conflict or another. No other social process threatens the stability and order of the international system more than conflict. No other social process threatens the complete elimination of another person, group or nation. Clearly, there is much to be learned about conflict and how best to resolve it, to avoid the undesirable and negative consequences associated with conflict. Knowledge about the conditions and causes of conflict, and an understanding of its dynamics and modes of termination can help us transform a potentially violent process into a more constructive one. This chapter purports to suggest a way, a method, of thinking about conflict management, and presenting some ideas for scholars and policy makers that might suggest how best to approach a conflict. Our focus here is avowedly practical, though our approach is strongly theoretical (Deutsch, 1973).

As is the case with other phenomena we study, different approaches and methods are used by different people to shed light on the question at hand. The single case study approach has been the dominant research strategy in conflict studies. This approach focuses on an in-depth study of a single case of conflict to highlight its dynamics or mode of termination. At times the single study is used to illuminate a hypothesis; at times it is a mostly descriptive

R. Trappl (ed.), Programming for Peace, 115–141.

account of what happened in any given conflict. Either way, a case study approach is useful to trace processes and to build up a reservoir of knowledge on comparative cases of conflict (see, for instance, Dahlitz, 1999).

As well as looking at conflicts in isolation, there has been a strong tendency among many scholars to view all international conflicts as discrete, single or isolated events. No patterns were looked for, nor was there any thought given to features such as continuing conflicts, repeated conflicts, same parties in conflict etc. The study of international conflict was thus mostly the study of one conflict, and its causes, evolution and termination were generally discussed in terms of unique features. Here we want to present a very different logic and a very different methodology.

There can be no doubt that international conflict, and how best to deal with it, is one of the most important issues social and behavioral scientists face. We are also convinced that if we are to make any progress in the study of conflict and its resolution, we have to adopt a different approach; an approach that recognizes that conflicts have many features in common, and that we can make better decisions about conflicts when we learn more about conflict in general, rather than about a specific conflict in particular. With that in mind we have been working on developing a high quality data set on international conflict and its resolution, and using statistical and computer software programs to seek out patterns and trends that may tell us something about the initiation of hostilities, consequences of conflicts, and the conclusion of a peace treaty or a compromise. We believe that the data set we present below (CONFMAN 2002) takes us a long way toward achieving these objectives.

2 CONFLICTS—AGGREGATE STUDY OF

For a very long time we had little or no aggregate data or information on social events. We may have had aggregate information on individual events, such as diseases or intelligence, for quite some time, but no general information on, say, wars, strikes, demonstrations, alliances, etc. These events were assumed to be too complex to study in the aggregate. No one collected information on such events; no one believed it could be a useful exercise.

In the late 1930s and early 1940s the first major efforts to collect data on social events in a scientific manner were undertaken. Pioneers like Sorokin, Richardson and especially Quincy Wright (1965) began studying and recording events such as conflicts and wars, using a systematic approach, and carefully evaluating and measuring every aspect of these social events. The main concern of these three great pioneers of aggregate studies in the social sciences was very much with the processes of conflict and political violence.

Their approach was predicated upon the belief that violence and wars can be studied systematically, and that it is possible to discover correlates of conflict and violence (e.g. how long they last, which party wins more conflicts, etc.), and to do so longitudinally (that is studying a number of years, not just a single year), and globally. Thus, we had the first intellectual attempts to develop knowledge on conflict using methods that had for long been common in the physical sciences, but hardly developed in the social sciences (Holsti, 1966).

In the 1960s and 1970s scholars such as Ed Azar (1980), Charles McClelland and Rudolph Rummel (1976) developed various data sets that deal with conflict behavior both domestically and internationally. These data sets examined interactive events in a sophisticated manner, and provided us with many insights on the dynamics of conflict and ways of forecasting international interactions (Bloomfield and Leiss, 1969). At about the same time we also had the development of two of the biggest data sets in the study of conflict, Singer's Correlates of War Project (1993, see Singer and Small, 1984), and Sherman's Sherfacs data (see Sherman, 1992). All these data sets built up a substantial and very credible body of information on the causes and dynamics of conflict. What we did not know much about was the subject of conflict termination or management. What happens to parties who do try and deal with a conflict in a non-violent manner? Which method do they adopt and with what success? Should parties accept a powerful mediator or a neutral one? Should they negotiate at home or in a neutral territory? Should they make quick or slow concessions? All these are interesting questions to which we have had no answers. Thus, in the mid- 1980s we started to collect data on international conflict management events.

Our approach was clearly influenced by the work of the earlier scholars mentioned above, and particularly the work of J. David Singer (Singer, 1979; Singer and Small, 1972, 1982, 1997; Maoz, 1982). We too use a longitudinal method, a global focus and the state as our basic unit of analysis. We too want to know more about international conflict and believe the best way to knowledge is through a systematic analysis of conflict interactions. Our data collection activity is informed by the desire to identify all cases of conflict since 1945, and more specifically, to enumerate all cases of conflict management in that period and to study their features and characteristics. That is the bold objective of our project.

The project, which we refer to as CONFMAN (short for conflict management) began initially at the University of Canterbury, under the direction of Professor Jacob Bercovitch, in the mid 1980s. Since then, its parameters expanded, and once Professor Trappl and his team joined the project in 1997, we were able to expand the data set very considerably, and apply different methods of analysis to the more than one million observations we have. Here we just want to present the basic ideas of the project and the logic behind it.

Our main concern was to provide a comprehensive, chronological account of international conflict 1945-2000 and to shed some light on its occurrence and management. The international conflict management dataset is an extension of our work and interests in the conditions which make international mediation and negotiation successful, and in the application of sophisticated data analysis methods to identify and predict conditions of conflict management. The objective of our work with CONFMAN is to both further our understanding of conflict in general, and to facilitate the comparative investigation of different conflict management mechanisms (Bercovitch and Jackson, 1997) (that is mediation, negotiation, etc.).

Prompted by dissatisfaction with previous studies, which have rested on ideographic or normative approaches, this research project was established with the aim of furthering the much needed empirical investigation of conflict management within a sound theoretical framework. We are not, it must be emphasized, engaged in some pure inductive exercise, in which we collect data and then look if it makes sense or creates some patterns. We work within a conceptual framework that highlights the reciprocal nature of conflict management, and recognizes that the outcomes of all social processes are influenced by the structure or context of that situation, and the actual process of behaviors that occurs within that structure. Our framework identifies all events within a time continuum where events have antecedents, current and consequent features and manifestations. We recognize that what happens in conflict management in any given moment may well be affected by what happened in the past between these two parties, or by their perception of the future. Thus our framework is both theoretically driven and dynamic in nature. We want to know something about the context of each conflict situation, the way it unfolds in practice and its consequences over a period of time. All these are innovative aspects of the approach.

Given our theoretical framework with its emphasis on context, process and outcomes, we felt it was important to collect information on antecedent events relating to the context of the conflict, information on the nature and characteristics of the parties in conflict, and information on conflict management activities undertaken by the parties. Numerous variables were developed, information was collected on each and thoroughly examined and analysed (in fact, the total number of independent variables is 218).

3 FEATURES OF THE DATA SET

3.1 On Conflict in General

Many datasets are only concerned with one set of activities, either "war" or "mediation" as separate issues of exploration. Here the intention is to present as inclusive as possible a collection of all relevant activities within our case criteria (including different types and levels of international conflicts and different management agents and approaches) that can then be utilised in a number of different avenues of research.

Clearly, our preliminary question was how to identify all conflicts that took place in the international environment since 1945. An original threshold of 100 fatalities was imposed on the data collection process (that is, we defined as conflicts only those situations which involved states and resulted in 100 or more fatalities). This was revised twice, extending the data to include lower fatality level (moving from 100 to 10 fatalities), and then to include as conflicts even those situations that entailed no fatalities, but had a significant component of threat to use force (i.e. military crises). Currently there is no minimum threshold placed on the number of fatalities for an event to be counted as a conflict. Thus, we moved from having 76 international conflicts in our data set to 295, to the current level of 333 international conflicts since 1945. This approach includes a broad scope of conflicts that pose a grave threat to international peace and security and had political effects and ramifications equal to that of full warfare.

"Conflict" may entail a variety of criteria and meanings from political quarrels and struggles, economic differences, large scale wars with fatality criteria, to small wars and skirmishes etc. Bloomfield and Moulton suggest that political differences "invariably start with a dispute" or quarrel over some issue (Bloomfield and Moulton, 1997:11-13). This develops into a conflict (or militarized interstate dispute) when one or both of the parties to the dispute consider force, threats, and military means as an option for settling the dispute. Hostilities mark the progress from the show of force and threats to outright fighting or violence, be it a recognizable warfare, destruction of property, ceasing of territory etc. (this is commonly where the casualty threshold comes into place in some dispute lists).

This project has thus adopted the generic term of "conflict" rather than "war" or "dispute" to denote our cases, as "conflict" recognizes the dynamic and diverse nature of international interactions and confrontations that characterize threats to international peace and stability.

Internationalized ethnic conflicts are included were there are verifiable and significant international aspects to the conflict and posing a major threat to international peace and security (from assistance by other states with foreign troops, military training, harboring refugees and subversives, supporting agitation etc.) CONFMAN also includes secession conflicts where the party seeking independence was accorded international recognition (regardless of whether successful in its efforts or not). Note that the terms civil, internal, domestic, intra-state are interchangeable. The effects outside (internationalization of a civil conflict) of a country of origin of civil disputes may be devastating. There may be threats to regional security, refugees (destabilizing the balance of power in a new country), inspiring strife in related countries and groups (exchanging experiences), all leading to the civil dispute diffusing into interstate implications and war.

The relevance of our selection criteria is confirmed by Dixon's view of international conflict:

> International disputes arise initially because two or more parties clash over competing interests or values. Transformation from dispute to crisis typically occurs when one or both of the parties perceives little prospect of a satisfactory resolution and decides to communicate the strength of its resolve by making explicit or implicit reference to the availability of military options. Once threats are made and armed forces are set in position, the step across the next threshold to military violence seems regrettably short. By this account, then, conflicts escalate by discrete movements across a series of steps, or thresholds, marking distinct levels of hostility and violence (Dixon 1996: 656).

The original intention of the project was to build up a databank of mediation and negotiation in international conflicts. In order to construct this, firstly we relied on established dispute lists (Butterworth, 1976; etc.), as a foundation for dispute information and preliminary descriptions of conflict management activities, as a basis for our search for further information. International conflict management activities had not been previously extensively recorded empirically. As a result the research had to be started from scratch through a series of systematic searches of various primary and secondary sources. We have subsequently extended these criteria to encompass not only mediation but other forms of conflict management such as: negotiation, arbitration, multilateral conferences, and management referrals. Note that many of the evaluations of what mediators (or other third parties) do is, on the whole, based on *ex post facto* reflections by mediators or other third party interveners and they may be quite reluctant to do so, or on reports about the intervention and inferences of their performance by observers or the media, with direct recording by researchers rarely available in international relations.

The international political system is a social system that is dynamic and composed of a number of core elements that characterize the situational, relational, and contextual milieu that define international interactions and conflict behavior. The dataset is composed of three interrelated elements or conceptual clusters that reflect our theoretical framework and belief that all social processes involve some actors, in some context, interacting in some specific manner. What we seek to do here is provide as much information as we can on each of the following three variable clusters.

- The parties—capabilities, relationships, status in international system
- The conflict—issues, fatalities, identity, incidence, extent, international constellation, how managed, and outcome, and
- The conflict management agents and activities—identity, behavior, where, when, how, outcome

Figure 6.1. indicates the theoretical parameters of our project, and how we locate our research efforts within a framework that highlights parties in conflict, the nature of a conflict, the nature of conflict management activity, and the outcomes of any such activities. (Bercovitch et al., 1991)

3.2 Operational Definition of Conflict

Different sources or datasets tend to organise and define conflicts differently. Conflicts may be split into parts or partial conflicts or treated as one ongoing event. Here we treat conflicts as a situation involving two parties, at least one of which is a state, where each has different objectives and interests which produce tensions or violent interactions between them, and these interactions may either cause fatalities or spill over into other territories. We identified conflicts by relying at first on some existing data sets, but then expanding upon them. Each conflict was accorded a code number, title detailing the principal parties in conflict (initiator always coded first), a brief description of the core issue and hostility activities, and the dates of the conflict (from the first to the last identifiable violence directly related to the conflict) (a variable coded 'conflict phases' accounts for the dispute and settlement history of the conflict before and after the major conflict period), thus providing a set of environmental parameters, reflecting the nature of the disagreement, and the level and type of conflict behavior emergent in the dispute.

A conflict starts from the initiation of some overt incidents in which one party indicates or pursues its demands. A conflict transforms into a crisis where there is a crossover from employing diplomatic, political means of addressing a conflict to using credible threats of military force. Where tensions are high, and the parties use coercive means that result in significant

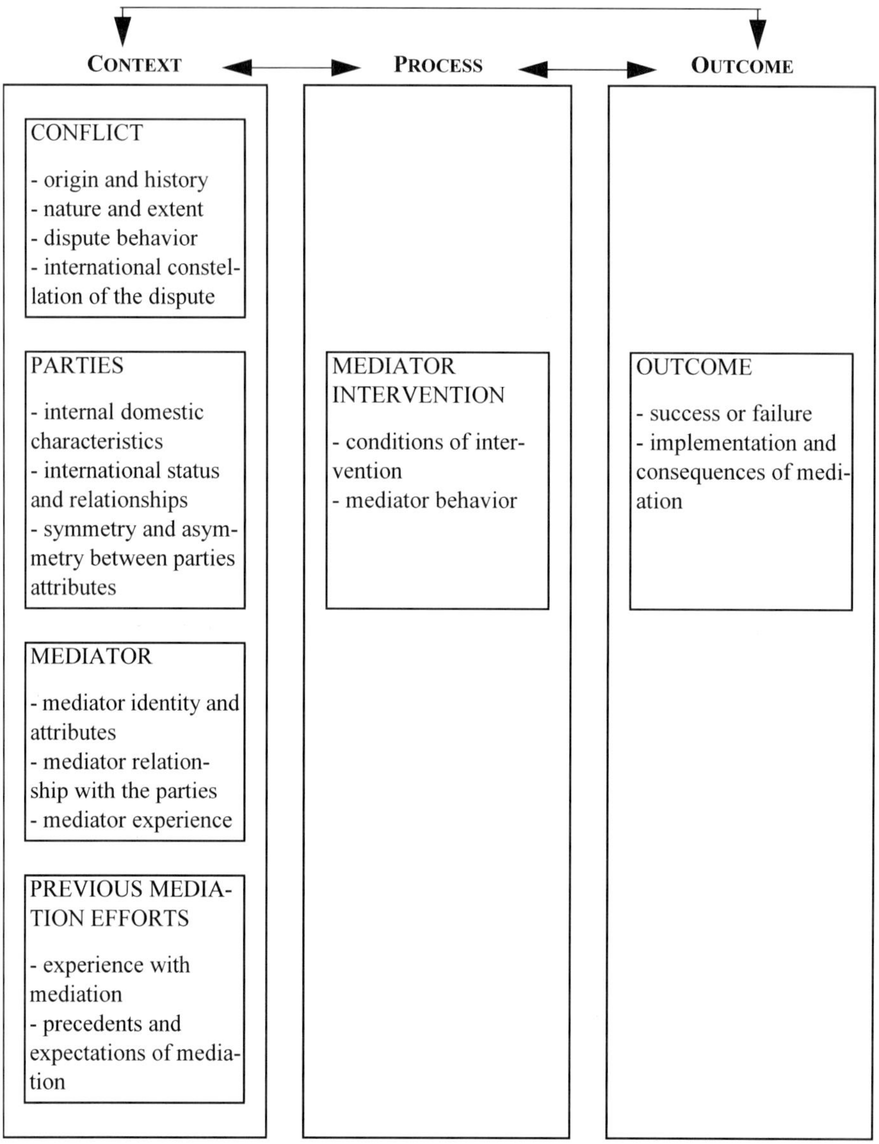

Figure 6.1. The conceptual framework of the project

fatalities, we have a war situation. Conflicts may escalate to wars, and often do, but there is no pre-ordained route for them to do so. How a conflict will evolve will depend in part on how it is managed.

Once we conceive of conflicts in operational terms, we see that they have a logical and identifiable structure of factors characterizing their fundamental features. These essential factors explaining a conflict can be evaluated on a number of different levels:

- Identifying the conflict
- Conflict behavior and evolution
- Nature of the conflict, its scope and intensity
- The issue substance of the conflict
- Type and impact of conflict management efforts in the eventual outcome of the conflict
- The key international constellations of the conflict. Organisational and major/superpower involvement in the conflict.

These features, on which we gathered much information, denote the nature of issues in conflict, its size and type, external influences and support, geographic factors influencing conflict behavior, communication, relationships, past relations, cohesion, time constraints and balance of power factors. All of these factors pre-exist intervention, and influence, enhance, and constrain the disputants' conflict actions and any conflict management behavior they may take.

For the most part, the 333 international conflicts we have identified relate in some way to the two main fault lines of conflict that have run throughout the post-war period. Namely, the East-West conflict which divided all states into the Communist camp and the Capitalist camp, and the North-South conflict which divided the rich "Northern" states from the poor third world or "Southern" states. The Cold War split the world into two spheres (bipolar alliances) of influence after the late 1940s, each dominated by one of the superpowers, the US or the Soviet Union. Both superpowers vied for influence, and many of the conflicts from 1950 to 1990 reflected this struggle. The other fault line, the North-South divide produced a whole series of conflicts related to the question of de-colonization. In some cases, the wars were fought in pursuit of independence from European colonial powers like Britain, France, Portugal, and the Netherlands. Since 1991 we have begun to note a new trend in conflict, and that is the increasing prevalence of internal or ethnic conflicts. The dissolution of one superpower produced a large increase in internal and ethnic conflicts. This is an important trend and we propose to examine it.

In other cases, war broke out when new states emerged from colonial domination and upset local power balances. Israel's war of independence (1948-49) and subsequent conflicts with its neighbors resulted directly from British de-colonization. In some instances, conflicts were the result of colonial policies which failed to take into account local sensibilities and conditions. The ethnic violence between the Hutu and Tutsi tribes which has plagued Rwanda and Burundi since their independence can be directly linked to colonial policies which not only played tribal animosities off each other, but which also took no account of tribal land settlement in drawing state boundaries. The drawing of state boundaries in a haphazard manner in the Pakistan-India demarcation in 1947 contributed in a large measure to the violence that followed in the years since.

The end of the Cold War in the late 1980s, when Gorbachev rose to power in the Soviet Union and began to seek peace with the West, led to the end of a number of Cold War conflicts. The US and Soviet Union both withdrew support from the warring parties, the Soviets withdrew from occupied countries, and the Western Alliance successfully intervened as partners in conflict management efforts. It seemed as if a new era of peace had begun, especially since the threat of global nuclear annihilation was gone, but it only seemed so!

Unfortunately, the collapse of the Soviet Union and the end of superpower rivalry did not produce a stable period of peace; instead it led to a whole new series of conflicts breaking out in the 1990s. These can be largely characterized as internal, ethnic conflicts where the parties fight over religion, identity, separateness or resources. In each case, ethnic groups vie for power and resources in a spiral of violence laced with hatreds and grievances that often go back centuries.

Another important characteristic of conflicts that have broken out since the end of the Cold War is that they are largely within states, and not between states. Since 1991 by far the largest majority of conflicts have been of this kind.

3.3 Parties in Conflict

The definition of a who or even what is a party to a conflict is not a straightforward matter. It incorporates formal states as well as distinct ethnic, cultural, religious, or socio-political groups or peoples which do not have a recognized 'state' structure but which nonetheless engage in conflict at the international level, e.g. Irian Jaya, the Kurds, the PLO, the Chechens, etc. and reflect the diversity of the international conflicts discussed above. Here we use as inclusive a definition of parties to a conflict as we can (we are not bound by states only).

The parties or participants are identified according to the level of involvement and actions in the dispute. A primary party is one who is directly involved in a conflict through its actions and behaviors. Secondary parties are those with an interest in the conflict, such as supporters or allies. And third parties are all those parties with an interest in the conflict be it a desire to resolve it, or a desire to benefit from its continuance. Thus, we have a range of parties with different degrees of involvement in any conflict. We tried to identify as many of these as we could.

Usually our primary party is a state. States after all are the main actors on the international stage. They still have a monopoly over the use of violence in today's world, and they are often organized to wage conflicts against other states. States have different power resources, different ideologies and different ways of acting on the international stage, but they are all deemed to be sovereign in international law, and all are able to act as they see fit. Here we have decided to examine all cases of conflict in which at least one of the primary actors was a state. The other actor may well have been another state, or, as is the case, more recently, an ethnic group within a state. We examine all these instances of conflict.

Parties in conflict are bounded by several factors, providing opportunities and constraints for action in the international arena. Such factors include previous or general relations between parties, international actor configurations, allies of the moment, superpower interests and actions, general external relations, military/strategic factors, international organisations, public opinion, ethnic, refugees, minorities, economic and resource factors, internal political factors, ideology, communication and information, and disputant actions in a disputed area. We sought to provide information on as many of these factors as we could.

The key actors in a conflict are evaluated according to a number of internal and external factors, such as material capabilities and diplomatic recognition, providing an assessment of their power, influence, and support within the conflict system. Internal factors or attributes relate to the domestic conditions, situation, and identity of the party, and their type of interest and interactions relative to the other actors. Power may be measured by structural and behavioural components such as resources, abilities, and experience as international actors. A party's autonomy of action is dictated by its access to power, resources, allies, and reliance on economic and military aid. Spheres of influence based on power, geo-strategic, historic, ideological interests can be crucial to national security and provide a basis to support, challenge or confront a certain party behavior.

These essential factors explain that parties to a conflict (the disputants) can be organised on a number of different levels: through this we can evaluate measures of equality/similarity and inequalities between the primary actors in the conflict:

- The identity and nature of the conflict initiator
- Factors comparing the identity of the secondary parties in dispute and their place in the international system
- The parties' power capabilities
- The internal (or domestic) characteristic of the parties: political systems, parameters of social structure and freedoms
- The parties' international systemic identity and relationships
- The parties' conflict history

3.4 Conflict Management

Essentially, the project we describe here is about conflict management. We wanted to know how it works, its features and why it succeeds or fails, and to do it all in a systematic, empirical fashion. Conflict management refers to all manners of efforts, both formal and informal, to affect or change the nature of a conflict, and the way the parties interact so as to reduce its violence while increasing any possible benefits from it. In particular we were keen to study how parties in conflict manage to start and sustain negotiations, even in conflict, and how often and with what degree of success, do outside third parties intervene in a conflict peacefully in order to reduce its violence and help settle it. Conflict management to us can be bilateral (e.g. negotiation) or multilateral (e.g. arbitration or mediation). We study both here.

There are a wide range of mechanisms and opportunities for conflict management. Our focus here was on the activities of outside third parties who intervene in conflict not as supporters or allies of one of the parties, but as actors who are keen to settle and terminate the conflict. We felt it was important to have information on the following dimensions of the process:

- Identifying the conflict management event and its occurrence
- Identifying characteristics of specific types of interveners (e.g. private mediators, organizational interventions, etc.)
- Recording the intervener's past experiences with conflict management (some third parties are more experienced than others in conflict management)
- The sequence and strategies of intervention events

- Identifying the parties' negotiators and the past relationship between the intervener and the current conflict parties
- Identifying the point of intervention (timing) in the conflict
- Establishing the key factors in the intervention process: who initiates, the environment, and method of conflict management
- The outcome (success or failure?) of the intervention process
- Identifying relevant information on the history of past intervention efforts in the conflict

Having identified a universe of international conflicts from 1945 to 2000, we then proceeded to look at all cases of conflict management that had taken place in these conflicts. Each conflict management event (that is each case of mediation or negotiation) is coded separately where possible. Many conflicts do of course involve multiple attempts at conflict management (e.g. the conflict in former Yugoslavia required more than 90 different mediation attempts). Each conflict management event or episode is recorded in full so that we have as much information on all aspects of the event as possible.

The outcome of a specific diplomatic effort or conflict management may mean continued conflict (still thinking in terms of a military relationship), but attempting to contain it (to reduce conflict behavior and levels and to avoid escalation), whereas conflict resolution refers to a change in the basic characteristics of the relationship between rival parties, that ends militarized means of the conflict (or resort to hostilities) in the form of settlement treaties etc. A sub-category of settlement is an agreement that ends disagreement on most disputed issues.

Thus there are short-term (cease-fire), medium-term (partial agreements) and long-term (termination of the dispute) consequences of management. There are also specific factors that provide feedback on how previous management events were carried out. This includes information, experience, learning and understanding gained by both the intervener and the disputants from previous efforts at dispute management, and their general understanding of a specific type of intervention as a tool of conflict management.

A conflict can be considered settled when destructive behavior has been reduced and hostile attitudes have been lessened. In contrast to that, a conflict is said to be resolved when the basic structure of the situation giving rise to destructive behavior and hostile attitudes has been re-evaluated, or re-perceived by the parties in conflict. Conflict management can, therefore, be directed toward conflict settlement, or it can be directed toward achieving the more complex, if enduring, outcome of conflict resolution.

First, states can try to solve their differences directly, or **bilaterally**. Here they may negotiate tacitly or explicitly, openly or in secret. Second, they can enlist the support of an outside or **third party**. Mediation, conciliation, adjudication, or referrals to the U.N. are all examples of various forms of conflict management by third parties. We need to have information on these activities and ensure it is as detailed as possible.

These three approaches are mirrored in dividing peaceful conflict management methods into **diplomatic** means, **legal** means, and **political** means (Merrills, 1991). Diplomatic or direct methods include traditional diplomacy, bargaining and negotiation, mediation, conciliation, and inquiry, and are methods decided upon and controlled entirely by the disputing states themselves. Legal methods include arbitration and adjudication, or judicial settlement. While there is usually some negotiation between the states about the terms, methods, interpretation of outcomes, and so on, once the legal method is under way, it is out of the hands of either state. Political methods refer to all efforts to manage conflict by submitting it to an international organization such as the UN, or a regional arrangement, such as the European Union (EU) or the African Union (AU).

4 METHOD

The present data set has been expanded considerably from previous versions to encompass more conflicts (from 72 international conflicts initially to 333 in our current set), more types of conflict management cases (from 240 initial conflict management attempts to more than 5,000 in our present data set) and many more new variables (from 46 independent variables to more than 300 in the Confman.2002 data set). However the basic structure, logic and way of coding the variables have not changed at all. What Confman.2002 purports to do is to offer the most comprehensive information on all aspects of conflict management in international conflicts from 1945 to 2000, and to answer the question of what works in conflict management, how and why. Answers to these questions are sought within a theoretical framework that basically states that the process, and its antecedent factors (e.g. nature of the parties in conflict and their leaders), affects actual behavior in conflict management (e.g. nature of communication and interaction, promises, threats etc.), and that the interaction between process factors and contextual factors determines the specific outcome (e.g. success or failure) of each conflict management effort.

Compiling a list of all conflict management events in international disputes is a complex and ambitious task (many mediation attempts are conducted in strict secrecy and not even reported on). We wanted to compile a data set that would be as comprehensive, global, longitudinal, and accurate as possible. We also wanted to ensure ease of use and replicability. With the help of a team of research assistants we went through each conflict and carefully consulted all the available information data sources to scan for any conflict management attempt (of course we could only study formal conflict management attempts that had been reported upon. There is no way we could study informal, and/or secret conflict management efforts, although we recognize these do take place). The data on conflict management attempts was actually generated by systematically searching such sources of current and historical events as *Keesing's Record of World Events*, the *New York Times*, the *New York Times Index*, the *London Times* and *Reuters*. These sources were supplemented by more detailed searches of specific conflicts by consulting the available secondary literature and participants' memoirs. From 1945 onwards, these sources were studied, analysed and the information they yielded was collated using a very detailed code book.

The data set was coded by graduate students with extensive knowledge of conflict management and training in mediation. Each term was defined conceptually and empirically. Each conflict management attempt was studied in terms of all the possible contextual factors that could affect it. Data was collected and cross-checked over our main sources and between coders, achieving inter-coder reliability across the variables of 95%. We went through the usual phases of designing, changing codebooks, pre-testing, reformulation etc. until we felt satisfied that we had all the information that we needed to have in the manner we wanted it. In Table 6.1. below we give some indication of the three clusters of variables we were looking for, and also suggest the manner of operationalizing them. We found information on more than 5,000 formal conflict management attempts in our 333 conflicts.

Table 6.1. Variables in the project

Characteristics of the Dispute	*Characteristics of the Parties*	*Conflict Management Variables*
Dispute Start/End Date	Party Initiator in Previous Disputes	CM Start/End Date
Duration	Identity Party A & B	CM Type i.e. Negotiation, Mediation, Referral to INO, Arbitration/adjudication, multilateral conference.
Fatalities	Party Alignment	Third Party Identity
Dispute Intensity	Member of UN - Party A & B	Mediator Rank

Highest Action	Power A & B (GDP, Military budget etc.)	Strategies-Primary
Hostility Level	Parties Previous Relations	Supplementary Strategies
Reciprocity	History Disputes with Other Parties	Previous Relationship of Parties With Mediator
System Period Dispute Start	Party Political System, Openness/Democracy, Closedness/Autocracy, Polity Type and Change	Previous Attempts Med/Neg this Dispute
Geographic Region	Leadership change during the dispute	Previous Attempts this Mediator
Geographical Proximity of Parties	Number Parties Supporting the Disputants	Timing (grouped)
Issue One	Characteristics of Previous Disputes between the parties – Initiator, Issues, Balance of Power, Highest Hostility Level, Outcome, Temporal Proximity to previous dispute, United Nations Operations	Timing (raw)
Issue Two		Dispute Phase Conflict Management
Issue Three		Initiated by
Final Outcome		Environment
Re-emergence of Dispute		Outcome
Type of Conflict		Hostilities Reported
Number Mediation Efforts		Durability Outcome
UN Involvement		Rank Negotiator Party A
Type of Super Power Involvement		Rank Negotiator Party B
UN Peacekeeping/Sanctions/Embargos		Number of Mediators Acting
Enduring Rivalries		Functional Mediator Identity
Characteristics of Ethnic Conflict - Ethnic Groups, Ethnic War, Revolutionary War, Abrupt/Disruptive Regime Change, Genocide/Politicide, Ethnic Issues, Origin and Internationalisation of Ethnic Rivalries		Mediation Type
Dispute Initiator		Mediator Experience
Type of Power Initiator		UN Mediator

Balance of Power Initiator		CM Duration Identifying INO Mediating Highest Rank of INO Mediator Number Mediators in INO Attempts Geographical Proximity of Mediator UNSC Permanent Members as State Mediators Polity of Mediator Polity Compared with Parties Characteristics of Previous Conflict Management Change in Negotiator Change in Mediator Number of Different Mediators in the Dispute so far Mediators Experience With These Parties In Other Disputes

Coding of cases was constructed on the basis of typologies of relevant variables forming a coding scheme of quantifiable data conforming to the conceptual map of the contingency model (outcomes are contingent upon interaction between process and context). The project has been research driven and guided by a specific set of concerns, namely identifying factors and dimensions that may affect the success or failure of conflict management. Rather than speculate on what makes conflict management successful, or offer anecdotal evidence, we felt it was important to study the issue systematically, and devise indices that explain such behavior, and hopefully predict situations where some mode of conflict management can succeed. If we can do that, we can offer policy makers the tools to work with in complex conflict situations.

The overall objective of the project is to build a cumulative map of conflict and conflict management, and trace many of the factors that may affect their development and termination. We also want to do that so as to generate hypotheses, and spur other scholars to further research. Our particular approach suggests the fruitful cooperation that may exist between political science and artificial intelligence methods for the study of social phenomena (see Chapters 9 and 11 in this volume). The conflict management data we have assembled, with its phase structure, easily lends itself to neural network analysis and other artificial intelligence methods. Such methods offer highly sophisticated approaches for analysing discrete events (that is nominal data, rather than interval data). In our work we endeavour to bring the intellectual traditions (that is the social and physical scientists) together.

5 SOME FINDINGS

In this section we provide some of our findings relating to the nature, patterns and trends of mediation and conflict management in international conflicts since 1945. Here we mostly present some findings on the occurrence of mediation, and its effectiveness, and we do in a reasonably simple format. In subsequent chapters we engage in more sophisticated systematic analysis where we examine interactive effects amongst a large number of independent variables.

We note first and foremost just how widespread the recourse to mediation has been, especially in the years since the end of the Cold War. Mediation is now without doubt the most important method of dealing with international conflicts. Not only is it adopted very frequently, mediation seems to achieve some positive effect in close to 40 % of all cases. Bearing in mind the strict criteria we have for coding mediation success, that strikes us as a pretty good gauge of the effectiveness of mediation. Mediation can hardly be described as being ineffective. Tables 6.2 to 6.5 below provide some interesting figures on the occurrence of international conflict in the 1945-2000 period. We draw attention to such features as conflicts per decades in Table 6.2., duration of international conflicts in Table 6.3., number of fatalities in conflict (Table 6.4.), and the geographic spread of conflict (Table 6.5.).

Many features can be highlighted by examining these tables and bar charts. Here we have examined only some simple structural features of the international system and frequency of conflict. Obviously, the data lends itself to more systematic examination of types of conflict, types of parties in conflict, issues and their impact on conflict duration, why some conflicts become violent, while others remain non-violent, what accounts for conflict duration and intensity and many similar questions. All these questions can of course be examined using our data set.

Table 6.2. International conflicts 1945-2000

System Period Dispute Start

		Frequency	Percent	Valid Percent	Cumulative Percent
Valid	1945-55	47	14.1	14.1	14.1
	1956-65	77	23.1	23.1	37.2
	1966-75	54	16.2	16.2	53.5
	1976-85	72	21.6	21.6	75.1
	1986-95	64	19.2	19.2	94.3
	1996-2000	19	5.7	5.7	100.0
	Total	333	100.0	100.0	

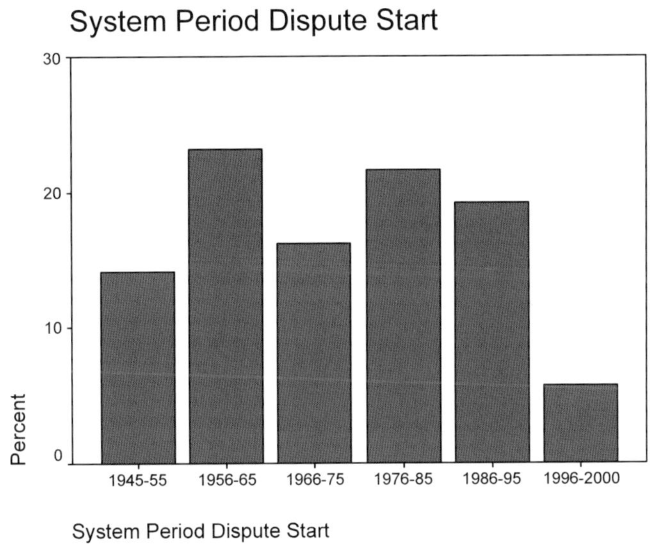

Table 6.3. International conflicts duration (in months)

Duration (grouped)

		Frequency	Percent	Valid Percent	Cumulative Percent
Valid	0-1	73	21.9	21.9	21.9
	1-3	31	9.3	9.3	31.2
	4-6	29	8.7	8.7	39.9
	7-12	42	12.6	12.6	52.6
	13-24	33	9.9	9.9	62.5
	25-36	23	6.9	6.9	69.4
	36+	102	30.6	30.6	100.0
	Total	333	100.0	100.0	

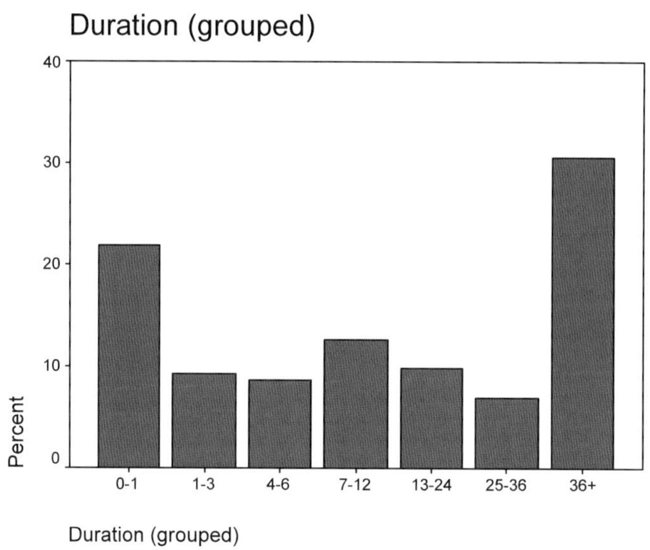

Table 6.4. Fatalities in international conflict

Fatalities (grouped)

		Frequency	Percent	Valid Percent	Cumulative Percent
Valid	0-500	192	57.7	58.9	58.9
	501-1000	24	7.2	7.4	66.3
	1001-5000	37	11.1	11.3	77.6
	5001-10000	9	2.7	2.8	80.4
	10000+	64	19.2	19.6	100.0
	Total	326	97.9	100.0	
Missing	unknown	7	2.1		
Total		333	100.0		

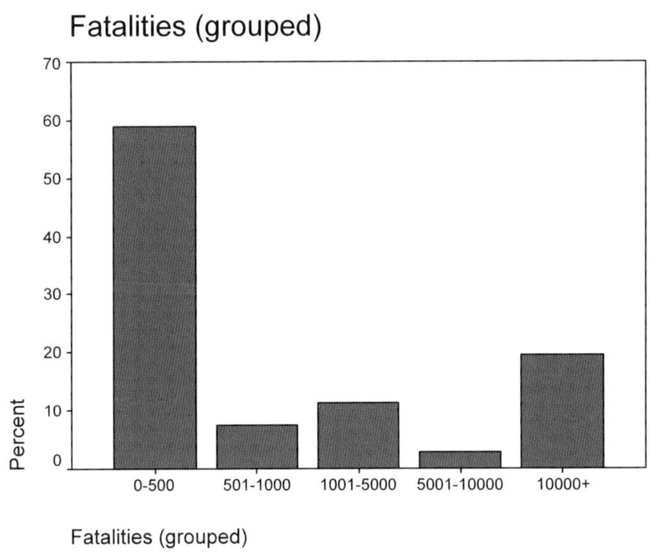

Table 6.5. Geographical spread of international conflict

Geographic Region

		Frequency	Percent	Valid Percent	Cumulative Percent
Valid	Central & S Amer	45	13.5	13.5	13.5
	Africa	93	27.9	27.9	41.4
	SW Asia	36	10.8	10.8	52.3
	E Asia & Pacific	62	18.6	18.6	70.9
	Middle East	72	21.6	21.6	92.5
	Europe	25	7.5	7.5	100.0
	Total	333	100.0	100.0	

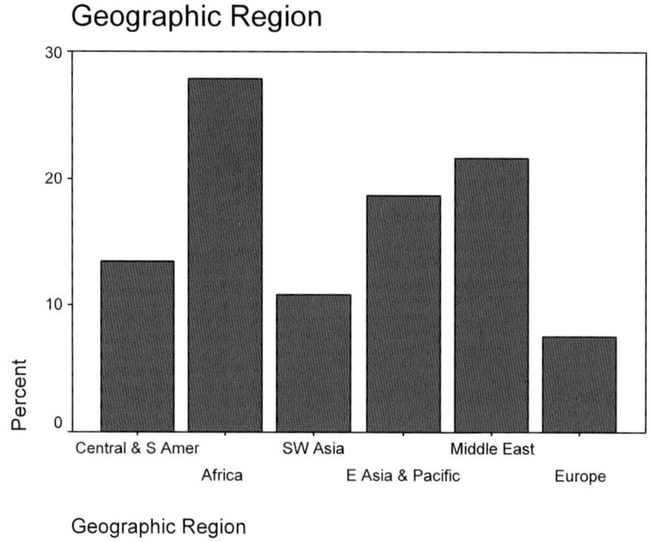

The most original and important part of the project related to the identification of conflict management events. Here we examined all the sources mentioned above in terms of our stipulated variables, and discovered 5,066 conflict management events in the 1945-2000 period. Most of the conflict management events related to mediation and negotiation, suggesting to us that these are the most important aspects of international conflict management. We studied all these cases extensively in terms of 218 independent variables to ascertain how each method worked, when was it used, why did it fail (or succeed?), who was involved, and how did they do it. Many papers and monographs were published presenting the information that relates to these issues (for a useful review, see Bercovitch and Regan, 2004). Some of the other chapters in this volume touch upon these questions. Here we merely propose to introduce the project logic and some of the findings.

Table 6.6. International conflict management events

	Frequency	*Percent*	*Valid Percent*	*Cumulative Percent*
No Management	66	1.3	1.3	1.3
Mediation	3005	59.3	59.3	60.6
Negotiation	1631	32.2	32.2	92.8
Arbitration	32	0.6	0.6	93.4
Referral	180	3.6	3.6	97.0
Multilateral Conference	152	3.0	3.0	100
Total	5066	100	100	100

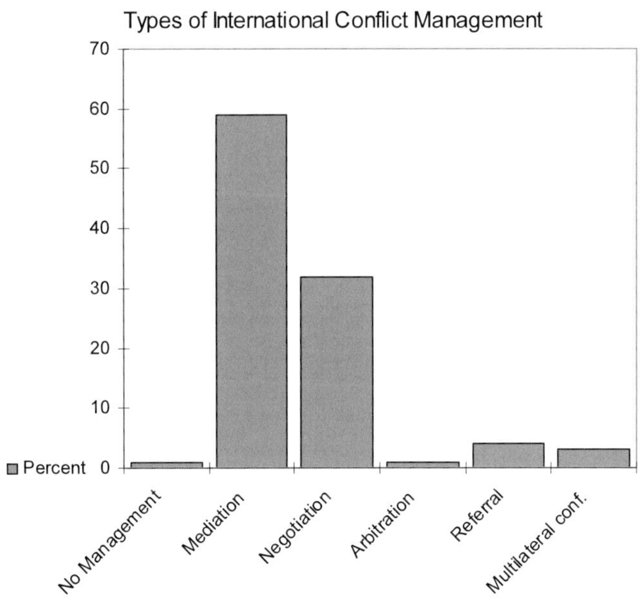

In Figure 6.2. we summarize the results of our analysis as far as mediation effectiveness is concerned. We suggest that there are four broad dimensions that affect its effectiveness: nature of the dispute, nature of the parties in the dispute, nature of the mediation process itself and nature of the mediator. The interaction of all these dimensions determines whether a given mediation will be successful or not.

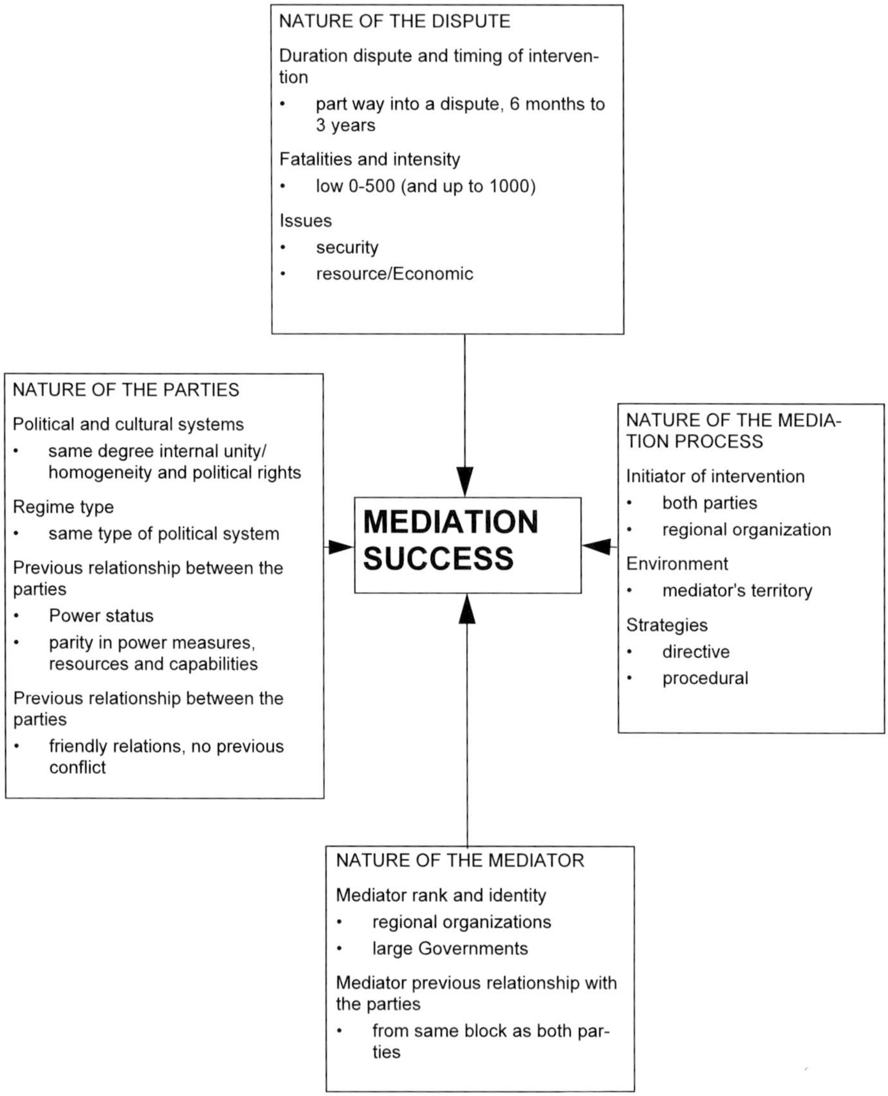

Figure 6.2. Conditions affecting mediation success in international conflict

What we find is that there are clear features that affect mediation. Relatively short conflicts with low fatalities are far more amenable to mediation than other kind of disputes. Conflicts over certain issues, involving parties of the same political system or parties with roughly the same degree of power and resources are more likely to be successfully mediated than other kinds of conflicts. We also find that mediators' strategies and identity have a significant impact on the course and likely outcome of mediation. High ranking mediators and those representing major powers are more likely to succeed as conflict managers. All these findings are very significant as they point the way to some policy guidelines and ideas for international mediators. We want to be able to offer advice to mediators, to policy makers and others involved in conflict on the best time and manner of managing or terminating their conflict. We believe that our project and the chapters in this volume take us a long way toward achieving this goal.

6 CONCLUSION

We are aware that improvements can be made to develop and enhance the data, its usefulness and application. More cases can be added, more variables can be coded, and more information can be provided on each of the methods. A more significant feature concerns our approach to conflict management 'success'. At present the data set has been designed to conform and support a specific conflict management framework, namely, the contingency approach to mediation. While this allows systematic and replicable analysis, the data presents conflicts and their mediation as linear concepts. Consequently, conflict management attempts are analyzed as discrete events and the cumulative effects of successive mediation, for instance, are neglected in the assessment of 'success'. A revised framework, inclusion of more 'raw' data and different methods of analysis are needed to view mediation effectiveness cumulatively across each conflict rather than considering each attempt as a discrete event with a discrete outcome. This is one of the goals of this volume.

By bringing together different scholars who use different methods and approaches, we hope to show how a substantive issue like conflict management can be given fresh impetus and new insights. We believe such an approach would add cumulatively to our knowledge, and strongly feel that the objective of any serious study is to add to existing knowledge. We hope we do so here.

In a recent publication Andrew Mack called for the creation of a data set on conflict that commands the consensus of the academic community and makes sense to the policy-making community (Mack, 2002). His call is timely and we must pay attention to it. We want policy makers and international civil servants to know of this data, to see it its potential, and above all to use it occasionally. This may mean that more resources may be needed to expand the data and realize its full potential. The study of international conflict and how it is managed is central to our age; we need good information on this issue. We believe our data set makes a good first stab at this direction; it commands considerable consensus, and it can be presented to policy makers in a way that makes sense to them. If we could go some way towards that, we would feel our efforts were amply justified.

References

Azar, E. E., 1980, The conflict and peace data bank (COPDAB) project, *Journal of Conflict Resolution* **24**:143-152.

Bercovitch, J., Anagnoson, J. and Wille, D. 1991, Some conceptual issues and empirical trends in the study of successful mediation in international relations, *Journal of Peace Research* **28** : 7-18.

Bercovitch, J., and Jackson, R., 1997, *International Conflict Management, 1945-1995: A chronological encyclopedia of conflicts and their management,* Congressional Quarterly, Washington, DC. .

Bercovitch, J., and Regan, P., 2004, Mediation and international conflict management: A review and analysis, in Maoz, Z., et al., eds., *Multiple Paths to Knowledge in International Relations,* Lexington Books, Lanahm, MD, pp. 249-272.

Bloomfield, L. P., and Leiss, A., 1969, *Controlling Small Wars: A Strategy for the 1970s,* Knopf; New York.

Bloomfield, L. P., and Moulton, A., 1997, *Managing International Conflict: From Theory to Policy. A teaching tool using CASCON.* St. Martin's Press, New York.

Brecher, M., Wilkenfeld, J., and Moser, S., 1988, *Crises in the Twentieth Century—Volume One and Two: Handbook of International Crises*, Pergamon Press, Pergamon Books Ltd, Oxford, England, UK.

Butterworth, R. L., 1976, *Managing Interstate Conflict, 1945-1974: Data with Synopses*, with Margaret E. Scranton, University of Pittsburgh Press, Pittsburgh.

Correlates of War Project, 1993, *Militarized Interstate Dispute Dataset. 1816-1990*, University of Michigan.

Dahlitz, J. (ed.). 1999, *Peaceful Resolution of Major International Disputes,* U.N. Publications, Geneva, New York.

Deutsch, M., 1973, *The Resolution of Conflict: Constructive and Destructive Processes*, Yale University Press, New Haven, Connecticut, USA.

Dixon, W. J., 1996, Third-Party techniques for preventing conflict escalation and promoting peaceful settlement, *International Organisation* **50**:653-681.

Haas, E. B., Butterworth, R. L., and Nye, J. S., 1972, *Conflict Management by International Organisations*, General Learning Press, Morristown, New Jersey, USA, pp.1-66.

Holsti, K.A., 1966, Resolving international conflicts: A taxonomy of behaviour and some figures on procedure, *Journal of Conflict Resolution* **10**:272-296.

Keesings Contemporary Archives, Monthly and weekly accounts of world events, 1931-1987, Keesings Publications, London.

Keesings Record of World Events, Monthly accounts of world events continue Keesings Contemporary Archives from 1987 onwards, Longman, London.

Kosimo Manual (1998-99) Heidelberg Institute for International Conflict Research, HIIK e.V. at: http// www.hiik.de

Mack, A., 2002, Civil wars: Academic research and the policy community, *Journal of Peace Research* **39**: 515-525.

Maoz, Z,. 1982, *Paths to Conflict: International Dispute Initiation. 1816-1976*, Westview Press, Boulder.

McCleland, C. A., 1969, Conflict patterns in the Interactions among nations, in *International Politics and Foreign Policy*, Rosenau, J., ed., The Free Press, New York, pp. 711-724.

Merrills, J. G., 1991, *International Dispute Settlement*, Grotious Publications, Cambridge.

Rummel, R. J., 1976, The state and political system, Chapter 31 from *Understanding Conflict and War: Vol. 2. The Conflict Helix*, Sage Publications, Beverly Hills, CA. http:// www2.hawaii.edu/~rummel/TCH.CHAP31.HTML#31.2

Sherman, F. L., 1992, *SHERFACS: Research Design, Operational Protocols, Data Representations and Paradox 4.0 Codebook*, School of international studies, The American University, Washington D.C.

Singer, J. D., ed., 1979, *The Correlates of War*, Free Press, New York, USA.

Singer, J. D., and Small, M., 1997, *COW Interstate System Dataset, 1816-1997.* Http:// pss.la.edu/intsys.html

Singer, J. D., and Small, M., 1972, *The Wages of War, 1816 - 1965: A Statistical Handbook*, Wiley, New York, USA.

Singer, J. D., and Small, M., 1982, *Resort to Arms: International and Civil Wars, 1816-1980*, Beverly Hills, California, USA.

Singer, J. D., and Small, M., 1984, *The Wages of War, 1816-1980*, Inter-University Consortium for Political and Social Research, Ann Arbor, Michigan.

Wright, Q., 1965, Approaches to the study of war, in *A Study of War, Second Edition*, Chicago University Press, Chicago, USA, pp. 423-437.

PART II

Chapter 7

Events, Patterns, and Analysis

Forecasting International Conflict in the Twenty-First Century

Devika Subramanian, Richard J. Stoll
Rice University, Houston, Texas, U.S. A.[1]

1 INTRODUCTION

It seems like a lifetime ago, but if one looks back to the heady days after the fall of the Berlin Wall, and the subsequent demise of the Soviet Union, there was certainly a great deal of speculation that the world in general, and the United States in particular, would experience a significantly lower amount of conflict than was the case during the Cold War. In many ways, the world is a safer place than it was during that era, but a quick glance at the experience of the United States since the end of the Cold War will demonstrate that conflict has been an important part of US foreign policy:

- The United States has engaged in four significant military conflicts: the Gulf War, the NATO campaign against Kosovo, the conflict against Afghanistan that led to the overthrow of the Taliban, and the Iraq War of 2003.
- The United States has been the target of a number of significant terrorist attacks, culminating in the events of September 11, 2001. This prompted the President to begin a world-wide campaign against terrorist groups, most prominently Al Qaeda (including but not limited to the above mentioned campaign against Afghanistan).
- At the same time, North Korean actions that facilitated a re-starting of its nuclear weapons program and recent events in Iran might involve the US in significant military conflicts.

While this list includes the most important conflicts experienced by the United States, it by no means exhausts the significant conflicts throughout the

1. Both authors are also affiliated with the Center for the Scientific Study of International Conflict and Co-operation

R. Trappl (ed.), Programming for Peace, 145–160.

world. Even if we restrict our attention to situations in which the current United States administration has taken a direct interest, at a minimum we would have to add the Israeli-Palestinian and Indian-Pakistani conflicts to the list. In short, despite the end of the Cold War, serious international conflicts—unfortunately—still exist.

A glance at the US conflict involvements shows that there are significant differences. The Gulf War featured both an air campaign and a ground campaign fought according to the doctrines of the US Air Force and the US Army. Kosovo is regarded by many as the first war decided by airpower alone. In the campaign in Afghanistan, a combination of indigenous opposition groups, selective air strikes, and US ground forces prevailed. Finally, the Iraq War was a swift blitzkrieg followed by a significant—and continuing—insurgency involving a continuing large-scale US presence.

While there were major differences in how each of these conflicts was prosecuted, there is one thing they have in common. Despite the unparalleled intelligence capabilities of the US government, to a significant extent, each situation (except the Iraq War) was unanticipated by US decision makers.

If the onset of serious conflicts can often surprise the US government, one can only assume that individuals, groups, organizations, and other states throughout the world (with fewer intelligence resources) are even more unlikely to anticipate conflicts. If conflicts cannot be anticipated, what chance do we have to prevent or stop them? Consequently, we see many uses for an increased ability to anticipate the outbreak of serious conflict.

This is the goal of our research: to improve the ability to anticipate serious international conflict. We will use a combination of online media sources, analytic techniques, and knowledge derived from research in international conflict to achieve this goal. Since we are at the beginning stages of our research, we are not in a position to present enough information to allow for a final judgment of our approach. However, we can provide enough of a descriptive to allow the reader to develop a good sense of what we propose to do, and to draw a preliminary conclusion about its worth.

2 CONCEPTUAL FOUNDATIONS

Any research in international conflict is guided by a conceptualization of the process by which it develops. Some researchers make this conceptualization very explicit through the use of formal theory. There are other researchers (usually traditionalists) who claim that they look at "everything," but this is misleading. They are guided by informal (and often unrecognized) conceptualizations. We believe that it is always better to make these conceptualizations explicit. So before we describe the plan of our research, we need to explain the conceptual foundation of our work. For purposes of our discussion, we will assume that there are only two countries involved in the conflict. This is merely to simplify the verbiage; our work can accommodate a larger number of actors.

We begin by introducing the concept of a *conflict of interest*. This is a situation in which each of two countries[2] seeks to influence the other to change or modify its position on at least one issue. Three conditions are necessary for these countries to have a conflict of interest:

1. There must be at least one issue over which the two parties have different preferences.
2. The two countries must both be aware of these different preferences.
3. Each party must decide that it is worthwhile to try to influence the other.

These conditions seem simple, even obvious, but they are important. If two countries have exactly the same preferences on all issues, there is no need for either party to try to influence the other, since they are in total agreement. Obviously, such complete and total agreement between two countries (or two individuals for that matter) is highly implausible. It is likely that for any pair of countries, there are a number of issues over which they have different preferences. But unless both parties are aware of these differences in preferences, they cannot consider doing anything about it.[3] Finally, even if two countries are aware of differences in preferences, they may not consider that it is worth an effort to influence one another. One can imagine that the governments of Great Britain and the United States have different preferences about which country's soccer team should win the next World Cup. But it seems highly unlikely that either government would try to influence the other to change that outcome.

Once an influence situation develops, we expect that both countries will take actions. Actions can be words, deeds, or a combination of the two. States have a variety of instruments at their disposal: diplomatic, economic, etc. Our research is restricted to influence situations in which military force is seriously contemplated, or actually used. That is, we are not trying to deal with the entire gamut of activities that comprise foreign policy.

2. Note: we use the words "country," "state," "party," and "actor" interchangeably in our discussion.

3. Think of two roommates meeting for the first time. At that point they do not know each other well enough to be aware of differences in preferences. That will come later.

Once the use of military force is considered, the influence situation has become a militarized interstate dispute (Jones et al., 1996). Disputes can be "resolved" in a variety of fashions. For example, some sort of written settlement that resolves the discrepancy in preferences between the parties might occur. On the other hand, both countries may simply cease to use military instruments without either side changing its preference ordering. Finally, the dispute may escalate to a war. A war is a continuous combat in which each state tries to inflict a military defeat on the other.

We see conflict as a series of steps or phases (Bremer, 1996). There is an implied sequence as countries move through a conflict of interest, a dispute, and a war. But not every conflict of interest represents a significant danger to the parties involved. Often the closest of countries go through periods of time that are characterized as "rocky" or "stormy" but despite this, the use of force may never be considered a viable instrument of policy by both sides. These situations are of little interest to us. But it does illustrate one of our challenges: to successfully separate those conflicts of interest with no potential for violence, from those that will spill over into increasing levels of violence.

This conceptual framework has a number of implications. First, conflicts of interest are *about something*. Countries do not try to influence one another, even to the point of using military instruments, unless there are one or more important issues at stake. This seems like a simple point, but it is important. We often have a tendency to think of conflict as "caused" by things such as the capability balance between two sides, but we need to remember before governments consider the chances of winning a military confrontation, they have to have a *substantive reason* for that confrontation.

Second, we do not expect the countries to be omniscient, all-knowing, and comprehensively rational actors. We do expect them to behave in a limitedly-rational, goal seeking manner. Their decisions will not be perverse or random. They try their best, given the constraints of the situation, problems with obtaining and correctly evaluating information, and limitations of time, to achieve their goals. But we do not expect them to make optimal decisions.

Third, in deciding on future actions, a state takes into account a variety (but a limited one) of considerations. It considers the recent actions of the other party (not individual actions, but rather an aggregation of recent events), its own recent actions, and a series of factors that play a significant role in evaluating which state is likely to prevail if the contest turns on the relative military capabilities of the two sides. The state forms a summary evaluation that combines these factors together in a fairly simple fashion.

Finally, the confluence of these assumptions will produce a flow of events. These events, when aggregated at the appropriate level, will provide a good trace of the ebb and flow of the interactions between countries. An analysis of these (aggregated) events, along with appropriate other factors will allow us to predict the onset of serious conflict.

3 FORECASTING INTERNATIONAL CONFLICT: THE BUILDING BLOCKS

The primary building block of our research is the event:

> ...an interaction, associated with a specific point in time, that can be described in a natural language sentence that has as its subject and object an element of a set of actors and as its verb an element of a set of actions, the contents of which are transitive verbs.(Gerner et al., 1994: 95)

The process by which events data are created is discussed below. Our analysis will not rely on individual events, but on *aggregations* of them, for reasons we will identify below. Given an aggregate set of events data, we need tools to analyze them. We will be using wavelet analysis as our primary tool. Finally, as a way to increase our understanding, we will move beyond the forecasting of serious international conflicts, to modeling the factors that play a critical role in the escalation and de-escalation of conflict.

Collecting Events Data. In the social sciences, critical information for research rarely appears in a useful form. Instead, social scientists must engage in the process of *data making* (Singer, 1965). Events data—nominal or ordinal codes recording the interactions between international actors – are a prime example of this. Events data are a common type of information used in quantitative international relations research. A single record or case of events data consists of the actor (the entity that initiated the action), the action itself, the target of the action, and the date of the action. Most collections also associate a scale score with each event; this score represents the degree to which the event is cooperative or conflictual.

Until recently, the collection of these data was only possible through the use of teams of trained human coders who read through media sources to extract the appropriate information. This approach was both slow and expensive. Consequently the most widely used events data collections, the Conflict and Peace Data Bank (COPDAB; see Azar, 1980) and the World Event Interaction Survey (WEIS; see Tomlinson, 1993) both cover only a limited period of time in the post-World War II era.

We propose to automate the extraction process. This process will require a variety of state of the art tools. Some of these are already developed. One important tool is the set of software programs developed by the Kansas

Events Data Project (KEDS; see Gerner et al., 1994), although we will also explore using similar tools that have been developed in the field of artificial intelligence (Craven et al., 1999). The creation of events data is basically a process of content analysis and involves three steps:

1. A source or sources of news about political interactions is identified. This could be an internationally-oriented newspaper such as *The New York Times*, a set of regional newspapers and newsmagazines, a news summary such as *Facts on File* or *Deadline Data on World Affairs*, or a newswire service such as Reuters, the Associated Press, or *Agence France Presse*.
2. A coding system is developed, or a researcher may decide to use an existing coding system such as the World Events Interaction Survey (WEIS), the Conflict and Peace Data Bank (COPDAB), or the Conflict and Mediation Event Observations (CAMEO) systems. The coding system specifies what types of political interactions constitute an "event", identifies the political actors that will be coded (for example, whether non-state actors such as international organizations and guerrilla movements will be included in the data set), specifies the categories of events and their codes, and specifies any information to be coded in addition to the basic event. For example, the COPDAB data set codes a general "issue area"—whether an action is primarily military, economic, diplomatic or one of five other types of relationship. WEIS, in contrast, codes for specific "issue arenas" such as the Vietnam War, Arab-Israeli conflict, and SALT negotiations. CAMEO was developed in part to evaluate the role of mediation in international conflict, and its event categories reflect that theoretical perspective.
3. In a machine-coding project, coding rules are implemented in a computer program such as Tabari (the program currently being used at the KEDS project) or WebKB (Craven et al., 1999) by using extensive dictionaries (corpora) that identify actors and events. Corpus-driven techniques are more robust than methods that attempt to parse and understand natural language sentences. Instead, corpus-driven techniques take advantage of implicit regularities in the structure of news sources. This allows us to create coding rules from samples of suitably marked up documents (Craven et al., 1999). Such an approach eliminates the need to manually formulate extraction rules.[4]

4. Researchers (Schrodt and Gerner, 1994; King and Lowe, 2003) have shown that machine-based events coding is as accurate as human coding.

KEDS has already been used to produce an extensive set of events data on various regions of the world (see for example, Schrodt and Gerner 1994, 1997), and it will be an important part of our effort to convert contemporary information into data. But we will also need to gather information from sources other than those that have been utilized previously by KEDS. We will extend the scope of KEDS-like data gatherers to more text sources on the internet. In this effort we will take advantage of the growing number of open media sources on the internet. These sources contain not only current stories, but also archives of past stories, allowing the possibility of updating the classic events data collections to the present.[5]

There are several issues that have to be addressed before we can proceed with the events data collection. First, which sources should we use? Media sources vary widely in their completeness and quality of reporting. We need to find a systematic way to pick the best set of sources. A second issue is the question of duplicate events. Different sources may report the same event in slightly different ways, so it is critical to find a reasonable way to eliminate duplicates.[6]

A third issue is aggregation of events. For several reasons, we believe it is unwise to analyze the events data as individual events. First, we believe that such a large number of events would contain a large amount of noise. This of course is a judgment on our part and other researchers may disagree.

But we believe there are other problems with using individual events in analysis. There is really no good way to order events within a day. Often news stories do not contain enough information to order events through time. Of course some stories will contain the time that the action took place. But it is less likely that the story will contain information as to when the *target* knew the act took place, and without that information, it is hard to see how one can make use of the sequencing of individual events.

Even if the times are available, we still have to consider just how quickly one can expect governments to react to actions. Consider the Cuban Missile Crisis. The time difference between Washington and Moscow was eight hours. But a reading of accounts of that crisis suggests that the time difference meant that each government responded not to individual actions of the other, but to the *accumulation* of events that took place in the previous day.

All of these problems have led us to conclude that, like generations of events data researchers, it is necessary to aggregate events data.[7] In a number of our preliminary analyses, we have used a two week aggregation period. In

5. We should note one minor impediment to using a wide variety of media sources from the internet. Virtually every source uses a different format to present stories. Consequently the software necessary to extract stories from online archives must be modified (at least a bit) for each different source.

6. A fairly common technique to achieve this is to code only one event of each type per dyad per day.

the analysis reported below, we used a one week aggregation period. Obviously the issue of the optimal aggregation period is one that needs additional study.

4 PLAN FOR ANALYSIS

We will pursue two paths of analysis. The first will involve attempting to predict the onset of serious international conflict strictly from patterns in previous events. The second path involves building models that will increase our understanding of the process by which conflict escalates.

To pursue the first path, we will treat the stream of aggregated events as a time series. In order to be successful, we must be able to demonstrate two things. First, serious interstate conflicts have to register as significant changes from the event stream prior to the outbreak of the serious conflict. That is, our measure of events should reflect the onset of serious conflicts as dramatic changes in the level of conflict in the event stream. Second, there must be enough information in the event stream *prior* to the onset of serious conflict to predict it. That is, the pattern of events prior to the onset should allow for the prediction of serious conflict without an excessive number of false positives or false negatives.

While the first path can be viewed as an exercise (albeit a sophisticated one—see below) in signal processing, in pursuing the second path we seek to increase our understanding of the process by which conflict breaks out. In some ways this is the easier task because international relations researchers have accumulated a number of strong findings at the dyadic level concerning the outbreak of conflict. But a good model is more than an accumulation of variables that have been significant in other studies. So this is likely to prove to be the more difficult task. On the other hand, it is also the more important task.

If we are successful in the first task, we will have created the foundation for an early warning system. By itself this would be an important step forward. But we would accomplish more if this is accompanied by advancing our knowledge about the process by which conflicts occur. We break down our research into a series of questions.

Step 1: Are serious conflicts visible through the analysis of events data? Our initial examination of conflict data from KEDS datasets leads us to conclude that these events series have significant levels of non-stationarity (singularities). This is both good and bad news. The good news is that it

[7]. A good discussion of issues involved in aggregation is Thomas (2000).

appears that significant conflicts are likely to be reflected in these non-stationarities. The bad news is that many statistical (and machine learning) tools do not handle these data well. Consequently we need to use an analysis technique that will be able to handle singularities. That is, it must be able to cope with and identify these singularities. Wavelet analysis is just such a technique. It is very useful because, unlike Fourier analysis (the standard tool of signal analysis for many years), it simultaneously decomposes a time series into time/ frequency space.

Step 2: Is there an unambiguous signal of the onset of serious conflict? Given that serious conflicts register as singularities in events data, the next question is whether these singularities are preceded by clear signals of the onset of conflict. Our initial efforts will also involve using wavelet analysis to detect these precursor signals. As noted above, to be successful, we have to find precursors that simultaneously do not produce too many false positives and too many false negatives.

Step 3: Can we develop compelling models of the onset of serious conflict? The final step in our research is to model the outbreak of conflict. In this effort we will build on the work of quantitative international relations scholars. There have been many studies through the years of what conditions are most frequently associated with the escalation (and de-escalation) of conflict. It would be too much to say that a single dominant model has emerged. But in recent years, there has been a convergence of findings, particularly those that account for the escalation of disputes to war; good summaries of the state of the discipline are in Bremer and Cusack (1996), and Vasquez (2000). The factors that are most often associated with the escalation or de-escalation of conflict—usually in situations involving a pair of countries—are (Vasquez, 2000:367):

- The presence of a territorial issue at stake between the two parties. Situations in which territorial issues are present are more likely to escalate; contiguous states are more likely to have territorial issues that states that do not share a common border.
- Some alliances promote war, while others promote peace. Alliances that settle territorial questions or which do not pose a great threat to a third party promote peace. Alliances that are formed by states that have fought a war recently and are dissatisfied with the status quo are likely to promote war (although the war does not break out immediately).
- Disputes involving states which are in an ongoing arms competition are more likely to escalate to war as long as the arms competition does not involve nuclear weapons.

- Disputes between parties that have had repeated conflicts are more likely to escalate to war.
- A dispute in which the parties bargain aggressively is likely to end in war; across a series of disputes, if the parties take on more and more aggressive bargaining strategies, a war is likely.
- Strong states are more war-prone than weak states. If the power balance between a pair of states rapidly moves towards parity, there is an increased chance of war.
- When major states establish norms or common expectations that reduce their freedom to take unilateral actions, the chances of war are reduced.
- Democratic states are very unlikely to go to war with one another.

These are all important findings that have turned up repeatedly in quantitative studies, and to this mix we will add the level of recent conflict within the dyad of states. Together, this is a set of empirical building blocks that we can use to increase our understanding. But we still need to formulate coherent models that combine sets of factors in a meaningful (i.e., theoretical) fashion. Otherwise, we have a set of interesting empirical relationships, but no real understanding of why conflict happens.

5 AN EXPLORATION: THE EBB AND FLOW OF THE COLD WAR, 1966-1978

Our research over the next few years will determine whether our approach helps to predict and to understand the onset of serious conflict. For now what we can offer is an exploration of a particular interaction: the United States and the Soviet Union from 1966 through 1978. This analysis uses the original (human coded) WEIS data; this determines the time frame of our study. We begin by selecting just those events from the WEIS data that involve both the United States and the Soviet Union. We then aggregate events to the weekly level, summing the scale scores for all the events during the week. This gives us a dataset with 678 observations. We analyze these data with a Haar wavelet (the simplest possible wavelet).

Figure 7.1. displays the results of the wavelet analysis.[8] For wavelet analysis to be a useful tool, the results must make sense. That is, there must be a correspondence between what we see in the wavelet analysis, and the ebb and flow of US-Soviet relations. To be sure, this is not a rigorous test of the validity of the analysis technique; we are in essence looking backwards from the wavelet results to the Cold War. On the other hand, if there is no correspondence between events and the wavelet analysis, then great doubt has been cast on the utility of this approach to identify conflicts.

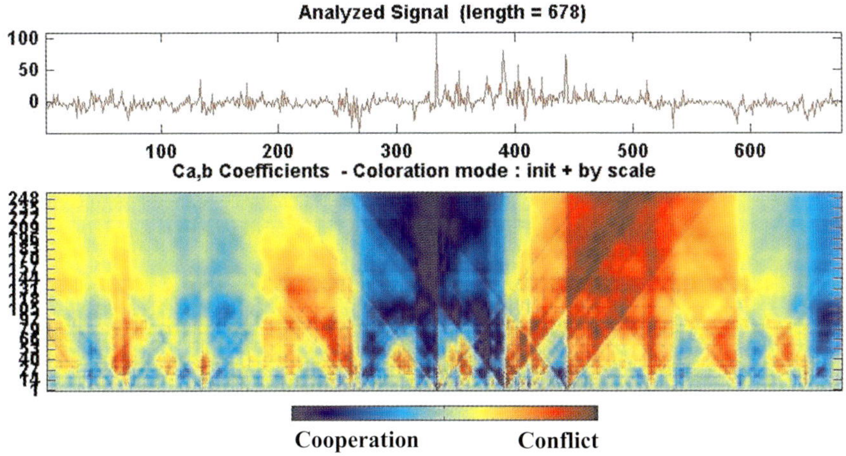

Figure 7.1. Wavelet analysis of US-Soviet interactions, 1966-1978

The top part of Figure 7.1. displays the "raw signal"; it is a plot of the summed scale scores, aggregated to the weekly level as noted above. The lower part of Figure 7.1. is from the wavelet analysis. The main areas of interest are colored in red and blue. Red areas should correspond to periods of time in which the US and the Soviet Union relations are going through a conflictual period. Blue areas should correspond to periods of time when the US and the Soviet Union are going through a cooperative period. At the present time, we are basically restricted to "eyeballing" the figure in order to identify the specific periods of time. Table 7.1. displays the identification value of the weeks bounding each area of red and blue, the year and month that corresponds to the weeks, and a list of important events that occurred during that time.

8. The wavelet analysis was done using MATLAB version 6.5, release 13, and version 2.2 of the Wavelet toolbox. A haar wavelet was used with a scale setting maximum of 256. Results were displayed with the jet colormap and the init + by scale coloration mode.

Table 7.1. Key Events During Extreme Red and Blue Periods[9]

Week(s)	*Date(s)*	*Comments*
56 – 83	67/1 – 67/8	[Red] Six Day War
132	68/7	[Red] Czech Crisis (138; 68/8), but NPT signed
187-265	69/8 – 71/1	[Red] Cienfuegos (Cuban sub base)
271-289	71/3 – 71/7	[Blue] Soviet ships leave Cienfuegos.
295-312	71/8 – 71/12	[Red] Soviets criticize Nixon trip to China, Moscow summit
316-334	72/1 – 72/5	[Blue] Moscow summit, SALT, ABM Treaties
341-363	72/7 – 72/12	[Red] US "Christmas bombing" of North Vietnam
364-390	72/12 – 73/6	[Blue] US-Soviet Summit (Brezhnev to US)
391-585	73/6 – 77/3	[Red] October War Crisis; Angola; Carter criticizes Soviets on human rights
620-649	77/11 – 78/6	[Red] Soviet UN employees arrested. Carter criticizes dissident trials. Soviet stage large maneuvers in Central Europe. Ginzburg & Shchransky sentenced.

An informal examination is not a definitive test of the utility of this approach to analysis. In fact, there are actually two parts to this informal examination. In the first part, the wavelet analysis figure is examined to delineate the red and blue zones. The second part involves examining Cold War chronologies, and determining what events took place during the zones. Aside from the informality of the process, it also involves working backwards from the identified zones to the events. But nevertheless, we believe this is a reasonable first step in our investigation.

6 SOME ISSUES IN ANALYZING EVENTS

We are generally pleased with the ability of wavelet analysis to identify significant periods of conflict and cooperation between the United States and the Soviet Union.[10] Obviously, we need to formalize the procedures by which we identify zones of conflict and cooperation.[11] But there are other issues that we need to address as well.

9. Sources used to identify key events were: Department of History, University of San Diego (2002), Goldstein and Freeman (1990), International Institute for Strategic Studies (1978), International Institute for Strategic Studies (1979), and Studenic (2002).

10. In previous work (Subramanian and Stoll, 2002) we have used wavelet analysis in a similar fashion to identify periods of conflict and cooperation among eight states in the Persian Gulf region from 1979 through 1999 and reached a similar conclusion.

What events coding scheme should be used? Much of the computer-generated events data has used the WEIS data, and this is therefore a reasonable choice. But the developers of KEDS have recently unveiled a new coding scheme called CAMEO (Conflict and Mediation Event Observations; see Gerner et al., 2002).[12]

Another issue is the particular type of wavelet analysis to be used. There are a large number of wavelets that can be applied to data, and there are additional parameters that must be specified. For the time being, we have been using the haar wavelet. This is a very simple wavelet and one that is excellent for data that contains singularities (which is why we choose to use it). But we need to determine which wavelet (or which wavelets) we should use for our analysis.

An additional issue is the difference in predicting the onset of serious conflict, and postdicting it. In our work to date, we have used an extended time series (for example, the 1966-1978 US-Soviet interactions explored above), and applied wavelet analysis to pick out the areas of high conflict and high cooperation across that entire series. But to build a good early warning system, we will have to predict areas of high conflict *before* they occur. This is a different matter. Consider walking across a field that has peaks and valleys. After walking across the entire field, we can look back and pick out the deepest valleys. But in doing this, we can take advantage of knowing the full extent of each peek and valley, and being able to compare them to pick out the deepest valleys. However, as we walk along and begin to descend that first valley, we don't have the additional information that we acquire in the course of entire journey. So how can we tell as we descend whether we are going down into a deep valley or a shallow one? This is the challenge of prediction that we face.[13]

Finally, there is the question of at what point we go beyond analyzing just events, to incorporating factors that represent the substantive reasons for the onset of conflict. While it would be intriguing to be able to predict the onset of conflict using only previous events, we think this is unlikely to happen. We believe that there is good chance that we will have to include substantive variables in order to generate accurate predictions. Since our initial goal is to

11. We are currently implementing a more systematic and precise way to identify these periods.

12. It should be noted that this scheme is optimized for mediation, which may not serve our purposes as well. In addition, currently there is no scale of conflict and cooperation associated with CAMEO events, although this should be available soon.

13. We have made a few informal attempts to investigate this problem. We have taken an events data time series, ended it after the first major valley in a series, then subjected this reduced series to wavelet analysis. The wavelet analysis still appears to detect the major valley. Of course we have only run a small number of informal tests, so the ability of this analysis technique to successfully identify conflicts as they occur remains an open question.

create an early warning system, this sort of approach (begin with a few variables, add what is needed to reach a particular level of accuracy) is acceptable. But ultimately we hope to shed additional light on the reasons *why* serious conflicts occur. When we move from prediction to explanation, we will have to build explanatory (as opposed to predictive) models. Predictive ability, while still of interest, will be less of a touchstone than developing explanation.

7 SUMMARY: COMPUTER-AIDED PREDICTION OF THE ONSET OF SERIOUS CONFLICT

International conflict remains a serious problem in the world of today, despite the end of the Cold War and the demise of the Soviet Union. With an increasing concern about the proliferation of weapons of mass destruction, it is very important that we are able to anticipate the outbreak of serious international conflict. In the future, any number of conflicts could escalate and produce extremely large numbers of casualties, particularly among civilians. The ability to anticipate conflict would be a valuable tool for those individuals, groups, countries, and organizations that would be willing to intervene to prevent or curtail the outbreak of conflict.

Unfortunately, if recent history is any guide, our current abilities are woefully inadequate. Even the United States, with its impressive collection of intelligence assets, has been repeatedly surprised at the outbreak of conflict. One can only assume that other actors have had an equally difficult time of anticipating conflicts.

So how shall we go about creating the tools that would facilitate the accurate anticipation of international conflict? There is no single answer to this question. But we believe that recent advances in information available on the internet, the computer processing of text, and signal processing can be married with existing knowledge about the factors associated with the outbreak of conflict.

The internet provides access to an increasing number of news sources, both to current stories and archives of older stories. The computer processing of text allows us to extract international events from news stories. We believe that the use of signal processing techniques will give us a good chance to both identify and predict the onset of international conflict. Finally, we can build on the foundation of results from international relations scholars to develop a more complete understanding of why conflicts occur.

How successful will we be with this approach? That remains to be seen (check back in a few years!). But we believe we have a good plan and some preliminary results that are promising.

Acknowledgement

The research discussed in this paper is funded by the National Science Foundation under its ITR program, grant number 0219673, and by INTEL.

References

Azar, E., 1980, The conflict and peace data bank (COPDAB) project, *Journal of Conflict Resolution* **24**:143-252.

Bremer, S., and Cusack, T., 1996, *The Process of War: Advancing the Scientific Study of War*, Gordon and Breach, Amsterdam, Netherlands.

Bremer, S., 1996, Advancing the scientific study of war, in *The Process of War: Advancing the Scientific Study of War*, Bremer, S., and Cusack, T., eds., Gordon and Breach, Amsterdam, Netherlands, pp. 1-33.

Craven, M., DiPasquo, D., Freitag, D., McCallum, A., Mitchell, T., Nigam, K., and Slattery, S., 1999, Learning to construct knowledge bases for the world wide web, *Artificial Intelligence* **118**:69-113.

Department of History, University of San Diego, 2002, *Cold war policies 1945-1991*, http://history.acusd.edu/gen/20th/coldwar0.html, accessed 1/21/03.

Gerner, D., Schrodt, P., Francisco, R. and Weddle, J., 1994, Machine coding of events data using regional and international sources, *International Studies Quarterly* **38**:91-119.

Gerner, D., Schrodt, P., Yilmaz, O., and Abu-Jabr, R., 2002, The creation of CAMEO (conflict and mediation event observations): an events data framework for a post cold war world, paper presented at the *Annual Meetings of the American Political Science Association*, 29 August – 1 September, 2002.

Goldstein, J. and Freeman, J., 1990, *Three-Way Street: Strategic Reciprocity in World Politics*, University of Chicago, Chicago.

International Institute for Strategic Studies, 1978, *Strategic Survey 1977*, International Institute for Strategic Studies, London, Great Britain.

International Institute for Strategic Studies, 1979, *Strategic Survey 1978*, International Institute for Strategic Studies, London, Great Britain.

Jones, D., Bremer, S., and Singer, J. D., 1996 Militarized interstate disputes, 1816-1992: rationale, coding rules, and empirical patterns, *Conflict Management and Peace Science* **15**: 163-213.

King, G. and Lowe, W., 2003, An automated information extraction tool for international conflict data with performance as good as human coders: a rare events evaluation design, *International Organization* **57**: 617-642.

Schrodt, P. and Gerner, D., 1994, Validity assessment of a machine-coded event data set for the Middle East, 1982-1992, *American Journal of Political Science* **38**:825-854.

Schrodt, Philip and Deborah Gerner. 1997. Empirical indicators of crisis phase in the Middle East, 1982-1995. *Journal of Conflict Resolution* 41(4): 529-552.

Singer, J. David, 1965, Data making in international relations, *Behavioral Science* **10**:68-80.

Studenic, R., 2002, *The Cold War Guide*, http://www.geocities.com/CapitolHill/Lobby/4907/Chron.htm, accessed 1/21/03.

Subramanian, D. and Stoll, R. J., 2002, Events, patterns, and analysis: forecasting international conflict in the twenty-first century, position paper presented at the *Computer-Aided Methods for International Conflict Resolution Workshop*, Vienna, Austria, Austrian Research Institute for Artificial Intelligence, October 25-26, 2002.

Thomas, G. D., 2000, The machine-assisted creation of historical events data sets: a practical guide, paper presented at the *2000 Annual Meeting of the International Studies Association*, Los Angeles, CA, March 14-18, 2000.

Tomlinson, R., 1993, *World Event/Interaction Survey (WEIS) Coding Manual*, manuscript, Department of Political Science, United States Naval Academy, Annapolis, MD.

Vasquez, J., ed., 2000, *What Do We Know About War?* Rowman and Littlefield, Lanham, MD.

Chapter 8

Forecasting Conflict in the Balkans using Hidden Markov Models[1]

Philip A. Schrodt
University of Kansas, Lawrence, Kansas, U.S.A.

This study uses hidden Markov models (HMM) to forecast conflict in the former Yugoslavia for the period January 1991 through January 1999. The political and military events reported in the lead sentences of Reuters news service stories were coded into the World Events Interaction Survey (WEIS) event data scheme. The forecasting scheme involved randomly selecting eight 100-event "templates" taken at a 1-, 3- or 6-month forecasting lag for high-conflict and low-conflict weeks. A separate HMM is developed for the high-conflict-week sequences and the low-conflict-week sequences. Forecasting is done by determining whether a sequence of observed events fit the high-conflict or low-conflict model with higher probability.

Models were selected to maximize the difference between correct and incorrect predictions, evaluated by week. Three weighting schemes were used: unweighted (U), penalize false positives (P) and penalize false negatives (N). There is a relatively high level of convergence in the estimates—the best and worst models of a given type vary in accuracy by only about 15 % to 20 %. In full-sample tests, the U and P models produce an overall accuracy of around 80 %. However, these models correctly forecast only about 25 % of the high-conflict weeks, although about 60 % of the cases where a high-conflict week has been forecast turn out to have high conflict. In contrast, the N model has an overall accuracy of only about 50% in full-sample tests, but it correctly forecasts high-conflict weeks with 88% accuracy in the 3- and 6-month horizon and 92 % accuracy in the 1-month horizon. The models are remarkably insensitive to the length of the forecasting horizon—the drop-off in accuracy at longer forecasting horizons is very small, typically around 2 % to 4 %. Some experiments with simplified models indicate that it is possible to use models with substantially fewer parameters without markedly decreas-

[1] This work was partially supported by an EPSCoR start-up grant from the National Computational Science Alliance and utilized the NCSA SGI/CRAY Origin2000 parallel computing system.

R. Trappl (ed.), Programming for Peace, 161–184.

ing the accuracy of the predictions; in fact predictions of the high conflict periods actually increase in accuracy quite substantially.

1 THE SEQUENCE RECOGNITION APPROACH TO POLITICAL FORECASTING

Event sequences are a key element in human reasoning about international events. Human analysts "understand" an international situation when they recognize sequences of political activity corresponding to those observed in the past. Empirical and anecdotal evidence point to the likelihood that humans have available in long-term associative memory a set of "templates" for common sequences of actions that can occur in the international system (and in social situations generally). When part of a sequence is matched, the analyst predicts that the remainder of the sequence will be carried out *ceteris paribus*. Sequences can be successfully matched by human analysts in the presence of noise and incomplete information, and can also be used to infer events that are not directly observed but which are necessary prerequisites for events that have been observed.

The use of analogy or "precedent-based reasoning" has been advocated as a key cognitive mechanism in the analysis of international politics by Alker (1987), Mefford (1985) and others, and is substantially different from the statistical, dynamic and rational choice paradigms that characterize most contemporary quantitative models of international behavior. Khong (1992) and Vertzberger (1990) review the general arguments in the cognitive psychology literature on use of analogy in political reasoning; May (1973) and Neustadt and May (1986) discuss it from a more pragmatic and policy-oriented perspective. As Khong observes:

> Simply stated, ... analogies are cognitive devices that "help" policymakers perform six diagnostic tasks central to political decision-making. Analogies (1) help define the nature of the situation confronting the policymaker; (2) help assess the stakes, and (3) provide prescriptions. They help evaluate alternative options by (4) predicting their chances of success, (5) evaluating their moral rightness and (6) warning about the dangers associated with options. (Khong, 1992: 10)

Analogical reasoning is an easy task for the human brain, one that is substantially easier than sequential or deductive reasoning. Most experimental evidence suggests that human memory is organized so that when one item is recalled, this naturally activates links to other items that have features in common, and these are more likely to be recalled as well (Anderson, 1983; Kohonen, 1984).

Because analogies are so prevalent in human political reasoning, it would be helpful to have some computational method for systematically assessing the similarity of two sequences of political events. In Schrodt (1991), I posed this problem in the following manner:

> In human pattern recognition, we have a general idea of what a category of event sequences look like—the archetypal war, the archetypal coup, and so forth. In a sense, ideal sequences are the centroid of a cluster of sequences, but that centroid is a sequence rather than a point. If a method could be found for constructing such a sequence, the cluster of behaviors could be represented by the single ideal sequence, which would substantially reduce computing time and provide some theoretical insights as to the distinguishing characteristics of a cluster. (Schrodt, 1991: 186)

The problem of generalizing sequences is particularly salient to the analysis of international political behavior in the post-Cold War because many contemporary situations do not have exact historical analogs. Yet human analysts are clearly capable of making analogies based on some characteristics of those behaviors. For example, because of its unusual historical circumstances, Zaire in 1997 had a number of unique characteristics, but nonetheless analysts pieced together sufficient similarities between Zaire and a variety of earlier crises in Africa and elsewhere to come to the correct conclusion that Zaire had entered a period of rapid political change. The key to this was the ability to use *general* analogies: if one insisted on matching all of the features of a case—which a human analyst would almost never do, but a computer might—then the Zairian situation would be nearly impossible to classify using analogies.

2 HIDDEN MARKOV MODELS

Techniques for comparing two sequences of discrete events—nominal-level variables occurring over time—are poorly developed compared to the huge literature involving the study of interval-level time series. Nonetheless, several methods are available, and the problem has received considerable attention in the past three decades because it is important in the problems of studying genetic sequences in DNA, and computer applications involving human speech recognition. Over the past fifteen years the hidden Markov model (HMM) has emerged as one of the most widely used techniques for the classification of noisy sequences into a set of discrete categories. While the most common applications of HMMs are found in speech recognition and comparison of protein sequences, a recent search of the World Wide Web found applications in fields as divergent as modeling the control of cellular phone networks, computer recognition of American Sign Language and—inevitably—the timing of trading in financial markets. The purpose of this project is to apply this technique to the problem of forecasting conflict in the former Yugoslavia.

A sequence is "noisy" when it contains missing, erroneous and extraneous elements, and consequently the sequence cannot be classified by simply matching it to a set of known "correct" sequences. A spelling program, for example, would always mark "wan" as an incorrect spelling of "one" because written English usually allows one and only one correct spelling of a word. Spoken English, in contrast, allows a wide variation of pronunciations, and in some regional dialects, "wan" is the most common pronunciation of "one". A computer program attempting to decipher spoken English needs to provide for a variety of different ways that a word might be pronounced, whereas a spelling checker needs only to know one.

An HMM is a variation on the well-known Markov chain model, one of the most widely studied stochastic models of discrete events (Bartholomew, 1975). The standard reference on HMMs is Rabiner (1989), which contains a thorough discussion of the estimation techniques used with the models as well as setting forth a standard notation that has been used in virtually all contemporary articles on the subject. Like a conventional Markov chain, a HMM consists of a set of n discrete states and an n x n matrix $[A] = \{a_{ij}\}$ of *transition probabilities* for going between those states. In addition, however, every state has a vector of *observed symbol probabilities* that combine into a second matrix $[B] = \{\mathbf{b}_j(k)\}$ corresponding to the probability that the system will produce a symbol of type k when it is in state j. The states of the HMM cannot be directly observed and can only be inferred from the observed symbols, hence the adjective "hidden." This is in contrast to most applications of Markov models where the states correspond directly to observable behaviors.

While HMMs can have any type of transition matrix, the model that I will focus on in this chapter is called a "left-right-left model" because it imposes the constraint that the system can only remain in its current state or move to adjacent states. The transition matrix is therefore of the form

$$\begin{matrix}
a_{11} & 1-a_{11} & 0 & 0 & \ldots & 0 & 0 \\
a_{21} & 1-a_{21}-a_{23} & a_{23} & 0 & \ldots & 0 & 0 \\
0 & 0 & a_{32} & 1-a_{32}-a_{34} & \ldots & 0 & 0 \\
\ldots & \ldots & \ldots & \ldots & \ldots & \ldots & \ldots \\
0 & 0 & 0 & 0 & \ldots & 1-a_{n-1,n-2}-a_{n-1,n} & a_{n-1,n} \\
0 & 0 & 0 & 0 & \ldots & a_{n,n-1} & 1-a_{n,n-1}
\end{matrix}$$

and the individual elements of the model look like those in Figure 8.1. A series of these individual elements form an HMM such as the 5-state model illustrated in Figure 8.2. The left-right-left model is a generalization of the "left-right" model commonly used in speech recognition, where transitions are only allowed to the next state.

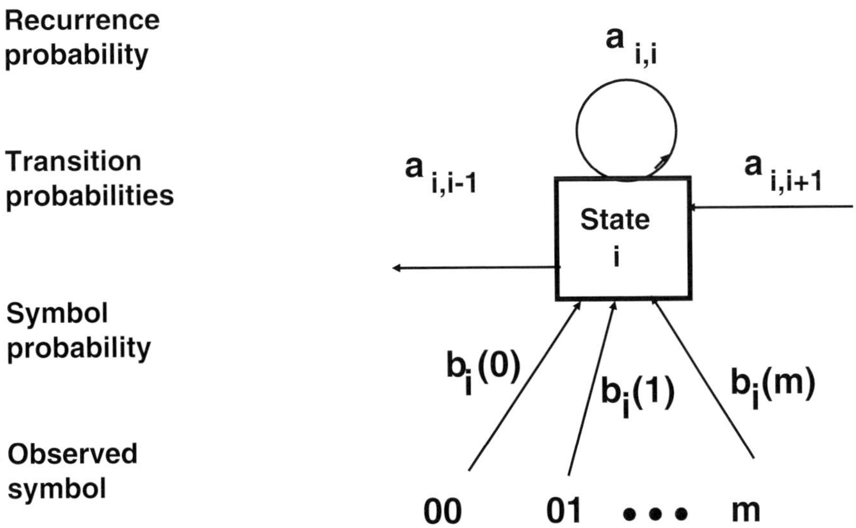

Figure 8.1. An element of a left-right-left hidden Markov model

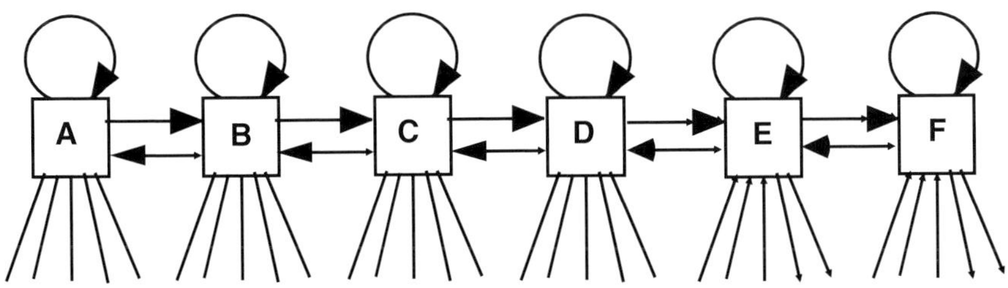

Figure 8.2. Schematic of a left-right-left hidden Markov Model

In empirical applications, the transition matrix and symbol probabilities of an HMM are estimated using an iterative technique called the Baum-Welch algorithm. This procedure takes a set of observed sequences (for example the word "seven" as pronounced by twenty different speakers) and finds coefficients for the matrices [A] and [B] that locally maximize the probability of observing those sequences. The Baum-Welch algorithm is a nonlinear numerical technique and Rabiner (1989:265) notes "the algorithm leads to a local maxima only and, in most problems of interest, the optimization surface is very complex and has many local maxima." In my experience with this problem, the variance of the parameter estimates found in these local solutions is very large, although a variety of differing parameters appear to yield roughly similar estimates for the joint probability of the sequences.

After a set of models has been estimated, that set can be used to classify an unknown sequence by computing the maximum probability that each of the models generated the observed sequence. This is done using an algorithm that requires on the order of N^2T calculations, where N is the number of states in the model and T is the length of the sequence. Once the probability of the sequence matching each of the models is known, the model with the highest probability is chosen as the one which best represents the sequence.

For example, in a typical speech-recognition application such as the recognition of account numbers, a system would have HMMs for the numerals "zero" through "nine". When a speaker pronounces a single digit, the system converts this into a set of discrete sound categories (typically based on frequency), then computes the probability of that sequence being generated by each of the ten HMMs corresponding to the ten digits. The HMM that has the highest probability—for example the HMM corresponding to the numeral "three"—gives the best estimate of the number that was spoken.

The application of the HMM to the problem of generalizing the characteristics of international event sequences is straightforward. The symbol set consists of the event codes taken from a political event data set such as WEIS (McClelland, 1976). The states of the model are unobserved, but have a close theoretical analog in the concept of crisis "phase" that has been explicitly coded in data sets such as the Butterworth international dispute resolution data set (Butterworth, 1976), CASCON (Bloomfield and Moulton, 1989; 1997) and SHERFACS (Sherman and Neack, 1993), and in work on preventive diplomacy such as Lund (1996). For example, Lund (1996:38-39) outlines a series of crisis phases ranging from "durable peace" to "war" and emphasizes the importance of an "unstable peace" phase. In the HMM, these different phases would be distinguished by different distributions of observed events found in the estimated $\mathbf{b}_j$ vectors. A "stable peace" would have a preponderance of cooperative events; the escalation phase of the crisis would be characterized by events such as accusations, protests, denials, and threats, and a phase of active hostilities would show events involving acts of violence. The length of time that a crisis spends in a particular phase would be proportional to the magnitude of the recurrence probability a_{ii}.

The HMM has several advantages over alternative models for sequence comparison. The model is stochastic rather than deterministic, and specifically designed to deal with noisy input and with indeterminate time; both of these are present in international event sequences. HMMs are *trained by example*—a model that characterizes a set of sequences can be constructed without reference to the underlying rules used to code those sequences. This provides a close parallel to the method by which human analysts generalize sequences: they typically learn general characteristics from a set of archetypal cases.

HMMs do not require the use of interval-level scales such as those proposed by Azar and Sloan (1975) or Goldstein (1992). These scales, while of considerable utility in conventional statistical time series analysis, assign weights to individual events in isolation and make no distinction, for example, between an accusation that follows a violent event and an accusation during a meeting. The HMM, in contrast, uses only the original, disaggregated events and models the context of events by using different symbol observation probabilities in different states. An event that has a low probability within a particular context (that is, a specific hidden state) lowers the overall probability of the model generating the sequence.

Finally, while most existing work with event data aggregates by months or even years, the HMM requires no temporal aggregation. This is particularly important for early warning problems, where critical periods in the development of a crisis may occur over a week or even a day. The HMM is relatively insensitive to the delineation of the start of a sequence. It is simple to prefix an HMM with an initial "background" state that reflects the distribution of events generated by a particular source such as Reuters when no crisis is occurring. A model can simply cycle in this state until something important happens and the chain moves into the later states characteristic of crisis behavior.

3 DATA AND FORECASTING MODEL

3.1 Data

The event data used in this study were coded using the 2-digit (22 category) WEIS system (McClelland, 1976) from the lead sentences in Reuters stories obtained from the NEXIS data service for the period January 1991 through May 1997 and the Reuters Business Briefing service for June 1997 through January 1999. These reports were coded using the Kansas Event Data System (KEDS) automated event data coding program (Gerner et al., 1994; Schrodt et al., 1994). Only the lead sentences—the first sentence in the story—were coded and a sentence was not coded if it contained six or more verbs or no actor was found prior to the verb (sentences meeting these criteria have a greater-than-average likelihood of being incorrectly coded by KEDS).

A 00 nonevent was added for each day in which no events were recorded in either direction in the dyad. Multiple events occurring in the same day are kept in the sequence. The four primary ethnic groups in the conflict—Serbs, Croats, Bosnians, and Kosovars—were defined as the actors for the purpose of the analysis. Figure 8.3. shows the general pattern of events in the data.

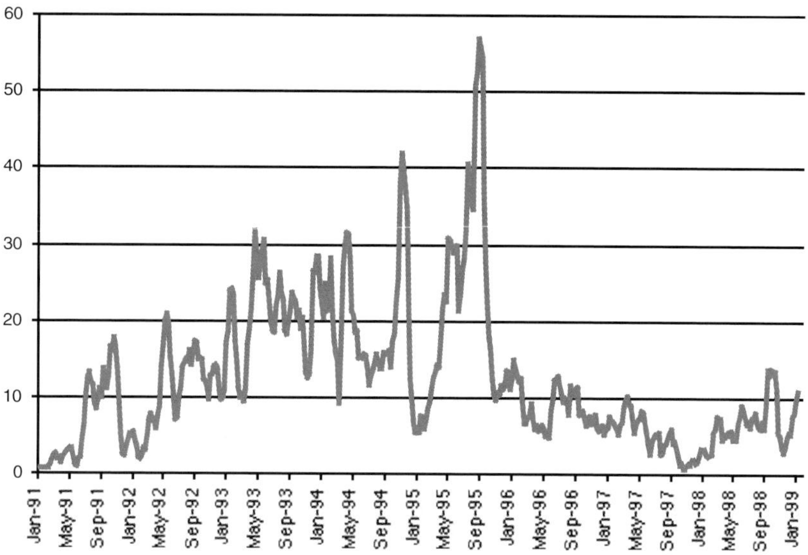

Figure 8.3. Number of WEIS 22 events per week (5-week moving average)

3.2 Forecasting Model

The accuracy of the model is evaluated on whether it can predict when violence will occur, with violence being defined as events coded into the WEIS 22—"use of force"—category. Given the diverse character of conflict in this region over the time period—violence having occurred between Serbs and Croats, Serbs and Bosnians, Serbs and Kosovars, but also occasionally between other groups (e.g. Croats and Bosnians)—the dependent variable of the model does not differentiate who was involved in the violence.

The forecast target was whether a week contained more or less than twenty WEIS category 22 events. The threshold of twenty events appears reasonable for differentiating periods when the Balkans were relatively quiet from those where there was substantial violence; approximately 20 % of the weeks in the data set satisfy the "high conflict" criterion.

Three forecast periods were used: 28 days, 91 days, and 184, corresponding to approximately 1, 3, and 6 months. The early warning sequence for each week consisted of the 100 events prior to the first day of the week minus the forecast period;[2] Figure 8.4. provides a schematic of this model.

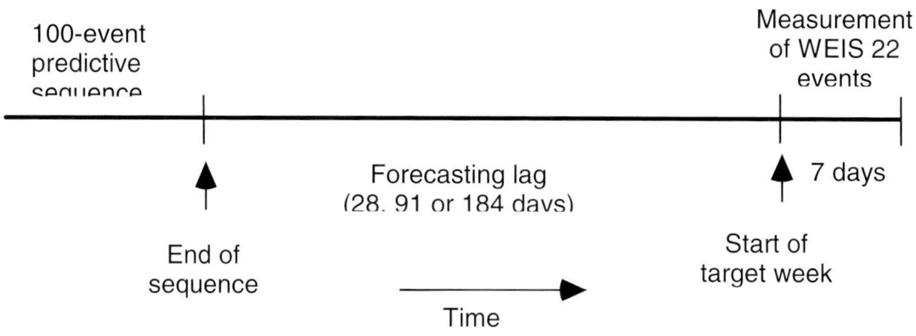

Figure 8.4. Prediction scheme

The HMMs were estimated using 16 "forecasting templates," eight for the high-conflict weeks and eight for the low-conflict weeks. A high-conflict template was created from the data by choosing a high-conflict week at random, then getting a 100-event sequence with the appropriate forecasting lag; low-conflict templates are created in a similar manner. Finally, prediction for a particular week is done by computing the fit of a 100-event sequence, obtained with a suitable lag prior to the beginning of the week, and then assigning the "high conflict" or "low conflict" prediction depending on which one of the two models had a higher probability of generating the sequence.

In this analysis, the templates have been chosen at random from *any* week in the data set, so while the computed *forecast* is strictly predictive (i.e. the prediction technique uses no information beyond that available at the beginning of the week minus the number of days in the forecast lag), the *estimation* of the predictive model is not, because the model can use templates that occurred after the time of the forecast. This approach was used because I anticipated that some periods of time would provide higher-quality templates than others, though this turned out not to be the case so far as I can determine.

The forecasting model used the following eight relationships

Serbia → any target   Croatia → any target

2. The length of the warning sequence is a free parameter and other values might work better, depending on the application. In previous work on the Middle East, I have done some experiments with sequences of 50 and 200 events; the results were roughly comparable to the results from 100 event sequences used here. Given the vagaries of timing in this region—for example the unpredictable and seasonally variable effects of weather on military operations, as well as the large number of diplomatic interventions during the course of the conflict—it is unlikely that the model will be very sensitive to the length of the sequence.

any source → Serbia	any source → Croatia
Bosnia → any target	Kosovo → any target
any source → Bosnia	any source → Kosovo

Following the approach in Schrodt (2000a), the multiple interactions were modeled by incrementing the WEIS code for the Nth dyad by (N-1)*22, so for example the {any source → Serbia} events have codes 23 through 44 (corresponding to the original WEIS codes 01 to 22) the {Croatia → any target} events have codes 89 through 110, and so forth. If no event occurred with either dyad, the 00 nonevent was assigned to the day. The resulting model contains 177 event codes (8*22 + 1). Consistent with the CASCON and SHERFACS approaches, and with earlier work that I did on the Middle East (Schrodt 1999, 2000a), the estimated models used 6 states.

3.3 Estimation Algorithm

The HMM parameters were estimated by extensively modifying the source code written by Myers and Whitson (1995). Their C++ code implements a left-right HMM and the corresponding Baum-Welch maximum likelihood training algorithm. I translated this code from the Solaris C++ environment to a Macintosh CodeWarrior ANSI C environment, in the process combining Meyers and Whitson's separate driver programs for training and testing into a single program, and modifying the input format to handle the WEIS sequences. I then extended the code to handle the left-right-left model, and implemented the Viterbi algorithm described in Rabiner (1989) in order to estimate the most likely state sequence. In the process of extending the model to the left-right-left form, I rewrote the estimation equations to correspond exactly to those in Rabiner—the Meyers and Whitson implementation differed slightly from Rabiner's equations, presumably because their models estimate a separate vector for "transition symbols." These new procedures produce estimates similar to those of Meyers and Whitson when all probabilities of a transition to the previous state are forced to zero.[3]

On average, estimating a single 177-code, 6-state HMM model using 8 template sequences required about 0.80 seconds on a 350 Mhz Apple Macintosh G3, and calculating the probability of a given sequence—i.e. doing a prediction—is practically instantaneous. Unfortunately, this speed is canceled out by the fact that the optimization surface of an HMM calculated using the Baum-Welch algorithm is characterized by a very large number of local maxima. This means that the resulting parameters—and the predictive

3. This source code is available on the KEDS project web site: http://www.ku.edu/~keds/software.html.

accuracy—of the model depend heavily on the initial approximation for those parameters. In order to explore this surface, I used a combination of Monte Carlo methods and genetic algorithms; these methods are described in detail in Schrodt (2000b). In the protocols used for this analysis, a standard run requires estimating 49,664 models (= 2* {[(24*64)+16]*16}) so it takes around 11 hours.[4]

3.4 Alternative Measures of Fitness

The fitness of the model-pairs is computed using

$$w_{TP} + w_{TN} - w_{FP} - w_{FN}$$

where the w_{aa} correspond to the weights for a

TP: true positive	high conflict predicted when high conflict occurs
TN: true negative	low conflict predicted when low conflict occurs
FP: false positive	high conflict predicted when low conflict occurs
FN: false negative	low conflict predicted when high conflict occurs

This is equivalent to a weighted "right minus wrong" criterion:

(#correct predictions) minus (#incorrect predictions)

The sum is over all of the weeks in the data set (from 1 January 1991 to 26 January 1999); each week is classified into one of these categories.

Because the data set is strongly skewed towards low-conflict weeks (80 % of the cases), this model will generally under-predict the occurrence of high-conflict weeks: in particular a null model that predicts *only* low-conflict for all weeks would have an impressive 80 % accuracy, but it will also be quite useless. This is the perennial early warning problem of balancing Type I and Type II errors: how should a model balance the possibility of false alarms with the possibility of missing actual cases of high conflict. One can create a trivial model with zero false alarms by *never* predicting high conflict, and one can also create an equally useless model that misses none of the cases of high conflict by *always* predicting high conflict. There is no simple way around this tradeoff.[5]

The simplest way of doing this is to differentiate reward and penalize some types of predictions over others. I experimented with the three different weighting systems described in Table 8.1.

4. Bond et al (2004) have recently implemented the Baum-Welch algorithm in *Mathematica* and with a combination of an alternative search strategy and presumably faster hardware (they do not provide details beyond noting that the processor was a Pentium IV), they reduced estimation time to about an hour.

5. A more sophisticated analysis, however, might use a receiver-operator characteristics (ROC) curve to determine the exact statistical trade-off between Type I and Type II errors. I did not compute these curves in this analysis but they could easily be done in principle.

Table 8.1. Weighting systems for measuring predictive accuracy

	true positive	true negative	false positive	false negative
Unweighted (U)	1.0	1.0	1.0	1.0
Entropy, false positives (P)	1.68	0.21	1.68	0.21
Entropy, false negatives (N)	1.68	0.21	0.21	1.68

The entropy-based weights are suggested by the information theory definition of the entropy of a sequence

$$E = -\sum_{i=1}^{C} p_i \ln(p_i)$$

where

p_i = the proportion of category i in the data,

C = the number of distinct categories,

and ln() is the natural logarithm. By taking only the log of the proportion, one gets the weights

$-\ln(0.186) = 1.68$ high conflict

$-\ln(0.814) = 0.21$ low conflict

These weights were used as the "reward" for a correct prediction for each type of week. I also looked at two different ways of weighting the incorrect predictions: one using the high-conflict weight to penalize false positives; the other uses the high-conflict weight on false negatives.[6]

4 RESULTS

Models were estimated for the three forecasting horizons and the three weighting systems, a total of nine models. At least sixteen Monte Carlo experiments were run for each model; in some cases there are a larger number of models in the sample due to the availability of results from additional experiments. In the tables and figures, the numerical prefix (1, 3, and 6) refers to the number of months in the forecasting horizon; the letter prefix (U, P, N) refers to the fitness weighting. In all of the analyses, the U and P models produce

6. The penalty for incorrect predictions does not need to have the same value as the reward for correct predictions, but this was used as a first approximation.

very similar results, with the N model being distinctive, therefore Table 8.3., 8.4 and 8.5 compare only the P and N models.

4.1 Overall Accuracy

The overall accuracy of the models is shown in Table 8.2. This table summarizes the number of models evaluated, the total number of observations (i.e. total number of weeks predicted across all of the models), and the average accuracy (true positive + true negative). The key result here is that the overall accuracy for the best U and P models consistently show around 77 % accuracy; the best N models somewhat less consistently show about 50 % accuracy.

Table 8.2. Overall accuracy of estimated models

Model	# Models	# Obsrv	% Correct
1-U	22	8998	78.5%
3-U	21	8400	76.9%
6-U	16	6176	75.9%
1-P	29	11861	77.6%
3-P	54	21600	76.0%
6-P	16	6176	76.9%
1-N	16	6544	54.2%
3-N	16	6400	49.0%
6-N	16	6176	47.7%

Quite surprisingly, there is very little drop-off in accuracy as the time horizon increases. This pattern of small decreases in accuracy—rather than accuracy increasing and decreasing randomly—has been found consistently in a number of different conflict regions, and may be due to the episodic character of violence in the Balkans and elsewhere. For example, this data set is characterized by two extended high-conflict periods—May-93 to June-94 and April-95 to October-95—with the remainder of the period having only sporadic conflict, often lasting only a couple of weeks. These gross characteristics may be predictable quite far in advance.

Table 8.3. shows the accuracy of the forecasts broken down by high-conflict and low-conflict weeks respectively. The "observed" column gives the percentage of the weeks that were correctly forecast: this proportion is TP/(TP+FN) for high conflict and TN/(TN+FP) for low conflict. It is the percentage of time that a high or low conflict week would have been predicted correctly.

The "forecast" column, in contrast, gives the percentage of the weeks that were forecast as having high or low conflict actually turned out to have the predicted characteristic. This is TP/(TP+FP) for high conflict and TN/(TN+FN) for low conflict. It is the percentage of time that a type of prediction is accurate.

Table 8.3. Observed and forecast accuracy

Model	High Conflict Weeks		Low Conflict Weeks	
	Observed	Forecast	Observed	Forecast
1-P	29.3%	40.8%	89.5%	83.7%
3-P	29.0%	37.9%	87.9%	82.9%
6-P	25.9%	42.6%	90.6%	82.0%
1-N	92.67%	28.1%	45.3%	96.4%
3-N	88.1%	25.9%	39.6%	93.3%
6-N	88.5%	26.3%	37.4%	92.8%

As indicated in the discussion of the weighting systems, the N-type models operate very differently than the U- and P-type models. As shown in Table 8.2., U and P models have a high overall accuracy. However, this accuracy comes almost entirely from correctly forecasting low-conflict weeks—P models predict about 90 % of these weeks correctly, but correctly predict only about 30 % of the high-conflict weeks.

N-type models, in contrast, predict about 90 % of the high-conflict weeks correctly (and 40 % of the low-conflict weeks). From the perspective of forecasting, the N-type models are best at warning against the possible "bolt out of the blue". However, this comes at a price of a lot of false alarms: when an N-type model forecasts a high-conflict week, there is less than a 30% chance that this will occur.[7] A high-conflict prediction by a P-type model will coincide with an actual high-conflict week in about 40 % of the cases.

7. Some of these false positives are "near misses" in the sense of predicting high conflict in weeks that fall just short of the 20-event threshold. Furthermore, many of these errors occur during the period of the implementation of the Dayton Accords, and if that period is eliminated from the analysis, the forecast accuracy of the N models is substantially higher.

5 PURELY PREDICTIVE MODELS

The analysis reported above used templates from the entire period to develop the models. This means that some of the "predictions" of the models—50 % of the period on average—are retrospective in the sense of being based on templates that occur after the week that is being classified. In contrast, this section will evaluate two sets of models that are purely predictive: the templates will be chosen from the period prior to the weeks being evaluated.

Two different schemes were used to do this. First, the entire time period was subdivided by calendar years: 1993, 1994, 1995, 1996, 1997 and 1998. Let C_k refer to the beginning of the first full week of year k.

- Prior Templates: templates were taken from any time prior to C_k; predictions were evaluated on all of the weeks greater than C_k.

- Recent Templates: templates were taken from the time period $C_{k-1} \geq t > C_k$; predictions were evaluated on the weeks $C_k \geq t > C_{k+1}$.[8]

In other words, the "prior" scheme takes templates from any time before the beginning of a year, and then evaluates the accuracy of the prediction on all of the remaining weeks in the data set, whereas the "recent" scheme takes templates only from the previous year (where possible) and evaluates accuracy on a single year. The relationship between these schemes is illustrated in Figure 8.5.

The results of this analysis are reported in Table 8.4. and 8.5. In general, the predictive analyses mirror the full-sample analysis in the sense that most of the results are within ±20 % of the statistics obtained using the full sample. The differences between the P- and N-models that were found in the full-sample analysis continue to be reflected in the predictive analysis, though it seems to be somewhat more attenuated. The 6-month forecast tends to be less accurate than the 1-month forecast, though these differences are frequently small (less than 10 %) and the pattern is not universal.

8. Because of the small number of high-conflict weeks at the beginning and end of the sequence, there were not enough high-conflict weeks to provide an adequate number of templates (8) for some years, so this was implemented by choosing high-conflict templates from 1991 and 1992 for the year 1993, and for 1996 to the beginning of the year for 1997 and 1998.

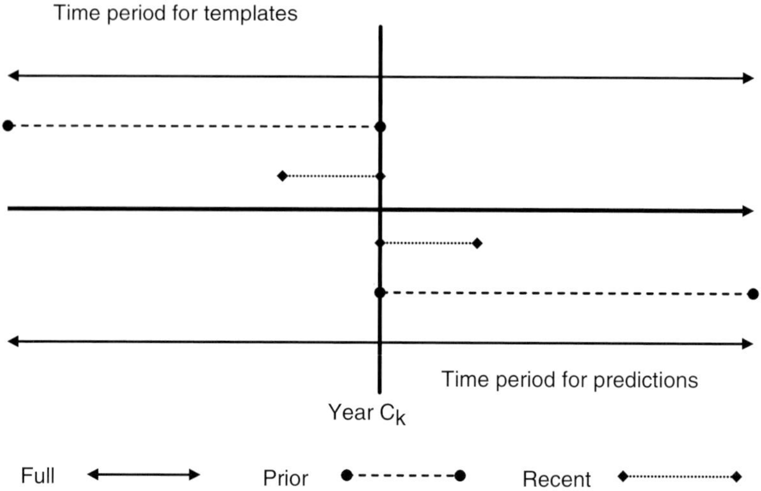

Figure 8.5. Prediction Schemes

Table 8.4. Accuracy for prior forecast templates and predictions computed on full period after year, 3-month forecast period

P-models	**1993**	**1994**	**1995**	**1996**	**1997**	**1998**
% Correct	60.73	61.86	61.38	81.21	82.75	90.85
% High Correct	29.11	31.52	35.19	33.75	31.25	0.00
% Low Correct	70.18	68.41	65.19	82.73	83.24	92.50
% High Forecast	22.61	17.70	12.79	5.90	1.71	0.00
% Low Forecast	76.79	82.25	87.39	97.50	99.23	98.07

N-models	**1993**	**1994**	**1995**	**1996**	**1997**	**1998**
% Correct	55.93	26.30	26.73	23.10	30.32	56.70
% High Correct	37.59	91.22	90.05	83.75	56.25	37.50
% Low Correct	61.42	12.30	17.54	21.15	30.08	57.05
% High Forecast	22.57	18.32	13.68	3.29	0.75	1.56
% Low Forecast	76.69	86.67	92.39	97.60	98.66	98.05

As expected, these results differ substantially over time, with the high-conflict years 1993, 1994 and 1995 generally having one pattern (consistently better or worse predictions, depending on the model), 1996 being an intermediate year, and 1997 and 1998 having a single pattern. There are a few exceptions to this—for example the "%High Forecast" indicator for the P-model is uniformly very low—but it holds more often than not. The sample sizes in the later years of the prior analyses are relatively small—particularly for the high-conflict weeks—so the accuracy fluctuates more wildly than it does in the full-sample analysis.

It should be noted that in many cases, the purely predictive models perform *better* than the full-sample model, which is frequently not the case in statistical analyses. This is probably due to the model being able to adapt to the changing characteristics of the system, for example the shift in the focus of the conflict from Croatia to Bosnia to Kosovo, as well as adapting to the periods of low conflict. In some situations, this adaptation can be counterproductive, notably as the prior model adapts to the high-conflict period prior to 1996 and then finds almost no conflict to predict after 1996. This can lead to situations where there is a great deal of difference between the relative accuracy in predicting high-conflict and low-conflict weeks. But in a majority of the cases, the short-term adaptation produces substantially better predictions. This will be discussed further in the next section.

5.1 Comparison of Forecast Accuracy by Year

The "recent" prediction scheme is the most sensitive to the changing character of the conflict. The annual statistics in Table 8.5. are also the most straightforward to evaluate, because each prediction is done on 52-weeks, in contrast to the variable number of weeks in the prediction period in the "prior" scheme.

Table 8.5. Accuracy for recent templates by year; 3-months forecast period

P-models	**1993**	**1994**	**1995**	**1996**	**1997**	**1998**
% Correct	48.80	52.16	47.60	75.12	93.87	97.96
% High Correct	16.83	55.94	27.27	28.12	0.00	0.00
% Low Correct	80.77	49.80	62.50	78.95	93.87	99.88
% High Forecast	46.67	41.06	34.78	9.84	0.00	0.00
% Low Forecast1	49.45	61.87	60.20	93.43	100.00	98.05

N-Models	**1993**	**1994**	**1995**	**1996**	**1997**	**1998**
% Correct	47.96	43.03	44.23	39.98	74.16	97.36
% High Correct	31.73	81.56	73.3	62.50	0.00	0.00
% Low Correct	64.18	18.95	22.92	38.14	74.16	99.26
% High Forecast	46.98	38.61	41.08	7.62	0.00	0.00
% Low Forecast	48.46	62.18	53.92	92.57	100.00	98.06

In order to get a systematic evaluation of the effect of changing the level of adaptation in the model, the results from the full-sample and prior analyses were re-analyzed on an annual basis: In other words, rather than assessing the accuracy on a period that extends to the end of the data set, the accuracy for each year (52 weeks) of the data was tabulated. (The *optimization* of the model was done as before—in fact this is simply a retabulation of the existing results, not a new set of estimations.)

Two features are evident in the data. First, there is generally a single rank ordering of the accuracy of the three methods across time: for example, if the recent and prior schemes (or full-sample and recent schemes) have roughly the same level of accuracy on one year, they will have this on all years. The exceptions that occur in this are usually at the ends of the data set, 1993 and 1998. There is quite a bit of variation in the patterns across the accuracy measures and estimation techniques, however.

Second, the full-sample scheme is almost always better than the prior scheme; when this is not true, the prior scheme and the recent scheme usually have about the same level of accuracy. In all cases, the prior scheme is either the least accurate of the three—in some cases dramatically less accurate—or else it is comparable in value to one of the other two measures.

These results suggest rather strongly that if one is in a predictive mode—as distinct from retrospectively analyzing a period of time or using one set of interactions to try to predict behavior in a different region—then it is best to use short-term adaptation. In many cases, the short-term model does also as well as the full-sample model, and at times it does substantially better in the later years. HMMs seem to work best when they can "forget"—in the sense of ignoring older information—as well as "learn."

6 SIMPLIFYING THE MODEL

Schrodt (2000b) presents the results of a number of additional experiments with the model, including determining whether the choice of a 6-state model is appropriate; determining whether there are significant differences in the parameter values for the high-conflict and low-conflict models, and seeing whether the model can be further simplified.

Three experiments were done in trying to simplify the model. First, instead of looking at the eight event sequences, only the two sequences involving Serbia—the dominant actor in the crisis—were analyzed. This model involved only 45 codes:

[any source] $\rightarrow$ Serbia Serbia $\rightarrow$ [any target]

plus the 00 nonevent code. The remainder of the forecasting design was the same as before.

In this model, the accuracy of the U and P models is almost identical to the results in the 4-dyad model, and the N model actually improves by about

10 %! In the analysis of the high and low-week errors, the U and P models gain between 5 % and 20 % observed accuracy in the high conflict week, while losing only about 2 % observed accuracy in low-conflict weeks. The forecast accuracy of the U and P models remains about the same. In the N model, the observed accuracy for high-conflict weeks increases slightly (about 5 % for the 3 and 6 months forecasts), and increases about 10 % for low-conflict weeks. Forecast accuracy increases about 7 % for high-conflict weeks and stays the same for low-conflict weeks. In almost none of these cases is there a serious loss of accuracy when moving to the simpler model.[9]

This analysis suggests that a simple Serbia-only model may be more appropriate than the more complex 4-dyad model, despite the fact that the original model uses much more information. There are at least three reasons that this might be true. First, simple models of social behavior are often more accurate, because the measurement errors in a more complex model add more noise than signal. This parallels the experience of the State Failures Project, which started by looking at several hundred variables, and found that all they really needed were half a dozen.[10] Second, an approach that emphasizes "watch the bad guys" is intuitively plausible—Serbia has been the initiator of much of the violence in this region, and when not the initiator, usually the target, so monitoring Serbia alone will provide most of the required information. Such an approach might not work in an area characterized by a truly multi-actor conflict such as central Africa, or the Afghan or Lebanese civil wars. Finally, the underlying theory of sequence matching suggests that models should not be overly specific—the point of the exercise is to generalize. In this case, the generalization is across all Serbian behavior, irrespective of target.

A second experiment involves simplifying the coding system. Earlier work on conflict in the Middle East (Gerner and Schrodt 1998) showed that in a cluster analysis, it was possible to substantially reduce the number of coding categories substantially without much loss in predictive power (in fact predictive power might even be gained by eliminating sources of noise). I therefore re-estimated the models using the following five-category system:

0. Non-event
1. Verbal cooperation (WEIS categories 02, 03, 04, 05, 08, 09,10)
2. Material cooperation (WEIS categories 01, 06, 07)

9. The Serbia-only model also shows a greater likelihood of being more accurate at longer horizons, which would be consistent with that model having reduced amounts of noise.

10. In the case of event data, coverage bias is probably the most important source of error: reporters go to where the action is, and when the action is in Sarajevo, few reports will come out of Kosovo.

3. Verbal conflict (WEIS categories 11, 12, 13, 14, 15, 16, 17)

4. Material conflict (WEIS categories 18, 19, 20, 21, 22)

This reduces the total number of codes in the 8-dyad Balkans model from 177 to 33, which also substantially reduces the number of low frequency code categories. It is also likely to reduce the effect of coding variance and coding error somewhat: several of the "verbal conflict" codes in WEIS are ambiguous even for human coders, and the automated coding probably generates some misclassification in those categories.

Once again, the results of the new analysis are comparable to those of the original analysis. As before, the drop-off in accuracy with the increasing forecasting lag is small—about 4 % from the 1-month to 6-month forecast lag—but there is consistently a small decrease. The overall accuracy measure decreases about 4 % for the P-models and *increases* about 8 % for the N-models. The largest difference in the results occurs with respect to the accuracy of the high-conflict predictions in the P-models—these average about 18 % better in the percentage of the observed high weeks that were correctly forecast, albeit at the cost of an 8 % decrease in the corresponding percentage of the observed low weeks that were correctly forecast. The N-model shows an 11 % increase in the percentage of the observed low weeks that were correctly forecast and a 5 % increase in the percentage of forecasts of high conflict that actually had high conflict. All of the remaining statistics differ from the original model by less than 3 %.

This analysis clearly supports the results found in Gerner and Schrodt (1998)—the use of simplified event coding systems at worst involves only a small penalty in terms of predictive accuracy, and at best can actually improve the accuracy, probably through the reduction of noise. This is particularly important when data produced via automated coding is being used, since automated coding is generally less capable of making subtle distinctions between event categories, but generally is quite good at making large distinctions such as the difference between cooperative and conflictual behavior.[11]

11. It should be noted that both this test and the earlier Gerner and Schrodt (1998) test use machine-coded data, so this effect might be due to the errors found in that type of coding. However, this seems somewhat unlikely given the magnitude of the effect, the fact that the overall error rate in machine coding is comparable to that of human coding, and the fact that many of the categories that are ambiguous in machine coding are also ambiguous to human coders.

7 CONCLUSION

The overall conclusion of this analysis is that hidden Markov models are a robust, though hardly flawless, method for forecasting political conflict, at least when applied to an area such as the former Yugoslavia where substantial information about political events is available. From the standpoint of pure prediction, the models are credible.

There are several likely reasons for this. First, these forecasting models have relatively long time horizons. The common-sense signs of short-term escalatory behavior such as demands, threats and small-scale incidents of violence will not necessarily be found at three and six months horizons or, in this data, even at one month. Instead the models seem to be picking up relatively diffuse indicators, and as often as not, simply increased attention to the area by the international media and the international community. For example, one would expect that if a NATO commander or UN representative called attention to some issue, Reuters would almost always report it, whereas if the mayor of a village made the same comment, this might be ignored.

Unfortunately, these models are less useful from the standpoint of *inference*; in particular, it is very difficult to figure out what information the HMM is using to make these predictions. An extensive analysis was done of the coefficient estimates in the full-sample model to determine what the model was "looking at" in order to make predictions. While a number of statistically significant differences exist between the high and low conflict models, these do not fall into any neat patterns. This is probably due to a combination of the large number of parameters being estimated, the multiple local maxima in the estimation surface, and the complications introduced by the presence of a number of very low probability event categories.

Some of these indicators may be indirect: for example some of the high-conflict models had high parameter values for indicators involving Kosovo, despite the fact that in most of the data, relatively few events involved Kosovo. I initially interpreted this as a statistical artifact, but these coefficients could be reflecting that fact that after 1991 or so, the international community consistently responded to aggressive moves by Serbia by warning Serbia not to do anything in Kosovo, and these activities probably were picked up in the data set. The presence or absence of non-events was clearly very important in most of the models, so the fact that the international media are reporting on an area is by itself a useful indicator (Gerner and Schrodt 1998).

This interpretation of the coefficients is further complicated by the problem of the indeterminancy of the estimates produced by the Baum-Welch algorithm. This indeterminancy does not seem to be dealt with in detail in the HMM literature—most HMM applications are solely concerned with prediction, not inference—but where it is mentioned, the experience that I have had estimating these models appears to be typical. I have done a series of additional unreported experiments to attempt to find ways to reduce the variance of the estimates—increasing the number of templates used, varying the parameters of the genetic algorithm, changing the convergence conditions of the Baum-Welch algorithm, and setting the initial observation probabilities in the vicinity of the marginal probabilities of events in the data set as a whole—and none of these had a major impact. There is some limited evidence that the variance in the *accuracy* of the models estimated with the 5-code system is less than that of the 22-code system, but the variance in the parameters is still quite high.

Bond et al. (2004) have recently experimented with an alternative approach that employs the "Kullback-Leibler (KL) distance measure. [This] gives the degree of statistical dissimilarity—in terms of symbol output—between two models and makes it easier to monitor the performance of the estimation procedures." (Bond et al., 2004:12). The Bond et al. models have a one-month forecast accuracy for cooperative and conflictual behavior in Indonesia 1999 that is comparable to the levels I found for the Balkans, but the estimation can be done much more quickly. This suggests that greater efficiency may be possible using methods more sophisticated than those I have explored so far.

Finally, the sheer number of parameter estimates generated by these HMMs complicates the problem of interpretation. The HMM models may be similar to neural networks in this regard: the diffuse coefficient structure is the model's way of dealing with the high degree of uncertainty in the underlying data, and the complexity of tradeoffs between the parameter values makes them almost impossible to interpret in a simple fashion. Doing a full interpretation would ideally involve five dimensions of comparison—WEIS category, dyad, Markov state, weighting scheme and high/low model—which are three dimensions more than most people can deal with. I have focused here on two weights, one or two Markov states, and a two-dimensional actor-by-code comparison, but that obviously leaves plenty of other possibilities that have not been explored.

References

Azar, E. E., and Sloan, T., 1975, *Dimensions of Interaction*, University Center for International Studies, University of Pittsburgh, Pittsburgh.

Bartholomew, D. J., 1971, *Stochastic Models for Social Processes,* Wiley, New York.

Bloomfield, L. P., and Moulton, A., 1989, *CASCON III: Computer-Aided System for Analysis of Local Conflicts,* MIT Center for International Studies, Cambridge.

Bloomfield, L. P., and Moulton, A., 1997, *Managing International Conflict,* St. Martin's Press, New York.

Bond, J., Petroff, V., O'Brien, S., and Bond, D., 2004, Forecasting turmoil in Indonesia: an application of Hidden Markov Models, paper presented at the *International Studies Association Convention*, Montreal, March 17-20, 2004. (Paper can be downloaded via http://archive.allacademic.com/publication/search.php)

Butterworth, R. L., 1976, *Managing Interstate Conflict,1945-74: Data with Synopses,* University of Pittsburgh University Center for International Studies, Pittsburgh.

Cimbala, S., 1987, *Artificial Intelligence and National Security,* Lexington Books, Lexington, MA.

Cyert, R. M., and March, J. G., 1963, *A Behavioral Theory of the Firm,* Prentice-Hall,Englewood Cliffs, NJ.

Gerner, D. J., Schrodt, P. A., Francisco, R. A., and Weddle, J. L., 1994, The machine coding of events from regional and international sources, *International Studies Quarterly* **38**:91-119.

Gerner, D. J. and Schrodt, P. A., 1998, The effects of media coverage on crisis assessment and early warning in the Middle East, in *Early Warning and Early Response*, Schmeidl, S., and Adelman, H., eds., Columbia University Press-Columbia International Affairs Online, New York.

Gurr, T. R., and Harff, B., 1996, *Early Warning of Communal Conflict and Humanitarian Crisis.* Monograph Series on Governance and Conflict Resolution, United Nations University Press, Tokyo.

Goldstein, J. S., 1992, A conflict-cooperation scale for WEIS events data, *Journal of Conflict Resolution* **36**: 369-385.

Hopple, G. W., Andriole, S. J., and Freedy, A, eds., 1984, *National Security Crisis Forecasting and Management* Westview, Boulder.

Hudson, V., ed., 1991, *Artificial Intelligence and International Politics*, Westview, Boulder.

Khong, Y. F., 1992, *Analogies at War*, Princeton University Press, Princeton.

Kruskal, J. B., 1983, An overview of sequence comparison, in *Time Warps, String Edits and Macromolecules,* Sankoff, D., and Kruskal, J. B., eds., Addison-Wesley, New York.

Lund, M. S., 1996, *Preventing Violent Conflicts: A Strategy for Preventive Diplomacy,* United States Institute for Peace, Washington, D.C.

McClelland, C. A., 1976, *World Event/Interaction Survey Codebook* (ICPSR 5211), Inter-University Consortium for Political and Social Research, Ann Arbor.

May, E., 1973, *"Lessons" of the Past: The Use and Misuse of History in American Foreign Policy,* Oxford University Press, New York.

Mefford, D., 1985, Formulating foreign policy on the basis of historical programming, in *Dynamic Models of International Conflict*, Luterbacher, U., and M. D. Ward, M. D., eds., Lynne Rienner Publishing, Boulder.

Myers, R., and Whitson, J., 1995, *HIDDEN MARKOV MODEL for automatic speech recognition (C++ source code)*, http://www.itl.atr.co.jp/comp.speech/Section6/Recognition/myers.hmm.html, accessed 25 January 1998.

Neustadt, R. E., and May, E. R., 1986, *Thinking in Time: The Uses of History for Decision Makers,* Free Press, New York.

Rabiner, L. R., 1989, A tutorial on Hidden Markov Models and selected applications in speech recognition, *Proceedings of the IEEE* **77,2**:257-286

Schrodt, P. A., 1991, Pattern recognition in international event sequences: a machine learning approach, in *Artificial Intelligence and International Politics*, Hudson, V., ed., Westview, Boulder.

Schrodt, P. A., 1993, Rules and co-adaptation in foreign policy behavior, paper presented at the *International Studies Association*, Acapulco.

Schrodt, P. A., 1994, Event data in foreign policy analysis, in Neack, L., Hey, J. A. K., and Haney, P. J., eds., *Foreign Policy Analysis: Continuity and Change,* Prentice-Hall, New York, pp. 145-166.

Schrodt, P. A., 1999, Early warning of conflict in Southern Lebanon using Hidden Markov Models, in *The Understanding and Management of Global Violence*, Starr, H., ed.,. St. Martin's Press, New York, pp. 131-162.

Schrodt, P. A., 2000a, Pattern recognition of international crises using Hidden Markov Models, in *Political Complexity: Nonlinear Models of Politics*, Richards, D., ed., University of Michigan Press, Ann Arbor, pp. 296-328.

Schrodt, P. A., 2000b, Forecasting conflict in the Balkans using Hidden Markov Models, paper presented at the *American Political Science Association meetings*, Washington, DC. Available at http://www.ukans.edu/~keds/papers.html.

Schrodt, P. A., and Gerner, D. J., 1994, Validity assessment of a machine-coded event data set for the Middle East, 1982-1992, *American Journal of Political Science* **38**: 825-854.

Schrodt, P. A., Davis, S. G., and Weddle, J. L., 1994, Political science: KEDS—a program for the machine coding of event data, *Social Science Computer Review* **12**: 561-588.

Schrodt, P. A., and Gerner, D. J., 1997, Empirical indicators of crisis phase in the Middle East, 1982-1995, *Journal of Conflict Resolution* **41**:529-552.

Sherman, F. L., and Neack, L., 1993, Imagining the possibilities: the prospects of isolating the genome of international conflict from the SHERFACS dataset, in *International Event-Data Developments: DDIR Phase II.* Merritt, R. L., Muncaster, R. G., and Zinnes, D. A., eds., University of Michigan Press, Ann Arbor.

Singer, J. D., and Wallace, M. D., 1979, *To Augur Well: Early Warning Indicators in World Politics*, Sage, Beverly Hills.

Vertzberger, Y. I., 1990, *The World in their Minds: Information Processing, Cognition and Perception in Foreign Policy Decision Making,* Stanford University Press, Stanford.

Chapter 9

Neural Computation for International Conflict Management

Georg Dorffner
Medical University of Vienna and Austrian Research Institute for Artificial Intelligence, Vienna, Austria

Jürgen Rattenberger, Erik Hörtnagl
Austrian Research Institute for Artificial Intelligence, Vienna, Austria

Jacob Bercovitch
University of Canterbury, Christchurch, New Zealand

Robert Trappl
Medical University of Vienna and Austrian Research Institute for Artificial Intelligence, Vienna, Austria

This chapter reports about the application of pattern recognition methods from the area of "neural computation" exploring their capabilities for finding structure in a data base of conflict management events since 1945 (Confman: Bercovitch and Langley, 1993; see Chapter 6). In particular, the following two methods were tested:

- So-called Multilayer Perceptrons (MLPs) as powerful nonlinear classifiers to predict the outcome of conflict management
- So-called Selforganizing maps (SOM) as a flexible clustering and visualization method enabling structured "browsing" through the data

Two explorations were performed using the previously available version of Confman, containing data from 1945-1995. A thorough analysis of non-linear classification revealed only minor differences as compared to linear classifiers. Yet, classification performance significantly above chance could be reached. Selforganizing maps, on the other hand, proved to be a viable technique for revealing interesting clusters and substructure in the data.

A third exploration was performed with an extended version of Confman, containing data from 1945-2000. Here, the focus was put on evaluating

R. Trappl (ed.), Programming for Peace, 185–225.

whether there are significant differences in the two subsets 1945-1989 and 1990-2000, assuming that 1990 marks the end of the cold war. Results show that this is indeed the case. Conflict management outcome is more predictable after 1989 using an MLP, and the SOM analysis leads to interesting interpretations.

1 INTRODUCTION

Work described in this chapter falls in the category of "intelligent data analysis" in the political sciences (see, e.g., Schrodt, 1991; 2000; Fürnkranz et al., 1997; Wickboldt and Bercovitch, 1996, for examples in literature). In particular, it is an attempt to apply advanced statistical methods to find structure possibly hidden in data collected about political conflicts in the world, in order to support decision makers or political scientists aiming at a deeper insight into such data. The scientific area the mathematical methods are drawn from is also usually called "pattern recognition" and comprises, among others, the following tasks (see, among others, Duda et al., 2000):

- Classification (or sometimes called "discriminant analysis"): This refers to the task of assigning one of several classes to a number of so-called "features" describing a case, by building a classifier based on one set of data (the "training set") and then applying it to new data, thus making predictions about the proper class.
- Regression (or sometimes called "function approximation"): This refers to the task of estimating a numerical variable (e.g. the number of fatalities in a conflict) based on other features describing the data. Again, an estimation (or usually called a "model") is build based on training data, then used to derive estimates for new data cases.
- Clustering (or sometimes called "unsupervised learning"): This refers to the task of finding significant groups of data (i.e. sets of similar cases that are distinctly different from other sets), such as to describe a data set in terms of such clusters.
- Visualization: This refers to the task of depicting high-dimensional data (i.e. data that is described by a high number of features, too high to be simply plotted as points) in a comprehensive manner, such as a low-dimensional "map" depicting cases as points in a 2-dimensional plane. By doing this, the structure of the data set, i.e. how cases relate

to each other in terms of similarity is revealed and can be used for further exploration.

- Forecasting: This refers to the task of analysing the time-course of changing data (i.e. observations of cases at several points in time) with respect to predicting the future.

The data to be considered originated in the database Confman (Bercovitch and Langley, 1993; Chapter 6, this volume), a comprehensive collection of conflicts since 1945 and their mediation attempts. The variables describing each conflict and mediation attempt—to be subsequently turned into "features" for pattern recognition—are grouped into three categories:

- The parties: capabilities, relationships, status in international system
- The conflict: issues, fatalities, identity, incidence, extent, international constellation, how managed, outcome, and
- The conflict management agents and activities: identity, behaviour, where, when, how, outcome

The entire database (Confman.2002) contains descriptions of 333 conflicts between 1945 and 2000 with altogether more than 5000 mediation attempts. At the beginning of this study, a smaller version (Confman.1995) was available containing only 248 conflicts and 3676 mediation events. Thus, some explorations were performed on this version, whereas the final questions could be tackled using the entire Confman.2002.

The main methods for intelligent data analysis to be explored are all from the area of Neural Computation. Neural Computation is concerned with advanced and powerful methods for pattern recognition, centered on the set of so-called artificial neural networks models (Bishop, 1995; Dorffner, 2000). Given sufficient amounts of data, these methods have been proven to show significant improvements over more classical, mostly linear, statistical techniques. While most successes of neural computation lie in engineering fields, neural computation has also proven feasible for pattern recognition in the social sciences (see, e.g., Garson, 1998). Therefore, it was natural to evaluate their potential in finding patterns in international conflict management.

Work concentrated on the following questions, selecting among the above-mentioned typical tasks of pattern recognition:

1. Classification: Can mediation attempts reliably be classified into "successful" vs. "unsuccessful" attempts? In other words, can the outcome of a mediation attempt be reliably predicted based on features describing the conflict and the properties of the mediation event?

Such a question had been addressed before, using earlier versions of Confman (Wickboldt and Bercovitch, 1996, Fürnkranz et al., 1997), with some success. Thus, the question in this study was whether classifiers from neural computation can outperform those earlier approaches including, in particular, simple linear discriminant analysis, in the context of richer data in more recent versions of the database.

2. Clustering and visualization: Can the database be meaningfully depicted as a 2-dimensional "map" revealing its intrinsic structure and similarities between cases?

3. Comparison: Can significant differences in pattern recognition be detected when splitting the data into two subsets 1945-1989 and 1990-2000? This was investigated under the assumption that 1989/1990 marked the end of the cold war and thus could have lead to a decisive change in the nature of conflicts and conflict management.

The first two questions were investigated using Confman.1995 (1945-1995). For the third question, the extended version Confman.2002 (1945-2000) was used.

Time series processing, as another potentially useful approach, proved to be infeasible, since temporal dependencies are too short in nature (i.e. time series do not reach sufficient length) to exploit neural computation algorithms.

2 METHODS

2.1 Multilayer perceptrons

The most widely neural computation method for classification is the so-called "multi-layer perceptron" (MLP). In neural network terms it consists of two layers of "units". Units in the first, the hidden, layer compute a weighted sum of input features and apply a sigmoid activation function that yields a value to be passed to the next layer:

$$h_j = f\left(\sum_{i=1}^{n} w_{ij} x_i\right)$$

$$f(z) = \frac{1}{1+e^{-z}}$$

where x_i is the i-th input feature, w_{ij} is the "weight" attached to the i-th feature by the j-th hidden unit, n is the number of features used, and h_j is the resulting (activation) value of the hidden unit. The units of the second, the output, layer again compute a weighted sum of the activation values of the hidden layer. For a two-class problem (here: "successful" vs. "unsuccessful"), a single output unit is sufficient computing the sigmoid function applied to the weighted sum:

$$c = f\left(\sum_{i=1}^{k} v_i h_i\right)$$

where v_i is the weight attached to the i-th hidden unit, k is the number of hidden units, and the output value c can be interpreted as the probability that the case with the input features x_i belongs to one of the classes (say, "successful").

The weights w_{ij} and v_i are the free parameters of the model to be estimated in the so-called "training" procedure. This is done by using a gradient-based optimization method to minimize an error function defined over a set of "training" cases, such as the so-called cross-entropy error

$$e = \sum_{i=1}^{N} t_i \log c_i + (1 - t_i)\log(1 - c_i)$$

where N is the number of training cases, and t_i is the "target" for the i-th training case (t_i=1, if the case belongs to the particular class; t_i=0 if it belongs to the other class).

Multilayer perceptrons have been proven to be able to solve arbitrary non-linear classification problems, provided a sufficient number of hidden units are supplied, where "non-linear" refers to the type of decision border one can draw if cases are represented as points in space. In other words, MLPs have the theoretical power to optimally solve any kind of classification problem, no matter how complex it might be; "solving", of course, means minimizing the error to the theoretical minimum that is possible by the data. Since for given classification problems, data usually is "noisy"—i.e. random variations with respect to the classes make errors unavoidable—a classification performance for new cases (i.e. cases that were not in the training set) of 100% is impossible. On the other hand, a classification performance on new cases above chance level is an indicator of some non-random structure in the data.

As powerful methods, MLPs usually should be compared to simpler (usually "linear") methods. The analogous linear version of the above classifier is the so-called logistic classifier obtained by using input features directly, without employing an intermediate hidden layer:

$$c^{\text{lin}} = f\left(\sum_{i=1}^{n} v_i x_i\right)$$

In terms of decision borders, this simpler classifier can only treat classes that can be separated by a “hyperplane” (e.g., a straight line in the 2-dimensional case). One can see that an MLP can be considered as computing new features from the original ones (through the hidden units), which are subsequently linearly classified.

2.2 Selforganizing Maps

The SOM algorithm (Kohonen, 1995) combines adaptive k-means clustering with a simple topographic mapping scheme. The result is a mapping of clusters in the original (high-dimensional) data space onto points in a (usually) two-dimensional plane. Similar clusters tend to be points that are close together in this plane. This way, cases can be explored by means of easy finding of similar cases in a Euclidean sense.

In its simple form, a selforganizing map consists of nxn units, each associated with a set of weights w_{ij}. Given an input vector $\boldsymbol{x}$ consisting of the input features x_i, a “winner” among the units is chosen, which is the unit whose weight vector is closest to the input vector according to the Euclidean distance. Weights of all units are then adapted according to the following equation

$$w_{ij}(n+1) = w_{ij}(n) + n(y_j, y_{win})(x_i - w_{ij})$$

where y_j is the j-th unit in the map, y_{win} is the winner, and $n(y_j, y_{win})$ is a neighborhood function defining how close the two units are to each other. This way, a clustering of the data (similarly to k-means) is achieved, with weight vectors as cluster centers, while similar clusters (i.e. clusters that are close to each other in the original feature space) tend to be represented by units that are close together in the map. By then highlighting units according to which type of case they respond to as the winner, a 2-dimensional visual “map” of originally high-dimensional data can be drawn.

2.3 Standard procedure

Since MLPs and SOMs are statistical techniques to deal with noisy data, several important guidelines must be followed when applying them:

- *Preprocessing and coding*: Due to their mathematical formulation, MLPs and SOMs need numerical features as input. Thus database attributes must be coded as such. Attributes that are numeric (e.g. the number of fatalities in the conflict) can be used directly. All other attributes must be mapped to a set of features, mostly of binary nature (i.e., taking values 0 or 1). Redundant attributes (containing no significant statistical information) or otherwise non-informative attributes must be removed.

- *Feature selection*: If the data set is of limited size, the number of features must be reduced to the minimum necessary for good results. Otherwise, the number of weights would grow too large, making a good statistical estimate impossible.
- *Validation*: Training must be repeated several times using different training sets to render statistically reliable results. For this purpose, n-fold cross-validation is an appropriate methodology. For this, the data set is randomly split into *n* parts, always using *n*-1 parts as training set and the remaining part as a test, or validation, set to check the performance on new cases. This is repeated *n* times, subsequently calculating the mean and standard deviation of performance results.
- *Testing*: All results obtained should be tested on another, hitherto unused test data set to confirm the performance.

The following sections describe the first two of these important steps, before the result sections report about the outcome of validation.

3 DATA PREPARATION AND CODING

This section describes the main analyses made that lead to the first selection and coding of attributes into features.

3.1 Target variable

Basically, the attributes *CM14* and *CM14a* are suitable as target variables for prediction, being the only attributes representing the whole conflict management outcome. They have the following meaning and values:

CM14 *The specific outcome of the conflict management attempt*

(0) No management	(2) Unsuccessful	(4) Partial agreement
(1) Offered Only	(3) Cease-fire	(5) Full settlement

CM14a CONFLICT MANAGEMENT OUTCOME

(1) Success (cease-fire, partial agreement, full settlement)

(2) Failure (unsuccessful)

It was decided to use attribute *CM14a*, since it leads to a dichotomic classification problem (i.e. a two-class problem, as opposed to the potential 6-class problem based on *CM14*), which is more easy to approach given the amount of data available.

3.2 Attributes used

The following attributes were deleted due to redundancy or other reasons:

- Attributes that had largely zero or otherwise redundant entries
- Double entries
- Indices, since they do not contribute to prediction
- Attributes containing extremely unbalanced value distributions (e.g. having 3000 entries of one class and 30 of another) and thus not having much information content

Furthermore, entries that contained missing or corrupt values (e.g. Null-Entries, or "Boolean" variables having three states) were deleted. The remaining attributes were coded into numerical values.

3.3 Coding

Attributes with numerical (e.g. fatalities) or binary values could directly be coded, after a normalization to restrict them to unit intervals was applied. Attributes with more than two symbolic values that cannot be ordered along an ordinal scale, provide a particular challenge. Three methods were used to cope with those kinds of attributes:

3.3.1 Split into several attributes

As an example, consider the coding of the attribute "political system":

P14a POLITICAL SYSTEM PARTY A
Original coding:
Nature of the POLITY of the Party at the start of the dispute.

(1) Democracy	(6) Military regime
(2) Totalitarian	(7) Non-state- becomes independent during the dispute
(3) Communist	(8) Non-state- ethnic/regional base
(4) Authoritarian	(9) Non-state- political/military base
(5) Monarchy	

The numbers in brackets show the code representing the entry in the database. As these numbers are not on an ordinal scale, the attribute has to be split up into nine Boolean attributes representing each value. For notational purposes, these new attributes were given a new name using an additional letter or digit indicating the value (e.g. P14ad represents *(1) Democracy*, P14at represents *(2) Totalitarian,* and so on).

3.3.2 Combination of values

Basically the goal should be to keep the number of features small (see section *Feature Selection*). Therefore, splitting one attribute into a large number of binary features might not be an efficient solution. Thus, a combination of values into one category was performed wherever feasible. A machine-learning algorithm (the J48 decision tree algorithm, Witten and Frank, 1999) was used to test whether such a combination leads to a loss in information with respect to classification outcome.

3.3.3 Recoding

In some cases, switching the numeric codes representing the attribute values could achieve a meaningful order. For instance,

if the original coding had values

(0) Not Applicable (1) Yes (2) No

this was modified to:

(1) Yes (0) Not Applicable (-1) No

The annex contains a list of all attributes used in the investigations and their coding as features.

3.4 Selection of the final data set

The structure of the database contains another challenge for pattern recognition. The database (Confman, version 1945-1995) contains data about 248 conflicts and altogether 3676 mediation events. This means that on average each conflict was accompanied by around 15 conflict management attempts. A set of 248 cases would be too small to perform useful classification with neural networks. In addition, predicting the outcome of a conflict management attempt only makes sense when considering each attempt separately. This, however, leads to the fact that on average 15 cases share the same subset of attributes describing the conflict and its involved parties. Since most pattern recognition methods assume independence of training cases, this can pose severe problems by adding a bias to all results. Unfortunately, there is no straight-forward way to cope with this problem, so it was ignored. The potential bias, nevertheless, must be kept in mind when interpreting the results.

In all experiments reported below, each conflict management was taken as a separate case, encoding attributes from all 3 classes D (demographic), P (parties), and CM (conflict management). The data was randomly divided into a test and a working set (used for all n-fold cross-validations reported below). The selection was done on conflicts. 100 conflicts (about a third of the data) were randomly assigned to the test set, the rest to the working set (consisting of all corresponding conflict management events).

4 FEATURE SELECTION

Since multilayer perceptrons are powerful classifiers with a potentially large number of degrees-of-freedom (weights), for limited data sets models must be kept as small as possible to arrive at useful estimations. The number of hidden units determines the model complexity and thus the degree of non-linearity that can be approximated. The only other way to keep models small is to reduce the number of input features actually used in model estimation. Therefore, a sensible step in every application of MLPs is to perform a statistically based feature selection to come up with the most compact and useful subset of features.

Literature on feature selection distinguishes between

- *filters* (e.g. correlation analysis) to select subsets prior to the use of the target classifier
- *wrappers*, which are methods employing the target classifier itself in feature selection

In addition, one can distinguish between

- *heuristic methods* that, for instance, employ domain knowledge to select proper subsets
- *search-based methods* that intelligently explore the space of all possible subsets
- *ranking methods* using a particular performance measure (e.g. the so-called Gini-index)

In this work, a mixture of heuristic and search- and rank-based wrappers was used to perform feature subset selection. Wrappers, however, did not employ the target MLP classifier but decision trees from the Weka data mining toolbox (Holmes et al., 1994); i.e. a pruned C4.5 Decision tree learner (Quinlan, 1993) termed “J48” (Witten and Frank, 1999) and the “ZeroR” naïve learner. The following sections describe the main methods used.

4.1 Important attributes from literature

A viable heuristics is to look at past similar work for proper attribute subsets. While this previous work is directly comparable to this endeavor (i.e. all authors have used the Confman database), it should be noted that results in literature were based on older versions of the database.

Fürnkranz et al.

According to Fürnkranz et al. (1997), the following attributes have turned out to be the most important ones:

* Previous relation of the parties with the mediator: CM7
* Power of parties: P10a, P10b
* Number of parties supporting: P19a,P19b
* Mediation environment: CM13
* Core issue: D14

In the same publication, a statistical analysis has lead to the following subset:

* Fatalities: D5a
* Mediation environment: CM13
* Mediation strategy: CM6
* Previous relation between the parties: P12
* Core issue: D14
* Mediator rank: CM5

Wickboldt and Bercovitch

According to Wickboldt and Bercovitch (1996), the most important attributes after feature selection are

* Duration: D4a
* Fatalities: D5a
* Power of parties: P10a,b
* Number of parties supporting: P19a,b
* Civil liberties of parties: P22a,b
* Mediation strategy: CM6
* Previous relationship of the parties with the mediator: CM7
* Number of previous Mediations: CM8
* Mediation environment: CM13

Bercovitch et al.

Bercovitch et al. (1991) and Bercovitch and Houston (1993) provide some discussion on important attributes for conflict mediation. According to that the most important attributes are:

* Political system of parties: P14a,b
* Power of parties: P10a,b
* Previous relations between the parties: P12
* Duration: D4a
* Dispute intensity: D5a
* Core issue: D14
* Third party identity: CM4
* Characteristics of the mediator
    - rank: CM5
    - strategy: CM6
    - relationship with parties: CM7
    - number of previous attempts: CM8

4.2 Ranking based on Weka

In this part of the work, the WEKA data mining toolbox (Holmes et al., 1994) was used to evaluate all coded attributes in order to get a rough picture about their possible relevance in classification. The tool uses a wrapper based on C4.5 decision trees, a ranker or a best-first search (greedy hill climbing augmented with a backtracking facility) and the following evaluators (selection measures):

1. ConsistencySubsetEval:
   Search: BestFirst
   Evaluates the validity of a subset of attributes by the level of consistency in the class values when the training instances are projected onto the subset of attributes.
2. CfsSubsetEval
   Search: BestFirst
   Evaluates the validity of a subset of attributes by considering the individual predictive ability of each feature along with the degree of redundancy between them.
3. InfoGainAttributeEval
   Search: Ranker

Evaluates the validity of an attribute by measuring the information gain with respect to the class.

4. GainRatioAttributeEval
   Search: Ranker
   Evaluates the validity of an attribute by measuring the gain ratio with respect to the class.
5. ReliefFAttributeEval
   Search: Ranker
   Evaluates the validity of an attribute by repeatedly sampling an instance and considering the value of the given attribute for the nearest instance of the same and different class.
6. SymmetricalUncertAttributeEval
   Search: Ranker
   Evaluates the validity of an attribute by measuring the symmetrical uncertainty with respect to the class.
7. OneRAttributeEval
   Search: Ranker
   Evaluates the validity of an attribute by using the OneR classifier.
8. ChiSquaredAttributeEval
   Search: Ranker
   Evaluates the validity of an attribute by measuring the chi-squared value with respect to the class.

The following tables depict the resulting attribute rankings for all 8 evaluators:

1	2	3	4	5	6	7	8
D5a	D5a	CM122	D5a	CM122	CM122	P10a	CM122
P10a	P10a	P21b	CM122	P18b	D5a	CM122	P21b
P10b	P10b	P10b	P22b	CM6m	P10b	D5a	P10b
P14bd	CM6p	D5a	P10b	CM15	P22b	P10b	CM1345
P14ak	CM134	CM1345	CM6p	CM1345	P21b	P21b	D5a
P14a9	CM122	P22b	P19b	CM12r	CM1345	P22b	P22b
CM6c	CM6c	P10a	P21b	CM121	P10a	CM6p	P10a
CM6p	CM121	P14Bd	CM1345	P19b	P14bd	D4a	P14Bd
CM1345	P21b	CM121	P14Bd	CM8	CM6p	P14a9	CM121
P21b	P22b	CM6c	P14a9	P21b	CM121	P18a	CM6p
CM121	P20a	CM6p	P10a	P18a	P19b	CM5	CM6c
CM122	1 D4a	P20a	CM121	CM6c	CM6c	P12	P20a
CM12r	P20b	CM12r	P20b	CM7r	P14a9	P21a	CM12r

Furthermore, the correlation coefficients between attributes and the class-attribute (CM14a) were calculated. The resulting correlation coefficients can be found in the following table. This corresponds to yet another ranking of the main attributes.

D25	0.15
P10b	0.14
P10a	0.14
P11bc	0.14
CM1345	0.13
P24	0.12
P14bd	0.11
D5a	0.11
P4a	0.11
P17bc	0.10
CM6p	0.10
D18a	0.10
CM6c	0.10
P8d	0.10
P19b	0.09

Based on the above evaluation certain trends with respect to attribute relevance can be deduced. The following table summarizes this ranking, sorted by the weights assigned in the evaluation and by the number of times the attributes were considered relevant by the different evaluators.

Attribute
D5a
P10b
CM122
P10a
CM6p
CM1345
CM6c
P21b
P22b
P14bd
P14a9
P19b
P14ak
CM121
P20a
P20b

CM131
CM12r
D4a
P14bt

4.3 Final subset selection

The aim was to use about 5-8 attributes to train the neural networks. Therefore, the decision tree J48 was used to test several subsets, pre-selected by the above ranking. The following lists sample results (only the best of the many subsets evaluated are reported here for brevity; the one in bold face corresponds to the subset finally selected):

All listed attributes:
J48 Classification rate: 60.4 %

Attributes from Fürnkranz et al.:
J48: 60.5%

Attributes from Wickboldt & Bercovitch:
J48: 60.5%

Attributes from Bercovitch et al.:
J48: 60.5%

Attributes: D5a, P10b, CM122, P10a, CM6p, CM1345
J48: 61.1 %

Attributes: P10b, CM122, P10a, CM6p, CM1345, D4a
J48: 60.2 %

Attributes: D5a, P10b, CM122, P10a, CM6p, CM1345, D4a
J48: 60.7 %

Attributes: P10b, CM122, P10a, CM6p, CM1345
J48: 60.2 %

Attributes: D4a, P10a, P10b, P21b, CM122
J48: 62.6 %

Attributes: D5a, P10a, P10b, P21b, CM122
J48: 60.7 %

Attributes: D5a, P10a, P10b, P21b, CM122, D4a
J48: 61.3 %

Attributes: P10a, P10b, P21b, CM122
J48: 62.5 %

Attributes: P10a, P10b, P21b, CM122, CM6p, CM1345
J48: 60.7 %

Attributes: D5a, P10a, P10b, P21b, CM122, CM6p, CM1345, D4a
J48: 60.4 %

It should be mentioned that the default accuracy acquired through a naive learner is 57.1%, meaning that 57.1% of the mediations were unsuccessful.

As a result, the following five attributes were selected:

DURATION (RAW) **D4a**,
POWER PARTY A (RAW) **P10a**,
POWER PARTY B (RAW) **P10b**,
POLITICAL RIGHTS PARTY B **P21b**,
CM INITIATED BY BOTH PARTIES **CM122**

4.4 Plausibility check of the chosen attributes

Observing the chosen attributes, it is noticeable that they contain only one conflict management attribute (CM122). This might look questionable considering the fact that the remaining attributes have the same value for all its conflict management events (see discussion above on the possible resulting bias). Therefore, additional tests concerning all the CM-attributes were performed.

Using only the CM-attributes, 59.3% of the cases were correctly classified. Using only P-attributes, 61.8 % of the instances were correctly classified. Finally, with only D-attributes, 60.1% of the cases were correctly classified. This indicates that the particular subset indeed appears to be a feasible selection.

5 EXPLORATION 1: NONLINEAR VS. LINEAR CLASSIFICATION

In this part of the work the goal was to explore MLPs as non-linear classifiers with respect to their ability to predict the outcome of conflict management.

5.1 Methods

All experiments were performed using Matlab 6 and the toolbox Netlab (Nabney, 2001). The model "mlp" was used for multiplayer perceptrons, and "glm" for linear classification, the chosen optimization algorithm was the quasi-Newton method. For model selection (choosing the number of hidden units) and the comparison to linear classifiers, 10-fold cross-validations were performed on the working data set. MLPs had one hidden layer, 5 input units and one output. For model selection, the number of hidden units was varied from 2 to 20. For comparison between cross-validation runs, the decision threshold was held constant at 0.5. Data was normalized to zero mean and unit variance, which is common practice in pattern recognition.

Four subsets of attributes were used to arrive at results:

- one set of five attributes selected as the most predictive ones (see above)
- three sets of attributes selected as being most predictive in previous literature (Fürnkranz et al., 1997; Wickboldt and Bercovitch, 1996; Bercovitch et al., 1991)

Results on the first set are considered as the main outcome of this work, while the other attribute sets were used for comparative purposes and for further validation of the results. Consequently, model selection was performed with the main subset of five attributes.

5.2 Results

Figure 9.1. depicts the results from model selection (average performances of cross-validation). Choosing more than 2 hidden units only leads to minor improvements. As a result, 5 hidden units were selected as being optimal. The performance of this network was 59.4%. Figure 9.2. depicts the range of performances when varying the decision threshold. The best overall performance was 62.3% on average (+- 3.1%).

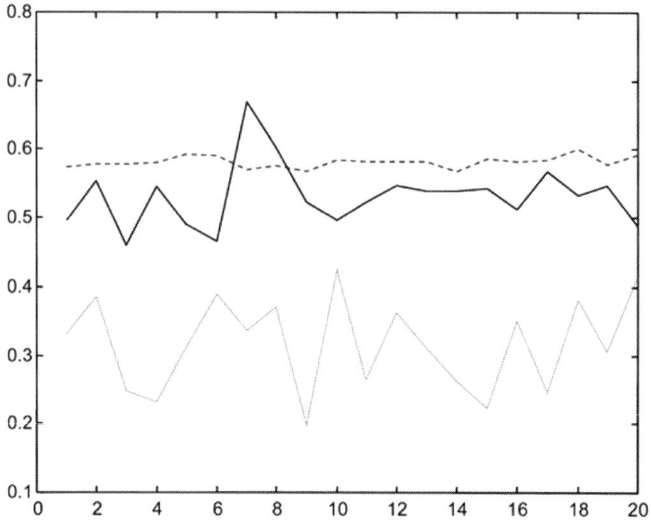

Figure 9.1. Results from model selection. Average overall classification results are shown by the dashed line, the threshold for the best overall performance is shown by the solid line, and the standard deviation of results are shown by the dotted line.

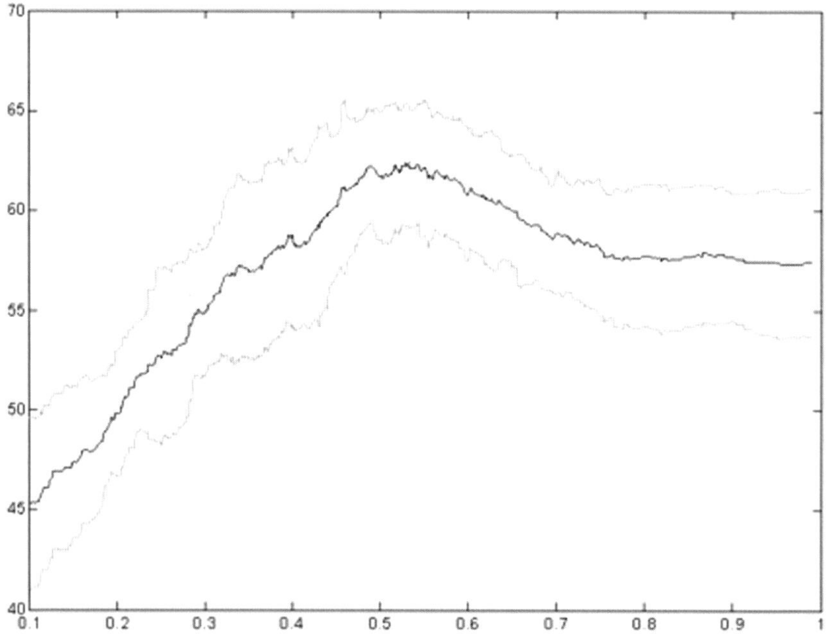

Figure 9.2. Classification performance (average and standard deviation) of the MLP with 5 hidden units, plotted against the decision threshold)

The performance of the corresponding linear classifier with 5 inputs is depicted in Figure 9.3. The best overall performance is 61.3% on average (+- 3.3%).

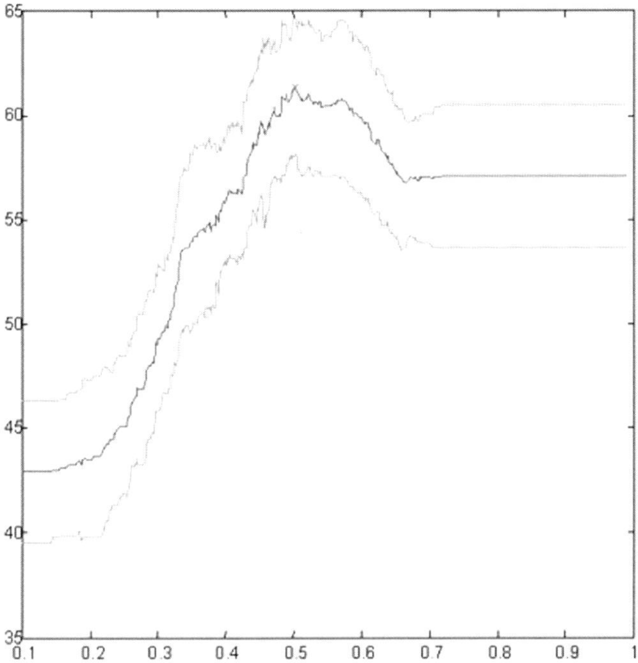

Figure 9.3. Classification performance (average and standard deviation) of linear classifier, plotted against the decision threshold)

Since the distribution of positive and negative cases is not even (i.e. naïve classification would achieve more than 50% correct performance), the best way of depicting comparative results is by showing the entire ROC (receiver operated characteristics) curve, plotting sensitivity (correctly classified positive cases, in this case "successful" mediation attempts) against specificity (correctly classified negative cases; in this case "unsuccessful").

Figure 9.4. depicts the ROC curve for MLP (black) and linear classification (grey). The results show a weak tendency of neural networks to improve classification performance, at least in some parts of the ROC curve. Depending on the desired sensitivity and specificity, this means that nonlinear methods seem to be able to extract slightly more information from the data. However, the difference is not statistically significant. What is significant, on the other hand, is the difference of both classifiers from the 45-degree line of a naive classifier, pointing to the general fact that classification can indeed be performed better than at random.

Figure 9.5. to Figure 9.7. depict the comparative ROC curves, when using the three attribute sets from literature (Fürnkranz et al., 1997; Wickboldt and Bercovitch, 1996; and Bercovitch et al., 1991). As can be seen, in none of

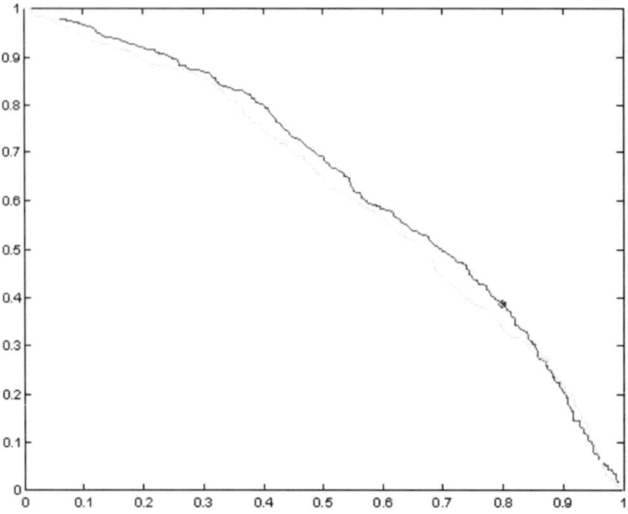

Figure 9.4. ROC curves - Sensitivity vs. Specificity – of MLP (black) and linear classification (grey). ⊗ marks the highest value of cases correctly classified (overall %)

these cases the nonlinear MLP achieves a decisive advantage over linear classifiers. The subsequent table confirms the superiority of the selected five attributes set by comparing best overall performances.

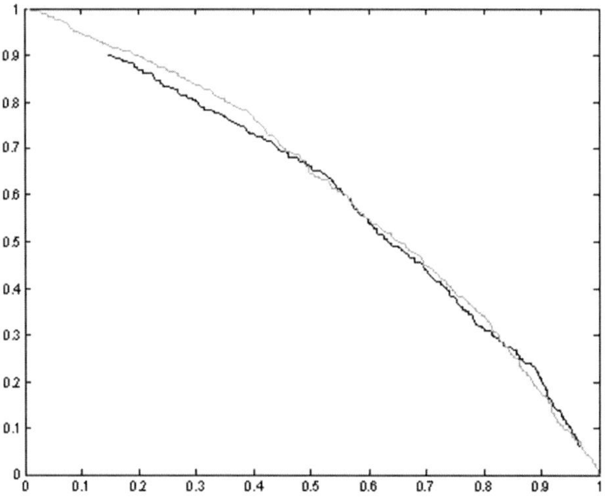

Figure 9.5. ROC curves - sensitivity vs. specificity - based on attributes suggested by Fürnkranz et al. MLP: black, linear: grey

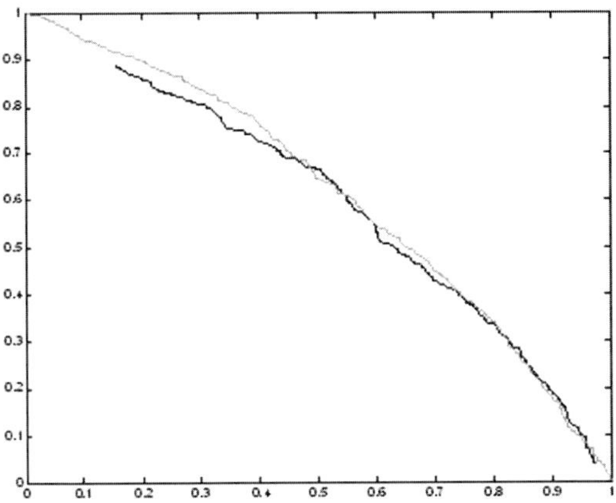

Figure 9.6. ROC curves – sensitivity vs. specificity – based on attributes suggested by Wickboldt et al. MLP: black, linear: grey

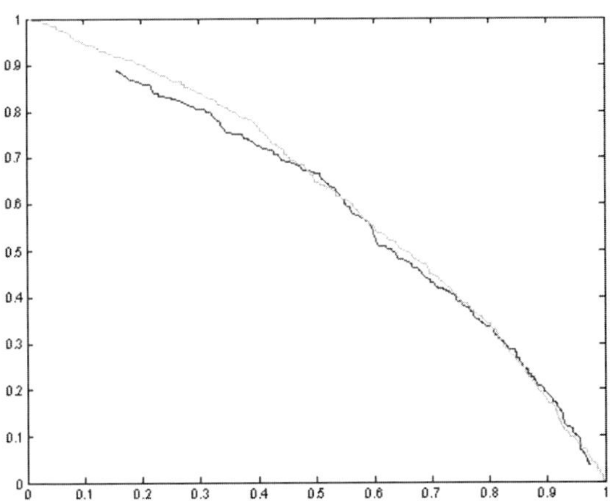

Figure 9.7. ROC curves – sensitivity vs. specificity – based on attributes suggested by Bercovitch et al. MLP: black, linear: grey

attributes	Performance linear classifier	Performance nonlinear classifier
Fürnkranz et al.	60.5%	59.9%
Wickboldt and Bercovitch	60.5%	60.8%
Bercovitch et al.	60.5%	60.4%
Our selection	61.3%	62.3%

Finally, a test including the independent test set was performed. Figure 9.8. depicts the results. The best overall performance was 60.5% for the linear classifier and 60.8% for the MLP. This test does not confirm the slight advantage of the nonlinear prediction.

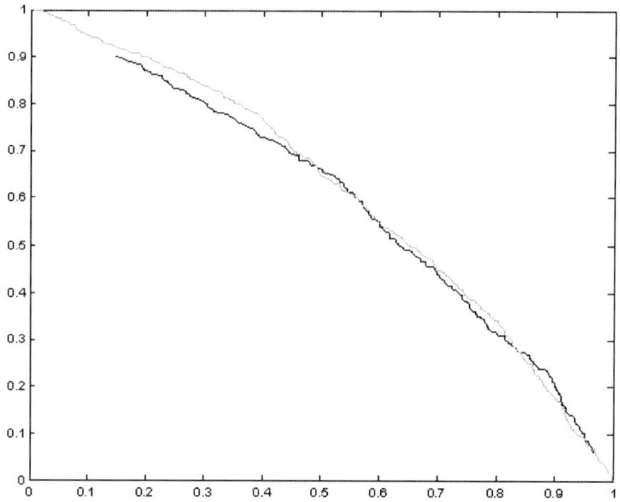

Figure 9.8. ROC curves for the best attribute set on the independent test set. MLP: black, linear: grey

6 EXPLORATION 2: CLUSTERING AND VISUALIZATION

In this part of the work, selforganizing maps (SOM, Kohonen, 1995) were applied in order to visualize the conflict management database, find relevant clusters in the data and other interesting structure. One purpose was to explore the capability of SOMs, by virtue of their visualization capability by mapping high-dimensional data into a 2-dimensional "map", to form a flexible visual interface to the database.

6.1 Methods

For all experiments in this section the SOM Toolbox 2.0 (Vesanto et al., 1999) was used. The size of the map was chosen to be 80x80 units. In order to make the structure revealed in the map more conspicuous, the U-matrix method (Ultsch, 1991) was employed. It depicts the distance between cluster centres through a colour-code, such as to make visible clear borders between larger clusters or areas of similarity. All conflict management cases in the Confman database (version 1994-1995) were used in the clustering and mapping task. The input consisted of the five attributes selected during feature selection (see above) plus the conflict management outcome (C14a) encoded as a binary attribute.

6.2 Results

Figure 9.9. depicts the resulting map of the entire data set 1945-1995. According to the U-matrix visualization, distances of units very close to each other (with very similar vectors) are represented with black and dark grey shades, and large distances are represented in light grey and white.

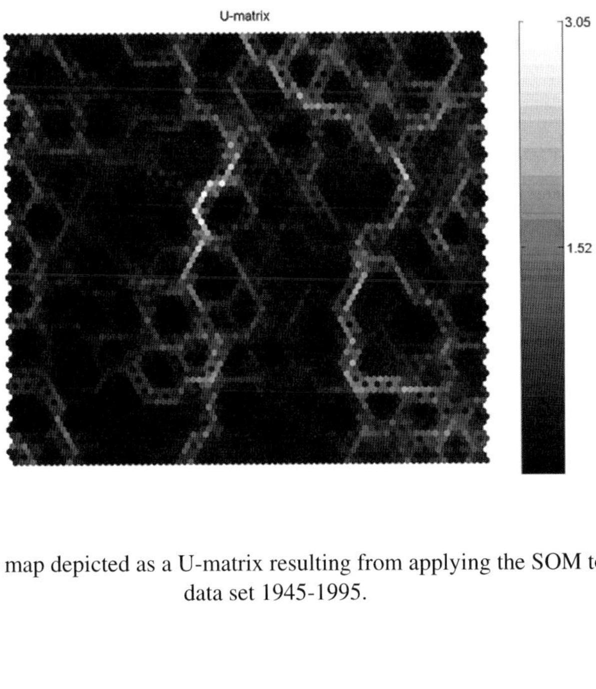

Figure 9.9. The map depicted as a U-matrix resulting from applying the SOM to the entire data set 1945-1995.

The U-matrix can also be represented separately be each component (feature). By comparing each feature map with the overall map, it becomes visible which features are mainly responsible for which significant border.

The following figures (9.10 to 9.15) show, on the right side, for each unit the value of the feature. The feature-vector contains the displayed value, which represents for each unit a certain number of similar vectors. On the left side a component-specific view of the U-matrix is shown, which can be interpreted as the first derivative of the respective matrix on the right.

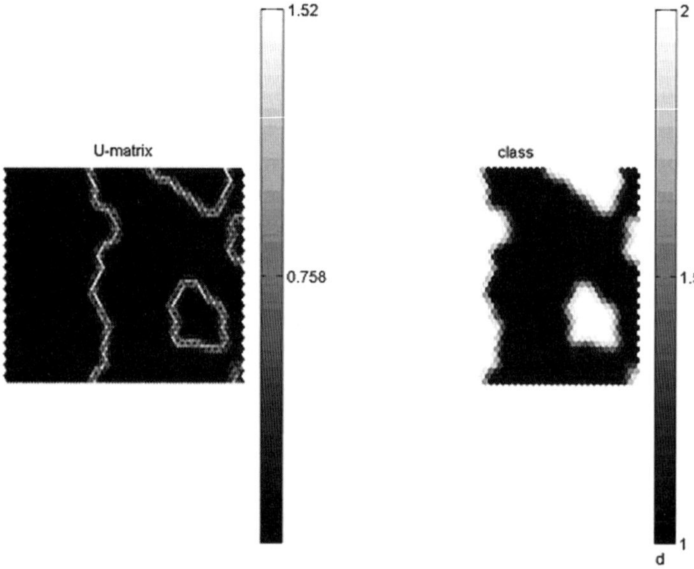

Figure 9.10. Feature-based U-matrix for conflict management outcome (CM14a)

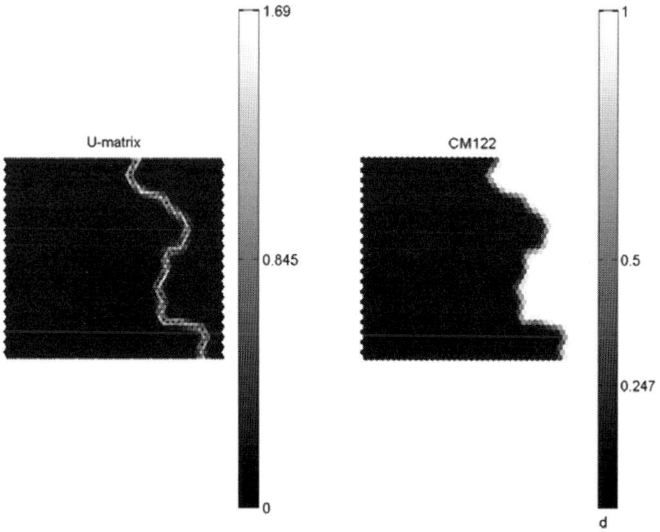

Figure 9.11. Feature-based U-matrix for whether conflict management was initiated by both parties (CM122)

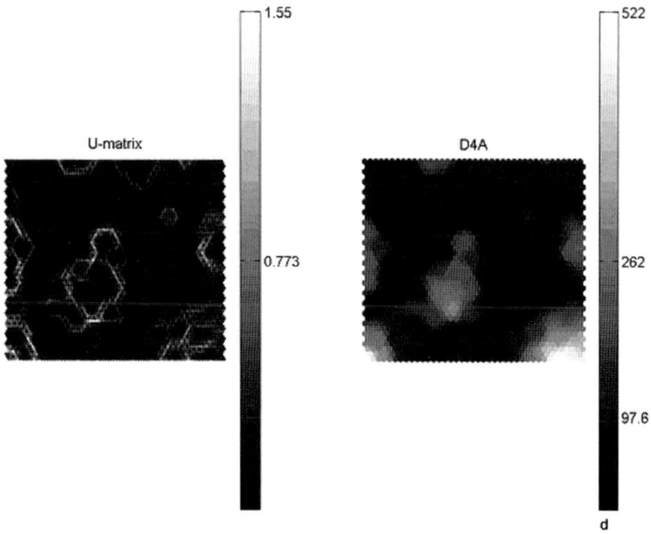

Figure 9.12. Feature-based U-matrix for conflict duration (D4a)

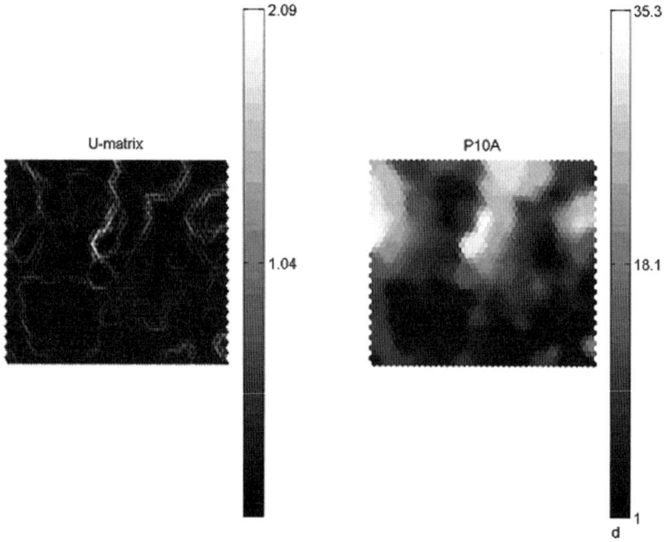

Figure 9.13. Feature-based U-matrix for power of party A (P10a)

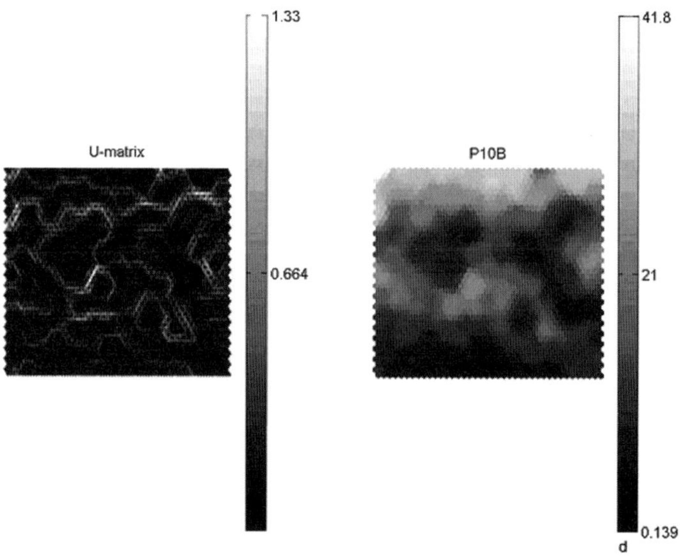

Figure 9.14. Feature-based U-matrix for power of party B (P10b)

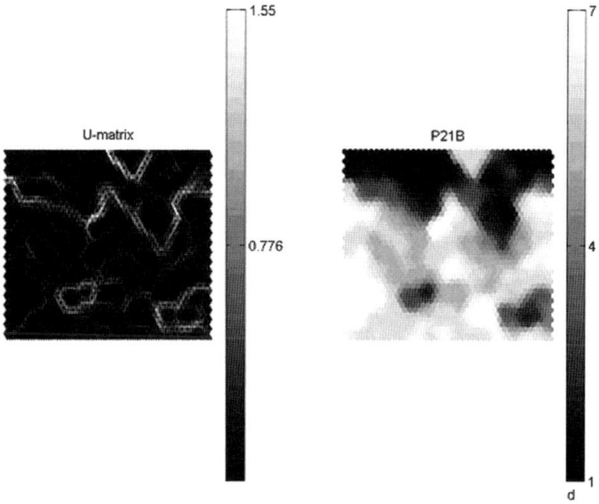

Figure 9.15. Feature-based U-matrix for political rights of party B (P21b)

Several important observations can be made:

- While the main clusters for successful conflict mediation outcome have vertical borders, most features are evenly divided across the horizontal dimension. This explains why overall prediction is generally rather poor.
- The clearest clusters are distinguished by mediation outcome (CM14a) and by whether the mediation was initiated by both parties (CM122).
- Duration of the conflict (D4a) and the power of party A (P10a) contribute to the most distinguished clusters. In particular, conflicts of high duration differ quite distinctly from other conflicts.

Figure 9.16. depicts another view on the U-matrix. This time, grey scale encodes the main responsibility of a feature for one of the borders in the matrix. Thus, by crossing a border, each grey scale encodes which feature changes the most between points on either side of the border.

The following observations can be made: Features that determine many boundaries in the U-matrix are a good basis for navigation, since they separate clusters rather clearly. Among the features used, some can be considered as *supporting features*, such as D4a and P10b, since they do not draw sharp

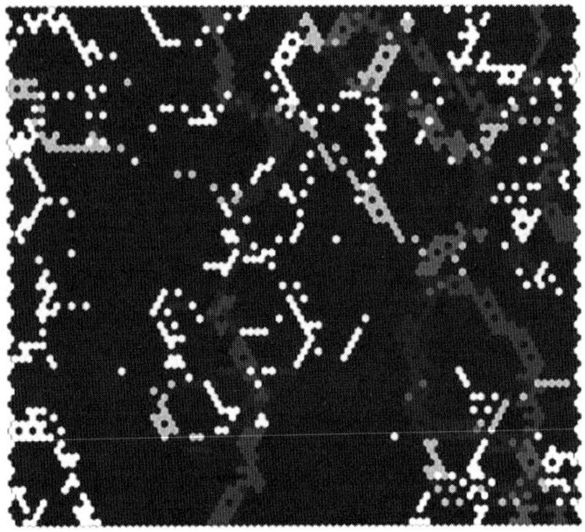

Figure 9.16. An "extended" U-matrix over the entire data set 1945-1995, depicting the responsible attributes for distinctive cluster borders.

boundaries, but due to their set of values, they restrict the more separating features.

Figures 9.17 through 9.20 give an example how the map can be used for data exploration. In particular, several steps can lead to an identification as to which ranges of feature values determines conspicuous clusters (sometimes called "islands").

We begin with identifying the island marked by the ellipse in Figure 9.17. The separating feature for the two marked boundaries is P21b (political rights party B). P21b is now continuously thresholded, and the corresponding areas in which the value exceeds the threshold are coloured in light grey. This is done until the island identified is covered clearly and distinguished from its

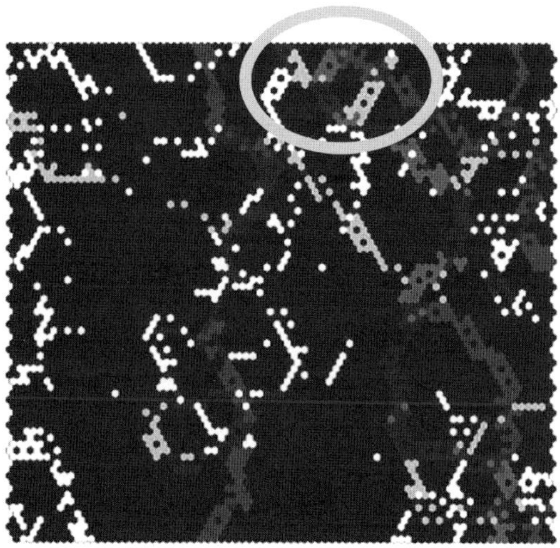

Figure 9.17. Identifying a distinctive "island" in the map (ellipse)

surroundings (see Figure 9.18.). Of course, other areas are also still light grey, since the island is not determined by this feature alone.

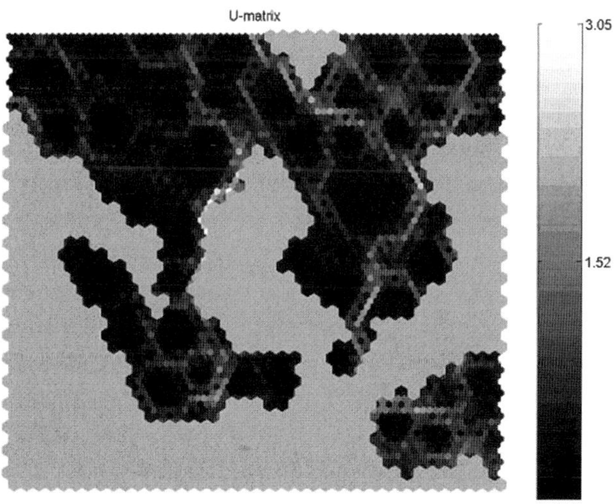

Figure 9.18. Areas obtained by thresholding attribute P21b (political rights of party B)

Therefore, in the next step another feature supporting the island in the U-matrix is chosen, in this case P10b (power party B). Thresholding it to value 0.4 leaves the areas marked in Figure 9.19. Here the island on top is no longer visible, but continuing the thresholding would leave an area smaller than the island.

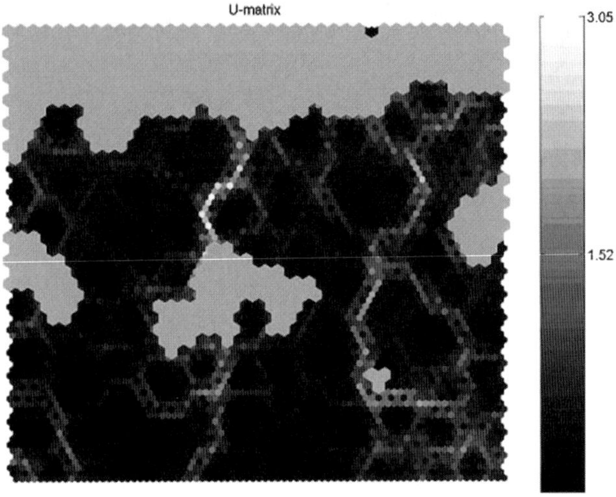

Figure 9.19. Areas obtained by thresholding attribute P10b (political power of party B)

Yet, a combination of these two features mainly leaves the target region (Figure 9.20.).

The remaining regions can be eliminated by exploring further features, as exemplified in the following example.

The target region here is the island encircled, like above (Figure 9.21.).

In the U-matrix one can see that the boundary-features forming the island are CM14a (conflict management outcome), CM122 and P21b (political rights, party B). When considering all three, still some other unwanted regions remain and therefore P10a was chosen as supporting feature. Finally the following combination of thresholded features leads to the marked area in Figure 9.22., almost exactly corresponding to the target island:

P10a < 21

P21b > 5.17

CM122 = 1 (binary value)

CM14a = 2 (binary value)

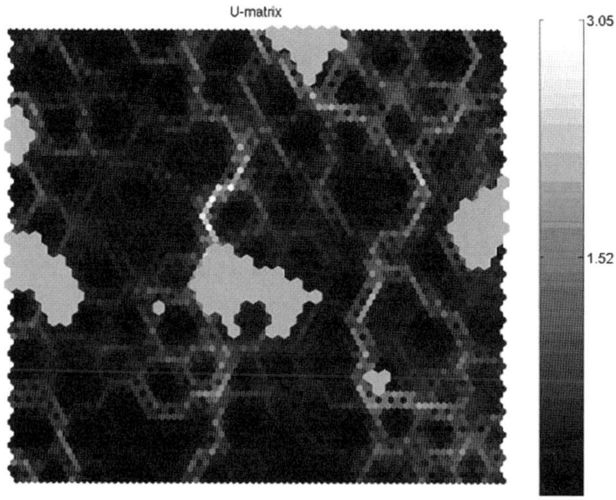

Figure 9.20. Areas obtained by combining the two thresholded attributes P21b (political rights of part B) and P10b (political power of party B)

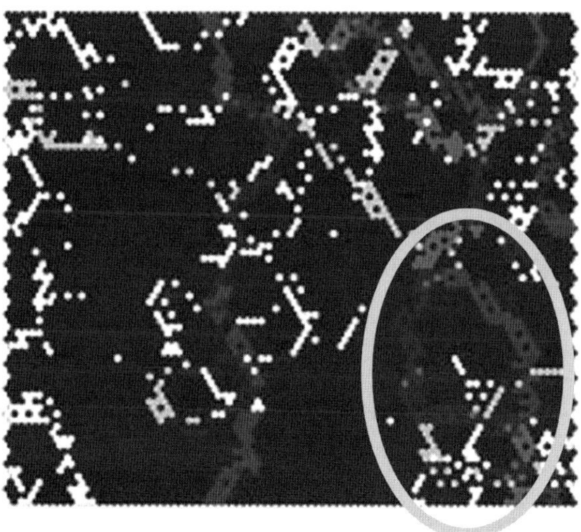

Figure 9.21. Identifying another conspicuous island (ellipse)

In this example, the island covers 60 cases in the database, although it is not completely unambiguous (e.g. the light grey spot in the right lower corner). It mainly corresponds to cases that

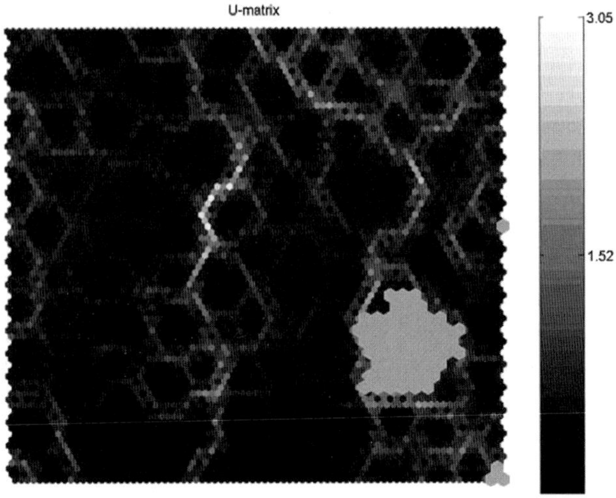

Figure 9.22. Identifying the island by thresholding several attributes

- are unsuccessful (CM14a)
- were initiated by both parties (CM122)
- are characterized by relatively large political rights of party B
- are characterized by relatively small power of party A

In summary, a SOM-based visualization of the database permits a host of ways for exploring the data, helping in identifying meaningful clusters of similar cases.

7 EXPLORATION 3: COMPARING PRE- AND POST-1990 DATA

In this part of the work, the methods from the first two explorations were employed to investigate whether there are significant differences in data before 1990 (1945-1989 including, to be precise) and after (1990-2000). The main motivation behind this exploration was the observation that 1989/1990 marked the end of the cold war period, which presumably would have a strong influence on the nature of conflicts and mediation attempts.

7.1 Methods

Both MLPs and SOMs were applied again in this task. Data was split into two data sets: 1945-1989, and 1990-2000, respectively, whereby the date of the conflict management was taken as the attribute for the split. This resulted in an almost even data split, leaving 2084 cases for the "before" period and 2159 cases for the "after" period.

Again, the five attributes selected as being the most predictive ones previously were chosen as input, and the size of the MLP was according to what resulted from the model selection described above (5 hidden units). The MLP was again subjected to a 10-fold cross-validation for either data set. The size of the SOM also remained the same.

7.2 Results

Figure 9.23. depicts the comparative results of prediction using the MLP and linear classifiers for both data sets, including error bars based on one standard deviation.

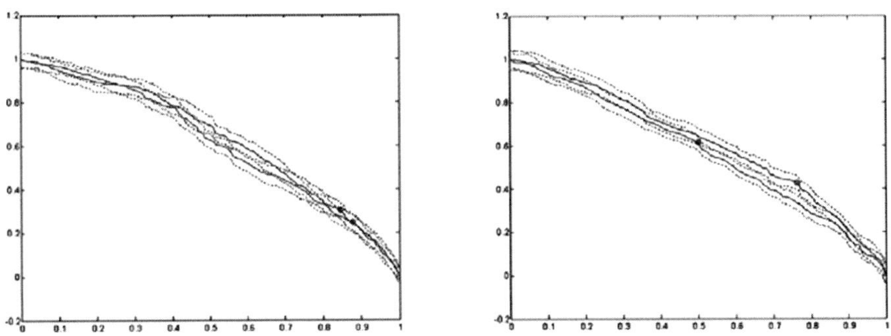

Figure 9.23. Comparative results of classification (predicting the conflict management outcome) with non-linear (MLP, top curve) and linear classifiers (lower curve) for the two data sets 1945-1989 (left) and 1990-2000 (right), in terms of ROC curves. Error bars depict standard deviation.

The performance results are depicted in the following table. Results from the naïve classifier (always predicting the class that has the higher number of cases) are also shown.

	1945-1989	1990-2000
MLP	61.5%	59.3%
linear	61.2%	56%
naive	57.4%	50.8%

This leads to the following interpretation:

- While the overall performance appears to be lower for the "after" period, compared to the naïve classification it is actually better. Given this observation, one can say that conflict management outcomes are slightly more predictable for the period 1990-2000.
- The difference between non-linear (MLP) and linear classifiers is bigger for the "after" period than for the "before" period. In fact, for the former the difference is statistically significant ($p < 0.05$), while for the latter it is not.

Figures 9.24 and 9.25 show the U-matrices and the corresponding attribute-wise maps for the two periods, respectively. Again, decisive differences can be observed, which can be interpreted the following way:

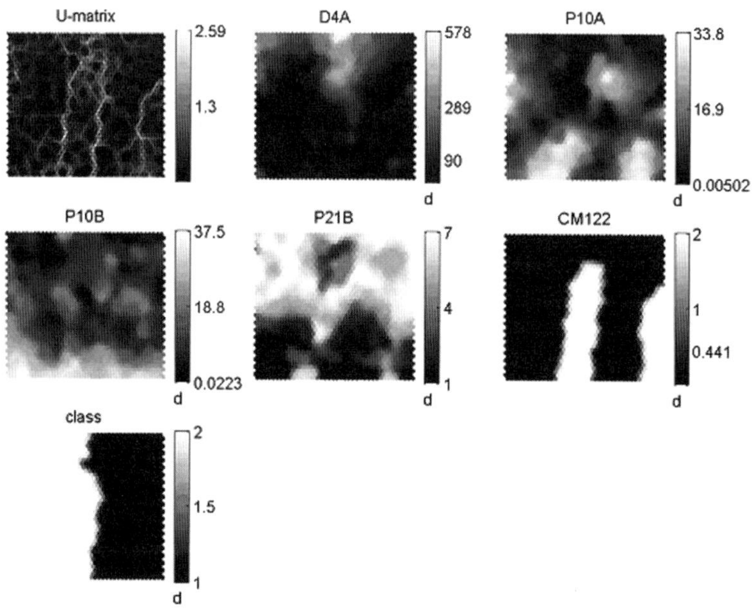

Figure 9.24. Overall and attribute-based U-matrices for the data set 1945-1989 ("before")

- While the maps for the "before" period have large similarity (topologically speaking) to the maps in the previous section, the visualization for the "after" period tends to show more fine-grained clusters. This means that in the period 1990-2000 there appear to be many more different types of conflicts and conflict management events.

- While long duration conflicts cluster together, as in the "before" period, medium duration events in the "after" period consist of several different types.
- Similarly, unsuccessful events seem to be of more different types in the "after" period than in the "before" period.
- Cases where mediation was initiated by both parties (CM122) appear more coherent in the "after" period than in the "before" period.
- The power of party A (P10a) appears to play a smaller role in forming clusters in the "after" period as compared to the "before" period.
- The political rights of party B (P21b) play a role in more clusters in the "after" period as compared to the "before" period.

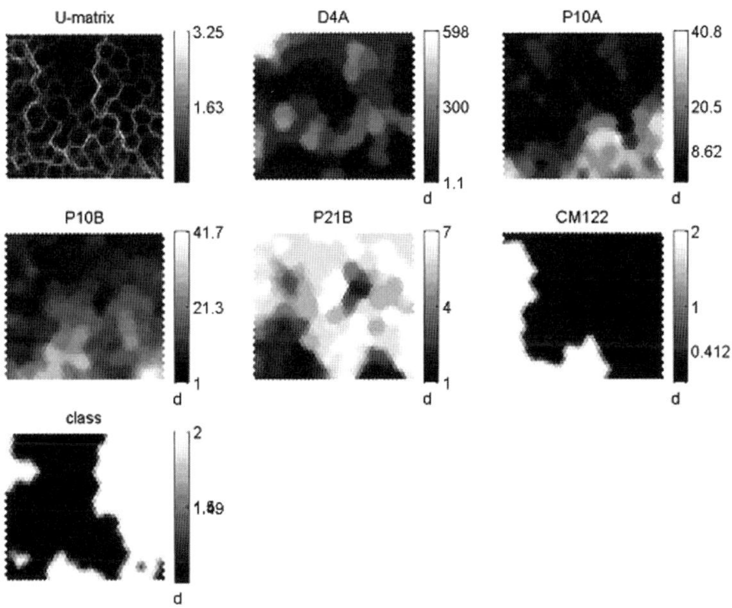

Figure 9.25. Overall and attribute-based U-matrices for the data set 1990-2000 ("after")

An even more interesting difference can be seen when depicting the distribution of actual cases in the maps. Figure 9.26. again depicts the map corresponding to the "before" period. The actual distribution of cases is depicted by dots of various sizes (black for cases in the "before" period, grey for cases in the "after" period). The size of the dots corresponds to the number of cases leading to the activation of the respective unit in the map (note that the SOM does not directly reflect the number of cases represented, since it tends to become more fine-grained in areas of large input density). Note also that cases from the "after" period become projected into the map built on cases from the "before" period. This way, cases become directly comparable. Figure 9.26. concentrates on unsuccessful events initiated by both parties (i.e. the conspicuous "peninsula" in the centre of the map).

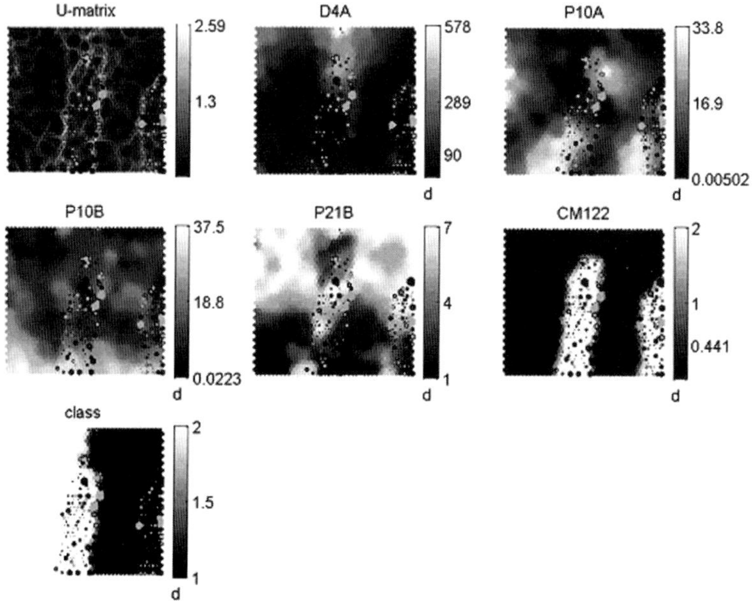

Figure 9.26. Clusters of cases "before" (black dots) and "after" (grey dots), superimposed over the overall and attribute-based U-matrices of the period 1945-1989 ("before").

After careful examination one important fact becomes visible: Large grey dots tend to lie in areas of higher political power of party A (map corresponding to P10a), as well as in areas of higher political power of party B (map corresponding to P10b). In other words, unsuccessful conflict management events in the period 1990-2000 are characterized by higher political power of either party involved, as compared to the period 1945-1989.

8 DISCUSSION

Overall, the results obtained can be interpreted in the following way:

- The predictability of conflict mediation outcome (dichotomous variable CM14a) is rather weak, i.e. hardly above 60%.
- However, predictability is significantly above chance, revealing some structure on the data.
- Non-linear classifiers from neural computation (MLPs) tend to slightly outperform linear classifiers; in some cases (see results on period 1990-2000) the difference is even statistically significant. Also, performance is slightly better than previously reported in literature.
- SOMs as a clustering and visualization technique prove to be a viable tool for navigation and exploration of the Confman database.
- Besides being able to help identify distinct clusters of cases with respect to certain attribute ranges, SOMs can help identify the most distinctive attributes in terms of clustering (e.g. CM122).
- There are significant differences in the data, when split into two subsets according to the date that marks the end of the cold war period (1945-1989 vs. 1990-2000).
- Conflict management outcome is slightly more predictable in the period 1990-2000 than in 1945-1989.
- Duration and political power of either power appears to play a more important role in the period 1990-2000, as compared to 1945-1989.
- SOMs might help identify subsets of cases with a higher predictability of conflict management outcome.

With respect to predictability of conflict management outcome, the overall ceiling is probably reached, unless more predictable subsets are identified. With respect to SOMs as a navigation and exploration tool, however, more investigations can be worthwhile, especially from the viewpoint of political scientists interpreting the visualizations.

9 SUMMARY

In the first part of this report we presented results on applying neural networks (in particular, multilayer perceptrons) to the task of predicting the mediation outcome based on features on each conflict event and mediation event. The actual comparison of the neural network with linear classifiers was preceded by

- a careful evaluation of the attributes in the database with respect to their suitability for the task, and their coding to be used in the neural net,
- the task of feature selection using machine learning methods
- and a determination of the optimal network parameters using an n-fold cross-validation

The results show a weak tendency of neural networks to improve classification performance, at least in some parts of the ROC curve. Depending on the desired sensitivity and specificity, this means that nonlinear methods seem to be able to extract slightly more information from the data. However, the difference does not appear to be statistically significant. What is significant, on the other hand, is the difference of both classifiers from the 45-degree line of a naïve classifier, pointing to the general fact that classification can indeed be performed better than at random.

The second part of the work was concerned with evaluation selforganizing maps as a clustering and visualization technique with respect to their ability to reveal useful structure in the data. It could be shown in several examples that this is indeed a viable method to investigate the data in-depth. Interesting and interpretable structure in the data was revealed.

The third part of the work was concerned with the investigation of differences in the data before and after the date that marks the end of the cold war period (1989/1990), using both methods from the first two parts. Indeed, significant differences could be discovered, both with respect to predictability of conflict management outcome and with respect to visible cluster structure.

In summary, tools from neural computation could be shown to be valuable tools for analyzing data from conflict management.

References

Bercovitch, J., and Houston, A., 1993, Influence of mediator characteristics and behavior on the success of mediation in international relations, *Journal of Conflict Resolution* **37**:297-321.

Bercovitch, J., and Langley, J., 1993, The nature of dispute and the effectiveness of international mediation, *Journal of Conflict Resolution* **37**:670-691.

Bercovitch, J., Anagnoson, J., and Wille, D. L., 1991, Some conceptual issues and empirical trends in the study of successful mediation in international relations, *Journal of Peace Research* **28**:7-17.

Bishop, C., 1995, *Neural Networks for Pattern Recognition*, Clarendon Press, Oxford.

Dorffner, G., 2000, *Neural networks in peace and conflict research: An overview of and proposals for possible uses*, Technical Report, Österreichisches Forschungsinstitut für Artificial Intelligence, Wien, TR-2000-03.

Duda, R., Hart, P., and Stork, D., 2000, *Pattern Classification*, 2nd ed., Wiley, New York

Fürnkranz, J., Petrak J., and Trappl, R., 1997, Knowledge discovery in international conflict databases, *Applied Artificial Intelligence* **11**:91-118.

Garson, G. D., 1998, *Neural Networks: An Introductory Guide for Social Scientists*, Sage, London.

Holmes, G., Donkin, A., and Witten, I. H., 1994, Weka: A machine learning workbench, In *Proceedings of the Second Australia and New Zealand Conference on Intelligent Information Systems*.

Kohonen, T., 1995, *Selforganizing Maps*, Springer, Berlin/New York.

Nabney , I., 2001, *NETLAB: Algorithms for Pattern Recognition*, Springer, New York.

Quinlan, R., 1993, *C4.5: Programs for Machine Learning*, Morgan Kaufmann, San Mateo, CA.

Schrodt, P. A., 1991, Prediction of interstate conflict outcomes using a neural network, *Social Science Computer Review* **9**:359-380.

Schrodt, P. A., 2000, Pattern recognition of international crises using Hidden Markov Models, in *Political Complexity: Nonlinear Models of Politics*, Richards, D., ed., University of Michigan Press, Ann Arbor, pp. 296-328.

Ultsch, A., 1991, *Connectionist Models and their Integration with Knowledge Based Systems*, Habilitationsschrift, Univ. Dortmund.

Vesanto, J., Himberg, J., Alhoniemi, E., and Parhankangas, J., 1999, Self-organizing map in Matlab: the SOM Toolbox, in *Proceedings of the Matlab DSP Conference 1999*, Espoo, Finland, November 16–17, pp. 35–40.

Wickboldt, A.-K., Bercovitch, J., 1996, Dynamics of international mediation: analysis using machine learning methods, *Conflict Management and Peace Science* **17**(1).

Witten, I. H., and Frank, E., 1999, *Data Mining: Practical Machine Learning Tools and Techniques with Java Implementations*, Morgan Kaufmann, San Mateo, CA.

ANNEX

The following contains a list of all attributes, for which a different coding scheme than in Confman was chosen. All other attributes used were coded according to the Confman coding sheet, or split as described in section 3.3.1.

P18a,b Leadership Change During the Dispute Party A, B

(1) Leadership Change (2) Unknown (3) No Leadership Change

Modification according to section 3.3.3. Recoding

D31a ETHNIC WAR

(0) Yes (1) No Applicable (2) No

Modification according to section 3.3.3. Recoding

D31b REVOLUTIONARY WAR

(0) Yes (1) No Applicable (2) No

Modification according to section 3.3.3. Recoding

D31c ABRUPT/DISRUPTIVE REGIME CHANGE

(0) Yes (1) No Applicable (2) No

Modification according to section 3.3.3. Recoding

D31d GENOCIDE/POLITICIDE

(0) Yes (1) No Applicable (2) No

Modification according to section 3.3.3. Recoding

D33 ETHNONATIONAL WAR

(0) Yes (1) No Applicable (2) No

Modification according to section 3.3.3. Recoding

CM8 NUMBER OF PREVIOUS MEDIATION/NEGOTIAION ATTEMPTS IN THIS DISPUTE

(0) 0 or No mediation/negotiation	(2) 3-4	(4) 7-8	(6) 11+
	(1) 1-2	(3) 5-6	(5) 9-10

Modification according to section 3.3.2. Combination of values

CM9 NUMBER OF PREVIOUS MEDIATION ATTEMPTS BY THIS MEDIATOR IN THE DISPUTE

(0) 0 or No mediation	(2) 2	(4) 4	(6) 6+
	(1) 1	(3) 3	(5) 5

Modification according to section 3.3.2. Combination of values

CM6 STRATEGIES - PRIMARY

Has been spitted:

CM6m coded with 1 if CM6 = (2), (3), (6) or (4) else 0 *There is a mediation strategy specified*

CM6c coded with 1 if CM6 = (2) else 0 *Communication-Facilitation*

CM6p coded with 1 if CM6 = (3) else 0 *Procedural*

CM6d coded with 1 if CM6 = (4) else 0 *Directive*

CM12 INITIATED BY

Request for conflict management initiated by

(0) No management	(2) Both parties	(4) Regional organisation
(1) One party	(3) Mediator/Third Party	(5) International organisation
(6) Unspecified		

CM12m coded with 1 if CM12 = (2) else 0 *Both parties*

CM12r coded with 1 if CM12 = (3), (4) or (5) else 0 *Regional organization Mediator/Third Party or International organisation*

The value (6) was overwritten by (0).

CM7 PREVIOUS PRELATIONSHIP OF THE PARTIES WITH THE MEDIATOR

CM7r. coded with 1 if CM7 = (2), (3), (4), (5) else 0 *Previous relationship*

CM73 coded with 1 if CM7 = (3) else 0

CM74 coded with 1 if CM7 = (4) else 0

Chapter 10

Modeling International Negotiation

Statistical and Machine Learning Approaches

Daniel Druckman
George Mason University, Fairfax, Virginia, U.S.A.

Richard Harris
RA Software, Chapel Hill, North Carolina, U.S.A.

Johannes Fürnkranz
Technical University Darmstadt, Germany

An earlier study by Druckman et al. (1999) showed that a variety of cases of international negotiation can be distinguished in terms of their objectives. A set of 16 features of negotiation effectively distinguished—by multidimensional scaling (MDS)—among the types of international negotiation objectives proposed by Iklé (1964). The features include aspects of the parties, issues, process, negotiating environment, and outcomes. The statistical analyses performed in that study showed a distinct profile for each of the Iklé categories: innovation, re-distribution, extension, normalization, and side effects. In addition, a sixth category was identified as being different than the others. This category was referred to as multilateral regime negotiations, a form that became prevalent twenty years after Iklés book appeared. These results were further supported by discriminant analysis classifications. When only information about the 16 features were known, 78 % (or 21 of 27 cases) were placed in the correct a priori category. These are impressive results. They provide empirical validation for this well-known typology of negotiation. In this chapter, an attempt is made to extend these analyses in several directions with the help of sophisticated methodological approaches not previously used to interpret data on negotiation.[1]

One direction concerns negotiation outcomes. Of particular interest in the negotiation literature are questions about the relative importance of different

1. These techniques have, however, been used to analyze a large number of historical cases of international mediation. Those cases focus primarily on various dimensions of the mediated interventions rather than on the negotiation process (Trappl et al., 1997).

R. Trappl (ed.), Programming for Peace, 227–250.

kinds of factors—such as relationships, issues, process, and the situation surrounding the talks—on the outcome. Each kind of factor has been shown to influence whether an agreement is achieved and the type of agreement as partial vs. comprehensive or as favoring one or another party (asymmetrical) vs. equal benefits (symmetrical). The question asked is which factor(s) is (are) the best predictors or discriminators of these outcomes? (For answers with laboratory studies see Druckman, 1993; 1994; for an application of these findings, see Druckman al., 2002). These questions are addressed here in the context of cases on international negotiation.

Another direction focuses on the Iklé categories. We want to know whether some features relate more strongly to (or provide better discriminations among) the various types of negotiation than others. Whereas previously we were interested in the profiles of characteristics (the largest set) that distinguish among the types, we are now interested in the smallest sub-set of those characteristics that accurately distinguishes among the Iklé categories. This entails a search for the particular features from the set of 16 that are the strongest discriminators. This is a search for the simplest model of negotiating objectives. It is conducted with the aid of both statistical and machine-learning approaches.

For both these directions—focus on outcomes and on negotiating objectives—we are interested in the extent to which the machine-learning approach adds value to the findings obtained with statistical methods. These approaches can be regarded as being similar in the sense that both model regularities in a dataset. But, there are also differences. Statistical approaches are based on assumptions about the distribution of data (e.g., parametric analyses assume normal distributions) while machine-learning approaches make few assumptions about the distributions. The borders between these approaches can, however, be fuzzy. In a recent paper, Breiman (2001) contrasts the algorithmic modeling of the machine-learning approach to the data-modeling culture of the statistical community. Many machine-learning algorithms are treated in the statistical literature, including decision or classification trees (Breiman et al., 1984; Quinlan, 1986) and inductive rule learning (Fürnkranz, 1999; Friedman and Fisher, 1999). In this chapter, we compare statistical findings, primarily correlational analyses, with two types of machine-learning approaches, decision trees and rule learning. Of interest is the extent to which the findings converge or are mutually reinforcing. As well, we are interested in diverging findings which may be either contradictory or complementary in the sense of added knowledge about the dataset. We return to this issue in the discussion section.

The analyses are conducted on a dataset of 42 cases. In the earlier study, we performed analyses on 30 cases, categorized initially into the five Iklé categories. These cases are listed in Table 1 of Druckman et al. (1999). The additional twelve cases used in these analyses were drawn from the Pew Case Studies in International Affairs and are shown by category in Table 10.1. below. As in the earlier study, each case was coded in terms of the 16 features —concerning parties, issues, timing, process, environment, and outcomes— described in Druckman et al. (1999: Table 2). In addition, the cases were coded into the appropriate Iklé category, resulting in a data matrix of 42 cases by 17 negotiation categories. This matrix was analyzed by both statistical and inductive machine learning methods. Many of the statistical analyses were presented in the earlier article. These results are summarized and extended with new analyses of the 42 cases before launching into a discussion of the machine-learning procedures and outputs.

Table 10.1. Additional Cases Categorized by Negotiation Type[2]

Normalization negotiation	
435-93-R[3]	Making Peace with Germany, 1918: The Pre-Armistice Negotiations (by Robert Randle)
Innovative negotiations	
105-92-R	The United States and Anastasio Somoza: Dealing with Friendly Dictators Who Are Losing Their Authority (by Douglas A. Chalmers)
208-93-R	Renegotiating International Debt: The Young Plan Conference of 1929 (by William C. McNeil)
462-94-N	The Clinton Administration and Multilateral Peace Operations (by Ivo H. Daalder)
454-93-N	Debt-for-Nature Swaps: Win-Win Solution or Environmental Imperialism? (by Vicki Golich and Terry Forrest Young)
Redistribution negotiation	
147-93-R	U.S.-E.C. Trade negotiations on the accession of Spain and Portugal (by Bradley B. Billings)
153-93-N	Shifting Winds and Strong Currents: George Bush Charts a Trade-Policy Approach to Japan (by Michael J. Fratantuono)

2. See Druckman et al. (1999: Table 1) for a listing of the other 30 cases categorized by negotiation type.

3. Number of the case in the 1999 ISD Compendium of Case Study Abstracts and Indexes, Pew Case Studies in International Affairs

Extension negotiations

365-94-N	Pakistan in the Bush Years: Foreign Aid and Foreign Influence (by Terry L. Deibel)
201-93-R	The 1982 Mexican Debt Negotiations (by Roger S. Leeds and Gale Thompson)

Regime negotiations

210-95-N	Money and Politics: The Iranian Asset Freeze (by Karin Lissakers)
327-88-O	The United States and Nicaragua: Anatomy of a Failed Negotiation for Regime Change, 1977-79 (by Alex Roberto Hybel)
443-92-R	The United States and South Africa: The 1985 Sanctions Debate (by Gregory F. Treverton and Pamela Varley)

1 STATISTICAL ANALYSES

As noted above, the results reported in Druckman et al. (1999) showed that the 30 cases were distinguished in terms of the Iklé categories. A variety of statistical analyses were performed, each demonstrating distinct empirical categories: Significance tests calculated on the coordinates produced by the MDS analysis showed strong differences between innovation and regime cases, innovation and normalization cases, redistribution and normalization cases, and innovation and redistribution cases. A cluster analysis revealed that innovation cases are quite distinct from re-distribution cases while regime and normalization cases are generally similar. And, discriminant analyses produced strong classification results indicating that more than three quarters of the cases are correctly classified based only on information about their 16 features. From these statistical findings, an attempt was made to develop profiles for each of the categories. For example, contrasting profiles were obtained for innovation (few parties and issues, bargaining processes leading to integrative or impasse outcomes, moderate media coverage) and regime talks (many parties, many issues, mixed processes, compromise outcomes, no media coverage).

Further correlational analyses on the extended dataset highlight the sub-set of variables that show significant relationships with the Iklé types (a categorical variable). Kendall's tau is the appropriate measure of association for this data. Significant correlations were obtained for four variables: type of relationship among the parties (.37), delegation status (.37), intra-party disagreement (.28), and changes in the political context (.30). (Kendall produces smaller correlations than other measures of association—Pearson, Spearman, Gamma—which are based on more stringent scaling requirements. A Pearson correlation of .30 is needed for significance with 40 df at the .05 level.) The cross-tabulations between the Iklé types and each of these variables reveal contrasting patterns of the four variables for the innovation and normalization categories. The innovation pattern is as follows:

- friendly relationships among the parties
- asymmetrical status among the delegations (one delegation sends higher-status delegates to the talks than the other)
- occur in generally stable political contexts, and
- symmetrical disagreements within the delegations (the delegations have generally the same amount of disagreement among their members)

The normalization pattern is as follows:

- unfriendly relationships among the parties
- symmetrical high status among the delegations
- occur in generally unstable political contexts, and
- asymmetrical disagreements within the delegations.

Thus, the significant variables impacted most clearly on these two types of negotiation. Not surprisingly, the earlier analysis showed that more breakdowns occurred in the normalization talks than in the innovation cases. These results are compared below to those obtained from the machine-learning analyses.

Five significant correlations were obtained with type of agreement (comprehensive, partial, no agreements) in the analyses reported in Druckman et al. (1999): number of parties (.40), relative power (.37), length of relationship (.36), type of relationship (.36), and number of issues (.35). (A Pearson correlation of .36 is needed for significance at the .05 level with 28 df.) When the cases were increased to 42, some of these correlations were stronger while others were weaker (A correlation of .30 is needed for significance with 40 df.) . Stronger correlations occurred with length of relationship (.42), number of issues (.44), and delegation status (from .26 to .32). The same correlation emerged with type of relationship (.36) and weaker correlations were found for number of parties (.23) and relative power (.22). More comprehensive agreements occurred for shorter-term and friendly relationships as well as when many issues were negotiated among high status delegations. Apparently, few issues were more difficult to resolve (among friendly parties) than many issues. Further insights into the way these variables operate with respect to agreements are generated from the decision-tree analysis presented in the next section.

It is interesting to note as well that two significant correlations were found with type of outcome: length of relationship (.46) and number of issues (.34). (Neither was significant in the earlier analysis of 30 cases.) More symmetrical, compromise agreements occurred in short-term relationships with many issues on the table. The Iklé categories did not correlate significantly with either of these outcome measures.

2 DECISION TREES

The induction of decision trees is one of the oldest and most popular techniques for learning discriminatory models, which has been developed independently in the statistical (Breiman et al., 1984) and machine-learning (Quinlan, 1986) communities. A decision tree is a hierarchical model that successively divides the example space into smaller and smaller regions that can be tackled by a constant predictor. Typically, the program selects the most discriminative attribute for the root of the tree, and splits the set of examples into disjoint sets, one for each outcome of the chosen test. This attribute is then turned into a *node* of the decision tree, and a *branch* is added for each possible outcome of the tree. Then, this procedure is repeated for each of the new subsets of the dataset, as long as splitting the data seems to be advisable. In the simplest case, the dataset is successively partitioned into smaller datasets until each set only contains examples of the same class. This class is then used for labeling a *leaf* of the tree. One can always find a tree that perfectly reproduces the classification of the original data unless they contain contradictory examples, i.e., examples with the same feature values but different class values.

The crucial step in decision tree induction is the choice of an adequate attribute for making the split. The attribute selection criterion that is most commonly used in decision tree induction algorithms is *information gain*. It measures the amount of information that can be gained about the class membership of the case examples by splitting the cases using attribute x_i. The formula for choosing the most promising attribute x_i is

$$x_r = \arg\max_i \left[-\sum_c p(c) \log p(c) + \sum_v p(x_i = v) \sum_c p(c \mid x_i = v) \log p(c \mid x_i = v) \right]$$

where c iterates over all class values and v iterates over all possible values of the attribute x_i. The first term measures the information content of the class distribution in the current set. From this term, the second term is subtracted (note that the sums are negative), which measures the weighted average of the information contents of the sets that result from splitting using attribute x_i. Maximising this difference results in the choice of the attribute which reduces the heterogeneity in the class distributions in the successor nodes the most. This enforces a fast convergence towards nodes where the majority of the examples belong to the same class. Of course, this "greedy" procedure will only find locally optimal choices for the attribute.

As discussed above, decision trees can be refined until the classification of all cases is 100 % correct. This, however, results in *over-fitting* of the data. The situation is quite comparable to fitting a curve to a number of points: The points can be fitted arbitrarily well if a polynom of an arbitrarily high degree can be used. Restricting the degree of the polynom results in models that have a worse fit on the data points, but will typically be better in capturing the inherent trend. These models will thus be better in making predictions for new, unseen points. This is similar also to the distinction made in anthropology and linguistics between emic and etic approaches (Headland et al., 1990). The former focuses on the details of particular cases in order to capture context. The latter compares many cases for general trends. The information requirements for these approaches are different: Emic approaches require immersion in the culture or case in order to produce a refined interpretation, which can lead to "over-fitting" the data; etic approaches require the collection of limited comparable data from many cases in order to "capture the inherent trend."

For a decision tree, the complexity of the model can be roughly measured with the number of leaves in the tree. Thus, state-of-the-art decision tree induction techniques employ a post-processing phase in which the learned tree is simplified by *pruning* branches and nodes near the leaves. In effect, this procedure replaces some of the interior nodes of the tree with a new leaf, thereby removing the sub-tree that was rooted at this node. The exact details of this procedure are beyond the scope of this paper, but it is important to note that the leaf nodes of the new tree are no longer *pure* nodes, i.e., they no longer contain cases that all belong to the same class. Typically, this is simply resolved by predicting the most frequent class at a leaf.

A decision tree can be used for classifying new cases by starting at the top node—the *root*—and the example follows the branch that corresponds to the outcome of the associated test, arriving at a new node with a new attribute. This process is repeated until we arrive at a leaf that predicts the class for the example.

2.1 Quality of trees

We have noted above that tree-based models can be made arbitrarily complex, and are therefore able to fit the data arbitrarily well. Thus, a simple resubstitution estimate, which computes how many of the existing cases are classified correctly by the tree, is typically not a good indicator for the quality of a tree. What we would like to know is how well the tree is able to predict the quality of unseen cases. A simple way for doing this is to hold out part of the data, construct the tree on the remaining data, and test its performance on the held-out part of the data. However, when only few cases are available, one typically resorts to leave-one-out cross-validation (see Stone, 1974; 1977; Kohavi, 1995). This means that n experiments are performed, and in each experiment (each *fold*), one example is held out and a model is fitted to the remaining n-1 examples. This model is then tested on the withheld example. This is repeated n times, each time holding out a different example. The total number of misclassified hold-out examples is then used as an estimate for the predictive accuracy of the tree that is grown from the full dataset of n examples. (This is similar to discriminant-function analysis; see Druckman et al., 1982, for an application of classification equations to new cases.)

It is important to note that often a different model will be estimated on each fold. Thus, the estimated average accuracy will be different than the accuracy resulting from testing a model that is learned on the same entire dataset, and typically more realistic.

In the discussion to follow, we will present two performance numbers: One is the estimate computed by re-applying the fitted model to the same data used for fitting the model (referred to as classification accuracy); the other estimate is the average performance of n models, each one fitted to n-1 data-points and applied to the nth data-point (referred to as predictive accuracy).

3 PREDICTING THE IKLÉ TYPOLOGY

Following the general approach used by Druckman et al. (1999), we employed induction of decision trees for learning a descriptive discriminator between the different types in Iklé's typology of negotiating objectives. We used the J48 implementation of the C4.5 algorithm (Quinlan, 1993) that is available within the Weka open source data mining library[4] (Witten and Frank, 2000).

4. Weka is freely available from http://www.cs.waikato.ac.nz/~ml/weka.

As noted above, the dataset we used contained 42 cases, 12 more than used in the earlier study. All 16 characteristics were used as possible descriptors for a categorization of the cases into the Iklé typology. One of the examples had a classification that did not follow the typology, so we ignored this example. Because of the small size of the dataset, predictive accuracy could be estimated using leave-one-out cross-validation.

An effort for generating a decision tree that perfectly discriminates all cases in the dataset results in a tree with 24 leaf nodes. Thus, on average, each leaf node describes less than two of the 41 cases in the dataset, which shows that the found patterns are hardly statistically significant. Consequently, the leave-one-out cross-validation estimate of the predictive performance of this tree is only 39.02 %, which is not much more than the 29.27 % accuracy that is achieved by the simple classifiers that always predict *re-distribution*, the most frequent type in the typology, occurring in 12 of the 41 cases.

Specifying that a node is no longer refined if it contains only two or less examples results in a tree that has only 13 leaf nodes, but only classifies 82.93 % of the training examples correctly. An estimate of its performance on unseen cases results is 48.78 %. Using pruning,[5] the tree can be reduced to a manageable tree with six leaf nodes (four of the Iklé types, two repeated). This tree is shown in Figure 10.1. Each leaf shows the number of examples that end up in this node, both the correct classifications (the first number indicating those that are of the type with which the leaf is labelled), and the incorrect classifications (the second of the two numbers).

The most important factor (root of the tree) for discrimination is the relationship between parties, in particular whether they are unfriendly or not (friendly and neutral). The second most significant factor is, in both successor branches, the delegation status. These two factors alone characterize several diverse groups. Situations with friendly or neutral relationships and a delegation status that is low or asymmetric occur five times in the data base, all five times with type *innovation*. Unfriendly relationships and a delegation status that is not high occur two times, both with type *re-distribution*. Unfriendly relationships with a delegation status *high* occur eleven times, in a clear majority of the cases (seven) with type *normalization*. The group of examples with a friendly or neutral relationship and a medium and high delegation status is more diverse. The majority of the cases are of type *re-distribution*, but subgroups that are mostly of type *innovation* and *multilateral regime* can be characterized using the length of the relationship and the breakdowns in negotiation. Further refinements are not very productive. For example, the two exceptions in the *multilateral regime* node are of type *innovation*. However,

5. J 48's pruning parameter -C was set to 0.01.

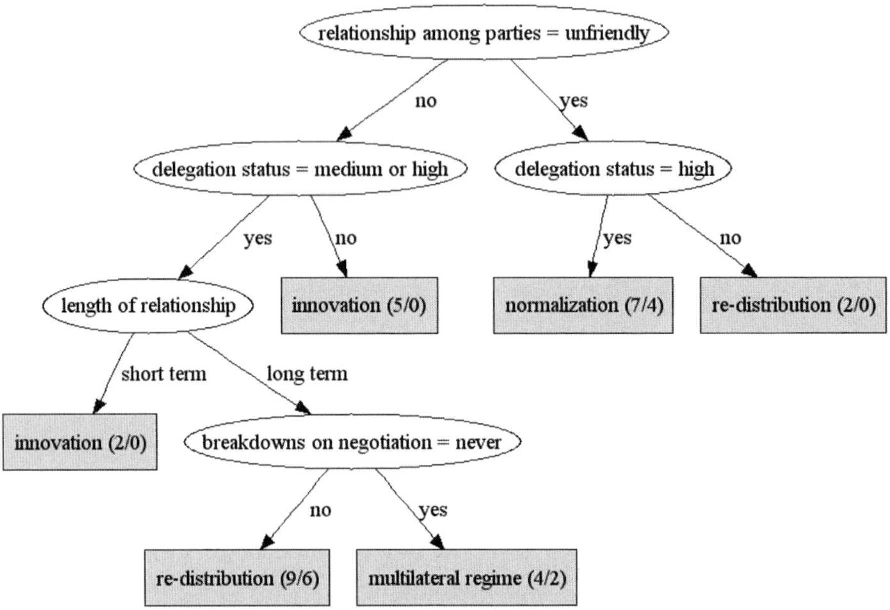

Figure 10.1. Decision tree for predicting the Iklé typology

they cannot be characterized with a single additional test. The best test, based on the number of issues, captures both cases, but also one additional *multilateral regime* case.

It is interesting to observe that the type *extension* is not at all used in the decision trees, which indicates that this type is particularly hard to characterize with the sixteen variables in the dataset. This may be due to the small number of cases in this category (n = 4).

Table 10.2. Confusion matrix for predicting Iklé type

	predicted type				
true type	*i*	*r*	*m*	*n*	*e*
innovation	7/5	2/2	1/3	0/0	0/0
redistribution	0/0	11/9	0/0	1/3	0/0
multilateral regime	0/0	1/2	4/3	2/2	0/0
normalization	0/0	0/0	0/2	7/5	0/0
extension	0/0	3/3	1/1	1/1	0/0

In total, this tree provides a correct classification for 29 and misclassifies 12 cases, most of which are cases that are mistaken as *normalization* and *re-*

distribution. This results in a dataset accuracy of 70.73 %. The estimated predictive accuracy of this model is considerably lower, namely 53.03 %, but it is much better than those of the other two, more complex models. Table 10.2. shows a matrix that illustrates which groups tend to be confused with each other: For example, of the 10 innovation cases, the tree classifies seven as innovation, two as redistribution, and one as multilateral regime. In the leave-one-out cross-validation procedure, only five of the cases were recognized as innovation, two as redistribution, and three as multilateral regime. If the learned tree (predictor) were entirely accurate, there would only be entries along the diagonal; in other words, there would be no confusion. It can be seen that redistribution cases are predicted quite accurately with only one misclassification as normalization; three are misclassified as normalization for the leave-one-out procedure. The normalization cases are also accurately predicted with only two misclassifications for the leave-one-out procedure.

Table 10.3. Performance summary of trees investigated

Model	*Number of leaves*	*Classification accuracy*	*Predictive accuracy*
unpruned tree	24	100.00 %	39.02 %
reduced splitting	13	82.93 %	48.78 %
pruning	6	70.73 %	53.66 %

Table 10.3. shows a brief summary of the results obtained with trees of various sizes (2nd column). Both the classification (3rd column) and predictive accuracies (4th column) are shown. The first row shows an unpruned tree that perfectly fits the data, the second a tree that prevented splitting of nodes with two or fewer examples, and the third row a pruned version of this tree. The results exhibit a typical pattern: simpler models provide less fit on the original data, but their estimated predicted accuracy is better, i.e., they are more likely to provide a correct characterization for new instances that have not been part of the original dataset. For comparison, Druckman et al. (1999) reported two discriminative models, one using all features, which obtained a perfect fit on the training data, and one using an average value for each of six groups of variables, which obtained a training accuracy of 78 %. No estimates of out-of-sample accuracy were given in that article. (See the earlier discussion of the distinction between context-specific [emic] and generalizable [etic] approaches to analysis.)

4 PREDICTING TYPE OF OUTCOME AND AGREEMENTS

Our next experiment aimed at evaluating whether it is possible to predict the outcome of the negotiation. Possible outcomes are symmetric benefits (14 cases), asymmetric benefits (8 cases), enlarged joint benefit (9 cases), impasse (6 cases), and mixed (5 cases). As independent variables we used all of the variables except the one that encodes the reached agreement, which carries information that is not known at the time where we want to predict the outcome.

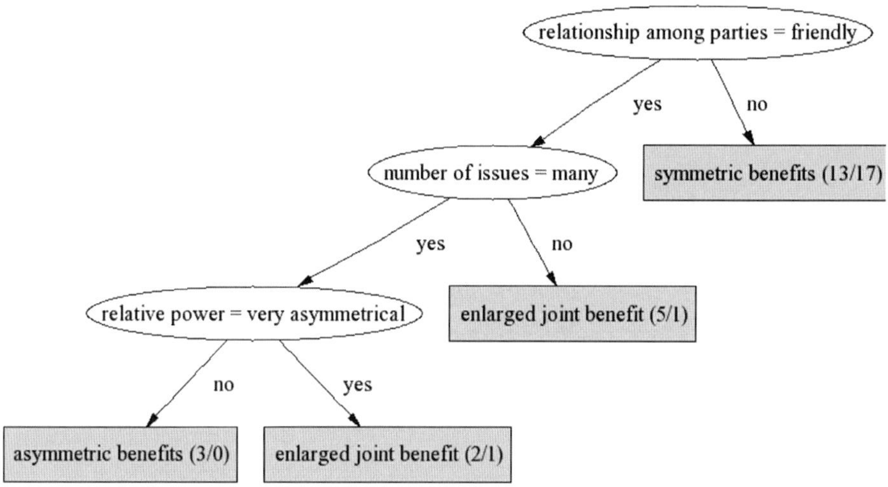

Figure 10.2. Decision Tree for predicting the type of outcome

Figure 10.2. shows the tree resulting for a pruning parameter -C 0.1. The tree has an accuracy on the dataset of 54.76 %, but only a 33.33 % accuracy (estimated again with leave-one-out cross-validation), which corresponds to 14 correctly classified test cases. This is exactly the same as the simple classifier that always predicts the majority class (symmetric benefits, in our case), classifying the 14 cases (33.33 %) correctly.

The problem is apparent when we look at the branch with unfriendly relationship among parties. Among the 30 cases that have this property, the most frequent outcome is symmetric benefits, which appears in 13 cases. However, 17 cases have one of the other outcomes. The learning algorithm was not able to detect properties that provide a significant discrimination between the different cases for this large group. As a consequence, this node alone (which classifies 30 of the 42 examples) produces an error rate that is above 50 %. If we force the algorithm to further discriminate between cases in this class (e.g., by lowering the pruning parameter to its default value -C 0.25), the algorithm adds a complex tree structure that involves the length of the relationship, whether there were breakdowns on negotiations, and the types of issues, but the estimated predictive accuracy of this tree falls even below 33 %. Thus, we may conclude that it is not possible to predict the outcome of the negotiation based on the variables coded in the input, at least not with decision tree methods.

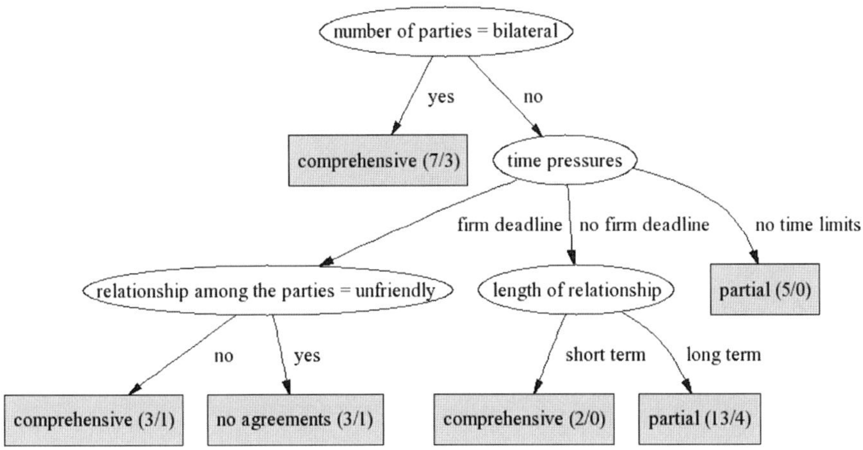

Figure 10.3. Decision Tree for predicting the reached agreements

Using a similar procedure, we also tried to predict the agreement reached, which can be comprehensive (15 cases), partial (22 cases), or no agreements (5 cases). Input variables were all variables except type of outcome. The resulting tree, shown in Figure 10.3., correctly classifies all but 9 of the examples in the training set (78 %). Its estimate for predictive accuracy is somewhat uncertain, because this tree is consistently learned across a wide range of pruning parameters (including -C 0.1 and -C 0.25). However, this stability does not hold for the dataset and test splits that are used for estimating the predictive accuracy in the leave-one-out cross-validation. As a result, the accuracy estimate for -C 0.1 is only 50 % (i.e., approximately the default accuracy), whereas for -C 0.25 it increases to 61.90 %.

Despite this uncertainty, it seems safe to conclude that it is easier to predict the reached agreements than the type of outcome, presumably because the number of possible agreements is smaller than the number of possible outcomes. This means that there are more case examples available for each class.

5 RULE LEARNING

Decision trees may also be interpreted as sets of rules, where each possible path through the tree, starting from the root and ending in one of the leaves, corresponds to a single rule. For example, the decision tree in Figure 10.3. can be re-written as a rule set in the following way:

if number of parties = bilateral
then comprehensive (7/3)

if number of parties ≠ bilateral
& time pressure = firm deadline
& relationship among the parties ≠ unfriendly
then comprehensive (3/1)

if number of parties ≠ bilateral
& time pressure = firm deadline
& relationship among the parties = unfriendly
then no agreements (3/1)

if number of parties ≠ bilateral
& time pressure = no firm deadline
& length of relationship = short term
then comprehensive (2/0)

if number of parties ≠ bilateral
& time pressure = no firm deadline
& length of relationship = long term
then partial (13/4)

if number of parties ≠ bilateral
& time pressure = no time limits
then partial (5/0)

It should be noted that the rules have a very rigid structure. For example, all rules have to start with a condition regarding the number of parties. The reason for this is that decision trees partition the space of examples so that each example is covered by *exactly* one rule.

If one relaxes this constraint and allows for the learning of rules that *overlap* (i.e., allow that a case is covered by more than one rule), very often simpler rules can be found. When this happens, mechanisms for tie breaking (i.e., which rule to choose when more than one covers the given case) and default classifications (what classification to choose when no rule covers the given case) are needed. Typically, one prefers rules with a higher ratio of correctly classified examples from the dataset.

It is beyond the scope of this paper to provide a detailed description of algorithms that learn such rule sets. However, the underlying ideas are quite similar to the ideas used in decision tree induction. The key idea in rule learning is that, instead of successively splitting the data into regions with increasingly uniform class distributions (in the literature, this strategy is also known as *divide-and-conquer* learning), rule learning algorithms immediately try to focus on regions in which a certain class prevails. This is done by learning a single rule first, removing all cases that are covered by this rule from the dataset, and repeating this procedure with the remaining examples (this strategy is also known as *separate-and-conquer* learning). Each rule is learned by picking the best condition (i.e., the test for the presence of a single factor value that identifies the subset of cases with the most uniform class distribution) and adding it to the rule until the conjunction of all conditions in the rule covers only cases from a single class. Again, pruning is a good idea for rule learning, which means that the rules only need to cover cases that are *mostly* from the same class. It turned out to be advantageous to prune rules immediately after they have been learned or before successive rules are learned (Fürnkranz, 1997). For a detailed survey of rule learning algorithms we refer the reader to Fürnkranz (1999).

Below, we show a rule set that has been generated with the state-of-the-art Ripper rule learning algorithm[6] (Cohen, 1995).

if number of parties = bilateral
then comprehensive (7/3)

if negotiation process = mixed
& number of issues = few
then partial (6/0)

if number of parties = large
& significant intra-party disagreement = symmetrical
then partial (5/0)

if time pressures = no time limit
then partial (5/1)

if relationship among the parties = unfriendly
& time pressures = firm deadline
then no agreements (3/1)

else comprehensive (7/9)

This rule set has a dataset accuracy of 71.43 %, and an estimated predictive accuracy of 59.52 %, which is approximately the same as the accuracy

6. Ripper is available from its author at http://www.cs.cmu.edu/~wcohen/.

that was estimated for the decision tree in Figure 10.3. In general, the rule set learned by Ripper is somewhat smaller than the set learned for the decision tree, which illustrates that a relaxation of the constraint for non-overlapping rules leads to simpler and more comprehensible theories. Nevertheless, some rules of the decision tree reappear in the same or a similar form, in particular the first rule regarding comprehensive agreements. In some cases, the differences are enlightening. For example, the rule regarding "no agreements" covers the same examples in both theories. However, the rule learner, not being restricted to non-overlapping rules, omits the test on the number of parties in formulating the rule. Apparently, this test is not necessary for a good discrimination, and was only added because it was needed at the top node of the decision tree for discriminating comprehensive agreements from all others based on the number of parties.

It is also interesting to observe that the algorithm found three very diverse rules for recognizing partial agreements, all but one of them being pure (i.e., covering only cases of that class in the dataset). The last of these rules, the only one that covers a single exception, is again a variant of a rule in the decision tree. Here, the addition of the condition on the number of parties, which is the top node in the decision tree, would exclude this single exception as can be seen from the decision tree. However, the relation was not estimated to be significant enough, so this condition was dropped as well.

One should also note that the sum of covered cases is 47. This means that 5 cases are covered by more than one rule. Moreover, 16 cases are not covered by any of the found rules. For these cases, the algorithm could not find any rule of significance and decided that the best thing to do is to assign all of them to the largest class among them, which is "comprehensive" (7 of the 16 cases).

6 ASSOCIATION RULES

The results in the previous section illustrate that parts of the dataset may be explained with interesting rules (e.g., the rules on partial agreements), while other parts seem to be hard to explain (e.g., the 16 cases that remained unclassified). Thus, it might be of interest to look for *local* patterns which describe relations that only hold for part of the data instances, instead of a global model for all of the data.

Association rules are the predominant technique for the discovery of local patterns that hold between the values of the variables in a database. They may be regarded as a generalization of pair-wise correlation tables, which uncover associations between pairs of variables (see Druckman et al., 1999, Table 5).

Association rules generalize this by analyzing the correlations between groups or conjunctions of variables.

Like other rules, association rules consist of a condition part, also called the *left-hand side (LHS)* of the rule, and a conclusion part, also called the *right-hand side (RHS)* of the rule. Typically, the quality of an association rule is characterized with two measures:

> **support:** The support of a rule is the number of cases that satisfy both the condition and the conclusion of a rule. This is a simple measure for the amount of evidence that backs up the rule.
>
> **confidence:** The confidence of a rule is the fraction of cases that satisfy the conclusion of the rule among those cases that satisfy the condition of the rule. This is a measure for the strength of the observed relationship. A rule with confidence 1.0 is always valid on the dataset.

The first rule of the previous section, covering 7 examples with comprehensive agreements and 3 examples with other agreements, has a support of 7 and a confidence of $7/(7+3) = 0.7$.

For a survey of commonly used association rule discovery algorithms we refer to Hipp et al. (2000). All of these algorithms implement an exhaustive search that finds *all* rules that have support and confidence values above a certain threshold. This complete search is performed in an efficient way, so that not all candidates have to be evaluated. The prototypical algorithm for such a search is the a priori algorithm (Agrawal et al., 1995), which is designed for efficient search of database systems. We employed an algorithm called MagnumOpus[7] (Webb, 2000), which is more flexible but only applicable to databases that are small enough to entirely fit into the main memory.

In principle all possible rules are tried out, which results in a large number of rules that satisfy the constraints, even for a small database like the one we are dealing with. In particular, often many variants of the same rule are found. For example, adding an irrelevant condition to an interesting rule will not change its coverage. Thus, the new extended rule will cover the same number of cases—and therefore have the same support and confidence values—but it will do so using one additional condition, which is not backed up by evidence. We have seen an example of this in the previous section when we compared the rule for "no agreement" found by the decision tree algorithm to that found by the rule learning algorithm. To deal with such cases, MagnumOpus has an option that filters rules that do not provide a significant improvement over

7. A demonstration version of MagnumOpus is available from http://www.rulequest.com/MagnumOpus-info.html.

their predecessor. Significance is evaluated with a binomial test at the .05 level.

We applied the algorithm for finding local patterns regarding the agreements and the type of outcome. We used a minimum support of 2, a minimum confidence of .5, and the significance filter with significance level at .05.

6.1 Agreements

For agreements, we only found two of the previously observed rules.

if number of parties = bilateral
then comprehensive (7/3)

if relationship among the parties = unfriendly
& time pressure = firm deadline
then no agreements (3/1)

6.2 Type of outcome

For outcome type, the following rules were found:

if relationship among parties = friendly
then enlarged joint benefit (7/5)

if relationship among the parties = unfriendly
& breakdowns on negotiations ≠ frequent
then asymmetric benefits (4/1)

if number of issues ≠ few
& time pressure = no firm deadline
& changes in political context = no
then symmetric benefits (4/0)

if number of parties = bilateral
& negotiation process primarily = mixed
then asymmetric benefits (3/0)

if relationship among the parties = unfriendly
& breakdowns on negotiations ≠ infrequent or less intense
then asymmetric benefits (3/0)

if relationship among the parties ≠ unfriendly
& breakdowns on negotiation = frequent or intense
& changes in political context = yes
then asymmetric benefits (3/1)

if significant intra party disagreement = asymmetrical
& length of negotiations < months
& negotiation process primarily = mixed
then symmetric benefits (3/0)

if relationship among the parties ≠ unfriendly
& types of issues = trade / economic
& breakdowns in negotiation = infrequent or less intense
& changes in political context = yes
then symmetric benefits (3/0)

if relationship among the parties ≠ unfriendly
& length of negotiations < weeks
& breakdowns in negotiation = frequent or intense
& exposure to mass media = high
then asymmetric benefits (2/0)

Unlike the rules for agreements, type of outcome provides a complex set of rules or fit that does not lend itself to an easy interpretation. We can, however, observe a few rules that highlight an unfriendly relationship among parties, which were summarized in a single node in the tree of Figure 10.2. On the other hand, there are also rules that use very different characterizations of some of the cases, such as the second rule for predicting symmetric benefits.[8]

7 DISCUSSION

The earlier statistical findings showing distinct profiles for the Iklé types of negotiation (Druckman et al., 1999) are reinforced by the results from the machine learning (ML) analyses reported in this chapter. Going beyond the earlier analyses, the ML results highlight particular variables from the set of 16 features of negotiation that impact on one or another type of negotiation. They also illuminate contingent effects of two or more variables on a type of negotiation: Normalization and re-distribution talks are characterized by unfriendly relationships and high delegation status; in contrast, innovation talks are likely to occur between friendly parties representing somewhat lower-status delegations. It is also the case that innovation talks are "predicted" from the conjunction of friendly parties, low or asymmetrical delegation status, and short-term relationships. A more complex set of contin-

8. The predictive validity of individual association rules cannot be tested as easily as the validity of complete theories. The question whether the local patterns observed in this dataset are generalizable remains to be judged.

gencies occur for multilateral regime negotiations: friendly relations, medium delegation status, long-term (friendly) relationships, and no breakdowns. Of particular interest are the dominant role of relationships and the distinction between innovation and normalization negotiations.

Relationship is a distinguishing feature between innovative and normalization talks in both the statistical and decision-tree analyses. It is also associated directly – rather than contingent on another variable—with symmetric benefits in the decision-tree analysis on type of outcome. Taken together, these analyses present a larger picture of what may be happening in many of these cases of international negotiation.

It is not surprising that normalization talks would be conducted between adversaries; after all, these talks are intended to end hostilities or to bring about a cease fire. Nor is it surprising that innovation talks are conducted between friends. Good relationships help to promote the trust that is needed to engage in problem solving leading to new, innovative solutions. What is less apparent, however, is that the impact of relationships on these types of negotiation depends (at least in part) on the status of the delegations and, to some extent for innovation talks, on the length of the relationship. An implication of this finding is that innovation talks may depend for their success on good relations among lower-status delegations. Further, enlarged joint benefits, a goal of innovation talks, is more likely to occur between friendly parties who discuss few issues (see Figure 10.2.). (It is noted that for the innovation cases that achieved enlarged benefits, friendly parties addressed only a few issues.) A typical outcome for the innovation cases is an integrative agreement (enlarged benefits) or an impasse. For normalization, either impasses or compromises (symmetrical benefits) typically occurred (see Druckman et al., 1999: Table 4). Relationship may be the key to these outcomes. It sets in motion processes that can lead to satisfying or unsatisfying outcomes. The decision-tree analyses show that these "processes" may depend also on a few other features of the negotiation (delegation status, length of relationship, number of issues). What remains to be learned is how these processes unfold. Some insights on this come from the experimental literature.

Experiments have shown that friends negotiate in a different way than non-friends, who may be strangers or adversaries. These findings show that friends are willing to make concessions rapidly in order to get an agreement (e.g., Halpern, 1994). However, if their expectations for the other's behavior are disappointed (e.g., a failure to reciprocate concessions) they toughen their stance, leading to impasses (e.g., Druckman and Bonoma, 1976). A key implication of these findings turns on the role of perceived trust: When it is high, friends reach agreements quickly; when it is low, impasse results with the attendant ramifications for the relationship. This may explain the split between impasse and integrative outcomes for the innovation cases. The impasses may have followed a loss of trust between the friendly parties. The integrative outcomes may have occurred because the friendly parties trusted each other to engage in an exchange of information needed to obtain those outcomes. Further, the process of exchanging information may enhance the trust needed for settling on comprehensive, integrative agreements as shown in Irmer's (2003) study of process-outcome connections. The symmetric benefit outcomes achieved by unfriendly parties—often in normalization talks—reflects a desire for fairness or strict reciprocity also found to characterize the behavior of laboratory bargainers (Bartos, 1995). Adhering to reciprocity norms seems to be more important for unfriendly (including strangers) bargainers. Additional analyses are needed to explore the role played by trust in the different types of negotiations, particularly the difference between a trusting relationship as a pre-condition for negotiation (innovation vs. normalization), as an impact on the way the process unfolds (expected vs. disappointed expectations between friends and non-friends), and as an influence on outcomes (partial or comprehensive agreements).

With regard to agreements, another variable emerges as being prominent. A smaller number of parties occurred in the decision-tree analysis with comprehensive agreements. This is a direct relationship, unmediated by other variables. A larger number of parties, on the other hand, impacts on agreements through time pressure, type and length of relationship: for example, friendly parties operating with a deadline occurs with comprehensive agreements (see Figure 10.3.). However, the more interesting finding is the direct relationship. Earlier case analyses and simulation data support the advantage of having only two parties at the table. In his analysis of 23 cases of negotiations involving Austrian delegations, Druckman (1997) found that the key discriminating variable (by MDS) was number of parties. Bilateral cases were distinguished from small and large multilateral negotiations on a number of features: for example, the smaller negotiations had less time pressure, less turnover of delegates, and were more likely to culminate in treaties. Of special interest is the relationship with treaties, which can be regarded also as comprehensive agreements. This is similar to the decision-tree finding shown in Figure 10.3. In their simulation of the Lausanne Peace Negotiations (1922-23), Beriker and Druckman (1996) showed that a symmetric power bilateral structure was more effective than two coalitional, multi-party structures: Bilateral-condition bargainers were more satisfied with the outcomes, achieved faster resolutions, disagreed less, and made fewer competitive statements during the discussions than those in the multi-party conditions.

The findings from the analyses reported in this chapter along with the earlier results support an observation made by Iklé: "In bilateral negotiations the 'available terms' can be described more simply. If a government is negotiating an agreement that is to be cast in the form of a treaty, the terms available at any particular time consist of the articles agreed to, articles offered by the opponent, plus those terms for articles not yet discussed that the government expects its opponent would be ready to grant" (1964: 60). Bilateral structures may facilitate choosing among the "available terms." They may also be a more cost-effective alternative to participation in multilateral forums because of fewer transaction costs and better, more comprehensive outcomes. It may also be the case that other factors lead to agreement in multilateral negotiations. These factors include time pressures and the length and type of relationship among the parties as shown in the analyses reported above.

Finally, what are we to conclude about the value added by machine-learning analyses to our understanding of negotiation? Three observations provide an answer to this question. One is that the statistical analyses are reinforced or bolstered by the decision-tree classification, both for the Iklé typology and for types of outcomes. With regard to the former, types of relationship and delegation status are shown to distinguish among the Iklé types in both analyses. The clearest discrimination in both analyses is between the innovation (friendly, medium or asymmetric status) and normalization (unfriendly, high status) categories. Concerning the latter, type of relationship and number of issues are associated with symmetric or enlarged benefits in both analyses: see the strong correlations (.46 and .34 respectively) and Figure 10.2.. However, the relationship between number of parties and comprehensive agreements, shown in the decision-tree and rule-learning analyses (Figure 10.3.), is not supported by a significant correlation between these variables.

Another observation is that the machine-learning analyses add knowledge about contingent relations among variables. The pair-wise correlations do not provide a window into the way the variables interact or are dependent on one another. The path-like feature of the decision trees and the "if ... then" feature of the association rules reveal hidden structures in the data: For example, enlarged joint benefits occur when friendly parties discuss only a few issues or when they discuss many issues in asymmetrical power structures. An advantage of this approach to analysis is that it produces a refined elucidation of the connections among factors that influence outcomes.

A third observation is that the combined approaches of statistical and machine-learning analyses yield a larger picture of what is happening in negotiation. This picture was described earlier in this section. It captures the 42 cases in this dataset but also has implications for other cases. The distinction between complex and simpler decision trees is relevant. As we noted earlier, very refined decision trees can be developed in order to achieve perfect classification of the cases in a dataset. The unpruned tree with 24 leaves produced such perfection. Trees with fewer leaves reduced the classification accuracy but improved the accuracy of predicting new cases (see Table 10.3.). Thus, while capturing the dataset in some detail (as would be done in ethnographic analysis), we also reduced the number of leaves (variables) in order to capture "trends" that are more general (as in large-N comparative analysis). The general trends are the key variables isolated in the pruned trees. Whether these particular variables (type of relationship, delegation status, number of parties) provide the best explanation for negotiation processes and outcomes in other cases remains to be discovered.

References

Agrawal, R., Mannila, H., Srikant, R., Toivonen, H., and Verkamo, A.I., 1995, Fast discovery of association rules, in *Advances in Knowledge Discovery and Data Mining*, Fayyad, U. M., Piatetsky-Shapiro G., Smyth, P., and Uthurusamy, R., eds., AAAI Press, Cambridge, MA.

Beriker, N. and Druckman, D., 1996, Simulating the Lausanne Peace Negotiations, 1922-1923: Power asymmetries in bargaining, *Simulation & Gaming* **27**: 162-183.

Bartos, O. J., 1995, Modeling distributive and integrative negotiations, *The Annals of the American Academy of Political and Social Science* **542**: 48-60.

Breiman, L., 2001, Statistical modeling: The two cultures, *Statistical Science* **16**: 199-231. (With comments by D. R. Cox, B. Efron, B. Hoadley, and E. Parzen, a rejoinder by the author.)

Breiman, L., Friedman, J., Olshen, R. and Stone, C., 1984, *Classification and Regression Trees*, Wadsworth & Brooks, Pacific Grove, CA.

Cohen, W. W., 1995, Fast effective rule induction, in *Proceedings of the 12th International Conference on Machine Learning (ML-95)*, Lake Tahoe, CA, Prieditis, A., and Russell, S., eds., Morgan Kaufmann, San Francisco.

Druckman, D., 1997, Dimensions of international negotiations: Structures, processes, and outcomes, *Group Decision and Negotiation* **6**: 395-420.

Druckman, D., 1994, Determinants of compromising behavior in negotiation: A meta-analysis, *Journal of Conflict Resolution* **38**: 507-556.

Druckman, D., 1993, The situational levers of negotiating flexibility, *Journal of Conflict Resolution* **37**: 236-276.

Druckman, D., and Bonoma, T. V., 1976, Determinants of bargaining behavior in a bilateral monopoly situation II: Opponent concession rate and similarity, *Behavioral Science* **21**: 252-262.

Druckman, D., Harris, R., and Ramberg, B., 2002, Computer-aided international negotiation: A tool for research and practice, *Group Decision and Negotiation* **11**: 231-256.

Druckman, D., Rozelle, R., and Baxter, J., 1982, *Nonverbal Communication: Survey, Theory, and Research,* Sage, Beverly Hills, CA.

Druckman, D., Martin, J., Allen Nan, S. and Yagcioglu, D., 1999, Dimensions of international negotiation: A test of Iklé's typology, *Group Decision and Negotiation* **8**: 89–108.

Friedman, J. H., and Fisher, N. I., 1999, Bump hunting in high-dimensional data, *Statistics and Computing* **9**: 1–20.

Fürnkranz, J., 1999, Separate-and-conquer rule learning, *Artificial Intelligence Review* **13**: 3–54.

Fürnkranz. J., 1997, Pruning algorithms for rule learning, *Machine Learning* **27**: 139–171.

Halpern, J., 1994, The effect of friendship on personal business transactions, *Journal of Conflict Resolution* **38**: 647-664.

Headland, T. N., Pike, K. L., and Harris, M., eds., 1990, *Emics and Etics: The Insider/Outsider Debate,* Sage, Newbury Park, CA.

Hipp, J., Güntzer, U., and Nakhaeizadeh, G., 2000, Algorithms for association rule mining—a general survey and comparison, *SIGKDD Explorations* **2**: 58–64.

Iklé, F. C., 1964, *How Nations Negotiate*, Harper, New York.

Irmer, C. G., 2003, *The Promise of Process: Evidence on Ending Violent International Conflict*, unpublished doctoral dissertation, George Mason University, Fairfax, Virginia.

Kohavi, R., 1995, A study of cross-validation and bootstrap for accuracy estimation and model selection, in *Proceedings of the 14th International Joint Conference on Artificial Intelligence (IJCAI-95)*, Mellish, C. S., ed., Morgan Kaufmann, Montreal.

Quinlan, J. R., 1993, *C4.5: Programs for Machine Learning*, Morgan Kaufmann, San Mateo, CA.

Quinlan, J. R., 1986, Induction of decision trees, *Machine Learning* **1**:81–106.

Stone, M., 1977, Asymptotics for and against cross-validation, *Biometrika* **64**: 29–35.

Stone, M., 1974, Cross-validatory choice and assessment of statistical predictions, *Journal of the Royal Statistical Society B* **36**:111–147.

Trappl, R., Fürnkranz, J., Bercovitch, J., and Petrak, J., 1997, Machine learning and case-based reasoning: Their potential role in preventing the outbreak of wars or in ending them, in *Learning, Networking, and Statistics,* Riccia, G. D., Kruse, R., and Lenz, H., eds., Springer, New York.

Webb, G. I., 2000, Efficient search for association rules, in *Proceedings of the 6th ACM SIGKDD International Conference on Knowledge Discovery and Data Mining (KDD-2000),* Boston, MA, ACM Press, New York.

Witten. I. H., and Frank, E., 2000, *Data Mining—Practical Machine Learning Tools and Techniques with Java Implementations*, Morgan Kaufmann, San Mateo, CA.

Chapter 11

Machine Learning Methods for Better Understanding, Resolving, and Preventing International Conflicts[1]

Robert Trappl
Medical University of Vienna and Austrian Research Institute for Artificial Intelligence, Vienna, Austria

Erik Hörtnagl, Jürgen Rattenberger
Austrian Research Institute for Artificial Intelligence, Vienna, Austria

Nicolas Schwank
University of Heidelberg, Germany

Jacob Bercovitch
University of Canterbury, Christchurch, New Zealand

1 MOTIVATION AND BACKGROUND

The main motivation guiding our research during the last 15 years, formulated as question, has been: Is it possible to aid decision-makers or their advisors who want to prevent the outbreak of hostilities/wars or to end them by means of negotiations or mediation, by giving them (interactively) recommendations as the result of applying Artificial Intelligence methods to existing war/crisis/mediation databases?

If the answer is at least partially "yes" then these results should definitely not only be made available to decision-makers from government but also to groups who may oppose a government heading, in their opinion, towards war.

Two methods from Artificial Intelligence, specifically machine learning, namely computing decision trees and case-based reasoning, have mainly been applied.

1. The research reported in this chapter was in part supported by the Austrian Federal Ministry for Education, Science, and Culture, and in part commissioned by the European Humanitarian Aid Office of the European Commission (ECHO). The authors would like to thank Johannes Fürnkranz for helpful comments on a draft version of this chapter.

R. Trappl (ed.), Programming for Peace, 251–318.

In the following "Insert" the basics of both methods will be briefly explained; the methodologically experienced reader is recommended to skip it.

Insert: Methodological Background

The basic idea behind decision trees is very simple, and shall be explained by an example that is based on Quinlan (1993).

Depending on the weather conditions, a person decides to go for a walk with her dog, or not.

The weather conditions and the outcome, i.e. if the person goes for a walk, have been recorded 12 times. These observations are listed in the following table:

Table 11.1. Database

No.	*Outlook*	*Temperature*	*Humidity*	*Windy*	*Walk?*
1	sunny	hot	high	false	no
2	sunny	hot	high	true	no
3	overcast	hot	high	false	yes
4	rain	mild	high	false	yes
5	rain	cool	normal	false	yes
6	rain	cool	normal	true	no
7	overcast	cool	normal	true	yes
8	sunny	mild	high	false	no
9	sunny	cool	normal	false	yes
10	rain	mild	normal	false	yes
11	sunny	mild	normal	true	yes
12	overcast	mild	high	true	yes
13	overcast	hot	normal	false	yes
14	rain	mild	high	true	no

Is it possible to predict from this albeit small database if, given specific weather conditions, the person will go for a walk or not? The program, originally ID3, now usually C4.5, tries to find the variable which reduces the uncertainty most. This is done by applying an information theoretic measure. When this variable is found, it is placed at the root of a tree. The number of values of this variable gives the number of branches going down from the root. Now for each of these values all remaining variables are tested which of them contributes most to the reduction of uncertainty of the prediction. The one which does it is placed at the end of this branch ("a leaf") and from this leaf all values of this variable define a branch. This procedure is continued until termination.

Figure 11.1. shows the resulting graph: the most important variable, therefore at the root of the tree, is "Outlook". Depending on "sunny", "overcast" or "rain", the user of this decision tree comes to another variable, where she/he has to decide on humidity or wind conditions, or she/he arrives directly at a node where she/he is informed if the prediction is "yes" or "no".

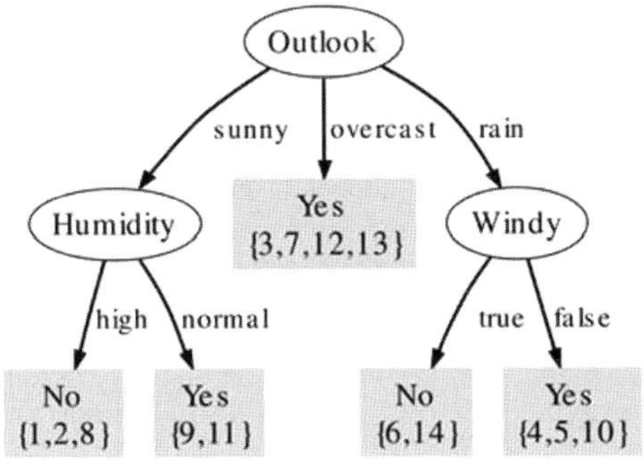

Figure 11.1. A decision tree, computed from the database above, to predict if a person will walk or not.

It is clear that the example was chosen in such a way that the decision tree is small and the prediction is certain. With real data, this is rarely the case. The decision tree may become very large; in order to keep it relatively small, special "pruning" methods were developed. At the end-nodes of such a tree there may be no "certain" answers but a probability for e.g. walk.

Three additional remarks: 1. The decision tree, by its structure, also gives information which variables are the most important ones. 2. It may help to reduce the efforts of collecting data: in the example above, the variable "temperature" does not show up in the decision tree, therefore it is no longer necessary to collect it. 3. All decision trees can be represented as a set of rules, e.g. "If the outlook is sunny and the humidity is normal, then the person will go for a walk."

In order to test the validity of a decision tree one is tempted to apply it on the original dataset.

However, that's the data from which it is computed. Therefore, the best solution would be to test it on an independent sample. Since it is often not possible to wait until new data is collected, the method of cross-validation was developed: The dataset is divided randomly into two sets, one of them, the so-called "training-set", comprising 90 % of the original dataset, and the other one, the "test-set", comprising 10 %. Then the decision tree is computed from the training-set and tested on the test-set. If this is done ten times, the procedure is called ten-fold cross-validation, if fifty-times, fifty-fold, etc. The mean of the percentages of the correct predictions on the test-sets is a measure of the validity of the predictions of this decision tree.

The second method from AI is case-based reasoning. The flow-chart of a case-based reasoning procedure is given in Figure 11.2.

The aim of this method is to find the most similar case(s) to a given case by comparing the values of the attributes of a given case with those in a case database, as indicated in the upper part of Figure 11.2. This is usually done by finding the case(s)

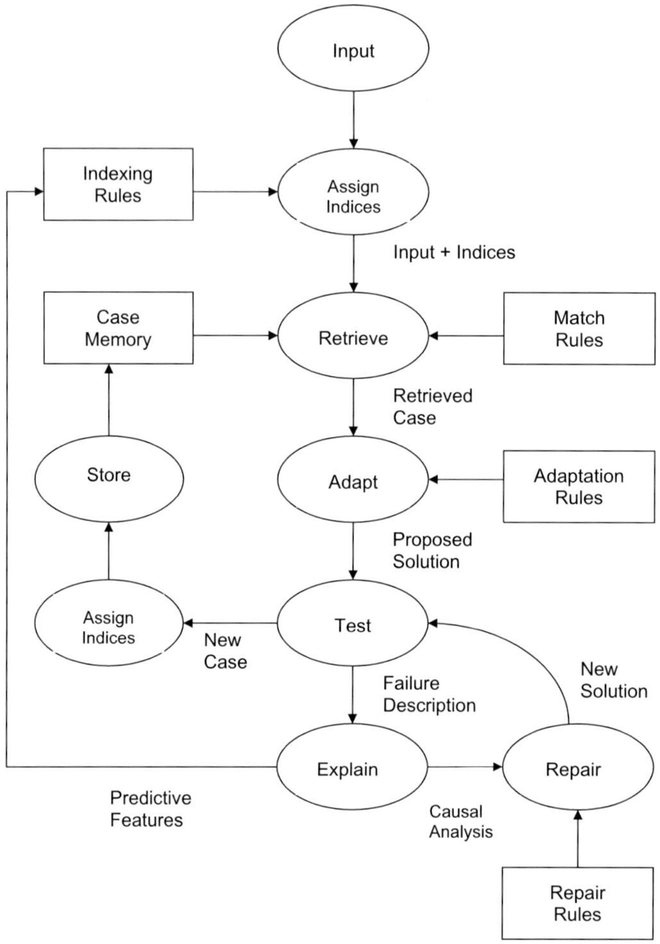

Figure 11.2. Flow-chart of case-based reasoning (modified after Kolodner, 1993).

with the smallest Euclidian distance(s). However, this is not always simple since many variables are measured not on a ratio or an interval scale but on an ordinal scale.

While the flow-chart may give the impression that all other tasks, e.g. case-adaptation, are also done by programs, this is usually done by the user her/himself.

(End of Insert)

Of the several projects we have undertaken at the Austrian Research Institute for Artificial Intelligence in Vienna, two will be briefly described, these two being the background of our recent work.

In the first project (Petrak et al., 1994; Trappl et al., 1997) Case-Based Reasoning was applied to the crisis and war database KOSIMO (Pfetsch and Billing, 1994; see Chapter 2 in this volume). In this context, the case(s) most similar to a given crisis situation can be found and the decision-maker can judge which means have helped to prevent the outbreak of war, or which have failed, in the (most) similar case(s). Several measures of similarity, some of them developed by using information from political scientists, were computed and tested against situations already known. By using the method of cross-validation, it could be shown that it was possible to predict e.g. the intensity level of war correctly in 90 % of the cases.

Even more importantly, the well-known situation of the Bosnia-Herzegovina conflict of the early nineties was tested. At the onset of this crisis, there were two opposing groups among politicians and political scientists: one group heavily warned against intervention because an intervention could result in a situation like the Vietnam war. The other group argued for intervening against the invasion by a dictator because not doing so would encourage him. Therefore, the main coder of the KOSIMO database was asked to code the case (it could have been easily done by any decision-maker). As a result of the computation, in the list of the similar cases (see Table 11.2.) the first and most similar one was the Munich Treaty, i.e. the wrong appeasement policy of Chamberlain and Daladier, and not, as many political scientists had stated and what the U.S. decision was based upon, the situation of the Vietnam war.

Table 11.2. List of similar cases to the situation in Bosnia-Herzegovina, in descending order.

Sim	Year	Conflict
		Bosnia-Herzegovina
0.62	1938	Germany-Czechoslovakia (Munich Treaty)
0.60	1948	Israel I (Palestine War)
0.57	1974	Cyprus IV (Turkish Invasion)
0.55	1965	India XVI (Kashmir IV)
0.54	1968	CSSR (Invasion)

The decision not to intervene resulted in a death toll of about 250 000 persons. The following Serbian aggression in 1999 was then halted by a military intervention.

Unfortunately, as often, a conflict has escalated into war, and therefore attempts have to be made to de-escalate the situation, i.e. conflict management attempts (CMAs). One of the most important is mediation. To gain a better understanding of the conditions of successful CMAs, in another study

(Fürnkranz et al., 1997) C4.5 was applied to the CONFMAN database (Bercovitch, 1996), the largest database on mediation attempts world-wide.

It could be shown that, with this method, better predictions were possible than with all other methods hitherto applied. Later, Wickboldt et al. (1999) obtained quite similar results.

The pruned decision tree as obtained by Fürnkranz et al. (Figure 11.3.) presents the conditions for successful CMAs).

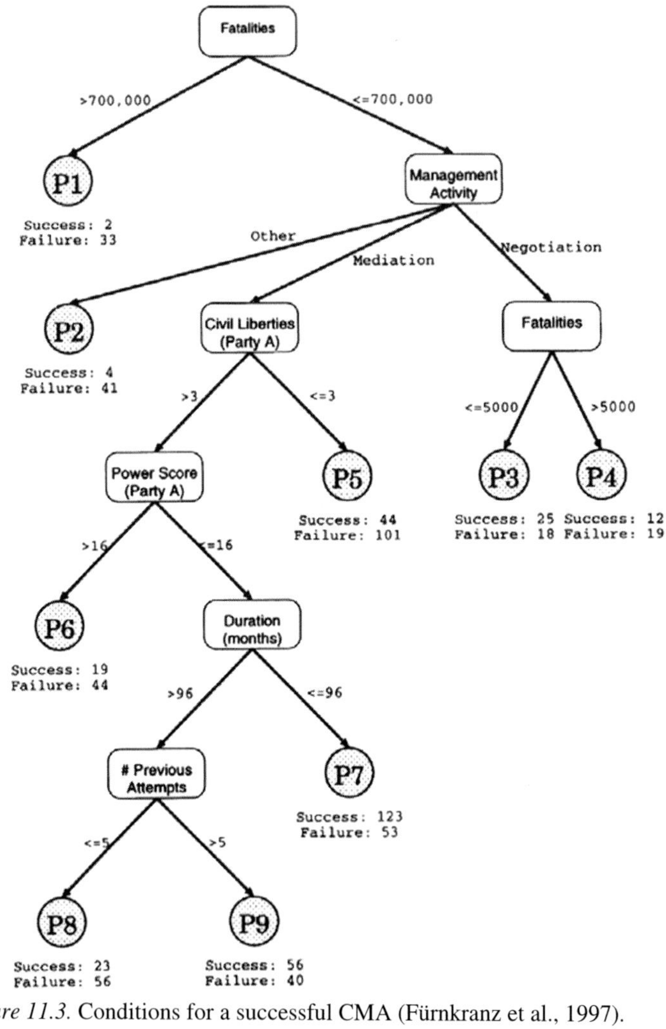

Figure 11.3. Conditions for a successful CMA (Fürnkranz et al., 1997).

Since mediation is one of the most important CM methods, we tried to find the rules that determine which mediation strategy had the greatest chance of success in a given situation. The resulting decision tree is presented in Figure 11.4.

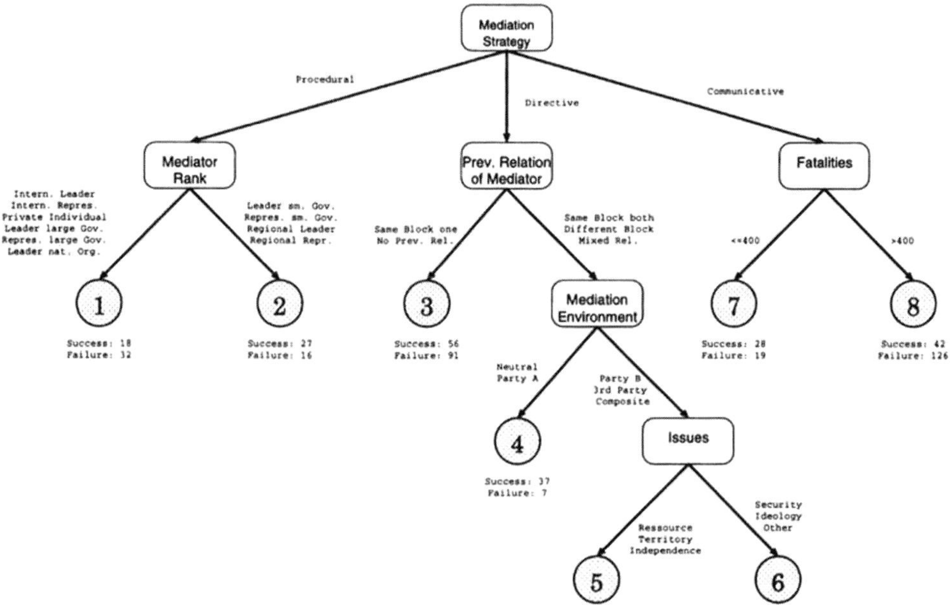

Figure 11.4. Recommendation, which mediation strategy has the greatest chances of success in a given situation.

Since completion of these projects, both databases have developed considerably: the CONFMAN database was enlarged from 241 disputes with 921 CMAs between 1945 to 1995 to 333 conflicts with 5066 CMAs until 2000, each one characterized by 218 variables (see Chapter 6, this volume), and KOSIMO with 301 conflicts between 1945 and 1998 (see Chapter 2, this volume) was transformed into KOSIMO 2 with 644 conflicts until June 2005 (see Section 5.2 of this chapter). Furthermore, hard- and software developments, especially the open source data mining library Weka (Witten and Frank, 2000) allowed us to raise (and attempt to answer) the following questions:

1. Is it possible to better predict the outcome of a conflict management attempt?
2. From two superpowers to only one: Is this reflected in the relevance of variables for successful conflict management?
3. Are there regional differences in the relevance of variables?
4. Is it possible to interactively study conflicts, and with which benefits?

2 PREDICTING THE OUTCOME OF A CONFLICT MANAGEMENT ATTEMPT

4570 conflict management attempts with 41 attributes from the CONF-MAN database were used for this analysis. Of these, 2045 were successful, 2525 were failures. The resulting decision tree contained 258 leaves, the pruned decision tree 10 leaves. For reasons of space, a pruned tree is given in Figure 11.5.

In order to predict the outcome, we have to identify the attributes of the variables in this graph. Then we can calculate the approximate probability of a successful outcome of the conflict management attempt.[1]

It naturally is of interest to know how accurate such a prediction will be. In order to test the reliability of this decision tree, a ten-fold cross-validation was performed. The percentage of correct predictions on the independent test data was 59.1%. This percentage, however, has to be compared with the default prediction, i.e. how good a person would be who always predicted the more likely outcome. Since 2525 conflict management attempts failed, the likely outcome is the quotient of the ratio 2525/4570 = 55.3%. Only 3.8% of the cases more were correctly classified, compared to the default prediction.

This result may look poor. But let us compare it to, e.g., the prediction of next day's weather which is usually in 75 % of the cases correct; hardly anybody compares it to the default "Weather tomorrow will be the same as today" which is correct in about 2/3 of the cases. That means the official weather forecast is only 8 % better than the default. Nevertheless the comparison with the default percentage is the only correct way to evaluate the improvement obtained by a forecasting method. However, in many cases even a small improvement may justify an application.

3 FROM TWO SUPERPOWERS TO ONLY ONE: IS THIS REFLECTED IN THE RELEVANCE OF VARIABLES FOR SUCCESSFUL CONFLICT MANAGEMENT?

Since the fall of the iron curtain the international political arena changed considerably. Have the factors, e.g. those expressed in the variables of conflict management databases, remained the same ones with regard to their influence on the success of a conflict management attempt, or do we now

1. The complete listing of the respective output from the program including the definition of the variables encountered in this decision tree and all the following ones can be found in the Appendix.

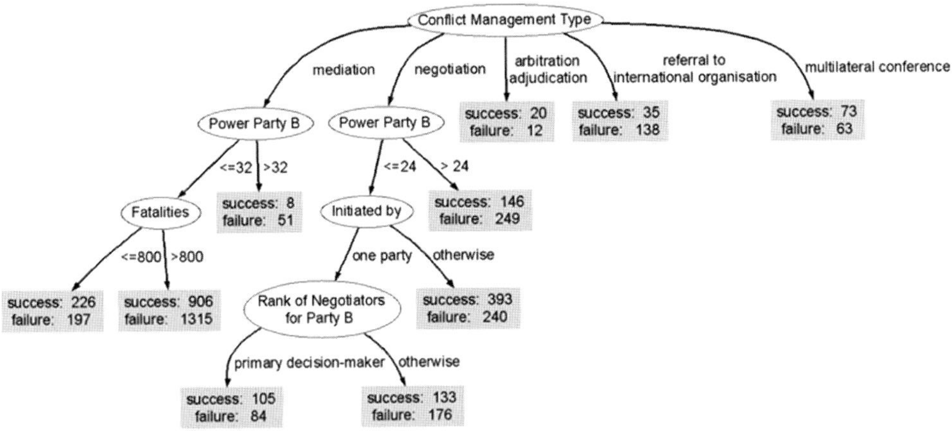

Figure 11.5. Predicting the success/failure of a conflict management attempt by the decision tree

need to consider other factors? Could this information be used to increase the predictive capacity of decision trees?

As late as in the mid-nineties, a question like this could not be tested (Fürnkranz et al., 1997; Trappl et al., 1996; 1997) since there were not yet enough recent cases in the CONFMAN database. The update of CONFMAN to the year 2000 made this feasible.

Therefore, in order to test this hypothesis, the database was divided into two subsets: Conflict management attempts of conflicts starting before and in the year of the fall of the Berlin Wall (1989) and attempts in 1990 and afterwards. The first subset, from now on called "before", contained 3420 attempts, of which 1477 were successful and 1943 failed, and the second subset, from now on called "after", contained 1150 attempts, 568 successful ones and 582 failures.

For both subsets decision trees were computed, using again C4.5. In order to test the reliability of these decision trees, a fifty-fold cross validation was computed for these subsets. This led again to indicators of the predictive validity of both the complete and the pruned trees.

Figure 11.6. gives the pruned decision tree for "before" and Figure 11.7. for "after". While in "before" the most important variable is "Conflict Management Type", as seen already in Figure 11.5. (decision tree of all conflicts), in "after" the most influential variable is "Conflict Duration". As can be seen easily, the trees do not only differ in their roots, but also most of the other influential variables are different.

The predictive value of the pruned tree in "before" is 59.8 % correct. Since the default value is 56.8 % (predicting always "failure"), the predictive value of the pruned tree is 3.0 %, i.e. only slightly higher.

In "after" the predictive value of the pruned tree is 57.7 %. Since the default value is 50.6 % (again predicting always "failure"), the predictive value is 7 % higher than the default one. The predictive value of the decision tree obtained with the "after" subset is considerably higher than the one from "before" (nearly as good as a weather forecast).

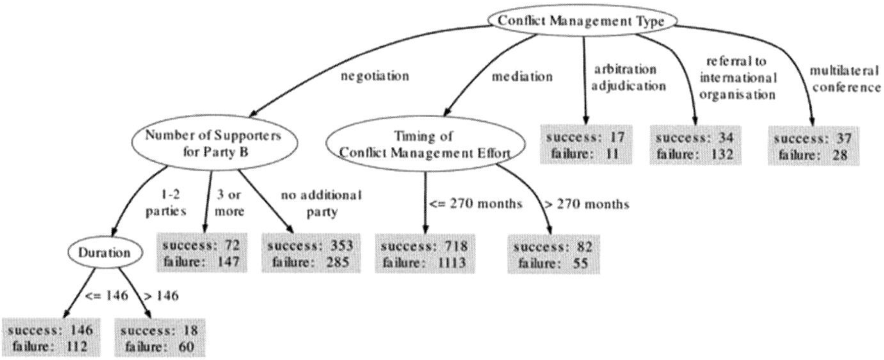

Figure 11.6. Pruned decision tree for the conflict management attempts of conflicts, starting before and in 1989.

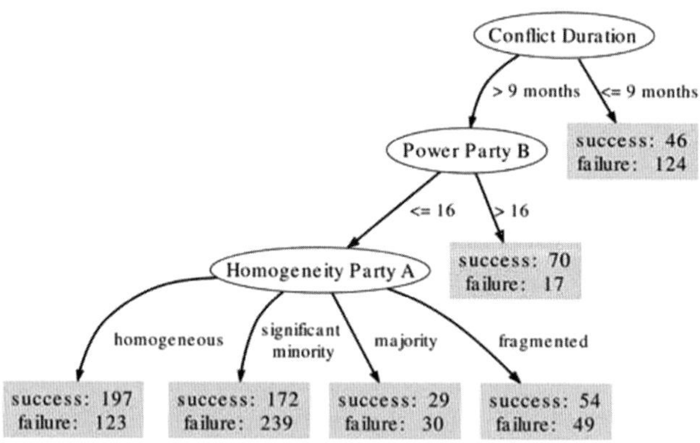

Figure 11.7. Pruned decision tree for the conflict management attempts of conflicts, starting 1990 and later.

In order to better compare the differences between the relevance of the variables—a first indication already are the different trees for "before" and "after"—in each of the 50 decision trees in each subset those variables that were among the 5 most influential ones were counted and the results compared between the two subsets. The following table shows the frequency of a variable being among the five most influential ones in the 50 decision trees obtained by cross-validation:

Table 11.3. Frequency of a variable being among the five most influential in the 50 decision trees obtained by cross-validation

Level, variable	*=< 89*	*> 89*
0, Conflict management type	50	0
0, Duration	0	50
1, Timing	50	0
1, Power B	0	50
1, No. of parties B	50	0
2, Initiated by	1	0
2, Negotiators B	21	0
2, Negotiators A	0	15
2, Duration raw	24	0
2, Homogeneity A	4	35
3, Initiated by	12	0
3, Negotiators B	0	6
3, Geographic region	0	10
3, Homogeneity A	0	3
4, Timing	0	2
4, Political system A	0	1

This table shows the extreme difference of the distribution of influential variables in "before" and "after". Considering the variables in level 0 and 1, a χ^2-test (df = 15) gives a probability $p < .0005$, thus the difference is highly significant.

The change of the geopolitical situation is significantly expressed in the differences of the variables which have an influence on the success of a conflict management attempt.

4 ARE THERE REGIONAL DIFFERENCES IN THE RELEVANCE OF VARIABLES?

The large number of conflict management attempts (from now on abbreviated with CMA) and the large number of attributes recorded with each CMA makes it possible to investigate differences in the relevance of attributes for successful CM.

In the CONFMAN database the world is divided into seven geographic regions:

1. North America, including the USA and Canada
2. Central and South America
3. Africa
4. South West Asia, i.e. Indian subcontinent and mountain areas to the North
5. East Asia and the Pacific, i.e. the western edge of the Pacific basin including Australia, New Zealand and Pacific Islands
6. Middle East, i.e. the ancient crescent from Egypt to Iran
7. Europe

For each of the seven regions—with one exception, see below—the following information was computed and some of it graphically represented:

- The number of conflict management attempts
- The percentage of successful CMs
- A graph showing the percentage of CMAs in this region of all CMAs world-wide, for each year
- A graph showing the absolute number of CMAs in each year (dotted line) und the absolute number of successful CM (full line), in this region
- A pruned decision tree for CMAs for the conflicts in the years 1945 to 2000
- The number of CMAs in the year 1990 and after, and the number of successful CM in the same period
- A pruned decision tree for "after", giving the conditions for the success/failure of a CM, presenting the variables and their influence (for a listing of the Weka output and a complete description of the variables please see the Appendix).

  Remark: Only the decision tree for "after" has a predictive value for current and future conflicts.

- The reliability of this decision tree, tested with tenfold cross-validation and compared with the default value (guessing always the most likely outcome)

No conflicts of the database have as their location North America, therefore no CMA was undertaken in this region.

4.1 Central and South America

397 conflict management attempts, 50.13 % successful (199 successful; 198 failed)

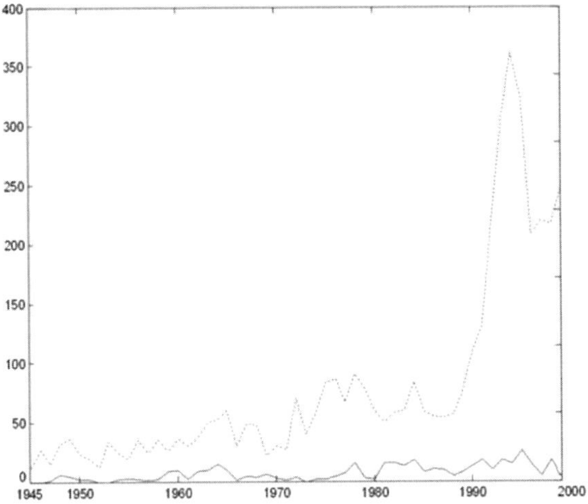

Figure 11.8. Percentage of CMAs of all CMAs world-wide. The dotted line represents all CMAs from 1945 to 2000 in all regions and the solid line represents those within Central and South America.

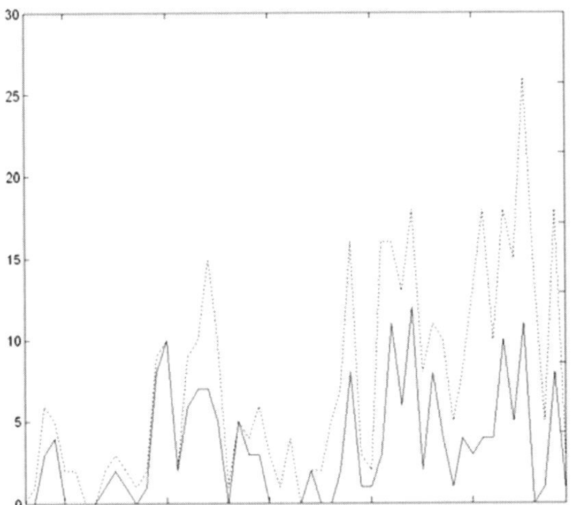

Figure 11.9. Absolute Number of CMAs (dotted line) vs. unsuccessful CMs (full line)

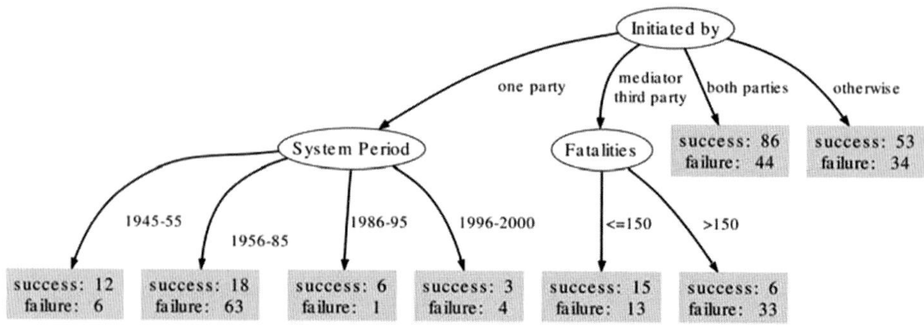

Figure 11.10. Pruned decision tree for CMAs from 1945 to 2000 in Central and South America

- Number of CMAs in the years 1990 and after: 140; successful 90
- Default: 64.29 % (prediction success)
- Predictive value of the decision tree: 63.57 %

As the predictive value of the decision tree is worse than the default, relying on the tree is not recommended. Nevertheless, for reasons of completeness the decision tree is plotted.

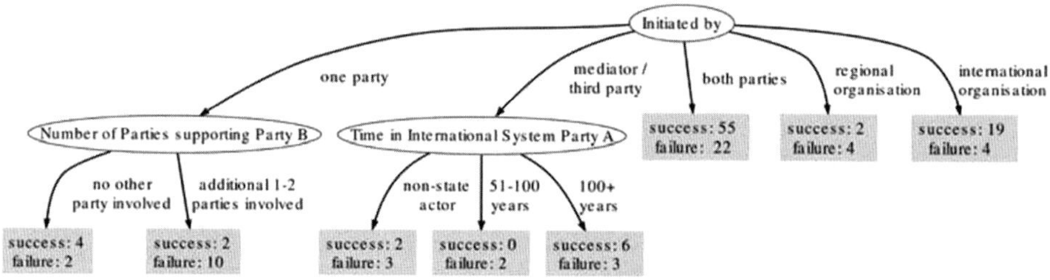

Figure 11.11. Pruned decision tree for CMAs in the years 1990 and after in Central and South America

4.2 Africa

1314 cases of conflict management attempts, 44.75 % successful

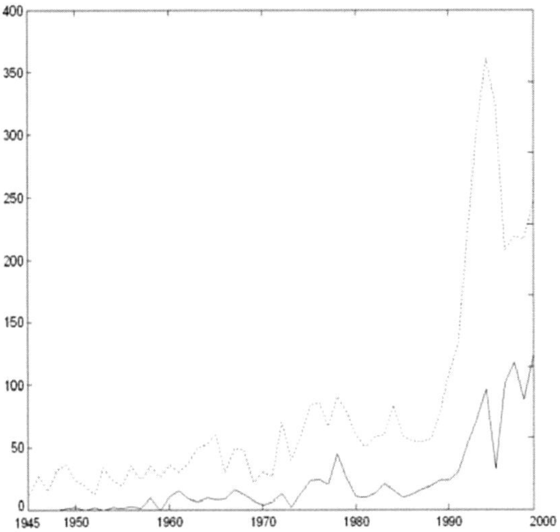

Figure 11.12. Percentage of CMAs of all CMAs world-wide. The dotted line represents all CMAs from 1945 to 2000 in all regions and the solid line represents those within Africa.

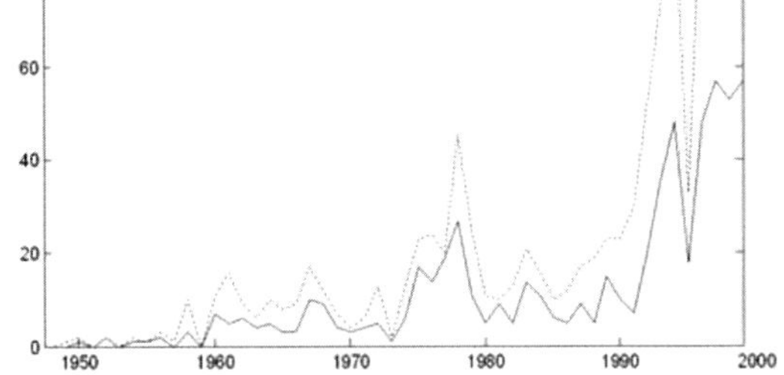

Figure 11.13. Absolute Number of CMAs (dotted line) vs. unsuccessful CMs (full line)

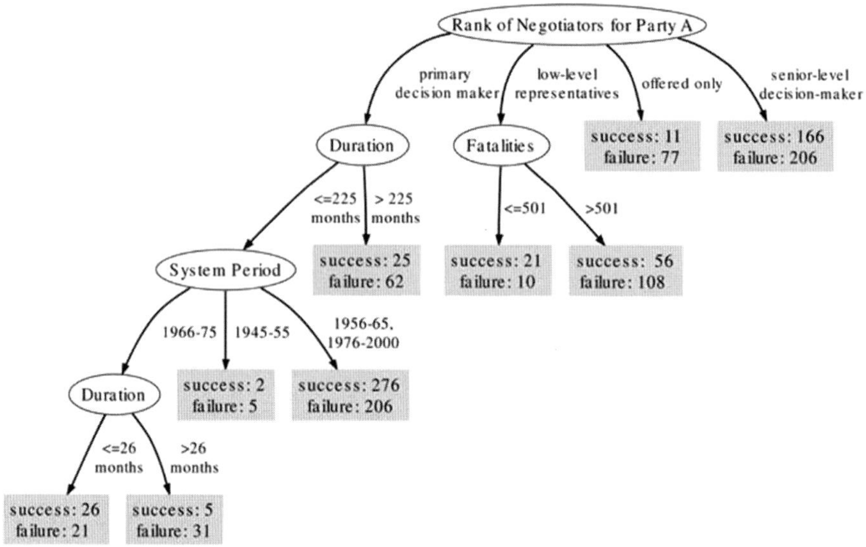

Figure 11.14. Pruned decision tree for CMAs from 1945 to 2000 in Africa

- Number of CMAs in the years 1990 and after: 739; successful 363
- Default: 50.88 % (prediction failure)
- Predictive value of the decision tree: 56.56 %

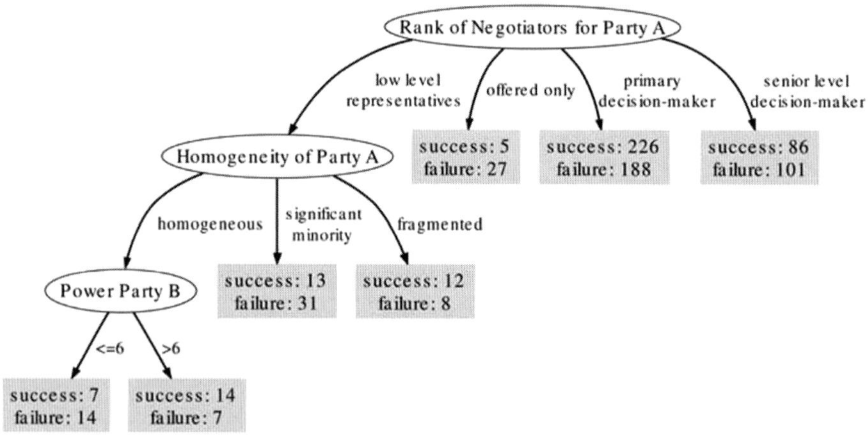

Figure 11.15. Pruned decision tree for CMAs in the years 1990 and after in Africa

4.3 South West Asia

466 conflict management attempts, 47.85 % successful (223 successful, 243 failed)

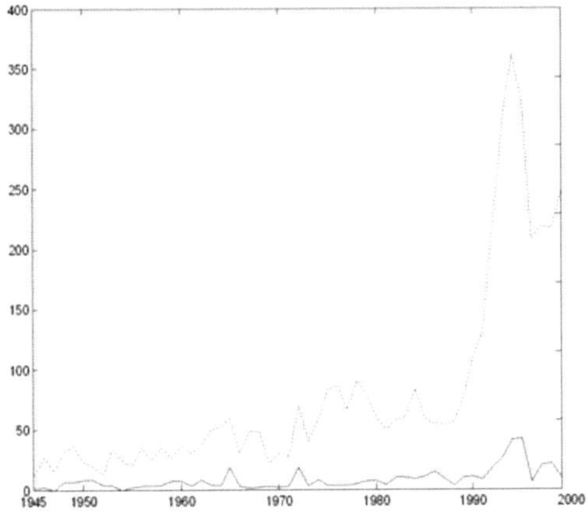

Figure 11.16. Percentage of CMAs of all CMAs world-wide. The dotted line represents all CMAs from 1945 to 2000 in all regions and the solid line represents those within South West Asia.

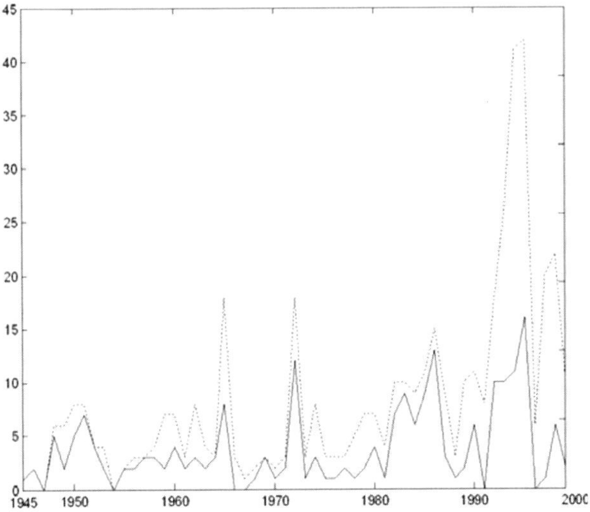

Figure 11.17. Absolute Number of CMAs (dotted line) vs. unsuccessful CMs (full line)

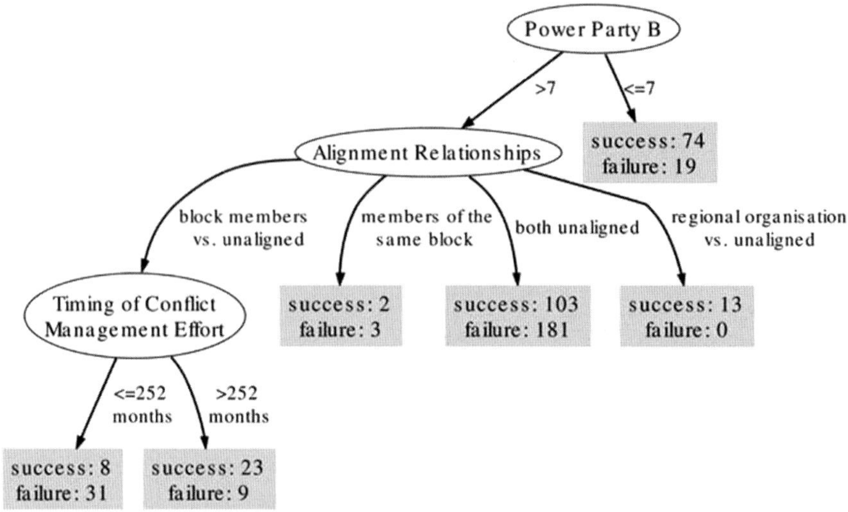

Figure 11.18. Pruned decision tree for CMAs from 1945 to 2000 in South West Asia

- Number of CMAs in the years 1990 and after: 204; successful 128
- Default: 62.75 % (prediction success)
- Predictive value of the decision tree: 73.53 %

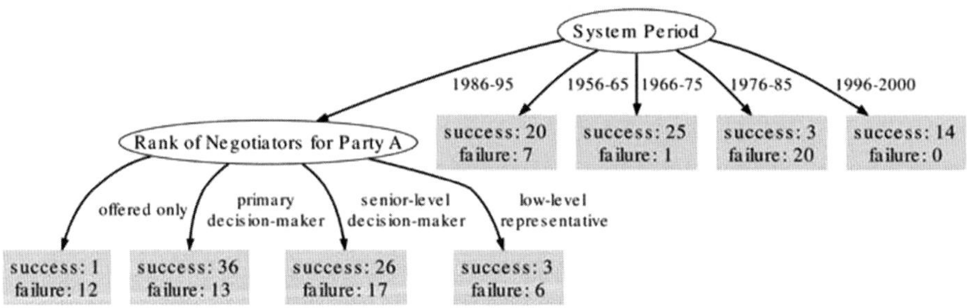

Figure 11.19. Pruned decision tree for CMAs in the years 1990 and after in South West Asia. The "system period" is the time period in which the dispute became an international conflict.

4.4 East Asia and the Pacific

621 conflict management attempts, 46.86 % successful (291 successful; 330 failed)

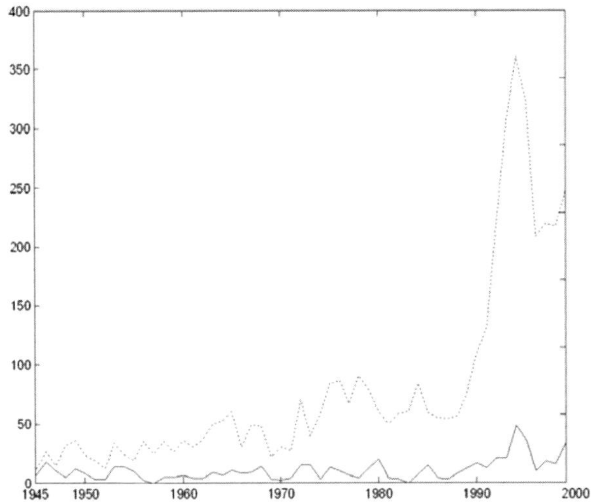

Figure 11.20. Percentage of CMAs of all CMAs world-wide. The dotted line represents all CMAs from 1945 to 2000 in all regions and the solid line represents those within the region of East Asia and the Pacific.

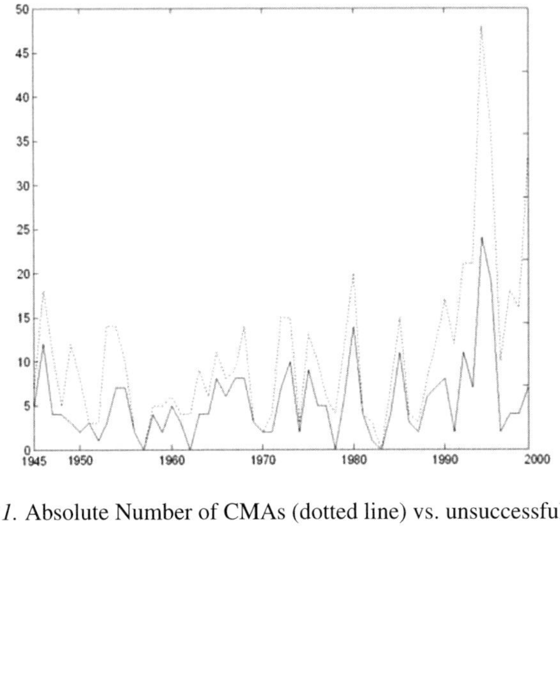

Figure 11.21. Absolute Number of CMAs (dotted line) vs. unsuccessful CMs (full line)

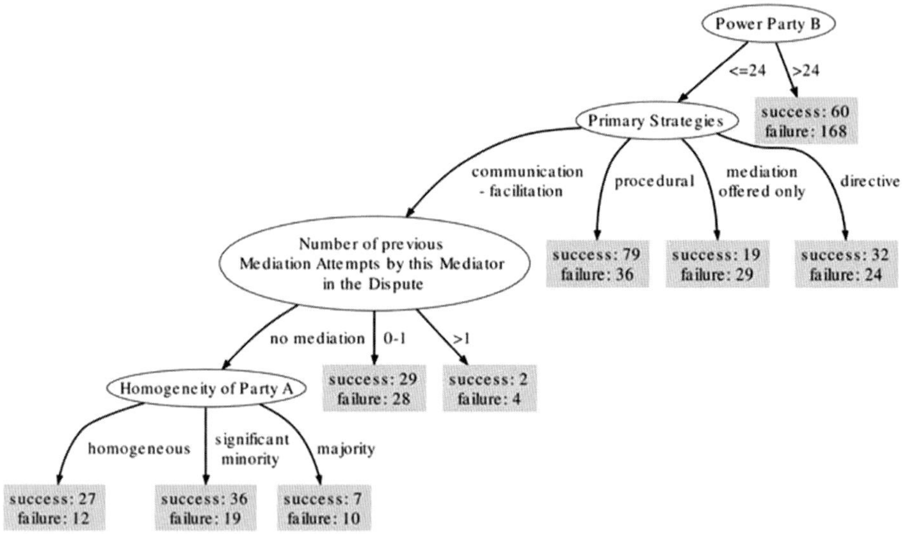

Figure 11.22. Pruned decision tree for CMAs from 1945 to 2000 in East Asia and Pacific.

- Number of CMA in the years 1990 and after: 232; successful 135
- Default: 58.19 % (prediction success)
- Predictive value of the decision tree: 63.36 %

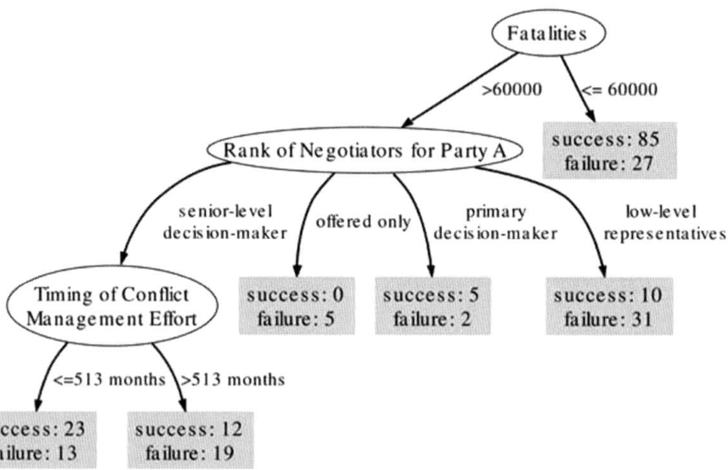

Figure 11.23. Pruned decision tree for CMA in the years 1990 and after in East Asia and Pacific

4.5 Middle East

883 conflict management attempts, 37.71% successful (333 successful; 550 failed)

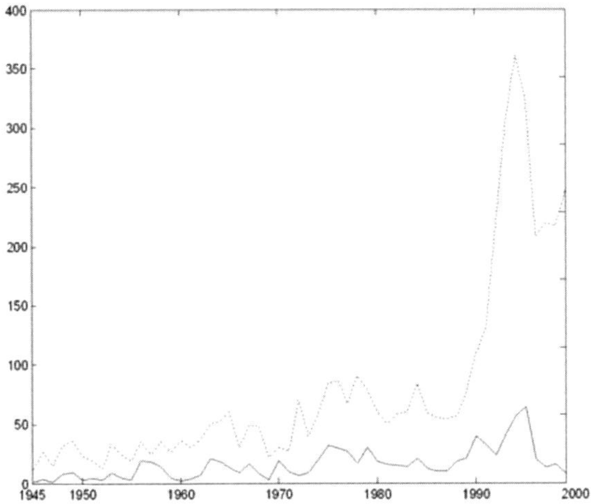

Figure 11.24. Percentage of CMAs of all CMAs world-wide. The dotted line represents all CMAs from 1945 to 2000 in all regions and the solid line represents those within the Middle East.

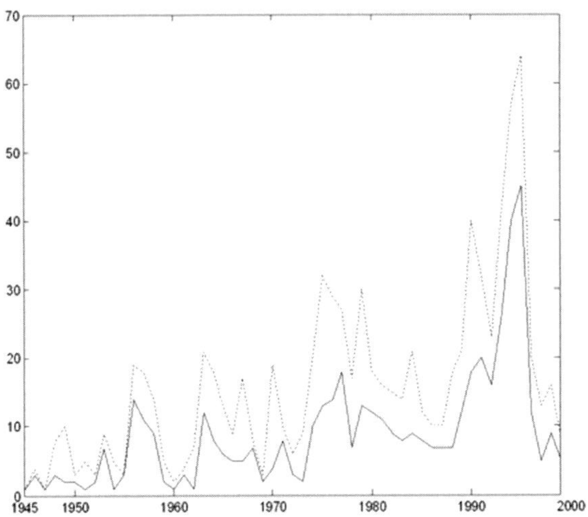

Figure 11.25. Absolute Number of CMAs (dotted line) vs. unsuccessful CMs (full line)

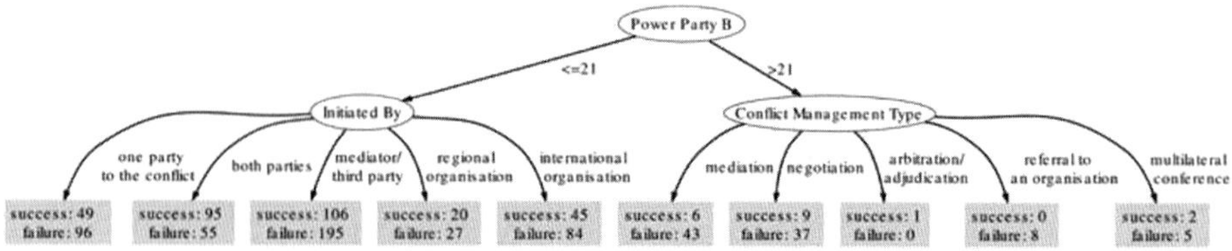

Figure 11.26. Pruned decision tree for CMAs from 1945 to 2000 in the Middle East

- Number of CMA in the years 1990 and after: 314; successful 100
- Default: 68.15 % (prediction failure)
- Predictive value of the decision tree: 64.97 %

As the predictive value of the decision tree is worse than the default, relying on the tree is not recommended. Nevertheless, for reasons of completeness the decision tree is plotted

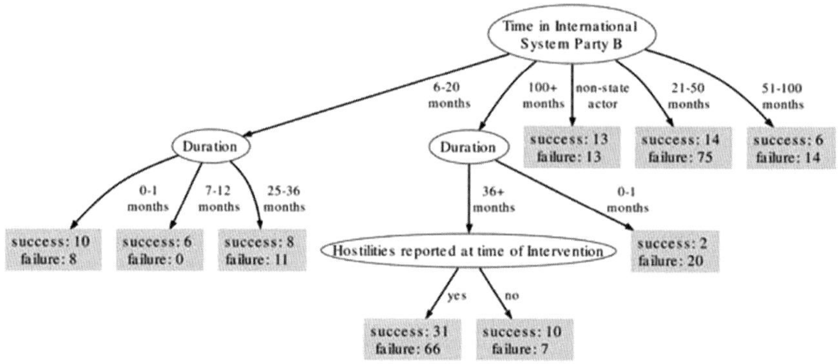

Figure 11.27. Pruned decision tree for CMAs from 1990 and after in the Middle East

4.6 Europe

European continent and adjacent islands, including Russia and Turkey.

889 conflict management attempts, 46.23 % successful (411 successful; 478 failed)

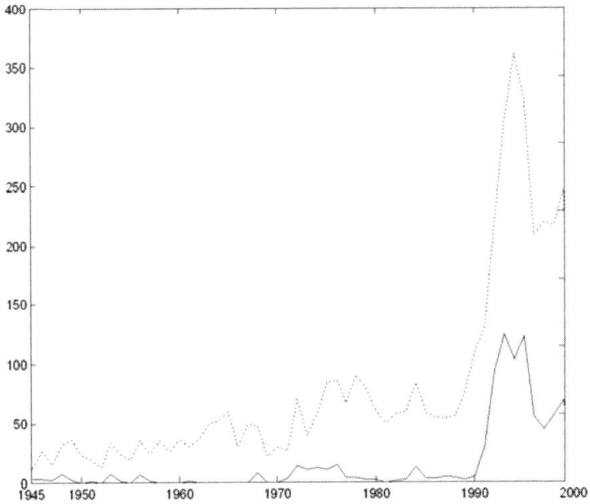

Figure 11.28. Percentage of CMAs of all CMAs world-wide. The dotted line represents all CMAs from 1945 to 2000 in all regions and the solid line represents those within Europe.

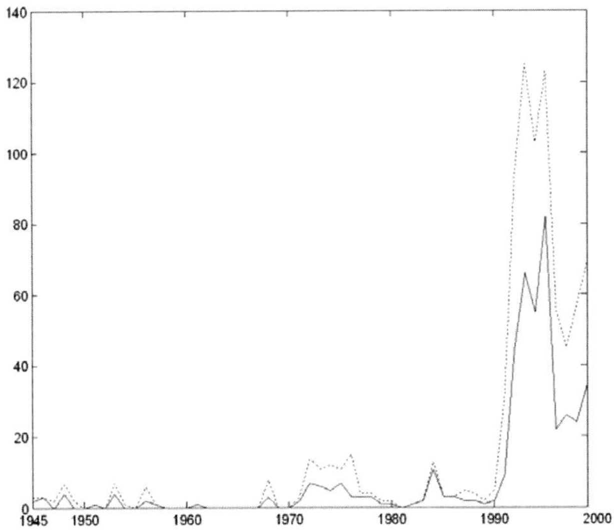

Figure 11.29. Absolute Number of CMAs (dotted line) vs. unsuccessful CMs (full line)

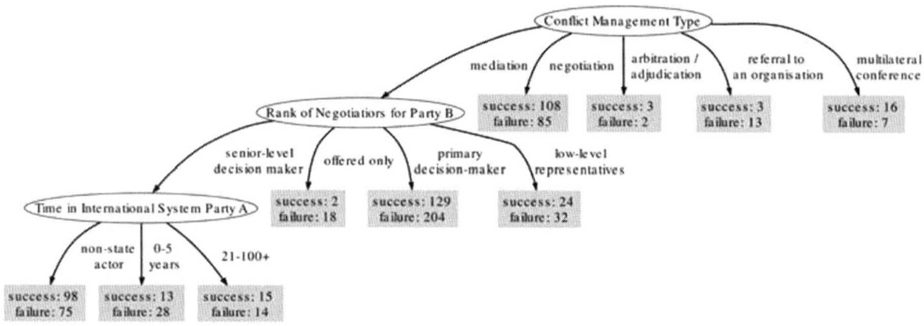

Figure 11.30. Pruned decision tree for CMAs from 1945 to 2000 in Europe

- Number of CMA in the years 1990 and after: 708; successful 333
- Pruned decision tree: 52.97 % (prediction failure)
- Predictive value of decision tree: 52.12 %

As the predictive value of the decision tree is worse than the default, relying on the tree is not recommended. Nevertheless, for reasons of completeness the decision tree is plotted.

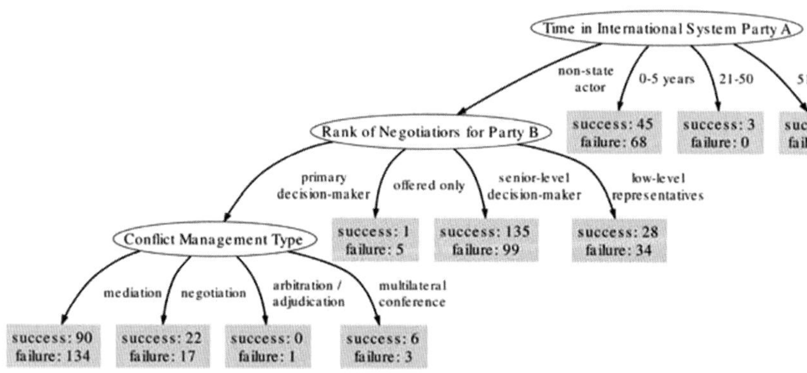

Figure 11.31. Pruned decision tree for CMA from 1990 and after in Europe

4.7 Summary of the regional differences of CMAs, their successes, and the predictive values of the decision trees

Table 11.4. Summary of the regional differences of CMAs, their successes, and the predictive values of the decision trees

					Correctly Classified Instances	
Geographic Region	*Conflict management attempts*	*Successful CMA*	*Cases after 1989*	*Successful CMA after 1989*	*Default*	*C4.5*
2 Central and South America	397	50.13%	140	64.29%	64.29%	63,57%
3 Africa	1314	44.75%	739	49.12%	50.88%	56.56%
4 South West Asia	466	47.85%	204	62.75%	62.75%	73.53%
5 East Asia and the Pacific	621	46.86 %	232	58.19%	58.19%	63.36%
6 Middle East	883	37.71%	314	31.85%	68.15%	64.97%
7 Europe	889	46.32%	708	47.03%	52.97%	52.12%
All Regions	4570	44.70%	2337	49.17%	50.83%	60.20%

It is interesting to note that the average predictive value of the decision trees for the period "after" is nearly 10 % higher than the default value.

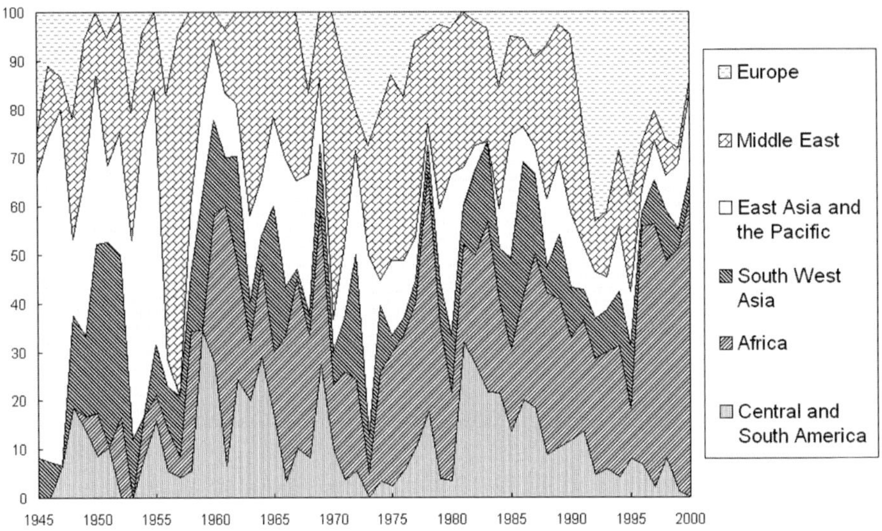

Figure 11.32. Geographic distribution of CMAs, from 1945 to 2000

5 IS IT POSSIBLE TO INTERACTIVELY STUDY CONFLICTS AND WITH WHICH BENEFITS?

In this section two interfaces will be presented which have one special quality in common: They use case-based reasoning for finding similar cases to a specific crisis situation.

They have different aims and therefore operate on different databases:

1. The first one aims at finding similar cases in order see which conflict management methods helped in situations similar to a current crisis situation and how good the chances are that a proposed conflict management attempt is successsful. This interface therefore operates on the CONFMAN database, the largest database on conflict management attempts.
2. The second one aims at finding similar cases to a current crisis situation to help assess the risk of its escalation in order to more efficiently prepare humanitarian aid. It therefore makes use of the database KOSIMO 2. More details also about this database are given also in Section 5.2.

5.1 Interface 1: For finding similar cases to a current crisis situation, in order to study which management attempts were successful

In order to make the CONFMAN database usable by the decision-maker, the political scientist or a student who wants or needs to study the relations between the different attributes, the interface which is described on the following pages has been developed.

Special concern was given to the decision-maker who is faced with a specific crisis situation and who wants to know which crisis situations are most similar to the current one in order to study which CMAs were successful in these similar situations, also considering differences between the current and these other situations in order to adapt her/his measures to the current circumstances. This is done by case-based reasoning, by finding the five most similar cases.

The functionality of the interface is explained in what follows, using screen-shots for illustration.

Figure 11.33. The start-page of the program. Options are displayed in the left-hand bar, with the Browse option activated and the others, namely Search, (Conflict) Details, and Case-Based Reasoning, at the bottom.

The Browse option allows browsing through the whole database, focusing on conflicts, mediators and a special region. The Search option offers more detailed ways of finding specific conflicts. Therefore a Search Assistant, SQL-queries and simple search queries are provided. The Details option provides all the details concerning a selected conflict. At the beginning, of course, this option cannot be accessed, as no conflict has been chosen. The Case-Based Reasoning option allows to retrieve the most similar case (or cases) comparing either a previously selected or a user-specified case to the database.

In the following we give a short introduction to these options and program functions.

5.1.1 Browse option

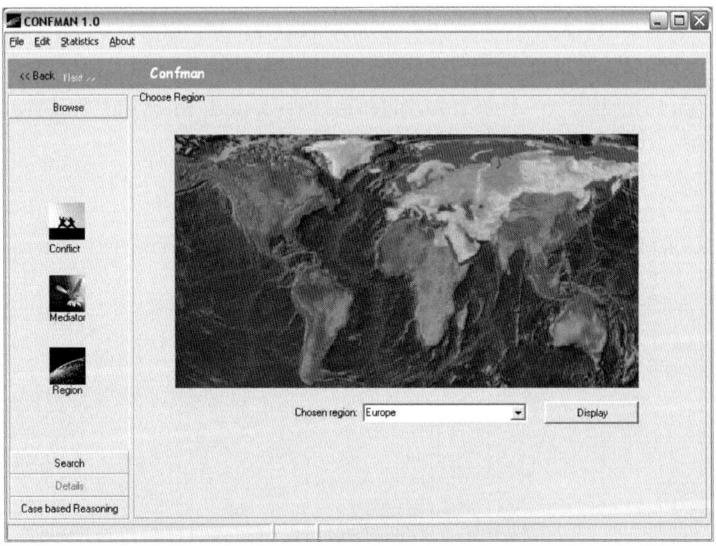

Figure 11.34. When clicking "Region", a map of the world is presented with the regions used in CONFMAN.

The user can click on any of the regions, e.g. Europe, and will get a list of all the conflicts from the specified region. Clicking on any conflict will access the Details option, providing an overview of the selected conflict and the possibility to access all information stored in the database about a specific conflict.

5.1.2 Details option

The following figure shows the Details option for a previously selected conflict. As already mentioned, this option is only available when a conflict from the database has been selected.

The Details option provides a general overview of the selected conflict, with the most important variables from the database describing the conflict, such as final outcome, core issue, brief party overview and all mediation attempts. The user can choose to see more specific details concerning the involved parties, the history of the involved parties, the management and the mediator.

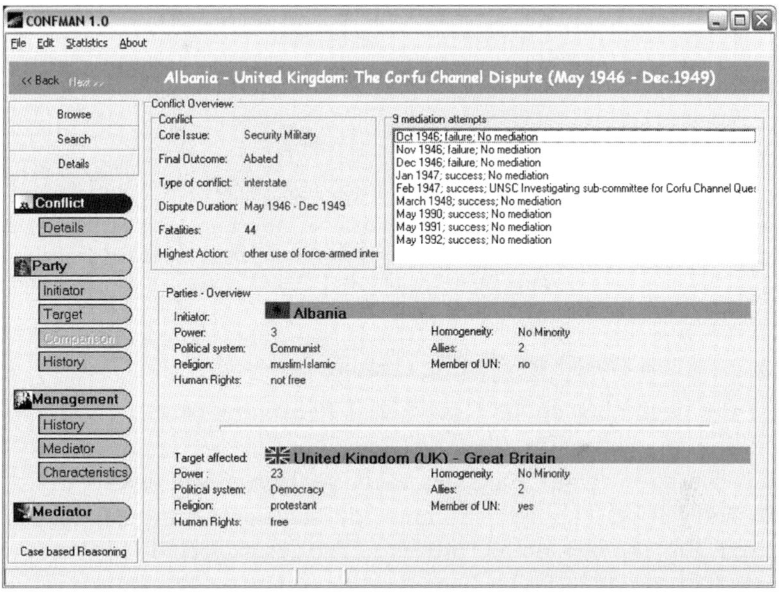

Figure 11.35. When selecting a conflict, essential information about this conflict is displayed. In the right window the Conflict Management Attempts (CMAs) are listed, clicking on a CMA brings up the details of this specific CMA.

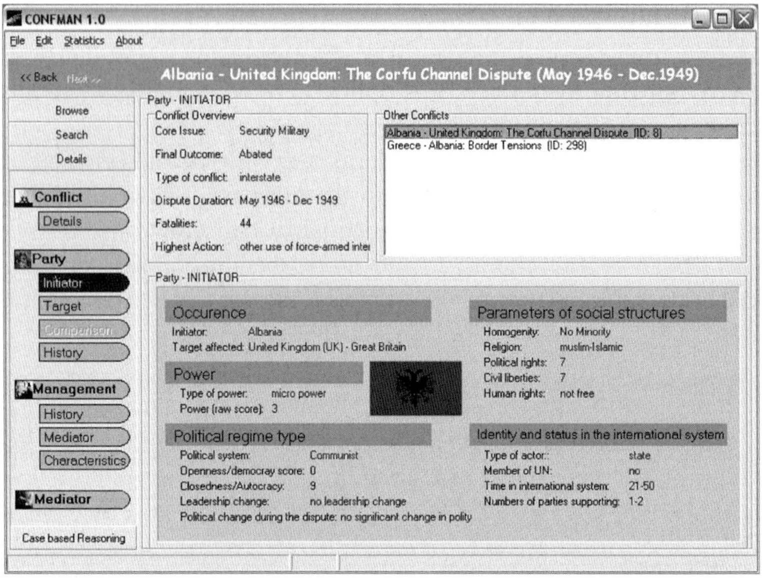

Figure 11.36. Detailed information on the initiator of the conflict. Other conflicts the initiator has been involved in are displayed and can be selected.

5.1.3 Case-Based Reasoning Option

At the beginning of the Case-Based Reasoning process, some variables describing the currently (user-)selected conflict are automatically added, namely Duration (D4a), Fatalities Party A (D5a) and Power Party A and B (P10a and P10b). The user can now add additional attributes that might be required for the reasoning process. The pre-selected attributes can be removed, in case the user wants to describe a new or different situation.

After selecting all attributes, the most similar cases to the current conflict situation are listed. When changing the desired similarity, more conflicts, which are less related to the conflict specified by the selected variables, are shown, by switching to the (Conflict) Details-Mode.

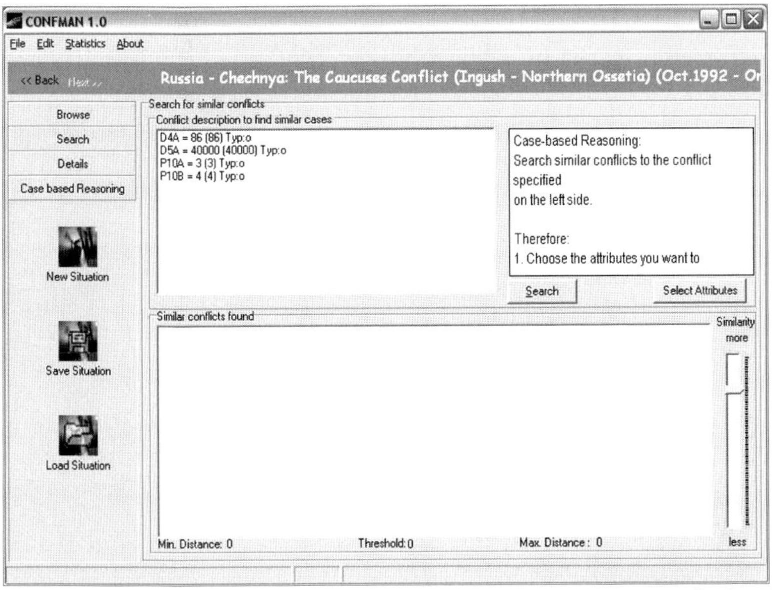

Figure 11.37. Start-menu for CBR. The instructions for the CBR-process are displayed.

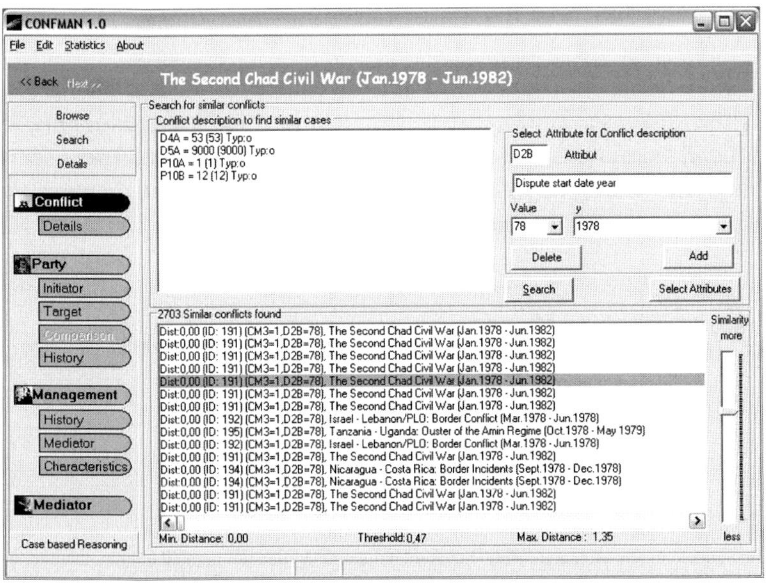

Figure 11.38. List of similar conflicts is shown

The Search option can be used for looking up a specific conflict.

5.1.4 Search Option

The Search option provides a Simple Search, a Search-Assistant and the possibility of stating SQL-queries for direct database access.

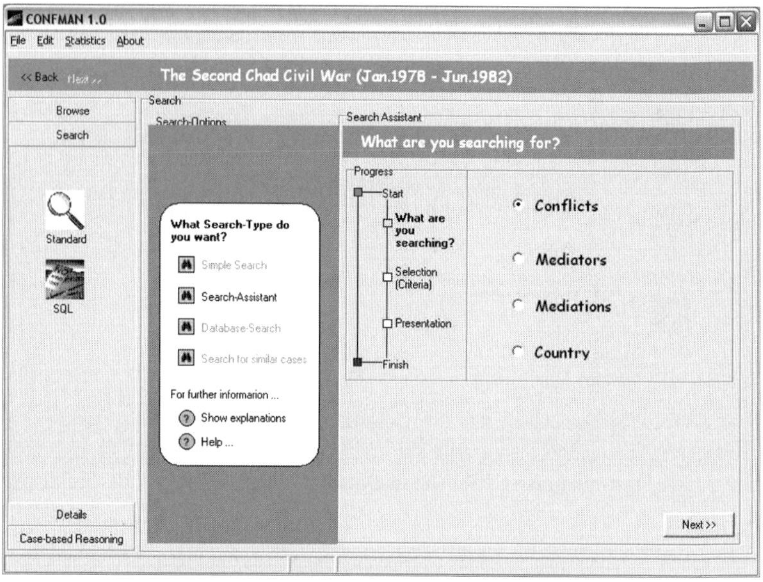

Figure 11.39. The search menu with the Search-Assistant selected

The Search Assistant has been developed for users who are unfamiliar with the database. The first step is to decide what you are looking for—either conflicts, mediators, mediation attempts or countries. The user is guided through the search process with a progress report which displays the remaining steps in the search process.

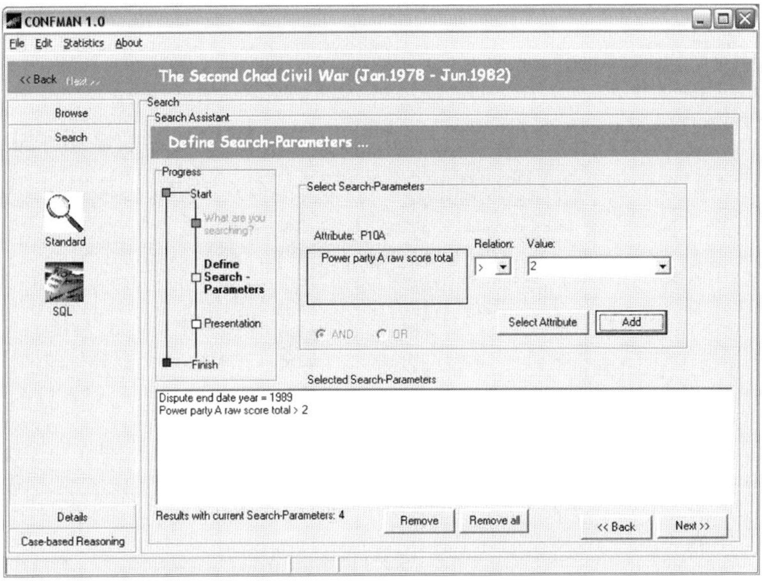

Figure 11.40. Defining search parameters

When selecting attributes, the Select Attribute dialogue introduced earlier is displayed, and variables can be chosen from the database and added to the search parameters. The selected search parameters are displayed and described in "natural language". Clicking on the "next" button advances the search process and leads to the specification of the search results. The user can then specify which attributes will be displayed in the search result. Pre-chosen attributes (recommended by the program) can be added from a drop-down menu, or more attributes can be selected, and finally the arrangement of the attributes can be modified. An abridged preview of the search result and the chosen attributes is displayed.

The following figure shows the Simple Search option.

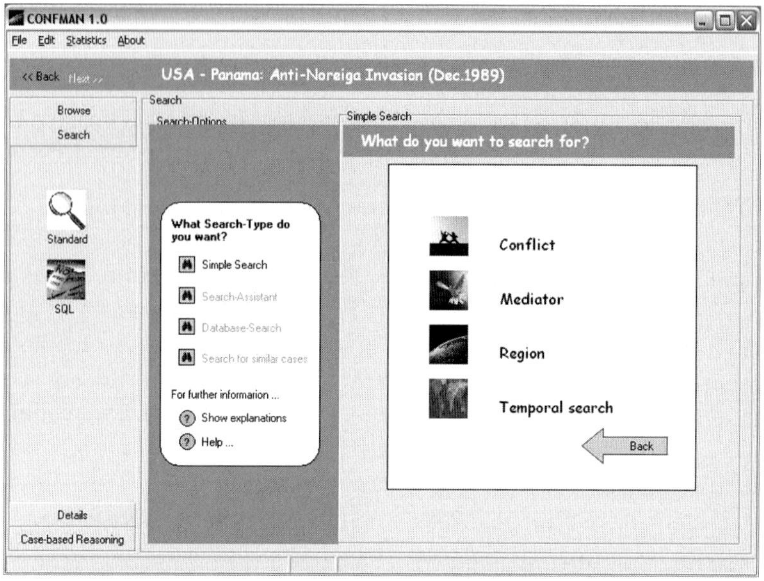

Figure 11.41. The Search Menu with simple search selected. All these search options can be accessed through the browse menu, but can also be directly accessed from this menu.

The search menu also provides access to a SQL-search which can be executed on the database, as shown in the following figure.

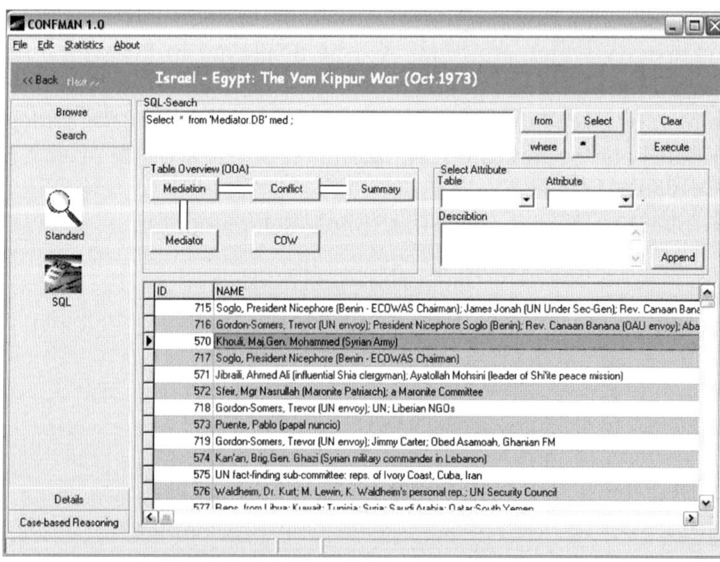

Figure 11.42. A simple SQL-search is given as an example. This function is for users who are already familiar with the database.

5.2 Interface 2: Preparing humanitarian aid by learning from history: Finding the most similar cases

Since the second interface is the result of a commissioned project, the considerations of the client which led to the project will be presented first:

Violent conflicts and wars still claim the lives of thousands of people every year, they devastate for years to come the infrastructure built up in developing regions with much effort, and deprive millions of refugees of their homes. However, the extent of violence and destruction caused by wars represents almost unsolvable problems also to those who want to help. Within the shortest amount of time, medical supply and foods have to be organized for the victims. This demands an enormous effort with regard to planning and organizing, which cannot be instantly afforded. Information and knowledge can make the difference here between life or death: the earlier humanitarian organizations learn of the place and extent of the catastrophe, the more effective help can be delivered. Yet, how is one supposed to know where the next war is going to drive tens or hundreds of thousands of people out of their houses?

Wars do not emerge out of thin air. They have a non-violent lead time during which participating actors threat with violence or use it only to a very small extent. A successful early-warning system for conflicts should identify these situations and differentiate them from those conflicts in which the likelihood for escalation is very low.

Although different attempts in developing such an early-warning system have been made in past years, none of them have been really convincing so far. These models were either too inexact, too time-consuming, or too expensive for the practitioners' demands. The European Humanitarian Aid Office (ECHO) of the EU Commission decided to follow a different path. According to the requirements set by the client, not a fully automated early-warning system was to be built, but an instrument that helps to assess the risk of escalation for new conflicts. ECHO commissioned the University of Heidelberg and the Austrian Research Institute for Artificial Intelligence (OFAI) with the creation of a conflict information system as simple but also as effective as possible. By entering some selected parameters of ongoing conflicts, the most similar conflicts from the past years should be found and listed. Based on the course of these similar conflicts, experts of the organization are then required to analyze and evaluate themselves the threat for escalation. In the following, the three essential elements of the project will be commented on: firstly, the provision of the dataset, secondly, the handling of the programme, and thirdly, the application of Artificial Intelligence.

5.2.1 The Creation of a Database

Already since the end of the 1980s, data regarding the present conflict events have been surveyed at the University of Heidelberg. What is specific about the Heidelberg approach is that here inter- as well as intra-national wars are recorded; also, in addition to this, the non-violent conflicts are being systematically observed. Thus an overview over the totality of conflict events could be achieved. The data were stored, similar to the Correlates of War Project with its wider circulation, in a list database, which was updated in irregular intervals between 1992 and 1998. Besides, a yearly conflict summary was created by the Heidelberg Institute for International Conflict Research (HIIK), where the conflicts observed worldwide were categorized with a methodology similar to the database. The most recent Conflict Barometer 2004 can be downloaded at http://www.hiik.de/en/main.htm.

The Acquisition of Conflict Dynamics

However, already prior to the start of the research project it had become obvious that the structure of the database so far showed substantial deficits regarding the acquisition and analysis of conflict dynamics. As for example changes in the actors‘ constellation, in the number and type of disputed items, and in the intensity with which a conflict has been carried out could only be understood in a very limited way. It was an essential requirement for the project, however, that the single conflict phases be recordable and offer the possibility to be put into a time sequence.

The Special Significance of Intra-national Conflicts

A further difficulty represented the exact acquisition of intra-national conflicts. The problem was two-fold: on the one hand, the perception of these conflicts has strongly changed since the end of the Cold War. While in earlier projects most attention focused on the international conflicts, the humanitarian catastrophes in Rwanda, Somalia, and Yugoslavia refocused research interest on the different rebel groups and their mode of warfare. The difficulty with the acquisition of these conflicts is that they are being carried out in a different way than international wars. Non-state actors avoid, as far as possible, large and continuous confrontations with their adversaries and prefer a “pinprick tactic“ instead: through frequent but limited attacks, mostly against the civil population. The primary aim of these attacks is often not to kill but to displace people, to deprive them of their goods and to control the raw materials. Identifying or evaluating these conflicts via the number of fatalities is, therefore, inapplicable. But in order to record this kind of conflicts in the database, nevertheless, other criteria than the specification of fatalities had to be consulted.

The second problem with intra-national conflicts is the multiplicity of actors involved in intra-national wars and their forming and changing of alliances. In contrast to international conflicts, dyads, i.e. conflicts between exactly two parties, are the exception, and a frequent change in the constellation is an essential feature of these conflicts. Up to now, however, only one dyad for each conflict could be recorded in the list database.

Insight into the Process Level and the Verifiability of the Data

One last issue in conceptualizing a database regards the deepening of information about a conflict. Since one of the most important aims of the database project has been the yield of insight into the dynamics of conflicts, all entries in the database have been provided with the date when they took place or with the time span for which they were valid. In order to keep all data and entries understandable also for external users, fields for stating the information source as well as for comments have been added.

The Relational Database Model

All in all one can say that the problems prior to the project start lay in the small amount of data and in the low explanatory power of the quantitative analyses so far. This was due to the form of the list database used up to that time. The solution to this problem lay in the development of a relational database model, which can, firstly, record significantly more diverse information about a conflict, and, secondly, permits a nearly unlimited number of information units. The following table provides an overview over the improvements attained. It shows that the amount of information available has clearly increased. Especially regarding the variable of "Conflict Measures", which is important for the analysis of causes and effects of conflict dynamics, data of a number and a quality unequalled so far could be stored, which permits totally new insights into the process level of conflicts.

Table 11.5. Progress from KOSIMO 1 to KOSIMO 2

	KOSIMO 1	*KOSIMO 2*
Temporal Coverage	1945 – 1998	1945 – 06 /2005
Number of Conflicts	301	644
Number of Conflict Dynamics Data Entries	693	3.400
Number of Conflict Instruments	1.800	23.200
Number of Recorded Non-State Actors	290	1.200

Number of Constellations	340	1400
Number of Supporters	0	870
Number of State Actor Describing Variables	210	6.700
Number of Non-State Actor Describing Variables	0	1.300

5.2.2 The Input Module

The project's second challenge was the client's requirement to keep the handling of the program as simple as possible. For the sequel of the first project, we decided to create the input modules on the basis of a Flash Program.

The handling of the program comprises three steps: 1) the input of the data on the ongoing conflict; 2) the output of the list of all similar conflicts and the selection of the most interesting conflicts; 3) the insight into the details of the respective conflict.

The Input of the Values about the Ongoing Conflict

In order to record the ongoing conflict situation as exactly as possible, all in all nine different variables can be entered. One can, but does not have to, use all nine input possibilities. According to the value entered, the most similar values are being searched by the program developed by OFAI. The input is menu-driven via drop-down menus. Multiple choice is possible. For all variables on-line help is available during the entry. This makes sure that the program requires only moderate training time to be usable by new coders.

The following variables can be recorded:

Affected Countries: not all states that participate in conflicts are also affected by these conflicts. As for example, the war between the USA and Iraq was being carried out exclusively on Iraqi territory. Vice versa, a lot of wars that are actually intra-national are being carried into neighbouring states through the withdrawal of rebel groups.

Restrict to Time Period: this variable expresses the duration since when the respective conflict situation has been observed.

Time Difference to Previous Conflict: the findings of our research have shown that a major part of violent conflicts occur in the same countries. Often previous conflicts destabilize the affected country so that this increases the threat for escalation of a new conflict.

Duration of Current Conflict: this variable checks since when the entire conflict has existed. Analyses of the dataset have shown that conflicts escalate with a different pace depending on the region where they occur and on the conflict issue. While in African conflicts the time span between the first utterance of a contrast of interests and the outbreak of violence averages to six years, in Asia, in contrast, it averages to nine years.

Direct Actors: hardly any other variable influences the outcome of a conflict as much as the number and type of directly participating actors. These are defined as parties which have articulated own interests within the conflict and have pursued them. Categorically to be differentiated are state and non-state actors. Both of them are recorded separately. While a lot of variables describing military or demographic structure are already stored in annual series, and while these can be used in finding most similar states, these have to be specifically recorded for non-state actors. As far as known, the following factors allow to specificy a non-state actor: the time elapsed since the organization's establishment; the size, i.e. the number of people avowing themselves to the actor; the degree of organization (from the unorganized mass-movement to the state-like organized rebel group); the actor's orientation (religious, cultural, or ethnic group); or the type of armament.

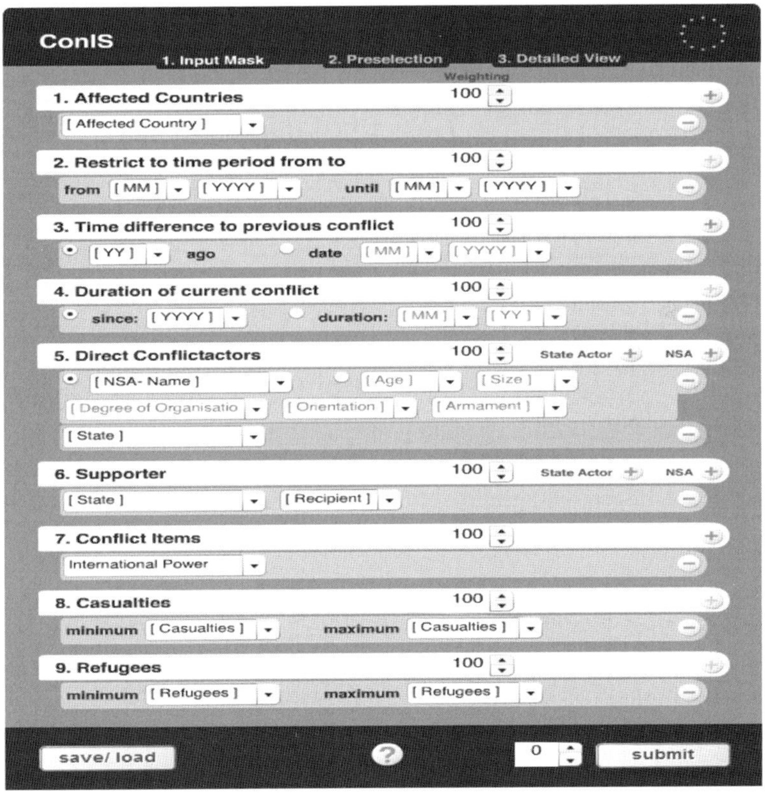

Figure 11.43. Input Mask

Supporter: third parties which support one of the conflict parties militarily, financially, or politically can exert decisive influence on the perseverance of directly involved actors.

Conflict Items: besides the participating actors, this is one of the variables with most decisive influence on the course of the conflict. The following conflict items can be selected: Autonomy, Decolonialization, Ideology/ System, Internal Power, International Power, Regional Predominance, Resources, Secession, Territory, and Others.

Casualties: even though the number of fatalities is more difficult to ascertain in intra-national than in international wars, and though many sources often strongly contradict each other in their statements, this variable is nevertheless an important factor in weighing the conflict. If fatalities could be observed at a specific moment, these can be indicated with maximum and minimum values.

Refugees: the number of refugees can also be an important indicator for further escalation. We know from our data analysis that in some conflicts a small wave of refugees is followed by mass flight. The entry takes place analogously to the previous item.

For later repetitions of the query, the scenario can be saved or a scenario previously recorded can be loaded. With the „Submit" button, the data are handed over to the Case Based Reasoning Programme.

The Output List of the Most Similar Conflicts

After acquisition of all existing or relevant data regarding the ongoing conflict, the data are handed over to the program created by OFAI. This program reports back a list of similar conflicts. Sorted by highest agreement, the following information can be read off the output list: 1) name of conflict; 2) the internal conflict identification number; 3) the conflict start; 4) information as to whether the conflict escalated at a later point in time (Yes/ No field); 5) information as to whether further refugee movements occurred (Yes/ No field); 6) the degree of agreement (stated in per cent).

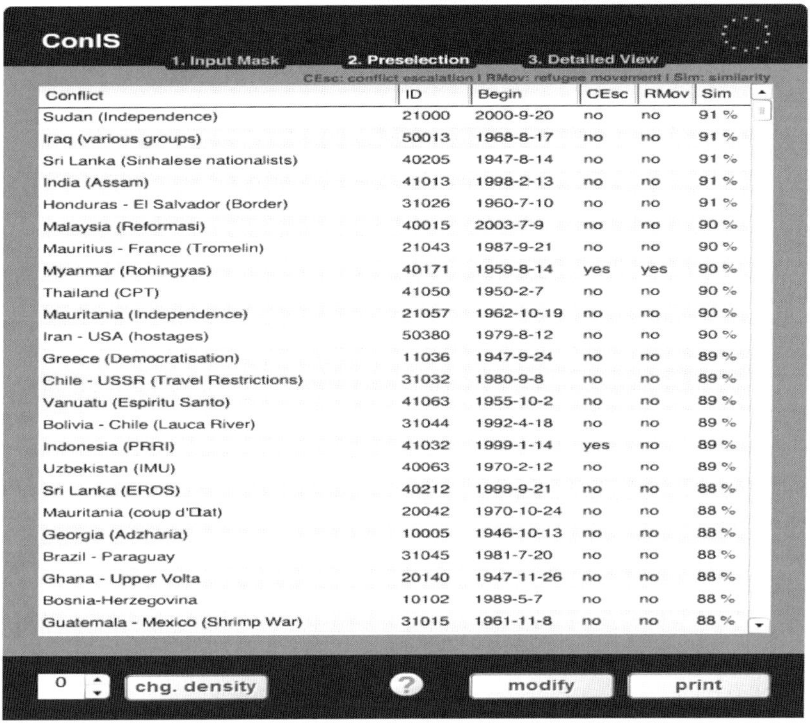

Conflict	ID	Begin	CEsc	RMov	Sim
Sudan (Independence)	21000	2000-9-20	no	no	91 %
Iraq (various groups)	50013	1968-8-17	no	no	91 %
Sri Lanka (Sinhalese nationalists)	40205	1947-8-14	no	no	91 %
India (Assam)	41013	1998-2-13	no	no	91 %
Honduras - El Salvador (Border)	31026	1960-7-10	no	no	91 %
Malaysia (Reformasi)	40015	2003-7-9	no	no	90 %
Mauritius - France (Tromelin)	21043	1987-9-21	no	no	90 %
Myanmar (Rohingyas)	40171	1959-8-14	yes	yes	90 %
Thailand (CPT)	41050	1950-2-7	no	no	90 %
Mauritania (Independence)	21057	1962-10-19	no	no	90 %
Iran - USA (hostages)	50380	1979-8-12	no	no	90 %
Greece (Democratisation)	11036	1947-9-24	no	no	89 %
Chile - USSR (Travel Restrictions)	31032	1980-9-8	no	no	89 %
Vanuatu (Espiritu Santo)	41063	1955-10-2	no	no	89 %
Bolivia - Chile (Lauca River)	31044	1992-4-18	no	no	89 %
Indonesia (PRRI)	41032	1999-1-14	yes	no	89 %
Uzbekistan (IMU)	40063	1970-2-12	no	no	89 %
Sri Lanka (EROS)	40212	1999-9-21	no	no	88 %
Mauritania (coup d'□at)	20042	1970-10-24	no	no	88 %
Georgia (Adzharia)	10005	1946-10-13	no	no	88 %
Brazil - Paraguay	31045	1981-7-20	no	no	88 %
Ghana - Upper Volta	20140	1947-11-26	no	no	88 %
Bosnia-Herzegovina	10102	1989-5-7	no	no	88 %
Guatemala - Mexico (Shrimp War)	31015	1961-11-8	no	no	88 %

Figure 11.44. List of the most similar cases. By clicking the respective buttons, the result summary can be either modified or printed.

Insight into Conflict Dynamics of Similar Conflicts: "Conflicts at a Glance"

With a double click on one of the conflicts in the summary list, the receives detail information regarding the single conflict "at a glance". In the example mentioned here, the conflict between Iran and Iraq, the summary extends over three pages in total.

Figure 11.45. shows the first page. Top left there is a little world map where the affected region is encircled; the conflict name appears in the middle, and the maximum intensity that the conflict reached is displayed on the right side of the headline.

Iraq - Iran

ID: 50004

5

Items

Periodstart	Periodend	Item	Comment
1969-04-19	1988-08-02	Territory	territorial conflicts along the Shatt el-Arab and several islands in the Persian Gulf; Iraq drops its territorial claims
1969-04-19	--	International Power	there needs to be a category "other" to code prisoners of war and reparations (since 2.8.1988)
1979-04-01	--	Ideology / System	Panislamism in Iran versus Panarabism in Iraq
1980-09-22	1988-08-20	Resources	not sure about item but some authors argue that one of the reasons for Iraq to invade Iran was to annex the oil-rich Iranian province of Khusistan in order to own most of the oil-sources in the region to gain dominance (see Mirzaie-Tahmizi 2002, p. 21 f.)

Constellations

Periodstart	Periodend	Actor 1	Actor 2	Comment
1971-01-01	--	Iraq	Iran	--

Supporter

Periodstart	Periodend	Actor	Adressee	Kind of Support	Comment
1980-09-22	1988-08-20	United States	Iraq	military support	--
1980-09-22	1988-08-20	Germany	Iraq	military support	--
1980-09-22	1988-08-20	United Kingdom	Iraq	military support	--
1980-09-22	1988-08-20	France	Iraq	military support	--
1980-09-22	1988-08-20	Italy	Iraq	military support	--
1980-09-22	1991-08-20	USSR	Iraq	military support	--
1985-09-14	1986-01-15	United States	Iran	military support	--
1980-09-22	1988-08-20	AL Arab League	Iraq	political support	--

Intervention

Periodstart	Periodend	Actor	Intervention	Comment
--	--	--	--	--

Intensities

Periodstart	Periodend	I	Intensity	Sparking Event
1969-04-19	1973-11-30	3	Crisis	--
1973-12-01	1974-03-06	4	Severe Crisis	--
1974-03-07	1974-03-18	3	Crisis	--
1974-03-19	1974-07-31	2	Manifest Conflict	--
1974-08-01	1975-03-05	4	Severe Crisis	--
1975-03-06	1979-02-01	1	Latent Conflict	Algier treaty
1979-02-02	1980-09-21	4	Severe Crisis	When Khomeini gains power in Iran, Iraq starts single combat operations in the borderland.
1980-09-22	1988-08-20	5	War	--
1988-08-21	2001-04-17	3	Crisis	--
2001-04-18	2001-08-01	3	Crisis	--
2001-08-02	2003-04-09	2	Manifest Conflict	--
2003-04-10	2004-07-26	1	Latent Conflict	--
2004-07-27	--	2	Manifest Conflict	The conflict intensity between Iraq and Iran has increased throughout the last weeks. TV station al-Arabija reported that the Iranian consul, Fereidun Jahani, was taken hostage by a group called "Islamic Army of Iraq". According to news agency Isna, more than 1,200 Iranians have been arrested in Kerbala at the end of July/ beginning of August. Iraq's minister of defense called Iran the "main enemy of Iraq".

< prev | next > | 1 of 3 | New Search | Print

Figure 11.45. "Conflicts at a Glance" 1st page

The first section under the headline provides information about the disputed items, the second about the conflict constellation (i.e. who acts against whom), the third about the supporting parties (each with specifications to the type and receiver of support); the fourth lists any intervening powers, and the fifth block on this page shows the conflict dynamics, i.e. through which intensity this conflict has already passed. For all entries, specifications regarding duration and validity of the values are given as well as any comments.

The second page starts with a graphical representation of the course of the conflict, which is derived from the last section of the first page. This chart shows exactly when the conflict became violent.

Further information to be obtained from page two refers to attempts by a third party to mediate between the conflict parties, and to specifications about negotiations between the actors. The program also shows the data recorded in the database concerning refugees and fatalities. These two items are recorded with additional specifications as to the source of information, beside the usual comments.

On the third page here, the specifications about the point in time and the number of fatalities are continued.

Iraq - Iran [ID: 50004]

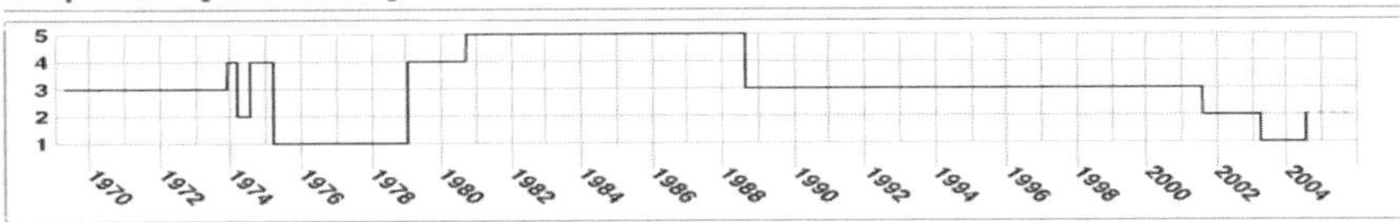

Mediation

Periodstart	Periodend	Actor	Meditationterm	Comment
1974-03-19	1974-03-19	UN - United Nations	Third parties are accepeted as mediators by all conflict parties	--
1975-06-13	1975-06-13	Algeria	Third parties are accepeted as mediators by all conflict parties	--
1987-09-13	1987-09-14	UN - United Nations	Third parties are accepeted as mediators by all conflict parties	--

Negotiations

Periodstart	Periodend	Negotiationterm	Comment
1988-02-11	1988-02-11	negotiations with a special objective with all of the conflict parties	unsuccessful
1988-04-20	1988-04-20	negotiations with a special objective with all of the conflict parties	unsuccessful
1988-08-18	1988-08-20	negotiations with a special objective with all of the conflict parties	--
1988-08-25	1988-08-25	negotiations with a special objective with all of the conflict parties	unsuccessful
1988-11-01	1988-11-02	negotiations with a special objective with all of the conflict parties	unsuccessful
1988-11-11	1988-11-11	negotiations with a special objective with all of the conflict parties	unsuccessful
1990-07-04	1990-07-04	no information available	--
2002-01-28	2002-01-28	preliminary negotiations without any special aims with all of the conflict parties	--

Refugees

Total Min:	81000	Max:	0		
Periodstart	**Periodend**	**Origin**	**Dest.**	**Source**	**Comment**
1969-04-20	1969-05-15	Iraq	Iran	Pfetsch; S. 114 ff.	Iranians who lived in Iraq were forced to leave and came to rest in Iranian border cities.
1970-01-01	1970-06-30	Iraq	Iran	Pfetsch; S. 114 ff.	exact dates unclear
1971-12-26	1972-01-03	Iraq	Iran	AdG; 16803	--

Casualties

Total Min:	557177	Max:	2054137
Periodstart	**Periodend**	**Source**	**Comment**
1972-01-03	1972-01-03	AdG; 16803	info probably biased
1973-12-24	1974-03-06	AdG; 18727	info probably biased
1973-12-24	1974-03-06	AdG; 18727	info probably biased

< prev   next >   2 of 3   New Search   Print

Figure 11.46. "Conflicts at a Glance" 2nd page

Iraq - Iran [ID: 50004]

Casualties

Periodstart	Periodend	Source	Comment
1980-09-22	1988-08-20	For minimum see: Mirzai-Tashnizi, Hossain: Der Konflikt Irak - Iran, Wien 2002, p. 22.	--
1980-09-22	1980-09-30	AdG; 23909	info probably biased
1980-09-22	1980-09-30	AdG; 23909	info probably biased
1980-09-22	1980-12-25	AdG; 25282	info probably biased
1980-09-22	1985-10-14	AdG; 29346	info probably biased
1986-02-12	1986-02-12	AdG; 29646	info probably biased
1986-12-24	1986-12-26	AdG; 30701	info probably biased
1986-12-24	1986-12-26	AdG; 30701	info probably biased
1987-01-09	1987-01-12	AdG; 30701	info probably biased
1987-01-09	1987-01-12	AdG; 30701	info probably biased
1987-01-15	1987-01-18	AdG; 30701	info probably biased
1987-01-15	1987-01-20	AdG; 30701	info probably biased
1987-05-17	1987-05-17	AdG; 31353	--
1988-03-17	1988-03-17	AdG; 32075	Iraq kills 5000 Kurds in Halabjah by the use of poison gas. The Kurds were suspected to support Iranian soldiers.
1988-05-04	1988-06-26	AdG; 32321	info probably biased
1988-05-04	1988-06-26	AdG; 32321	info probably biased
1988-07-03	1988-07-03	AdG; 32321	--
1988-07-29	1988-07-31	AdG; 32477	info probably biased
1988-08-03	1988-08-03	AdG; 32477	--

Figure 11.47. "Conflicts at a Glance" 3rd page

6 DISCUSSION

The decision trees obtained from the subset with conflict data in 1989 and before and the subset with conflict data from the years 1990 and after not only look very different, the relevance of the variables for predicting successful outcome of a CMA, obtained by a fifty-fold cross-validation, are significantly different.

However, one should not ignore the possibility that due to the inputting of the information about the conflicts between 1995 and 2000 by other persons with other implicit coding criteria than the ones before, a potential bias could enter the database, and these differences could be their result.

Therefore another database, the International Crisis Behavior (ICB) was used to see if also in this database differences would show up. Since the variables are, evidently, differently coded, as a variable corresponding to success or failure of a CMA in CONFMAN, we chose the variable EXSAT (Extent of satisfaction about outcome). Its values (1) All satisfied, and (2) Mostly satisfied were taken as corresponding to "success" and the values (4) Mostly dissatisfied, and (5) All dissatisfied, to "failure".

CRISMG (Crisis managemnet technique) was used as variable corresponding to CM3 (Conflict management type) in CONFMAN. CRISMG has eight values: (1) Negotiation, (2) Adjudication or arbitration, (3) Mediation,

(4) Multiple not including violence, (5) Non-military pressure, (6) Non-violoent military, (7) Multiple including violence, and (8) Violence.

In order to have enough cases for a comparison in the "after" time period, 1985 was chosen as "cutting year", this being even less favorable for showing a difference than the comparison with the CONFMAN data.

The resulting comparison is presented in the following table:

1918-1985

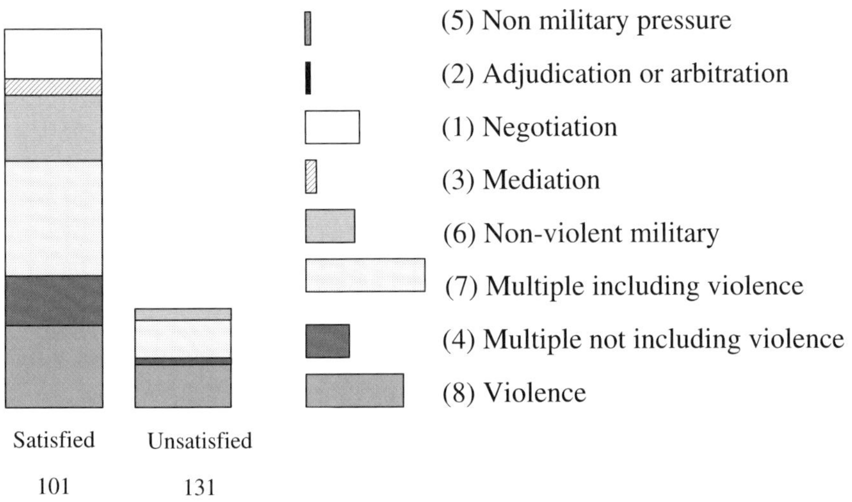

1986-2001

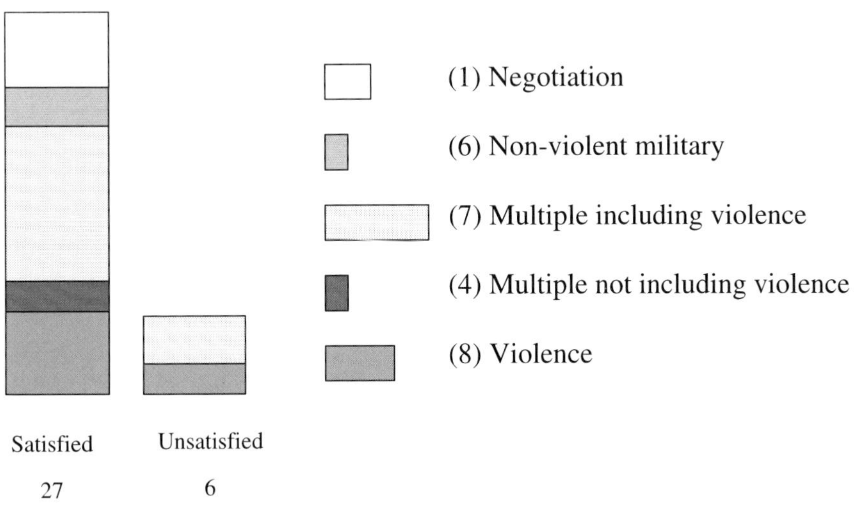

This result is in concordance with the difference found when using the CONFMAN database and demonstrates that the global political situation, at least with regard to conflict management, *is* different.

A comparison of the accuracy of the decision trees obtained under the different conditions is shown in Table 11.6.

Table 11.6. Comparison of interstate and internal conflicts.

				Correctly classified instances	
		Conflict management attempts	*Successful CMAs*	*Default*	*C4.5*
Interstate conflict	all	1917	43.77 %	56.2 %	65.0 %
	after 1989	537	47.49 %	52.5 %	60.3 %
Civil / international conflict	all	2653	45.46 %	54.5 %	61.1 %
	after 1989	1800	49.67 %	50.3 %	57.6 %

In the future, decision trees for different subsets of the database will be computed and their validity checked by cross-validation. In addition to this specificity of the decision trees, it can be assumed that by this pre-selection of variables—if there are structural differences between the subsets—a higher predictive validity of the decision trees should be achieved. However, it could also happen that the entries in the variables of these subsets are too few to justify the application of these methods.

Turning back to CONFMAN, from the differences in the decision tress, at least two questions arise:

1. When *today* predicting the outcome of conflict management attempts, does it make sense to rely on data from before 1990 when it was shown that there is such a difference in the influence of variables "before" and "after"? And when it even was shown that the prediction quality of the "after" data is better than that from "before?

   Probably the answer must be "no", however, these data still remain very valuable, e.g. for this study, but also for other historical, retrospective or developmental studies. The same seems to hold also for ICB.

2. Can the variables chosen about 15 years ago still be relevant when the international arena has changed so much?

   Here the answer can be "yes", since their prediction quality in the time since 1990 is even considerably *better* than before.

The reason for the difference between "before" and "after" may not only be the gradual shift from a bipolar to a unipolar system of politics, it may also be the result of the shift from a majority of conflicts between states to a majority of internal conflicts, as can also be seen in the following picture (data used from CONFMAN): This other possible cause will be tested in the next step of the project.

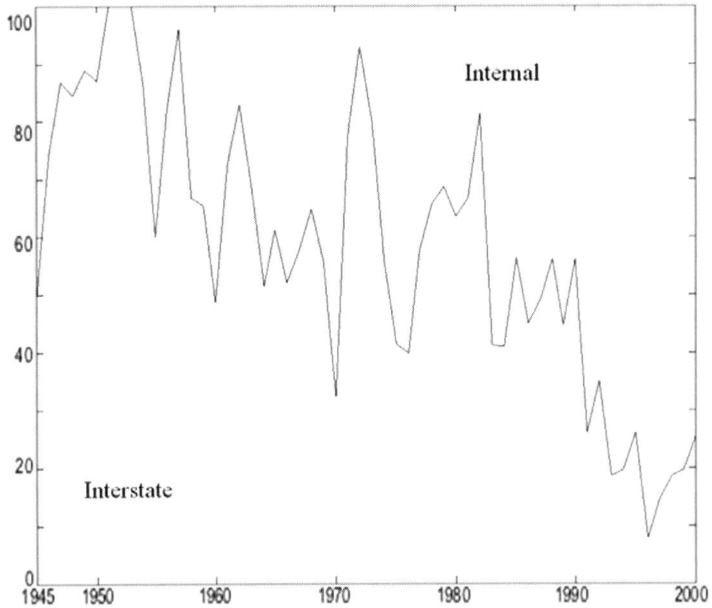

Figure 11.48. Temporal development of the ratio of interstate and internal conflicts

One can also question if 1989 really is *the* year which separates the "before" and the "after" sets best. It was not arbitrarily chosen, e.g. Wallensteen (2002) writes that "the Cold War may have ended somewhere between 1987 and 1991", thus 1989 seems to be a well-chosen year. However, some political scientists argue that the global influence of the USSR had decreased already considerably in the eighties. Others argue that it took some time after the dissolution of the USSR until its global influence diminished. As a further step, the "border" year shall be moved from 1950 to 1995 (excluding the years near the end of the time scale) to search maximum differences between the decision trees in both subsets, testing them with cross-validation.

It may also be of interest to move to two borders because one could imagine that there are more then two distinguishable time periods to be found, e.g. the time before the onset of the so-called cold war and the cold war period itself. However, it is not yet clear how this should be managed from a technical point of view.

Regarding regions, it was attempted to compute decision trees for the time period "1990 and after" for each region. Clearly, the validity of these decision trees is very low compared to the default values. The reasons may be the small number of cases that is further reduced by 10 % in the case of the cross-validations, and the fact that in some regions many conflicts started not long before 2000, so that the number of successful CMAs is even smaller than the average. However, the clear differences between the decision trees may be of interest.

Regarding the interface, a first version, using a commercial database system, was developed which was as general as possible. This version, probably because it gave no guidance, did not allow to key in a current conflict situation, sometimes had horrible response times, and turned out to be more of interest to computer nerds than to political scientists.

The first of the two interfaces was designed after studies of two interfaces that were developed originally for small databases with far less attributes (Bloomfield and Moulton, 1997, Brecher and Wilkenfeld, 2000; for an updated version see http://www.cidcm.umd.edu/icb/). It is really a version 0.1, i.e. it has to be improved in several aspects and then has to be tested by experts with respect to its usability before it can be made available for a larger audience. Owing to the fact that the CONFMAN database is the largest database of conflict management attempts, its usefulness for recommendations in current crisis situations could be expected.

The second interface was recently delivered to the European Humanitarian Aid Office (ECHO). Its aim is a different one, and it therefore also operates on data from another database, namely KOSIMO 2. The field test will show its benefits (or not).

At least to our knowledge, these are the only two interfaces which make use of case-based reasoning.

References

Bercovitch J., Langley J., 1993, The nature of dispute and the effectiveness of international mediation, *Journal of Conflict Resolution* **37**:670-691.

Bercovitch J., ed., 1996, *Resolving International Conflicts*, Lynne Rienner Publ., Boulder and London, 1996.

Bloomfield, L. P., Moulton, A., 1997, *Managing International Conflict*, St. Martin's Press, New York.

Brecher, M., Wilkenfeld, J. 2000, *A Study of Crisis*, Univ. of Michigan Press, Ann Arbor.

Fürnkranz J., Petrak J., Trappl R., 1997, Knowledge discovery in international conflict databases, *Applied Artificial Intelligence* **11**:91-118.

Kolodner J. L., 1993, *Case-Based Reasoning*, Kluwer Academic Publishers, Boston/Dordrecht/London.

Petrak J., Fürnkranz J., Trappl R., 1994, *The Potential Contribution of AI to the Avoidance of Crises and Wars: Using CBR Methods with the KOSIMO Database of Conflicts*, Oesterreichisches Forschungsinstitut fuer Artificial Intelligence, Wien, TR-94-32.

Pfetsch F. R., Billing P., 1994, *Datenhandbuch nationaler und internationaler Konflikte*, Nomos, Baden-Baden, Germany.

Quinlan, J. R., 1993, *C4.5: Programs for Machine Learning*, Morgan Kaufmann, San Mateo, CA.

Trappl R., Fürnkranz J., Petrak J., 1996, Digging for peace: Using machine learning methods for assessing international conflict databases, in Wahlster W., ed., *Proceedings of the 12th European Conference on Artificial Intelligence (ECAI-96)*, Wiley, Chichester/London/New York, pp. 453-457.

Trappl, R., Fürnkranz, J., Petrak, J., Bercovitch, J., 1997, Machine learning and case-based reasoning: their potential role in preventing the outbreak of wars or in ending them, in Della Riccia, G., Kruse, R., and Lenz, H.-J., eds., *Learning, Networks, and Statistics*, Springer, Vienna and New York.

Wallensteen, P., 2002, *Understanding Conflict Resolution. War, Peace and the Global System*, Sage, London.

Wickboldt A.-K., Bercovitch J., Piramuthu S., 1999, Dynamics of international mediation: analysis using machine learning methods, *Conflict Management and Peace Science* 17:49-68.

Witten, I. H., Frank, E., 2000, *Data Mining—Practical Machine Learning Tools and Techniques with Java Implementation*, Morgan Kaufmann, San Mateo, CA.

APPENDIX

In this Appendix the complete listings of the respective output from the weka-program http://www.cs.waikato.ac.nz/~ml/weka (last checked 22 September 2005) is presented, together with the abbreviations of the variables and their possible values in the CONFMAN database. This output was used to draw the decision trees in the main body of this chapter.

The number in brackets in the listings have the following interpretation: The first number is the total number of cases, the second number is the number of cases which do not fall in the category (success/failure) given before the bracket. E.g, in the first decision tree below: If the CM3 (conflict management type) is 1 (mediation) and P10b (power of party B) is less or equal 32 and D5a (number of fatalities) is less or equal 800, then D5a <= 800: success (423.0/197.0) means in 226 cases (423-197) the CMA was a success, in 197 cases it was a failure (opposite of success). Since these numbers are the result of a 10-fold cross-validation, fractions can occur

In order to make finding the respective decision tree easier, each listing is preceded by the respective figure number and caption.

Figure 11.5: Predicting the success of a CMA by the decision tree

```
CM3 = 1
|  P10b <= 32
|  |  D5a <= 800: success (423.0/197.0)
|  |  D5a > 800: failure (2221.0/906.0)
|  P10b > 32: failure (59.0/8.0)
CM3 = 2
|  P10b <= 24
|  |  CM12 = 1
|  |  |  CM17b = 0: failure (10.6/0.62)
|  |  |  CM17b = 1: success (189.35/84.7)
|  |  |  CM17b = 2: failure (234.84/109.63)
|  |  |  CM17b = 3: failure (63.57/23.41)
|  |  |  CM17b = ?: failure (0.0)
|  |  CM12 = 2: success (613.26/230.66)
|  |  CM12 = 3: failure (12.46/5.98)
|  |  CM12 = 4: success (2.77/0.33)
|  |  CM12 = 5: failure (4.15/1.66)
|  |  CM12 = ?: success (0.0)
|  P10b > 24: failure (395.0/146.0)
CM3 = 3: success (32.0/12.0)
CM3 = 4: failure (173.0/35.0)
CM3 = 5: success (136.0/63.0)
```

CM3 CONFLICT MANAGEMENT TYPE

Management type

0 No management activity

1 Mediation
2 Negotiation
3 Arbitration/Adjudication
4 Referral to an organisation
5 Multilateral conference

P10b POWER PARTY B RAW SCORE TOTAL

The absolute value of the difference in the power of Party A and Party B is calculated (ranging from 0 to 34)

compute P10c=abs(P10a-P10b)

D5a FATALITIES RAW

CM12 INITIATED BY

Request for conflict management initiated by (i.e. suggested, appealed for, or offered).

CM17b RANK OF NEGOTIATORS FOR PARTY B

Negotiators in the conflict management attempt for Party A or B
0 Offered Only
1 Primary Decision-Maker
2 Senior-level Decision-Maker
3 Low-level Representatives
6 Unspecified
9 No Conflict management - Not Applicable

Figure 11.6: Pruned decision tree for the CMAs of conflicts starting before and in 1989

CM3 = 1
| CM10b <= 270: failure (1831.0/718.0)
| CM10b > 270: success (137.0/55.0)
CM3 = 2
| P19b = 1: success (638.0/285.0)
| P19b = 2
| | D4a <= 146
| | | CM12 = 1: failure (129.0/59.0)
| | | CM12 = 2: success (122.8/39.47)
| | | CM12 = 3: success (3.72/1.32)
| | | CM12 = 4: success (2.48/1.21)
| | | CM12 = 5: success (0.0)
| | | CM12 = ?: success (0.0)
| | D4a > 146: failure (78.0/18.0)
| P19b = 3: failure (53.0/15.0)
| P19b = 4: failure (166.0/57.0)
CM3 = 3: success (28.0/11.0)
CM3 = 4: failure (166.0/34.0)

CM3 = 5: success (65.0/28.0)

Correctly Classified Instances	1363	61.039 %
Incorrectly Classified Instances	870	38.961 %

CM3 CONFLICT MANAGEMENT TYPE

Management type

0 No management activity
1 Mediation
2 Negotiation
3 Arbitration/Adjudication
4 Referral to an organisation
5 Multilateral conference

P10b POWER PARTY B RAW SCORE TOTAL

The absolute value of the difference in the power of Party A and Party B is calculated (ranging from 0 to 34)

compute P10c = abs(P10a-P10b)

D5a FATALITIES RAW

P19b NUMBER OF PARTIES SUPPORTING PARTY B

Number of additional parties allied with Party B

CM10b TIMING OF CONFLICT MANAGEMENT EFFORT RAW

D4a DURATION RAW

The actual number of months the conflict is in length recorded in a 3 digit code.

CM17b RANK OF NEGOTIATORS FOR PARTY B

Negotiators in the conflict management attempt for Party A or B

0 Offered Only
1 Primary Decision-Maker
2 Senior-level Decision-Maker
3 Low-level Representatives
6 Unspecified
9 No Conflict management - Not Applicable

Figure 11.7: Pruned decision tree for the CMAs of conflicts starting 1990 and later

Pruned decision tree for CMA after 1989:

D4a <= 9: failure (170.0/46.0)
D4a > 9
| P10b <= 16

```
| | P20a = 1: success (320.3/123.08)
| | P20a = 2: failure (410.52/172.14)
| | P20a = 3: failure (58.79/28.59)
| | P20a = 4: success (0.0)
| | P20a = 5: success (103.39/49.35)
| | P20a = ?: success (0.0)
| P10b > 16: success (87.0/17.0)
```

Correctly Classified Instances	663	57.6522 %
Incorrectly Classified Instances	487	42.3478 %

D4a DURATION RAW

The actual number of months the conflict is in length recorded in a 3 digit code.

P10b POWER PARTY B RAW SCORE TOTAL

The absolute value of the difference in the power of Party A and Party B is calculated (ranging from 0 to 34)

compute P10c=abs(P10a-P10b)

P20a HOMOGENEITY OF PARTY A

Index of internal homogeneity (Freedom House Scale)

1 Homogeneous No
2 Significant minority
3 Majority
4 Plurality
5 Fragmented

Figure 11.10: Pruned decision tree for CMAs from 1945 to 2000 in Central and South America

```
CM12 = 1
| D10 = 1: success (17.69/5.56)
| D10 = 2: failure (40.85/6.28)
| D10 = 3: failure (3.0/1.0)
| D10 = 4: failure (36.95/10.26)
| D10 = 5: success (7.36/1.28)
| D10 = 6: failure (6.24/2.54)
CM12 = 2: success (130.78/44.6)
CM12 = 3
| D5a <= 150: success (28.99/13.54)
| D5a > 150: failure (38.73/5.36)
CM12 = 4: success (53.71/21.3)
CM12 = 5: success (32.69/11.4)
CM12 = ?: success (0.0)
```

Correctly Classified Instances	257	64.74 %

Incorrectly Classified Instances	140	35.26 %
Kappa statistic	0.2942	
Mean absolute error	0.4399	
Root mean squared error	0.4796	
Relative absolute error	87.97 %	
Root relative squared error	95.91 %	
Total Number of Instances	397	

CM12 INITIATED BY
Request for conflict management initiated by (i.e. suggested, appealed for, or offered).

0 No management
1 One party to the conflict
2 Both parties
3 Mediator/Third Party
4 Regional organisation
5 International organisation
6 Unspecified

D10 SYSTEM PERIOD
The system period in which the dispute became an international conflict (as defined by our criteria).

The 50 year period of post-WWII 1945 to 1995 has been split into six 10-year groupings.
1 1945-55
2 1956-65
3 1966-75
4 1976-85
5 1986-95
6 1996-2000

D5a FATALITIES RAW
The actual number of fatalities recorded in a 7 digit code

Figure 11.11: Pruned decision tree for CMAs in the years 1990 and after in Central and South America

CM12 = 1
| P19b = 1: success (6.17/2.13)
| P19b = 2: failure (11.68/1.53)
| P19b = 3: failure (0.0)
| P19b = 4: failure (0.0)
CM12 = 2: success (76.86/21.49)
CM12 = 3
| P6a = 0: failure (5.35/2.41)
| P6a = 1: success (0.0)

| P6a = 2: success (0.0)
| P6a = 3: success (0.0)
| P6a = 4: failure (2.12)
| P6a = 5: success (9.0/3.12)
CM12 = 4: failure (5.49/2.1)
CM12 = 5: success (23.33/4.67)
CM12 = ?: success (0.0)

Correctly Classified Instances	89	63.57 %
Incorrectly Classified Instances	51	36.43 %
Kappa statistic	0.1335	
Mean absolute error	0.4273	
Root mean squared error	0.489	
Relative absolute error	92.94 %	
Root relative squared error	102.06 %	
Total Number of Instances	140	

CM12 INITIATED BY
Request for conflict management initiated by

(0) No management
(1) One party
(2) Both parties
(3) Mediator/Third Party
(4) Regional organisation
(5) International organisation
(6) Unspecified

P6a TIME IN INTERNATIONAL SYSTEM PARTY A
Length of time in the international system as a legitimate state actor

(0) Non-State actor
(1) 0-5 years
(2) 6-20
(3) 21-50
(4) 51-100
(5) 100+

P19b NUMBER OF PARTIES SUPPORTING PARTY B
Number of additional parties allied with Party B

(1) No other party involved
(2) Additional 1-2 parties involved
(3) Additional 3-5 parties involved
(4) More than 5 parties involved

Figure 11.14: Pruned decision tree for CMAs from 1945 to 2000 in Africa

CM17a = 0: failure (87.89/11.24)
CM17a = 1
| D4a <= 225
| | D10 = 1: failure (7.01/2.0)
| | D10 = 2: success (27.03/9.02)
| | D10 = 3
| | | D4a <= 26: success (47.55/21.03)
| | | D4a > 26: failure (36.0/5.0)

```
| | D10 = 4: success (62.52/17.52)
| | D10 = 5: success (328.06/148.82)
| | D10 = 6: success (64.62/31.07)
| D4a > 225: failure (87.09/25.04)
CM17a = 2: failure (371.72/166.53)
CM17a = 3
| D5a <= 501: success (30.84/10.92)
| D5a > 501: failure (163.66/55.95)
CM17a = 6: failure (0.0)
CM17a = ?: failure (0.0)
```

Correctly Classified Instances	784	59.67 %
Incorrectly Classified Instances	530	40.34 %
Kappa statistic	0.1554	
Mean absolute error	0.4655	
Root mean squared error	0.4833	
Relative absolute error	94.14 %	
Root relative squared error	97.21 %	
Total Number of Instances	1314	

CM17a RANK OF NEGOTIATORS FOR PARTY A
Negotiators in the conflict management attempt for Party A or B

0 Offered Only
1 Primary Decision-Maker
2 Senior-level Decision-Maker
3 Low-level Representatives
6 Unspecified
No Conflict management - Not Applicable

D4a DURATION RAW
The actual number of months the conflict is in length recorded in a 3 digit code.

D5a FATALITIES RAW
The actual number of fatalities recorded in a 7 digit code
This is the highest approximate reported or calculated number of fatalities.

D10 SYSTEM PERIOD
The system period is the time period in which the dispute became an international conflict (as defined by our criteria).

The 50 year period of post-WWII 1945 to 1995 has been split into six 10-year groupings.
1 1945-55
2 1956-65
3 1966-75

4 1976-85
5 1986-95
6 1996-2000

Figure 11.15: Pruned decision tree for CMAs in the years 1990 and after in Africa

CM17a = 0: failure (31.65/5.1)
CM17a = 1: success (413.02/187.51)
CM17a = 2: failure (186.73/86.07)
CM17a = 3
| P20a = 1
| | P10b <= 6: failure (21.24/7.44)
| | P10b > 6: success (22.29/7.68)
| P20a = 2: failure (44.42/12.98)
| P20a = 3: success (0.29/0.15)
| P20a = 4: failure (0.0)
| P20a = 5: success (19.37/8.22)
| P20a = ?: failure (0.0)
CM17a = 8: failure (0.0)
CM17a = ?: failure (0.0)

Correctly Classified Instances	418	56.56 %
Incorrectly Classified Instances	321	43.44 %
Kappa statistic	0.1301	
Mean absolute error	0.4878	
Root mean squared error	0.4937	
Relative absolute error	97.59 %	
Root relative squared error	98.75 %	
Total Number of Instances	739	

CM17a RANK OF NEGOTIATORS FOR PARTY A
Negotiators in the conflict management attempt for Party A or B

0 Offered Only
1 Primary Decision-Maker
2 Senior-level Decision-Maker
3 Low-level Representatives
6 Unspecified
No Conflict management - Not Applicable

P20a HOMOGENEITY OF PARTY A
Index of internal homogeneity (Freedom House Scale)
1 Homogeneous No
2 Significant minority

3 Majority
4 Plurality
5 Fragmented

P10b POWER PARTY B (RAW)
Raw power score from International Actor Power Indicator

Figure 11.18: Pruned decision tree for CMAs from 1945 to 2000 in South West Asia

P10b <= 7: success (93.0/19.0)
P10b > 7
| P7 = 1: failure (0.0)
| P7 = 2: failure (5.0/2.0)
| P7 = 3
| | CM10b <= 252: failure (39.0/8.0)
| | CM10b > 252: success (32.0/9.0)
| P7 = 4: failure (284.0/103.0)
| P7 = 5: failure (0.0)
| P7 = 6: failure (0.0)
| P7 = 7: success (13.0)

Correctly Classified Instances	308	66.09 %
Incorrectly Classified Instances	158	33.91 %
Kappa statistic	0.3189	
Mean absolute error	0.4087	
Root mean squared error	0.4611	
Relative absolute error	81.89 %	
Root relative squared error	92.30 %	
Total Number of Instances	466	

P10b POWER PARTY B (RAW)
Raw power score from International Actor Power Indicator

P7 ALIGNMENT RELATIONSHIPS
The political/security alignment of the disputing parties most salient and relevant to the parties international interactions at the time of the conflict.

A measure of formal international affiliations and status of the parties, provides an indicator of prestige and potential influence of the parties, and their political/security association with super powers and regional organizations that are critical parts of regional and national security and stability.

1 Members of opposing blocs
2 Members of the same bloc

3 Blockmember vs. Unaligned
4 Both unaligned
5 Different regional organisation
6 Same regional organisation
7 Regional organisation vs. Unaligned

CM10b TIMING OF CONFLICT MANAGEMENT EFFORT RAW

A 3 digit code recording the exact number of months elapsed in the conflict at the time of intervention initiation.

This is taken from the start data of the conflict as specified in D2a D2b in the Conflict section of the dataset.

Figure 11.19: Pruned decision tree for CMAs in the years 1990 and after in South West Asia

D10 = 1: success (0.0)
D10 = 2: success (27.0/7.0)
D10 = 3: success (26.0/1.0)
D10 = 4: failure (23.0/3.0)
D10 = 5
| CM17a = 0: failure (12.54/0.66)
| CM17a = 1: success (49.02/13.44)
| CM17a = 2: success (43.32/17.04)
| CM17a = 3: failure (9.12/3.48)
| CM17a = 8: success (0.0)
| CM17a = ?: success (0.0)
D10 = 6: success (14.0)

Correctly Classified Instances	150	73.53 %
Incorrectly Classified Instances	54	26.47 %
Kappa statistic	0.4183	
Mean absolute error	0.3391	
Root mean squared error	0.4286	
Relative absolute error	72.46 %	
Root relative squared error	88.64 %	
Total Number of Instances	204	

D10 SYSTEM PERIOD

The system period is the time period in which the dispute became an international conflict (as defined by our criteria).

(1) 1945-55 (2) 1956-65 (3) 1966-75 (4) 1976-85
(5) 1986-95 (6) 1996-2000

CM17a RANK OF NEGOTIATORS FOR PARTY A

Negotiators in the conflict management attempt for Party A or B

0 Offered Only
1 Primary Decision-Maker
2 Senior-level Decision-Maker
3 Low-level Representatives
6 Unspecified
No Conflict management - Not Applicable

Figure 11.22: Pruned decision tree for CMAs from 1945 to 2000 in East Asia and Pacific.

Pruned decision tree for CMA from 1945 to 2000 in the region of East Asia and the Pacific

```
P10b <= 24
|  CM6 = 1: failure (47.72/19.31)
|  CM6 = 2
|  |  CM9 = 0: failure (45.89/21.89)
|  |  CM9 = 1: success (11.44/4.44)
|  |  CM9 = 2: failure (3.0)
|  |  CM9 = 3: success (1.0)
|  |  CM9 = 4: success (1.0)
|  |  CM9 = 5: failure (1.0)
|  |  CM9 = 6: success (0.0)
|  |  CM9 = 9
|  |  |  P20a = 1: success (38.53/11.51)
|  |  |  P20a = 2: success (54.91/19.04)
|  |  |  P20a = 3: failure (17.27/6.64)
|  |  |  P20a = 4: success (0.0)
|  |  |  P20a = 5: success (0.0)
|  |  |  P20a = ?: success (0.0)
|  CM6 = 3: success (115.09/35.53)
|  CM6 = 4: success (56.14/24.43)
|  CM6 = ?: success (0.0)
P10b > 24: failure (228.0/60.0)
```

Correctly Classified Instances	407	65.54 %
Incorrectly Classified Instances	214	34.46 %
Kappa statistic	0.3134	
Mean absolute error	0.4395	
Root mean squared error	0.4704	
Relative absolute error	88.24 %	
Root relative squared error	94.26 %	
Total Number of Instances	621	

P10b POWER PARTY B (RAW)
Raw power score from International Actor Power Indicator

CM9 NUMBER OF PREVIOUS MEDIATION ATTEMPTS BY THIS MEDIATOR IN THE DISPUTE

An indicator of a specific mediator's association with the dispute and familiarity with the parties' conflict management efforts.

0 0
1 1
2 2
3 3
4 4
5 5
6 6+
9 No mediation

CM6 STRATEGIES - PRIMARY

The primary strategy employed by the mediator.

0 No mediation
1 Mediation Offered Only
2 Communication-Facilitation
3 Procedural
4 Directive
6 Unspecified

P20a HOMOGENEITY OF PARTY A

Index of internal homogeneity (Freedom House Scale)

1 Homogeneous No
2 Significant minority
3 Majority
4 Plurality
5 Fragmented

Figure 11.23: Pruned decision tree for CMAs in the years 1990 and after in East Asia and Pacific

```
D5a <= 60000: success (112.0/27.0)
D5a > 60000
| CM17b = 0: failure (5.26/0.18)
| CM17b = 1: success (7.37/2.12)
| CM17b = 2
| | CM10b <= 513: success (35.76/13.55)
| | CM10b > 513: failure (30.55/12.0)
| CM17b = 3: failure (41.05/10.37)
| CM17b = ?: failure (0.0)
```

Correctly Classified Instances 147 63.36 %

Incorrectly Classified Instances	85	36.64 %
Kappa statistic	0.221	
Mean absolute error	0.4263	
Root mean squared error	0.4741	
Relative absolute error	87.57 %	
Root relative squared error	96.10 %	
Total Number of Instances	232	

D5a FATALITIES RAW
The actual number of fatalities recorded in a 7 digit code

This is the highest approximate reported or calculated number of fatalities

CM17b RANK OF NEGOTIATORS FOR PARTY A
Negotiators in the conflict management attempt for Party A or B

0 Offered Only
1 Primary Decision-Maker
2 Senior-level Decision-Maker
3 Low-level Representatives
6 Unspecified
9 No Conflict management - Not Applicable

CM10b TIMING OF CONFLICT MANAGEMENT EFFORT RAW
A 3 digit code recording the exact number of months elapsed in the conflict at the time of intervention initiation.
This is taken from the start data of the conflict as specified in D2a, D2b in the conflict section of the dataset

Figure 11.26: Pruned decision tree for CMAs from 1945 to 2000 in the Middle East

```
P10b <= 21
|   CM12 = 1: failure (145.25/49.41)
|   CM12 = 2: success (149.83/55.12)
|   CM12 = 3: failure (300.79/105.48)
|   CM12 = 4: failure (46.89/20.04)
|   CM12 = 5: failure (129.24/45.37)
|   CM12 = ?: failure (0.0)
P10b > 21
|   CM3 = 1: failure (49.0/6.0)
|   CM3 = 2: failure (46.0/9.0)
|   CM3 = 3: success (1.0)
|   CM3 = 4: failure (8.0)
|   CM3 = 5: failure (7.0/2.0)
```

Correctly Classified Instances	564	63.87 %
Incorrectly Classified Instances	319	36.13 %
Kappa statistic	0.1522	
Mean absolute error	0.4328	
Root mean squared error	0.4692	
Relative absolute error	92.11 %	
Root relative squared error	96.80 %	
Total Number of Instances	883	

P10b POWER PARTY B RAW SCORE TOTAL

CM12 INITIATED BY

Request for conflict management initiated by (i.e. suggested, appealed for, or offered).

0 No management
1 One party to the conflict
2 Both parties
3 Mediator/Third Party
4 Regional organisation
5 International organisation
6 Unspecified

CM3 CONFLICT MANAGEMENT TYPE

Management type

0 No management activity
1 Mediation
2 Negotiation
3 Arbitration/Adjudication
4 Referral to an organisation
5 Multilateral conference

Figure 11.27: Pruned decision tree for CMAs from 1990 and after in the Middle East

P6b = 0: success (26.0/13.0)
P6b = 1: failure (0.0)
P6b = 2
| D4 = 1: success (18.0/8.0)
| D4 = 2: success (0.0)
| D4 = 3: success (0.0)
| D4 = 4: success (6.0)
| D4 = 5: success (0.0)
| D4 = 6: failure (19.0/8.0)
| D4 = 7: success (0.0)

P6b = 3: failure (89.0/14.0)
P6b = 4: failure (20.0/6.0)
P6b = 5
| D4 = 1: failure (22.0/2.0)
| D4 = 2: failure (0.0)
| D4 = 3: failure (0.0)
| D4 = 4: failure (0.0)
| D4 = 5: failure (0.0)
| D4 = 6: failure (0.0)
| D4 = 7
| | CM15 = 1: failure (97.0/31.0)
| | CM15 = 2: success (17.0/7.0)
| | CM15 = 3: failure (0.0)
| | CM15 = 8: failure (0.0)
| | CM15 = ?: failure (0.0)

Correctly Classified Instances	204	64.97 %
Incorrectly Classified Instances	110	35.03 %
Kappa statistic	-0.0255	
Mean absolute error	0.4239	
Root mean squared error	0.4802	
Relative absolute error	97.5562 %	
Root relative squared error	103.0728 %	
Total Number of Instances	314	

P6b TIME IN INTERNATIONAL SYSTEM PARTY B
Length of time in the international system as a legitimate state actor from date of independence

0 Non-state actor
1 0-5 years
2 6-20
3 21-50
4 51-100
5 100+

D4 DURATION GROUPED
Total duration of the conflict in months from star to end dates given above in D2a to D3b

NB: The measure of duration is approximate in some cases due to lack for specific information, thus a raw score and a grouped measure is coded.

1 0-1months
2 1-3
3 4-6
4 7-12

5 13-24
6 25-36
7 36+
9 Unknown

CM15 HOSTILITIES REPORTED AT TIME OF INTERVENTION
Military hostilities present during conflict management attempt.

1 Yes
2 No
9 No Conflict Management

Figure 11.30: Pruned decision tree for CMAs from 1945 to 2000 in Europe

```
CM3 = 1
| CM17b = 0: failure (19.96/2.08)
| CM17b = 1: failure (332.65/129.69)
| CM17b = 2
| | P6a = 0: success (172.8/75.28)
| | P6a = 1: failure (41.46/13.12)
| | P6a = 2: failure (0.75)
| | P6a = 3: success (0.37)
| | P6a = 4: success (2.0/1.0)
| | P6a = 5: success (26.12/12.75)
| CM17b = 3: failure (55.89/23.83)
| CM17b = ?: failure (0.0)
CM3 = 2: success (193.0/85.0)
CM3 = 3: success (5.0/2.0)
CM3 = 4: failure (16.0/3.0)
CM3 = 5: success (23.0/7.0)
```

Correctly Classified Instances	507	57.03 %
Incorrectly Classified Instances	382	42.97 %
Kappa statistic	0.1143	
Mean absolute error	0.4862	
Root mean squared error	0.4958	
Relative absolute error	97.80 %	
Root relative squared error	99.45 %	
Total Number of Instances	889	

CM3 CONFLICT MANAGEMENT TYPE
Management type
0 No management activity
1 Mediation
2 Negotiation

3 Arbitration/Adjudication
4 Referral to an organisation
5 Multilateral conference

CM17b RANK OF NEGOTIATORS FOR PARTY B
Negotiators in the conflict management attempt for Party A or B

0 Offered Only
1 Primary Decision-Maker
2 Senior-level Decision-Maker
3 Low-level Representatives
6 Unspecified
9 No Conflict management - Not Applicable

P6a TIME IN INTERNATIONAL SYSTEM PARTY A
Length of time in the international system as a legitimate state actor from date of independence

0 Non-state actor
1 0-5 years
2 6-20
3 21-50
4 51-100
5 100+

Figure 11.31: Pruned decision tree for CMAs from 1990 and after in Europe

```
P6a = 0
| CM17b = 0: failure (5.78/0.89)
| CM17b = 1
| | CM3 = 1: failure (223.88/90.02)
| | CM3 = 2: success (38.67/16.65)
| | CM3 = 3: failure (1.42/0.47)
| | CM3 = 4: failure (0.0)
| | CM3 = 5: success (9.07/3.32)
| CM17b = 2: success (234.05/98.82)
| CM17b = 3: failure (62.12/27.62)
| CM17b = ?: failure (0.0)
P6a = 1: failure (113.0/45.0)
P6a = 2: failure (0.0)
P6a = 3: success (3.0)
P6a = 4: failure (2.0)
P6a = 5: failure (15.0/3.0)
```

Correctly Classified Instances	369	52.12 %
Incorrectly Classified Instances	339	47.88 %

Kappa statistic	0.0267
Mean absolute error	0.4925
Root mean squared error	0.5076
Relative absolute error	98.85 %
Root relative squared error	101.69 %
Total Number of Instances	708

P6a TIME IN INTERNATIONAL SYSTEM PARTY A
Length of time in the international system as a legitimate state actor from date of independence

0 Non-state actor
1 0-5 years
2 6-20
3 21-50
4 51-100
5 100+

CM17b RANK OF NEGOTIATORS FOR PARTY A
Negotiators in the conflict management attempt for Party A or B

0 Offered Only
1 Primary Decision-Maker
2 Senior-level Decision-Maker
3 Low-level Representatives
6 Unspecified
9 No Conflict management - Not Applicable

CM3 CONFLICT MANAGEMENT TYPE
Management type
0 No management activity
1 Mediation
2 Negotiation
3 Arbitration/Adjudication
4 Referral to an organisation
5 Multilateral conference

PART III

Chapter 12

New Methods for Conflict Data

Will Lowe
Harvard University, Cambridge, Massachussetts, U.S.A.

This chapter sketches out some new ways to look at conflict data sets. Since political scientists have more computer power available to them than at perhaps any point in the past, the paper emphasizes methods whose principle feature is that they purchase substantive realism at the cost of more compute cycles, not more advanced statistics. Existing statistical theory is sufficient to perform much more realistic analyses than are typically performed, but it is not necessarily found in the standard location. Most of the models and methods described here can be found in other guises in the field of machine learning. Political methodology is often accused of importing techniques wholesale from other disciplines, particularly econometrics, and by introducing machine learning as another field worth mining, this paper continues a long tradition.[1]

The sections below consider new approaches to two important sources of information about conflict: event data and conflict databases. Event data remain underused in international relations, in part because of the apparently narrow range of inferences they license using existing methods. Hopefully, widening the range of available methods should earn this sort of data a wider audience, and help integrate them more fully into quantitative international relations research. Conflict data sets, e.g. the State Failure, and Correlates of War datasets (Esty et al., 1998; Singer and Diehl, 1990), in contrast, are widely used to provide data for regression analysis and this application is well-understood. Trappl and colleagues have recently applied case-based reasoning methods to making predictions (see Chapter 11 in this volume). We describe how this work might itself be generalized in a way that allows it to be integrated back into regular statistical methodology using probabilistic expert systems.

[1]. But it is a good one; methodology should always be about ensuring a model represents your theory, not somebody else's, so ultimately it is the theory that matters, and any model that effectively represents it is good enough, wherever it came from.

R. Trappl (ed.), Programming for Peace, 321–334.

1 EVENTS DATA

Event data analysis is motivated by McClelland's observation that international interactions can be understood as the cumulative effects of large numbers of stereotypical dyadic actions, or events (McClelland, 1978; Gerner et al., 1994). Three aspects are important to this view of international relations: first, events are stereotypical because they come in a finite number of possible types. They are also relatively unambiguous. Theoretically this is because although the typology is typically hierarchical with a single root action node (e.g. IDEA[2]) or a set of root nodes (e.g. WEIS, McClelland, 1978; CAMEO, Gerner et. al, 2002), no leaf action can be a child of more than one parent. Thus there is no typological ambiguity as to the meaning of an event. They are also practically unambiguous because events, in contrast to the intentions of the actors involved, are in principle observable. The second aspect is that event data sets are focused around the country dyad. This contrasts with case study methods that concentrate on the multilateral relations of one actor. The third aspect is that, given their definition, the natural numerical summary of event data is the count.

Much event data analysis involves regressing sets of counts, or more usually sets of scaled counts, on each other. This practice makes event data analyses a natural target for critique, from two directions. From one side, researchers immersed in case studies and historical research object to the reduction of subtle cultural and institutional processes to a universal set of decontextualized actions and reactions. From the other side, game theorists, who may not be so averse to reductive theories, complain that the strategic choices, reputation effects, and successful deterrence that occurs in international politics is necessarily hidden from the event level of analysis. Consider, for example, the event series generated by successful mutual deterrence between two heavily armed countries: nothing happens on Monday, nothing happens on Tuesday, etc. This is a caricature certainly, but answers to the more serious question of how to match strategic theory to statistical data sources, and when such theories are in fact identifiable, remains underdeveloped.

Both types of objection are often reasonable, but that is not because of any inherent flaw in event data itself as a way of decomposing international politics. It can be difficult to see what else an international system might reduce to, at its lowest observational level, except a set of discrete events that are the actions and choices of agents, however those agents are understood. The problem is more about forcing events into models that were not meant for

[2] See http://www.vranet.com/IDEA

them. And the solution is surely to expand the models to fit already existing substantive theory. The first step is to quantify what substantive assumptions current methods are implicitly already making.

1.1 Scaling, Summing, and Equivalence Classes

Current work using event data sets typically uses methods that were designed for real-valued time series data. This requires that events, which are discrete, need to be massaged into variables that are real-valued and (possibly) normally distributed. The standard approach is to first pick a start time, an aggregation period, e.g. seven days, and a scaling, e.g. Goldstein's conflict-cooperation scale (Goldstein, 1992), and then transform each seven days worth of events in the life of a country dyad into a single real number defined as the sum of the conflict-cooperation scores of each event. There are two sets of problems associated with this approach, the first associated with scaling, and the second associated with summing of an aggregation period.

Event scaling necessarily loses information to the extent that more than one event can be assigned the same conflict-cooperation score. Subsequent summing loses information about the order of events in a particular aggregation period. The combination may also generate strange equivalences. To see this, notice that 2 complaints (WEIS code 131), one denial (140) and a neutral comment (023) are equivalent (in summed conflict-cooperation terms) to an expulsion of personnel (201), or a seizure (210). If we observe, in addition to the complaints, comment and denial, a formal protest (132) and two requests for policy change (096), then we have an event set that is equivalent to an attempted coup d'état.

It is possible that the level of conflict generated by these events is equivalent to that generated by an attempt to change the government by force. Indeed, that is exactly the substantive assumption that would justify scaling this way. But they are clearly very different sorts of events, and for many purposes they probably should not be treated as equivalent.

The problem of strange equivalences is recognized in the literature (e.g. Schrodt, 2004), but it is important to see that equivalence classes in themselves are important for any method of analysis since they make generalization possible across otherwise completely unique events. And they are essential for statistical analysis because they correspond to exchangeability assumptions, and answer the fundamental question 'what are the units in this analysis?' (King et al., 1994)

An important special case of equivalence classes is Most and Starr's notion of foreign policy substitutability (Most and Starr, 1984). When policies are substitutable they are equivalent with respect to the strategic situation an actor finds itself in, and any statistical model of foreign policy outcomes should ideally know (or attempt to infer) what these classes are. Foreign policy substitutability is more nuanced than the aliasing generated by event scaling schemes because two policies may be substitutable in one context and not in another, but the importance of finding the correct equivalences is the same.

1.2 Summing and Scaling: An Illustration

The strange equivalences above depend on both scaling and summing, but perhaps the moral is that it would be better not to sum. One prima facie plausible alternative is to average rather than sum over the relevant aggregation unit. In this scheme, each event moves an average Goldstein score up or down depending on how conflictual it is, but the final score always remains on [-10:10]. And if we assume, as the Goldstein scale suggests, that actors harbor a constant amount of enmity towards one another, at least within the relevant unit of aggregation, then the more events that are gathered together in the average, the more accurate our estimate of the true conflict or cooperation level.

There are a number of statistical problems with this scheme relating to the variance of each average, but the real problem lies elsewhere: we (King and Lowe, unpublished) attempted to replicate Goldstein and Pevehouse's work on reciprocity and bullying in Bosnia (Goldstein and Pevehouse, 1997). Everything about our analysis was the same as the original, except for the use of averaged rather than summed events data. Unfortunately, the averaged model produced very few reliable or interpretable estimates for parameters of substantial theoretical interest.

In an attempt to understand why this model performed so badly, we noted that a scaled summed Goldstein score can be factored into two parts. One part is the average Goldstein score for a week of events, and might be interpreted as the average level of hostility shown that week; this is what we used in the alternative model. The other part is the number of events of any kind that Reuters reported in that week. Multiplied together, they reproduce the original data.

It seemed to us that all the conflict information must be contained in the average, and that N was a measure of media interest. However, the same model, run with N rather than the average, gave a fitted model that was extremely similar to the published paper.[3] It is, we think, theoretically problematic that the number of events of any kind that Reuters reports in a week

3. This would be less surprising if Reuters tended to make more reports when events were more conflictual. Then N would be informative about the conflict. However this does not seem to be so: N is uncorrelated with the average.

should constitute the statistical evidence for reciprocity and bullying in the Bosnian conflict.

Rather than conclude from this that event data cannot help us illuminate the question, the failure of this kind of analysis suggests that we may be radically misusing event data by forcing it into the shape of a real-valued time series.

The success of N in replicating the analysis suggests one final problem. The Bosnia conflict was very densely reported; similar conflicts in, for example, West Africa, are not so densely reported by Reuters. This implies that if we continue to use summed event data to describe conflicts then we must conclude that the levels of conflict involved in West African wars are smaller. But this seems unlikely to be true in general.

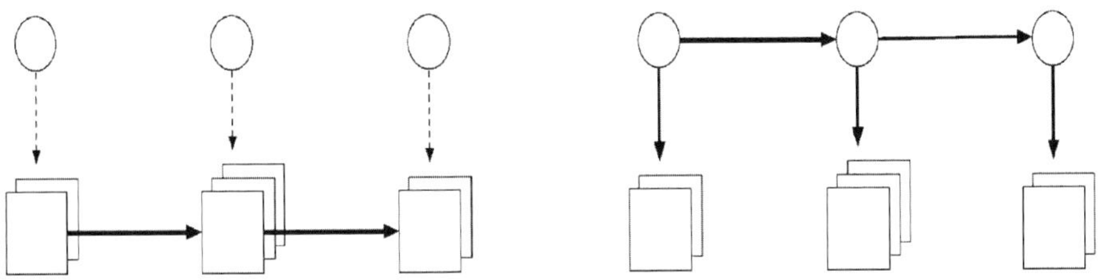

Figure 12.1. Regression model (left) and true causal structure/state space model (right)

1.3 The Data Generating Process

Another problem for regression models of event data occurs irrespective of the manipulation used to acquire data for the time series analysis. When building a model of some process, we hope to reflect the actual data generating process as closely as possible. Or at least we try not to postulate a model that directly contradicts something we know to be true and potentially important.

There are two basic classes of data generating processes for ongoing conflict and its reporting. In the first, Reuters provides a transparent and complete description of the conflict; in statistical terms the conflict is assumed to be observed directly. This is almost certainly false and some reasons are presented below.

The second possible data generating process is one where at each time step, each actor gauges the hostility or cooperativeness of the other's action as described by Reuters news reports that describe what they did and what was done to them in the past, and then decides, using only this information, how hostile or cooperative to be toward its neighbors. Although this captures media-aware combatants, it does not respect our basic understanding that military actions in the field or diplomatic actions in international forums are the main external force driving another actor's behavior.

Each conflict process has its own dynamics; Reuters is essentially an observation process that maps an unobserved conflict onto news coverage. The causal story is roughly this: a conflict is observed directly by reporters in the field. Their reports are sent to editors who decide which of many reports to run. Statistically then, the news stories provided by Reuters in a day is a set of noisy observations at a particular point in time on a conflict process that has its own dynamics.

In particular, although reports occur at particular times and similar reports may not appear in the data set the next day, the events that they describe often span a much longer time period. For example, when Sarajevo was under siege by Serbian forces from April 1992 to March 1996 we did not get reports of the form: "Sarejevo is under siege" every day for the length of the event. This fact ensures that even if news reports are accurate, they are not transparent. At best they provide indicators of state changes in the conflict process e.g. beginnings and ends of military action and individual diplomatic moves.

Various alternative sources for event data do exist e.g. a document like the United Nations' report after Resolution 780 (UN, 1992) has sufficient detail to reconstruct substantial portions of the civil war in Bosnia. Several groups, including the Swiss Peace Foundation[4] (see Chapter 4 in this volume) also collate precoded events data from local sources across the world.

1.4 State space models and regression

The more realistic data generating process is described on the right hand side of Figure 12.1. This conditional independence diagram shows three time steps in the evolution of a conflict and its reporting. At each time step the conflict itself (circle) generates events, and these events generate news reports (overlapping sheets). In the next time step the conflict continues, but statistically the reports written in one time period are conditionally independent of those written the period before, given knowledge of the current state of the conflict. This is the generic form of a state space model (Harvey, 1991; Durbin and Koopman, 2001)

A model of this data generating process therefore needs to have two parts: one to model conflict dynamics (the horizontal arrows) and another to model the observation process (vertical arrows). This distinction is important if we are interested only in the conflict, e.g. when planning a mediation, or only in the observation process, e.g. if we want to measure media interest or reporting

4. http://www.swisspeace.org, see also Chapter 4 in this volume.

bias. The importance of distinguishing between these processes is shown by Krummenacher's finding that levels of conflict reported by Swiss Peace personnel and media sources can differ considerably (see Chapter 4 in this volume).

The left hand side of the figure does not make much substantive sense as a story about how the data were generated (although it might if Reuters were a transparent reflection of the conflict). It does, however, reflect the assumptions of standard regression models using event data in which this time period's media reports are regressed on those in the past.

Although the state space model is preferable, both models are of course considerable simplifications. Actors may be acutely sensitive to what is written in the media (e.g. Rose, 1998). But it is unlikely that this could be the only factor that drives their actions.[5]

There are other advantages besides substantive realism to developing state space models. The primary statistical advantage is that dealing with missing data becomes straightforward (Harvey, 1991). If there is a sudden lull in reporting, a holiday, or a technical failure, then reports may not be generated for some time periods. In a state space model this will not bias our inference about the conflict process; in the absence of observations we need not alter our view of the conflict at all, so it advances on its internal dynamic as specified in the process model, albeit with increasing amounts of uncertainty surrounding our estimates. In the regression model, by contrast, we either map a time period containing no reports to zero (meaning no conflict in Goldstein's conflict scale), or attempt to deal with a pervasive missing data problem affecting both independent and dependent variables. The missing data problem is exacerbated by the fact that missingness may well depend on the value (e.g. there is no report because fighting is so severe that reporters have evacuated) so 'missing at random' assumptions may not hold (Little and Rubin, 1987).

Similarly if we decide to deal with event data as counts of event types, rather than real numbers, then zero counts are not problematic. In a regression framework they are, at least for count data, an unsolved research problem (Cameron and Trivedi, 1998).

1.5 New methods: Particle filters

At the beginning of the 1990s there were considerable practical and theoretical difficulties to fitting models with arbitrarily specified process and

5. In this case we would also want to model a third relationship, schematically this would entail another arrow between the reports at t and the unobserved conflict process at t+1, and a corresponding probability distribution.

observation models. Two tractable alternatives were the Kalman Filter, and the Hidden Markov Model. The former has been widely used in econometrics and in real-valued time series analysis with missing data (Durbin and Koopman, 2001; Harvey, 1993). The Hidden Markov Model has been used recently by Schrodt (see Chapter 8 in this volume). In that work a specific conflict model is encoded in the structure of the hidden variables (the circles of Figure 12.1.) and a separate observation model maps the state of the conflict to the observation of different WEIS event categories.

Currently, however, there is less need to be concerned with mathematical tractability because sequential Monte Carlo methods known as 'particle filters' make it possible to fit arbitrary models using sampling methods (Doucet et al., 2001). Particle filters are a convenient intermediate between tractable but inaccurate linear models, and those that are more faithful, but that require full Markov Chain Monte Carlo methods to use. Despite being well-suited to Bayesian methods, in a particle filtering framework the researcher does not need to decide large numbers of prior distributions or intuit suitable Markov Chain parameters; the sampling element serves only to make an otherwise mathematically intractable likelihood practical to deal with.

The class of state space models is extremely large and is only just beginning to be explored using these methods. Political scientists therefore have a unprecedented opportunity to specify models that truly reflect detailed substantive theories of conflict.

2 CONFLICT DATABASES

Recently Trappl and colleagues have presented a very interesting set of applications of machine learning to the problem of pattern recognition in databases of international crises. This work has used primarily decision trees and case-based reasoning tools (Trappl et al., 1997, 1996; Fürnkranz et al., 1994; see Chapters 9, 10 and 11). This is a promising line of enquiry and the next section suggests some future directions for research.

2.1 Case-based Reasoning

Other important work has used case-based reasoning (CBR) systems to infer similarities between crises from various conflict databases.

CBR assumes that each event, crisis, or generically 'case', is coded according to a range of attributes. A similarity metric is then imposed which maps any two sets of attribute values onto a number expressing how similar the cases are (Mitchell, 1997). It is often argued that foreign policy decision making and analysis do proceed by finding a previously similar set of situations and making decisions based on this more limited set: e.g. "Afghanistan was Russia's Vietnam".

CBR systems can be used as descriptive tools, to suggest precedents, or as prediction devices. To use a set of cases for prediction, one picks an attribute of interest, say mediation outcome (successful/unsuccessful), and a new case for which the value of this attribute is not known. The new prediction is now either the value of that attribute in the most similar case, or a majority vote from several of the most similar cases.

First, CBR systems are vulnerable to uninformative attributes: if three quarters of the attributes measured in a conflict database have significant variance yet are unrelated to the attribute that a prediction is required for, then this extraneous variability may swamp the effect of the relevant attributes in the similarity computation. On average the prediction may be correct, but in smaller samples accidental correlations tend to be problematic. Weights can be assigned to attributes, but there is no acknowledged optimal scheme. As a prediction system, CBR has the advantages and limitations of N-nearest neighbor algorithms. The advantages are that prediction is straightforward and that the principle cost is storage of the cases. However there are some important limitations.

Second, missing data has no clear solution. In particular, it is not reasonable to treat a missing datum as another special value of the variable. If the data is missing at random then predictions may be compromised by using this variable, because it will be pure noise. Also, in many older cases some attribute values are not available; this is true of several of the data sets Trappl and colleagues study. But to treat missingness as distinct value suggests it will be a proxy for something like 'age of case', another violation of the 'missing at random' assumption. Finally, it is hard to take seriously any missing data treatment which would allow a prediction of the form "if the GDP is more than X and the ideological differences are missing, and we don't know the population size, then ...".[6]

2.2 New Methods: Probabilistic Expert Systems

Both of these problems can be solved in a principled way by using probabilistic expert systems (Castillo et al., 1999), sometimes referred to as graphical models, or Bayes nets. The move from cases to expert systems is relatively straightforward, particularly when the case attributes have discrete categories, or can be plausibly considered to be normally distributed.

6. Certainly we would like to make marginal predictions, but they ought to be based on marginals, not the result of conditioning on a 'don''t know'.

In a probabilistic expert system, the attributes are treated as random variables and a set of conditional independencies is specified between them. This allows causal relationships to be more easily expressed without resorting to an attribute weighting scheme. In particular, it is possible to use such a system in confirmatory mode by encoding any causal structure that is believed to relate the attributes and looking at the probability of all cases under this assumption and under competing theories.

As an example of the advantages of a probabilistic expert system approach, Figure 12.2. shows three simplified and hypothetical relationships between gross domestic product (G), polity (P), arms purchase (A) and use of force (F).

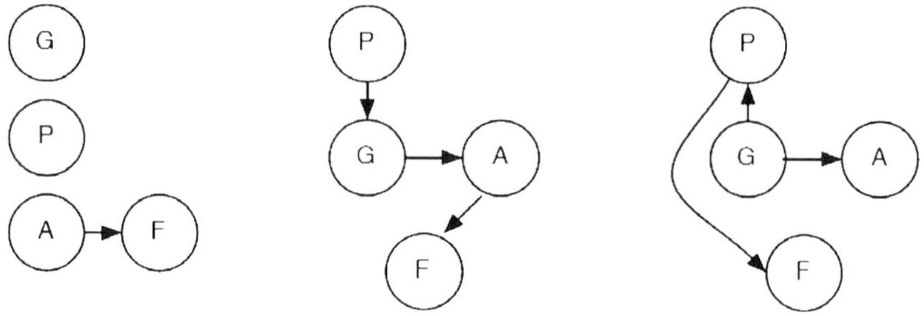

Figure 12.2. Three possible models of the relationship between gross domestic product (G), polity (P), arms purchasing (A) and use of force (F)

In the first model, arms purchases affect use of force and the other two variables are independent. Whether arms purchase decreases or increases the risk of force is reflected in a conditional distribution represented by the arrow. This distribution would be inferred from the set of cases. If the model holds, then a CBR system that includes GDP and polity in its similarity computation risks being misled by irrelevant variance in these attributes. (Likewise, regressions that use GDP and Polity as independent variables will be inefficient.) To get a prediction for a new case under this model we fix A to its value in the new case and plug that into the conditional distribution. For a discrete-valued variable the result is a probability, interpreted in the same way as a logistic regression output. For a real-valued variable the result is the predicted value and error bar, as in standard regression.

The second, more conventional model asserts that the type of polity drives GDP, that GDP drives arms purchasing, and that arms purchasing drives the use of force. Here the effect of GDP on use of force is always mediated by arms purchases and has no independent leverage. This is expressed probabilistically as: GDP is conditionally independent of use of force, given arms purchasing, and reflected by the absence of a direct arrow from G to F. In the third model, GDP drives the choice of polity and arms purchasing, but it is the polity that directly drives the use of force. If we believed that there were a separate direct effect of arms purchasing on the use of force, one that was not mediated via GDP or polity, we would add another conditional distribution represented by an arrow from A to F.

The advantage of this conditional independence formulation is that it provides another way to test models against existing cases: there is a likelihood associated with each of these models when a data set is specified. Some will be more likely than others, and model comparison occurs in a familiar statistical framework (e.g. AIC, Akaike, 1973; or marginal probability, Gelman et al., 2000) Finally, there is no problem with missing data because standard inference algorithms marginalize with respect to the unknown quantities (Castillo et al., 1999).

Case-based reasoning systems correspond approximately to a degenerate form of network in which all variables are connected to each other. Note that the circles that represent random variables in Figure 12.2. are intended to resemble those in Figure 12.1.; state space models are simply special cases of the probabilistic expert system framework described above.

Using probabilistic expert system models also allows a wider perspective on explanation in conflict databases. Usually, one specifies a dependent variable of interest, and then regresses most of the other available variables on it. In terms of the Figure, we might use regression to estimate the conditional distribution $p(F \mid G , P, A)$. However, in the expert system we attempt to model the tougher but potentially more informative joint distribution $p(F, G , P, A)$. This is potentially more informative because it allows us to compute any other conditional, e.g. $p(A \mid G , P, F)$, or bivariate relations, e.g. $p(A, F \mid P)$ where here in addition, the effects of GDP are optimally accounted for by marginalization.

Learning the joint distribution is tougher because it is inevitably more highly parameterized than any regression conditional. However this potential explosion of parameters is modulated (hopefully) by a relatively sparse conditional independence structure. Then a distribution needs to be fitted to each arrow, not between every value of every variable and every other, which is implicitly the model the CBR works with.

The expert system formulation comes into its own when some of the variables are unobserved, as in the state space model described earlier. Case-based systems cannot operate with latent variables because they make no distributional assumptions and so cannot express posterior distributions of the latent variable, or marginalize them out when making predictions over observables. Because of their links to regression analysis (each arrow specifies is a mini-regression), expert systems also provide a partial unification of the regression methods typically used by political scientists, and the latent variable models more common in psychology (Everitt, 1984).

Finally it would be very useful to be able to learn the dependencies that are just stipulated in Figure 12.2.. This is an active area of research in artificial intelligence (Glymour and Cooper, 1999), but there exists some theory and limited implementation to help curious political scientists.

Recently a handful of free software implementations of probabilistic expert systems have become available, suitable for varying levels of statistical expertise.[7] Inference in these models is computationally expensive, but is hidden from the user, and typically requires no mathematical skills to perform. Even the specification of arrows in the Figure can almost always be considered to specify causal connections (rather than simply conditional independence relationships).

3 CONCLUSION

This paper has explored some of the methods international relations researchers apply to event data and conflict databases, and suggested improvements. These have mostly been probabilistic reformulations and developments. Increased computer power, rather than more sophisticated statistical theory, has made it easier than before to fit models that reflect substantive theory. State space models should allow more realistic models to be fitted to events data, and probabilistic expert systems should extend the range of theories testable with conflict databases. Hopefully, together these suggestions will help methods keep up with the theories they need to represent.

References

Akaike, H., 1973, Information theory and an extension of the maximum likelihood principle, in Petrov, B. N., and Caski, F., eds., *Second International Symposium on Information Theory*, Akademiai Kaido, Budapest, pp. 267-281. Reprinted in *Selected Papers of*

7. For those with some programming ability in matlab, Kevin Murphy's Bayes Net Toolbox (see http://www.ai.mit.edu/murphyk/) is a highly developed free set of functions for building and learning probabilistic expert systems.

Hirotugu Akaike, Parzen, E., Tanabe, K., and Kitagawa, G., eds., 1998, Springer Verlag, New York.

Cameron, A. C., and Trivedi, P. K., 1998, *Regression Analysis of Count Data. Econometric Society Monographs*, Cambridge University Press, Cambridge.

Castillo, E., Guitierrez, J. M., and Hadi, A. S., 1999, *Expert Systems and Probabilistic Network Models*, Springer Verlag, New York.

Doucet, A., de Freitas, N., and Gordon, N., 2001, *Sequential Monte Carlo Methods in Practice*, Springer Verlag, New York, NY.

Durbin, J., and Koopman, S. J., 2001, *Time Series Analysis by State Space Methods*, Oxford University Press, Oxford.

Esty, D. C., Goldstone, J., Gurr, T. R., Harff, B., Surko, P. T., Unger, A. N., and Chen, R., 1998, The state failure project: Early warning research for US foreign policy planning, in Davies, J. L., and Gurr, T. R., eds., *Preventive Measures: Building Risk Assessment and Crisis Early Warning Systems*, Rowman and Littlefield, Boulder, CO.

Everitt, B. S., 1984, *An Introduction to Latent Variable Models*, Chapman and Hall, London.

Fürnkranz, J., Petrak, J., Trappl, R., and Bercovitch, J., 1994, *Machine Learning Methods for International Conflict Databases: A Case Study in Predicting Mediation Outcome*, Technical Report OEFAI-TR-94-33, Austrian Research Institute for Artificial Intelligence, Vienna.

Gelman, A., Carlin, J. B., Stern, H. S., and Rubin, D. R., 2000, *Bayesian Data Analysis*, Chapman and Hall/CRC, Boca Raton, FL.

Gerner, D. J., Abu-Jabr, Schrodt, P. A., and Yilmaz, O., 2002, Conflict and Mediation Event Observations (CAMEO): A new event data framework for the analysis of foreign policy interactions, paper presented at the *Annual Meeting of the International Studies Association.*

Gerner, D. J., Schrodt, P. A., Francisco, R. A., and Weddle, J. L., 1994, The analysis of political events using machine coded data, *International Studies Quarterly* **38**:91-119.

Glymour and Cooper, 1999, *Computation, Causation and Discovery*, MIT Press, Cambridge, MA.

Goldstein, J. S., 1992, A conflict-cooperation scale for WEIS events data, *Journal of Conflict Resolution* **36**:369-385.

Goldstein, J. S., and Pevehouse, J. C., 1997, Reciprocity, bullying and international cooperation: Time-series analysis of the Bosnia conflict, *American Political Science Review* **91**:515-529.

Harvey, A. C., 1991, *Forecasting, Structural Time Series Models and the Kalman Filter*, Cambridge University Press, Cambridge.

Harvey, A. C., 1993, *Time Series Models*, Harvester Wheatsheaf, Hemel Hempstead.

King, G. and Lowe, W., 2003, An automated information extraction tool for international conflict data with performance as good as human coders: a rare events evaluation design, *International Organization* **57**: 617-642.

King, G., Keohane, R. O., and Verba, S., 1994, *Designing Social Inquiry: Scientific Inference in Qualitative Research*, Princeton University Press, Princeton, NJ.

Little, R., and Rubin, D., 1987, *Statistical Analysis with Missing Data*, Wiley, New York.

McClelland, C., 1978, *World Event/Interaction Survey, 1966-1978. WEIS Codebook ICPSR 5211*, Inter-university consortium for political and social research, University of Southern California.

Mitchell, T. M., 1997, *Machine Learning*, McGraw-Hill, Singapore.

Most, B. A., and Starr, H., 1984, International relations, foreign policy substitutability, and "nice" laws, *World Politics*, 36:383-406.

Rose, M., 1998, *Fighting for Peace*, Harvill, London, UK.

Schrodt, P. A., 2004, *Patterns, Rules and Learning: Computational Models of International Behavior*, available from http://www.ku.edu/~keds/papers.dir/Schrodt.PRL.2.0.pdf.

Singer, J. D., and Diehl, P., 1990, *Measuring the Correlates of War*, University of Michigan Press, Ann Arbor, MI.

Trappl, R., Fürnkranz, J., and Petrak, J., 1996, *Digging for Peace: Using Machine Learning Methods for Assessing International Conflict Databases*, Technical Report OEFAI-TR-96-10, Austrian Research Institute for Artificial Intelligence, Vienna.

Trappl, R., Fürnkranz, J., Petrak, J., and Bercovitch, J., 1997, *Machine Learning and Case-Based Reasoning: Their Potential Role in Preventing the Outbreak of Wars or in Ending Them*, Technical Report OEFAI-TR-97-10, Austrian Research Institute for Artificial Intelligence, Vienna.

UN, 1992, *Final Report of the Commission of Experts (Siege of Sarajevo)*, United Nations Security Council.

Chapter 13

Information, Power, and War [1] [2]

William Reed
Rice University, Houston, Texas, U.S.A.

Ultimatum bargaining models of international interactions suggest that when conflict is costly and the actors are fully informed, the probability of conflict goes to zero. However, conflict occurs with some positive probability when the challenger is uncertain about the defender's reservation value. I employ a simple ultimatum game of bargaining to evaluate two traditional power-centric theories of world politics, balance of power and power transition theory. The formal and empirical analyses demonstrate that as states approach power parity, information asymmetries are greatest, thus enhancing the probability of militarized conflict. Uncertainty is a central cause of conflict emergence and is correlated with the distribution of observable capabilities. Recognizing the relationship between the distribution of power and uncertainty offers a more sophisticated interpretation of power-centric explanations of world politics.

Why is there a tendency for states with an equal distribution of observable military capabilities to engage in militarized conflict? Why might an equal balance of power cause bargaining to break down? Is the empirical relationship between power parity and conflict an artifact of the relationship between uncertainty about who is likely to win a war and equal distributions of power? These were important questions during the Cold War as the distribution of power between the United States and the Soviet Union was posited by some to maintain the peace but to promote conflict by others. These questions remain relevant today as China approaches parity with the United States, as

1. American Political Science Review, Vol. 97 (2003), pp. 633-641. Reprinted with the permission of Cambridge University Press.

2. For their feedback on this project I am grateful to seminar participants at Rice University, the University of Illinois, Texas A & M University, Binghamton University, and the Austrian Research Institute for Artificial Intelligence. In addition I received valuable suggestions from David Clark, Justin Fox, Scott Gates, Jeff Gill, Kristian Gleditsch, Jim Granato, Indridi Indridason, Mark Jones, Jiyoung Kwon, Ashley Leeds, Jim LeSage, Doug Lemke, Andrew Martin, Cliff Morgan, Karoline Mortensen, Irfan Nooruddin, Kevin Quinn, Dan Reiter, Eric Reinhardt, Mark Souva, Randy Stevenson, Ric Stoll, Suzanne Werner, Ken Williams, and Rick Wilson.

R. Trappl (ed.), Programming for Peace, 335–354.

Pakistan pursues nuclear parity with India, and as tensions on the Korean peninsula deepen.

In his seminal work on bargaining and war, Fearon (1995) specifies three conditions that may lead to war in cases such as these.[3] The conditions include uncertainty about the distribution of power, the inability to commit to a bargained outcome short of war, and the indivisibility of the stakes of war. Paramount among these conditions is that there may be disagreement between the two sides (challenger and defender) about the balance of power. Uncertainty about the balance of power can cause the challenger to demand too much from the defender. Likewise, uncertainty about the distribution of power can cause the defender to underestimate the challenger's willingness to fight. During the Cold War, foreign policy makers speculated about the willingness of the Soviet Union and the United States to fight. This condition is an issue today as analysts' opinions about the war fighting capabilities of China vary widely and there is substantial uncertainty about the maturity of North Korea's nuclear weapons program. Moreover, in the dispute over the Kashmir territory it is unclear how Pakistan's nuclear capabilities balance India's apparent overwhelming conventional military advantage.

Abstracted away from many of the everyday details of world politics, a related theoretical debate highlights the effect of balanced power versus power preponderance on the likelihood of war. With few exceptions, the scholarly consensus is that pairs of states with relatively equal amounts of observable capabilities are more likely to experience conflict (Kugler and Lemke, 1996). However, traditional explanations for this empirical pattern are unconvincing. I offer bargaining theory as a structure for examining the relationship between the distribution of power and conflict. I tie together traditional treatments of power and conflict with recent research about bargaining and conflict to provide an alternate explanation for the observed relationship between the balance of power and conflict caused by the challenger's uncertainty about the distribution of power (i.e., the expected outcome of a conflict).

In contrast to the conventional argument that the distribution of power causes conflict, I maintain that uncertainty about the distribution of power is as important a predictor of the probability of conflict as is the observed balance of power (Wittmann, 2001). I use a bargaining model to explore these questions formally and use Bayesian statistics to evaluate the empirical credibility of that bargaining model.

3. For a summary and review of bargaining theory as it has been applied to world politics see Reiter, 2003.

1 POWER AND CONFLICT

Many theories of international politics rely on the concept of power to explain international interactions. Early work claims that the probability of war is enhanced by unequal distributions of power. This "balance of power" approach asserts that the likelihood of conflict is lowest when there is an equal distribution of power (Morgenthau, 1948). The logic underlying the balance of power perspective is that equality of power makes it impossible for opponents to believe in assured victory and thus causes states to proceed with caution, thereby avoiding conflict. Since the balance of power approach associates equal distributions of power with uncertainty, the *distribution of information* is central. Even the earliest theoretical work implicitly connects uncertainty to power distributions.

In studies examining dyadic interactions between challengers and defenders, a recurring empirical pattern has emerged. Specifically, balances of power within dyads are conflict enhancing rather than inhibiting (Bremer, 1992). An explanation for this pattern is found in early work on power transition theory. Countering balance of power claims, power transition theorists assert that parity makes conflict more likely because dissatisfied states are willing to tolerate the risk of defeat in light of the possibility of victory, which offers the opportunity to modify the status quo to suit their tastes. This relationship is especially robust in the context of interactions between dissatisfied challengers and defenders of the status quo. For example, Lemke and Werner (1996) claim that pairs of states relatively equal in observable capabilities are more conflict prone because they have an opportunity to engage in conflict. Dissatisfaction with the status quo provides the incentive or *willingness* to wage war (Werner, 2000). For power transition theory, uncertainty in the form of asymmetric information about who might prevail in a potential conflict makes conflict more likely. Importantly, the challenger is uncertain about the outcome of a militarized conflict because it is unsure about the true distribution of power.[4] Nevertheless, if the challenger values its expected value for war more than the status quo distribution of benefits, it is willing to fight.

In sum, balance of power theory and power parity theory agree that an equal distribution of power enhances uncertainty about the outcome of a militarized clash. Specifically, this uncertainty can be conceptualized in terms of asymmetric information about the distribution of military capabilities. What these theories disagree over is *how* uncertainty affects the prospects for militarized conflict. Balance of power approaches assume that uncertainty makes

[4] It is also important to note that the hegemonic defender may be uncertain about the outcome of a conflict because of uncertainty about the balance of power and uncertainty about the challenging state's preferences for or against the prevailing status quo.

states cautious, thus reducing conflict. Power parity theorists believe that uncertainty makes dissatisfied states more likely to use force to alter the status quo.

2 INFORMATION AND CONFLICT

My emphasis on information is not novel. Influential research demonstrates various ways in which information asymmetries can affect the probability of conflict (Powell, 1999).[5] Information is asymmetric when states hold different beliefs about the context of an international interaction. For example, one state may hold private information about its chances for victory in the event of conflict. Most relevant to this argument is the notion that states are uncertain about their opponent's military capabilities (see, e.g., Blainey, 1973; Morrow, 1989; and Fearon, 1995).

When states are uncertain about their opponent's capabilities, they may either overestimate or underestimate their own bargaining leverage. Such miscalculation may enhance the probability of a militarized clash by shrinking the range of acceptable non-violent agreements. Conversely, if both states are fully informed and militarized conflict is costly, the probability of conflict is zero. The challenger knows what the defender is willing to concede (i.e., the disagreement point or reservation value), and likewise the defender knows precisely how much it must give to appease the challenger and thereby avoid the costs of a militarized clash. In such a scenario, the challenger makes a demand exactly equal to the maximum concession the defender is willing to make. The bargain is made by the defender accepting the challenger's initial offer. However, when information asymmetries arise about relative capabilities, the challenger may overestimate its bargaining leverage and demand more than the defender is willing to concede. This may lead the defender to reject the challenger's offer, thereby making militarized conflict more likely. Asymmetric information may also lead the challenger to overestimate the defender's capabilities and thus make an inadequate opening offer, resulting in the defender's acceptance of the initial offer.

In the second scenario, asymmetric information decreases the probability of militarized conflict, just as balance of power theory suggests. In the first one, asymmetric information increases the probability of conflict, just at power transition theory suggests. Thus, the relationship between information

5. I am specifically interested in uncertainty about the distribution of power, but actors could also be uncertain about the stakes or the costs of the conflict, the beliefs their opponents have about them, their opponent's preferences for different outcomes, etc. For a detailed discussion of different types of uncertainty that could cause conflict see (Jervis, 1968).

and militarized conflict is not as clear as might be expected based on existing theories. It is important to consider how the expectations of these existing theories relate to bargaining arguments about the effect of uncertainty. What can be said is that in the ultimatum bargaining framework, asymmetric information is necessary for the emergence of militarized conflict. That is, when conflict is costly and states are fully informed, the probability of militarized conflict is zero.[6]

3 BASIC INGREDIENTS

A concrete example of the operation of asymmetric information may be useful at this point. The Russo-Japanese War emerged from the competing interests of Russia and Japan over Manchuria and Korea, and arguably was heavily influenced by Russia's inability to assess Japan's military capabilities accurately. Russia's eventual goal was the occupation of Korea. Japan also sought to extend its realm of influence to Korea and to extract revenge for Russia's interference during the 1894-95 Sino-Japanese War, in which Russian troops had seized Port Arthur and limited Japanese occupation of the Liaotung Peninsula. Between 1900 and 1903, Russian soldiers covertly moved across the Yalu River into northern Korea and prepared to fight the Japanese for control of the country. Russia's refusal to withdraw from Manchuria and subsequent penetration into North Korea were countered by Japanese attempts to negotiate a division of the disputed area. Russia remained inflexible and confident that it could defeat Japan in a military contest. However, Japan estimated that it had an even chance of defeating Russia and, on the basis of this information, ended negotiations and terminated domestic relations with Russia on February 6, 1904. Two days later Japan attacked Port Arthur, where the Russian Pacific fleet lay. A series of quick Japanese victories culminated in the fall of Port Arthur in January 1905. The Japanese successes continued under General Oyama at Shenyang in March of the same year. Admiral Togo destroyed a second Russian fleet at Tsushima in May. Russia's inability to estimate Japan's military might resulted in a disastrous outcome that paved the way for the Russian Revolution of 1905 (Nish, 1985). This historical example fits the claim that war is commonly the outcome of a crisis in which states' opinions about the distribution of power (i.e., thus about bargaining power) differ (Blainey, 1973). Although the Russo-Japanese example seems to support such a claim, the question remains of whether

6. This conclusion is consistent with several formal treatments of the bargaining process in both the formal theory literature, and applications of bargaining models to international interactions (Fearon 1995). For an important paper critical of this result, see Slantchev (2003).

uncertainty about the distribution of power is a general cause of conflict or matters only in particular historical instances.

To illustrate these claims formally, consider a fully informed risk-neutral challenger (*C*) and status quo defender (*D*) in a dispute with stakes, π, where $\pi > 0$. For the sake of simplicity, I assume $\pi = 1$.[7] The stakes could be territorial, as they were in the Russo-Japanese War, or more ideological, as they were between the United States and the Soviet Union during the Cold War.

The model here is a bargaining problem in which the outside option is a costly lottery, specifically militarized conflict. Bargaining begins when the challenger makes a demand ϑ that would leave the defender with $-\vartheta$. I assume that if a conflict breaks out, the challenger will prevail with likelihood p, and in the event of militarized conflict the winner gets π. The challenger's expected value for such a militarized conflict is $p - \delta_C$, and the defender's is $-p - \delta_D$. The costs of conflict are indexed by δ_i, $i \in (C,D)$ and κ denotes the sum of the challenger's and defender's costs of conflict.

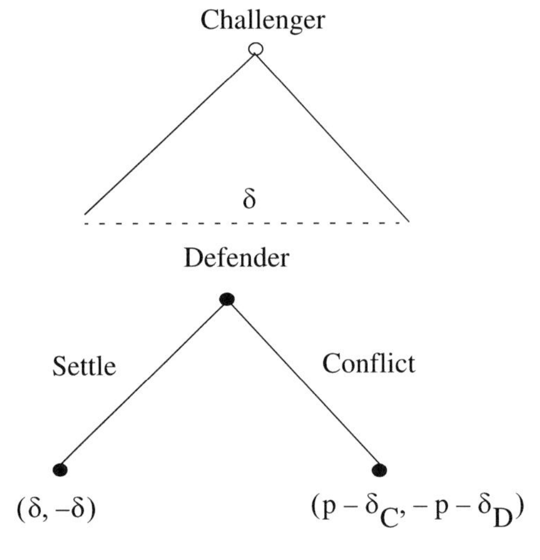

Figure 13.1. A simple bargaining game

The structure of the interaction between the challenger and defender is a take-it-or-leave-it bargain with the outside option of the costly lottery that is militarized conflict. If the defender rejects the challenger's demand, some

7. This formalization draws on previous work on international politics by Fearon (1995) and parallels work on law and economics by (Bebchuk, 1984). Moreover, it is the simplest possible bargaining model. Much richer formal models appear in the literature (Powell, 1999; Filson and Werner, 2002). My choice of the simplest model is useful for motivating the statistical analysis reported in the empirical section of the manuscript.

form of militarized force is used to settle the disagreement. I assume that the challenger's expected value for conflict is greater than zero—the status quo payoff. Conflict always occurs if the defender rejects the challenger's demand, and the defender rejects the demand only if it values the challenger's demand less than its expected value for conflict. Because the actors are fully informed, the challenger and defender know each other's reservation values. As a result, the challenger makes a demand equal to the defender's disagreement point, $\vartheta^* = p + \delta_D$. This is the subgame perfect equilibrium of the game because such an offer makes the defender indifferent between its expected value for militarized conflict and for appeasing the challenger. Thus, when the costs of conflict and the odds of success are known to both the challenger and defender, they are always able to settle their differences without a militarized clash.

However, it is unrealistic to assume that the challenger and defender are completely informed. Instead it is more reasonable to assume that the challenger is uncertain about the disagreement point. In many cases the challenger is unsure about the defender's costs of conflict, the quality of the defender's military, and the defender's resolution with respect to the issue at stake (Morrow, 1989). I assume that the challenger has only a rough estimate of the disagreement point, and is faced with the dilemma of either making a demand that is too small, which would be inefficient as it would let the defender keep too much of the stakes, or too large, which would lead to a militarized clash. I introduce uncertainty by assuming that the defender has some private information about the challenger's likelihood of prevailing in a militarized clash or about the distribution of power, p.[8] The defender may be better equipped to assess the likelihood of the challenger winning because of private information that the defender holds about its own military forces. On the basis of its private information, the defender estimates p. A defender with an estimate of p is referred to as being of type p, where defenders with low estimates of p have a higher expected value for conflict than defenders with high estimates of p. The challenger does not know the defender's type. However, it does know that p is distributed with a density function $f(\cdot)$ and a distribution function $F(\cdot)$. I assume that $f(\cdot)$ is positive in the interval (a,b), $0 < a < b < 1$, and zero outside that interval. Finally, I assume that $f(\cdot)$ is continuous and twice differentiable throughout with some neighborhood of b where $f(\cdot)$ is non-increasing.

Because the defender will accept an offer if, and only if, its utility for the offer is greater or equal to its expected value for militarized conflict, it gives

8. Asymmetric information of this sort is the most common approach to introducing uncertainty. It may be that the defender and the challenger are both uncertain about the balance of power. See Gartzke et al. (2001) for a treatment of two-sided uncertainty.

in to the challenger's demand only if $\vartheta \leq p + \delta_D$. Equivalently, the defender accepts the challenger's offer only if $p \geq \vartheta - \delta_D$. Therefore, the defender will accept the challenger's offer only if its type p is equal to or greater than $q(\vartheta)$, where

$$q(\vartheta) = \vartheta - \delta_D \tag{13.1}$$

The value of $q(\vartheta)$ represents the borderline type of challenger associated with an offer ϑ, and splits defenders into two groups. Defenders of type higher than $q(\vartheta)$ give in to the challenger's demand, whereas defenders of type less than $q(\vartheta)$ fight. An increase in the challenger's demand raises the borderline type and increases the probability of conflict. It is also useful to note that $q(\vartheta)$ and ϑ are linearly related. Therefore the challenger's problem can be seen as choosing an optimal demand or selecting an optimal borderline type. The challenger is faced with a difficult decision. The challenger knows that if it makes a demand ϑ, the probability that the defender will accept the offer is $1 - F[q(\vartheta)]$ and the probability of conflict is $F[q(\vartheta)]$. If the defender rejects the offer, its type is lower than $q(\vartheta)$, and a militarized clash will occur. The challenger makes a conditional probability calculation to determine the probability of winning such a conflict. Given that the defender fights, the probability that the challenger wins is $\frac{\int_{\alpha}^{q(\delta)} xf(x)dx}{F[q(\delta)]}$, the average probability of defender types lower than $q(\vartheta)$. Thus, the challenger's expected value for a demand ϑ is

$$E(\delta) = \{1 - F[q(\delta)]\}\delta + F[q(\delta)]\left\{\frac{\int_{\alpha}^{q(\delta)} xf(x)dx}{F[q(\delta)]} - \delta_C\right\} \tag{13.2}$$

The first part of (13.2) is the product of the probability that the defender gives in to the challenger's demand, $(1 - F[q(\vartheta)])$, and the value of the challenger's demand, (ϑ). The second part of (13.2) is the product of the probability that the defender rejects the challenger's offer, $(F[q(\vartheta)])$, and the challenger's expected value for a militarized clash. The challenger chooses ϑ to maximize this function. Using Leibniz's rule to differentiate the right hand side of (13.2) with respect to ϑ and rearranging slightly shows:

$$\frac{\partial E(\delta)}{\partial \delta} = \{1 - F[q(\delta)]\} - \{f[q(\delta)]\kappa\} \tag{13.3}$$

The first expression in (13.3) represents the benefits the challenger receives with a marginal increase in ϑ. The challenger can expect to receive this marginal increase with probability $1 - F[q(\vartheta)]$. The second expression in

(13.3) represents the costs to the challenger of a marginal increase in ϑ. An increase in ϑ raises the likelihood of conflict. This is the case because, if the defender's type is equal to $q(\vartheta)$, it will accept any demand ϑ but will reject a higher demand. That is, a marginal increase in ϑ increases the probability of conflict by $dF[q(\vartheta)]/d\vartheta = f[q(\vartheta)]$.

Let ϑ^* solve the challenger's problem (13.3), and let q^* denote $q(\vartheta^*)$. This is the perfect Bayesian equilibrium of the game. Note that the challenger's choice of ϑ^* determines the probability that the defender will accept the settlement offer. I denote the probability of conflict:

$$W^* = F[\vartheta^* - \delta_D] \equiv F[q^*] \tag{13.4}$$

This suggests that the defender's decision to accept or reject any demand is a function of its private information. Therefore, in contrast to the complete information result, there is a positive probability of conflict. In this model, uncertainty is necessary but not sufficient for militarized conflict. A numerical example illustrates the predictions of the model. Consider a challenger and defender bargaining over \$ 1,000. I assume that the costs of conflict are \$ 100 for both challenger and defender. A triangular distribution over the range of 0.4 and 0.8 describes the challenger's beliefs about the distribution of power. In such a scenario, the challenger makes a demand of about \$ 646 and the probability of conflict is about 26%.

4 COMPARATIVE STATICS

This simple model, while consistent with several analyses that adopt the bargaining framework (see, e.g. Reiter, 2003), illustrates the relationship between the probability of conflict and the stakes of the contest, the magnitude of the challenger's demand, and the actors' costs of conflict. But unlike most previous research, I use it to explore the relationship between characteristics of the challenger's information about the distribution of power and the probability of conflict (Bueno de Mesquita and Lalman, 1992; Bueno de Mesquita et al., 1997; Wittmann, 2001). I operationalize the challenger's uncertainty as variance in their belief about the distribution of power (e.g., variance in $f(\cdot)$ and $F(\cdot)$). Thus, the formalization combines scholarly interest in the relationships among uncertainty, conflict, and the distribution of power in a novel way.

4.1 Distribution of Information

Most bargaining research focuses on the effect of asymmetric information on the probability of a militarized clash. Here the important difference is that the probability of militarized conflict is affected by characteristics of the distribution describing the challenger's beliefs about the defender's odds of winning a militarized clash (i.e., the distribution of power).

Consider the effect of expanding or contracting the range of the distribution of the challenger's information about the distribution of power without altering the mean. What effect does a change in the variance in the challenger's estimate of the distribution of power have on the probability of a militarized clash? To assess the effect of such incremental changes, I denote μ to be the mean of the distribution $f(\cdot)$, and assume that p is distributed in the interval $(\mu - \sigma(\mu - a), \mu + \sigma(b - \mu))$, with a density function $h(\cdot)$ and a cumulative distribution function $H(\cdot)$ defined by

$$h(x) \equiv \frac{1}{\sigma} f\left\{\mu + \frac{x-\mu}{\sigma}\right\} \tag{13.5}$$

and

$$H(x) \equiv F\left\{\mu + \frac{x-\mu}{\sigma}\right\} \tag{13.6}$$

Varying the values of σ gives a family of distributions with the same mean, but with different higher moments. This allows me to assess the impact of variance in the challenger's estimate of the distribution of power on the probability of conflict. For $\sigma = 1$, $h(\cdot)$ is equivalent to $f(\cdot)$. However, for $\sigma > 1$, $h(\cdot)$ is an expanded version of $f(\cdot)$ and for $\sigma < 1$, $h(\cdot)$ is a contracted version of $f(\cdot)$.

> **Proposition 1:** *A marginal expansion in the variance of the challenger's estimate of the distribution of power has an indeterminate effect on the challenger's demand, and will increase the probability of conflict.*

Likewise, as σ goes to zero, so does the probability of conflict. As the variance in the challenger's estimate of the distribution of power goes to zero, the incomplete information result converges on the complete information result. If there is no variance in the challenger's estimate of the distribution of power, the challenger is able to select an optimal demand, thereby making the defender indifferent between its expected value for conflict and its utility for the challenger's demand.[9]

Consider a numerical example. When the challenger's estimate of the distribution of power is bounded by 0.5 and 0.7, the probability of conflict is about 10 %. However, when the distribution ranges from 0.2 to 1.0, the probability of conflict is 50 %. When there is greater uncertainty about the distribution of power, the probability of conflict is significantly higher.

Increasing the variance in the challenger's estimate of the distribution of power enhances the likelihood of conflict because it increases the differences among types in the expected outcome of a militarized clash. This comparative static is consistent with Wittman (2001), and central to my argument. The effect of variance in the distribution of types of defenders on the probability of conflict provides a rational explanation for the recurring empirical pattern that relates equal distributions of observable capabilities to the onset of militarized conflict.[10]

In order to interpret the relationship between power distributions and the emergence of militarized conflict, it is important to consider what types of power distributions are most likely to affect the variance in the challenger's estimate of the distribution of power. As discussed earlier, this is a topic upon which the balance of power and power transition approaches concur. These traditional theories claim that uncertainty about the outcome of militarized conflict is greatest when states are relatively equal in power. That is, at parity, the distribution of defender types is likely to have the greatest variance. States can observe much of their opponent's capabilities, through the size and technological sophistication of the opponent's military. Thus, information asymmetries about the distribution of power are most likely to come from such unobservable factors as resolve or military tactics. Resolve is an important component of military power, but resolve goes only so far against an opponent whose observable military power is great. For example, regardless of Denmark's resolve, in a crisis with the United States its resolve would do little to make its expected leverage greater than whatever demand the United States might make. However, when two states with relatively equal observable capabilities bargain, unobserved resolve is an important factor for them to estimate their bargaining leverage. In such situations, information asymme-

9. Of course the probability of conflict only goes to zero if the uncertainty about the defender's reservation value is focused only on a disagreement about the distribution of power. It is certainly possible for the challenger to be uncertain about other important variables such as the defender's costs of conflict. In this case, conflict would still occur with some positive probability.

10. Proof of Proposition 1: The proposition is proved by differentiating the first-order condition, using h and H instead of f and F, with respect to σ: $\frac{\delta(1-F(q^*))}{\delta\sigma} = -\frac{\kappa f(q^*)}{\sigma^2}$. The effect of σ on q^* and as a result on the size of the challenger's demand is ambiguous.

tries arise naturally, and states have an incentive to bluff in order to secure a better deal.

Following Wittman (2001), I incorporate this dynamic into the bargaining model by assuming that σ is a function of the distribution of power. As states approach parity, σ increases, leading to an expanded distribution of defender types. Likewise, as the distribution of power moves away from parity, σ approaches zero, and the variance in the challenger's estimate of the balance of power shrinks. *Ceteris paribus*, I expect the probability of conflict to be greatest at equal distributions of power specifically due to the relationship between equal distributions of power and variance in the challenger's estimate of the distribution of power. This explanation for conflict emergence is consistent with power transition arguments as well as with the wealth of empirical evidence pointing to the conflict-enhancing effect of equal distributions of power. It implies a rational explanation for the observed conflict-enhancing effect of equal distributions of power, while remaining consistent with the logic of both balance of power and power transition theories. If one equates power distributions with σ, two testable hypotheses can be deduced from the bargaining model.

> **Hypothesis 1:** *The more equal the distribution of power, the more variable the distribution of defender types.*

The first hypothesis follows from the logic of the traditional international politics theories and from the expectation that σ is a function of the distribution of power.

> **Hypothesis 2:** *The greater the variance of the distribution of defender types, the greater the probability of militarized conflict.*

The second hypothesis is deduced directly from the bargaining model. I analyze historical data to examine the empirical validity of the hypotheses. To facilitate comparison with previous research, I use data from Oneal and Russett (1997). These data contain observations on 20,990 pairs of states, 1950-1985. The unit of analysis is the dyad year, and there is information on 827 politically relevant dyads. Each dyad is observed once for every year it appears in the data file. The dependent variable is the existence of a militarized dispute. The coding of this dependent variable and the collection of the militarized interstate dispute data are discussed in Jones et al. (1996). In this sample there are 947 disputes, resulting in a average value of .045 for the dependent variable. The crucial independent variable is the distribution of power, indexed as the ratio of the stronger state's power to the weaker state's power with the Correlates of War composite capabilities index (Singer, 1987). At parity, this variable is equal to one.[11] Drawing on past research and the logic of the bargaining model, I expect the effect of this variable to be negatively related to militarized conflict. Measures of joint democracy, economic growth, alliance membership, territorial contiguity, and economic interdependence are included as controls. The measurement of these control variables is discussed in Oneal and Russett (1997). I also include a spline to correct for temporal dependence in the data (Beck et al., 1998).

5 STATISTICAL ANALYSIS

The goal of the statistical analysis is to estimate the relationship between the distribution of power and σ from equations (13.5) and (13.6). In previous statistical studies the onset of conflict has been modeled using special cases of generalized linear models for indicator variables (Oneal and Russett, 1997). These models are ill-equipped to assess heterogeneity in conflict behavior as a function of the distribution of power. One weakness of previous treatments is their assumption that there is no observed heterogeneity in the conflict data. The current literature considers variation in conflict behavior only in the mean rather than in the variance. Not only is this an unrealistic practical assumption, it is also at odds with international relations theories whose explanations rely on power distributions.

It is standard practice to pool pairs of states such as the United States and Canada or India and Pakistan and assume that the variation in their conflict behavior is identical. These models further assume that the variance among Western European dyads is the same as that among African dyads. This seems highly unrealistic. Bargaining models anticipate heterogeneous behavior as a function of asymmetric information and, specifically, variance in the challenger's estimate of the distribution of power. I expect the variance of the error in the challenger's estimate of the defender's type (its unobservable capabilities) to vary with the distribution of power. As the challenger and defender approach power parity, the variance in the challenger's estimate of the defender's power is expected to be greatest. This leads to an enhanced probability of mistakes and a non-zero probability of conflict onset. To address this deficiency in the standard models and to evaluate my claims about variance in the challenger's estimate of the defender's unobserved capa-

11. It is also possible to operationalize this variable as the ratio of the weaker state to the stronger state. The weaker to stronger index lies between zero and one. I use the stronger to weaker measure to be consistent with Oneal and Russett (1997). Moreover, normalizing the index makes the visual presentation in the second figure difficult to interpret. This is because pairs of states characterized by substantial preponderance are drawn back toward the values of dyads with less significant preponderance.

bilities, I incorporate heteroscedasticity in the probit model as given in the following hierarchical specification:

$$\begin{aligned} y &= X\beta + \varepsilon \\ \varepsilon &\sim N(0, \sigma^2 V) \\ V &= \mathrm{diag}(v_1, v_2, \ldots, v_n) \\ \beta &\sim N(0, 100) \\ \sigma &\sim (1/\sigma) \\ r/v_i &\sim ID\chi^2(r)/r \\ r &\sim \Gamma(14, 2) \end{aligned}$$

where y is a $n \times 1$ vector containing information on conflict onset. The matrix X represents the explanatory variables in the analysis. I assume that ε is an $n \times 1$ vector of normally distributed errors with non-constant variance. The prior on β is normal and diffuse. The relative variance terms (v_1, v_2, ..., v_n) are assumed to be fixed but unknown parameters that have to be estimated. Estimating n variance parameters in addition to β and σ using n observations seems problematic. However, Bayesian methods do not encounter the standard degrees of freedom constraints because informative priors are placed on the parameters. Because I assign the v_i terms an independent $\chi^2(r)/r$ prior, the prior is centered on one with a variance $2r$, and only a single parameter r is added to the estimation procedure. The parameter r is updated based on the Γ prior.

The hypotheses I deduced from bargaining theory anticipate that the variance in the challenger's estimate of the distribution of power is greatest at parity, and that this variance will enhance the likelihood of a militarized clash. Therefore, the presence of heteroscedastic errors that are related to different distributions of power is consistent with the expectations derived from bargaining theory and provides some support for my hypotheses.

The multiple integrals in the reparameterized probit likelihood function make computation difficult. To minimize the computational costs of evaluating the likelihood function, I analyze the conflict data with Bayesian tools. Utilizing Bayesian simulation (MCMC), I am able to make inferences based on the posterior. I use the Gibbs sampler to obtain posterior samples.[12] Obtaining samples directly from the posterior is difficult because of the presence of several integrals and the probit function Φ in the likelihood. To

12. The Gibbs sampler is the most widely used MCMC method. If one can express each of the coefficients in the model conditioned on all of the other coefficients, the Gibbs sampler can cycle through these conditional statements and eventally find the true distribution of interest. See Jackman (2000) for a discussion of the Gibbs sampler in a political science context. A more general discussion may be found in Carlin and Lewis (1996) and Gelman et al. (1995)

overcome these difficulties, I use the auxiliary variable technique of Albert and Chib (1993).[13] This approach augments the observed data with a quantity Z. From both the observed data and Z, it is possible to calculate the posterior density. Because the data are augmented with $Z = (z_1, z_2, ..., z_N)$, the likelihood is equivalent to the standard linear model. As a result, the posterior is computationally manageable. I ran 10,000 Gibbs samples to recover the posterior densities with a burn-in period of 1,000 samples.[14]

6 RESULTS AND INTERPRETATION

Results from the estimation are presented in Figure 13.2. and in Table 13.1. In the first column of the table, I report the means of the posterior densities for each explanatory variable. These mean values are comparable to conventional maximum likelihood estimates and are consistent with results reported elsewhere (Beck et al., 1998). I report the results from a standard maximum likelihood probit model in the second column of Table 13.1. for comparison.

Table 13.1. Bayesian Heteroscedastic Probit of Dispute Onset

Variable[a]	*Posterior/(SD)*	*MLE/(SE)*
Capabilities	-0.000141	-0.001131
	(0.000034)	(0.000155)
Joint Democracy	-0.006811	-0.024078
	(0.002058)	(0.003721)
Trade	-2.010337	-5.116253
	(1.829739)	(4.435773)
Growth	-0.002323	-0.007404
	(0.003592)	(0.004738)
Alliance	-0.085877	-0.185617
	(0.028794)	(0.043635)
Contiguity	0.192059	0.380107
	(0.030424)	(0.044104)
Intercept	-0.494545	-0.591197
	(0.035718)	(0.047177)

13. For an alternate approach to modeling heterogeneity in the context of a probit regression, see Alvarez and Brehm (1995). To check the robustness of my result, I also estimate the model they suggested. The results from this analysis also suggest that the variance in the model of conflict onset is correlated with the distribution of power.

14. See Smith (1999) for a discussion of estimating the posterior of β though data augmentation in the context of crisis escalation

Burn-in Iterations	1,000
MCMC Iterations	10,000
Observations	20,990

a. MATLAB was used to obtain these results. The mean and standard deviation of the samples produced by the Gibbs sampler are reported in the first column. For comparison, maximum likelihood estimates and their standard errors appear in the second column.

Inspection shows that the maximum likelihood estimates and the means of the posterior distributions are similar. Past research reporting a negative relationship between power preponderance and militarized conflict is confirmed. The mean of the posterior density of the relative power variable is negative and credibly different from zero. As states approach power parity, the probability of militarized conflict increases. The effects of the control variables are also consistent with the empirical patterns reported in the literature. Jointly democratic dyads are less likely to experience militarized conflict. States sharing a border are more likely to fight. States sharing an alliance, experiencing economic growth, and engaged in trade are all moderately less prone to conflict. The effect of alliances on bargaining is an especially fruitful area of emerging research. For a detailed discussion of alliances in the context of bargaining and militarized conflict onset, see (Leeds, 2003). These results are consistent with the comparative statics from the bargaining model in terms of the effect of the stakes and the costs of conflict on the probability of a militarized clash.

Inspection of Figure 13.2. illuminates the relationship between information and power distributions. This figure plots the mean of the posterior densities of the variances against the distribution of power. Each plotted point is the mean of the draws from the posterior distribution of v_i. Following research that equates increasing uncertainty with greater error variance (Downs and Rocke, 1979; Alvarez and Brehm, 1995), the relationship between power distributions and variance in the distribution of types of defenders is striking. Variance in the distribution of types of defenders and its proxy, the mean of the posterior distributions for the variances, increases as states approach an equal distribution of power. These results indicate that there is more variance in the model as the ratio of power approaches parity and that a strong positive correlation exists between power parity and greater variance in the challenger's estimate of the distribution of power. This illustration thus provides support for the first hypothesis. I refer to the Figure 13.2. to evaluate the credibility of the hypothesis about the relationship between variance in the distribution of types of defenders and the distribution of capabilities. I plot the means of the posterior samples of v_i against different distributions of power in order to assess the possibility that the posterior means of v_i are a function of the distribution of power. The assumption of

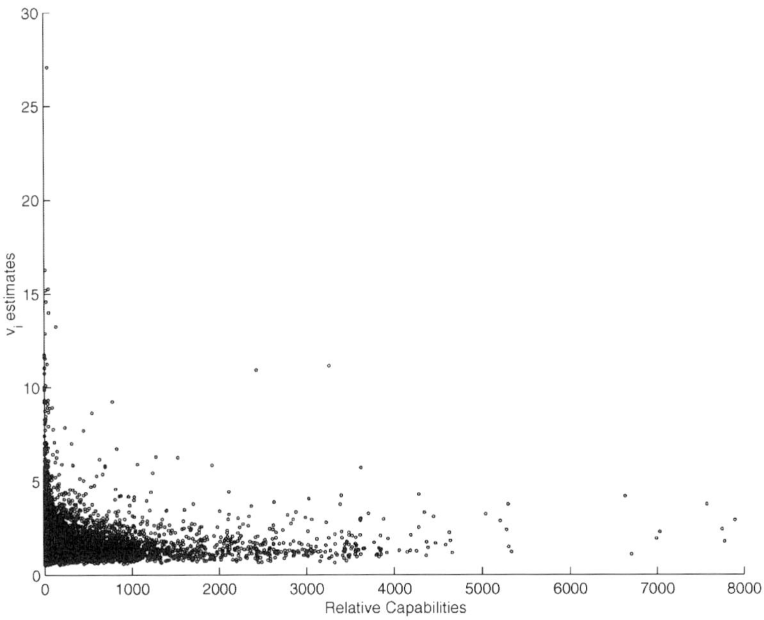

Figure 13.2. Capabilities and information

constant variance in the errors and independence between the errors and the explanatory variables can be evaluated visually. The formalization suggests that the variance will increase as the distribution of power approaches parity, and increases in the variance will be associated with the onset of militarized conflict.

Not only is there a significant amount of unexplained heterogeneity in the data, but the heterogeneity is correlated with the distribution of power. Because the probit model is known to be inconsistent and the covariance matrix may be incorrect when the variance of the errors is heteroscedastic (Yatchew and Griliches, 1985), the implications of this analysis are far reaching. Specifically, analyses that fail to address the relationship between the variance in the error and the distribution of power may be incorrect. Although I demonstrate a potential source of the heterogeneity, a much richer model is needed to model the heterogeneity explicitly. Additionally, this result provides support for formal bargaining models of international interactions. Increases in the variance of the distribution of types of defenders appear to exhibit the expected effect of creating the conditions for bargaining to break down, leading to the use of force to settle disputes. States with relatively equal amounts of power, knowing the similarity between their observable capabilities and those of their opponent, have an incentive to misrepresent their unobservable capabilities in order to strike a better bargain. The paramount role that these unobservable capabilities play in the bargaining process and the clear incentive to bluff about them result in an enhanced probability of militarized conflict.

7 CONCLUSION

Is there greater uncertainty about the distribution of power when observable military capabilities are relatively balanced between two states? Is the observed relationship between the distribution of power and conflict an artifact of the relationship between uncertainty about the distribution of power and conflict? In the context of the Russo-Japanese War of 1904, the evidence suggests that Russia's inability to assess the distribution of power accurately led Russia to refuse to bargain with the Japanese, and thus was a central cause of the war. The relatively equal distribution of observable capabilities probably also enhanced Russia's uncertainty about the distribution of power. The bargaining model illustrates this dynamic formally, and the statistical analysis suggests that this pattern operates more generally. Pairs of states with equal distributions of power exhibit greater variance, and greater variance is correlated with the onset of conflict.

These results suggest that a focus on observable power alone is insufficient. Instead, the distribution of information and its relationship to power are important determinants of international interactions. I illustrate the effect of information formally and provide a rational explanation for the assertions of more traditional power-centric theories of world politics. While balance of power theorists and power transition theorists disagree about the relationship between specific power distributions and war, they agree that uncertainty is greatest when power is distributed equally. Their convergence on the topic of uncertainty is consistent with bargaining models of international interactions. Further, bargaining models provide an exciting opportunity to subsume balance of power and power transition assertions within a single theoretical framework. The results I report provide encouraging support for the use of a bargaining framework to understand such international interactions.

My arguments and results are consistent with those of others utilizing a bargaining framework and suggest a much richer relationship between power distributions and the probability of militarized conflict than do the traditional power-centric theories. I find that asymmetric information and greater variance in the distribution of types of defenders are related to power parity. I claim that the often debated relationship between power parity and militarized conflict may, at least to some extent, be an artifact of the relationship between power distributions and the distribution of information. Evidence is building to suggest that heterogeneous data are the norm in international politics (Lemke, 2002). As a result, it seems essential that future research start to recognize the threat that such heterogeneity poses for inferences about international interactions.

References

Albert, J. A., and Chib, S., 1993, Bayesian analysis of binary and polytomous response data, *Journal of the American Statistical Association* **88**: 669–679.

Alvarez, R.. M., and Brehm, J., 1995, American ambivalence towards abortion policy: Development of a heteroscedastic probit model of competing values, *American Journal of Political Science* **39**: 1055–1082.

Bebchuk, L. A., 1984, Litigation and settlement under imperfect information, *Rand Journal of Economics* **15**: 404–415.

Beck, N., Katz, J. M., and Tucker, R., 1998, Beyond ordinary logit: Taking time seriously in binary time-series cross-section models, *American Journal of Political Science* **42**: 1260–1288.

Blainey, G., 1973, *The Causes of War*, Macmillan, London.

Bremer, S. A., 1992, Dangerous dyads: Conditions affecting the likelihood of interstate war, 1816-1965, *Journal of Conflict Resolution* **36**: 309–341.

Bueno de Mesquita, B., and Lalman, D., 1992, *War and Reason*, Yale University Press, New Haven.

Bueno de Mesquita, B., Morrow, J. D., and Zorick, E., 1997, Capabilities, perception, and escalation, *American Political Science Review* **91**: 15–27.

Carlin, B. P., and Lewis, T. A., 1996, *Bayes and Empirical Bayes Methods for Data Analysis*, : Champman and Hall, London.

Downs, G. W., and Rocke, D. M., 1979, Interpreting heteroscedasticity, *American Journal of Political Science* **23**: 816–828.

Fearon, J. D., 1995, Rationalist explanations for war, *International Organization* **49**: 379–414.

Filson, D. and Werner, S., 2002, *Bargaining and Fighting*, Mimeo Emory University.

Gartzke, E., Li, Q., and Boehmer. C., 2001, Investing in the peace: Economic interdependence and international conflict, *International Organization* **55**: 391–438.

Gelman, A., Carlin, J. B., Stern, H. S., and Rubin, D. B., 1995, *Bayesian Data Analysis*, Champman and Hall, London.

Jackman, S., 2000, Estimation and inference are missing data problems: Unifying social science statistics via Bayesian simulation, *Political Analysis* **8**: 307–332.

Jervis, R., 1968, Hypotheses on misperception, *World Politics* **20**: 454–479.

Jones, D., Bremer, S. A., and Singer, J. D., 1996, Militarized interstate disputes, 1816-1992: Rationale, coding rules, and empirical patterns, *Conflict Management and Peace Science* **15**: 163–213.

Kugler, J., and Lemke, D., 1996, *Parity and War: Evaluations and Extensions of 'The War Ledger'*, University of Michigan Press, Ann Arbor.

Leeds, A., 2003, Do alliances deter aggression? The influence of military alliances on the initiation of militarized interstate disputes, *American Journal of Political Science* forthcoming.

Lemke, D., 2002, *Regions of War and Peace*, Cambridge University Press, Cambridge, UK.

Lemke, D., and Werner, S., 1996, Power parity, commitment to change, and war, *International Studies Quarterly* **40**: 235–260.

Morgenthau, H. J., 1948, *Politics Among Nations*, Alfred A. Knopf., New York.

Morrow, J. D., 1989, Capabilities, uncertainty, and resolve: A limited information model of crisis bargaining, *American Journal of Political Science* **33**: 941–972.

Nish, I., 1985, *Origins of the Russo-Japanese War*, Longman, London.

Oneal, J. R., and Russett, B. D., 1997, The classic liberals were right: Democracy, interdependence, and conflict, 1950-1985, *International Studies Quarterly* **41**: 267–294.

Organski, A. F. K., 1958, *World Politics*, Alfred Knopf, New York.

Powell, R., 1999, *In the Shadow of Power*, Princeton University Press, Princeton, NJ.

Reiter, D., 2003, Exploring the bargaining model of war, *Perspectives on Politics* **1**: 1–17.

Singer, J. D., 1987, Reconstructing the Correlates of War dataset on material capabilities of states, 1816-1985, *International Interactions* **14**: 115–132.

Slantchev, B. L., 2003, The power to hurt: Costly conflict with completely informed states, *American Political Science Review* **97**: 123–133.

Smith, A., 1999, Testing theories of strategic choice: The example of crisis escalation, *American Journal of Political Science* **43**: 1254–1283.

Werner, S., 2000, The effects of political similarity on the onset of militarized disputes, 1816-1985, *Political Research Quarterly* **53**: 343–374.

Wittman, D., 2001, War or peace?, paper presented at the *Political Economy of Conflict Conference*, Yale University, 2001.

Yatchew, A., and Griliches, Z., 1985, Specification error in probit models, *Review of Economics and Statistics* **67**: 134–139.

Chapter 14

Modeling Effects of Emotion and Personality on Political Decision-Making

Application to International Conflict Prevention and Resolution

Eva Hudlicka

Psychometrix Associates, Inc., Blacksburg, Virginia, USA

The ability to see the world from another person's perspective is critical for mutual understanding and conflict prevention and resolution. It allows us to understand others' subjective perspectives, and to predict, to some extent, their reactions to particular situations or events. This then allows us to identify specific situations or actions which are likely to trigger desirable (or undesirable) behavior, and thereby aid in the prevention and resolution of potential conflicts. A key component of these capabilities is the understanding of the other individuals' values and motivations, patterns of reasoning, and behavior determined by their personalities, and individual reactions that may occur as a result of specific emotions. This type of understanding in turn necessitates understanding how different emotions and traits influence decision-making, and how these influences may result in specific decision-making styles or biases. This chapter describes a generic methodology for representing the effects of multiple, interacting emotional states and personality traits on decision-making, and an associated computational cognitive architecture which implements this methodology. I present results of an evaluation experiment that demonstrates the architecture's ability to model individual tactical decision-making and produce observable behavior differences resulting from distinct individual profiles. I then discuss how the methodology and architecture would be extended to model strategic, political decision-making, and how it could support a variety of activities geared towards international conflict prevention and resolution. I conclude with specific theoretical and pragmatic challenges associated with this approach to computer-aided conflict prevention and resolution.

R. Trappl (ed.), Programming for Peace, 355–411.

1 INTRODUCTION

The ability to see the world from another person's perspective is an essential component of the mutual understanding necessary for preventing and resolving conflict. This ability is essential regardless of the type of conflict in question: family misunderstandings and organizational feuds with relatively limited scopes, or international conflicts with significant long-term consequences for entire nations and world peace.

Many factors make this task challenging. Not only must we step outside of our own, deeply-engrained mode of perceiving the world, and see it from a distinct perspective—to 'get inside the other person's head'. We must also understand the other person's distinct modes of thinking and decision-making, specific decision-making biases, and the various emotions they may experience in response to particular events, which profoundly influence both their subjective perceptions and their decision-making. We must understand the values and motivations that guide their goal priorities and goal selection, and the subsequent choice of the best means to accomplish those goals (e.g., Levy, 2003; Jervis, 1976; George, 1979; Kahneman et al., 1982; Forgas, 2003; Loewenstein and Lerner, 2003; Williams et al., 1997). Such in-depth understanding of another individual (or a group of individuals, whether a family or an entire nation) requires not only 'getting inside the other person's head', but equally importantly, 'getting inside their heart'.

Recent emotion research has identified the crucial role of affective states in influencing, often profoundly, perception and decision-making (LeDoux, 1992, 1996; Damasio, 1994, 2003; Williams et al., 1997; Matthews et al., 2000; Matthews and Dreary, 1998l; Forgas, 2003; Loewenstein and Lerner, 2003). These influences span the full spectrum of perceptual and cognitive processes that mediate decision-making and determine behavioral choices. Emotion effects range from the mundane (a sudden, intense urge for a particular meal or piece of music) to the significant (choice of one's spouse), and include influences on decisions that are made instantaneously and almost automatically, as well as those which may take days, months or even years. These effects are not limited to the more dramatic expressions of extreme emotions (e.g., table bashing with shoes), but include internal, often subtle, effects on attention (anxiety-induced attentional narrowing and threat focus), on working memory (anxiety-induced reduction in working memory capacity), and inhibition or activation of particular interpretive schemas in long-term memory, which influence problem-solving and decision-making.

Depending on the type and intensity of the affective state, these effects range from necessary, appropriate and adaptive, through maladaptive, to destructive and dangerous. We are generally not surprised that emotions can be maladaptive, since, until recently, emotions and 'emotionality' have had rather negative connotations. What is striking about the empirical findings over the past decade is the evidence that emotions are necessary for adaptive decision-making, and that without an emotional input, even simple day-to-day decisions may become impossible (e.g., deciding what to wear or how to accomplish basic daily chores (Damasio, 1994)). Thus regardless of whether we wish to model 'good' or 'bad' decision-making, it is clear that effects of states and traits must be incorporated, if we are to develop realistic models of human decision-making.

While such effects may be subtle in terms of their external manifestations, they are profound in terms of their influence on the internal processes mediating decision-making. They determine what information is processed, which goals are given priority, what conclusions are derived, and ultimately determine the decisions made and actions taken.

If we think of emotions as triggering transient shifts in perception and decision-making strategies, or, as Minsky has recently put it, distinct ways of thinking (Minsky, forthcoming), we can think of personality traits as representing established long-term patterns of such distinct modes of perceiving and thinking, as well as distinct modes of affective responses (e.g., rapid and intense vs. slow and mild reactions to events; people vs. task orientation).

A rather dramatic illustration of these state and trait effects can be found in an analysis of Woodrow Wilson's decision-making and behavior during the Treaty of Versailles ratification process in the US senate in 1919. Wilson's vehement opposition to any amendments to the treaty resulted in a failure to obtain the desired senate ratification, and led to a less effective League of Nations. Some political psychologists attribute Wilson's intransigence to his 'need for power' and 'need for achievement' traits, and associated affective states of fear (of loss of power), and anger (at those who would oppose him), which prevented him from making the necessary political compromises during the ratification process (Walker, 1995). While we may question the theoretical focus of this particular analysis of Wilson's decision-making (psychodynamic depth psychology), there is no doubt that whatever the distal causes of Wilson's personality, it had a profound impact on his decision-making, the outcome of a crucial senate vote, and quite possibly on the state of the world. Recent history has taught us that a multinational governing body is no guarantee against aggression, yet one wonders whether World War II might have been avoided had a fully-functional League of Nations been in place in the 1940s.

In short, to fully understand another person's or group's perspective, and perhaps to predict their reactions or behavior, we need to know something about their personalities, the types of emotions they are likely to experience in different situations, and their decision-making biases. This knowledge, coupled with a knowledge about the generic effects of emotions (states) and personality characteristics (traits), may then allow us to see the world through their eyes, minds, and 'hearts'. And this capability may allow us to predict specific reactions in particular circumstances, as well as long-term strategic decision patterns. Together, these capabilities may then contribute in preventing and resolving conflicts, large and small, among individuals, groups, and entire nations.

In this chapter I describe a computational approach for modeling multiple, interacting effects of states and traits on decision-making. The approach consists of a generic modeling methodology for modeling state and trait effects within a computational cognitive architecture, and the associated cognitive architecture that implements this methodology. The architecture supports the mapping of specific state / trait configurations onto particular values of the parameters controlling the architecture structures (e.g., long-term memory clusters), and processing (e.g., speed and capacity of individual processing modules). Specific state/trait profiles can then be defined to represent particular decision-maker types, their decision-making can be simulated within the cognitive architecture, and the resulting behavioral outcomes can be observed within the simulated environment. This allows the construction of explicit computational models of how specific decision biases might arise in individual decision-making, how they might manifest themselves within the distinct stages of the decision-making process and, eventually, in terms of distinct behavioral outcomes.

The resulting computational model can then be used to construct simulated agents to model the decision-making of particular types of individuals, across a range of external contexts (e.g., peace negotiations, specific decisions within an existing conflict) and internal contexts (e.g., low- vs. high-anxious decision-maker). Such simulations can then be used for a variety of applied and research purposes within the broad area of international conflict resolution and prevention, including improved understanding of the decision bias mechanisms, simulation-based behavior prediction for a variety of decision-maker stereotypes and their reactions to particular political situations, as well as simulation-based training and assessment environments.

The chapter is organized as follows. First, I provide background information on the variety of decision-biases that have been identified, and on the effects of states and traits on decision-making (section 2), and on computational models of decision-making, motivating the current emphasis on explicit models of emotions in decision-making (section 3). I then describe a generic methodology for modeling the effects of states and traits within cognitive architectures (section 4), and describe its demonstration in a specific operational context: modeling individual, short-term tactical decision-making within a peacekeeping scenario (section 5). Next, I describe how the existing methodology and architecture would be applied to model long-term strategic decision-making (section 6). I then outline specific applications of this cognitive modeling approach to international conflict resolution and prevention (section 7), and conclude with a summary and an outline of specific theoretical and pragmatic challenges (section 8).

2 DECISION MAKING: BIASES AND STATE / TRAIT EFFECTS

This section provides an overview of the variety of biases and heuristics that have been identified in decision-making (section 2.1), and the empirical evidence regarding the specific effects of states and traits on decision-making (section 2.2). This background information serves several purposes: *first*, to demonstrate the pervasive and profound effects of decision-making biases on behavior; *second*, to motivate the need for improved understanding of the etiology, mechanisms and consequences of decision biases, and *third*, to provide the necessary background for the computational model described in sections 4 through 6.

2.1 Biases and Heuristics in Decision-Making

Judgment and decision-making research has identified a number of *biases* in decision-making. Since under some circumstances particular biases can in fact serve as useful shortcuts (e.g., reasoning by analogy, confirmation bias), the term *heuristics* is frequently used (Tversky and Kahneman, 1974).

Judgment and decision-making research focuses on what can be categorized as *process* biases; that is, biases resulting from the misapplication of the reasoning processes, or from errors in perceptual and reasoning processes. In addition to these process biases, we can also consider *content* biases. Content biases refer to the biasing effects of specific contents of the knowledge structures (schemas) that mediate decision-making. These include specific values and goals, beliefs and assumptions about the world, and beliefs and perceptions of the decision-maker's own behavior capabilities and options. These content-oriented biases, though generally not termed as such, are frequently explored in clinical, organizational, social and political psychology. Both of these types of biases and heuristics are discussed below.

2.1.1 Process-Based Decision-Making Biases

A variety of biases have been identified by a number of researchers (e.g., Howard et al., 2003). The seminal work in this area was done by Kahneman, Tversky and colleagues (Kahneman et al., 1982; Tversky and Kahneman, 1974; 1981) in the context of individual decision-making. A number of specific judgment and decision-making biases were identified, including the following: *availability bias* (the tendency to base decisions on the most readily available evidence, rather than the most appropriate evidence, hence the *primacy* and *recency* bias resulting from biased memory recall), *confirmation bias* (the tendency to prefer, or actively seek out, evidence that supports one's hypotheses, expectations and goals), and *framing effects* (the tendency to be influenced by, and respond differently to, the wording (as opposed to the substance) of a question or a decision). When we enlarge the focus from the individual to the social realm, another important bias emerges which is endemic in decisions made by groups: the *groupthink bias* (Janis, 1972). Groupthink is characterized by several factors including pressure to conform, illusion of morality, and illusion of consensus, and has been studied extensively by organizational, social and political psychologists.

A number of attempts have been made to classify the identified biases. For example, Levy (2003), refers to 'unmotivated' and 'motivated' biases, the former arising from errors in cognitive processing with no connections to particular needs, whereas the latter arising from particular psychological needs such as desires, fears, reduction of anxiety, etc. (I will return to the motivated biases during the discussion of state effects in section 2.2.2.) An interesting comprehensive classification of bias types was developed by Howard and colleagues (Howard et al., 2003), who divided biases into five categories: *comfort zone biases* (e.g., resistance to change, focus on what is easy rather than what is important); *motivational biases* (e.g., escalating commitment bias, wishful thinking), *perception biases* (e.g., anchoring), *reasoning fallacies* (e.g., misunderstanding of statistical principles), and *groupthink* (e.g., illusion of consensus, pressure for conformity). Approaching the bias literature from a computational perspective, I have expanded this categorization, provided additional differentiating subcategories (e.g., memory and perception, meta-cognition, statistical principles), and re-categorized some of the biases. Table 14.1. lists a number of the identified biases in terms of this augmented categorization scheme. This organization begins to provide a basis for a more differentiated type of thinking about biases, which lays the ground work for a computational cognitive modeling approach, and for a systematic identification of the effects of states and traits on the emergence of the observed biases.

When considering the prevalence of process biases across different decision-making contexts, it is important to realize that the original research of Kahneman and Tversky was conducted in artificial, highly-controlled laboratory settings, using situations explicitly designed to demonstrate the manifestations of these biases and heuristics. As decision-making research has expanded from controlled laboratory settings into more naturalistic contexts, the ubiquity of these biases has begun to be questioned. Some researchers studying decision-making in more naturalistic settings, or in laboratory settings designed to emulate naturalistic contexts, have not found strong evidence for, or large impact of, these biases (e.g., Klein, 1996). Questions are thus emerging regarding the strength and prevalence of these biases in settings where a wide variety of evidence is available, and where decisions are made over longer periods of time, in contrast to the relatively simple, time-constrained and highly-controlled experiments that have traditionally been used to demonstrate these biases (Cohen, 1993). These findings are directly relevant to strategic decision-making.

Table 14.1. Examples of process-based judgment and decision-making biases and errors (expanded and modified based on a bias categorization provided by Howard et al. (2003))

Perception and Memory	*Reasoning: Meta-Cognitive*
Anchoring (anchor judgment on information easily-recalled information—recency, primacy, unusual events, trusted sources) Make insufficient adjustments of initial anchors Framing effects Availability	Overestimation of knowledge Lack of awareness of causal contradictions (Tetlock, 1992) Lack of ability to reach integrative conclusions(Tetlock, 1992)
Reasoning: General	*Reasoning: Violation of statistical principles*
Reasoning by analogy and premature closure (Vertzberger, 1990) Substitute relative comparisons for absolute measures Form false beliefs based on random effects Inability to perform simple statistical reasoning Intransitivity of judgments Inadequate generation of alternative hypotheses Confirmation bias (prior hypothesis bias) Prospect theory	Base-rate neglect Sample size neglect Ignoring regression to the mean Gambler's fallacy—insensitivity to prior probability Misconceptions of chance Illusory correlation Representativeness

Motivational and Affective	*Interpersonal: Groupthink*
Escalating commitment bias (sunk cost)	Jump to premature conclusions
Illusion of control	Never reach consensus
Overestimates of positive events	Fear of dissent
Confirmation bias (prior hypothesis bias)	Illusion of consensus
Avoidance of contradictory information	Illusion of morality
Overconfidence	Pressure for conformity
Loss aversion (prospect theory)	

2.1.2 Content-Based Decision-Making Biases

In contrast to the *process-based* biases above, a number of biases result from the knowledge used to make decisions, that is, the *content* of the knowledge structures (schemas) mediating the decision-making processes. These *content-based biases* determine the decision-maker's *values* and *beliefs*, which *goals* are considered important; and which *behaviors* are expected to achieve those goals. Together, these schemas then guide the decision-maker's perceptions, determine the expectations, and influence the selection of goals and actions. A variety of biases are possible, depending on the prevalence (or absence) of particular schema in the decision-maker's long-term memory (e.g., trait anxiety individuals will have more threat-related schemas making the retrieval of these schemas more likely), and the decision-maker's current affective state. The influences of states and traits on these schemas are outlined in section 2.2 below.

Given the potentially infinite specific pieces of knowledge we may hold in long-term memory, it is impossible to categorize these types of biases into specific content categories. We can however discuss them in terms of the categories of the affected knowledge structure types. Below we briefly discuss several categories which are particularly relevant to the analysis and modeling of strategic political decision making: 1) *values, beliefs, and attitudes*; 2) *situation assessments and expectations*; and 3) *goals and behavior scripts.*

Values, Beliefs, and Attitudes: There is considerable terminological overlap between 'values' and 'beliefs', but in general *values* tend to reflect more established, and often more affect-linked, preferences (e.g., how much we value human life, nature, material comfort, democracy, etc.), influencing both long- and short-term goal selection, the choice of behavior to accomplish those goals, and the biasing of attitudes towards self, others and the world in general. The term 'belief' refers to distinct constructs in the literature. Here we use the term to refer to the stable propositional knowledge the decision-maker associates with particular objects, individuals or groups, or events. Levy refers to the existing beliefs as "the most basic unmotivated bias [...] on the observation and interpretation of information" (Levy, 2003: 19). Within the context of strategic and political decision-making, researchers often use the term operational codes (George, 1979) to describe the decision-maker's beliefs. It should be noted that operational codes are not limited to cognitive constructs, but include an integration of cognitive-motivational (affective) factors. Extensive research literature exists on *attitudes* (e.g., Ajzen, 1988; Ajzen and Fishbein, 2000). Some researchers have identified attitudes as key factors in behavior prediction (e.g., Ajzen's theory of planned behavior (Ajzen, 1988) identifies the decision-maker's attitudes and beliefs about available behavioral choices as the critical determinants of the action selected to accomplish the most critical goals).

Situation Assessments and Expectation Generation: In contrast to values, attitudes, and beliefs, which reflect stable, long-standing knowledge biases, *situation assessments* and *expectations* represent the decision-maker's *dynamic, on-going, immediate* assessment of the current and future state of the world, self, and others. These assessments represent the integration of the current in-coming external and internal stimuli with the stable knowledge stored in the long-term memory schemas (Endsley, 1995).

Goals and Goal Behavior Scripts: A critical set of knowledge-structures determining behavior is the decision-maker's goal set, and the associated behavior scripts used to achieve these goals. The choice of a particular goal at a given time is influenced by all of the knowledge structures described above, by the structure and contents of the decision-maker's goal hierarchy, and the associated goal scripts and behavioral repertoire, and by the environmental circumstances which may facilitate or hinder the execution of particular scripts.

In dynamic decision-making, whether short- or long-term, the content of all of the knowledge structures outlined above determines the final behavioral outcome, influenced by the specific reasoning taking place, and subject to the biases of the decision-maker's personality and affective state. Several additional features of these knowledge structures bear highlighting: first, they are *highly idiosyncratic,* making behavior prediction challenging; second, they are *dynamic* and thus subject to change, which may be rapid in the case of situation assessments and expectations, or gradual in the case of attitudes, some values, some goals; third, they are *not necessarily globally coherent,* thereby allowing room for choices that may appear contradictory over time.

2.2 State and Trait Effects on Decision-Making

Affective states and personality traits influence decision-making via a variety of distinct effects on perception and cognition, both transient and long-term. A number of these influences have been identified, at varying levels of specificity and generalizability. Effects exist both at the low-level, *elementary cognitive task level*, influencing attentional and memory processes (e.g., attention orientation during an acute fear episode, increased working memory capacity correlated with positive affect), and at more *complex cognitive processing levels*, involving goal selection and planning, situation assessment and expectation generation, and the processes mediating learning and judgment. The low-level processes at the periphery of the information processing apparatus (perception and motor control) are more readily studied and measured than the more internal processes and constructs such as goals, expectations, self-schemas, etc., and thus correspondingly more concrete empirical data exist about the effects of states and traits on these processes.

As might be expected, states tend to produce transient changes that influence the dynamic characteristics of a particular cognitive or perceptual process (e.g., attention and WM capacity, speed, and accuracy, situation assessment and goal selection biases), whereas traits tend to exert their influence via more stable structures (e.g., types of schemas stored in long-term memory over time, preferential processing pathways among functional components of the decision-making process), and general characteristics of specific affective responsiveness). Below we briefly outline some of these effects.

2.2.1 State Effects

Effects of emotional states on decision-making and behavior have been studied extensively over the past 15 years (refer to Table 14.2. for examples of specific findings). Studies have focused on both short term *emotions* and longer-term *moods,* considering primarily the effects of *basic emotions*[1] such as fear, sadness, happiness, anger but also the effects of more *complex emotions* such as pride, shame, jealousy, guilt. Some of the more robust findings include the effects of anxiety and fear, anger and frustration, and positive and negative mood. These effects include altering the nature of attentional processing (e.g., changes in attention capacity, speed and bias); influencing the speed and capacity of working memory; and activating (or inhibiting) particular perceptual and cognitive schemas that enhance (or inhibit) the perception and processing of specific stimuli. Examples of specific effects identified include: *perceptual categorization biases* towards threats associated with fear and anxiety; *memory encoding and recall* effectiveness and mood-congruent biases associated with positive and negative affect; and a variety of additional

[1] It should be noted that not everyone subscribes to the notion of basic emotions (e.g., Ekman, 1994), and that the issue remains somewhat controversial, with a number of researchers disputing its terminological usefulness, or the assumption that a small set of basic emotions can be identified.

specific influences on reasoning, judgment, and decision-making (Williams et al., 1997; Eysenck, 1997; Mineka and Sutton, 1992; Isen, 1993; LeDoux, 1992; MacLeod and Hagan, 1992; Blaney, 1986; Bower, 1981). Table 14.2. below provides a list of identified effects.

Existing empirical data provides the basis for linking specific affective states with some of the decision-making biases outlined in section 2.1. For example, Mellers points out the association between positive affect and lack of anchoring, overestimation of positive events, underestimation of negative events (Mellers et al., 1998). At more abstract levels of description, data indicate that anxious individuals tend to exhibit avoidance behavior: avoiding risk, being cautious, being more accurate; tend to focus on possible failures, and choose strategies that attempt to 'minimize losses'. In general, anxious individuals tend to be more accurate and slower than their non-anxious counterparts, and appear to be more sensitive to the negative influence of punishment, rather than to the positive influence of reward (Matthews and Dreary, 1999).

Within the context of strategic decision-making, researchers recognize that emotion has an intermittent, but powerful impact (e.g., Simon, 1967), triggering the types of effects outlined above (e.g., misperceptions, loss of data, etc.), and also acknowledge the difficulties of identifying the detailed mechanisms of these processes. For example, Levy points out the likely increase in motivated biases associated with high-stakes decisions, but does not go beyond this to identify the cognitive-affective mechanisms mediating these biases within the decision-making process (Levy, 2003). One of the more frequently cited specific effects in political decision-making is the impact of emotions on framing, and the resulting series of biases, including loss aversion effects (Walker, 1995; Levy, 2003).

Table 14.2. Effect of emotions on attention, perception and decision-making: Examples of empirical findings

Anxiety and Attention & WM	*Obsessiveness and Performance*
(Williams et al., 1997; Mineka and Sutton, 1992) Narrowing of attentional focus Reduced responsiveness to peripheral cues Predisposing towards detection of threatening stimuli Reduced capacity of working memory	(Persons and Foa, 1984) Delayed decision-making Reduced ability to recall recent activities Reduced confidence in ability to distinguish among actual and imagined actions and events Narrow conceptual categories

Arousal and Attention (Edland, 1989)	*Affective state and Memory*
Faster detection of threatening cues Slower detection of non-threatening cues	(Bower, 1981; Blaney, 1986) Mood-congruent memory phenomenon (positive or negative affective state induces recall of similarly valenced material)
Positive Affect and Problem Solving	*Negative Affect and Perception, Problem-Solving, Decision-Making*
(Isen, 1993; Clore, 1994; Kahn and Isen, 1993; Mellers et al., 1998; Gasper and Clore, 2002) Promotes heuristic processing (Clore, 1994) Increased likelihood of stereotypical thinking, unless held accountable for judgments (Mellers) Increased estimates of degree of control Overestimation of likelihood of positive events / Underestimation of likelihood of negative events Increased problem solving Facilitation of information integration Promotes variety seeking Promotes less anchoring, more creating problem solving (Mellers) Longer deliberation, use of more information, more re-examination of information Promotes focus on 'big picture'	(Williams et al., 1997; Streufert & Streufert, 1981; Gasper and Clore, 2002) Depression lowers estimates of degree of control Anxiety predisposes towards interpretation of ambiguous stimuli as threatening Use of simpler decision strategies Use of heuristics and reliance on standard and well-practiced procedures Decreased search behavior for alternatives Faster but less discriminate use of information - increased choice accuracy on easy tasks but decreased on more difficult tasks Simpler decisions and more polarized judgments Increased self-monitoring Promote focus on details

2.2.2 Trait Effects

A variety of traits have been identified in different disciplines within psychology (e.g., biological, personality theory, clinical, social, political, and organizational) using a variety of techniques (e.g., neuroscience methods, factor analysis of self-report data, linguistic analysis, clinical observations, cultural analysis, etc.), and yielding trait sets with varying degrees of reliability and validity (e.g., extensive validation and reliability studies exist for descriptive personality trait sets such as the five factor model, but fewer studies exist for clinically-derived traits (e.g., narcissism), or for high-level traits identified in political psychology (e.g., authoritarianism)).

The two most extensively studied trait sets emerged from academic personality theory over the past 20 decades: the five factor model[2] ("Big 5") (extraversion/introversion, emotional stability, openness, conscientiousness, and agreeableness) (Costa and McCrae, 1992), and the three factor model ("Giant 3") (extraversion/introversion, emotional stability, and psychoticism) (Eysenck, 1991). Both sets of factors were derived from factor analyses of descriptive data from self-reports and observations. A number of researchers provide evidence for the biological bases of the "Giant 3"; specifically, the Behavioral Approach System (BAS) corresponding to the extraversion factor and mediating approach behaviors, the Behavioral Inhibition System (BIS) corresponding to the emotional stability factor and mediating avoidance behaviors, and the Fight / Flight System (FFS) corresponding to the psychoticism factor and mediating aggressiveness and its expression (Gray, 1994).

A number of other trait sets exist, less formally defined and studied, notably in clinical psychology (e.g., narcissism, obsessive-compulsive, need for power, need for achievement, need for affiliation) and political psychology (e.g., nationalism, leadership, authoritarianism). Within these disciplines, researchers have generally focused on traits defined at more aggregated levels than the "Big 5". For example, Holsti (1977) developed a typology of decision-makers based on the traits 'need for power', 'need for affiliation', and 'need for achievement', and linked the distinct decision-maker types to a number of key beliefs influencing political decision-making (e.g., nationalism, etiology and permanence of international conflict, predictability of future outcomes, etc.). Others have studied high-level traits such as "loss aversion" and "risk tolerance", and their influence on framing (Jervis, 1992; Walker, 1995). The effects of traits on decision-making can be grouped into three broad categories: 1) effects on the *content and organization of long-term memory schemas*; 2) *effects on the dynamic characteristics of affective states*; and 3) *effects on preferential processing pathways, and data and knowledge use.* Examples of some of these effects are briefly outlined below and examples of specific empirical findings are listed in Table 14.3.

Trait Effects on Memory Schemas: To the extent that traits represent long-term tendencies to experience particular affective states, and be subject to the associated perceptual and cognitive biases, an individual's trait profile strongly influences the content and organization of the long-term memory schemas, as well as any associated processing biases. For example, high-extraversion individuals tend to have more task- and people-related schemas vs. self-related schemas; low emotional stability individuals tend to have a predominance of self-focused and negatively-valenced schemas; high emotional stability and extraversion individuals tend to have a predominance of

2. The "Big 5" factors appear to be applicable across multiple cultures, although some controversy exists regarding their cross-cultural validity.

positively-valenced schemas, etc. (Matthews and Dreary, 1998; Matthews et al., 2000).

Trait Effects on Dynamic Characteristics of Affective States Traits contribute to the dynamic characteristics of the affective states, that is, their generation (latency and ramp-up rates), intensity, duration, decay rates, and expression (Revelle and Born, 1999). Traits also interact with situational valence to affect current mood: extraverts respond to positive situations with positive emotions, but show much smaller reactions to negative situations; neurotic individuals respond to negative situations with negative moods, but show much smaller responses to positive situations (Larsen and Ketellar, 1991).

Table 14.3. Effect of traits on attention, perception and decision-making: Examples of empirical findings

Low Emotional Stability and Attention / Perception	*High Extraversion / Low Emotional Stability and Behavior Preferences*
Preference for self and affective state stimuli Bias toward negative appraisal (self and non-self) Bias towards threat cues (Matthews et al., 2000)	High extraversion preference for approach / active behavior Low emotional stability preference for avoidance / passive behavior
Behavioral approach system and Attention and Working Memory	*Traits and Reward / Punishment Behaviors*
High BAS correlates with increased attention and working memory speed (Matthews et al., 2000)	High extraversion and reward seeking Low emotional stability and punishment avoidance Risk tolerance (Matthews and Deary, 1998)

3 COMPUTATIONAL MODELS OF DECISION-MAKING

Decision-making has been formally studied for several centuries (e.g., Bernoulli proposed a measure of the expected value of a decision in the 18th century (Pew and Mavor, 1998: 152). Both the methodologies and the underlying assumptions have been changing, with evolving technology supporting increasingly computationally-intensive modeling methods. In addition, emerging findings from experimental psychology and neuroscience are motivating a refinement of both the underlying assumptions, and the structure of the computational models implementing the hypothesized decision processes.

Existing theories and models can be examined from two overlapping perspectives: (1) *assumptions made about the decision-maker*, and the *factors influencing decision making*, and (2) *computational methods used to implement the model.* In terms of the assumptions about the decision-maker, researchers have gradually shifted away from assumptions of the *idealized decision-maker*, with perfect knowledge, flawless reasoning capabilities, and ability to explore all possible options, to a more *realistic decision-maker* with limited knowledge, subject to the influences of a variety of biasing factors, and typically unable to explore a large segment of the decision-space. In terms of the computational methods, focus has been shifting from table-lookup approaches (e.g., decision tables and decision trees), to simulation-based approaches (including gaming), and more recently to models of the decision-makers' cognitive apparatus itself (cognitive architecture or agent-based models).

Below I summarize decision-research from these perspectives (sections 3.1 and 3.2). I then briefly discuss recent efforts to incorporate state and trait effects in decision-models (section 3.3), as a lead-in to the description of the MAMID modeling methodology and architecture in section 4.

3.1 Assumptions About the Decision-Maker

For didactic purposes, we can divide existing decision-modeling approaches into three categories, based on the assumptions they make about the decision-maker, and the context within which the decision-making is taking place:

1. Optimal decision making (classical, rational behavior models)
2. Satisficing decision making (bounded rationality models)
3. Naturalistic decision making (bounded rationality experts in field settings)

3.1.1 Classical Rational Decision Making (Prescriptive)

The earliest formal models of decision-making (the *rational decision making* models) assumed an 'optimal' decision-maker, with perfect knowledge of the world, flawless logic used to arrive at the final decision, and the ability to exhaustively generate and evaluate all possible alternatives. An 'optimal' decision was selected by the decision-maker based on evaluation of each option in terms of expected value, or expected utility (hence the term 'utility theory' models). This approach to decision-making research was prevalent between the 50s and the 70s and was applied in both single decision-maker context with non-competing goals, in contexts where competing or conflicting objectives existed (multi-attribute utility theory), and in contexts where multiple agents were involved, either in a collaborative or in a competitive context (game theoretic settings) (Pew and Mavor, 1998: 150-171; Collyer and Malecki, 1998).

However, as the rational models began to be applied to modeling 'real humans' in realistic decision-making environments, a number of drawbacks emerged. *First*, the lengthy analysis and structuring of the decision space required made this approach ill-suited for modeling fast tempo decisions (Collyer and Malecki, 1998). *Second*, more importantly, these models made a number of unrealistic assumptions about the human decision-maker. As a result, when the rational decision-making models were applied to predict actual human decision-making, they often failed to account for observed results, particularly decision biases (Kahneman et al., 1982).

3.1.2 Bounded Rationality Models (Descriptive)

In an attempt to account for the discrepancies between the idealized models and actual human decision-makers, researchers began to develop models reflecting the limitations of the human information processing apparatus; that is, imperfect information, inability to generate all possible alternatives, and inability (or unwillingness) to search the entire decision space before selecting the optimal alternative. This approach, originally proposed by Simon (1957), was termed the *bounded rationality model*. Rather than assuming the evaluation of all possible outcomes, Simon proposed that the decision-maker examines the possible outcomes and selects the first one which satisfies some set of criteria. The resulting bounded rationality model was therefore termed 'satisficing', to contrast it with the optimal, complete search assumed by the earlier rational decision models. This approach, while still cast in the classical rational model of decisions as a search through alternative options, relaxed the assumptions regarding the decision-maker, and served as basis for a number of empirical studies of decision-making between the 60s and 80s (Collyer and Malecki, 1998).

3.1.3 Naturalistic Decision Making Models

Both the rational decision-making models and the bounded rationality models were most often investigated in highly-controlled laboratory settings. As researchers began to be more interested in real-world decision-making, field studies revealed that neither of these models could fully account for actual behavior of expert decision-makers 'in the field'.

Research conducted in field settings revealed that experts do not make an explicit, exhaustive list of all possibilities, nor do they then systematically evaluate all possible options, as postulated by the rational decision models, nor do they appear to use a similar, but less complete process, hypothesized by the bounded rationality models. Rather, they appear to form a rapid assessment of the current situation, by integrating the available cues with existing memory schemas of similar situations encountered in the past. An associated action is then selected that represents the most appropriate response. This recognize-act approach to decision-making was termed *recognition-primed decision-making*, and the general approach of focusing on real-world decision-makers making real decisions led to a formulation of the *naturalistic decision-making model* (NDM) (Klein, 1997; Zsambok, 1997). NDM models were developed in the 90s, and aimed to address the shortcomings of both the rational and the bounded rationality models, and to account for observable data of real-world decision-makers in naturalistic settings (i.e., 'in the field') (Zsambok, 1997). These models have been broadly applied in expert decision-making research and as the theoretical basis for the development of training systems (Zsambok and Klein, 1997; Cannon-Bowers and Salas, 1998).

One of the key distinguishing characteristics of the recognition-primed decision-making models is their shift from formalized structures (e.g., decision trees, utility functions) to models of processes, and components, that more closely correspond to the hypothesized perceptual and cognitive processes that mediate decision-making, and associated structures (e.g., long-term memory, working memory). Figure 14.1. shows a schematic diagram of the recognition-primed decision-making model, explicitly showing both the mental constructs involved (cues, situations, expectations and goals), and the sequence of processing (cues map onto situations which generate expectations, goals influence all stages of this process and feedback exists between the distinct constructs). This shift in modeling perspective sets the stage for applying artificial intelligence and cognitive science methods to models of decision-making, as outlined below.

3.2 Computational Methods Used to Implement Decision Models

Much as the assumptions about the decision-maker and the resulting models have evolved, so have the method and techniques used to implement the proposed models. The rational and bounded rationality models were most often implemented in terms of decision-trees or decision-tables, using table-lookup mechanisms to determine the selected decision, based on the results of the various utility evaluation functions. These methods were applied both in

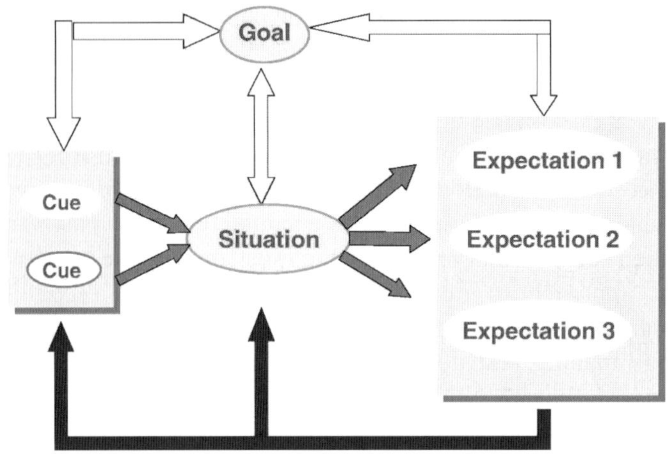

Figure 14.1. Diagram of the recognition-primed decision-making process

single decision-maker contexts, and in situations when two agents were modeled in the context of game-theoretic simulations (Myerson, 1991). Within the bounded rationality models, additional functions or heuristics were employed to select the 'satisficing' choice, and, analogously, in gaming situations, to limit the search horizon of the game trees.

Cognitive science and Artificial Intelligence (AI) computational modeling approaches provide a recent addition to the methodological repertoire available for decision-making research. These methods provide the type of modeling resolution required to construct more cognitively- and process-oriented models, such as the recognition-primed models mentioned above, and begin to allow the explicit integration of state and trait effects to model decision-making biases.

Rather than abstracting the decision process into a series of formal, static structures, these methods use an explicit model of the decision-maker's perceptual and cognitive processes, and associated memory structures, that mediate the decision-making process. Depending on the level of resolution required, either a single process may be represented (e.g., attention, situation assessment), or the entire 'end-to-end' decision-making process can be modeled. This latter approach is termed a cognitive architecture or an agent architecture approach.

The cognitive architecture based approaches have several advantages over decision-trees and decision-tables. *First* and foremost, they attempt to emulate the actual processes and structures that mediate decision-making. *Second,* the exercise of constructing a computational cognitive architecture model requires a degree of operationalization of the structures and processes which often reveals gaps in existing theories or data. Such gaps can then serve as stimulus for further empirical research. *Third*, the development of a computational model implementing a particular theory, or attempting to account for particular data, provides an opportunity for validation of an existing theory, and for the generation of alternative hypotheses explaining specific data or phenomena.

3.3 Modeling State and Trait Effects in Decision-Making

None of the decision-modeling approaches or methods discussed so far has explicitly addressed the influence of affective states and personality traits on the decision-maker. While the rational and bounded rationality utility models can represent some traits (e.g., risk tolerance, aggressiveness vs. passivity, optimism vs. pessimism) in terms of the shapes of the various utility evaluation functions (Pew and Mavor, 1998: 163), the effects of states are generally ignored in these models, and the decision-maker is assumed to be deterministic; that is, given the same external information the decision-maker will always produce the same decision. (It should be noted that these modeling formalisms are capable of modeling some state effects, albeit at highly abstracted levels. For example, the number of available attributes can be reduced to model reduced attention capacity due to stress, or to bias particular types of input or expected output; e.g., fear might increase the weight of negative consequences (Busmeyer and Townsend, 1993)).

Naturalistic decision making models, while acknowledging the effects of some states, most notably stress (e.g., Orasanu, 1998; Klein, 1996), also generally do not provide explicit means of integrating state effects. In addition, until very recently, these models have also not been implemented, and were instead used as theoretical basis for decision-aiding and training system design and evaluation, and cognitive task analysis.

Examples of current efforts to incorporate state and trait effects on decision-making include the following: work of Lisetti and Gmytrasiewicz (2002) to provide a framework for integrating affective factors into classical decision models, in terms of specific transformations of the constituent utility functions; Hudlicka's augmentation of the recognition-primed decision model with affective and trait factors (Hudlicka and Pfautz, 2002); and the generic approach to modeling state and trait effects described in sections 4 and 5 (Hudlicka, 2002; 2003). A number of researchers are also modeling the effects of emotion on decision-making and behavior in the broader context of robot, agent, and cognitive architecture research (e.g., Velasquez, 1998; Sloman, 2000; Breazeal, 2003).

4 METHODOLOGY AND ARCHITECTURE FOR MODELING STATE AND TRAIT EFFECTS ON DECISION-MAKING

In this section I describe a generic approach to modeling state and trait effects on decision-making (section 4.1), the associated cognitive architecture that implements this approach (section 4.2), and the parameter space available for encoding effects of states and traits on decision-making (section 4.3).

4.1 MAMID Generic Modeling Methodology

The core component of the modeling approach is a *generic methodology* for modeling individual differences within symbolic cognitive architectures, via parametric manipulations of the architecture *processes* and *structures*. The underlying thesis of this approach is that the combined effects of a broad range of states and traits, as well as a variety of cognitive and individual history factors, can be modeled by varying the *values of these parameters*.

Distinct individual types (e.g., anxious vs. aggressive) are represented by distinct individual differences profiles, in terms of specific values of the selected traits, states, and cognitive characteristics. These profiles are then mapped onto specific configurations of the architecture parameters, which then lead to distinct behavioral manifestations under the same external circumstances (e.g., anxious individual is passive and withdrawing, aggressive individual is active and engages in 'approach' behavior, etc.). Figure 14.2. provides a schematic illustration of the general relationship among a representative set of individual differences, the architecture parameters, and the architecture itself. We have termed this methodology MAMID (Methodology for Analysis and Modeling of Individual Differences, Hudlicka, 1997, 2002, 2003; Hudlicka and Billingsley, 1999).

A key objective of the methodology is to provide flexibility regarding the *types of factors* selected for inclusion in a model, the *nature of their influence* on cognitive, perceptual, and decision-making processing, and the *degree of this influence*. Such flexibility then supports an experimental, exploratory approach to the development of computational models of particular theories of specific individual difference (states, traits, cognitive) influences on perception, cognition and behavior. This approach is necessitated by the fact that few definitive theories exist regarding the exact mechanisms of these influences, particularly so with respect to the more complex, internal processes of situation assessment, expectation generation, and goal selection. In addition, new data regarding these effects continue to emerge. The MAMID methodology, and the computational modeling testbed that implements it, were designed with the explicit purpose of facilitating a rapid accommodation of these emerging findings.

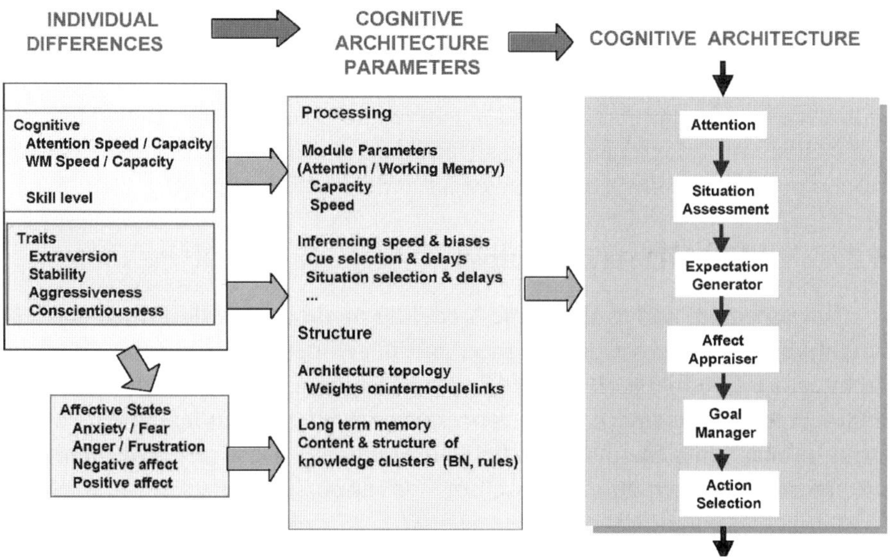

Figure 14.2. Schematic illustration of MAMID state & trait modeling approach and architecture

The modeling methodology achieves this flexibility through a high-degree of parameterization of the processes and structures that comprise the distinct architecture modules, and the analyst's interactive access to these parameters and their weights. The distinct individual differences factors are mapped onto distinct configurations of the cognitive architecture parameters, which in turn produce different processing within the model, and ultimately produce different behavioral outcomes for the associated simulated agent.

There are several advantages of this methodology for modeling state and trait effects, as well as a broad range of additional individual differences. *First,* it facilitates rapid modeling of a broad range of distinct individual profiles. *Second*, the rich architecture parameterization allows the definition of additional high-level individual characteristics (see section 6). *Third*, it provides a means of integrating the possibly conflicting effects of multiple, interacting behavior moderators, much as these influences interact in humans. *Fourth*, it is psychologically grounded, with both the behavior moderators themselves, and the architecture parameters, selected on the basis of empirical data and psychological theory.

MAMID Individual Differences: The individual differences modeled within MAMID are divided into three broad categories: cognitive, affective, and personality. The specific factors included in the initial MAMID implementation are as follows: *cognitive factors* include attention and working memory capacity and speed, skill level (high / low), and specific skills and experience encoded in long-term memory belief nets and rules; *affective states* include anxiety, anger, and negative and positive affect, as well as the dimensions of valence and arousal; and *personality traits* include extraversion, emotional stability, aggressiveness and conscientiousness.

4.2 MAMID Architecture

To implement and evaluate the modeling methodology described above, a cognitive architecture was designed and developed: the MAMID cognitive architecture (Hudlicka, 2002; 2003). MAMID is a sequential 'see-think-do' architecture, consisting of seven processing *modules* which map the incoming stimuli (cues) onto the outgoing behavior (actions), via a series of intermediate internal representational structures (situations, expectations, and goals). We term these internal structures *mental constructs*. The remainder of this section describes the MAMID cognitive architecture and the parameter space available for encoding behavior moderators.

Architecture Modules: The MAMID modules consist of the following: *sensory pre-processing*, translating the incoming raw data into high-level task-relevant perceptual cues; *attention*, filtering the incoming cues and selecting a subset for further processing; *situation assessment*, integrating individual cues into an overall situation assessment; *expectation generation*, projecting the current situation into one or more possible future states; *affect appraiser* deriving the affective state from the variety of influencing factors: static (traits, individual history) and dynamic (current affective state, current situation, goal, expectation); *goal selection*, selecting the most relevant goal for achievement; and *action selection,* selecting the most suitable action for achieving the current goal within the current context. Figure 14.3. illustrates the MAMID cognitive architecture, its constituent modules (excluding sensory pre-processing), and the mental constructs that comprise the input and output of these modules; that is, cues, situations, expectations, goals and actions.

The modules execute in a fixed sequence, with a single cycle consisting of the transformation of the incoming cues into an agent action. The mental constructs represent this progressive transformation of the cues (input data) into high-level schemata corresponding to the current situation, and further into a set of expectations regarding the state of the world. At that point sufficient information is available for the agent to derive the next affective state, and

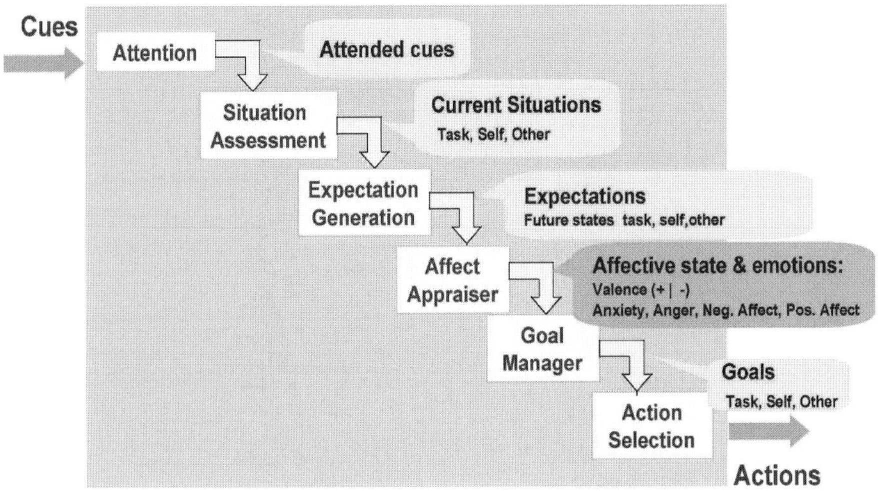

Figure 14.3. MAMID cognitive architecture and mental constructs that comprise input / output of the architecture modules

immediately following this, to select the most critical goal as the focus of the next action. Finally, during the last step of this sequence, all of the current constructs, plus the affective state, contribute to action selection.

While the basic processing cycle is sequential, the results of previous cycle's processing are available, which makes it possible to implement processes such as priming and goal-directed perception, and in effect allows a simulation of a limited degree of parallel processing.

4.3 Architecture Parameter Space

Two broad categories of parameters are available for encoding the effects of individual differences within the MAMID cognitive architecture: those affecting the *module processing*, and those affecting the *structure and contents of the agents' long term memory* (belief nets and rules) (refer toFigure 14.2.). The processing parameters themselves fall into two subcategories: those determining the *modules' speed and capacity*, and those affecting the *values of the mental construct attributes* (e.g., threat level, salience, desirability, etc). Table 14.4. summarizes the architecture parameters.

Table 14.4. Summary of MAMID architecture parameters available for encoding the effects of states and traits

Parameter Category	*Examples of Parameters*
Processing	
Module parameters	Module speed
	Capacity limit
Mental Construct Attributes (subset of attributes)	Time requirements
	Capacity requirements
	Threat level
	Salience
Structural (Structure and content of LTM)	Distinct belief net clusters, net topology, conditional probabilities
	Distinct rule clusters, antecedent and consequent clauses

Both the module speed and capacity limits, and the mental construct attribute values, are calculated using normalized linear combinations of the weighted constituent factors. Each factor contributes positively or negatively to the attribute value, and the magnitude of this effect is further modified by an associated weight. These weights, along with the factors, thus provide an additional means of encoding the effects of individual differences. For example, an agent whose behavior is strongly influenced by his affective states, will have a higher weight associated with the affective states factors within the goal and action selection functions. The user (analyst) can manipulate these functions by changing the weights of individual factors, or the values of the factors themselves.

The effects of individual differences are thus modeled by translating the individual profile values into specific values of the available architecture parameters. These parameters then determine which mental constructs are activated (function of stable long term memory structures and dynamic processing context), what subset of these are considered relevant (highly ranked), which subset of these is selected for processing (function of construct capacity requirements and module capacity limits), and how fast they are processed (function of construct time requirements and module speed). Thus, for example, an agent whose emotional stability trait is low, and who is in a high-state of anxiety, both favoring the selection of high-threatening and self-relevant cues, will preferentially process these types of cues, derive corresponding situations, and preferentially engage in self- and anxiety-related activities (e.g., anxiety-reducing coping strategies) vs. task-relevant activities.

5 MAMID MODEL OF STATE AND TRAIT EFFECTS IN TACTICAL DECISION MAKING

The MAMID architecture and methodology were evaluated by modeling agent decision-making in the context of a peacekeeping scenario. The behavior of several agent types (anxious, aggressive, normal) was modeled by instances of the cognitive architecture. During the experiment described here, a series of surprise events occur, to which the unit commanders must react. These events represent high-stress or novel situations, which provide opportunities for interesting expressions of the commander's individual profiles, and results in different reactions from the distinct commander types. The simulated humans (peacekeeper unit leaders / commanders) were exposed to these 'surprise' situations (e.g., destroyed bridge, hostile crowd), designed to elicit different reactions as a function of the distinct state and trait profiles.

The decision-making modeled here is typical of a tactical situation; that is, rapid-tempo decisions taking place in the course of seconds or minutes (e.g., move fast vs. slowly, attack hostile crowd vs. negotiate; repair bridge vs. attempt to ford river, etc.). The detailed description of MAMID's current functional context below provides the necessary background for understanding the enhancements necessary to model state and trait effects on strategic decisions, described in section 6. It should be noted that while the demonstration below models commander behavior in a peacekeeping scenario, the modeling methodology is generic and the architecture is domain-independent, and both can thus be readily adapted to distinct scenario contexts.

The agent-commanders interact with a simulated environment, and with each other within this environment. Each commander model receives data about the environment (e.g., locations and activities of other friendly units, adversary units, etc.), and communications from other units, in terms of high-level abstracted cues. These data represent the input to the associated MAMID cognitive architecture, and, in conjunction with data representing the commander's internal state during each time frame of the simulation, provide the basis for deriving the commander's behavior during the next time frame of the simulation. The results of the behavior are then displayed on an animated map display, showing unit movement and agent communication (refer to Figure 14.5.).

5.1 Agent Individual Differences

Individual differences in the agents' long-term memories (LTM) are reflected in the content and structure of both the rules and the belief nets comprising the agents' LTM (e.g., the propositions associated with individual nodes within the belief net nodes, their topologies, and the conditional probability tables; contents and structure of the rule antecedents and consequents). For example, empirical evidence indicating that high-introversion / low-stability individuals have more self-focused schemas in LTM is translated into correspondingly larger numbers of self-focused propositions in the belief nets mediating situation assessment and expectation generation in these types of individuals; e.g., an anxious commander has a belief net cluster for deriving an explicit assessment of his level of control over a situation (see Figure 14.4.), whereas the normal commander has no such structures elaborated in his LTM, reflecting the lack of self focus schema elaboration in his long-term memory. Similarly, the rules for goal and action selection differ both in the complexity of the constructs triggering a particular rule, and in their specific content.

The agents' affective states are dynamically generated by the affect appraisal module, in response to each surprise situation, and the results vary as a function of the agents' emotional state, trait profile, as well as the current mental constructs representing the internal dynamic processing context (i.e., cues, situations, expectations, and goals). The resulting emotions then influence processing within each of the architecture modules, as outlined above (e.g., contribute to lower or higher processing capacities, threat bias, etc.). Figure 14.6. shows the fluctuating anxiety levels of a normal and a trait-anxious commander, during the course of the simulation scenario. The different emotions, together with the trait-related differences in both processing and memory, then result in differences in behavior, in response to the identical set of external circumstances produced by the scenario simulation (Figure 14.7.).

Thus, for example, an anxious commander used inappropriate force against a hostile crowd, moved more slowly, and spent more time in situation assessment than the 'normal' commander. Below we focus in more detail on one such specific event: the peacekeeping unit encountering a hostile crowd, which blocks the unit's route.

5.2 Detailed Description of 'Hostile Crowd' Surprise Event

The 'normal' commander realizes that this event does not represent imminent danger to the unit. It must, however, be dealt with so that the unit can proceed along the route and reach the objective. The commander therefore implements non-lethal crowd control and asks for PSYOP assistance to disperse the crowd. In contrast, the 'high anxious' commander assumes that the crowd represents a real danger to the unit, and to himself, and overreacts by firing into the crowd (lethal crowd control), which is an inappropriate action under the current rules of engagement. His primary focus is on reducing his

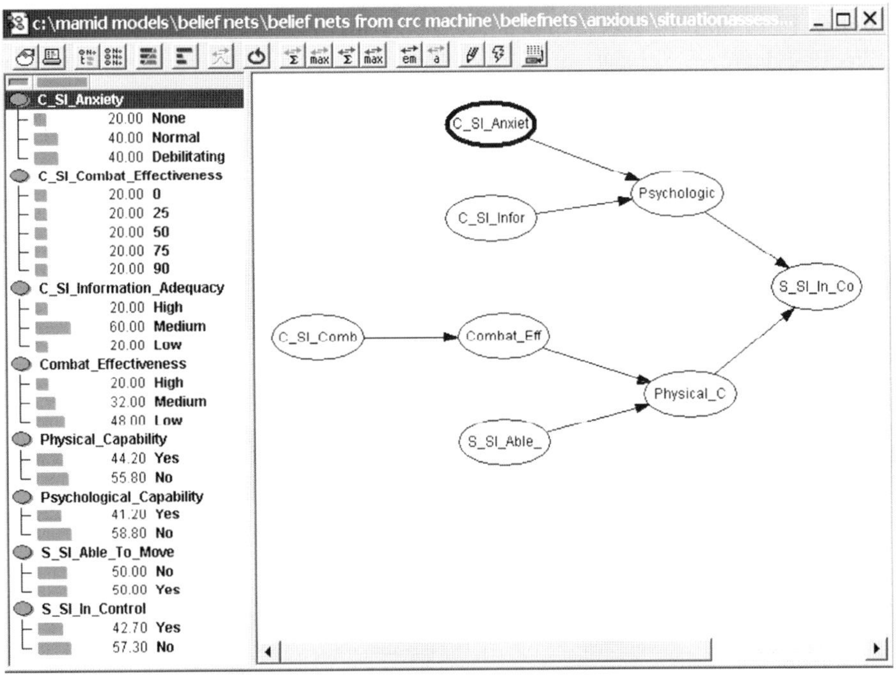

Figure 14.4. Situation assessment belief net for deriving 'in control' self situation for anxious commander

own level of anxiety, by engaging in several 'coping strategies' (e.g., excessive communication and requests for help). These alternative behaviors are generated due to the distinct situations and expectations derived by the distinct commander stereotypes, differences in affective states, and differences in triggered goals and rules. MAMID provides a variety of alternative pathways to these results, allowing for multiple sequences of mental constructs to result in the same final outcome, depending on the exact structure of LTM, the mental constructs derived in the current context, the affective states, and the module processing parameters. For example, the 'lethal crowd control' may be triggered due to a specific goal to implement lethal crowd control, or due to a rule which triggers this behavior in response to an 'under attack' situation and 'high anxiety'. This type of redundancy is consistent with empirical evidence and allows the exploration of alternative mechanisms through which individual differences effects are expressed. Figure 14.5. shows these contrasting behaviors for the normal and anxious commanders for this situation. Figure 14.6. provides a view of the contrasting internal processing for the normal and the anxious commanders when encountering the hostile crowd.

Figure 14.6. and 14.7 below provide additional comparative behavioral and affective data.

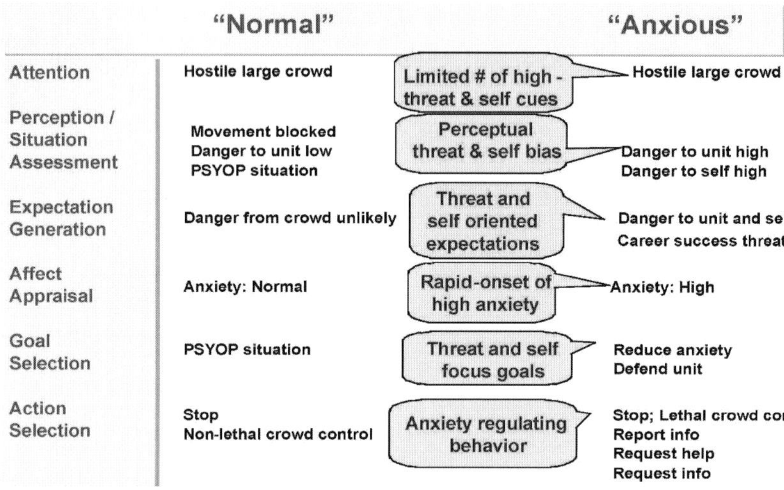

Figure 14.5. Contrasting behavior exhibited by normal commander (left) and anxious commander (right), in response to encountering a hostile crowd

5.3 Performance Modeling Results

As shown above, the distinct instances of the MAMID architecture modeling the different commander types produce different decision-making sequences and, eventually, distinct observable behaviors. Here we summarize these differences, focusing again on the normal and anxious commanders, but also including a behavior summary and comparison for the aggressive commander.

Figure 14.6. focuses on the affective state changes over time, as generated by the Affect Appraiser module, in response to the changing situation. The figure shows the level of anxiety for the normal and anxious commanders, and also indicates the occurrence of the surprise events in the associated 'stickies'. Thus the normal commander begins with a lower baseline level of anxiety, and while he does experience two anxiety 'peaks', one at the bridge and one at the hostile crowd, his anxiety level never goes above .2. In contrast, the high anxious commander's baseline anxiety level is higher, and his reactions to the surprise events are reflected by the maximum level of anxiety intensity (1.0). Note also that due to his delay at the bridge, he experiences two surprise events at the same time (bridge and illumination). These types of emergent interactions further demonstrate the richness of possible variations due to the interacting state and trait effects.

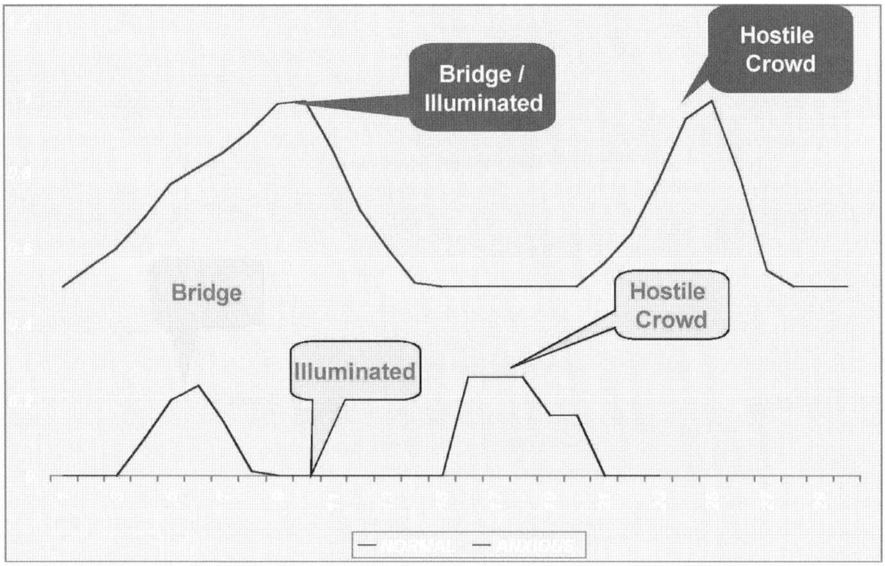

Figure 14.6. Anxiety level changes over time for the normal (lower line) and anxious (upper line) commanders

Figure 14.7. provides behavior summaries for the aggressive vs. anxious vs. normal commanders, over the course of the scenario. Note that the normal commander's behavior set is rather sparse: he does what he needs to at a normal pace. In contrast, the anxious commander engages in a number of non-essential behaviors (e.g., communication, assessing, defending, attacking), and even inappropriate and damaging behavior (lethal crowd control). The aggressive commander's behavior sequence is sparse, similar to the normal commander, but inappropriate, similar to the anxious commander; he also selects lethal crowd control, although for different reasons than the anxious commander.

The MAMID prototype implementation was able to demonstrate the ability of the architecture to generate distinct differences in individual commander behavior, as a function of their individual profile, and consequent significant differences in the final mission outcome. These results indicate the ability of the modeling methodology to effectively represent the selected states and traits in terms of the parameters controlling the architecture structures and processing.

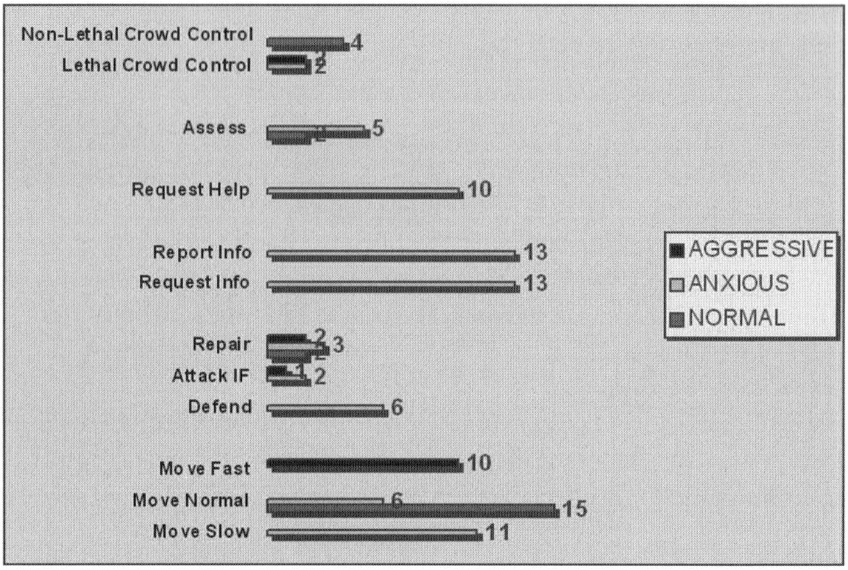

Figure 14.7. Behavior exhibited by normal vs. anxious vs. aggressive commanders

6 MODELING BIASES AND STATE / TRAIT EFFECTS IN STRATEGIC DECISION MAKING

In this section I outline how the MAMID methodology and architecture would model decision-making biases and state / trait effects in strategic political decision-making. The resulting enhanced MAMID architecture could then be used to model the behavior of individual decision-makers, and thereby simulate the evolution of political situations, the effects of changing interpersonal and information environments, and the consequences of specific political, diplomatic or economic interventions. These simulations could then be used to explore particular conflict resolution and prevention strategies, within the broader context of computer-aided international conflict prevention and resolution. Examples of several possible applications are discussed in section 7. A number of issues and open questions related to the modeling effort, both research-oriented and applied, are then discussed in section 8.1.

This section is organized as follows. First, I outline categories phenomena relevant to strategic, political decision-making that could be modeled and explored in terms of the MAMID methodology and cognitive architecture, namely: (1) *effects of traits, attitudes and beliefs*; (2) *effects of decision-mak-*

ing biases; and (3) *effects of transient emotional states* (section 6.1). Next, I outline in detail how MAMID would model these types of effects (sections 6.2 through 6.4). I conclude with a concrete example of a specific decision-making sequence illustrating the modeling approach (section 6.5).

6.1 Candidate Strategic Decision-Making Phenomena to Model

The first stage of any cognitive modeling effort is the definition of a sufficiently narrow scope of the problem, in terms of specific phenomena, to allow the construction of a computational model. Below I outline three categories of phenomena which could be modeled within MAMID.

First, since strategic decision-making takes place over longer time frames, the primary focus should be on *modeling the effects of stable, static factors* (e.g., traits, attitudes, beliefs, and cultural factors), which are likely to have a more profound and persistent influence over longer time intervals. This is in contrast to the influence of transient emotional states, whose effects on strategic decisions are less well documented, and may even 'cancel out' over time. (However, their effects should by no means be disregarded, and I will discuss possible roles of affect in strategic decisions, and an approach for modeling affect, in section 6.4 below.) The focus on traits has the additional advantage that some high-level, empirical (or at least anecdotal) data are available, most notably from political psychology analysis of political decision-making and behavior (e.g., Walker, 1995; Levy, 2003; Holsti, 1977). Specifically, I will describe how MAMID would be applied to model the following:

1. Effects of several representative traits considered important by political psychologists, some of which have also been identified as useful for characterizing distinct cultures; specifically: *optimism / pessimism*, *need for power*, *activity orientation* and *uncertainty avoidance* (Hermann; Post and Shaw, 1999; Walker, 1995; Holsti, 1977; Hofstede, 1991).
2. Effects of established attitudes and 'world views' or 'operational codes' (e.g., George, 1979; LeFebvre, 1977) which include both cognitive and affective/motivational elements (Walker, 1995), and effects of values and attitudes (Ajzen, 2001).

Second, I will outline how MAMID would model one of the more prevalent *decision making biases* identified in the judgment and decision-making empirical literature: *confirmation bias.* In addition to describing a computational mechanism for modeling confirmation bias, I will also show how the effects of specific affective states could be integrated with this bias model, thereby demonstrating how a computational model could be applied to modeling hypothesized mechanisms of the affective influence in decision-making biases.

Finally, to explore the *effects of emotional states*, both transient emotions and longer-term moods, I will show how MAMID would model the interaction of the transient influences of these states with the more long-term influences of the static factors outlined above, during decision processes that extend over hours, days or weeks. Unfortunately, concrete data demonstrating these effects are very limited. In this example I will therefore draw upon available anecdotal evidence and on extrapolations of existing empirical data from studies of fast-tempo decisions. The underlying working assumption is that transient emotional states can in fact exert a profound effects on strategic decision-making, by influencing the perceptual and cognitive processes during critical stages of the decision-making process. I will focus on describing the mechanisms through which such effects might take place.

An important caveat must be stated at the outset regarding availability of supporting empirical data for this type of a modeling endeavor. A lack of systematic studies of the cognitive and perceptual mechanisms mediating strategic decision-making, not to mention a lack of empirical data regarding the effects of traits and states on these mechanisms, necessitates a reliance on anecdotal evidence and on 'educated guesses', based on extrapolations of existing empirical data regarding fast-tempo decision-making, to define both the type and magnitude the state and trait effects, and the mechanisms implementing these effects.

6.2 Modeling Effects of Traits, Attitudes and Beliefs on Political Decision-Making

Traits represent more or less permanent temperamental tendencies. Attitudes and beliefs, while not immutable, also tend to persist over long periods of time. This suggests that these factors should be modeled primarily in terms of the *structural features* of the cognitive architecture, specifically, in terms of the *memory contents and organization*. Representing these persistent effects within the MAMID architecture thus involves primarily the definition and construction of the long-term memory (LTM) schemas associated with the different modules of the cognitive architecture, which mediate the distinct phases of strategic decision-making (refer to Figure 14.3.); that is: Situation Assessment, Expectation Generation, Affect Appraisal, Goal Selection, and Action Selection.

These structures, residing in declarative knowledge-bases which are external to the architecture proper, are constructed by the model developer to reflect the particular configuration of traits, beliefs, attitudes and values of the individual or stereotype being modeled, as well as the specific task domain. They include trait-related biases; attitudes towards self and others; beliefs and expectations about self, others, and the world; goal hierarchies; and links among beliefs, goals, and goal scripts.

Two specific features of the memory structures can be manipulated to represent distinct configurations of these constructs:

1. *Relative prevalence (or absence) of specific memory schemas in long-term memory,* which makes it more (or less) likely that a particular schema will be activated during a particular decision-making sequence, and exert its associated influence.
2. *Connectivity patterns among related schemas,* which reflect established patterns of thought and behavior. These connections capture the individuals' mental models of the world, including expected causal sequences among observed events (cues) and internal states (situations, expectations), and goals and goal scripts.

Since both rules and belief nets used to represent LTM in MAMID are generic knowledge representation mechanisms, they are capable of representing any of these required variations. No enhancements to the existing MAMID architecture or processing are therefore necessary, beyond the construction of the LTM clusters themselves, which are required for any new domain.

Several concrete examples are outlined below. The discussion is organized by the distinct decision-making stages, represented by the individual cognitive architecture modules. Note that different traits, attitudes and beliefs, are likely to exert distinct types and magnitude of effects on the different stages of decision-making sequence.

Recall that the **situation assessment** module integrates the current low-level cues into a high-level situation assessment. The long-term memory associated with this module thus explicitly links these cues to the situations, via a number of intermediate processing stages (refer to Figure 14.4. for an illustration of this representational structure). Trait effects, as well as values, attitudes, and predominant beliefs are reflected in the *type* and *frequency* of particular cues and situations represented, and the *connectivity patterns* among them, which determine which cues will trigger which situations. Thus *optimism* would be reflected in a predominance of situations that are generally positive, possibly even distorting reality to derive an overly-optimistic situation assessment (e.g., an optimistic leader might underestimate the likelihood of defeat, and fail to take the appropriate precautions). Analogously, *pessimism* would be reflected by a predominance of negative assessments of the world, self, and others, and an associated ease of triggering these situations, perhaps based on limited cues. Thus a pessimist might require only a single negative cue for a triggering of a comprehensive negative assessment of an entire situation. *Need for power* would be reflected in a presence or predominance of schemas that relate to situations where own power is enhanced, maintained, or threatened. Thus an individual with high need for power would be more likely to detect, and focus on, situations relevant to power maintenance, which might not be noticed or recognized by an individual with low need for power; e.g., early indicators of possible rivals emerging, of factions being created and alliances formed. An individual with high *activity orientation* would have a predominance of cues and situations related to tasks and outcomes, whereas an individual with high people- and process-orientation would have a predominance of cues and situations related to the people involved in the accomplishment of these tasks. For example, the LTM of a leader focused on individuals would include schemas representing the needs of the population and risks to individual lives, whereas a leader with high activity orientation would be more likely to have schemas focusing on favorable task outcomes (e.g., winning a war), with diminished regard for the 'human element'. A high *uncertainty avoidance* decision-maker would require high-certainty cues, and might ignore cues with low levels of certainty, or, conversely, might focus excessively on low-certainty cues and expend inappropriate amounts of effort to enhance their certainty and reliability.

Specific values, attitudes and beliefs about the self, others, the task and the world in general would also be represented in the types of cues and situations represented in the Situation Assessment long-term memory, and the links among them. These would reflect the individual's history, training, key relevant experiences as well as long-term affective and temperamental factors influencing what information is stored in memory and how it is organized. Thus, for example, an attitude of *nationalism* would be reflected in a predominance of schemas that involve considerations of the national interests (vs., for example, an ethnic group's interest or 'world peace'), and assumptions about the superiority of the decision-maker's nation.

Expectation generation module processes and memory structures are similar to the Situation Assessment module, but rather than mapping cues onto situations, they map derived situations onto expected future developments, that is, expected future states of the world, self and other individuals or groups. The trait effects on memory schemas would be analogous to those outlined above, capturing preferences for situation-to-expectations mappings reflecting particular individual biases. Thus, as above, the trait of *optimism* would be reflected in a higher frequency of positive situations and expected favorable outcomes, and an associated ease of triggering such expectations. For example, an optimistic leader might expect even an unfavorable situation to turn out well. In contrast, a pessimistic decision-maker would be more likely to focus on negative situations, and to then map those onto further negative expectations of future outcomes. *Need for power* would again be reflected in a predominance of expectations regarding the further developments of these situations. Here, interesting interactions between the optimist / pessimist traits, and affective states, would be likely to occur. For example, consider an *optimistic, high-need for power* individual vs. a *pessimistic, high-need for power* individual. In both cases there would be a predominance of schemas relating to power (gaining, maintaining, re-gaining - via a variety of means). However, in the optimist's case, there would be predominance of positive schemas (e.g., conditions reflecting expectations of having or gaining the desired degree of power), whereas in the pessimist's case there would be a predominance of negative schemas (e.g., expectations of loss of power, or threats of such loss).

Recall that a critical component of the **affect appraisal** process is the secondary appraisal, which generates distinct emotions based on current situation assessments and expectations. This process is influenced by specific traits as well as individual history, beliefs, attitudes, and values, encoded within the affect appraisal memory LTM structures. The idiosyncratic organization of these memory schemas within a particular decision-maker's LTM then gives rise to the individual affective responsiveness and generates possibly 'biased' affective assessments, of individuals, groups, situations, and the decision-maker's own prospects. Within the affect appraisal module, the set of activated situations and expectations, reflecting the current assessment of the present and future, is then be mapped onto specific emotions, reflecting the decision-maker's priorities and needs (as well as the idiosyncratic beliefs and attitudes, individual history, and the personality traits).

Thus an *optimist's* affect appraisal memory would have a predominance of positively-valenced situations and expectations, which would be easily triggered and would map onto positive emotions. In contrast, a *pessimist* decision-maker's predominance of negative situation and expectation schemas would map onto negative emotions (e.g., fear / anxiety, anger / frustration, and negative affect), thus increasing the a priori likelihood of the pessimist being in a negative affective state. Recall that the LTM of an individual with high *need for power* would have a predominance of situations and expectations representing power-enhancement, power-maintenance, or the threat of loss of power. Depending on the interaction with other traits and states, different subsets of these schemas would be activated at a given point in time, resulting in specific affective reactions. For example, suppose that a high *need for power* decision-maker has repeatedly experienced a situation where a specific individual attempted to usurp his leadership role. Any situation (or expectation) involving that individual would then trigger a negative affect (e.g., anxiety, anger or sadness), the exact affective reaction depending on the overall temperament and attitudes. The trait of *uncertainty avoidance* would also play a key role in affect appraisal. A decision-maker with high uncertainty avoidance would have affect appraisal memory schemas focusing on the certainty level of the current situations and expectations, and mappings linking these schemas with corresponding affective states. High uncertainty situations and expectations would trigger anxiety / fear, frustration or negative affect, depending on the exact trait profile of the decision-maker, whereas situations and expectations with low levels of uncertainty would reduce anxiety and frustration levels and increase positive affect.

The affect appraisal LTM also allows for the representation of highly idiosyncratic individual experiences and preferences (attitudes, values) and their contributions to particular affective states, and reflects the motivational-affective aspect of the decision-makers 'operational code'.

The **goal selection** module integrates current situations, expectations and affective states, and selects the most important goal to achieve within the current context. The memory schemas containing the decision-maker's goals are influenced by traits, but reflect primarily the decision-maker's stable value set, which determines both the specific goals represented, and their priority within the decision-maker's goal hierarchy. Thus, for example, high *need for power* would be reflected in the decision-maker's preference for selection of goals corresponding to gaining or maintaining power. Depending on the specific scenario and context, these might involve goals such as: 'Achieve higher position within group', 'Gain support from powerful individuals', 'Take over another group / nation', etc. Some of these goals might be more or less permanent (e.g., 'Achieve higher position within group'), whereas others might be triggered by a particular combination of situations and expectations. For example, 'Gain support from powerful individuals' goal might only be selected if a concrete threat to own power were detected in terms of specific adversaries forming alliances. A decision-maker with high need for certainty (high *uncertainty avoidance*) would select goals that either implicitly or explicitly focus on uncertainty reduction, or that reflect situations with low levels of uncertainty. For example, such a decision-maker might explicitly search for additional supporting information that would increase the certainty of his situation assessment. Exactly how these goals would be accomplished would then be determined in the action selection module, discussed below. The decision-maker's *activity orientation* would play a critical role in goal selection and action focus, with those focused on outcomes preferring task-related goals, whereas those focused on process preferring goals that involved the well-being, or manipulation, of the human participants.

In the **action selection** module, the entire current dynamic context (i.e., situations, expectations, affective state, and goals) is brought to bear on the selection of a specific behavior to accomplish the selected goals within the current context. The memory schemas associated with this module reflect the individual's attitudes and values associated with the distinct approaches to achieving the individual's specific goals, within a given internal and external context. This in turn allows for distinct configurations of the specific triggers for the selection of a particular action. Thus an individual with a high *need for power* but strong ethical principles would select legal and ethical actions to attempt to achieve his goals, presumably avoiding dissembling, not to mention underhanded behavior or violence. In contrast, the behavioral repertoire of an unscrupulous individual with high-need for power would have a broad range of unethical, and possibly violent, means of achieving his goal. A decision maker with high *uncertainty avoidance* would be more likely to select actions associated with low-risk and designed to increase his level of certainty in a particular situation. As with goals, activity orientation would play a critical role here, with task-oriented individuals selecting actions that focused on the environment and the task, perhaps neglecting personnel issues, whereas process- and individual-orientation decision-makers focusing on actions directly affecting the human participants. Ajzen's research is particularly relevant here, indicating the importance of the individual's attitudes towards particular behaviors in determining the likelihood of their selection. These attitudes would be represented in the Action Selection memory schemas by differential weighting of the various action options, thereby making it more or less likely that a particular action would be selected in a given context.

6.3 Modeling Decision-Making Biases

Decision biases, while influenced by the structural features of the cognitive apparatus, are inherently dynamic. A number of factors acting together contribute to, and determine, the exact nature and expression of a particular bias. Below I outline how the MAMID architecture would model one of the more common decision biases identified in the judgment and decision-making empirical studies: confirmation bias.

Recall that confirmation bias is the tendency to actively seek and emphasize the importance of evidence that is consistent with the decision-maker expectations or desires. Confirmation bias may be classified as both a cognitive (reasoning) bias, and an affective (motivational) bias (refer to bias classification in Table 14.1.). Within the cognitive realm, this phenomenon has been most extensively studied in perception, where the currently activated situational schemas prime incoming cues that confirm those schemas, raising their relative salience. This then results in a positive-feedback cycle, eventually leading to the preferred selection of the associated schema, which may or may not reflect the actual situation. However, confirmation bias is also evident in the subsequent, more internal, stages of decision making, for example, expectations can 'prime' situation construals (e.g., if a leader expects his nation to be attacked, he will be more likely to interpret ambiguous cues as representing an impending attack and react accordingly).

Within the affective / motivational realm, confirmation bias serves to maintain beliefs and attitudes, both short- and long-term, which serve some desired function or meet a particular need. Many examples of this phenomenon exist in clinical psychology (e.g., the need to maintain ego-syntonic self image and various types of projective identification). In extreme cases, when an individual's desire or habit is very strong, confirmation bias can lead to 'seeing things'; for example, cases where we may think we have seen an absent person in a crowd, or heard their voice. In general, it is difficult, if not impossible, to separate the cognitive and motivational factors in the confirmation bias, much as it is difficult to separate these two distinct realms of cognitive and affective information processing (LeDoux, 1992; 1996).

The essence of the confirmation bias mechanism thus appears to be priming (facilitated activation) of cues or mental constructs by already activated mental constructs further along the information processing sequence. In understanding how these priming effects take place, it is helpful to use the spreading activation metaphor for memory and processing, where the most important schemas in memory, reflecting actual, expected, or desired states of self, others or the world, are the most highly activated ones. The 'energy' from these activated schemas then spreads through to other related schemas via the connecting links, thereby increasing *their* level of activation, and making them more likely to be selected for processing. If we think of a decision sequence implementing a simple stimulus-response model as a forward sequential data flow within the cognitive model, progressing from cues to situations to expectations to goals to actions (refer to Figure 14.3.) in a data-directed manner, we can think of the various priming effects associated with the confirmation bias as implementing this sequence in the reverse direction, in what is sometimes referred to in AI as goal-directed or top-down processing (refer to Figure 14.1.).

MAMID's processing sequence, parameter space, and mental constructs allow the modeling of the confirmation bias, both its cognitive and its affective components. Recall that whether or not a particular construct (e.g., cue, situation, expectation, goal) is activated within a module, processed, and passed on to the next stage of decision-making, depends on that construct's rank. This rank is a function of a number of factors, including salience, valence, threat level etc., with the exact set of factors varying by construct type. Implementing confirmation bias within the MAMID architecture requires two enhancements: first, the explicit representation of the necessary construct-to-construct links, which would allow the construct ranking functions to also consider the importance and rank of the *related, priming constructs*, and second, the augmentation of the rank-calculating function to include the rank of the related constructs. In this way, a highly-ranked (activated) situation could increase the rank (activation level) of its triggering cues, highly-rated expectation could increase the rank of its triggering situations, and highly-ranked goals could increase the rank of their triggering expectations and situations. A schematic diagram of this process is shown in Figure 14.8., along with links representing the influences of traits and states on the distinct mental constructs involved.

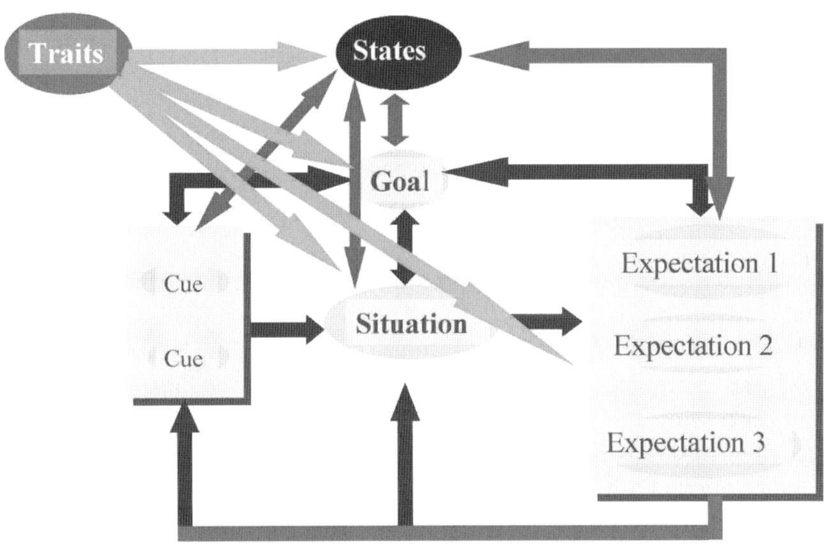

Figure 14.8. Recognition-primed decision-making model, augmented with explicit effects of states and traits on the distinct model components

6.4 Modeling Effects of Emotions

Unlike traits, emotions exert transient effects on processing, which can vary from seconds and minutes, in the case of transient fear or anger episodes, to hours, days and weeks, in the case of long-lasting moods or affective pathologies (e.g., anxiety disorders, paranoid fears). A number of specific effects identified in empirical studies have been outlined in section 2. Two of the more robust effects, both associated with acute fear episodes, are: 1) attentional narrowing and working capacity reduction, and 2) threat bias.

It is extremely difficult to predict the effects of transient emotions on long-term decision-making, since the exact effects depend on interactions of the individual, social and specific situational factors. While we know that episodes of anxiety will lead, *in general*, to heightened threat focus and reduced attentional and working memory capacities, the *exact* consequences of these effects on a long-term decision-making process cannot be predicted, without knowing the exact sequence of cues available, and the anxiety levels, at each stage of the decision process.

Nevertheless, computational cognitive models can still be useful, by simulating these effects across a large number of scenarios and contextual factor variations, and thereby quickly generating a large space of possible decision and behavioral outcomes. These can then be analyzed for emerging patterns of biases, and for specific triggering factors, in particular stereotypes or individuals being modeled. Thus, for example, we can generate behavior sequences for 'anxious leader' stereotype and compare these with 'aggressive leader' or 'non-anxious leader' stereotypes. Such analysis can then help establish the distributions and ranges of these transient effects for the distinct types of decision-makers, and provide a basis for improved understanding and development of de-biasing or intervention strategies.

MAMID's existing parameter space and mental constructs can currently model four of the basic emotions and some of their effects, as well as the dynamic interaction of specific emotions and traits (refer to sections 4 and 5 above). For example, fear and anxiety directly affect the capacity parameters of the processing modules, thereby reducing the number of constructs processed. Fear and anxiety also contribute to a higher-ranking of cues, situations and expectations with high threat levels, making it more likely that these will be processed. These features thus implement the attention and working memory capacity reduction, and attention and perceptual threat bias, associated with these emotions.

Modeling the effects of these emotions on strategic decision-making would require the following: 1) creation of the knowledge-bases representing the agent's memories within the associated task domain (e.g., foreign policy decision-making), as outlined in section 6.2. above; 2) definition of the domain-dependent 'absolute' factors contributing to the mental construct rank values (e.g., threat level and salience of particular types of situations and expectations encountered within the particular strategic domain, such as the threat-level associated with an unfavorable reaction from leader x, or possible economic boycott by country y, etc.), and, most importantly, 3) the 'tuning' of the numerous weights associated with the factors comprising the parameter and rank-calculating functions, to achieve desired model performance within the new domain. None of these require changes to the architecture proper, additions to the existing parameter space, or new mental construct or construct attributes. The weight tuning of the parameter and rank functions can be done via the analyst graphical user interface, and does not require changes to code. The definition of the domain-dependent 'absolute' factors requires the editing of constants in several external files. Limiting the model to the existing four basic emotions (fear, anger, positive affect, and negative affect) would thus not require any additions to the MAMID architecture processing algorithms, parameter space, or mental construct structures. It would however require extensive weight 'tweaking' and might require modifications on the functions calculating the parameter and mental construct values (e.g., change from linear weighted combinations to logistical functions).

Expanding beyond this set of emotions to include additional basic emotions (e.g., surprise, disgust), as well as more complex and cognitively-involved emotions (e.g., pride, shame, guilt), which are likely to play a greater role in strategic decision-making, would require some enhancements. *First*, additional affect appraisal knowledge clusters would need to be defined, specifying which combinations of situations and expectations trigger these emotions, and how their triggering is influenced by the personality traits (e.g., low emotional stability may facilitate shame and guilt, aggressiveness may facilitate disgust, etc.). This would also require extensive review of the existing literature to determine the exact facilitating and inhibiting effects of the selected traits on the different emotions, and, more likely, extensive educated guesses regarding these effects, since it is likely that the required empirical data would not be available. *Second,* the LTM clusters associated with the Goal Management and Action Selection modules would need to be augmented, to include the new emotions in their LTM rule preconditions (e.g., if a particular goal is triggered by a combination of disgust and fear, then these emotions would need to be added to the rule activating that goal). *Third*, the exact effects of the additional emotions on the perceptual, cognitive, and memory processing mechanisms would need to be identified. This would also require extensive review of the existing literature and an operationalization of what are generally rather high-level theories and observations regarding the effects of the more complex emotions on low-level cognitive mechanisms. Additional architecture parameters might need to be defined, as well as additional mental construct attributes, depending on the emotions and phenomena selected. It is also likely that representing the effects of some of these emotions and phenomena might require an augmentation of the MAMID architecture with additional processes, such as meta-cognitive capabilities, planning, and internally-oriented actions; that is, actions directed towards the manipulation of the internal constructs, rather than actions directed at the external world (for example, what-if simulations of alternative actions).

6.5 Example

I conclude this section with two brief illustrations of a MAMID model of strategic political decision making, in the context of a hypothetical scenario involving the leaders of two countries at the brink of war. The focus will be on modeling two key decisions of the two presidents.

Within the hypothetical scenario, a tense situation exists between two nations, Atlantia and Pacifica. Both nations have nuclear arms and an arsenal of chemical and biological weapons. While Atlantia is a democracy, and Pacifica a secular totalitarian dictatorship, both leaders are ambitious autocrats, surrounded by loyal advisors, and exercising their power to the maximum extent possible within the political systems of their country. Within this high-level strategic scenario, we assume that the behavioral repertoire of the decision makers includes actions in four categories of activities: *diplomatic* (e.g., negotiate, build / break alliances, etc.), *economic* (e.g., impose / lift trade sanctions, offer / withdraw particular goods, etc.), *military* (e.g, attack, defend, withdraw, etc.), and *domestic* (e.g., punish / reward/ appease / manipulate etc. particular individuals or segments of population).

Atlantia's president has recently accused Pacifica of hiding weapons of mass destruction and providing aid to terrorist organizations. In an attempt to force Pacifica to disclose and destroy its weapons, Atlantia has amassed vast armies at Pacifica's borders. Pacifica's leader is becoming isolated, his people are worried about war, his economy is devastated, and his army weak. In addition, his formerly unified and supportive advisors are beginning to express a desire to avoid war, which, at this point, would require the leader to step down. Within the past week, two additional massive troop movements have occurred, with Pacifica now surrounded on all sides by over 250,000 of Atlantia's troops, massively outnumbered in terms of air and land military capabilities. A World League, consisting of multi-national council, has attempted to mediate, but with little success. On the contrary, a number of long-standing coalitions among nations have been damaged as member countries and their leaders take sides in the conflict.

The first example illustrates alternative decision sequences for two possible types of Pacifica leaders, demonstrating the effects of distinct traits on decision-making and the resulting behavioral outcome. The second example illustrates the priming effects in Atlantia leader's decision to attack Pacifica, demonstrating the effects of confirmation bias on decision-making.

Alternative Decision Sequences for Two Types of Pacifica Leaders: Consider a decision-sequence that could occur in response to the recent deployment of Atlantia's troops by two types of hypothetical Pacifica leaders. Type 1, an ambitious individual, but one who is able to recognize when he can no longer control his people and in the end, values his people more than his own ambition. Type 2, an aggressive, ruthless individual, with a history of fits of unrestrained rage, and a pathological desire to maintain power and 'save face' at all costs. Figure 14.9. shows the decision sequence, and the behavioral outcome, for these two individuals, as it would be generated by the augmented MAMID architecture. The figure illustrates for each module of the architecture the data it would be processing and generating, at each stage of decision-making sequence.

	PACIFICA LEADER Type 1 "Normal Need for Power" "Normal Aggressiveness"	PACIFICA LEADER Type 2 "High Need for Power" "High Aggressiveness"
Attention (cues)	Massive Atlantiatroop movement Dissenting advisors Devastated country Weak army	Massive Atlantiatroop movement Dissenting advisors
Perception / Situation Assessment	Pacifica army vastly outnumbered Pacifica people demoralized Loss of support among advisors	Pacifica vastly outnumbered Advisors in service of the enemy
Expectation Generation	Unrestrained war Pacifica will be devastated 'Bad conscience' if does not avoid conflict	Conventional means unlikely to succeed Loss of power Loss of 'face'
Affect Appraisal	Fear for own people Fear for world peace	Fear for self Rage
Goal Selection	Avoid armed conflict Save people's lives Save the country	Preserve power for self 'Save face' Discharge aggression
Action Selection	Sends diplomats Engages UN Steps down	Executes dissenters Launches nuclear attack

Figure 14.9. Augmented MAMID processing representing two types of Pacifica leaders' response to an impending Atlantia attack

Priming Effects in Atlantia Leader's Decision-Making Sequence: Consider again the current scenario, specifically, the decision by Atlantia's president whether or not to launch the attack on Pacifica. Suppose that the chain of constructs depicted in Figure 14.10. represents a sequence of schemas in Atlantia's president's memory. Suppose that Atlantia's president's situation schema "Pacifica has weapons of mass destruction (WMD)" has been activated by rumors of Pacifica having WMD's. Suppose that his goal schema 'Defend Atlantia' is also strongly activated, for a variety of additional reasons (e.g., recent attacks against Atlantia, personal individual history / affective motivations). Depending on the exact nature of the links connecting these constructs, this goal activation may 'spread backwards' to the expectation 'Pacifica will attack with WMD', and the situation 'Pacifica has WMD', and finally to incoming cues, emphasizing the currently ambiguous cues indicating possible presence of WMD's (e.g., mobile laboratories). The resulting increased importance of these cues will then propagate forward again, further increasing the importance of the subsequent situations, expectations and goals, in a mutually-reinforcing positive-feedback cycle. Note also the multiple points within this decision sequence where distinct personality traits can be expressed. For example, the same cue-situation-expectation-goal sequence might result in a very different action for a different personality (e.g., negotiate, invoke sanctions, etc.). Obviously a large number of possible variations exist regarding the exact types of cues, situations, expectations and goals represented in the decision-maker's memory and the links among them.

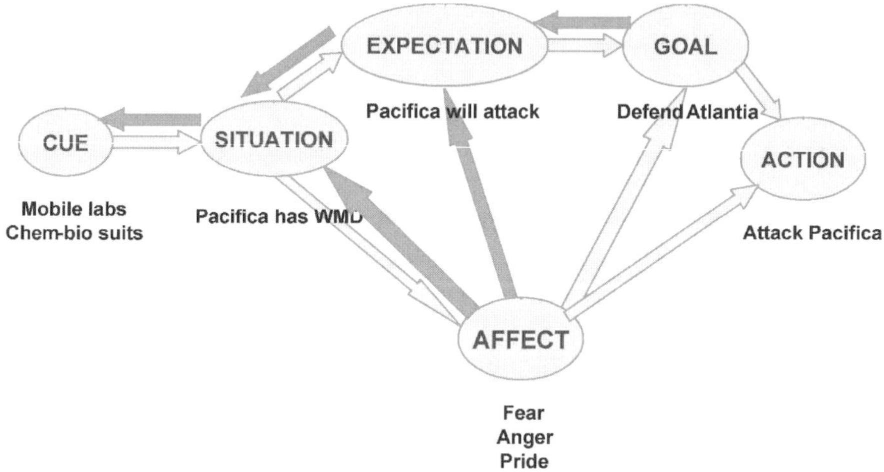

Figure 14.10. MAMID's model of Atlantia's president's confirmation bias during the 'attack vs. no attack' decision (data-directed information flow is shown by light Arrows; priming information flow is shown by dark grey arrows)

MAMID's capability to represent many of these additional factors in its current configuration indicates the ability of the MAMID *parameter space* to model additional high-level traits and cultural factors, as well as the ability of the MAMID *mental constructs* to represent the values, attitudes and beliefs ('operational codes') that guide strategic decision-making and behavior selection. The domain independence of the MAMID cognitive architecture would facilitate a transition to a distinct domain, from a tactically-focused peacekeeping scenario to a strategically-focused international conflict scenario. The key challenges in the extensions outlined above would be any necessary changes required in the modeling of the affect appraiser, including the development of a parallel-process appraisal approach, and the implementation of additional complex emotions, as well as identifying the necessary empirical data and the mapping functions implementing the translation of the state / trait profiles onto the architecture parameters.

7 APPLYING COMPUTATIONAL MODELS OF DECISION-MAKING TO INTERNATIONAL CONFLICT RESOLUTION AND PREVENTION

We now return to the core topic of this volume: computer-aided international conflict prevention and resolution. How can we apply the methods and models described above to this seemingly intractable problem? Below I outline a number of possible options, both in terms of specific applications, and also in terms of basic research. The applications discussed cover a broad spectrum of possibilities, ranging from *behavior modeling and prediction systems*, to *training and assessment* environments, and including examples of several *futuristic 'visions'*. The possible research directions also cover a range of areas, since computational models of decision-making, coupled with the ability to model state and trait effects and decision biases, are relevant for any domain concerned with the understanding and improvement of decision-making, and with the feasibility of individual and group behavior prediction.

7.1 Applications

The military establishment has begun to see the value of modeling cognition, and even emotion and personality (e.g., Pew and Mavor, 1998), to improve human and human-machine performance. Recent trends in this area include the application of video gaming to training and assessment, and extensive emphasis on virtual reality technologies (see, for example, the research efforts at the Institute for Creative Technologies (www.ict.usc.edu/). These same methods are equally applicable (although, unfortunately, not equally well funded) to the understanding, prevention, and resolution of international conflict situations, although the associated methods and technologies have not yet been adopted by this community. Interestingly however, the problems currently being addressed by the Western military establishment such as asymmetric warfare environments and management of multinational coalition teams, are very similar to the problems that must be addressed to prevent and resolve international conflict.

Below I outline examples of cognitive modeling applications in two broad areas relevant to international conflict resolution and prevention: *behavior prediction*, and *training and assessment*. I conclude with an example of a *futuristic application* of the modeling methods described here.

7.1.1 Behavior Prediction

Behavioral and social science literature reports mixed success in predicting behavior and forecasting change in political systems (e.g., Tetlock, 1992), and some researchers doubt that we will ever be able to predict human behavior (Dawes, 1995). In spite of this skepticism, several arguments can be made for guarded optimism regarding the application of cognitive models to model-based behavior prediction.

First, as Meehl points out, machines and associated algorithmic behavior prediction have been shown to do at least as well as human clinical judgment (Meehl, 1954; Grove and Meehl, 1996). While this may not appear to be an exciting proposition, given the notoriously low rates of successful behavior prediction by highly-trained human experts (e.g., 15-20 % of variance accounted for in predicting recidivism and occupational choices, Tetlock, 1992), it should be noted that until very recently, detailed human behavior models in terms of cognitive architectures were not available. It remains to be seen whether this new tool in the behavioral scientist's repertoire can be developed to a sufficient level of complexity and reliability to surpass the existing methods, human or machine.

Second, while predicting individual behavior with reasonable accuracy is not currently within the state-of-the-art of behavior models, computational cognitive models do have a distinct advantage over their human counterparts, and over the types of correlational, 'mechanistic' systems discussed by Meehl (1954; Grove and Meehl, 1996). These models allow a rapid generation of large spaces of possible behavioral alternatives, under a variety of changing internal and external conditions. The resulting behavior spaces then provide samples from which patterns of behavior can be determined, to identify regularities associated with particular configurations of specific factors; that is, traits, states, situational factors, etc.

Third, while current state-of-the-art high-level behavior models do not permit individual behavior prediction, we should not assume that this will continue to be the case in the future. Developments in cognitive science and neuroscience, coupled with improved computational technologies and the ability for extensive individual assessment, hold much promise for improving individual behavior models and their predictive abilities. Whether relying on deep theories of the mind, or on vast quantities of individual data collected over time, it may one day be possible to predict the behavior of specific individuals, albeit most likely within highly restricted contexts (e.g., predict behavior of team members in highly-constrained environments such as long-term space flights).

The ability to predict individual or group behavior, whether specific instances or ranges of possibilities, and whether for specific individuals or for stereotypes, necessitates the ability to model the effects of states, traits, and decision biases discussed above. Below is a list of two applications of these capabilities to the problem of international conflict prevention and resolution.

Predict possible reactions of specific leaders (or types of leaders) to particular situations

Whether during contemplation of possible national policies or actions, or during active conflict resolution, the ability to predict another leader's (or nation's, population's, advisor's, etc.) reaction is essential. To the extent that such reactions are likely to be highly idiosyncratic, and to reflect the individual's operational codes, traits and current affective states, it is essential to explicitly include these factors. In this type of application, a simulation environment could be constructed with multiple agents, each agent representing a key world leader (or other relevant decision-maker or influential group). Distinct personality and background profiles would then be specified for each simulated agent, either attempting to reflect actual individuals, or reflecting identified stereotypes (e.g., Holsti's typology (1977)). These profiles would be translated into the necessary model memory structures and an external scenario would be defined, capturing the situation of interest (e.g., impending war, on-going negotiations, etc.). A simulation would then be initiated, with an instance of the cognitive architecture associated with each agent generating distinct decisions and behavioral outcomes as a function of the distinct profiles. Over time, this simulation would produce a subset of the complete game tree, as the simulated agents would react to each other's behavior. A number of factors could then be varied, including the agent profiles (e.g., change agent A from anxious to aggressive), the scenario and associated environmental events (e.g., change an outcome of an election, introduce a natural disaster), as well as more fundamental aspects of the cognitive architecture (e.g., broaden or modify effects of particular emotions on specific cognitive processes, augment the model with additional emotions or traits). The resulting space of behaviors and interactions could then be examined to identify specific decision-points that are particularly dangerous (e.g., crisis escalations), or particularly favorable. The proximal behaviors of the agents, as well as the associated situational factors, would then be examined to determine what caused the situation to arise. This would then support a more systematic analysis of both the possible triggers of crises, and of interventions that might prevent them, and help identify situations conducive to negotiations and reduction of conflict. Both adversarial and cooperative gaming simulations could be defined to represent a variety of decision-makers or groups. In addition to aiding in conflict resolution, such predictive simulations could be applied in a number of additional areas, including predictions of the evolution of domestic policies.

If such systems were available to legislators, advisors, or voting citizens, they could be used to predict possible behaviors of elected or appointed officials, and would help provide additional evaluation data for such individuals. For example, such a simulation might demonstrate that a rigid decision-maker, with low cognitive complexity and a brittle personality, is likely to have an adverse impact on world events, regardless of his particular political convictions.

Explore different means of inducing a specific leader to make a particular decision

The simulation outlined above could also be used to 'reason backward', to generate hypotheses about the types of states or stimuli that would induce a particular decision or behavior in a specific individual or individual type. Here again, the modeling of traits and states is essential, since states in particular can have a strong biasing effect on decision-making. The behavior space generated above could be analyzed to determine specific agent states leading to particular decisions. Additional modeling could then be performed to determine how such states might be induced, and to determine the range of external stimuli that could induce them. This would then provide a political leader or a conflict mediator with concrete information regarding the possible interventions. For example, returning to the Wilson "League of Nations" example outlined in the introduction: we could imagine conducting several what-if simulations to determine what types of events might induce a more conciliatory attitude, facilitate more effective negotiations with the Senate, and eventually yield a ratification of the treaty. The simulation environments could then also be used to simulate the effects of such possible interventions, to confirm whether or not they would induce the desired states and behavior.

7.1.2 Simulation-Based Training and Assessment

Training and assessment represent another important set of applications of the modeling methods outlined in this chapter. The multi-agent simulation environments outlined above could be used to provide more realistic training scenarios for a variety of individuals and variety of specific purposes, including political leaders engaged in foreign and domestic policy decision-making, and diplomats and mediators engaged in peacekeeping efforts.

By explicitly modeling individual behavior variations due to personality traits and emotional states, these simulations would provide more realistic depictions of actual (vs. idealized) behavior, in both friendly and adversarial contexts. Specific scenarios and situations of interest could be 'role played' with simulated agents, providing opportunities for 'experiencing' particular situations, and practicing appropriate behavioral strategies. The ability to define the simulated agents to correspond to a variety of personality types, exhibiting various emotional states, would make it possible to expose the trainee to a variety of situations which would be difficult, costly or simply infeasible to construct in real-life. For example, negotiators could be exposed to a variety of specific dialogues, with varying degrees of hostility, to practice particular decision-making and negotiating strategies in conditions with varying degrees of stress. This would be particularly useful for identifying specific decision-making biases influencing the decision-maker, identifying the triggers activating their use (e.g., anxiety, frustration, exposure to particular event or individual, etc.), and for training specific '*debiasing' strategies and strategies for coping with undesirable affective states*, such as dialectical thinking, meta-cognitive integrative skills, etc. (see, for example, Tetlock (1992: 526)).

A key component of successful social interaction is the ability to see the world from another individual's point of view. This capability has recently been identified as a core component of *emotional intelligence* (Mathews, Zeidner and Roberts, 2002). Emotional intelligence refers to our ability to understand the emotional makeup of others, and ourselves, which is critical for effective interpersonal interactions, and functions at all levels of social interactions. The simulation environments described above could provide opportunities not only for simulating a variety of trait and state influenced behaviors, but also for examining the reasons for those behaviors, by visualizing the internal processing of the simulated agents' cognitive architectures. These capabilities would thus allow the trainees to 'view' an adversary's (or teammate's) internal operational codes and motivational factors, and would promote improved empathy, or at least improved understanding, of a variety of problematic behaviors.

The same set of tools could be also be applied to dynamic assessment of the trainee's initial capabilities and progress during training. Rather that filling out the standard psychological self-assessment instruments, trainees' performance could be evaluated within a series of immersive, realistic scenarios, over the course of hours or even days. A number of variables could be assessed, including possibly physiological correlates of stress and that trigger undesirable reactions in the trainee. The ability of the environment to re-create the same difficult situation repeatedly would then provide opportunities for repeated training runs and possibility for additional skill acquisition and improved performance.

Coupling the modeling tools described here with virtual reality technologies and immersive environments, would provide additional levels of realism and would enable the development of powerful and flexible training and assessment tools for improving decision-making and interpersonal understanding. Improvements in these skills have direct relevance for conflict resolution.

7.1.3 Futuristic Visions

What types of possibilities might exist if we brought together the state and trait modeling capabilities, with the simulation-based behavior prediction and training and assessment systems outlined above, including virtual reality technologies and physiological assessment? Currently our political leaders, whose decisions influence the lives of millions of individuals, are elected or appointed on the basis of very limited knowledge of their internal world models, motivations and behavior. Citizens in democratic societies have relatively little information upon which to base judgments that influence the fate of nations, and, increasingly, the entire world.

Imagine instead a scenario where a political candidate would not be elected on the basis of costly advertisements and few scripted debates. Instead, candidates for office (or applicants for the job of a peace negotiator, political advisor, cabinet member, etc.) would be evaluated in the types of virtual simulation environments described above. A presidential candidate would be presented with a variety of scenarios and his behavior, and its consequences, would be available to the voters. While this might be considered intrusive by some, it is likely to be no more intrusive than some recent instances of public scrutiny of private presidential behavior. And, unlike such scrutiny, such simulations would have direct relevance for informed voter decisions.

7.2 Research

The availability of computational modeling tools capable of modeling effects of states, traits and decision biases would contribute towards an understanding of the fundamental processes mediating a variety of decision-making types, under a variety of intrapsychic and interpersonal conditions, and across a broad range of situational contexts. Such understanding is valuable in its own right, and increasingly critical for the development of effective international political institutions and policies, as well as for the design and development of human-machine systems that increasingly pervade most aspects of our lives (e.g., medicine, transportation, telecommunication). The use of computational cognitive models represents an important tool for exploring and understanding the unique capabilities, as well as the limitations, of the human cognitive apparatus, across a broad range of contexts. Such understanding can serve as basis for the development of appropriate aiding technologies, that would enhance the existing human capabilities and limit the consequences of human biases and errors.

8 SUMMARY, CONCLUSIONS AND CHALLENGES

I described a methodology for modeling the effects of biases, affective states, and personality traits on decision-making, and an associated computational cognitive architecture that implements this methodology, the MAMID architecture. MAMID is unique in its focus on modeling the interacting effects of traits and states on decision-making in terms of parametric manipulations of the architecture processes and structures. This facilitates a rapid definition of distinct personality types, and simulation of the effects of states, traits and biases on decision-making across a wide range of contexts. Following a description of an evaluation experiment within a tactical, short-term decision-making context, I described how MAMID could be extended and applied to model strategic political decision-making. I concluded with examples of possible applications in the broad area of computer-mediated international conflict resolution and prevention.

The work described here is a research prototype. While computer aiding in general, and computational cognitive modeling in particular, have a tremendous potential for understanding decision-making and improving international (and interpersonal) interactions, many theoretical and pragmatic challenges exist. I therefore conclude this chapter with a brief outline of some of these challenges.

A number of questions must be addressed to effectively model the influences of states and traits on strategic, political decision-making. These include:

1. Strategic vs. Tactical decision-making

- * How is the process of strategic decision making different from tactical decision making?

* What are the differences among the memory structures, and the perceptual, cognitive, and affective processes, that mediate and influence these types of decisions?

* Which theoretical perspective is most appropriate to model strategic decision-making? Can the recognition-primed decision-making model be applied to strategic decision-making?

2. Factors influencing strategic political decision-making

* Which emotional states and personality traits are most critical to consider in modeling strategic decision-making?

* What other individual factors play a role?

* How do cultural and situational factors interact with individual characteristics to shape the decision-making process and outcome?

3. Effects of states and traits:

* What types of influences do transient emotional states exert on decisions that evolve over longer periods of time? How are these effects different from those observed in fast, one-shot decisions?

* What are the mechanisms of these effects?

* What types of empirical studies need to be conducted to collect the necessary data to enable computational modeling? What are the limits of empirical data when internal states are being modeled?

4. Modeling strategic decision-making

* When is it necessary to model the detailed mechanisms of state / trait effects to effectively model their influence, and when are black-box, input-output mappings adequate? What criteria can be used to decide which method is more appropriate for a particular situation?

* To what extent can a cognitive architecture capable of modeling tactical decision making be applied to strategic decision-making? Are additional components necessary (e.g., planning, learning)?

* Are the modeling methods appropriate for modeling tactical decision-making also suitable for modeling state / trait effects on strategic decision-making?

5. Modeling individuals vs. groups

* Can models of individual decision-making be applied to model the decision processes of larger groups (e.g., governments, political constituencies, etc.)?
* Can we identify distinct group stereotypes, similar to individual stereotypes, and are such stereotypes useful in modeling groups?
* Can we identify types of groups or decision situations for which this type of modeling would be appropriate?

Addressing the questions above would require an extensive research program, where researchers using computational models of decision-making would collaborate closely with social, political and cognitive psychologists, and emotion and personality researchers. Such collaborations would allow an implementation of a systematic research program, where existing empirical data would be used to construct computational models, which in turn would be used to evaluate the plausibility of hypothesized decision-making mechanisms, and generate empirical hypotheses for further testing. The resulting improved understanding of decision-making and decision biases would then provide a scientific basis for constructing focused training programs for conflict resolution at multiple levels of interpersonal interaction, which could contribute to international conflict resolution.

References

Ajzen, I., 2001, Nature and operation of attitudes, *Annual Review of Psychology* **55**:27-58.

Ajzen, I., and Fishbein, M., 2000, Attitudes and the attitude-behavior relation: reasoned and automatic processes, in *European Review of Social Psychology*, Stroebe, W., . Hewstone, M., eds., Wiley, Chichester, England.

Ajzen, I., 1988, *Attitudes, Personality and Behavior*, Dorsey Press, Chicago.

Blaney, P. H., 1986, Affect and memory, *Psychological Bulletin* **99**:229-246.

Bower, G. H., 1981, Mood and memory, *American Psychologist* **36**:129-148.

Breazeal, C., 2003, Emotion and sociable humanoid robots, *International Journal of Human-Computer Studies* **59**:119-155.

Busemeyer, J. R., and Townsend, J. T., 1993, Decision field theory: a dynamic-cognitive approach to decision making in an uncertain environment, *Psychological Review* **100**:432-459.

Cannon-Bowers, J. A., and Salas, E., 1998, *Making Decisions Under Stress*, Americal Psychological Association, Washington, DC.

Clore, G. L., 1994, Why emotions require cognition, in *The Nature of Emotion*, Ekman, P., Davidson, R. J. eds., Oxford University Press, Oxford.

Cohen, M. S., 1993, Three paradigms for viewing decision biases, in *Decision Making in Action: Models and Methods*, Klein, G. A., Orasanu, J., Calderwood, R., and Zsambok, C. E., eds., Ablex, Norwood, NJ.

Collyer, S. C., and Malecki, G. S., 1998, Tactical decision making under stress: history and overview, in *Making Decisions Under Stress*, Cannon-Bowers, J. A., and Salas, E., eds., American Psychological Association, Washington, DC.

Costa, P. T., and McCrae, R. R, 1992, Four ways five factors are basic, *Personality & Individual Differences* **13**: 653-665.

Damasio, A. R., 1994, *Descartes' Error: Emotion, Reason, and the Human Brain*, Putnam, New York.

Damasio, A. R., 2003, *Looking for Spinoza: Joy, Sorrow and the Feeling Brain*, Harcourt Brace Jovanovich, New York.

Dawes, R. M., 1995, The nature of human nature: an empirical case for withholding judgment—perhaps indefinitely, *Political Psychology* **16**: 81-97.

Deckert, J. C., Entin, E. B., Entin, E. E., MacMillan, J., and Serfaty, D., 1994, *Military command decision making expertise*, Report 631, Alphatech, Inc., Burlington, MA.

Edland, A., 1989, *On cognitive processes under time stress: A selective review of the literature on time stress and related stress*, Reports from the Dept. of Psychology, University of Stockholm.

Endsley, M .R., 1995, Toward a theory of situation awareness in dynamic systems, *Human Factors* **37**: 32-64.

Eysenck, M. W., 1997, *Anxiety and Cognition: A Unified Theory*. Psychology Press, Hove, E. Sussex.

Eysenck, H. J., 1991, Dimensions of personality: the biosocial approach to personality, in *Explorations in temperament,* Strelau, J., and Angleitner, A., eds., Plenum, London, pp. 87-103.

Forgas, J. P., 2003, Affective influences on attitudes and judgments, in *Handbook of Affective Sciences*, Davidson, R. J., Scherer, K. R., Goldsmith, H. H., eds., Oxford University Press, Oxford.

Gasper, K. and Clore, G. L., 2002, Atttending to the big picture: mood and global versus local processing of visual information, *Psychological Science* **13**:34.

George, A., 1979, Cognitive beliefs and decision-making behavior, in *Psychological Models in International Politics*, Falkowski, L., ed., Westview Press (Praeger), Boulder, CO.

Grove, W. M., and Meehl., P. E., 1996, Comparative efficiency of informal (subjective, impressionistic) and formal (mechanical, algorithmic) prediction procedures: the clinical-statistical controversy, *Psychology, Public Review, and Law* **2**: 293-323.

Hermann, M. G., 1986, *Political Psychology: Contemporary Problems and Issues*, Josey-Bass Inc., Publishers, San Francisco, CA:

Hermann, M., Unpublished, *A Handbook for the Measurement of Leader Personality.*

Hofstede, G., 1991, *Cultures and Organizations: Software of the Mind*, McGraw Hill, NY.

Holsti, O. R.., 1977, The 'operational code' as an approach to the analysis of belief systems, *Final report to the National Science Foundation*, Grant # SC 75-15368, Duke University, Durham, NC.

Howard, R., Meyer, J., and Spetzler, C., 2003, Garbage in, garbage out: reducing biases in decision-making. http://www.sdg.com/home.nsf/sdg/eBriefings--eBriefingArchive--Reducing Biases.

Hudlicka, E., 2003, Modeling effects of behavior moderators on performance: evaluation of the MAMID methodology and architecture, in *Proceedings of BRIMS-12*, Phoenix, AZ.

Hudlicka, E., 2002, This time with feeling: integrated model of trait and state effects on cognition and behavior, *Applied Artificial Intelligence* **16**: 1-31.

Hudlicka, E., and Pfautz, J., 2002, Once more with feeling: augmenting recognition primed decision making with affective factors, in *Proceedings of the 46th meeting of the HFES,* Baltimore, MD.

Hudlicka, E., and Billingsley, J., 1999, Representing behavior moderators in military human performance models, in *Proceedings of the 8th CGF-BR.*

Hudlicka, E., 1997, *Modeling behavior moderators in military HBR models*, TR 9716, Psychometrix Associates, Inc., Lincoln, MA. (see also Pew and Mavor, 1998)

Humphreys, M. S., and Revelle, W., 1984, Personality, motivation, & performance, *Psych. Review* **91**:153-184.

Isen, A. M., 1993, Positive affect and decision making, in *Handbook of Emotions*, Haviland, J. M., and Lewis, M., eds., The Guilford Press, New York.

Janis, I., 1972, *Victims of Groupthink*, Houghton Mifflin, Boston, MA.

Jervis, R., 1992, Political implications of loss aversion, *Political Psychology* **13**: 187-204.

Jervis, R., 1976, *Perception and Misperception in International Politics,* Princeton University Press, Princeton, NJ.

Kahn, B. E., and Isen, A. M., 1993, The influence of positive affect on variety seeking among safe, enjoyable products, *Journal of Consumer Research* **20**:257-270.

Kahneman, D., Slovic, P., and Tversky, A., 1982, *Judgment Under Uncertainty: Heuristics and biases*, Cambridge University Press, Cambridge, UK.

Klein, G., 1997, RPD model: looking back, looking forward, in *Naturalistic Decision Making*, Zsambok, C., and Klein, G., eds., Lawrence Erlbaum Ass., Mahwah, NJ.

Klein, G., 1996, The effects of acute stressors on decision making, in *Stress and Human Performance*, Driskell, J. E., and Salas, E., Eds., Lawrence Erlbaum Ass., Mahwah, NJ.

Larsen, R. J., and Ketellar, T., 1991, Personality and susceptibility to positive and negative affect, *Journal of Personality and Social Psychology* **61**:132-140.

LeDoux, J. E., 1992, Brain mechanisms of emotion and emotional learning, *Current Opinion in Neurobiology* **2**: 191-197.

LeDoux, J. E., 1996, *The Emotional Brain*, Simon and Schuster, New York.

Lefebvre, V., 1977, *The Structure of Awareness: Toward a Symbolic Language of Human Reflection*, Sage Publications, Beverly Hills, CA.

Leites, N., 1951, *The Operational Code of the Politburo*, McGraw-Hill, New York.

Lesser, I. O., Hoffman, B., Arquilla, J., Ronfeldt, D., Zanini, M., 1999, *Countering the new terrorism*, RAND Corporation, Santa Monica, CA.

Levy, J. S., 2003, Political psychology and foreign policy, in *Handbook of Political Psychology,* Sears, D. O., Huddy, L., .Jervis, R., eds., Oxford University Press, New York.

Lisetti, C. L., and Gmytrasiewicz, P., 2002, Can a rational agent afford to be affectless? *Applied Artificial Intelligence* **16**: 577-609.

Loewenstein, G., and Lerner, J. S., 2003, The role of affect in decision making, in *Handbook of Affective Sciences*, Davidson, R. J., Scherer, K. R., Goldsmith, H. H., eds., Oxford University Press, Oxford.

Matthews, G., Derryberry, D., and Siegle, G. J., 2000, Personality and emotion: cognitive science perspectives, in *Advances in personality psychology,* Hampson, S. E., ed., Vol. 1, Routledge, London.

Matthews, G., and Dreary, I. J., 1998, *Personality Traits*, Cambridge University Press, Cambridge, UK.

Matthews, G., Zeidner, M., and Roberts, R., 2002, *Emotional Intelligence: Science and Myth,* MIT, Cambridge, MA.

MacLeod, C. and Hagan, R., 1992, Individual differences in the selective processing of threatening information, *Behav. Res. Ther.* **30**: 151-161.

Meehl, P. E., 1954, *Clinical vs. Statistical Prediction*, University of Minnesota Press, Minneapolis, MN.

Mellers, B. A., Schwartz, A., Cooke, A. D. J., 1998, Judgment and decision making, *Annual Review of Psychology* **49**: 447-477.

Michel, R. R., and Reidel, S. K., 1988, *Effects of expertise and cognitive style on information use in tactical decision making,* US ARI Report 806, US Army Research Institute, Alexandria, VA.

Mineka, S., and Sutton, S. K., 1992, Cognitive biases and emotional disorders, *Psychological Science*, **3**: 65-69.

Minsky, M., 2004, *The Emotion Machine.* (forthcoming)

Myerson, R., 1991, *Analysis and Conflict,* Harvard University Press, Cambridge, MA.

Napier, R. W., and Gershenfeld, M. K., 1993, *Groups: Theory and Experience*, Houghton Mifflin Co., Boston, MA.

Orasanu, J., 1998, Stress and naturalistic decision making: strengthening the weak links, in *Decision Making Under Stress: Emerging Themes and Applications*, Flin, R., Salas, E., eds., Avebury, Aldersho, Hants, UK.

Pearl, J., 1986, Fusion, propagation, and structuring in belief networks, *Artificial Intelligence* **29**: 241-288.

Persons, J. B. and Foa, E. B., 1984, Processing of fearful and neutral information by obsessive-compulsives, *Behavior Res. Ther.* **22**: 260-265.

Pew, R. W. and Mavor, A. S., 1998, *Representing Human Behavior in Military Simulations,* National Academy Press, Washington, DC.

Post, J., and Shaw, E., 1999, *Review of commander information and interaction profile: recommendations for operationalization*, Political Psychology Associates, Ltd., Washington, DC.

Post, J., 1999, Hussein of Iraq: a political psychology profile, *Political Psychology* **13**(4).

Revelle, W., 1995, Personality processes, *Annual Review of Psychology* **46**: 295-328.

Scherer, K., 1993, Studying the emotion-antecedent appraisal process. *Cognition and Emotion*, 7:325-355.

Simon, H., 1985, Human nature in politics: the dialogue of psychology with political science, *American Political Science Review* **79**: 293-305.

Simon, H., 1967, Motivational and emotional controls of cognition, *Psychological Review* **74**:29-39.

Sloman, A., 2000, Architectural requirements for human-like agents both natural and artificial, in *Human Cognition and Social Agent Technology*, Dautenhan, K., ed., John Benjamins, Amsterdam.

Smith, C. A., and Kirby, L. D., 2001, *On the Elicitation, differentiation, and organization of emotions*, TR FS-01-02, AAAI Press, Menlo Park, CA.

Streufert, S., and Streufert, S. C., 1981, *Stress and information search in complex decision making: effects of load and time urgency*, Technical Report 4, Office of Naval Research, Arlington, VA.

Tetlock, P. E., 1992, Good judgment in international politics: three psychological perspectives, *Political Psychology* **13**: 517-539.

Tversky, A., and Kahneman, B., 1981, The framing of decisions and the psychology of choice, *Science* **211**:453-458.

Tversky, A., and Kahneman, B., 1974, Judgments under uncertainty: heuristics and biases, *Science* **185**: 1124-1131.

Velasquez, J. D., 1998, Modeling emotion-based decision-making, in *Proceedings of "Emotional and Intelligent: The Tangled Knot of Cognition",* AAAI Fall Symposium Series, TR FS-98-03, AAAI Press, Menlo Park, CA

Vertzberger, Y., 1990, *The World in Their Minds*, Stanford University Press, Palo Alto, CA.

Walker, S. G., 1995, Psychodynamic processes and framing effects in foreign policy decision-making: Woodrow Wilson's operational code, *Political Psychology* **16**: 697-717.

Williams, J. M. G., Watts, F. N., MacLeod, C., and Mathews, A., 1997, *Cognitive Psychology and Emotional Disorders*, John Wiley, NY.

Zsambok, C. E., 1997, Naturalistic decision making: where are we now? in *Naturalistic Decision Making*, Zsambok, C. E., and Klein, G. K., eds., Lawrence Erlbaum Ass., Mahwah, NJ.

Zsambok, C. and Klein, G. A., eds., 1997, *Naturalist Decision Making*, Lawrence Erlbaum Ass., Mahwah, NJ.

Chapter 15

Peacemaker 2020

A System for Global Conflict Analysis and Resolution; A Work of Fiction and A Research Challenge

Kirstie Bellman
Aerospace Corporation, Los Angeles, California, U.S.A.

Our knowledge of physics, chemistry, engineering, even psychology have all been used to develop weapons and approaches for winning armed conflicts. Especially the information sciences have been developed with a tremendous amount of funding and much of the initial motivation stemming from military needs and later developed with its funding. Robert Trappl has posed to the wider research community a fascinating question: Have our technologies and scientific approaches grown to the point that they can be applied to the much more difficult question of supporting the peaceful resolution of conflicts among nations? He has dubbed such technology "peacefare". Sometimes it is easier to design a complex system by starting with a solution and working backwards. Hence I wrote a story. Since I am a computer scientist and technologist, my story is about the technology that could provide some enhanced basis for analysis of growing international tensions and possible mediation. This story also is a way of eliciting from our broad research community our goals, our assumptions, and the success criteria for a system like "Peacemaker 2020."

1 THE STORY PEACEMAKER 2020: A SYSTEM FOR GLOBAL CONFLICT ANALYSIS AND RESOLUTION

The year is 2050. The setting is a large auditorium in Brussels. Although a huge screen dominates the room, a number of listeners are also attending to small flat panels in their tables and listening intently through the simultaneous translation with earphones. Some are already exploring System 2020 software at their tables, while others are comparing notes with those listening to the lecture in Virtual

R. Trappl (ed.), Programming for Peace, 413–439.

Worlds (Bellman, 1999; Bellman and Landauer, 2000b). The lecture today has been long awaited. Prof. Hope Field's group has spent over two years analyzing the thirty years of performance of the Peacemaker System 2020. She has been speaking for about a half hour on the history of, the motivation for, and the technical development of the Peacemaker System 2020, starting of course with the historical Vienna meetings in the early part of the 21st century.

She continues, "As one can see thus far, a lot of the impetus for data analysis in the early days of these technologies was to essentially learn the lessons of history and apply them, via intelligent decision aids, to human mediation that would decrease growing world conflicts or would mitigate ongoing conflicts. But now I come to the point in this talk where we have to ask ourselves 'What are our lessons learned? What have we learned over the last 30 years about this type of technology? What have we accomplished? What challenges do we still face?'

The hardest part was to recognize that the very technologies we had developed in the information sciences had amplified the ability of small, only partly connected groups of individuals to wage 'war' on major world cultures. That is, in the early part of the 21st century, we were just recognizing how much traditional warfare among nation states was changing into warfare waged by small groups loosely connected across nation states. Therefore we realized that the databases we had collected that had emphasized the political actions of nations had to be greatly enhanced in order to provide the basis for conflict resolution methods relevant to these small groups."

Immediately a question appeared on a sidewall in large red font, "What about groups of one, like the so-called 'snipers' or deranged individuals?"

She sighed, "Yes, I will get to that in my 'continual challenges' section. Realizing that we needed to expand to handle small groups and that we needed large and small group mediation techniques radically changed our notions of the technology we employed. In other words, we needed a much broader base of data and we needed a much broader base of methods to reach those small groups who were unlikely to be available to us through conventional means. Hence in a very controversial move, especially to certain security organizations in the US and in Europe, we decided to develop some handies with untraceable communication paths. That is we chose the longer-term goal of acquiring communication and information from disenfranchised groups—what in some Arab media were called the 'basement groups' as opposed to the 'street groups'—over the shorter term one of tracking down such groups.

Ironically we discovered that these devices were very effective in allowing people under dictatorial regimes to be polled as to their beliefs and desires, which aren't reflected often in those regimes' official polls. Does one remember some of the 100 % referendums from those regimes?"

While a small laughter went through the audience and 'ha-has' appeared on the sidewall from electronic listeners, a short series of slides appeared showing the small handheld devices being used by different populations around the world. One striking one showed young Nigerian girls posing questions to their newly elected national president.

She continued, "Of course there were several difficult challenges we had to overcome. First was bringing ubiquitous computing to desolate or rural areas. As you may know, in the early part of the century, for example, the costs to rural Alaska in the United States were paid for by their space agency since it cost over $ 30,000 a month per site for Internet connectivity which they used for some then novel cybermedicine applications. Happily, those costs although still expensive for several nations are now in the hundreds of Euros and are paid for out of an international UN fund.

Second, and by far the most difficult, we had to invent the means of having secure, untraceable communication from handheld wireless devices. To understand the importance of this is difficult for many of us, but it turned out to be critical in situations where tracing communication back to even a village could mean putting that entire village at risk. The solution to this problem is a fascinating technical story in itself, combining the capabilities of autonomous vehicles, new sophisticated methods in signal detection, encryption and in handheld devices. As you know, the autonomous vehicles, the so-called Doves because of the peaceful motivation behind them, traverse through countrysides in a nearly random fashion, act as wireless receivers and uplink the communications to the small satellites network. By both sending and receiving messages, they make it extremely difficult for anyone to determine whether a message was sent from any location. The on-board software applies the advanced techniques for sorting it all out. For those of you who are curious I will elaborate more technically after this talk. And of course hardware played its role when it became cheap and reliable enough to drop handies from other Doves for those who didn't have them."

She sighed again, "Now the purpose of all this effort was to allow average citizens of a region to not only answer questions (be polled) but to address questions to whomever they wanted to and to interact, when desired, in the international games and conversations I will discuss in a moment. Of course, we found out the hard way that corrupt governments could still 'pack the polls' by entering false entries supporting their policies. However, it did nonetheless greatly increase the visibility of the internal opinions of a region. In the now famous New Zealand study in 2030, Ragit showed that when people in one country were able to ask the peoples of another country directly whether or not they really wanted to exterminate them or end their nation, hearing the polled results, even with false entries or multiple entries by individual groups, helped greatly to decrease the average person's fears and hence their willingness to engage in aggressive action towards that other country.

Of course that leads to the second major lesson learned in our retrospective of Peacemaker 2020. The first was that we had to greatly broaden our ability to poll populations and to gather their attitudes, opinions (and as we'll see in a moment their solutions for a growing conflict). The second is that we needed not only much better broad translation capabilities—something that we called 'de-Babeling' after the biblical story of the Tower of Babel—but what we now call 'emotional' and 'cultural' translation. For example, at the beginning of the 21st century it was very difficult when reading a newspaper to know, when text was translated from a foreign language, whether or not the phrasing translated from another language was hyperbole, cultural flourish and style, or a threat? That's because the words in a text use to be translated literally and not semantically and idiomatically, and there were no emotional or cultural shading cues provided. We even had trouble in those days translating among different notational systems and scripts." Several of the younger members of the audience looked very surprised and Prof. Field laughed and said, "You can immediately tell who was born before 2010 here. Now in our results it is quite clear that emotional and cultural translation does not eradicate differences. That is we can understand each other but still disagree vehemently. But at least in understanding each other, we have a better chance of having successful dialog and mediation.

She continued, "The third lesson learned has to do with what we learned in analyzing this flood of individual and world opinion. To summarize, we are going to discuss three major ways of taking in the information and analyzing it that became, as those college majors among you know, separate fields of study although they are of course highly dependent upon each other. These three fields are role-playing simulations, social worlds, and story-based analysis. Each of these approaches collects slightly different kinds of information and involves different analysis techniques. On your screens you see an example of the first approach." She waited while some listeners shifted through the windows on their screens.

"As you can see, in these types of Virtual Worlds, we conduct situated role-playing simulations that replicate to some extent the current situation between groups or nations, according to the viewpoint and assumptions provided in the right hand corner of your screen." She laughed as a flurry of VW versions appeared on the side walls of the auditoriums, "yes, as many of you already know, users can change the carefully scripted scenarios in any way—the appearance of the players, their roles, their attitudes, the settings, the actions—because that is also information that we analyze and it is also as revealing as how any individual plays the game. To continue, users can play the scenarios as defined—acting out what they would do and say and what needs to be done—in any of the roles and as many times as they want to. Or they can change them as you all started to do and make comments on why they did so. They can play them individually with agents acting out the other roles or in small groups of other humans and agents. Small of course means something different from what it meant twenty years ago and we can now comfortably handle the activities and results from over 220 thousand simultaneous players. Of course, Peacemaker system 2020 can now handle over a hundred million users a day in terms of analysis and services. Luckily we are beginning to learn how to coordinate among Peacemaker systems much like the old Internet service backbones in order to provide even more scalability. The only condition we require in this technique—or at least that we really try to get the users to do—is that they stay with a scenario all the way through. What we mean by that is that if they declare war, they stay through the reconstruction period after the war. If they have resolved conflict in some non-aggressive fashion then they stay through the likely pattern of events following those decisions. Of course, as you all are familiar with, the likely pattern of events in these simulations is based on the Vienna work identifying and analyzing common patterns in politically tense interactions collected through the 1990s through the late 2020s.

The analysis of this data (which we will discuss momentarily) led to essentially a continuous set of worldwide Monte Carlo experiments, with the additional advantage of allowing individual disparate groups to poll others in the world implicitly. That is, one could see how many people in the world would resolve their situation in different common ways. Of course, it also added many novel solutions to the plans of decision makers.

Okay now go to the second major method of collecting and analyzing data, which are social Virtual Worlds." She paused and again allowed the room to open and close windows. Two people got up and strolled over to a corner CAVE where they could sign to other deaf participants in the Virtual World (which were also translated of course to the hearing participants).

"As you know, the same people who play the simulation games often go on to the social worlds in order to discuss their experiences so there is a great deal of overlap in these different approaches. However, the major thing I want to point out here is that in the social worlds, we are now not analyzing the conversation and behavior of users within a scripted simulation but in free form conversation and behavior within a virtual world. Hence we are not analyzing as much for problem-solving and both usual and novel solutions as for trends in attitudes, issues, and concerns. The results of the conversational analyses are used by mediators the world over to identify some of the issues and motivations before going into a conflict resolution situation. This technique has also been useful in allowing individuals in distressed populations to pose questions or concerns to the world. Now the big difference between System 2020 and the intent of the early peacemaking systems of this century is two-fold:

First, the data analysis system here is based not on static databases of largely national actions but on broad based databases of individuals and nations that are continually updated. To continually update the system we use an extension of the early idea by Bellman and Landauer of "continuous contemplation" introduced in the early part of the century. The concept of continuous contemplation is that the system has both domain data (data coming in from external sensors and users and analyzed in various ways within the system) and its own performance data (including its 'reflection' on its own analysis and problem-solving) that is continually being modified by ongoing exploratory data analysis and reasoning by the system. In the case of system Peacemaker 2020 this means that questions posed by an individual user are immediately analyzed for similarity to other questions (along with the relevant material associated with any discussions), and are fed back both to the user and added to the continually updated database of questions, concerns, themes, etc.

Second, the data analysis system heavily relies on emotional and cultural translation technology that was not available when the early New Zealand databases were being put together. To analyze free dialog in social worlds requires much more sophisticated emotional and cultural translation than even the situated role-playing games that we described earlier. That is because even rudimentary role-playing games provide a cultural context in how they describe the players, settings (or places of actions) and the actions. Early experiences with Virtual Worlds showed that even such minimal context could convey some emotional context for human users. In social worlds, even in ones that are situated and reveal behavior, expressions and body language within places, the issues and questions brought up by users cover every conceivable context of human experience and hence required a much more sophisticated translation of human meaning, culture and emotional reasoning.

The third field that emerged as part of the analysis technology needed for peacefare technology and that is reflected in Peacemaker 2020 is that the system is story-based. That is, both the simulated games and the free dialog in social worlds become potentially analyzable when they are collected and analyzed using the story grammars and story or scenario-based logics that first started emerging in 2000 with most notably the work of Joseph Goguen in San Diego and others. Actually there were three trends that came together that provided the necessary representational and analytic power needed by Peacemaker technology: story-based logics, 'domain-specific languages (DSLs),' and emotional agents. The story-based logics came from a number of new mathematical developments occurring at the turn of the century and are covered in a recent Spanish book, which I will gladly discuss in detail after this talk. The domain-specific languages were largely based on the US and European work around the turn of the century that extended well-known specification programming languages combined with more expressive mathematical logic-based languages. This allowed one to go beyond databases of declarations and separate facts into much more detailed and expressive stories, e.g. facts with actions, goals, viewpoints, attitudes and players computationally analyzable because of the language grammars and semantics.

At the same time, the work on emotional agents, especially in Europe, and the worldwide work on multi-agent systems at the turn of century started to give us the necessary experience in modeling emotional and interactive behavior and communication that became part of the properties successfully captured in the DSLs and later story languages. Story based analysis has allowed us to create databases with a great deal more cultural, emotional, and individual data than before and it has provided a springboard for techniques that allow more revealing profiling of the storyteller and their viewpoint. This last point means that we not only ask for the story tellers to tell us about themselves, answer questions, and to freely annotate their communications (through whatever medium they enter the system) but we can also learn more about the user implicitly by analyzing the similarity of the attitudes and viewpoint of the story to other users."

At this point, the lecturer stopped and looked earnestly around the room. She continued, "Now after thirty years of development what can I tell you about the successes and failures—or should we say future challenges—of Peacemaker 2020?

First, sadly, we have not done away with all wars or acts of terrorism. Although we have made great gains in understanding and modeling normal human emotions and quasi-rational decisions, we have recently realized that we are far short still of modeling the range of human minds. This goes back to the issue raised about an hour ago on 'snipers' and other individual humans who murderously act out against their entire world. However, we can say that we have begun with System 2020 a successful process for collecting much more detailed information from a much wider groups of individuals within both the role-playing simulations and the social worlds. The key importance of that is that we are beginning to accumulate tremendous databases on the decisions, actions, comments, and questions from unusual individuals. These individuals could be considered 'unusual' because of religious fervor, social traumas, mental illness, different belief systems, or other factors we are trying to characterize with the help of a number of social and theological experts. However, we have a tremendous amount of work needed still on understanding the dynamics of how such individuals impact those around them."

Immediately on the sidewall, a question bellowed out in red print, "that assumes that small groups always start with a cluster around an individual!"

Immediately Prof. Field nodded, "Yes, you are right. Let me correct my remark and add to it. I mean we need to understand more about how individuals can affect others around them. But of course as you rightly point out based on your own work, Dr. Wong, small group dynamics creates clusters of their own—some with no clear or necessary 'chief', which has led to some of the most difficult problems for mediators in crisis situations if I remember correctly." Dr. Wong nodded and smiled from his video head near his remark.

The second current shortfall in Peacefare technology is that, although we are getting better and better at modeling and analyzing unforeseen circumstances, we still have a long way to go in understanding how there are both positive and negative effects on mediation events due to naturally occurring events like earthquakes or epidemics, as well as unexpected impacts from the decisions of groups distant to those of the conflict regions. At first we thought this might be the result of the interdependencies clearly existing in globalization of so many products and areas of life. Although certainly true, it turns out that it involves a much more cognitive basis that we thought. As Anders of Norfolk University showed in 2028, people using Peacemaker 2020 gained more from analogous situations and from modeling the problem-solving processes in those analogous situations than we had expected when we first set up the games and social worlds to collect information on their use of Peacemaker on their own crisis situations. Of course if we had thought about it more, we would have realized that this was part of the original insight of Trappl and early researchers that such analogous historical situations could be used through data analysis for current situations. We just hadn't realized how much individuals would be affected by identifying with the stories from others into patterning their behavior after those others or how much individuals would make use of this information in their own game-playing and comments. Okay I see that several cognitive psychologists and cultural anthropologists in the audience are frowning as if to say, of course, that is the way humans reason and cultures grow, but it was a discovery for the computer scientists building this system.

Because of these first two points, we have not yet built any successful automated mediators yet." She continued, ignoring a number of protesting comments on the sidewall, "However, we have supported human mediation greatly, as seen by the fact that some version of Peacemaker 2020 is now used by most governments of the world, the United Nations, and even some multi-national large corporations. And I know that several of you object to my blanket statement about automated mediators, but in this case I will maintain I am correct. There are a number of good agents now aiding users of Peacemaker, and although they are certainly acting autonomously in acquiring information and even in pointing out relevant new information to users, they are still not directly involved in the acts of mediation. Partly because some would say, that other human beings still don't trust them to represent human ethics and values.

Before I close with an edifying usage case, let me remark on a somewhat unexpected result of peacemaker technology. Although we aimed the ubiquitous, two way media and wide-based polling technology at conflict resolution, we found that in fact all countries of the world today are increasingly sensitive to the opinions of their populations. That is, what started as conflict resolution has spread to the role of voicing popular opinion in every type of decision in different countries. Hence, much like the media technologies of the 1990s greatly impacted the behavior of even rogue groups to present a better act on the stage of world opinion, so peacemaker technology has made even dictatorial nations more sensitive to the results of electronic polls in their country. We are glad to say that this has especially amplified the ability of disenfranchised groups to speak out in different countries, e.g. minorities, women, children, and the poor.

Lastly, I must end this talk with a case example—as anecdotal as it is. In a recent impasse between the Columbian government and indigenous separatists, it was a group of teenagers on both sides of the issue who designed together eventually a scenario, played it a small number of times (in this case only a 100,000 times with the 1300 teens involved) until they found a reasonably proven solution. Then bolstered by these results and historical documents (also found through the help of Peacemaker) on 2000 similar resolutions, they approached the leaders of both the separatists and the Columbian government. Six months later, an electronic referendum based on that set of solutions in the game scenario was voted on by the Columbian people and accepted with an overwhelming vote of 63 %. Furthermore and perhaps most important, those agreeing to it had the full agreement of the leaderships in both groups. It is true that some mountainous regions are still hostile to either group, but the Doves have recently been dropping handies like mad in those regions and local Columbians are hoping to open up dialog and discussions with them soon.

So as you can see, although we have a long way to go in developing helpful technologies and new approaches in peacefare, we have nonetheless come a long way from the beginning of this century.

Thank-you for attending to my story."

Prof. Hope Field stepped down from the platform.

2 DISCUSSION OF THE TECHNOLOGY AND ISSUES UNDERLYING PEACEMAKER 2020

There are of course several assumptions underlying the viewpoint of this story of Peacefare technology. First of all, as difficult as it is to imagine a system capable of supporting negotiations among nations, we are increasingly faced with an even more difficult problem. The growth of worldwide terrorism means that peace negotiations increasingly involve small groups as well as nations. This tests both political and social science theory, as well as placing new demands upon the technologies used to support negotiations. For example, in the story, there is the need for technologies that can hide the location of participants in a discussion or negotiation. Unlike the story, in which the hiding was used to allow participants under tyrannical regimes the opportunity to participate in worldwide discussions and to be part of data gathering exercises on strategies and viewpoint, the hiding in negotiation with small (possibly terrorist) groups would have to involve both authentication and hiding. An odd combination indeed!

Small, loosely connected groups require not only new technologies but new mediation approaches, e.g., there may be no spokesman representative of all groups. More worrisome to many social and political scientists is that the motivations for agreeing to mediate appear to be very different from that of nation states. That is, how does one negotiate in good faith with groups that do not have the same stable properties and investments as nation states?

Part of the reason for assuming that we must in fact develop peacefare to include small non-state groups is that our current technologies amplify the capabilities of small groups to declare 'war' on other cultures. Whether we like it or not, small disenfranchised groups will make use of our current technologies to impact the world at large. This leads to the second major assumption underlying the story: future peacefare technology requires us to widely poll and include multitudes of individuals in the peacemaking processing.

My assumption is that fearful human beings tend to react more aggressively; technologies that lessen fear among populations through meaningful communication will decrease the likelihood of war or acts of violence. This assumption is reasonable given the large amount of anecdotal and experimental ethological and psychological literature (for example, as a start, see Lorenz, 1963; Freud, 1989). What is less proven is the solution taken in the story, which is that providing the capabilities for millions of human beings to learn more about each other's views will decrease their fear and decrease their willingness to attack each other. This is not as naively optimistic as it might first appear. The solution in the story was not based on the current media technology in which sound bites make momentary heroes of anything that catches the attention of the media and allows it to sell newspapers or airtime. To the contrary, as described below, the technology would allow sophisticated summarization of the attitudes, beliefs, and solutions for conflict resolutions of large populations, and at the same time provide the means for individuals relating as individuals to each other.

2.1 Discussion of Peacefare Needs

2.1.1 Technology Need #1: Pervasive Computing

In order to realize Peacemaker 2020, we need technology capabilities that introduce the analytic capabilities required for extraordinarily large and continually growing databases. However, the technology capabilities needed require more than data analysis; access and broad base communication is essential. Realizing the dream of "pervasive computing" is essential. We need omnipresent computing/ pervasive computing in rural, remote areas, and more difficultly, secure untraceable communication from handheld wireless devices in both remote and urban environments. In the story, the solution was to have:

- "Doves", Unmanned Aerial Vehicles (UAVs) drop handies and act as wireless receivers while they elaborately fly random patterns over countries.

- Reliable cheap handies airlifted to remote or inaccessible areas.
- "Handies" that are hardened enough and simple enough to be readily used after being airlifted to these areas.

Although this solution may seem somewhat glamorous, the issue of cheap and protected pervasive access is in fact the most nearly realized of any of the story's technology solutions (based on today's development of cheaper electronics and miniaturization, secure wireless technologies, and UAVs) and hence, will not be discussed here. However, the issue of how to deal with the misuse of such widespread polling technologies is definitely not solved and will be discussed in more depth in the analysis approaches described below. Based on the analysis approaches proposed, it is our contention that although one could still "pack the polls" so that it would not correctly represent the population being polled, it would nonetheless permit more of the population to express a range of opinions and attitudes.

2.1.2 Technology Need #2: Sophisticated "de-Babeling"

Part of pervasive access requires language translation. As surprising as it may seem to many, we have a long way to go for worldwide translation of even a modest sort, e.g., the notational systems underlying many languages are still not adequately represented in ASCII and hence even the translation of simple text presents barriers to communication (Reeder, 2001; Reeder and Harper, 2000). Even if the access is by visual or auditory interfaces, language translation is needed in order to network and analyze the communication. This ventures into the very difficult work of making images analyzable (Goguen, 2001; 2002).

However, as difficult as the above language notation issues are, the research and development community is faced with the more formidable issue of translating the semantics of languages—of translating meanings and placing them in a computational context that makes them actionable by both human and machine processes (Bellman, 1997; Landauer and Bellman, 1998; Norman, 1997; Suchman, 1987). In order to do so, we critically need emotional and cultural translation, so that one can understand for example the translation of colorful hyperbole versus that of a threat. Although there is not yet the necessary work in indexing language translation with emotional and cultural cues, the recent work on emotional and cultural agents is a step towards a better understanding of the type of information that would need to be conveyed in order to coordinate the actions of humans and agents in computer-mediated environments (Trappl et al., 2003).

New mediation methods go hand in hand with this required sophisticated cultural and emotional translation. That is, to understand is not necessarily to agree, but understanding is certainly a significant step in reaching agreement. It has traditionally been difficult enough to arrive at some common basis among nation states, with the usual stakes in negotiation, e.g., territory, responsibility for national governance of a population, economic motivations, and so forth, when values differ vastly. However, being able to translate emotional and cultural values—to convey values and meanings—becomes essential in negotiating with small non-national groups. This is because without the usual stakes in negotiation for nation states finding a common basis for negotiation may in fact end up depending on only our understanding of each other's values and beliefs.

2.1.3 Technology Need #3: New Database Construction and Analytic Techniques

The intent of this section is not to describe the current work in widely available Virtual Worlds (Bellman, 2001a; Bellman and Landauer, 2000b) or in the enormously popular Internet games (Herz, 1997). The point here is to propose some new approaches for collecting and analyzing the data available from such environments for Peacefare. However, for those perhaps unfamiliar with the current scale of both Virtual Worlds (VWs) and games, it may seem unlikely that one could collect as the story suggests, massive amounts of data from the millions of participants comprising significant parts of global populations.

However, in fact, the story was very conservative in suggesting that in the types of massive VWs and games that would be available by 2020 the data collection could occur for millions of players. The Virtual Worlds that evolved out of the old multi-players Dungeons and Dragons games ("MUDs") have hundreds of small online virtual communities (some numbering in the thousands), and with some that have been relatively stable societies for over ten years.

Recently the online games have flourished. For example, J. C. Herz recently reported (Herz, 1997; and in a recent talk at VWSIM '03) that the *Lineage* online game has 3 million players in Korea (out of a population of roughly 48 million), with even college scholarships offered for outstanding players. *Everquest* now supports a real world economy on *e-bay* selling objects acquired from playing for a worldwide group of players numbering in the millions. Guilds within *Everquest* have often 5000 participants, with leaders, governing boards, and so forth. These large online games already host large numbers of servers; the only difference is that in the story they would be integrated into more of a grid-like computing infrastructure. Hence the proposal of supporting 100 million players for several games in the story was actually rather modest, and was based not on the availability of the environments or on the growing databases, but rather on the ability of the future online analytic capabilities. That is, what is not currently available at such scale is the analytic capabilities that would make use of rapidly growing databases based on such VWs or games.

In the story, we proposed three new uses of such online analyses for Peacefare.

2.2 The Use of Role-playing simulations

First, based on role-playing simulations (much like the online games, but with more of the authoring capabilities seen in Virtual Worlds "quests"), one could define scenarios that describe at different levels of fidelity an ongoing or growing conflict. Authoring is a critical feature of VWs. In the story, Professor Hope Field describes authoring,

"… yes, as many of you already know, users can change the carefully scripted scenarios in any way—the appearance of the players, their roles, their attitudes, the settings, the actions—because that is also information that we analyze and it is also as revealing as how any individual plays the game. To continue, users can play the scenarios as defined—acting out what they would do and say and what needs to be done – in any of the roles and as many times as they want to. Or they can change them as you all started to do and make comments on why they did so. They can play them individually with agents acting out the other roles or in small groups of other humans and agents. Small of course means something different from what it meant twenty years ago and we can now comfortably handle the activities and results from over 220,000 simultaneous players."

There would be two major classes of data collected: first, there would be the ways in which a participant *played* out a scenario; second, there would be the ways in which a participant chose to *change* the scenario. The first case essentially would be much like the growing area of multi-agent simulations used for strategic and contingency planning, except instead of attempting to devise better models of the human and social behaviors, it would employ human-directed characters in the defined settings and scenarios. The results would become massive ongoing 'Monte Carlo' experiments that could help Peacefare researchers reason about the likelihood of different tactics, behaviors, and outcomes with more realistic probabilities based on the decision making and behaviors of real humans situated (Suchman, 1987) in the Virtual Worlds.

Also this would not detract from the growing field of human and social modeling, since the human-driven behaviors within the VWs could be compared with the results of the multi-agent architectures. Additional experimentation could allow one to replay the multi-agent simulations with different parameters and theoretical models.

The second type of data collected would be how the humans changed the scenarios. This would lead to new ideas on solutions not thought of by the scenarios or VWs developers. It could add valuable detail on the everyday reality of the populations involved in the conflicts, since in other VWs people often elaborate the world descriptions and the objects descriptions based on their everyday descriptions. Especially the characterization of the "enemies" or others in the conflict could help negotiators gain insight into how to start in the mediation process.

The idea in these human Monte Carlo experiments is to understand better the range of human behaviors, decisions, and outcomes that would occur under a range of scenarios involving a conflict. The statistics collected and the analysis of these statistics would speak to the range of observed behaviors and outcomes and the likelihood in a rough sense of the different events. When authoring is allowed, this authoring by participants could be used continually to elaborate that range of behaviors and outcomes in fixed scenarios.

If the game is designed with a judicious use of uncertainty built into it, such that identical activities do not always end up in identical results, then the same player playing the game any number of times would still result in a valid test of the game and the scenarios. That is, a single person or small group that would attempt to stack the deck or skew the results for whatever reasons, would certainly make the results not necessarily representative of a total population. However, such manipulation by individuals and groups would still be of use in testing the results of a scenario. They would be essentially flipping the dice for those setting up the scenarios.

However, in the story, I claim that even if there is massive manipulation of these games by small groups there will be nonetheless better representation of the range of attitudes, beliefs and behaviors in a given population if as the story assumes, one provides protected wide-spread access to the games for all parts of the population regardless of geography or language. With such access, even if governments or other groups attempt to overwhelm genuine population representation, those interpreting such results would quickly become sensitive to the difference between even small numbers versus zero. For example, in one opinion poll recently held in a small middle-eastern country, the questionable referendum results were 100 % for the government with zero against them. Against such a backdrop, even small percentages of different opinions would be significant.

Of course in the cases where one could guarantee a representative and large number of participants in a population playing out scenarios then one could make stronger claims to the role-playing simulations reflecting to some extent the attitudes of the population. An interesting question would be how to target a population into playing the game. Also, we would be faced with the technical challenge of ensuring that different individuals are playing (an odd version of authentication), while protecting the identity of those individuals. However, even then one should be cautious because how people perform in a Virtual World or in a game does not necessarily reflect their usual behavior or their beliefs. In fact one of the benefits of such worlds is that they can explore different roles and different behaviors from ones that they actually believe in or desire. In addition, it is an open question in the simulation training and education community how much one transfers from different virtual worlds to the external real world (Bellman, 2001a; Bellman and Landauer, 2000b).

All of the above argues that one should best use the role-playing games to test the models and the outcomes of the scenarios and to enrich those scenarios (through authoring) with more authentic details. One would use such results as indications of populations only in carefully controlled experiments or at best, in an exploratory manner that would be considered along side other sources of data.

In our discussion thus far we have not emphasized education as one of the chief benefits of role-playing simulations. In the story, we emphasized that "The only condition, we require in this technique—or at least that we really try to get the users to do—is that they stay with a scenario all the way through. What we mean by that is that if they declare war, they stay through the reconstruction period after the war. If they have resolved conflict in some non-aggressive fashion then they stay through the likely pattern of events following those decisions. Of course, as you all are familiar with, the likely pattern of events in these simulations is based on the Vienna work identifying and analyzing common patterns in politically tense interactions collected through the 1990s through the late 2020s."

Part of the reason in the story for urging a person to play through the consequences of decisions was to increase that learning by having them experience both long term (and often secondary effects) and short term impacts of their decisions and behaviors within the game. Role-playing remains a powerful way of teaching about other viewpoints and cultures. Similarly, there is mounting evidence (Bellman, 2001a; Mataric, 1997) that situated learning is more effective than many traditional methods in which the students are presented with verbal material. These situations also are an implicit way of polling populations that allows their behavior in the games (in the situated context) to speak louder than political slogans alone. With the caveats already noted above, this may be an effective for people to report beliefs and attitudes in addition to direct questioning.

2.3 The Use of Social Worlds

The second major approach to first amassing and then analyzing a continually growing body of data would occur in social worlds. As introduced in the story, Professor Field says,

"As you know, the same people who play the simulation games often go on to the social worlds in order to discuss their experiences so there is a great deal of overlap in these different approaches. However, the major thing I want to point out here is that in the social worlds, we are now not analyzing the conversation and behavior of users within a scripted simulation but in free form conversation and behavior within a virtual world. Hence we are not analyzing as much for problem-solving and both usual and novel solutions as for trends in attitudes, issues, and concerns. The results of the conversational analyses are used by mediators the world over to identify some of the issues and motivations before going into a conflict resolution situation. This technique has also been useful in allowing individuals in distressed populations to pose questions or concerns to the world."

As one can see from this description, the purpose of using social worlds is to both establish individual one-on-one relationships among diverse groups and to collect themes, issues and concerns through the analysis of unstructured dialog and behavior in the virtual worlds. The analysis of unstructured conversation is still in its infancy and will depend greatly on the de-Babeling technology noted above—especially in the advancement of sophisticated cultural, emotional, and semantic analysis.

However, the patterns of concerns and issues that could be discovered in these ongoing and constantly accumulating databases would greatly add to the potential knowledge and strategies of mediators. This approach would be especially important for those small non-nation groups who could participate directly or through sympathizers in these small discussions.

Furthermore, there could be a number of additional analysis capabilities that complement the analysis of the conversations and behaviors. For example, intelligent agents with the use of new capabilities could match conversational partners depending upon the user profiles (built both by explicit expression on the part of participants and by automatic analysis of their behaviors in the social worlds and in games); could discover resources to answer questions, could summarize the conversations so far, the polling, the games, etc.

So far we have emphasized several times the idea of continually updating and making use of those updated databases of participants, behaviors and conversations. Let us expand on that idea now.

By making use of the reflective knowledge captured through Wrappings (Bellman and Landauer, 1995; 2000a; Landauer and Bellman, 1993; 1996a; b;

1999) or other computationally reflective approaches (Duran, 1999; Kennedy, 1999; Maes, 1987; Maes and Nardi, 1988; Smith, 1986), one could develop a style of processing we have called "continual contemplation". In this approach, there is continual exploratory data analysis not only on external or domain knowledge introduced to the system through sensors or data sources, but also continual exploratory data analysis on the system's own state and its own use of its resources as it attempts to support user requests and to solve problems. The original purpose of our work on reflective architectures was to provide the means of integrating and using appropriately extremely large systems of models, databases, analyses, and other software and hardware resources (Bellman et al., 1993). In the Wrappings approach, one processes machine-interpretable descriptions of the problems, contexts for and uses of a resource in order to select, assemble, integrate, adapt and explain those resources to either human or other machine processes. This has led to a great deal of flexibility in the incorporation of diverse resources, selection and adaptation of such resources during the ongoing operation of the system, and the appropriate retention of context and problem information. The purpose for noting this system capability here is that this type of fluid self-contemplation and flexible infrastructure allows large complex systems to help us as the developers to develop and manage that system (e.g. in its configuration management, its record keeping, its reporting of state etc.). This is critically needed for very large and very complex systems such as the proposed Peacemaker 2020.

However of equal importance here is that the system could actually help reason about the appropriate methods, groups, and resources to provide to different users on a continual basis.

In order to apply Wrappings, or some other computationally reflective approach, the community will need to develop much better methods than currently exist for updating and changing the currently static meta-knowledge descriptions and user profiles etc. This would be just one of the critical potential roles for the emerging family of story logics, meta logics, domain specific languages and other higher level description logics described below.

2.4 Story logics become a fundamental key to analysis

In the story, we emphasize how critical new types of logics are to the future technology supporting Peacefare.

"The third field that emerged as part of the analysis technology needed for peacefare technology and that is reflected in Peacemaker 2020 is that the system is story-based. That is both the simulated games and the free dialog in social worlds become potentially analyzable when they are collected and analyzed using the story grammars and story or scenario-based logics that first started emerging in 2000 with most notably the work of Joseph Goguen in San Diego and others. Actually there were three trends that came together that provided the necessary representational and analytic power needed by Peacemaker technology: story-based logics, 'domain-specific languages (DSLs),' and emotional agents. The story-based logics came from a number of new mathematical developments occurring at the turn of the century and are covered in a recent Spanish book, which I will gladly discuss in detail after this talk. The domain-specific languages were largely based on the US and European work around the turn of the century that extended well-known specification programming languages combined with more expressive mathematical logic-based languages. This allowed one to go beyond databases of declarations and separate facts into much more detailed and expressive stories, e.g., facts with actions, goals, viewpoints, attitudes and players computationally analyzable because of the language grammars and semantics."

Many of the approaches proposed in this chapter depend on the advancements we have made and will continue to make in new formally based representational systems and analyses. Let us step back for a moment and discuss why this is so critical to our efforts here.

Science and technology have always depended upon the systems of representations it uses to both describe and reason about their systems of theories, processes, and objects of interest. In a general way, one always sees enormous growth in new types of representational systems—mathematics, logics, taxonomies, modeling notations, methodological schemas and so forth—whenever the scientific culture is faced as it is now with enormously complex and challenging new types of problems and issues. This has never been more true or necessary than in the current "information revolution" for several key reasons (Bellman, 2001b). Information architectures are not limited to the formidable complexity of large numbers and varieties of computational processes and the results of such processing. Rather information architectures are the integrative network and middleware ("the caulking material of modern intellectual life" as I have sometimes called it) of systems composed of software components, hardware components, robots, satellites, and other external effectors and displays, sensors (and now sensornets), and, most difficult of all, us—the humans.

These systems of humans and artifacts mean three key challenges to the development of suitable notations and analyses: first, more than ever the notations and formalisms we design in order to represent and reason about such systems must represent our human interactions with our systems of artifacts and with each other. This means that increasingly the representational notations and analyses must stretch to express difficult qualitative aspects of our individual reasoning, intents, values, and concerns, as well as our social and cultural collections of intents, values, and concerns.

This is especially true for Peacefare.

In addition, because these information architectures are so complex, we noted above that we want to have parts of the system helping us to monitor its state and performance, helping us to keep track of our goals and interactions with it, managing with us the use of its resources and so forth. This emphasis on autonomy (for example, helpful information agents that would discover and refine resources for users) and reflection presents additional challenges to our representations.

Third, again because of the complexity of the system, we must have as much analytic power as possible. Part of this power has traditionally come from the more formal and powerful languages of mathematics. As always then we strain as a scientific community between the power of formal analytic methods and the expressiveness of such descriptive languages as natural human language.

Over the last thirty years, we have seen this representational struggle presented on many scientific fronts. In Artificial Intelligence, the field struggled from its inception on how to best represent and make use of human-like cognitive capabilities, starting with the early work on the often qualitative expertise of humans, expressed as expert systems and production rules, to case-based reasoning, and schemas, to more recently, emotional agents and social agent architectures and more sophisticated knowledge interchange 'languages' of several sorts. In mathematics and logic, there has been an increasing emphasis on creating logics that could reason about other logics formally: meta-logics (Clavel et al., 1999; Duran, 1999; Kiczales et al., 1991; Meseguer, 1989; 1993), logics that could violate many set-theoretic assumptions, including the prohibition against self-representation (Aczel, 1988; Barwise, 1989; Barwise and Etchemendy, 1987; Barwise and Moss, 1966), and logics that sought to insert new types of properties useful to human qualitative reasoning, such as Zadeh's Fuzzy logic or Goguen's algebraic semiotics (Goguen, 1999; 2001; 2002).

In computer science, the last thirty years has seen a progression of strategies that would allow the human user to program at increasingly abstract and high levels and to use more of the terminology and the operations associated in the language of their own domain of knowledge. This started with parsers, compilers, and operating system design, some of the most successful technical triumphs of modern computer science, and has continued through first "higher level specification languages" to later domain specific languages (van Deursen et al., 1996; Hudak, 1996; IEEE, 1999; Luckham, 2002) and domain specific software architectures (Allen and Garlan, 1997; Hayes-Roth et al.,

1995; Shaw and Garlan, 1996). Starting twenty years ago, the development of many new logics became increasingly intertwined with the development of domain specific languages and higher-level specification languages with formal foundations. One exciting trend has been capabilities and tools that build domain specific "little languages" on top of an emerging class of executable languages (architectural description languages) that are combining more expressive capabilities with better analytic foundations. Another exciting trend is the work by J. Goguen and others on "algebraic semiotics", which is extending formal approaches to the difficult and qualitative area of visualizations, and recently to story structure and narration.

Although it is out of scope for this chapter to describe each of these developments, the purpose of bringing this family of new computational methods (such as emotional agents etc.) and new mathematical and logical developments into the discussion is for the following qualities they would add to Peacefare technology:

First, better representational systems will allow us to better model the emotional and social behavior of both our computational agents and ourselves. They will potentially allow us to express our goals, intentions, and meanings in terms that can be computationally carried out and verified. They will also allow us to better model and design systems with reflection and other cognitive capabilities. Such expressiveness when combined in representational systems that permit better analytic capabilities will allow us to build the types of sophisticated services that we need for "continual contemplation" or for services that can build user profiles (based on the analysis of behavior and conversation) and then match such user profiles to other users and resources. Lastly, languages are potentially a compact way of representing large amounts of detail in a computational form and could greatly supplement both our ability to build and to analyze enormous and varied databases.

As suggested in the story, the growing area of story logics is especially important to our ability to collect and analyze the behavior of participants in the role-playing simulations, of the Peacefare mediators and the mediation process, and even for the free ranging conversation and behavior occurring in the social virtual worlds. A number of researchers have been emphasizing for some time now the importance of narration and stories in individual cognition, society, and culture. The attitude expressed in the story is that the idea of stories will supplant the current emphasis on generating scenarios. The term scenario originally came from the simulation community, in which a sequence of events would drive the simulation. Later the term scenario came to mean more than just a sequence of events; it now came with enough of a 'cover story' to motivate students or trainees engaged with the simulation system. In the planning and logistics community, scenarios have become associated with the events that would lead to different contingencies and plans with associated results or outcomes. Stories not only have the structure and order associated with scenarios, they also include motivations, values (as Barry Kort has pointed out repeatedly), characters, emotions, and viewpoints. All of these latter characteristics are critical to reasoning about conflict and conflict resolution. A better analytic basis to stories will allow us to develop enormous numbers of stories that could be validated or discarded based on the "continual contemplation" of incoming data sources and the results of the reflective information architecture. In addition, such a story logic would allow us to better develop both the role-playing games and allow us to offer to participants better authoring tools for expressing their modifications of the games. It has been my experience that building domain specific languages can be useful as a community-building experience. That is, it allows a small disparate group to start discussing often vague and difficult concepts by allowing them to start defining the objects and actions allowed in a domain specific language, which in turn is immediately executable for experimentation on initial models. This helps to resolve some of the small group dynamics of having the most powerful personality or "squeakiest wheel" dominate the early modeling or discussion or degenerating into aggressive competition among personalities. The relevance here would be to have participants (especially if it was feasible to match people from the many sides of a growing conflict) start by defining the domain specific language that would be used to create the role-playing games that model their conflict in a Virtual World (e.g., build the descriptions, the settings, objects, behaviors of characters, etc.).

Lastly the story logics would be critical for analyzing and compactly representing the accumulating databases based on the participants in Peacemaker 2020. As an immediate result the current mediation databases currently collected could be enhanced with more qualitative information (e.g. the "facts with actions, goals, viewpoints, attitudes and players computationally analyzable because of the language grammars and semantics" noted in the story.) These new databases of "stories" would form a much more powerful base for analysis than databases composed of individual facts.

3 REMAINING CHALLENGES NOT SOLVED BY 2050

In addition to the many challenges to the technologies noted in the above story, it is clear that there are many formidable issues remaining. Professor Hope Field touched on two of the critical ones that she claims were not solved by 2050.

First, it is my opinion that even as our ability to model 'normal' human minds and emotions, social networks (Carley, 2002), diverse societies and cultures improves, we will still have an enormous distance to go in modeling abnormal psychology, and the destructive effect that disturbed individuals have on small groups around them, and the destructive effect that small groups have on the larger web of communities to which they are attached.

Although it is quite clear that there are culturally defined concepts within any group for what is to be considered normative or abnormal, the goal of our science should not necessarily be to define what is normative across all cultures. Rather, the scientific challenge will be to understand both the good and destructive dynamics of the outsider, of the magnetic leader, of the discontent, and all the myriad labels we have for distinguishing among the ways in which an individual can conform its social group.

Another modeling challenge raised in the story is to model and analyze the impacts of unforeseen circumstances and events on the negotiated outcomes we desire. One tactic of course is to develop methods for developing billions of scenarios and then to prune those depending on incoming information (as suggested in the story logics described above). Certainly one could explore large numbers of global interdependencies in that manner. However, it is also clear that no matter how much we model, we cannot nor should we model everything. Recent work on biological models of relevancy and saliency offers perhaps some new approaches for the future but more will need to be done on automating summaries, stories, relevancy, priorities, etc.

The last issue raised in the story was in a sense the starting point of this paper, which is to define and to develop the correct role for computer-mediated approaches to Peacefare. In the story, Professor Field declares that Peacemaker 2020 still has no automated mediators and notes that part of the reason reported in the story is that humans still don't trust the intelligent agents or other computer-based programs to correctly reflect their human ethics and values. The purpose of this paper was to stimulate a discussion that will help us answer basic questions on what we want computer-based approaches to do for Peacefare, for populations of human beings who still would rather war with each other than negotiate. It is my belief that knowledge always helps, that including more people in the discussions and in the mediation process could help to lessen fear and violence, and that technology is capable (eventually) of supporting such participation in a flexible and analyzable fashion. These beliefs are as yet unsupported by experimentation or experience. Hopefully, this paper and its companion papers in this volume will start the discussion towards both experimentation and experience in Peacefare.

References

Allen, R., and Garlan, D., 1997, A formal basis for architectural connection, *ACM Transactions on Software Engineering and Methodology*.

Aczel, P., 1988, *Non-well-founded Sets*, CSLI Lecture Notes No. 14, Center for the Study of Language and Information, Stanford University Press, Stanford.

Barwise, J., 1989, *The Situation in Logic*, CSLI Lecture Notes No. 17, Center for the Study of Language and Information, Stanford University Press, Stanford.

Barwise, J., and Etchemendy, J., 1987, *The Liar: An Essay on Truth and Circularity*, Oxford University Press, Oxford.

Barwise, J., and Moss, L., 1966, *Vicious Circles: On the Mathematics of Non-Wellfounded Phenomena*, CSLI Lecture Notes No. 60, Center for the Study of Language and Information, Stanford University Press, Stanford.

Bellman, K. L., 2001a, Building the right stuff: Challenges in developing better computer-based technology for education, in *Smart Machines in Education: The Coming Revolution in Educational Technology*, Forbus, K. D., and Feltovich, P. J., AAAI Press.

Bellman, K. L., 2001b, The challenge for a new type of computational semiotics: The roles and limitations of diverse representations in virtual worlds, in *Proceedings of VWsim'01: The 2001 Virtual Worlds and Simulation Conference, WMC'2001: The 2001 SCS Western MultiConference, 7-11 January 2001*, Landauer, C., and Bellman, K., eds., Phoenix, SCS.

Bellman, K. L., 1999. Towards a theory of virtual worlds, in *Proceedings of VWsim'99: Virtual Worlds and Simulation Conference, SCS Western Multi-Conference, 18-20 January 1999*, Christopher Landauer C., and Bellman, K., eds., San Francisco, SCS, pp. 17-21.

Bellman, K. L., 1997, Sharing work, experience, interpretation, and maybe even meanings between natural and artificial agents, invited paper, in *Proceedings of SMC'97: the 1997 IEEE International Conference on Systems, Man, and Cybernetics*, 12-15 *October 1997, Orlando, Florida*, vol. 5, pp. 4127-4132.

Bellman, K. L., Gillam, A., and Landauer, C., 1993, Challenges for conceptual design environments: The VEHICLES experience, *Revue Internationale de CFAO et d'Infographie*, Hermes, Paris.

Bellman, K. L., and Landauer, C., 1995, Designing testable, heterogeneous software environments, in *Special Issue: Software Quality in Knowledge-Based Systems*, Plant, R., ed., *Journal of Systems and Software*, **29**:199-217.

Bellman, K. L., and Landauer, C., 2000a, Towards an integration science: The influence of Richard Bellman on our research, *Journal of Mathematical Analysis and Applications* **249**:3-31.

Bellman, K. and Landauer, C., 2000b, Playing in the MUD: virtual worlds are real places, in *Proceedings ECAI'98: the 1998 European Conference on Artificial Intelligence*, Workshop w14 on Intelligent Virtual Environments, 25 August 1998, Brighton, England, U.K.; revised and extended version in *Special Issue of J. Applied Artificial Intelligence*, Luck, M., Aylett, R. S., eds., **14**:93-123.

Carley, K., 2002, De/stabilizing cellular networks, in *Proceedings of VWsim '02: The 2002 SCS Western MultiConference, 27-31 January 2002, San Antonio, Texas.*

Clavel, M., Duran, F., Eker, S., Meseguer, J., and Stehr, M.-O., 1999, Maude as a formal meta-tool, in *World Congress on Formal Methods* (FM '99), Lecture Notes in Computer Science, Vol. 1709, Springer, Heidelberg. pp. 1684-1703.

Duran, F., 1999, *A Reflective Module Algebra with Applications to the Maude Language*, Ph.D. Thesis University of Malaga, Malaga.

Freud, S., 1989, *Civilization and Its Discontents*, Strachey, J., ed., reissue edition, W.W. Norton & Company.

Goguen, J., 1999, An introduction to algebraic semiotics with applications to user interface design, in *Computation for Metaphor, Analogy, and Agents*, Nehaniv, C., ed., Springer Lecture Notes in Artificial Intelligence, vol. 1562, Springer, Heidelberg, pp. 242-291.

Goguen, J., 2001, Towards a design theory for virtual worlds: algebraic semiotics with information visualization as a case study, in *Proceedings of Virtual Worlds and Simulation Conference*, Landauer, C., and Bellman, K., eds., pp. 298 –303.

Goguen, J. 2002, Information visualization and semiotic morphisms, in *Proceedings Second International Conference on Visual Representations and Interpretations*, Liverpool UK, 9-12 September.

Hayes-Roth, B., Pfleger, K., Lalanda, P., Morignot, P., and Balabanovic, M., 1995, A domain-specific software architecture for adaptive intelligent systems, *IEEE Transactions on Software Engineering*, Vol. **SE-21**:288-301.

Herz, J.C., 1997, *Joystick Nation: How Videogames Ate Our Quarters, Won Our Hearts, and Rewired Our Minds*. Little Brown & Company.

Hudak, P., 1996, Building domain-specific embedded languages, *ACM Computing Surveys* **28 (4)**.

IEEE, 1999, *Special Issue on Domain Specific Languages*, IEEE Transacations on Software Engineering **25(3)**.

Kennedy, C. M., 1999, Distributed reflective architectures for adjustable autonomy, in *Proc. IJCAI-99 Workshop on Adjustable Autonomy Systems*, 1 August 1999, Stockholm, Sweden, Kortenkamp, D., Gregory , G., Myers, K. L., eds.

Kiczales, G., Rivieres, J., and Bobrow, D. G., 1991, *The Art of the Meta-Object Protocol*, MIT Press, Cambridge, MA.

Landauer, C., and Bellman, K. L., 1996, Active integration frameworks: The Wrapping theory, *Systems Development Management* **34-10-25**, Auerbach, and Building and maintaining systems using the Wrapping theory, *Systems Development Management* **34-10-26**, Auerbach.

Landauer, C., and Bellman, K. L., 1996, Knowledge-based integration infrastructure for complex systems, *International Journal of Intelligent Control and Systems* **1**:133-153.

Landauer, C., and Bellman, K. L., 1999, Computational embodiment: agents as constructed complex systems, in *Human Cognition and Social Agent Technology*, Dautenhahn, K., ed., Benjamins, New York

Landauer, C., and Bellman, K. L., 1993, The role of self-referential logics in a software architecture using Wrappings, in *Proc. ISS'93: the 3rd Irvine Software Symposium*, 30 April 1993, U. C. Irvine, California.

Landauer, C., and Bellman, K. L., 1998, Language formation in virtual worlds, in *Proc. SMC'98:the 1998 IEEE International Conference on Systems, Man, and Cybernetics*, 11-14 October 1998, San Diego, California. pp. 1365-1370.

Lorenz, K., 1963, *On Agression,* Harcourt, Brace, and World, Inc., New York.

Luckham, D., 2002, *The Power of Events: An Introduction to Complex Event Processing in Distributed Enterprise Systems*, Pearson Education, Inc.

Maes, P., 1987, Concepts and experiments in computational reflection, in *Proceedings OOP-SLA'87,* pp. 147-155.

Maes, P., and Nardi, D., 1988, Meta-level architectures and reflection, in *Proc. Workshop on Meta-Level Architectures and Reflection*, 27-30 October 1986, Alghero, Italy, North-Holland.

Mandler, J. M., 1984, *Stories, Scripts, and Scenes: Aspects of Schema Theory*, Lawrence Erlbaum Associates, Mahwah, NJ.

Mataric, M. J., 1997, Studying the role of embodiment in cognition, *Cybernetics and Systems: An International Journal* **28:**457-470.

Meseguer, J., 1989, General logics, in *Proc. Logic Colloquium'87,* Ebbinghaus, H., et al., eds., North-Holland, pp. 275-329

Meseguer, J., 1993, A logical theory of concurrent objects and its realization in the Maude language, in *Research Directions in Object-Based Concurrency*, Agha, G., Wegner, P., Yonezawa, A., eds., MIT Press, Cambridge, MA, pp. 313-389.

Norman, D. A., 1997, How might people interact with agents?, in *Software Agents,* Bradshaw, J. M., ed., ,AAAI Press, pp. 49-55.

Reeder, F., 2001, Do what I mean: Issues in cross-lingual collaboration, in *Proceedings of the Virtual Worlds and Simulation Conference,* 2001, Landauer, C., and Bellman, K. L., eds., San Diego, SCS, Inc., pp. 266 –271.

Reeder, F. and Harper, L., 2000, Parlez-vous francais? Multilingual interaction in virtual worlds/communities, in *Proceedings of VWSIM 2000, Virtual Worlds and Simulation Conference,* Landauer, C., and Bellman, K. L., eds., SCS Intl. San Diego, CA.

Shaw, M., and Garlan, D., 1996 *Software Architecture: Perspectives on an Emerging Discipline*, Prentice-Hall.

Smith, B. C., 1986, Varieties of self-reference, in *Proc. TARK'86:the 1986 Conference on Theoretical Aspects of Reasoning about Knowledge,* 19-22 March 1986, Monterey, California, Halpern, J. Y., ed.

Suchman, L. A., 1987, *Plans and Situated Actions: The Problem of Human-Machine Communication*, Cambridge U. Press, Cambridge.

Trappl, R., Petta, P., and Payr, S. 2003, eds., *Emotions in Humans and Artifacts,* MIT Press, Cambridge, MA.

van Deursen, A., Heering, J., and Klint, P., 1996, *Language Prototyping: an Algebraic Specification Approach*, AMAST Series in Computing, vol. 5, World Scientific Publishing Co.

Concluding Remarks: And Terrorism?

Robert Trappl

Vienna Medical University and Austrian Research Institute for Artificial Intelligence, Vienna, Austria

When searching in the subject index of this volume for "terrorism", only one entry can be found for all the preceding fifteen chapters. Why?

There are probably two reasons:

1. While in the terrorist attacks in New York, Madrid, and London about 3000 persons were killed, in the civil war in Congo alone approximately 3.3 million persons lost their lifes since 1998. Thus, if all human beings are of equal worth, the 3000 represent less than 0.1 % of those killed in "other" wars.

2. The databases developed for many years with great efforts by many scientists are practically useless for these attacks. It was already difficult to switch from interstate conflicts with well-defined actors with well-defined properties to internal conflicts. But even in these, at least groups, tied together by language or racial identity, could be defined. But terrorist groups?

Nevertheless, these terrorist attacks in the capitals in the "western" world are threatening. It's where also most of the researchers who contribute chapters like the ones for this book, live and work. Thus, computer-aided methods are being developed to better understand what's happening and, in consequence, help to better prevent future terrorist attacks.

Since, as already mentioned, "conventional" databases are practically useless, new databases focusing on terrorist attacks had and have to be developed. Three of them may be mentioned:

- ITERATE (International Terrorism: Attributes of Terrorist Events), developed on behalf the US Department of State, with an international focus. ITERATE records the incident date, type of event, number of people killed, number of people wounded, host country, the terrorist group, and other variables (Mickolus et al., 2004),

- the Terrorism Knowledge Base, developed by the Memorial Institute for the Prevention of Terrorism (MIPT), which catalogs events in the USA (http://www.tkb.org/Home.jsp, last checked 23 Sept 2005), and

R. Trappl (ed.), Programming for Peace, 441–444.

- the TWEED (Terrorism in Western Europe) data set which catalogs domestic and international events in Western Europe over nearly fifty years (Engene, 2004).

Recently, a large database was "detected", the "Pinkerton database" with more than 69.000 terrorist events worldwide which had been collected by a private company, the Pinkerton Corporation's Global Intelligence Services (PGIS) (LaFree, 2005). This data has been coded and computerized meanwhile and is therefore by far the largest database publicly available. Unfortunately, while beginning in 1970, it ends in 1997.

Of the increasing research published, two efforts will be presented which are paradigmatic for the application of computerized methods. Sandler and Enders (2002) analyzed the ITERATE database with time-series. In particular, they investigated if 9/11 constitutes a crucial structural break, and if post-9/11 defensive measures in rich countries altered the pattern of transnational terrorism, e.g. if these measures shifted terrorist attacks from rich to poor countries as terrorists sought soft targets. As a result, they could show that little has changed in the time-series of overall terrorist incidents. "Thus the stressed al-Qaeda network and other terrorist groups responded to the greater risk that they faced by the war on terror by eschewing difficult and costly attacks for simple bombing with high body counts." (Sandler and Enders, 2005).

The only lone structural break which they found (Enders and Sandler, 2005) occurred in the post-Cold War era in 1994 when transnational terrorist events fell strongly in number with the disappearance of many leftist terrorists and reduced state support. To summarize, there are two notable changes in pattern (Sandler and Enders, 2005): (1) deadly bombings are more prevalent, whereas hostage missions are less prevalent, and (2) there is a geographical transfer of attacks to the Middle East and Asia.

Terrorist networks can be viewed in the light of the "Eight R's" (Stohl and Stohl, 2005) used to understand global organizing (quoted from Stohl, 2005):

"(1) Relationships—What is the organization's network? (2) Rules—How do systemic structures affect the organization, its network, and its opportunities? (3) Resources—What are the organization's resources, and who are its potential opponents? (4) Record—What is the history of the organization and the history of the region in which it operates? How do these affect the organization's choices? (5) Region—Where is the organization's zone of operation, and who are its referents? (6) Readings—How does the organization perceive and interpret its and its opponents' "reality", "symbols", and "routines"? (7) Rationales—What provides meaning and understanding for the organization? (8) Responsibility—How does the organization justify its actions to itself and to potential supporters and others?"

Carley (2003) views terrorist organizations as such dynamic however covert networks and searches for means to destabilize them. She approaches the problem in 7 stages: (1) By identifying key entities and the connections among them, (2) by identifying key processes by which entities or connections are added or dropped or in the case of connections changes in their strengths (3) by collecting data on the system, the covert network, (4) by determining its performance characteristic, (5) by determining performance characteristic of a possible optimal system, (6) by locating vulnerabilites and selecting destabilization strategies, and (7) by determining performance characterization in the short and long term after a destabilization strategy has been applied.

She exemplifies her procedure by using data which were collected from an embassy bombing in Tanzania. For representing the key entities she uses a Meta-Matrix which relates people, resources, and tasks. Second she represents these variables in a social network. To measure performance it is simulated by DyNet, a multi-agent network system for assessing destabilization strategies on dynamic networks (http://www.casos.cs.cmu.edu/projects/DyNet/index.php, last checked 22 Sept 2005). DyNet is an interactive desktop tool which a user therefore can apply everywhere.

These simulations show that, while the removal of individuals leads to a "self-healing" of the covert network, the isolation of entire cells is considerably more devastating. She can further show that the removal of a critical person (e.g. in centrality, cognitive load, tasks exclusivity) can make a covert network less adaptive but even more efficient. In order to find that out each network has to undergo an analysis of its own.

Carley (2004) has recently extended her approach by reducing uncertainty by using two types of data, running the model in a Monte-Carlo simulation to determine the robustness of the results, and to examine the robustness of the results under adding and dropping nodes and edges in the underlying network. She illustrates this approach by contrasting the differential predictions of al-Quaeda and Hamas as the top leaders are removed.

As already mentioned, these are but a few examples of research taken from the increasing amount of publications in this area. In any case, several other methods, e.g. the ones introduced in the chapters of this volume and up to now "only" applied to "conventional" databases could, when applied to databases of terrorist events, prove to be useful in helping to reduce the severity and/or number of terrorist attacks.

References

Carley, K. M., 2004, *Estimating Vulnerabilities in Large Covert Networks*, www.dodccrp.org/events/2004/CCRTS_San_Diego/CD/papers/249.pdf (last checked 23 Sept 2005).

Carley, K. M., Domroski, M., Tsvetovat, M., Reminga, J., and Kamneva, N., 2003, *Destabilizing Dynamic Covert Networks.* In Proc. 8th Int. Command and Control Research and Technology Symp., Evidence Based Research, Vienna, VA.

Enders, W., and Sandler, T., 2005, After 9/11: Is it all that different? *Journal of Conflict Resolution* **49**:259-277.

Engene, J. O., 2004, *Terrorism in Western Europe: Explaining the Trends since 1950*, Edward Elgar, Cheltenham, UK.

LaFree, G., Dugan, L., and Franke, D., 2005, The interplay between terrorism, nonstate actors, and weapons of mass destruction: an exploration of the Pinkerton database, *International Studies Review* **7**:155-158

Mickolus, E. F., Sandler, T., Murdock, J. M., and Flemming, P., 2004, *International Terrorism: Attributes of Terrorist Events, 1968-2003*, Vinyard Software, Dunn Loring, VA.

Sandler, T., and Enders, W., 2005, September 11 and its aftermath, *International Studies Review* **7**:165-168.

Stohl, M., 2005, Is the past prologue? Terrorists and WMD, *International Studies Review* **7**:146-148.

Stohl, C., and Stohl, M., 2005, *Approaching Global Organizing*, Sage, London.

Contributing Authors

Kirstie L. Bellman is head of the Aerospace Integration Sciences Center (AISC), which serves as a research and development capability for a number of DoD and government agencies. AISC's focus is on the development of advanced system and model integration methods, new analytic techniques, and evaluation tools for assessing the impacts of new technologies. Kirstie Bellman has over 35 years of academic, industrial and consulting experience in both laboratory research and the development of models and information architectures for large military and government programs. Her published research spans a wide range of topics in Cognitive Science, Neuroscience, and Computer Science. Recently she became a Fellow for the American Association for the Advancement of Science, for work in complex systems and Virtual Worlds.

kirstie.l.bellman@notes.aerospace.org

Jacob Bercovitch is Professor of International Relations at the School of Political Science and Communication at the University of Canterbury in Christchurch, New Zealand. He received his Ph.D. from the London School of Economics. His main interests are in the areas of international conflict and mediation. He is widely regarded as one of the leading scholars in these fields, having published many books and professional articles on these issues. He is currently Vice President of the International Studies Association.

jacob.bercovitch@canterbury.ac.nz

Margit Bussmann received a Ph.D. in political science at the University of Alabama. She is currently a research associate at the University of Konstanz. Her research interests include causes of international and domestic conflict, economic interdependence, development and income inequality.

margit.bussmann@uni-konstanz.de

David Carment is a Professor at the Norman Paterson School of International Affairs. David Carment also serves as Principal Investigator for the Country Indicators for Foreign Policy project. His research interests include conflict prevention, conflict resolution, ethnic conflict, peacekeeping, Internet technology and Canadian foreign affairs.

dcarment@ccs.carleton.ca

Caroline Delany has a Bachelor of Science, with an Arts Minor in Political Science, from the University of British Columbia. Caroline recently completed a Masters of Arts from the Norman Paterson School of International Affairs in Ottawa, Canada and now works for the Canadian International Development Agency.

carolinedelany@sympatico.ca

Daniel Druckman is the Vernon M. and Minnie I. Lynch Professor of Conflict Resolution at George Mason University in Fairfax, Virginia where he has also coordinated the doctoral program at the Institute for Conflict Analysis and Resolution. He has been a visiting professor at National Yunlin University of Science and Technology in Taiwan and at the University of Queensland in Brisbane, Australia. He is also a member of the faculty at Sabanci University in Istanbul, Turkey. He has published widely on such topics as negotiating behavior, nationalism, peacekeeping, political stability, human performance, nonverbal communication, and methodology. He is a board member or associate editor of eight Journals. He received many awards for his research and teaching and is the recipient of the 2003 Lifetime Achievement award from the International Association for Conflict Management. His most recent book, *Doing Research: Methods of Inquiry for Conflict Analysis* was published by Sage in 2005.

dandruckman@yahoo.com

Johannes Fürnkranz studied at the Technical University Vienna, the University of Chicago, and at Carnegie Mellon University. In 2004, after several years at the Austrian Research Institute for Artificial Intelligence (OFAI) and a prestigious APART scholarship from the Austrian Academy of Sciences, he became Professor for Knowledge Engineering at the Technical University Darmstadt, Germany. His research interests are machine-learning, in particular inductive rule learning, and its applications to game-playing, web mining, and the social sciences. He is action editor of the journal *Machine Learning*, editorial board member of several AI-related journals, and a frequent member of program committees of prestigious conferences in the field.

juffi@ke.informatik.tu-darmstadt.de

Georg Dorffner is associate professor at the Dept. of Medical Cybernetics and Artificial Intelligence, Center for Brain Research, at the Medical University of Vienna, and heads the Neural Computation Research Group at the Austrian Research Institute for Artificial Intelligence. Among his main research interests are pattern recognition, signal and time series processing, connectionist cognitive modeling, simulation of intelligent agents and cognitive neuroscience. He has been in numerous national and EU-funded projects as a leading scientist and has, as the coordinator, successfully led one of them (Biomed-2 SIESTA) into a spin-off company. He has authored or co-authored more than 100 scientific publications.
georg.dorffner@ofai.at

Richard Harris is the president of RA Software, a consulting firm specializing in negotiation computer software. He has collaborated with Daniel Druckman and Bennett Ramburg on a grant from the US Peace Institute for computer negotiation software and on an interactive web negotiation program called Negotiator which has been used for conflict resolution research studies. He has also written several joint papers with Daniel Druckman.
harr3088@bellsouth.net

Erik Hörtnagl holds a diploma in computer science, with a focus on Artificial Intelligence, from the Technical University of Vienna. He is currently working as a researcher at OFAI (Austrian Research Institute for Artificial Intelligence).
erikh@a1.net

Eva Hudlicka is a Principal Scientist and President of Psychometrix Associates, Blacksburg, VA. Her research focuses on computational models of emotion, with emphasis on models of affect appraisal and state/trait effects on cognition and decision-making. She received her BS in Biochemistry from Virginia Tech, her MS in Computer Science from the Ohio State University, and her PhD in Computer Science from the University of Massachusetts-Amherst. Prior to founding Psychometrix Associates in 1995, Dr. Hudlicka was a Senior Scientist at Bolt Beranek & Newman, Cambridge, MA.
evahud@earthlink.net

Heinz Krummenacher received his M.A. (1982) and Ph.D. (1985) in political science from the University of Zurich. He started his professional career with the Swiss Defense Department where he directed a study group dealing with the re-definition of Swiss security policy (1985-1989). Between 1990 and 1992 he served as foreign editor with the newspaper "Der Bund". Before joining swisspeace in 1998 he was head of the social research department at IHA-GfM, the leading market research institute in Switzerland (1992-1998).

At swisspeace he is the acting director and head of the early warning unit FAST (Early Recognition of Tension and Fact Finding). In addition, he is a member of the UN staff college's Early Warning Preventive Measures training unit and of the advisory board of the UNDP Regional Early Warning System for Southeast Europe.

krummenacher@swisspeace.unibe.ch

Will Lowe is currently working at Trinity College, Dublin, on a new methodology for automatically assigning policy position to political texts. His interests center on statistical text analysis and on the role of identity and rationality in international relations. By training he is a philosopher who quickly lapsed into empirical work by starting a PhD on neural networks and natural language processing at the Centre for Cognitive Studies of Edinburgh University. In his dissertation, he used unsupervised neural networks and statistical methods from information retrieval to build a computational model of human semantic memory. After a time as visiting fellow at Danial Dennett's center for Cognitive Studies at Tufts University, he cooperated in the development of a new evaluation methodology which was applied to an information extraction system that generated events data directly from newswire.

wlowe@latte.harvard.edu

Frank R. Pfetsch is Professor of Political Science at the Ruprecht-Karls University of Heidelberg and Jean Monnet-Professor of European Political Science. He studied economics and political science at the universities of Karlsruhe, Paris, Turin, Heidelberg, and Harvard University. In 1964 he received his Ph.D. from Heidelberg University. From 1964 to 1976 he worked in research institutes and was a consultant to the West German Ministry for Scientific Affairs, to UNESCO for various science policy administrations in South America, Africa, and Asia as well as to the Commission of the European Union. His main research interests are in the field of International Relations and, more particularly, in conflict analysis, negotiation theory and European Integration. He has widely published on Science Policy, Foreign and Constitutional Policy, International Relations, Political Theory, especially Negotiation Theory and is author of several books and articles on these subjects.

frank.pfetsch@urz.uni-heidelberg.de

Jürgen Rattenberger holds a diploma in computer science from the Technical University of Vienna, with a specialization in Artificial Intelligence. He is currently researcher at the OFAI (Austrian Research Institute for Artificial Intelligence).

juergen.rattenberger@ofai.at

William Reed is an assistant professor in the political science department at Rice University. His research examines international politics using econometric and formal models. His current project explores the sources and influences of uncertainty on bargaining and war in international relations. Dr. Reed has published widely in such journals as *American Political Science Review, American Journal of Political Science, Journal of Politics, Journal of Conflict Resolution*, and *International Interactions.*
wlreed@rice.edu

Harald Scheuthle received his master in public administration from the University of Konstanz in 2002 and a master in political science from Rutgers University in 2001. He is currently working for the European University Association in Brussels.
email

Gerald Schneider is Professor of International Politics and Executive Editor of *European Union Politics.* He has published widely on applied bargaining theory, decision making, economic causes and consequences of armed conflict, conflict management and foreign policy analysis.
gerald.schneider@uni-konstanz.de

Philip A. Schrodt is a professor of political science at the University of Kansas. His major areas of research are formal models of political behavior, with an emphasis on international politics, and political methodology. Schrodt's current research focuses on predicting political change using statistical and pattern recognition methods. He has published more than 75 articles in political science, and his Kansas Event Data System computer program won the "Outstanding Computer Software Award" from the American Political Science Association 1995.
schrodt@ku.edu

Nicolas Schwank M.A. is research assistant at the Institute for Political Science at the University of Heidelberg. From 2002 to 2004, he created the new conflict databank KOSIMO 2 and was deputy project manager of two research projects for the European Union. Until 2005 he was also member of the board of directors of the Heidelberg Institute for International Conflict Research (HIIK) and editor of the *Heidelberg Conflict Barometer.* His main research interest is in improving methods for quantitative conflict research. He is presently completing his doctoral thesis on conflict dynamics.
nicolas.schwank@urz.uni-hd.de

Richard J. Stoll received his Ph.D. in political science from the University of Michigan in 1979. He is currently professor of political science and associate dean of social sciences at Rice University in Houston, Texas. His research

interests lie in the study of international conflict and American national security policy. He has published six books (most recently co-editing *Multiple Paths to Knowledge in International Relations: Methodology in the Study of Conflict Management and Conflict Resolution,* published by Lexington Books) and numerous articles and book chapters.
stoll@rice.edu

Devika Subramanian obtained her undergraduate degree in eclectrical engineering and computer science from the Indian Institute of Technology, and her PhD in computer science from Stanford University in 1989. Her research interests are in artificial intelligence and machine learning and their applications in science and engineering. She has been at Rice University since 1995 where she is now a professor of Computer Science. She was co-program chair of the National Conference of the American Association of Artificial Intelligence (AAAI) in 1999. Her research is currently funded by the NSF.
devika@rice.edu

Robert Trappl is professor and head of the Department of Medical Cybernetics and Artificial Intelligence, Center for Brain Research, Medical University of Vienna, Austria. He is head of the Austrian Research Institute for Artificial Intelligence in Vienna, which he founded in 1984. He has published more than 150 articles, he is co-author, editor or co-editor of 31 books, the most recent being *Emotions in Humans and Artifacts*, MIT Press, 2003, *Cybernetics and Systems 2004*, 2 vols., ASCS, Vienna, and *Agent Culture. Human-Agent Interaction in a Multicultural World*, Lawrence Erlbaum, 2004. He is Editor-in-Chief of *Applied Artificial Intelligence: An International Journal* and *Cybernetics and Systems: An International Journal*, both published by Taylor & Francis, USA. His main research focus at present is the investigation of the potential contributions of Artificial Intelligence methods to the avoidance of outbreaks of wars or in ending them, and the development of emotional personality agents both for synthetic actors in films, television and interactive media.
robert.trappl@meduniwien.ac.at

Name Index

A

B

C

D

Subject Index

D

I

J

K

L

M